PAUL

PAUL

His Life and Teaching

John McRay

Baker Academic
Grand Rapids, Michigan

© 2003 by John McRay

Published by Baker Academic
a division of Baker Book House Company
P.O. Box 6287, Grand Rapids, MI 49516-6287
www.bakeracademic.com

Paperback edition published in 2007

ISBN 10: 0-8010-3239-3 (pbk.)
ISBN 978-0-8010-3239-4 (pbk.)

Printed in the United States of America

The Library of Congress Cataloging-in-Publication Data has cataloged the hardcover edition as follows:

McRay, John.
     Paul : his life and teaching / John McRay.
          p.   cm.
     Includes bibliographical references and indexes.
     ISBN 0-8010-2403-X (cloth)
     1. Paul, the Apostle, Saint. I. Title.
 BS2506.3 .M37 2002
 225.9′2—dc21
     [B]   .   2002018588

Unless otherwise indicated, Scripture quotations are taken from the Revised Standard Version of the Bible, copyright 1946, 1952, 1971 by the Division of Christian Education of the National Council of the Churches of Christ in the USA. Used by permission.

Scripture quotations marked NRSV are taken from the New Revised Standard Version of the Bible, copyright 1989 by the Division of Christian Education of the National Council of the Churches of Christ in the USA. Used by permission.

Scripture quotations marked NIV are taken from the HOLY BIBLE, NEW INTERNATIONAL VERSION®. NIV®. Copyright © 1973, 1978, 1984 by International Bible Society. Used by permission of Zondervan Publishing House. All rights reserved.

To my sons,
Rob, David, and Barrett,
who share with me a love
for Paul and with whom I have
excavated and explored the world of Paul

Contents

Illustrations

Preface

In his masterful volume *Paul: Apostle of the Heart Set Free,* F. F. Bruce wrote that "no single event, apart from the Christ-event itself, has proved so determinant for the course of Christian history as the conversion and commissioning of Paul" (75). I share this conviction, which has motivated and guided my life as a college professor. I have taught courses on Paul for forty-five years, written a doctoral dissertation on one of his letters (1 Corinthians), and traveled extensively in the Mediterranean world since 1967, tracing out the routes Paul traveled. It has been my goal to explore every city of the approximately fifty he visited, and I have done that with the exception of only three or four. I have lived in Israel and Greece for extended periods of time researching the life of Paul and supervising teams in archaeological excavations in cities of Israel, including Caesarea Maritima, where Paul was imprisoned for two years. In addition, I have written more than 140 articles in eighteen dictionaries and encyclopedias, many of these articles on Paul. So when I completed my book on *Archaeology and the New Testament* for Baker Book House in 1991 and was asked to write this book on Paul, I was happy to accept the invitation because of my deep and abiding interest in the great apostle.

At the publisher's request, I have written this book on the level of a college text and not for the scholarly world of professors and critics. Therefore, the use of foreign languages is minimal, and reference to contemporary critical views is usually placed in the notes and summarized in chapter 18 ("Paul in Recent Study"). It has been my aim to produce a volume that essentially reflects the content and method of my college courses on Paul and the results of my twenty-seven trips to the Holy Lands studying Paul's world. As I exhort my students to do, I have tried to "put on my first-century glasses," look at Paul in his Jewish and Hellenistic world of the Mediterranean, and see him not as a fourth-century church father, a sixteenth-century Protestant reformer, or a twenty-first-century evangelical missionary, but as what he was, a first-century Jewish rabbi who accepted Jesus as his Messiah and became an ardent, dedicated Messianic Jew.

In this volume, I have tried to emphasize that Paul was not the founder of Christianity, that he never ceased to be a Jew, and that Christianity is not a Gentile religion. There has never been a greater advocate of the universal composition of the Christian faith than Paul, who emphatically asserted that in Christ "there is neither Jew nor Greek, there is neither slave nor free, there is neither male nor female; for you are all one in Christ Jesus" (Gal. 3:28). This means that when people place their trust in Jesus, neither Jews nor Gentiles have to abandon their ancestry, neither males nor females have to abandon their gender, and neither slaves nor free people have to abandon their sociological status. Paul's central focus in his preaching was that Gentiles do not have to become Jews any more than Jews have to become Gentiles, for as he went on to say, "If you are Christ's, then you are Abraham's offspring, heirs according to promise" (Gal. 3:29). Monotheism as seen in the faith of Abraham was the foundation of the Judeo-Christian faith Paul proclaimed, and God is thus the Father of all believers. This means that wherever God has a son or daughter, I have a brother or sister (Jew or Gentile, male or female). The impact of this truth can be nothing short of revolutionary in a world filled with religious division, if the teaching of Paul is accepted and applied with love to everyday life. It is my prayer that this book may make some contribution to the realization of that goal.

Numerous individuals, organizations, and foundations contributed to my travel and research from 1967 to the publication of my book *Archaeology and the New Testament* in 1991. These have been acknowledged in the preface to that volume, and my research continues to benefit from their generosity. Since that time other contributors have made possible my further travel and research on the life and times of Paul, and I owe a deep debt of gratitude to all who have assisted in this project. At the risk of overlooking some who have participated with me in various ways, I want to thank the following partners in this ministry: the faculty, staff, and administration of Wheaton College; Don Edwards; Rob McRay; Bering Drive Church of Christ in Houston, Texas; Wheaton Bible Church in Wheaton, Illinois; David Sveen and the Domanada Foundation in Wheaton; and the G. W. Aldeen Memorial Fund at Wheaton College. I am also grateful for the friendship and financial support of the following individuals: Mac and Vonla Airhart, Randy and Therese Tomassi, Robert and Dawn Cavalco, Joseph and Patricia Dodson, Dr. Paul and Janet Jorden, Dick and Mary Norton, Martha Purdy, and Julie Stahler.

It has been a rare and blessed privilege for me to have my three sons—Rob, David, and Barrett—travel with me in the world of the Mediterranean and Middle East. They have lived in Israel, excavated with me at various sites in that country, and traveled through most of the other countries included in Paul's travels. Teaching them and, in later years, their families about the life of Paul in the geographical settings where he lived has been one of the greatest joys and blessings of my life. They physically labored with me in archaeological excavations, challenged my thinking, and contributed to my research.

The greatest supporter and contributor in every way to my work, not only in this volume but in everything I have written, is my wife, Annette. She has been a source of inspiration, insight, and encouragement in difficult times and the proofreader for everything I have done. Without her professional expertise and genuine interest, this book would not have been completed. I cherish the wonderful memories of our living again in the Mediterranean in 2001— doing five months of further research in Greece and Israel and spending a month working together in the little third-floor "crow's nest" of our apartment in Elie, Scotland, where I wrote and she proofread the final portions of the book. And so this volume was written *amore Pauli*, for love of Paul, but with the love of Annette.

I also wish to acknowledge the important contribution my students have made to the composition of this volume by their research, papers, discussions of lectures, and the general interest and encouragement they have shown in my classes on the life and teaching of Paul. To the editorial staff at Baker Academic and especially to Jarl Waggoner I owe a special debt of gratitude. They meticulously checked my manuscript, offered valuable suggestions, and corrected my mistakes, while allowing me the freedom to express my viewpoints. Therefore, any failure to deal adequately with the overwhelming subjects of Paul's life and teaching is mine.

John McRay
Wheaton College Graduate School
Wheaton, Illinois

Abbreviations

General

ABD	*Anchor Bible Dictionary*, ed. David Noel Freedman, 6 vols. (New York: Doubleday, 1992)
Abraham	Philo, *On the Life of Abraham*
Ag.	Aeschylus, *Agamemnon*
AJA	*American Journal of Archaeology*
Ann.	Tacitus, *Annales*
ANRW	*Aufstieg und Niedergang der römischen Welt: Geschichte und Kultur Roms im Spiegel der neueren Forschung,* ed. Hildegard Temporini and Wolfgang Haase (New York: de Gruyter, 1972–)
Ant.	Josephus, *Jewish Antiquities*
ANT:LJ	Jack Finegan, *The Archeology of the New Testament: The Life of Jesus and the Beginning of the Early Church,* rev. ed. (Princeton, N.J.: Princeton University Press, 1992)
ANT:MW	Jack Finegan, *The Archeology of the New Testament: The Mediterranean World of the Early Christian Apostles* (Boulder, Colo.: Westview, 1981)
1 Apol.	Justin Martyr, *Apologia i*
ASOR	American Schools of Oriental Research
ASV	American Standard Version (1901)
Aug.	Suetonius, *Divis Augustus*
b.	Babylonian Talmud
BA	*Biblical Archaeologist*
BAFCS	The Book of Acts in Its First Century Setting
BAGD	W. Bauer, W. F. Arndt, F. W. Gingrich, and F. W. Danker, *A Greek-English Lexicon of the New Testament and Other Early Christian Literature,* 2d ed. (Chicago: University of Chicago Press, 1979)
BAR	*Biblical Archaeology Review*
Barn.	*Barnabas*
BASHH	*The Book of Acts in the Setting of Hellenistic History,* ed. Conrad Gempf, Wissenschaftliche Untersuchungen zum Neuen Testament 49 (Tübingen: Mohr, 1989)
BASOR	*Bulletin of the American Schools of Oriental Research*
BBR	*Bulletin for Biblical Research*
Bis. acc.	Lucian, *Bis accusatus*
BR	*Biblical Research*
c.	*circa,* about
CBQ	*Catholic Biblical Quarterly*
Cels.	Origen, *Contra Celsum*

CIG	*Corpus inscriptionum graecarum,* ed. A. Boeckh, 4 vols. (Berlin, 1828–77)
CIL	*Corpus inscriptionum latinarum*
Claud.	Suetonius, *Divus Claudius*
1 Clem.	*1 Clement*
Contempl. Life	Philo, *On the Contemplative Life*
Descr.	Pausanias, *Graeciae description*
Dial.	Justin, *Dialogus cum Tryphone*
Did.	*Didache*
Dreams	Philo, *On Dreams*
Ecl.	Clement of Alexandria, *Eclogae propheticae*
EEC	*Encyclopedia of Early Christianity,* ed. Everett Ferguson (New York: Garland, 1990)
Ep. Tra.	Pliny the Younger, *Epistulae ad Trajanum*
ET	*Expository Times*
EvQ	*Evangelical Quarterly*
Geogr.	Strabo, *Geographica*
Herm. *Sim.*	Shepherd of Hermas, *Similitude*
Herm. *Vis.*	Shepherd of Hermas, *Vision*
Hist.	Tacitus, *Historiae*
Hist. eccl.	Eusebius, *Historia ecclesiastica*
Hom. Act.	John Chrysostom, *Homiliae in Acta apostolorum*
HTR	*Harvard Theological Review*
IDB	*Interpreter's Dictionary of the Bible,* ed. G. A. Buttrick, 4 vols. (Nashville: Abingdon, 1962)
IDB Supplement	*Interpreter's Dictionary of the Bible: Supplementary Volume,* ed. K. Crim (Nashville: Abingdon, 1976)
IEJ	*Israel Exploration Journal*
Ign. *Eph.*	Ignatius, *To the Ephesians*
Ign. *Magn.*	Ignatius, *To the Magnesians*
Ign. *Phld.*	Ignatius, *To the Philadelphians*
Ign. *Pol.*	Ignatius, *To Polycarp*
Ign. *Smyrn.*	Ignatius, *To the Smyrnaeans*
Ign. *Trall.*	Ignatius, *To the Trallians*
JB	Jerusalem Bible
JBL	*Journal of Biblical Literature*
JETS	*Journal of the Evangelical Theological Society*
JNES	*Journal of Near Eastern Studies*
JRS	*Journal of Roman Studies*
JSNT	*Journal for the Study of the New Testament*
JTS	*Journal of Theological Studies*
J.W.	Josephus, *Jewish War*
KJV	King James Version
KNOX	*The Holy Bible,* trans. Ronald Knox (New York: Sheed & Ward, 1950)
LB	Living Bible
Legat.	Philo, *Legatio ad Gaium*
Life	Josephus, *The Life*
LSJ	H. G. Liddell, R. Scott, and H. S. Jones, *A Greek-English Lexicon* (Oxford: Clarendon, 1968)
LXX	Septuagint
m.	Mishnah
Marc.	Tertullian, *Adversus Marcionem*

MOFFATT	*The Bible: A New Translation,* trans. James Moffatt (New York: Harper & Row, 1954)
NASB	New American Standard Bible
Nat.	Pliny the Elder, *Naturalis historia*
Nav.	Lucian, *Navigium*
NEB	New English Bible
NICNT	New International Commentary on the New Testament
NIDNTT	*New International Dictionary of New Testament Theology,* ed. Colin Brown, 4 vols. (Grand Rapids: Zondervan, 1971)
NIV	New International Version
NRSV	New Revised Standard Version
NTS	*New Testament Studies*
Onom.	Eusebius, *Onomasticon*
Paen.	Tertullian, *De paenitentia*
PEQ	*Palestine Exploration Quarterly*
PG	Patrologia graeca, ed. J.-P. Migne, 162 vols. (Paris, 1857–86)
PHILLIPS	*The New Testament in Modern English,* trans. J. B. Phillips (New York: Macmillan, 1960)
Pis.	Cicero, *In Pisonem*
Princ.	Origen, *De principiis*
Prom.	Aeschylus, *Prometheus vinctus*
Pyth.	Pindar, *Pythionikai*
Quaest. conv.	Plutarch, *Quaestionum convivialium libri IX*
RSV	Revised Standard Version
Sat.	Horace, *Satirae*
SJT	*Scottish Journal of Theology*
TEV	Today's English Version (= Good News Bible)
Tib.	Suetonius, *Tiberius*
TynBul	*Tyndale Bulletin*
Vesp.	Suetonius, *Vespasianus*
Vir. ill.	Jerome, *De viris illustribus*
Vit. Apoll.	Philostratus, *Vita Apollonii*

Biblical

Old Testament

Gen.	Genesis	Neh.	Nehemiah	Hos.	Hosea
Exod.	Exodus	Esth.	Esther	Joel	Joel
Lev.	Leviticus	Job	Job	Amos	Amos
Num.	Numbers	Ps.	Psalms	Obad.	Obadiah
Deut.	Deuteronomy	Prov.	Proverbs	Jon.	Jonah
Josh.	Joshua	Eccles.	Ecclesiastes	Mic.	Micah
Judg.	Judges	Song	Song of Songs	Nah.	Nahum
Ruth	Ruth	Isa.	Isaiah	Hab.	Habakkuk
1–2 Sam.	1–2 Samuel	Jer.	Jeremiah	Zeph.	Zephaniah
1–2 Kings	1–2 Kings	Lam.	Lamentations	Hag.	Haggai
1–2 Chron.	1–2 Chronicles	Ezek.	Ezekiel	Zech.	Zechariah
Ezra	Ezra	Dan.	Daniel	Mal.	Malachi

New Testament

Matt.	Matthew	1–2 Thess.	1–2 Thessalonians
Mark	Mark	1–2 Tim.	1–2 Timothy
Luke	Luke	Titus	Titus
John	John	Philem.	Philemon
Acts	Acts	Heb.	Hebrews
Rom.	Romans	James	James
1–2 Cor.	1–2 Corinthians	1–2 Pet.	1–2 Peter
Gal.	Galatians	1–3 John	1–3 John
Eph.	Ephesians	Jude	Jude
Phil.	Philippians	Rev.	Revelation
Col.	Colossians		

Part 1

PAUL'S LIFE

ONE

Background and Biography

Paul once wrote that "when the fulness of the time was come, God sent forth his Son" (Gal. 4:4 KJV). This means that God waited until the time was suitable before providing the Jews with their Messiah. Also included within the scope of God's purposes was the selection of a man who would be chiefly responsible for carrying out the postresurrection commission of Jesus to the Twelve by proclaiming the fulfillment of the promise to Abraham. That man was Paul of Tarsus (Gal. 1:15–16); the promise was that God would bless all the nations (Gentiles) through Abraham's seed, the Jews (Gen. 12:1–4);[1] the commission was that the apostles should "teach all nations" (Gentiles as well as Jews) about the resurrected Lord (Matt. 28:18–20 KJV).

"I Am a Jew, from Tarsus in Cilicia" (Acts 21:39)

Paul was born and spent his earliest years in the Diaspora, the dispersion of the Jews outside the borders of the Holy Land. He once remarked to a Roman tribune that he was "a Jew, from Tarsus in Cilicia, a citizen of no ordinary city" (Acts 21:39 NIV). The population of Tarsus has been estimated at a half-million.[2] The city lay on the Cydnus River, about ten miles north of the

---

1. This gospel (that the Gentiles would receive the blessing of God) was preached even to Abraham (Gal. 3:8).
2. Hubert Rex Johnson, *Who Then Is Paul?* (Lanham, Md.: University Press of America, 1981), 11.

Photo 1.1. Cydnus River in Tarsus

southeastern coast of Turkey (ancient Asia Minor). Tarsus impresses one with the beauty of its geography, lying in rolling hills covered with wheat fields rippling in the afternoon breeze. Near the city is an abundantly flowing river that forms delightful miniature waterfalls between verdant shores. The locals can be seen washing their carts in the midst of its shallows, while one's imagination fancies a young Paul splashing knee-deep in water, unable to hide a childish expression of delight.

A great international highway, connecting the west coast of Asia Minor to Syria-Palestine and points east, ran through Tarsus and on to the north through the narrow Gates of Issus in the Taurus Mountains. Tarsus was the most important city of Cilicia, which was made a province under Pompey in 67 B.C. The province consisted of a western mountainous portion, Cilicia Tracheia ("Rough Cilicia"), and an eastern level portion, Cilicia Pedias ("Flat Cilicia"). Syria, the large country to the east, became a Roman province in 64 B.C. under Pompey, and about 25 B.C., for administrative purposes, it was joined with Cilicia's eastern portion, which included Tarsus; so throughout Paul's lifetime, Tarsus was a part of Syria-Cilicia. Paul once spoke of going into "the regions of Syria and Cilicia" after a visit to Jerusalem (Gal. 1:21 KJV). It was not until A.D. 72 that eastern Cilicia was detached from Syria and rejoined to western Cilicia, thus forming the province of Cilicia.

Tarsus was indeed "no ordinary city." When Julius Caesar visited the city in 47 B.C., the residents called it Juliopolis (the city of Julius) in his honor.

After defeating Brutus and Cassius, leaders in the assassination of Caesar, Mark Antony spent time in Tarsus, where on one memorable occasion in 41 B.C., he had a rendezvous with Cleopatra, the Egyptian queen, who was rowed up the Cydnus River dressed as the goddess Aphrodite.

Tarsus was an important educational center in the ancient world. Strabo, a first-century geographer, wrote that its citizens were fervent in the pursuit of culture and that most of its university students were from Tarsus itself, unlike Athens and Alexandria, which drew students from throughout the empire.[3] One may assume from this that there was not as much cross-cultural activity in Tarsus as in these other university cities. Interestingly, Strabo noted that the students who left Tarsus to complete their education in other cities rarely returned to live there. Nevertheless, the city did provide Paul with a rich educational milieu in his early years. His later writings are saturated with images from the Greco-Roman world in which he lived. These images play an important role in Paul's communication and interaction in his Jewish-Gentile environment.[4]

"I Was Born a Citizen" (Acts 22:28)

The prosperity of Tarsus was partially based on the manufacture of a material woven from goat hair and known as cilicium, the name given to the province. It was used at times in the making of tents, though not exclusively so. Paul was a tentmaker. However, the term "tentmaker" (σκηνοποιός, skēnopoios) more likely means "leatherworker" than tentmaker, and in Paul's day most tents were made of leather.[5] We are probably unjustified in assuming that he was a weaver of tent cloth from either goat hair or linen, and the relation of his profession to the cilicium industry of Cilicia is coincidental.[6]

We do not know how Paul's family became Roman citizens, but it is not unreasonable to postulate that Paul's grandfather and/or great-grandfather

3. *Geogr.* 14.5.12ff.

4. David Williams discusses a wide variety of Paul's metaphors that are based on architecture, law, commerce, health care, and education in his book *Paul's Metaphors: Their Context and Character* (Peabody, Mass.: Hendrickson, 1999).

5. Shimon Applebaum, "The Social and Economic Status of the Jews in the Diaspora," in *The Jewish People in the First Century: Historical Geography, Political History, Social, Cultural, and Religious Life, and Institutions,* ed. S. Safrai and M. Stern, Compendia rerum Iudaicarum ad Novum Testamentum, section 1 (Assen: Van Gorcum, 1974–76), 2:716–17; R. F. Hock, *The Social Context of Paul's Ministry: Tentmaking and Apostleship* (Philadelphia: Fortress, 1980), 21, and sources cited on p. 73 n. 16.

6. See Brian Rapske's arguments against Paul as either a weaver of goat hair, a worker of linen, or a tanner of hides. The latter profession was socially stigmatized. He argues that Paul, instead, worked with leather that had already been processed (*The Book of Acts and Paul in Roman Custody,* BAFCS 3 [Grand Rapids: Eerdmans, 1994], 106–7).

was also a tentmaker at the time Pompey (67–64 B.C.), Julius Caesar (47 B.C.), or Mark Antony (41 B.C.) was in the area and visited Tarsus. Paul's ancestor could well have provided one of them with tents for the Roman army, a service that might have been rewarded by a grant of citizenship.[7] The Roman franchise of citizenship could be obtained in several ways: (1) by being born a citizen, (2) by completion of military service, (3) by reward, (4) by *en bloc* grant, or (5) for financial considerations.[8] Paul was born a citizen (Acts 22:28; cf. 22:3).

It has been suggested that Paul's ancestors were a part of a Jewish colony that had been settled here by the Seleucid kings of Antioch of Syria in order to strengthen their hold on Tarsus, which Antiochus IV (175–164 B.C.) renamed Antiocheia.[9] Alternately, it has been argued that the close connection between Paul's family and the land of Judea makes descent from an old Diaspora family improbable.[10]

Whatever their origin,[11] it is clear that Paul's father was a Roman citizen, because Paul was "born a citizen" (Acts 22:27–28).[12] Even though Cilicia-Syria had been placed under Roman administration, citizenship was not automatically conferred on its inhabitants. Even those who were granted citizenship for special service to Rome, a privilege field commanders could bestow, had to own property worth five hundred drachmae (about seventy-five dollars). Luke affirms that Paul was not only a Roman citizen but also a citizen of Tarsus (Acts 21:39). According to Dio Chrysostom,[13] in the time of the empire citizenship in Tarsus could be bought for this same amount of money, which was the income of an ordinary day laborer for two years.[14] This appears to have been the policy since the time of Augustus.

Paul used his Roman citizenship to his advantage on three occasions. The first of these was in Philippi, a city in Macedonia, where he and Silas were imprisoned unjustly (Acts 16:37). Why he allowed himself to be beaten without revealing his citizenship, which would have prevented it, we do not know. Perhaps it was be-

---

7. F. F. Bruce, *Paul: Apostle of the Heart Set Free* (Grand Rapids: Eerdmans, 1977), 37.

8. Rapske, *Paul in Roman Custody*, 86.

9. Sir William Ramsay, *St. Paul the Traveller and the Roman Citizen* (London: Hodder and Stoughton, 1908), 32.

10. Martin Hengel, *The Pre-Christian Paul* (London: SCM Press; Philadelphia: Trinity Press International, 1991), 5.

11. For answers to objections leveled at Paul's citizenship, see Simon Légasse, "Paul's Pre-Christian Career according to Acts," in *The Book of Acts in Its Palestinian Setting*, ed. Richard Bauckham, BAFCS 4 (Grand Rapids: Eerdmans, 1995), 369ff.

12. A. N. Sherwin-White raises the question posed by Mommsen as to whether the phrase ἐγὼ δὲ καὶ γεγέννημαι ("I was born") means "born" or "became." In the latter case, the words meant that "Paul's father became a citizen when Paul was a child, and that Paul became a Roman as his father's legitimate son, which was the custom." He thinks this is "less probable than the more obvious rendering: 'I was born a citizen'" (*Roman Society and Roman Law in the New Testament* [Oxford: Oxford University Press, 1963; reprint, Grand Rapids: Baker, 1978], 151).

13. *Discourses* 34.21–23 (Second Tarsic Discourse).

14. Hengel, *Pre-Christian Paul*, 98 n. 43.

cause it would have been for purely personal reasons. Furthermore, Paul was trying to maintain his Jewish identity as he began his work in the synagogues. But when his very presence and ministry in Philippi were threatened by an air of disreputability, he used his citizenship to correct the impression.

The second occasion was in Jerusalem after the completion of his third missionary journey (Acts 22:25–29). The Roman officer who delivered Paul from a Jewish mob in the Court of the Gentiles at the temple had mistaken him first for an Egyptian and subsequently for a Hebrew-speaking Diaspora Jew whom he had no reason to believe was a citizen of Rome. Paul made his citizenship known as he was being prepared to receive a whipping and thus avoided the "interrogation" that would have cast an air of disrepute over him and his work.

The final occasion when Paul used his citizenship was at Caesarea, about two years later (Acts 24:27), when he stood before Festus and, by appealing to Caesar, thwarted the new Roman procurator's plans to return Paul to the Jews in Jerusalem (Acts 25:11). This appeal, which guaranteed Paul's right to have a hearing before the emperor, was one of the privileges of Roman citizenship and was not enjoyed by other inhabitants of the empire.

A citizen's rights were guaranteed by the Julian law on the use of public force, a law known as *lex Julia de vi publica*.[15] The law has been dated to the emperor Augustus in 23 B.C.[16] These rights included a fair public trial for a citizen who had been accused of a crime, protection against execution without legal formalities being conducted, and exemption from certain ignominious forms of punishment, such as crucifixion. The law would not allow any official to kill, scourge, chain, or torture a Roman citizen, or even to sentence him ("in the face of an appeal") or prevent him from going to Rome to make his appeal there within a specified time frame. From the early second century A.D., we have a piece of correspondence from Pliny, a governor of the Roman province of Bithynia in northern Asia Minor, to the Emperor Trajan, which states that he sent citizens who were accused of a crime directly to Rome.[17] Thus, by the second century, an appeal was not even required; accusations (at least some types of them) automatically entitled one to appear in Rome.

"Saul, Who Is Also Called Paul" (Acts 13:9)

It is often mistakenly asserted that the missionary changed his name from the Hebrew Saul to the Greek Paul shortly after his conversion. In reality, Paul

15. Sherwin-White, *Roman Society and Roman Law*, 57f.

16. A. H. M. Jones, *Studies in Roman Government and Law* (Oxford: Oxford University Press, 1960), 97ff.

17. *Ep. Tra.* 96. See the document in J. C. Ayer, *A Sourcebook for Ancient Church History* (New York: Scribners, 1941), 20ff.; H. Bettenson, *Documents of the Christian Church*, 2d ed. (London: Oxford University Press, 1963), 3–6.

had both names from birth, because it was required of Roman citizens that they be registered with the *tria nomina,* the three names that consisted of a *praenomen* (forename), a *nomen gentile* (family name), and a *cognomen* (given or additional name). We only know Paul's Roman *cognomen.* If we knew his family name, we might learn something more about the source of his citizenship, because a new citizen frequently took his patron's forename and family name.[18] For example, the Roman tribune Claudius Lysias, who rescued Paul from the temple mob, had taken the name of the Claudian family when he purchased his citizenship (Acts 21:31; 22:26, 30; 23:26). The Jewish general and historian Flavius Josephus took the name of the Flavian family to which Vespasian belonged. In his autobiography, Josephus wrote that when he arrived in Rome with Titus, the Emperor Vespasian "honored me with the privilege of Roman citizenship."[19] He was also given a pension, which Vespasian, whom Suetonius called "a devoted patron of the arts," customarily paid some teachers and other practitioners of the arts.[20]

Even though Jews in the empire who were Roman citizens would have been required to register that citizenship with three names for official records, they would not have been expected to use those names in all circumstances, especially in situations where the importance of ethnic identity transcended that of political affiliation. For example, the five hundred Jewish funerary inscriptions found in Rome, 10 percent of which indicate Roman citizenship, do not contain even one with the *tria nomina* on it.[21]

Thus, from the ninth day of his birth,[22] Paul would have had the Latin name *Paullus* ("the little"), which appears in the New Testament in the Greek form *Paulos* (Παῦλος, *paulos*). Since it was given to him at birth, the name is no indication of Paul's stature. Names like Little or Small (German *Klein;* French *Petit*), do not necessarily have anatomical significance, just as names like Brown, Black, and White carry no racial connotations. Although an older child might be affectionately called "little one," Paul's name was chosen at birth and perhaps selected because it sounded like Saul, his Hebrew name, which was worn by the first king of Israel, who, like Paul, was a member of the tribe of Benjamin (Rom. 11:1; Phil. 3:5). Paul is not the Roman or Greek form of the name Saul. They are two entirely different names. The name Saul, which derives from the Hebrew word *sha'al* ("to ask"), is spelled in various ways in the Bible:

18. William Smith, ed., *Dictionary of Greek and Roman Antiquities* (London: John Murray, 1878), 802.

19. *Life* 423.

20. *Vesp.* 17–18.

21. G. Fuks, "Where Have All the Freedmen Gone? On an Anomaly in the Jewish Grave Inscriptions from Rome," *Journal of Jewish Studies* 36 (1985): 25–32.

22. Smith, ed., *Dictionary of Greek and Roman Antiquities,* 801. Girls were named on the eighth day.

Saoul (Σαούλ)—in the Septuagint and in the New Testament only in the conversion accounts of Acts (Acts 9:4, 17; 22:7, 13; 26:14)[23]

Saoulos (Σαοῦλος)—in Josephus[24]

Saulos (Σαῦλος)—the most common form in the New Testament; a Hellenized form of the Hebrew *Sha'ul* (Acts 7:58; 8:1, 3; 9:1, 8, 11, 22, 24; 11:25, 30; 12:25; 13:1, 2, 7, 9; 22:7 in Codex D; 26:14).

The name Paul (Παῦλος, *Paulos*) in Latin (*Paulus*, or variantly *Pallus*, *Polus*, and *Pollus*) is simply a Roman *cognomen*, an extra name, like modern middle names. It was a common name at the time, one which, for example, was worn by a family of the gens Aemilia, two well-known members of which are cited in *Cassell's Latin Dictionary*.[25] Paul wore both names, Paul and Saul, from birth and no doubt utilized them selectively in various cultural settings. During his sojourn among Gentiles, he was probably called Paul, in either Greek or Latin, while his Jewish colleagues and brothers in Jerusalem would have known him as Saul. His letters, written to churches that were predominately composed of Gentiles, use the name Paul. Its first occurrence in the Book of Acts is when Paul confronts a Roman proconsul on Cyprus who is also named Paul (Sergius Paulus, Acts 13:7).[26] Luke, at this time, refers to him as "Saul, who is also called Paul" (Acts 13:9).

It is interesting that no Roman mentioned in the New Testament is referred to by all three of his names. And not everyone who wore a Roman name was a Roman. Some New Testament characters are referred to by their Roman forenames (*praenomina*, e.g., Gaius, Lucius, Titus) and some by their extra names (*cognomina*, e.g., Aquila, Crispus, Justus Rufus). However, we cannot know whether people were Romans unless the context determines this or their Roman citizenship is otherwise known (e.g., in the cases of the *cognomina* of Agrippa, Felix, Festus, Gallio). Pontius Pilate is referred to by his *cognomen* and *nomen*. One of Paul's Jewish Christian companions, Silvanus, wore a Roman *cognomen* (2 Cor. 1:19; 1 Thess. 1:1; 2 Thess. 1:1) but is better known in Acts only by his Greek name "Silas" (Acts 15–18). We know he was a Roman citizen, not because he had a Roman *cognomen*, but because Paul called him a Roman citizen (Acts 16:37).

23. The Chester Beatty manuscript of the Gospels and Acts ($\mathfrak{P}^{45}$) uses it throughout Acts.

24. *Ant.* 6.74.

25. L. Aemilius Paulus, a Roman military commander, and L. Aemilius Paulus Macedonicus, his son, who conquered Perseus, King of Macedonia (*Cassell's Latin Dictionary*, rev. J. R. V. Marchant and J. F. Charles [London and New York: Cassell, n.d.], 396).

26. See further, Colin Hemer, "The Name of Paul," *TynBul* 36 (1985): 179–83; F. C. Synge, "Acts 13.9: 'Saul Who Is Also Paul,'" *Theology* 63 (1960): 199–200. See a discussion of the evidence for possibly identifying this man with one of the same name found in three inscriptions (Alanna Nobbs, "Cyprus," in *The Book of Acts in Its Graeco-Roman Setting*, ed. David W. J. Gill and Conrad Gempf, BAFCS 2 [Grand Rapids: Eerdmans, 1994], 282–89).

Only twice in the New Testament are citizens referred to by their *nomina* (the centurions Cornelius, Acts 10:1ff., and Julius, Acts 27:1, 3), a practice carried over into the empire from the old Republican period of Roman history and practiced only in the military during the Julio-Claudian period.[27]

A study on the name of Paul says that "in Paul's case, as in that of enfranchised provincials generally, the *cognomen* will have been his ordinary personal name in the Gentile world, his formal designation by *praenomen, nomen,* father's *praenomen,* Roman tribe and *cognomen* being reserved for official documents and remaining unknown to us."[28] Since the possibilities of Paul's family having been granted Roman citizenship probably lie in the generosity of Pompey, Julius Caesar, or Mark Antony, as we noted above, Paul's Roman name could possibly have been Gnaeus Pompeius Paulus, Gaius Julius Paulus, or Marcus Antonius Paulus.[29] The second of these might be preferred on the basis of an inscription found at Naples,[30] which reads in full translation:

> To the spirits of the dead. L. Antonius Leo, also called Neon, son of Zoilus, by nation a *Cilician,* a soldier of the praetorian fleet at Misenum, from the century to the trireme "Asclepius," lived twenty seven years, served nine years. *Gaius Julius Paulus* his heir undertook the work [of his burial].[31]

This man, like Paul, was from Cilicia. Like Paul he had an extra name (*supernomen,* or *cognomen*); his was Leo, Paul's was Saul. And he had an heir whose name indicates that he or an ancestor had been enfranchised by Julius Caesar.[32]

"A Hebrew Born of Hebrews" (Phil. 3:5)

Of greater importance than his Roman citizenship was Paul's Jewish heritage. He twice mentioned that he was from the tribe of Benjamin (Rom. 11:1; Phil. 3:5), the small tribe whose territory encompassed the city of Jerusalem and bordered the northern side of the land allotted to the tribe of Judah. These two tribes remained faithful to God after the death of Solomon, when the northern ten tribes broke away and began worshiping idols (1 Kings 12). King Saul was from this tribe, and it was a matter of pride to be from Benjamin, and especially to be named after a king from this tribe. Even after the two southern tribes also fell into idolatry and were carried off into Babylonian

27. Hemer, "Name of Paul," 183.
28. Ibid.
29. Ibid., 179.
30. *CIL* 10.3377 = *Inscriptiones Latinae Selectae,* ed. H. Dessau (Zürich: Weidmann, 1997), 2839.
31. Hemer, "Name of Paul," 180.
32. Hemer says this name "may possibly have been Paul's own" (ibid., 182).

captivity, the people kept their tribal identities alive, so that the generation that came back from captivity were able to identify members of the tribe of Benjamin. Nehemiah 11:7–9 and 11:31–36 refer to the people "of Benjamin." Paul undoubtedly could trace his descent through the records preserved by these exiles.

However, early Christian writers did not always think favorably of the tribe of Benjamin. Recalling that the patriarch Jacob, on his deathbed, referred to his son Benjamin as a "ravenous wolf" (Gen. 49:27), Hippolytus related Paul's activities in persecuting the church to this statement (prophecy?) by Jacob.[33]

Defending the genuineness of his Jewish ancestry against his critics at Corinth, Paul wrote: "Are they Hebrews? So am I. Are they Israelites? So am I. Are they descendants of Abraham? So am I" (2 Cor. 11:22). Similarly, he wrote to the Philippians that he was "circumcised on the eighth day, of the people of Israel, of the tribe of Benjamin, a Hebrew born of Hebrews" (Phil. 3:5). The term *Hebrew* in this context denotes a Jew who maintained the traditional Hebrew culture rather than succumbing to the temptations of Diaspora hellenization. Such a person, who probably emigrated from Israel to the Diaspora (or was a descendant of one who did), attended a synagogue where Aramaic, rather than Greek, was spoken and resisted an incursion of Greco-Roman culture into his religion and way of life. An inscription in stone mentioning a "Synagogue of the Hebrews" was found in Corinth in 1898[34] and probably dates no earlier than the second century A.D.[35]

By contrast, a Hellenist was a Jew who embraced the Greco-Roman culture and was thus hellenized (ἑλληνίζω, i.e., "to make Greek"). Philo, a Jewish author who was contemporary with Jesus and called himself a Hellenistic Jew, used the term *Hebrew* to denote one who spoke "Hebrew" (i.e., Aramaic).[36] The two words are placed in juxtaposition in Acts 6:1, where Luke says the Hellenists complained against the Hebrews because their widows were being neglected.[37] One might assume that these Hellenists were from the Diaspora, perhaps converted to Christ and still in Jerusalem after Passover and Pentecost (cf. Acts 2:5–11). The Gospel of John seems to call such Jews "Greeks" (John 12:20). On the other hand, they may well have been residents of Syria-Palestine who had broken with traditional orthodoxy and embraced Greco-Roman ways.

33. Hippolytus, *De benedictionibus Isaaci et Jacobi* at Genesis 49:27.

34. It was published by Benjamin Powell, "Greek Inscriptions from Corinth," *AJA,* 2d series (1903): 60–61.

35. John Kent, *Corinth: Results of Excavations Conducted by the American School of Classical Studies at Athens* (Cambridge, Mass.: Harvard University Press, 1929–), 8.1:79.

36. *Dreams* 2.250; *Abraham* 28.

37. See further, Henry J. Cadbury, "The Hellenists," in *The Acts of the Apostles,* ed. F. J. Foakes-Jackson and Kirsopp Lake, The Beginnings of Christianity, part 1 (London: Macmillan, 1920–33), 5:59–73.

Jerome maintained that Paul's family originated in Gischala of Galilee[38] before moving to the Diaspora. The site is now known as Gush Halav, and its synagogue has been excavated by Eric Meyers and James Strange, with stratum V dating to the Early Roman Period (50 B.C. to A.D. 135).[39]

Paul Went to the Synagogue As Was His Custom (Acts 17:2)

The synagogue was the "religious, cultural and social center of the Jewish community in every settlement of the Roman and Byzantine Period."[40] Although several have been found in the Diaspora from the Byzantine period, only a couple date to the time of Paul.[41] More than one hundred have been found in Israel since 1905, over half of which are in Galilee and the Golan Heights. More than fifty of these one hundred have a discernable plan that is still visible, and no two of them are identical in size or interior plan.

The number constructed was determined by the size of the Jewish population, and large cities often had many synagogues. The Talmud reported, perhaps exaggerating, that there were "four hundred and eighty synagogues in Jerusalem . . . and Vespasian destroyed them all."[42] It has been noted that there were 365 synagogues in Jerusalem in the late Second Temple period, which includes the time of Paul.[43] By the third and fourth centuries, Tiberias was reported to have had 13 synagogues, Sepphoris 18, and Rome 11.[44]

Remains of synagogues in Israel dated prior to the third century A.D. are sparse. Perhaps this is because the economy of the Jewish population was so damaged in

38. *Vir. ill.* 5.

39. E. M. Meyers, "Excavations at Gush Halav in Upper Galilee," in *Ancient Synagogues Revealed,* ed. Lee Levine (Jerusalem: Israel Exploration Society, 1981), 75–77.

40. A. Kloner, "Ancient Synagogues in Israel: An Archaeological Survey," in *Ancient Synagogues Revealed,* ed. Levine, 11.

41. Two from the time of Paul have been found at Ostia and Delos. See Rachel Hachlili, "Diaspora Synagogues," *ABD,* 6:260–63. See also John McRay, *Archaeology and the New Testament* (Grand Rapids: Baker, 1991), 65–72; A. T. Kraabel, "Unity and Diversity among Diaspora Synagogues," in *The Synagogue in Late Antiquity,* ed. Lee Levine (Philadelphia: ASOR, 1987), 49–60; idem, "The Diaspora Synagogue: Archaeological and Epigraphic Evidence since Sukenik," *ANRW,* 2.19.1:477–510; G. Foerster, "A Survey of Ancient Diaspora Synagogues," in *Ancient Synagogues Revealed,* ed. Levine, 164–71; E. Meyers, "The Cultural Setting of Galilee: The Case of Regionalism and Early Judaism," *ANRW,* 2.19.1:686–702; see also articles on individual Diaspora synagogues in Levine, ed., *Ancient Synagogues Revealed;* Geoffrey Wigoder, *The Story of the Synagogue: A Diaspora Museum Book* (San Francisco: Harper and Row, 1986).

42. Jerusalem (Palestinian) Talmud, *Megillah* 3.1.73d.

43. J. Wilkinson, "Christian Pilgrims in Jerusalem during the Byzantine Period," *PEQ* 108 (1976): 76–77.

44. Lee Levine, "Ancient Synagogues—A Historical Introduction," in *Ancient Synagogues Revealed,* 4.

the first and second revolts (A.D. 70–135) that it took a very long time to recover and build the kind of synagogues whose remains we are now excavating.

The term συναγωγή (*synagōgē,* synagogue) originally referred to a gathering of people, as well as a building or institution.[45] Therefore, the New Testament and other early literature are not always clear as to which is meant. Archaeological excavations, however, are providing important information about how early the Jews constructed buildings for use as synagogues.

Most gatherings in small villages were probably held in private homes, as was undoubtedly true with early Christian assemblies. Information on the phenomena of Christian synagogues is sparse, but accumulating gradually.[46]

Clearly, a building used as a synagogue before A.D. 70 is evidenced by a stone inscription in Greek found in Jerusalem, which states that the building was constructed specifically for synagogue use:

> Theodotus, son of Vettenos, priest and ruler of the synagogue, son of a ruler of the synagogue, grandson of the ruler of a synagogue, built the synagogue for the reading of the Law and for the teaching of the commandments; furthermore, the hospice and the chambers, and the water installation for lodging of needy strangers. The foundation stone thereof had been laid by his fathers, and the elders, and Simonides.[47]

The water installation referred to is the *miqveh,* which was a pair of pools used for religious ritual washings.[48] Such pools have been found adjacent to first-century synagogues at Herodium and Masada. The synagogue, however, chiefly functioned in the first century as a place for prayer and the reading and study of the Torah. A common designation for a synagogue at this time was "a prayer place" (Acts 16:16; Josephus, *Life* 280–93).

We know a good deal about synagogues of the fourth century and later, but there is still little archaeological evidence about synagogues of the New Testament period.[49] The ones found in Israel at Gamla, Jericho, Herodium, Masada, Capernaum, and Magdala constitute our best examples. There is no uniformity of construction discernable in any of these as to interior layout. They all had main prayer halls with benches against one or more of the walls to seat the participants. Some had preserved portions of a *bema,* or platform, on

45. Lee Levine, "The Second Temple Synagogue: The Formative Years," in *The Synagogue in Late Antiquity,* ed. Lee Levine (Philadelphia: American Schools of Oriental Research, 1987), 9.

46. E. W. Saunders, "Christian Synagogues and Jewish Christianity in Galilee," *Explor* 3 (1977): 70–78.

47. Adolf Deissmann, *Light from the Ancient East,* English translation from the 4th German ed. (New York: George H. Doran, 1927), 439–41; Kloner, "Ancient Synagogues in Israel," 11.

48. William Sanford LaSor, "Discovering What Jewish Miqva'ot Can Tell Us about Christian Baptism," *BAR* 13.1 (Jan./Feb. 1987): 58.

49. John McRay, "The Place of Prayer: What Exactly Took Place in a Synagogue Service?" *Christian History* 17.3, issue 59 (1998), 24–25.

which the ark of the covenant containing the sacred scrolls stood and on which the speaker stood or sat. Jesus sat to teach after reading from a scroll in Nazareth (Luke 4:20). The "best seats in the synagogues" (Matt. 23:6) were undoubtedly those nearest the speaker. One special seat, found in excavations of synagogues at Delos and Chorazin,[50] was made of stone and had carved inscriptions on it. This seat may have been the point of reference by Jesus in Matthew 23:2, when he spoke of "Moses' Seat."[51] Most, if not all, were renovated buildings that had previously served a different function.

By the fourth century these synagogues were aesthetically appealing in their generous use of Greek architectural decoration.[52] Some had mosaic floors containing impressive works of art such as pictures of the Torah ark, a zodiac, and figures, both human and animal.[53] On the other hand, synagogues in upper Galilee were more conservatively done, using menorahs, eagles, and other simple elements of decoration that rarely included colored mosaics.[54]

Many of the numerous synagogues uncovered in Galilee and Judea[55] contain inscriptions in mosaic floors that shed considerable light on the comparative use of Greek and Hebrew in these communities. We now have about 125 Greek inscriptions from synagogues in the Mediterranean area, approximately 50 of which are from Palestine. There are about 110 Aramaic and Hebrew synagogue inscriptions known today, most of which were found in the area extending from upper Galilee and the Golan Heights in the north to Beersheba in the south.[56] Some synagogues have inscriptions in more than one language. In lower Galilee about 40 percent of the synagogue inscriptions are in Greek, 40 percent are in Hebrew, and 50 percent are in Aramaic. In upper Galilee, few of the inscriptions are in Greek, about 40 percent are in Hebrew, and 66 percent are in Aramaic.[57] Some of these inscriptions are repeated in more than one language; thus the totals exceed 100 percent.

Diaspora synagogues do not manifest this same degree of linguistic diversity, especially regarding the use of Aramaic. Considerable work is being done now among these synagogues, and the picture will gradually become clearer.[58] In the meantime, it is safe to postulate that Paul, as a "Hebrew born of Hebrews,"

50. For pictures of these, see Levine, ed., *Ancient Synagogues Revealed,* 135 and 166.

51. See Jack Finegan, *ANT:LJ,* 97.

52. Some examples are Beth Shearim, Capernaum, and Chorazin.

53. For example, Beth Shan, Beth Alpha, Hammath-Tiberias, Eshtemoa, Susiya, and Gaza.

54. Eric Meyers, "Galilean Regionalism as a Factor in Historical Reconstruction," *BASOR* 221 (February 1976): 99.

55. See the articles on various Galilean synagogues in Levine, ed., *Ancient Synagogues Revealed.* See also Hershel Shanks, *Judaism in Stone: The Archaeology of Ancient Synagogues* (San Francisco: Harper and Row, 1979). On Judean and Galilean synagogues, see the several articles in *Ancient Synagogues Revealed.*

56. J. Naveh, "Ancient Synagogue Inscriptions," in *Ancient Synagogues Revealed,* 133.

57. Meyers, "Galilean Regionalism," 97.

58. See sources cited in note 41.

probably spent his earliest years in an Aramaic-speaking synagogue in the midst of a Greek-speaking university city of the Diaspora. In Palestine, the pattern revealed from excavations indicates that Aramaic was used more widely in the mountains of northern and northeastern Galilee in rather isolated communities, whereas Greek predominates in inscriptions of synagogues in the major valleys and on trade routes where hellenization and commercial interests were greater. Except for several inscriptions and one ostracon, all the Aramaic texts dated between 150 B.C. and A.D. 70 come from Qumran.[59] It should be noted that Paul used Aramaic in addressing a Jerusalem audience in the temple's Court of the Gentiles (Acts 21:40; 22:2) and was addressed in Aramaic by the divine voice on the road to Damascus (Acts 26:14). This may indicate that his mother tongue was Aramaic. Aramaic was the language most commonly spoken in Palestine during the New Testament period.[60]

"A Young Man Named Saul" (Acts 7:58)

Paul was probably born around the time of the birth of Jesus.[61] Evidence of this is found in the fact that he is called a "young man" (νεανίας, *neanias,* Acts 7:58) at the time of the death of Stephen and shortly before Paul's conversion. However, we cannot be certain as to the precise age indicated by that word. An inscription in which the age groups of those who played in the gymnasium are categorized has been found in excavations in Beroea, Greece. Beroea was a city in Macedonia visited by Paul in Acts 17:10. One of the groups is designated by this same word, *neaniskoi,* and includes those aged eighteen to twenty-two.[62] However, other ancient sources indicate that the age range suggested by this word includes anyone from twenty-four to forty years of age.[63]

59. J. Murphy-O'Connor, "Qumran and the New Testament," in *The New Testament and Its Modern Interpreters,* ed. Eldon J. Epp and George W. MacRae (Philadelphia: Fortress; Atlanta: Scholars Press, 1989), 55.

60. J. A. Fitzmyer, "The Languages of Palestine in the First Century A.D.," *CBQ* 32 (1970): 501–31. Also printed in Fitzmyer, *A Wandering Aramaean: Collected Aramaic Essays,* Society of Biblical Literature Monograph Series 25 (Missoula, Mont.: Scholars Press, 1979), 29–56.

61. Most chronologies of Paul date his birth just prior to that of Jesus, at the same time, or shortly thereafter.

62. The two other categories of participants include (1) *paides,* up to age fifteen, and (2) *epheboi,* ages fifteen to seventeen. The inscription has been published by J. M. R. Cormack under the title "The Gymnasiarchal Law of Beroea," in *Ancient Macedonia II: Papers Read at the Second International Symposium Held in Thessaloniki,* Institute for Balkan Studies 155 (n.p.: Institute for Balkan Studies, 1977), 139–49; Jeanne and Louis Robert, *Bulletin Epigraphique* 9 (1978): 430ff.

63. BAGD, 534.

If Paul was a member of the Sanhedrin when Stephen was killed, he must have met the minimum age requirements for membership in that body. The Babylonian Talmud gives the minimum age as forty for the ordination of a rabbi.[64] Paul was, of course, a rabbi trained by Gamaliel in Jerusalem. This might suggest that Paul was at least forty, but we cannot assume this without further confirmation that the Talmud, written several hundred years later, preserves accurate information on conditions prevailing in the first century. I will say more about the Sanhedrin question later.

Several years before Paul's death, which is attested in early Christian literary sources as occurring in Rome during the reign of Nero (thus before A.D. 68, when Nero died),[65] he referred to himself as a presbyter (πρεσβύτης, *presbytēs,* Philem. 9). This usually means an "older person"[66] above fifty years of age,[67] but it is taken by many to be merely an alternative spelling of *presbeutēs* (πρεσβεύτης), which means "ambassador" and is so translated in the NEB, TEV, and RSV.

The general pattern of Paul's life can be imagined from what was traditional among Jews of his time and later. While it is not possible to reconstruct every aspect of Jewish life in the first century from later talmudic sources, a trap that writers often fall into,[68] we can well imagine that the basic lifestyle changed little across the centuries among a people who desperately tried to preserve it unchanged. A rabbi at the end of the second century said the following of a Jewish boy: "At five years old he comes to the reading of the Scripture, at ten to the Mishnah, at thirteen, to the practice of the commandments [Ten Commandments], at fifteen to the Talmud, at eighteen to marriage, at twenty to pursuing a calling."[69]

In his earliest years at home, Paul would have learned to recite the Shema (Deut. 6:4–9). From the age of five, he would have begun memorizing at least

64. *b. Sotah* 22b. See Hermann L. Strack and Paul Billerbeck, *Kommentar zum Neuen Testament aus Talmud und Midrasch,* 6 vols. (Munich: Beck, 1922–61), 2:647–61.

65. Eusebius, *Hist. eccl.* 2.25.5 ("Nero . . . in his time Paul was beheaded in Rome itself, and . . . Peter likewise was crucified. . . ."); *Acts of Paul,* "Martyrdom," 10.4, in *Apocryphal New Testament,* trans. M. R. James (Oxford: Clarendon, 1955), 295; etc. See further on Paul's place of death in chapter 8 on the voyage to Rome.

66. As in the case of the adjective used in Titus 1:5 and 1 Peter 5:1. Ronald Hock argues for the translation "old man" in "A Support for His Old Age: Paul's Plea on Behalf of Onesimus," in *The Social World of the First Christians: Essays in Honor of Wayne A. Meeks,* ed. L. Michael White and O. Larry Yarbrough (Minneapolis: Fortress, 1995), 67–81.

67. BAGD, 700.

68. See Anthony Saldarini, "Judaism and the New Testament," in *The New Testament and Its Modern Interpreters,* ed. Epp and MacRae, 27ff.

69. Rabbi Judah b. Tema in *m. Avot* 5.21. See Herbert Danby, trans., *The Mishnah* (Oxford: Oxford University Press, 1933), 458. He also added that a Jewish boy is fit "at thirty for authority, at forty for discernment, at fifty for counsel, at sixty for to be an elder, at seventy for grey hairs, at eighty for special strength, at ninety for bowed back, and at a hundred a man is as one that has [already] died and passed away and ceased from the world."

parts of the Hallel (Ps. 113–18). This portion of the Psalms was used at the Feast of Passover. When he was about six, he would have been sent to synagogue to learn reading and writing. The only textbook in an orthodox synagogue school was the Scriptures, which the Jews believed contained everything one needed to know about the world, whether in the realm of science, art, religion, or law. This kind of pedagogy in ancient Jewish culture, based on the all-sufficiency of Torah, a view that is still held by orthodox Jewry, is graphically portrayed by Chaim Potok in his captivating novel *The Chosen*.[70]

At about the age of ten, Paul would have begun memorizing large portions of the "traditions of the elders," orally transmitted teachings that would not be codified until A.D. 200 by Judah ha-Nasi in Sepphoris, Galilee. These traditions were known as the Mishnah, or "oral law," which is defined as follows:

> a deposit of four centuries of Jewish religious and cultural activity in Palestine, beginning at some uncertain date (possibly during the earlier half of the second century B.C.) and ending with the close of the second century A.D. The object of this activity was the preservation, cultivation, and application to life of "the Law" (Torah), in the form in which many generations of like minded Jewish religious leaders had learnt to understand this Law.[71]

The law, it was felt, had to be supplemented by rules (*halakoth*) in order to make it applicable to the constantly changing circumstances of life. These rules were not allowed to be written down at first; they had to be transmitted by memorization. By the time of Paul, they had become so numerous and burdensome that Hillel I tried to systematize them but without success. Johanan ben Zakkai, after the fall of Jerusalem in A.D. 70, probably collected a number of these, as Hillel had done, and certainly after the Bar-Kokhba revolt in A.D. 132–35, great efforts must have been made to gather and codify these traditions. However, as noted above, it was not completed until about A.D. 200 by Judah ha-Nasi.

At the age of twelve or thirteen, Paul would have been given the rite of bar mitzvah (son of the commandment) or its ancient counterpart by the elders of the synagogue. This rite of passage for a Jewish young man, also practiced in Reform Judaism today for young women (bat mitzvah), was the means by which Paul would have been declared an adult. This qualified him to be one of the minyan of ten required to constitute a synagogue and made him accountable as an adult for the full penalty of breaking the commandments. This may have been the occasion to which he referred in Romans 7:9, where he wrote that the law "came" into his life with disastrous results for his own perception of sin. "When the commandment came, sin revived and I died,"

---

70. Chaim Potok, *The Chosen* (Greenwich, Conn.: Fawcett, 1967). See also the sequel, *The Promise* (New York: Fawcett Crest, 1969).
71. Danby, *Mishnah,* xiii.

he wrote, probably meaning that when he committed sin after this event, he found himself transgressing a specific commandment of God that now applied to him with full force.

At this transition point in his life, a young modern Jewish male begins to wear *tefillin* (the Hebrew word *tefillah* means prayer), or phylacteries, during morning prayers on weekdays. They are not worn on Sabbaths or festival days,[72] which are themselves reminders of God's commandments, and the extra reminder provided by the *tefillin* on weekdays is not needed during these special days. Young men may be observed putting on the *tefillin* at the Western Wall of the temple mount in Jerusalem. They consist of two small black leather boxes containing small scrolls of parchment upon which are written four biblical passages that speak about the wearing of *tefillin* (Exod. 13:1–10, 11–16; Deut. 6:4–9; 11:13–21). One of these is strapped to the left upper arm, and the other is attached to the forehead, both by long leather straps attached to the boxes.[73] How long this custom has been observed is not clear, but the practice has been attributed to "ancient times,"[74] and young Paul may well have worn these symbols, as well as the *tallit,* or prayer shawl, with *tzitzit* (fringes) on the four corners containing blue threads (Num. 15:37–41; Deut. 22:12).

The only recorded activity of Jesus during the thirty years between his birth and baptism was the occasion when, at the age of twelve, he stayed in the temple with the rabbis during the Passover and demonstrated unusual maturity. He may have experienced bar mitzvah or its ancient equivalent on this occasion (Luke 2:41–52). This is probably the reason the story was included in the Gospel of Luke.

The pedagogical procedure in Paul's synagogue probably differed little from that which I have observed in a Samaritan synagogue on the northern slopes of Mount Gerizim near the Palestinian city of Nablus. A teacher sat in front of the rather small class of students with only a book and a cane on his desk. The students recited in unison and almost in musical cadence.

At age fifteen, Paul would have begun in earnest to study the oral traditions that were later codified in the Talmud, which contained the Gemara in addition to the Mishnah. Whereas the Mishnah represented the views of the early rabbis, the Tanaaim, whose opinions cover the period from about the birth of Christ until A.D. 200,[75] the Gemara represented the views of the Amoraim, rabbis who commented on the Mishnah from about A.D. 200 to 500.[76] There was both a

---

72. Hayim Halevy Donin, *To Be a Jew: A Guide to Jewish Observance in Contemporary Life* (New York: Basic Books, 1972), 146.

73. See the pictures in ibid., 147.

74. Ibid., 144.

75. Moses Mielziner gives A.D. 10 to 220 as the time frame (*Introduction to the Talmud,* 5th ed. [New York: Bloch, 1968], 23).

76. Ibid., 54.

Jerusalem, or Palestinian, Talmud and a Babylonian Talmud, the latter more influential. Much of the study of modern rabbis is concentrated on the Talmud.

At about the age of eighteen, as we noted above, a Jewish young man, especially one who was training to be a rabbi, was expected to marry. Whether Paul married is uncertain, but he did become a rabbi. Further evidence of marriage has been found by some in his reference to casting his vote (ψῆφον, *psēphon*)[77] against early Christians when they were put to death (Acts 26:10). Casting a vote for capital punishment required membership in the Sanhedrin, and marriage may have been a prerequisite for membership. If Paul were married, his later references to his marital status, which seem to imply that he was not married, would mean that he was not married at the time he wrote. He could have been either divorced or widowed by then.

From this perspective, Paul's comment in 1 Corinthians 9:5 ("Do we not have the right to be accompanied by a wife, as the other apostles and the brothers of the Lord and Cephas?") would not mean that Paul was not married, but only that he and Barnabas did not "lead about" (περιάγειν, *periagein*) wives as did Peter and others; that is, their wives did not accompany them on their arduous journeys. And his statement in 1 Corinthains 7:7 ("I wish that all were as I myself am. But each has his own special gift from God, one of one kind and one of another") would only suggest that Paul's control of his sexual appetites was such that he felt no compulsion to either marry or remarry. And especially during the "present distress" (ἐνεστῶσαν ἀνάγκην, *enestōsan anangkēn*, 1 Cor. 7:26 KJV) that afflicted the church, Paul considered being single an advisable posture to maintain.

The case for Paul's having belonged to the Sanhedrin depends largely on what he meant when he said he "cast his vote" against Stephen (Acts 26:10). This may mean that Paul cast one of the votes for capital punishment, and since such ballots could only be given by a member of the Sanhedrin, this would necessarily imply membership and thus marriage.

On the other hand, it is possible that what Paul meant by this statement in Acts 26:10 (in his defense before Agrippa) is best understood by a parallel but more generic remark he made earlier to the crowd on the temple grounds. On that occasion, recounting the same incident, Paul said "I also was *standing by* and *approving,* and keeping the garments of those who killed him" (Acts 22:20, italics added). There is, of course, a difference between merely approving what is happening and casting an official vote for capital punishment. But the use of the Greek term ψῆφος (*psēphos,* vote) makes it more likely that the voting is official, because this is the standard term used in formal casting of ballots.[78] Two such uses occur in Josephus.[79]

77. Metal ballots used for voting in classical Greece had the words ψῆφος δημοσία, "ballot of the people," written on them.

78. See ψῆφος in BAGD, 892; and James H. Moulton and George Milligan, *The Vocabulary of the Greek New Testament* (reprint, Grand Rapids: Eerdmans, 1952), 698.

79. *Ant.* 2.163; 10.60.

"In Person He Is Unimpressive" (2 Cor. 10:10 NIV)

We cannot help but wonder about the physical appearance of the great apostle. His opponents at Corinth referred to his bodily presence as "weak" (2 Cor. 10:10). The Greek word used here (ἀσθενής, *asthenēs*) often means weak or feeble (i.e., without strength), but it also means sick or sickly, referring to bodily disability.[80] Luke uses the word in Acts to refer to a lame man God healed through Peter (Acts 4:9; compare also Acts 5:15–16). Paul's remark at the close of his letter to the Galatians ("See with what large letters I am writing to you with my own hand," Gal. 6:11) possibly indicates a physical impairment that necessitated his use of secretaries for his written correspondence. Tertius, for example, wrote the Roman letter (Rom. 16:22). Paul uses this same Greek word in Galatians 4:13 when he reminds the Galatians that it was because of a "weakness of the flesh" ("bodily ailment," RSV) that he first preached to them.

Paul also wrote to the Galatians that "you would have plucked out your eyes and given them to me" (Gal. 4:15). While this may be no more than an expression indicating the regard the Galatians had for him, Paul may have chosen this particular imagery because there was actually something wrong with his eyesight. If so, this might provide an explanation for the fact that he did not recognize Ananias as the high priest during his appearance before the Sanhedrin in Jerusalem (Acts 23:5).

Contrariwise, it has been argued that a special characteristic of Paul's personality was his practice of staring intently at people (Acts 13:9; 14:9; 23:1). "This suggests that his fixed, steady gaze was a marked feature in his personality, and one source of his influence over them that were brought into relations with him."[81] In a similar way, Peter stared intently at the heavenly vision that sent him to Cornelius (Acts 11:6), Cornelius stared at the angel who appeared to him (Acts 10:4), and Peter stared at the lame man in the temple before healing him (Acts 3:4). Stephen stared intently into heaven before his death (Acts 7:55), his audience stared intently at him while he spoke (Acts 6:15), and the synagogue congregation in Nazareth stared at Jesus as he spoke (Luke 4:20). The Greek verb used in all these instances (ἀτενίζειν, *atenizein*)[82] is also used by Paul when speaking of the Israelites' inability to stare at Moses' glowing face when he descended the mount (2 Cor. 3:7, 13). Nevertheless, one with a visual impairment could stare just as intently as one who had good vision, and perhaps even with added incentive—the desire to see more clearly.

---

80. G. Abbott-Smith, *A Manual Greek Lexicon of the New Testament* (Edinburgh: Clark, 1950), 64.

81. Ramsay, *St. Paul,* 38.

82. The word is defined by BAGD, 119, as to "look intently at something or someone."

In any case, it seems best to understand Paul's "thorn in the flesh" as some kind of physical impairment he received at the time of his revelatory experience described in 2 Corinthians 12:7.[83] There is no question that Paul was a sick man. Others have considered his problem to be a human opponent who followed Paul around and harassed him, but nothing else in his letters or Acts seems to point to the existence of such a person.

On the other hand, there is a remarkably detailed description of Paul that appears quite early in Christian literature and portrays him not as feeble, but as possessing a "good state of body." It is in the beginning part of the *Acts of Paul,* which Tertullian, writing in the late second century, said was composed shortly before his time "from love of Paul" by a presbyter of Asia who confessed to writing it and was convicted and removed from his office.[84] The editor of *The Apocryphal New Testament* calls the author of the *Acts of Paul* an "orthodox Christian" and dates the book to about A.D. 160.[85] The author of a significant work on Paul holds that the account of Paul's appearance in the book "was originally written, probably in the latter part of the first century,"[86] a viewpoint not shared by a prominent authority on early church history.[87] An eminent papyrologist cautiously remarked that "perhaps the best thing to be said for it is that it is hardly likely to have been invented."[88] To modern readers, the description does not seem flattering.

In the setting of the story, Paul arrives in Iconium, a city in central Asia Minor, where Christian people are gathered to welcome him. One of these, Onesiphorus, who may or may not be the individual named in 2 Timothy 4:19, has never seen Paul but has been given a description by which he would be able to recognize him. When Paul finally appears, he is described as follows:

> And he saw Paul coming, a man little of stature, thin-haired upon the head, crooked in the legs, of good state of body, with eyebrows joining and nose somewhat hooked, full of grace: for sometimes he appeared like a man, and sometimes he had the face of an angel.[89]

83. Other possibilities have been advocated: epilepsy (like Julius Caesar and Napoleon), Malta fever, malaria, overstrung emotions with hallucinations, and a speech impediment. For documentation see Bruce, *Paul,* 135 n. 3.

84. Tertullian, *De Baptismo,* 17.5, in *I Tertulliani Opera: Pars I,* Corpus Christianorum: Series Latina (Turnholti: Typographi Brepolis Editores Pontifici, 1954), 292. The English translation is "On Baptism," in *The Ante-Nicene Fathers,* ed. A. Roberts and J. Donaldson (Grand Rapids: Eerdmans, n.d.), 3:677.

85. James, ed., *Apocryphal New Testament,* 270.

86. Ramsay, *St. Paul,* 151.

87. Adolf Harnack, *Geschichte der altchristlichen Literatur bis Eusebius* (Leipzig: Heinrichs, 1897) 2.1:505.

88. James Hope Moulton, *From Egyptian Rubbish Heaps* (London: Charles H. Kelly, 1917), 50.

89. *Acts of Paul* 3, *The Acts of Paul and Thecla,* paragraph 2, in J. K. Elliott, *The Apocryphal New Testament* (Oxford: Clarendon, 1993), 364.

A slightly different translation appears in M. R. James's edition of *The Apocryphal New Testament:*

> And he saw Paul coming, a man small in size, bald-headed, bandy-legged, of noble mien, with eyebrows meeting and nose somewhat hooked, full of grace. Sometimes he seemed like a man, and sometimes he had the face of an angel.[90]

This description may not have seemed as unflattering to ancient readers as it does to modern ones.[91] A second-century passage from Archilochus reads: "I love not a tall general nor a straddling one, nor one proud of his hair nor one part-shaven; for me a man should be short and bowlegged to behold, set firm on his feet, full of heart." The author of the *Acts of Paul* may have used this second-century passage by Archilochus to describe Paul because he admired him.[92] Suetonius, second-century biographer of the Roman emperors, described Augustus Caesar in terms that include the following: "His *eyebrows met above the nose;* he had ears of normal size, a *Roman nose* [i.e., it was a bit long and crooked, JM], . . . his height 5 feet 7 inches . . . how *small a man* he was. . . ."[93] Another author suggests that the author of the *Acts of Paul* took his description of Paul from several early authors, including Plutarch and Philostratus, who describe the Greek hero Herakles as having a hooked nose, meeting eyebrows, and bowed legs.[94] Thus, these early descriptions of Paul were intended to be flattering and represent him as a hero. Early pictures of Paul in the catacombs and elsewhere portray him as bald, as does the *Acts of Paul.* This may reflect a current tradition rather than an assumption based on the shaving of his head at Cenchreae (Acts 18:18) and probably in Jerusalem (Acts 21:24).

"I Am a Pharisee" (Acts 23:6)

Among Paul's recorded self-descriptions, he three times calls himself a Pharisee. Before Agrippa he said, "According to the strictest party of our religion I have lived [ἔζησα, *ezēsa*] as a Pharisee" (Acts 26:5). To the church in Philippi, Paul wrote that he was "as touching the law, a Pharisee" (Phil. 3:5 KJV), meaning that his perspective of the Torah was that of a Pharisee. And before the Sanhedrin in Jerusalem, he declared, "I am [ἐγὼ εἰμί, *egō eimi*] a Pharisee" (Acts 23:6),

90. James, ed., *Apocryphal New Testament,* 273.

91. See further the discussion in E. Margaret Howe, "Interpretations of Paul in *The Acts of Paul and Thecla,*" in *Pauline Studies: Essays Presented to Professor F. F. Bruce on His 70th Birthday,* ed. Donald A. Hagner and Murray J. Harris (Exeter, England: Paternoster; Grand Rapids: Eerdmans, 1980), 33–49.

92. This is the opinion of R. M. Grant, "The Description of Paul in the *Acts of Paul and Thecla,*" *Vigiliae Christianae* 36 (1982): 1–4.

93. *Aug.* 2.79 (italics added).

94. Abraham Malherbe, "A Physical Description of Paul," *HTR* 79.1–3 (1986): 170–75.

which, stated in the present tense, affirms that he had not forsaken that affiliation, even after three missionary journeys among the Gentiles!

The Pharisees were one of three "sects of philosophy," as Josephus called them,[95] that were prevalent in Judea before and during the time of Paul. The other two were the Sadducees and the Essenes. Sadducees were pro-Roman at this time and controlled appointments to the high priesthood. They denied a physical resurrection of the human body and the existence of both angels and spirits, all of which the Pharisees affirmed (Acts 23:8).[96] Essenes were the smallest of the groups and were almost certainly the group that produced the Dead Sea Scrolls. Their teaching is described in some detail by Josephus.[97] The Pharisees, Josephus wrote, were "the most accurate interpreters of the laws, and hold the position of the leading sect."[98] Paul was thus affiliated with the largest and most influential sect of the Jewish religion at the time, one that he himself called "the strictest party of our religion" (Acts 26:5). Since Paul maintained that he remained a Pharisee even after his conversion (Acts 23:6), it is important to understand something of the background of this group and its approach to understanding the Torah.

The origins of the Pharisees are hidden in obscurity. They appear in history by name after the Maccabean revolt in the mid–second century B.C. However, their approach to the law is as old as the time of Ezra and the return from exile. Among other things, they believed that the Torah, written and oral, contained the complete law. There were not two laws but one; the oral and the written law were of complementary and equal authority. The claim was that the extracanonical traditions, called the oral law or Mishnah, were handed down from the time of Moses along with the written Torah. The Mishnah declares:

> Moses received the Law from Sinai and committed it to Joshua, and Joshua to the elders [cf. Josh. 24:31, JM], and the elders to the prophets [cf. Jer. 7:25, JM], and the prophets to the men of the Great Synagogue [a body of 120 elders, including many prophets, who came up from the exile with Ezra, JM]. They said three things: Be deliberate in judgment, raise up many disciples, and make a fence around the Law.[99]

The Mishnah records the opinions of the Pharisaic party,[100] which was the only party to survive the destruction of Jerusalem in A.D. 70. These opinions have become the basis of modern forms of the Jewish faith. The value of the Mishnah in representing the views of Judaism in the time of Paul is not uniform because much of it reflects later opinions and emendations that were necessary for dealing with the inevitable changes in religious practices among Jews after

---

95. *Ant.* 18.11; cf. 13.171–73; *J.W.* 2.119.
96. See the teaching of the Sadducees in Josephus, *J.W.* 2.164–66; *Ant.* 18.16–17.
97. *J.W.* 2.119–61; *Ant.* 18.18–22.
98. *J.W.* 2.162.
99. *Avot* 1.1 (Danby, *Mishnah,* 446).
100. Danby, *Mishnah,* xiv.

the destruction of the temple. On the other hand, certain tracts of the Mishnah that preserve a knowledge of the customs dealing solely with Jerusalem and the temple[101] "were preserved and handed down," often in the very words of the men who had lived under the law in pre-destruction days and had known the full experience of living in temple times. Since these tracts no longer applied to daily life after the temple fell, "they have been less overlaid with comment and argument by later generations of teachers, and less exposed to the possibility of revision under the influence of later fashions of interpretation."[102]

However, there is no mistaking the basic claim under which these opinions that were codified into the Mishnah developed. The claim was expressed in the tract *Sanhedrin* 11.3: "Greater stringency applies to the observance of the words of the Scribes than to the observance of the words of the written Law." The significance of this claim is clearly enunciated by Danby:

> The Mishnah, in other words, maintains that the authority of those rules, customs, and interpretations which had accumulated around the Jewish system of life and religion was equal to the authority of the Written Law itself, even though they found no place in the Written Law. This, again, is but an assertion (known also in other religious and legal systems) that side by side with a written code there exists a living tradition with power to interpret the written code, to add to it, and even at times to modify it or ignore it as might be needful in changed circumstances, and to do this authoritatively. Inevitably the inference follows that the living tradition (the Oral Law) is more important than the Written Law, since the "tradition of the elders," besides claiming an authority and continuity equal to that of the Written Law, claims also to be its authentic and living interpretation and its essential complement.[103]

Moses had memorized this oral law and passed it on to Joshua, and so it had been passed down through the centuries by reliable authorities to succeeding generations, and its authenticity was beyond suspicion.[104] The men of the Great Synagogue had advised their disciples to "make a fence around the Law" in order to prevent breaking the law itself. The Torah was viewed as *Torah Shelemah,* that is, all-embracing. It "signified the fullness of the revealed tradition which is to say the oral and written stipulations and all the deductions, inferences, and case decisions authoritatively derived from them."[105] American constitutional law offers a rough secular parallel. "It includes not only the Constitution itself (the written law), but also the many aspects of oral law, i.e., naturalized traditions from older legal systems, two centuries of accumulated case decisions, theoretical writing on Consti-

101. Especially *Yoma, Middot, Tamid,* and parts of *Bikkurim* and *Sheqalim.*

102. Danby, *Mishnah,* xv n. 4.

103. Ibid., xvii.

104. D. J. Silver and B. Martin, *A History of Judaism* (New York: Basic Books, 1974), 1:224.

105. Ibid., 1:225.

tutional issues, and the implicit assumption that a consistent attitude toward the organization of human affairs exists within the Law."[106]

The problem facing a Torah scholar like Paul was how the all-embracing law, which was eternal and immutable, could be applied to Jews who no longer lived in circumstances for which that law was designed. The revision of such a law was theoretically impossible by definition, but pragmatically it was a necessary fact of life, especially for those Jews who lived in the Diaspora. How could a poor Jewish male living in Italy or Spain appear three times a year[107] in Jerusalem when he could barely afford to feed his family and had no money with which to travel such distances? Indeed, by the reign of the Roman emperor Hadrian (A.D. 117–38), the temple was destroyed, and Jews were not even permitted to enter the city of Jerusalem. How could Jewish worshipers, even in Palestine itself, keep the commandments related to worship in the temple/tabernacle when it had been destroyed?

Although the Torah scholar would adamantly deny that he was doing anything more than interpreting and elaborating on the law, applying the specifics of the law or at least its evident spirit to a particular case, the truth was that "the Pharisaic scholar in fact made law."[108] This scenario is all too familiar to those whose religious experience includes teachers and officials who see no difference between the Word of God and their interpretation of the Word of God!

Ancient rabbis differed in the methods they used to apply the law of Moses—given in the desert to a collection of Jewish tribes—to an urbanized and sedentary population. Even among the Pharisees, there were both stringent and lenient interpreters. It is one of the perplexing unknowns of New Testament study how Paul, the ardent defender of the "strictest party of [his] religion" (Acts 26:5)—who was "extremely zealous . . . for the traditions of [his] fathers" (Gal. 1:14), who was "educated according to the strict manner of the law of [his] fathers" (Acts 22:3), and who undoubtedly was brought up in an orthodox Hebrew-speaking synagogue in the Diaspora[109]—could have fallen under the influence of the lenient, if not liberal, theology of Gamaliel in Jerusalem.

"At the Feet of Gamaliel" (Acts 22:3)

Paul was "brought up" in Jerusalem "at the feet of Gamaliel" (Acts 22:3).[110] Later traditions associate Gamaliel with the eminent contemporary

106. Ibid.
107. At the Feast of Unleavened Bread, the Feast of Weeks, and the Feast of Booths (Deut. 16:16).
108. Silver and Martin, *Judaism,* 1:225.
109. Paul said he was a "Hebrew born of Hebrews" (Phil. 3:5).
110. Gamaliel I. See Bruce, *Paul,* 50. This Gamaliel is mentioned in the Mishnah, *Gittin* 4.2, in connection with liberalizing remarriage after divorce. See Danby, *Mishnah,* 310–11.

of Jesus, the rabbi Hillel, as successor to his school and possibly even his grandson,[111] though this is uncertain.[112] The translation of the word ἀνατρέφω (*anatrephō*) as "brought up" (RSV, NIV, etc.) is not to be taken as indicating anything more than that Paul was educated in Jerusalem under Gamaliel when he came to that city for his professional training. It need not mean that he was nurtured there from infancy as was Moses by Pharaoh's daughter (cf. *anatrephō* in Acts 7:21). We do not know at what age Paul was sent to Jerusalem from Tarsus. He did have a sister who lived there at the time of Paul's arrest, and perhaps he had relatives who had lived in Jerusalem earlier (Acts 23:16).

The influence of Hillel, whose approach to Jewish law was more lenient than that of his noted contemporary Shammai, is reflected in the moderating view expressed toward Christians by Gamaliel in Acts 5:33–39. Unlike Shammai, who was a Palestinian Jew, Hillel, as a young man, came to Jerusalem from Babylonia, where an important school of Jewish thought had existed for centuries—the one that produced the Babylonian Talmud. It has been argued that Hillel was schooled in Babylonia.[113] Even though the ancient city of Babylon was still in ruins in the time of Paul, there were small cities in the vicinity that contained flourishing communities of Jews. Nehardea, a city not far to the south of Babylon, was the chief center of Babylonian Jewry and has been considered the residence of the Head of the Exile, the leading rabbi among the Jews exiled in Babylonia (called the Exilarch).[114] Other important centers of education in Babylonia were Nisibis, Pumbedita, Sura, Mehoza, and Nersh.[115]

The name of Hillel is associated with certain hermeneutic norms of juristic deduction and analogy, which are called Hillel's *Seven Rules.*[116] These rules, which Hillel received and worked into a method, defined "certain ways in which logically valid conclusions in the juristic field are derivable from the written law."[117] For example, Deuteronomy 15:1–12 stipulates that all loans are to be canceled when the Sabbatical Year arrives. In Hillel's urban society, this would have produced chaos in the economic system, because no one would lend money in the months preceding the arrival of the Sabbatical Year, knowing that the loan would be canceled before it could be repaid. It has been

---

111. This is accepted by E. P. Blair, "Gamaliel," *IDB,* 2:351.

112. See Jacob Neusner, *The Rabbinic Traditions about the Pharisees before 70* (Leiden: Brill, 1971), 1:341–37; Bruce, *Paul,* 50. The tradition is evidently rejected by Bruce Chilton, who makes no mention of Hillel in his rather extensive article on Gamaliel in *ABD,* 2:903–6.

113. George Foot Moore, *Judaism in the First Centuries of the Christian Era: The Age of the Tannaim* (Cambridge, Mass.: Harvard University Press, 1962), 1:77.

114. Ibid., 1:105 n. 3.

115. Ibid., 1:102–5.

116. These seven rules may be found in the Tosefta (*Sanhedrin* 7.11) or more conveniently in Emil Schürer, *A History of the Jewish People in the Time of Jesus Christ* (New York: Scribners, n.d.), 2.1:336.

117. Moore, *Judaism,* 1:78.

argued that Hillel "unabashedly devised a legal subterfuge" that had the impact of voiding the requirements of the written law. He instituted a *takkanah*, an emergency decree, that allowed such late loans to be made over to the courts, a third party that was not a person and thus not specifically covered by the biblical text, which is framed in terms of one person lending to another. This allowed the loan to remain uncanceled despite the demands of the law. Thus, Hillel "did not repeal Torah or nullify it; he simply set it aside by interpretation."[118] After all, life took precedence over the letter of the law, he reasoned, for the Torah was a "law of life."

The reason Hillel's school became the more lenient one in treating law undoubtedly lay in the fact that he came from Babylonia, where the situation in the Diaspora was different from that in Jerusalem. Hillel realized that the law must take account of actual conditions rather than imposing regulations and making demands on people that are impossible for them to fulfill. More than three hundred conflicting interpretations of the two schools of Hillel and Shammai on matters of law and observance are reported in one connection or another in the Talmud.[119]

Paul, too, was from the Diaspora. His teacher, Gamaliel, was a representative of the Hillel point of view, and Paul's approach to Jewish law seems to have been the same. In dealing with the question of divorce among believers, Paul could draw on Jesus' teaching to Jews, and so he wrote: Now this says the Lord, not I (see 1 Cor. 7:10). But in dealing with mixed marriages, those in which one of the partners had converted to Christianity, Paul could only say, as Gamaliel or Hillel would have said: "To the rest I say, not the Lord . . ." (1 Cor. 7:12). Jesus never taught on the subject, since marriage outside the Jewish religion was not permitted (Ezra 10:11; Neh. 13:25). Paul, facing a new situation, the inclusion of Gentiles in the new faith, which the law did not envision, had to make the necessary adjustments to embrace the new circumstances.

Like Hillel, Paul would take a more commonsense approach to matters. The law did specify that an ox should be taken out of the ditch, even on the Sabbath. For Hillel this meant also that one *could* eat an egg laid by a chicken on the Sabbath. One *could* offer Passover sacrifice, even if the day for the sacrifice fell on a Sabbath. It was this mind-set, this more lenient approach to matters of law and grace, that eventually won out for Paul, overcoming his more strident background of strictness in biblical interpretation. Providence is an altogether marvelous thing. How different history might have been had Paul come under the influence of the Shammai school rather than that of Gamaliel. Saul of Tarsus was just the man for whom God was looking at this point in history, the fullness of time.

118. Silver and Martin, *Judaism,* 1:226.
119. *Jewish Encyclopedia,* ed. I. Singer et al. (New York: Funk & Wagnalls, 1912), 3:115f.

TWO

Conversion, Call, and Commission

The single most important element in understanding the ministry of Paul is his commission at the time of his conversion and call. His charge to preach to Gentiles, given during his Damascus Road experience (Acts 26:17) and repeated while Paul was in the temple in Jerusalem (Acts 22:17–21), constituted the driving force of his life, the purpose of his existence, and the central focus of his theology (cf. Rom. 1:13–17; 15:8, 16; Gal. 1:16). The fact that there is a triple account of Paul's conversion in Acts is remarkable when one considers the brevity of the book.[1] Luke's decision to record the conversion himself (Acts 9) and then add two accounts of it from the mouth of Paul (Acts 22 and 26) can only be explained by the importance he attached to the event in understanding Paul's ministry. Luke's accounts are supplemented by details Paul himself supplies in Galatians.[2]

Paul was traveling from Jerusalem to Damascus with letters from the high priest authorizing him to arrest Jewish Christians and imprison them for accepting this blasphemous new teaching. That Paul should go so far on such a mission lends added meaning to his comment that he was "extremely zealous" for the traditions of his fathers (Gal. 1:14). Before reaching his destination, Paul was blinded by the Christophany, and his life was changed. The risen Lord, Jesus Christ, spoke to him in Hebrew (or Aramaic) and called him to

---

1. See Charles W. Hedrick, "Paul's Conversion/Call: A Comparative Analysis of the Three Reports in Acts," *JBL* 100.3 (1981): 415–32.

2. See George Howard's informative discussion in *Paul: Crisis in Galatia* (Cambridge: Cambridge University Press, 1979).

Photo 2.1. Street Called Straight in Damascus

be one of his apostles. At this time Paul was commissioned to go to the Gentiles and proclaim to them the Christian faith (Acts 26:16–18; cf. 9:15). He was told to go into Damascus to receive further instructions (Acts 22:10; 9:6), which he got from a Jewish believer named Ananias. Paul describes him as "a devout man according to the law, well spoken of by all the Jews who lived there" (Acts 22:12). After three days of blindness and fasting, Paul was immersed by Ananias for the "washing away of his sins" and received his sight again (Acts 9:9, 18; 22:16). He then spent a period of time in Damascus and then in Arabia,[3] the purpose of which is not recorded, before returning first to Damascus and then to Jerusalem (Gal. 1:17).

"I Am a Jew" (Acts 21:39)

There are indications that Paul underwent a full conversion in the normal sense of that term: he stopped persecuting the followers of the faith he now embraced; he experienced the "washing away of his sins" (Acts 22:16); he became an ardent disciple of Jesus of Nazareth (Gal. 2:20); he gave evidence of genuine repentance by asking Jesus, "What will you have me to do?" (see Acts 22:10). However, an increasing number of scholars are now arguing that what

3. See J. Murphy-O'Connor, "Paul in Arabia," *CBQ* 55 (1993): 732–37.

Paul experienced was not a *conversion,* in the usual sense of a change of religion, but rather a *call,* such as the prophets of Israel experienced.[4] Pointing out that Paul never actually gave up his Jewish faith, one author concludes that "the usual conversion model of Paul the Jew who gives up his former faith to become a Christian is not the model of Paul but of ours."[5]

It is demonstrably true that Paul did not cease to regard himself as a Jew after he became a Christian. Such a dichotomy between his Jewishness and his acceptance of the Jewish Messiah would be foreign to the thought of Paul. This is easily shown by Paul's explicit references to his own Jewishness after his Damascus experience. He considers himself to be still a Pharisee (Acts 23:6),[6] a Jew (Acts 21:39), and one of God's Jewish vessels to carry the promise made to Abraham to the Gentiles (Rom. 9–11). He attended synogogue services and even had Timothy circumcised, *after Timothy became a Christian,* "because of the Jews" (Acts 16:3). Timothy's mother and grandmother were Jewish, but his father was not. Luke calls Timothy's father a "Greek," meaning probably a "God-fearer," a Gentile who accepted Jehovah as God and probably worshiped in the synagogue with his family without becoming a proselyte to the Jewish religion. Timothy, therefore, had not been circumcised as a child. The Book of Acts seemingly uses the word *Gentile* most frequently to refer to pagans and the word *Greek* at times to refer to God-fearers (Acts 10:22; 13:16, 26, 43; 16:14; 17:4, 17; 18:7).[7]

The most striking evidence of Paul's self-perception as a Jew is found in Acts 21. After the completion of three missionary journeys among the Gentiles, Paul acquiesced to the request of Jewish Christian leaders in Jerusalem and took an oath in the temple for the precise purpose of proving that he lived "in observance of the law" (Acts 21:24) and did not teach that Jewish Christians must "forsake Moses" and cease to "circumcise their children" and "observe the customs" (Acts 21:21).

---

4. Edwin Freed says, "Paul remained a Jew, even after becoming a Christian one" (*The Apostle Paul, Christian Jew* [Lanham, Md.: University Press of America, 1994]). See also Krister Stendahl, *Paul among Jews and Gentiles and Other Essays* (Philadelphia: Fortress, 1976), 7ff.; James D. G. Dunn, "'A Light to the Gentiles,' or 'The End of the Law'? The Significance of the Damascus Road Christophany for Paul," in *The Glory of Christ in the New Testament: Studies in Christology in Memory of George Bradford Caird,* ed. L. D. Hurst and N. T. Wright (Oxford: Clarendon, 1987), 251–66 (available also with an additional note in James D. G. Dunn, *Jesus, Paul and the Law: Studies in Mark and Galatians* [Philadelphia: Westminster, 1990], 89–107); Philip A. Cunningham, *Jewish Apostle to the Gentiles: Paul As He Saw Himself* (Mystic, Conn.: Twenty-Third Publications, 1986).

5. Stendahl, *Paul among Jews and Gentiles,* 9.

6. Jacob Jervell argues that Paul "remains a Pharisee afer his conversion and never becomes an ex-Pharisee" (*The Unknown Paul: Essays on Luke-Acts and Early Christian History* [Philadelphia: Fortress, 1979], 71). See also Brian Rapske, *The Book of Acts and Paul in Roman Custody,* BAFCS (Grand Rapids: Eerdmans, 1994), 99; and Brad H. Young, *Paul, the Jewish Theologian: A Pharisee among Christians, Jews, and Gentiles* (Peabody, Mass.: Hendrickson, 1997).

7. See my discussion of the terms *Gentile, Greek, God-fearer,* and *proselyte* in chapter 5.

If Paul had not wanted to remain a Jew, he certainly would not have endured the five whippings of thirty-nine lashes each given him by the Jews (2 Cor. 11:24) *in the synagogues.* Jesus had anticipated such treatment for his disciples, telling them that the Jews would flog them "in their synagogues" (Matt. 10:17).[8] It is argued by some that had Paul "really broken with his people he would not have submitted to this punitive discipline."[9]

The punishment was abusive and humiliating. Josephus called it a "disgraceful penalty" (αἰσχίστην, *aischistēn*),[10] but its humiliation is not often appreciated by moderns who study the life of the great apostle. The punishment was inflicted for such offenses as failing to share one's harvest with strangers as well as Israelites and falsely accusing one's wife of infidelity.[11] Such people were beaten with the "forty stripes save one,"[12] the punishment specified in Deuteronomy 25:3. The scenario, which had become so familiar to Paul, can probably be reconstructed from the Mishnah,[13] written centuries later, and transpired as follows: He was taken before the synagogue officials, who consigned him to what Josephus calls the "public lash" (δημοσίω σκύτει, *dēmosiō skytei*),[14] administered by the "minister of the synagogue."[15] An estimate was made of how many stripes one could bear (never more than forty). It had to be a number divisible by three (hence the thirty-nine);[16] if more than forty were given, the one administering it had to escape into exile. One third of the stripes were given on the chest and two thirds on the shoulder, while the person was bending low, never while standing or sitting. The person's two hands were bound to pillars on either side, and a leather strap was used to administer the lashes, which was made of calf hide doubled and re-doubled, to which two strips of ass hide were attached.

At this point in the punishment, Deuteronomy 28:58–61 was read, which added insult to injury. "If you are not careful to do all the words of this law, . . . the LORD will bring on you and your offspring extraordinary afflictions, afflictions severe and lasting. . . ." If, during the beating, a man befouled himself with excrement, or a woman with urine, he or she would be exempted from the rest of the punishment.

One can only imagine how Paul's upper torso must have looked and sense the rebuke he gave his opponents when he said, "Henceforth let no man trouble me; for I bear on my body the marks of Jesus" (Gal. 6:17). In the context

---

8. Cf. *m. Makkot* 3.12.

9. Richard Rubenstein, *My Brother Paul* (New York: Harper and Row, 1972), 121; Rapske, *Paul in Roman Custody,* 99.

10. *Ant.* 4.238.

11. Ibid., 4.238, 248.

12. Ibid.

13. *m. Makkot* 3.10–15.

14. *Ant.* 4.238.

15. *m. Makkot* 3.12.

16. However, Rabbi Judah, in the Mishnaic period, insisted on the full forty, the last stripe to be administered between the shoulders, perhaps reflecting Zech. 13:6 (*m. Makkot* 3.10).

of this statement in Galatians, Paul may have considered these marks in his flesh as a kind of second circumcision, showing that he belonged to Christ. Clearly, then, Paul continued to regard himself as a Jew, but equally clearly, as one who experienced fulfillment by accepting Christ as Messiah and Savior.

The Book of Acts is filled with evidence that Paul was not alone in retaining his Jewishness—ethnically, culturally, and religiously—after becoming a Christian. All Jewish Christians remained Jews after accepting Jesus the Jew as their Jewish Messiah. Paul went to Damascus to ferret out Christians from the synagogues there (Acts 9:2).[17] None felt they had become Gentiles by following Jesus; conversion for them, as for Paul, did not require a change of religion, because Christianity was Judaism internationalized.

The disciples remained involved with the temple and synagogue. The evidence from Acts is extensive:

1. The disciples spent much time together in the temple (Acts 2:46).
2. Peter and John kept the Jewish hour of prayer in the temple (Acts 3:1, 3).
3. Peter and John were arrested as Jews (Acts 4:1–3).
4. Peter and John were tried as Jews (Acts 4:6, 15, 21) by the Sanhedrin (συνέδριον, *synedrion,* Acts 4:15), which included the chief priests and elders (Acts 4:5, 8, 23).
5. Special attention is drawn to the fact that Barnabas was a Levite (Acts 4:36).
6. Disciples were meeting in Solomon's Portico in the temple (Acts 5:12; cf. 2:46; 3:11).

Colin Hemer states, "It is implicit that Solomon's Porch was a meeting place of the Christians in the Temple, as according to John 10:23, Jesus had walked there with his disciples."[18]

F. F. Bruce, commenting on Acts 2:46 says:

In the weeks that followed the first Christian Pentecost, the believers met regularly in the temple precincts for public worship and public witness, while they took their fellowship meals in one another's homes and "broke the bread" in accordance with their Master's precedent. The part of the temple precincts where they seem to have gathered habitually was Solomon's colonnade. . . . The common meal could not conveniently be eaten in the temple precincts, so they ate "by households. . . ."[19]

17. See further A. J. Hultgren, "Paul's Pre-Christian Persecutions of the Church: Their Purpose, Locale, and Nature," *JBL* 95 (1976): 101–4; R. A. Stewart, "Judicial Procedure in New Testament Times," *EvQ* 47 (1975): 99f.
18. *BASHH,* 190.
19. *The Book of the Acts,* rev. ed., NICNT (Grand Rapids: Eerdmans, 1988), 74. The meaning of "by households" for κατ᾽ οἶκον is attested in the papyri.

Peter's sermon on Pentecost may have been preached here. F. F. Bruce, in his commentary on the Greek text of Acts, writes:

> This seems to have been their habitual public meeting place. Certainly no ordinary building would have sufficed for their increasing numbers, and it was necessary that their ministry of witness should be fulfilled in the open. Probably this is the part of the temple complex indicated in 2:46, as it may have been the place where Peter addressed the crowd on the day of Pentecost. The breaking of bread took place privately, in various homes.[20]

7. The apostles were arrested by the high priest and those with him (Acts 5:17–18). They were brought before the Jewish Sanhedrin (Acts 5:27).
8. Peter's message was about Jews in the context of Israel (Acts 5:32).
9. The apostles were flogged by Jewish authority (Acts 5:40).
10. The apostles preached in the temple (Acts 5:42).
11. A great many (πολὺς ὄχλος, *polys ochlos*) priests were obedient (Codex Sinaiticus has Ἰουδαίων [*Ioudaiōn,* Jews] instead of ἱερέων [priests]) (Acts 6:7).
12. After his conversion, Stephen was still involved with the synagogue (Acts 6:8–9) when he was brought before the Sanhedrin (Acts 6:12). He was killed by Jewish authority (Acts 7:58).
13. The persecution of the church after Stephen's death was a Jewish persecution—conducted by Paul (Acts 8:1–3).
14. Paul asked for letters to the *synagogues* of Damascus, where Christians were to be found (Acts 9:2).
15. Ananias, who baptized Paul, was a "brother" of Paul (Acts 9:17) and a "disciple" (Acts 9:10; cf. v. 26). He was "a devout man according to the law, well spoken of by all the Jews who lived there" (Acts 22:12).
16. Paul preached in the *synagogues* of Damascus (Acts 9:20).
17. Jewish believers (cf. "circumcised believers" NRSV—οἱ ἐκ περιτομῆς, *hoi ek peritomēs,* Acts 11:2) in Jerusalem continued their Jewish way of life; they criticized Paul for eating with uncircumcised men (Acts 11:3).
18. Some (τινες, *tines*) from Jerusalem went to Antioch and taught that circumcision according to the custom (ἔθει, *ethei*) of Moses was necessary for salvation (Acts 15:1).
19. Some who had believed were still of the Pharisees' sect (τινες τῶν ἀπὸ τῆς αἱρέσεως τῶν Φαρισαίων πεπιστευκότες, *tines tōn apo tēs haireseōs tōn Pharisaiōn pepisteukotes,* Acts 15:5).

---

20. *The Acts of the Apostles: The Greek Text with Introduction and Commentary,* 3d rev. ed. (Grand Rapids: Eerdmans, 1990), 167.

20. Timothy was circumcised by Paul's direction *after* his acceptance of Christ (Acts 16:3). His mother is referred to as "a Jewish woman who was a believer" (Acts 16:1).

21. The fact that Jews continued to practice elements of the Jewish faith not required of Gentiles is seen in the delivering to the churches of Asia Minor the essentials (Acts 15:28) of Jewish observance that Gentiles in these churches were expected to keep (Acts 16:4).

22. Priscilla and Aquila evidently became Christians (Acts 18:2, 18). The implication is that they were among the believers whom Paul left in Ephesus (Acts 18:18). But later in Ephesus, they were attending synagogue when they heard Apollos speak (Acts 18:26). He evidently became a Christian too (Acts 18:27–28).

23. When Paul was rejected in the synagogue in Ephesus after three months, he left it "taking the disciples with him." These must have been believing Jews (Acts 19:9).

24. Thousands of believers among the Jews were "all zealous for the law" (Acts 21:20). They circumcised their children and observed the customs (Acts 21:21).

25. Paul went through a rite of purification in the temple (Acts 21:24–26), paid for the shaving of the heads of four others (Acts 21:24), and proved that he "observed" (στοιχεῖς, *stoicheis*) and "guarded" (φυλάσσων, *phylassōn*) the law (Acts 21:24).

26. Paul said that the people he imprisoned and beat who believed in Jesus *were in every synagogue* (κατὰ τὰς συναγωγάς, *kata tas sunagōgas,* Acts 22:19).

27. Paul said before the Sanhedrin: "I *am* a Pharisee" (ἐγὼ Φαρισαῖός εἰμι, *egō Pharisaios eimi,* Acts 23:6).

28. Paul told Agrippa that he punished the saints (ἁγίων, *hagiōn*) who were "in all the synagogues" (κατὰ πάσας τὰς συναγωγάς, *kata pasas tas sunagōgas,* Acts 26:10–11).

"Called Me through His Grace" (Gal. 1:15)

On the other hand, it is not true that Paul never experienced a "conversion," as some have maintained. Conversion need not imply, nor does it necessitate, a change of religion—the most obvious example of this being children of dedicated Christian parents who eventually make their own commitment to Christ. There are also many adults who have accepted the Christian religion intellectually and socially but have never really been converted. Their lives have never undergone a radical transformation; they have never become "new creatures" (2 Cor. 5:17).[21] What such people need now is conversion to Christ—

---

21. Cf. Jesus' statement to Nicodemus in John 3:5.

not a change of religion but a change in their practice of religion. Paul experienced such a change.

It is also clear that Paul simultaneously received a "call" to apostleship, not unlike the call of the prophets in the Old Testament. The account of his conversion in the Greek text of Galatians (Gal. 1:13–16) contains echoes of the calls of both Isaiah and Jeremiah (Isa. 49:1–6; Jer. 1:1–11). Phrases like "he called me from my mother's womb" and the commission to be a "light to the Gentiles" appear in the accounts of both of these prophets as well as in Galatians. The brightness of the Christophany recalls the vision of Ezekiel at his call to prophethood (Ezek. 1:27–28; 2:1–3; cf. also Isa. 35:5; 42:7, 16; 61:1; Jer. 1:17). Parallels do exist between the calls of prophets and apostles; God appointed both. Even in the church, God called both to service (Eph. 4:11).

But it is not, therefore, necessary to conclude, as some have,[22] that Paul was so unaware of a "conversion" that the meaning of his experience had to be interpreted for him later in Damascus by Ananias (Acts 22:14–15). Ananias need only be understood as reinforcing Paul's understanding by demonstrating that God had appeared to him also and had told him of Paul's commission to go to the Gentiles. There is nothing in Ananias's comments to Paul that suggests the apostle was being informed for the first time of what had happened to him. Paul's insistence in Galatians that he did not receive his gospel from human beings militates against any suggestion that Ananias imparted it to him.[23] This was the very charge that Paul's opponents were making and that Paul was refuting in Galatians 1. The account of Paul's conversion in Acts 26:16 supports the fact that his commission came at the time of this Christophany.

Accounts of Paul's Conversion

Nevertheless, there are some differences between the three accounts in Acts that require some explanation. By one account (Acts 9:7), Paul's companions heard the voice (ἀκούοντες τῆς φωνῆς, *akouontes tēs phonēs*), but according to another (Acts 22:9), they did not hear the voice (τὴν φωνὴν ἤκουσαν, *tēn phonēn ēkousan*). The Greek text indicates that the companions only *heard* (genitive case) the sound but did not *understand* (accusative case) what they heard. Paul *understood* (Acts 9:4) the voice (ἤκουσεν φωνήν, *ēkousen phonēn*—accusative case), which was speaking

22. E.g., Stendahl, *Paul among Jews and Gentiles,* 9.
23. Kirsopp Lake, "The Conversion of Paul and the Events Immediately Following It," in *The Acts of the Apostles,* ed. F. J. Foakes-Jackson and Kirsopp Lake, The Beginnings of Christianity, part 1 (London: Macmillan, 1920–33), 5:190.

in Hebrew.[24] The situation may be parallel to the one in John 12:27–29, where Jesus understood God's voice speaking to him while the crowd standing nearby only heard the sound and thought it was thunder.

Another difference in the accounts is that in one (Acts 9:4) Paul fell to the ground, but in another (Acts 26:14) they all fell down. This does not require the conclusion[25] that in chapter 9 the companions remained standing. Nothing is revealed about their posture in that chapter. The expression, "The men . . . stood speechless" (εἰστήκεισαν ἐνεοί, eistēkeisan eneoi, Acts 9:7), is probably used metaphorically or figuratively here in the sense of "stand firm"[26] and is not mentioned in Acts 22:7. The idea may be that they "had stood firm and stayed still after they fell"; that is, they did not try either to run away or to interfere but held their ground.

It is probable that Luke knew the story of Paul's conversion from three different sources: (1) Paul himself, with whom Luke traveled (2 Tim. 4:11); (2) the church in Jerusalem, from which Luke obtained information about events in the city before Paul's conversion that he used in writing Acts 1–6; and (3) the church in Antioch, where Paul based his ministry (Acts 11:25; 13:1–3; 14:26–28; 15:22, 30; 18:22–23). Some see chapter 22 as the most original of the three accounts in Acts, and the most Jewish.[27] Chapter 9 is a hellenized version by Luke, they argue,[28] and chapter 26, which agrees closely with Galatians 1, was written to harmonize with Paul's own account of his conversion.[29] The reason for this is that Luke knew Paul rejected the Ananias story, which was prevalent in Jerusalem and which played into the hands of Paul's opponents there who wanted to attribute the apostle's conversion and

24. This explanation was argued by J. L. Lilly, "The Conversion of Saint Paul: The Validity of His Testimony to the Resurrection of Jesus Christ," *CBQ* 6 (1944): 183–84. A. T. Robertson considers the difference in cases to be significant (*A Grammar of the Greek New Testament in the Light of Historical Research* [Nashville: Broadman, 1934], 506); also suggested by R. G. Bratcher, "ἀκούω, akouō, in Acts ix.7 and xxii.9," *Expository Times* 71 (1960): 243–45.

25. This is Lake's conclusion ("Conversion of Paul," 190).

26. See ἵστημι in BAGD, 382 §II.c.α.

27. This is the view of Kirsopp Lake. Expressions like "the God of our fathers," Jesus as "the righteous one," baptism for "the washing away of sins," and the lack of mention of the Spirit indicate Jewishness, according to Lake ("Conversion of Paul," 191).

28. Lake (ibid.) notes that the phrase "Lord Jesus" is used and that baptism is equated with the gift of the Holy Spirit. See also Johannes Munck, *Paul and the Salvation of Mankind,* trans. Frank Clarke (Atlanta: John Knox, 1977), 17.

29. Charles Hedrick argues that chapter 26 was based on 9 and 22 ("Paul's Conversion/ Call," 426f.). He sees chapter 9 as written to introduce an account of the healing of Paul, while chapters 22 and 26 were written to emphasize Paul's commission. For other examinations of the chapters from the standpoint of Luke's literary methods, see B. J. Hubbard, "The Role of Commissioning Accounts in Acts," in *Perspectives on Luke-Acts,* ed. Charles Talbert (Danville, Va.: Association of Baptist Professors of Religion, 1978), 187–98; and T. Y. Mullins, "New Testament Commission Forms, Especially in Luke-Acts," *JBL* 95 (1976): 605–14.

call to Ananias rather than God. Acts 26, like Galatians 1, emphasizes that Paul's message came without human instrumentality.

However, this view does not consider the likelihood that the "Jewishness" of the account in Acts 22 is to be accounted for by Paul's interest in making the story of his conversion conform to the understanding of the Jewish audience at the temple and might thus have been more the product of Paul than of Luke. As noted in the first chapter, Paul's Jewish name, Saul, rather than his Roman name, Paul, is used in all three conversion accounts.

"From My Mother's Womb" (Gal. 1:15 KJV)

In the account of his conversion in Galatians, Paul spoke of God's having set him apart from his mother's womb, which the Revised Standard Version translates "before I was born." The Greek phrase used by Paul (ἐκ κοιλίας μητρός μου, *ek koilias mētros mou*) has been thought by many, since Augustine and Calvin wrote on the subject, to mean that Paul considered himself predestined, with no option to reject the call of God. The phrase appears to be used that way in Psalm 22:9–10 (= 21:10–11 LXX) and Psalm 71:6 (= 70:6 LXX). However, the psalmist may only be expressing gratitude to God for the providence extended to him through his life. The phrase is used elsewhere in the Septuagint to simply specify a period of time. Samson, for example, told Delilah, "I have been a Nazirite to God from my mother's womb" (Judg. 16:17). The expression is used twice in Isaiah 49:1–6, where the context shows that "Israel," rather than Isaiah, is God's servant (Isa. 49:3) who has been called from the womb (Isa. 49:1) to be a servant (Isa. 49:5) to the Gentiles (Isa. 49:6). The same idea, though not the exact phrase, is used in Jeremiah 1:5 of the author's having been "*appointed . . . a prophet to the nations.*"

Paul is probably using the expression, then, not just of his personal conversion, but of God's preparation for the salvation of the Gentiles. Paul had been called to "preach him among the Gentiles" (Gal. 1:16), and this was the purpose of his call at Damascus. His conversion account before Agrippa II includes a statement that God had appointed Paul to "open the eyes" of the Gentiles, so that they might turn to God (Acts 26:18). This expression refers to the conversion of Gentiles in Isaiah 42:7 and 16. The heavenly voice in Acts 9:15 referred to Paul as "a chosen instrument [σκεῦος ἐκλογῆς, *skeuos eklogēs*] to carry the Lord's name "before the Gentiles and kings and the sons of Israel." The word used in Acts 22:14 to refer to Paul's call is προεχειρίσατο (*proecheirisato*), "appoint." The voice said to Paul, "The God of our fathers appointed you to know his will . . . for you will be a witness for him to all men" (Acts 22:14–15). Some argue that the word *appointed* refers here to a choice made anterior to his conversion rather than to the post-conversion appointment specified by the term in Acts 26:16,[30] but such a distinction

---

30. E.g., Munck, *Paul and the Salvation of Mankind*, 28.

is not clear, and one expects the same word in accounts of the same event to retain the same meaning.

In the accounts in both Acts and Galatians, Paul probably intends to say that he was called by God, just as were the ancient prophets, to be a messenger to the Gentiles, and that this was God's intent for Paul from the time Paul was born. This, however, does not mean that the call of Paul was irresistible. For example, God chose Israel to be a light to the Gentiles, but the nation steadfastly refused the mission, eventually falling into such idolatry that the entire nation was taken into captivity because of its idolatry.[31] It was because Israel failed in this task earlier that Christ "became a servant [δι-άκονον, *diakonon*] to the circumcised *to show God's truthfulness, in order to confirm the promises given to the patriarchs, and in order that the Gentiles might glorify God"* (Rom. 15:8–9, italics added). It was also for this same reason that Paul was appointed to be a "minister [λειτουργόν, *leitourgon*] of Christ Jesus to the Gentiles" (Rom. 15:16). Through his ministry, he completed "what is lacking in Christ's afflictions" (Col. 1:24) by extending Christ's foundational work among Jews ("Go nowhere among the Gentiles," Matt. 10:5–6; 15:24) to include Paul's work "among the Gentiles" (Col. 1:24).

"It Hurts You to Kick against the Goads" (Acts 26:14)

To the modern reader, one of the most enigmatic phrases in Paul's conversion accounts is the comment by the divine voice that "it hurts you to kick against the goads" (σκληρόν σοι πρὸς κέντρα λακτίζειν, *skleron soi pros kentra laktizein*). This is often taken to mean that Paul was offending his conscience, a notion bolstered by reading Paul through the eyes of Martin Luther, whose troubled conscience hastened the Reformation movement to a climax. But it could not have meant that to Paul, because he declared to the Sanhedrin in Jerusalem, "I have lived before God in all good conscience up to this day" (Acts 23:1).

Considerable evidence has been cited from Greek classical literature that shows the phrase to be a familiar proverb with the meaning "it is folly to resist what is inevitable."[32] Munck thinks the proverb refers to Paul's *future* relation to Christ, rather than looking to his *past* experience. The import of the words is, he says, "From now on you will have no discharge from the service that I, Christ, have laid on you," and in the context of the phrase in Acts 26:14 no reference is made to Paul's previous history.

31. Israel, the northern ten tribes, in 722 B.C., and Judah, the southern two tribes, in 587 B.C.

32. Munck, *Paul and the Salvation of Mankind,* 20, 21 n. 2. E.g., Aeschylus, *Prom.* 323; v. 322; *Ag.* 1624; Pindar, *Pyth.* v. 95.

However, this line of reasoning assumes that the account in Acts 26 is to be understood in isolation from what precedes it in chapters 1 through 25. Clearly, Paul's previous history as a persecutor of Christians is deeply involved in the development of Acts up to the time of his conversion and cannot be isolated from the conversion accounts. Perhaps the phrase is best taken to mean to Paul that his recent troubled life must be telling him that God has something more in mind for him and that it would be folly to resist further his inevitable acceptance of the risen Jesus as the Jewish Messiah and Son of God.

"Arise and Be Immersed and Wash Away Your Sins" (Acts 22:16)

The immersion of Paul in water, in obedience to the command of Ananias, is not mentioned in the accounts of Acts 26 and Galatians 1. Both seem to avoid all possible reference to the human agency involved in his experience, perhaps because of the efforts of his opponents in Jerusalem to stress human involvement against Paul's claims of a divine commission. In Acts 9 there is only a passing statement that Paul was immersed (v. 18), in the same sentence that says he took food and was strengthened, giving little emphasis to the importance of what had happened.

But in Acts 22, the more Jewish account, the *purpose* of immersion is stated as that of washing away his sin (Acts 22:16). The immersion was administered by a Jewish Christian, Ananias, who used terminology familiar to Jewish people of the time from the practice of John the Immerser/Baptist, who, because the kingdom was at hand, immersed Jews in water "for the forgiveness of sins" (Mark 1:4). An identical statement of the purpose for immersion, "for forgiveness of . . . sins" (εἰς ἄφεσιν ἁμαρτιῶν, *eis aphesin hamartiōn*), was used by Peter on Pentecost (Acts 2:38).

The practice of immersion "in living water" (i.e., in running water) was important in Jewish religious thought of the period. Excavations at Jerusalem,[33] Masada, Jericho, Herodium, and Qumram[34] have uncovered numerous *miqva'ot* (baptistries) that were constructed to provide running water from a storage cistern to the immersion tank during the time of immersion.[35] The Mishnah specifies that one should be immersed in running water, and that if such is not obtainable it may be provided by bringing water "directly from a river or a spring, or from rain-water that is led directly into the Immersion-

33. Ronny Reich, "Two Possible Miqwa'ot on the Temple Mount," *IEJ* 39.1–2 (1989): 63–66.

34. W. S. LaSor, "Discovering What Jewish Miqva'ot Can Tell Us about Christian Baptism," *BAR* 13.1 (Jan./Feb. 1987): 58.

35. See John McRay, *Archaeology and the New Testament* (Grand Rapids: Baker, 1991), 48–49.

pool."[36] It must be brought from the storage cistern into the immersion tank through a hole large enough "to contain two fingers doubled up."[37]

Danby, the translator of *The Mishnah,* points out that the person had to be "totally immersed" and that pools constructed for the purpose had to "contain forty *seahs* (approximately 60 gallons or 270 litres) of water, and at the same time be of such depth that the whole body can be covered."[38] Water standing in ponds, cisterns, ditches, caverns, and rain-ponds and pools holding less that sixty gallons could be used only while it is raining. The reason is that the water must be running. This is one reason why John the Immerser, whom I think was associated at one time with the Essenes at Qumran,[39] used the Jordan River. It was ritually pure for the Jews who came to him. This also explains the statement in the Gospel of John that John the Immerser was immersing "at Aenon near Salim, *because there was much water there"* (John 3:23, italics added).

It is my opinion that the first recorded departure from the practice of immersion in ancient Christian literature reflects this Jewish background and accommodates it. The *Didache* (*Teaching of the Twelve Apostles*) is a Jewish Christian document, compiled in the early second century, that describes the practices and ethical standards of those Jewish disciples who compiled it. Commenting on baptism, it states:

> Immerse in the name of the Father and of the Son and of the Holy Spirit, in running [ζῶντι, *zōnti,* living] water; but if you have no running water, immerse in other water, and if you can not in cold, then in warm. But if you have neither, pour water three times on the head "in the name of the Father, Son, and Holy Spirit."[40]

The intent is to produce *running* water by pouring, a symbol of purity. Paul received immersion, undoubtedly in running water, at the hands of the Jewish Christian Ananias. Whether it was done in a river or a *miqveh* is not stated.

Paul was also told to call on the name of the Lord (Acts 22:16), a phrase that may or may not have meant to recite the Shema of Deuteronomy 6:4–6. Peter told his Jewish audience on Pentecost to be immersed "in the name of Jesus Christ" (Acts 2:38). This is a new element that John's immersion did not include, because Jesus had not yet been raised from the dead when John was

36. Herbert Danby, trans., *The Mishnah* (Oxford: Oxford University Press, 1933), 732 n. 5.

37. *m. Mikwa'ot* 7.1.

38. Danby, *Mishnah,* 732 n. 5.

39. John McRay, "John the Baptist and the Dead Sea Scrolls," *Restoration Quarterly* 4 (1960): 80–88. For an opposing view, see W. S. LaSor, *The Dead Sea Scrolls and the New Testament* (Grand Rapids: Eerdmans, 1972), 142–53.

40. *Didache* 7, in *The Apostolic Fathers,* ed. Kirsopp Lake (Cambridge, Mass.: Harvard University Press, 1952), 1:319ff.

preaching. After his resurrection and just before his ascension, Jesus had charged his apostles that "repentance and [or for] forgiveness of sins (ἄφεσιν ἁμαρτιῶν, *aphesin hamartiōn*) should be preached *in his name* to all nations [i.e., Gentiles], beginning from Jerusalem" (Luke 24:47, italics added). The new commission, as compared to the restricted one in Matthew 10:5 that excluded the Gentiles, now includes them on the basis of Jesus' resurrection. The apostles had been charged at the transfiguration of Jesus to tell no one what they had just experienced "until the Son of man is raised from the dead" (Matt. 17:9). After his resurrection, the name of the crucified and risen Savior became an essential ingredient in their preaching and in the confession of new converts.

The importance of immersion to Paul is seen in his comments on it in later letters. To the Romans he wrote:

> Do you not know that all of us who have been baptized [immersed] into Christ Jesus were baptized [immersed] into his death? We were buried therefore with him by baptism [immersion] into death, so that as Christ was raised from the dead by the glory of the Father, we too might walk in newness of life. For if we have been united [σύμφυτοι, *symphytoi*, literally, "planted with or made to grow together"] with him in a death like his, we shall certainly be united with him in a resurrection like his (Rom. 6:3–5). [41]

---

41. See the end of chapter 16 below for a further discussion on baptism.

THREE

Toward a Chronology of Paul's Ministry

What happened in Paul's life immediately after his conversion/call is not clear. In fact, Pauline chronology is one of the most baffling problems of New Testament study, due primarily to the remarkable fact that Luke makes no mention of any of Paul's letters in Acts, even though he covers the period of time in which several of them were written. Efforts to construct a chronology have therefore centered primarily around two major considerations: (1) the concrete "pinpoints" of datable events in connection with Paul's ministry that are provided by literary and archaeological evidence; and (2) the number of visits Paul is recorded as having made to Jerusalem. This latter consideration is important because it provides a direct connection between Luke's writing and the letters of Paul. Acts mentions several visits to Jerusalem (Acts 9:26–27; 11:29–30; 15:1–29; 18:22(?); 21:15ff.), and Galatians records two (Gal. 1:18–19; 2:1–10). The problem is in correlating them. The major difficulty in dealing with this chronology is that virtually no date involved is uncontested, and even though the margin of difference in some cases is only a matter of weeks, current scholarship is able to do no more than establish tentative chronologies that may serve as a basis for better understanding the life and letters of Paul. These postulated chronologies will necessarily differ from one another based on the degree of credibility assigned to the Book of Acts and the letters of Paul as well as the degree of exactness demanded from ancient statements, whose contexts may be specialized or generic, official or unofficial, authoritative or unauthorative.

In this chapter, I will first make a condensed chronological outline of the life and journeys of Paul and then proceed to discuss the four chronological pinpoints on which the chronology rests. After that, the detailed exegesis of the biblical historical data involved in constructing the chronology will be presented, followed by a look at recent studies on Pauline chronology.

Table 3.1 Condensed Outline of Pauline Chronology

Event	Date
Conversion	34
Paul in Tarsus	37–43
Paul in Antioch	43–47
First Journey	47–48
Paul in Antioch	48–49
Jerusalem Conference	49
Second Journey	49–51
Third Journey	51–54
Imprisonment in Caesarea	54–56
Journey to Rome	56–57
First Imprisonment in Rome	57–59
Later Travels	59–67
Death in Rome	67

Pinpoints of Pauline Chronology

There are four historical/archaeological pinpoints that must be considered in working with Pauline chronology. These provide us with a comparatively secure basis on which to build our understanding of Paul's movements.[1] Following is a list of the pinpoints and a discussion of each.

1. The death of Aretas IV, king of Nabatea—between A.D. 38 and 40 (2 Cor. 11:32–33; Acts 9:23–25).
2. The expulsion of Jews from Rome by Claudius—A.D. 49 (Acts 18:2).
3. Gallio's proconsulship in Achaia—began in May/June, A.D. 51 (Acts 18:12).
4. Procuratorship of Festus in Judea—began in May/June, A.D. 56 (Acts 24:27).

1. See further the discussion of these visits in the chapters below on Paul's journeys.

Death of Aretas IV

Paul visited Jerusalem three years after his conversion, acccording to Galatians 1:18. In A.D. 37, the Roman general Vitellius deposed Caiaphas during the Feast of Passover,[2] replacing him with Jonathan, the son of Ananus the high priest. A few weeks later, during Pentecost, Vitellius deposed Jonathan and replaced him with Jonathan's brother Theophilus.[3] This would have allowed Paul to return to Jerusalem without having to confront the man (either Caiaphas or Jonathan) who had given him letters of authority for his mission.

A *terminus ad quem* for Paul's visit would be A.D. 40, because Aretas IV died in that year, according to coins and inscriptions.[4] Paul had escaped from Damascus and gone to Jerusalem while Aretas was still alive (Acts 9:25; 2 Cor. 11:32), thus before A.D. 40. Aretas IV ruled over Nabatea, a kingdom that at various times reached from the Euphrates to the Red Sea.[5] During the time of the Roman general Pompey, the Nabateans in northern Arabia occupied Damascus. In 63 B.C. Pompey launched an expedition against them and restored order. The Nabatean territory lay astride the caravan trade routes from the ports in Arabia to Syria and Palestine. Its capital, Petra, was a center of the spice and perfume trade, and the Romans monitored this important commercial route. Pompey allowed the Nabatean king to retain control of Damascus.[6]

Damascus was later removed from the jurisdiction of the Nabateans, but in the time of Paul they again usurped control of the city, and Tiberius, who discouraged the reign or free movement of independent client kings,[7] sent Vitellius on a punitive expedition against Aretas IV.[8] Aretas IV would obviously

---

2. *Ant.* 18.95. See Harold Hoehner's reconstruction of these events in *Herod Antipas* (Grand Rapids: Zondervan, 1980), 316. See also Michael Avi-Yonah, ed., *The World History of the Jewish People, First Series: Ancient Times,* vol. 7, *The Herodian Period* (Jerusalem: Masada, 1975), 131f.

3. *Ant.* 18.123.

4. George Ogg, *The Chronology of the Life of Paul* (London: Epworth, 1968), 16. The A.D. 40 date for the death of Aretas is also accepted by Jack Finegan, *ANT:MW,* 57; Colin Hemer, "Observations on Pauline Chronology," in *Pauline Studies,* ed. Donald Hagner and Murray Harris (Grand Rapids: Eerdmans, 1990), 4; and Dale Moody, "A New Chronology for the Life and Letters of Paul," in *Chronos, Kairos, Christos,* ed. Jerry Vardaman and Edwin Yamauchi (Winona Lake, Ind.: Eisenbrauns, 1989), 224. Aretas's dates are 11 or 9 B.C. to A.D. 40. Michael Grant gives 9 B.C. in *Herod the Great* (London: Wiedenfeld and Nicolson, 1971), 246; Jack Finegan gives 11 B.C. (*ANT:MW,* 57).

5. *Ant.* 1.221.

6. M. Cary, *A History of Rome Down to the Reign of Constantine,* 2d ed. (London: Macmillan, 1962), 356.

7. S. A. Cook, F. E. Adcock, and M. P. Charlesworth, *The Cambridge Ancient History* (Cambridge: Cambridge University Press, 1971), 10:744ff.

8. See the account in Josephus, *Ant.* 18.109–26. See also Emil Schürer, *A History of the Jewish People in the Time of Jesus Christ* (New York: Scribners, n.d.), 1.2:357. It was during this expedition that Vitellius visited Jerusalem and replaced the high priests, as mentioned above.

not have had a governor of Damascus (ὁ ἐθνάρχης, *ho ethnarchēs,* 2 Cor. 11:32) serving under his kingship at this time.

However, while Vitellius was in Jerusalem, he received news of the death of Tiberius (March 15, A.D. 37), and so his commission to punish Aretas was no longer valid. He therefore disbanded his army for the winter and awaited orders from the new emperor, Caligula (A.D. 37–41),[9] who in this first year of his reign put parts of Syria and other eastern regions under client kings and Roman officials.[10] Undoubtedly Aretas was given rights to Damascus for several years.[11] Aretas IV could have been ruling over Damascus as king from this time until his death, as 2 Corinthians 11:32 indicates, and thus during the time Paul was there.

In 2 Corinthians 11:32, Paul writes that an ethnarch (governor or viceroy) of Aretas was in charge of Damascus during this time. Aretas seems to have governed his Nabatean kingdom on a tribal basis, and inscriptions from the area use the word ethnarch (ἐθνάρχης, *ethnarchēs*) for the head of a tribal district.[12] Jewish governors in Palestine and Alexandria also had the title.[13]

Expulsion of the Jews from Rome by Claudius

A second important pinpoint in Pauline chronology is provided by Luke's statement in Acts 18:2 that when Paul arrived in Corinth on his second journey, he found Aquila and Priscilla, Jews who had "lately" (προσφάτως, *prosphatōs*) come from Rome "because Claudius had commanded all the Jews to leave Rome." This expulsion is also referred to in other ancient sources and can be dated to A.D. 49. Suetonius, chief secretary to the emperor Hadrian (A.D. 117–38), wrote a biographical account of the twelve caesars, in which he said, "Because the Jews at Rome caused continuous disturbances at the instigation of Chrestus, he expelled them from the City."[14] The Latin spelling of Christ (Christus) as Chrestus is found in ancient

9. *Ant.* 18.124.

10. Cook, et al., *The Cambridge Ancient History,* 10:750ff.

11. Finegan, *ANT:MW,* 57; Stewart Perowne, *The Journeys of St. Paul* (London and New York: Hamlyn, 1973), 18.

12. Alfred Plummer, *The Second Epistle of Paul the Apostle to the Corinthians,* Cambridge Greek Testament (Cambridge: Cambridge University Press, 1903), 188. Jones suggests the possibility that the Nabatean kings, organizing their kingdom on a centralized Hellenistic model, gave the title of "governor" to their local sheikhs (A. H. M. Jones, *Cities of the Eastern Roman Provinces* [Oxford: Clarendon, 1937], 292). For other evidence of the possibilities for this word, see Louis Feldman, trans., *Josephus: Jewish Antiquities,* Loeb Classical Library (Cambridge, Mass.: Harvard University Press, 1965), 12:79 n. 3 (*Ant.* 18.112).

13. Simon is called "high priest and ethnarch of the Jews" in 1 Maccabees 14:47; 15:1–2. Archelaus, the son of Herod the Great, was given the title ethnarch of Judea and Samaria, according to Josephus, *J.W.* 2.94.

14. *Claud.* 25.4.

Greek manuscripts of the New Testament.[15] The reference is probably to the disturbances in Rome caused by the making of Jewish converts to Christ.

Orosius, another early Roman author,[16] dates the expulsion to the ninth year of Claudius, which Finegan shows to be A.D. 49.[17] About the same time,[18] *The Teaching of Addai*[19] was written. This work refers to an expulsion of the Jews by Claudius after his wife Prontonice visited Jerusalem and became a Christian.[20] She is stated to have returned to Rome and informed the emperor about the Jews' refusal to allow Christians access to Golgotha, the cross, and the tomb of Christ. As a result Claudius banished the Jews from Italy. The text reads: "When Caesar heard it, he commanded all the Jews to leave the country of Italy, since in this whole region this event was spoken of by many."[21]

Some confusion exists about this expulsion, however, because Dio Cassius, about A.D. 230, published an eighty-volume history of Rome, which states that Claudius "did not drive them out . . . but ordered them not to hold meetings."[22] George Howard suggests that the occasion referred to by Dio Cassius probably coincides with Claudius's favorable attitude toward the Jews, an attitude referred to by Josephus,[23] who records two favorable edicts about the Jews given by Claudius at the beginning of his reign.[24]

I should also note that a huge cemetery of a Jewish family was excavated on the western borders of Jericho, in Palestine, which contains a sarcophagus

---

15. Χρηστιανος (*Chrēstianos*) in Codex Sinaiticus at Acts 11:26; 26:28; 1 Pet. 4:16. See F. Blass and A. Debrunner, *A Greek Grammar of the New Testament and Other Early Christian Literature,* trans. R. Funk (Chicago: University of Chicago Press, 1961), 14. The form Χρειστιανος (*Chreistianos*) is also found in Codex Bezae (G. Abbott-Smith, *A Manual Greek Lexicon of the New Testament* [Edinburgh: Clark, 1950], 484).

16. Orosius, *Seven Books of History against the Romans* 7.6.15–16 (written in A.D. 416–17).

17. *Handbook of Biblical Chronology,* rev. ed. (Peabody, Mass.: Hendrickson, 1998), 393.

18. Around A.D. 400, according to George Howard, *The Teaching of Addai* (Chico, Calif.: Scholars Press, 1981), vii.

19. Addai is taken by Eusebius to refer to Thaddeus, one of the seventy disciples of Jesus (*Hist. eccl.* 1.13.11ff.).

20. The document states that she was converted after her daughter, who had suddenly and painlessly died upon entry into the tomb of Christ, was restored to life by contact with the true cross of Christ (Addai 9b). See Howard, *Teaching of Addai,* 29.

21. Addai 10b. See Howard, *Teaching of Addai,* 33.

22. Dio Cassius, *History of Rome* 60.6.6 (see the seven volumes of extant fragments in the Loeb Classical Library series: *Dio's Roman History,* trans. Earnest Cary [Cambridge, Mass.: Harvard University Press, 1914–27]).

23. *Ant.* 19.290–91.

24. George Howard, "The Beginnings of Christianity in Rome: A Note on Suetonius, *Life of Claudius* XXV.4," *Restoration Quarterly* 24.3 (1981): 175–77. On the question of the relation of Dio Cassius's account and that of Suetonius, see Rainer Riesner, *Paul's Early Period: Chronology, Mission Strategy, Theology,* trans. Doug Stott (Grand Rapids: Eerdmans, 1998), 158–79, where he sees them referring to two different events.

with the inscription "Theodotus, a freedman of Agrippina."[25] Agrippina became the wife of Claudius in A.D. 49,[26] and her favorable attitude toward Jews, evident in her granting freedom to this Jewish slave,[27] supports the situation depicted by Josephus. Howard is probably correct in assuming that the expulsion of Jews from Italy by Claudius occurred later in his reign, represents a different mind-set, and involves a different wife.

Gallio's Proconsulship in Achaia

After spending eighteen months in Corinth on his second missionary journey (Acts 18:11), Paul was brought before Gallio, the proconsul of Achaia, by his Jewish opponents, who were presumably taking advantage of Gallio's recent appointment as a fresh opportunity for a "united attack" on the apostle (Acts 18:12). Their charge had to do with Paul's supposed violations of Jewish law, a matter about which Gallio was little concerned (Acts 18:15). The discovery of four fragments of an inscription carved in stone at Delphi, across the Corinthian Gulf from Corinth, that contain information about the accession of Gallio helps us to determine the date of his tenure in office.[28]

The fragments are from a copy of a letter sent from Claudius to the city of Delphi, either to the people of Delphi or to Gallio's successor,[29] and although it is fragmentary, it contains the name of Gallio, in addition to that of Claudius, with dates for his reign. Below is a selection from the reconstructed Greek fragments followed by Deissmann's restoration of the full text:

Τιβέρ[ιος Κλαύδιος Κ]αῖσ[αρ Σεβαστ]ός Γ[ερμανικός]. . . . [καθὼς Λούκιος Ἰού]νιος Γαλλίων ὁ φ[ίλος] μου κα[ὶ ἀνθύ]πατος [τῆς Ἀχαίας ἔγραψεν. . . .

Tiberius Claudius Caesar Augustus Germanicus (Pontifex Maximus, of tribunican authority for the 12th time, imperator the 26th time, father of the country, consul for the 5th time, honorable, greets the city of the Delphians. Having long been well disposed to the city of the Delphians. . . . I have had success. I have observed the religious ceremonies of the Pythian Apollo . . . now it is said also of the citizens . . .) as *Lucius Junius Gallio, my friend, and the proconsul of Achaia* wrote . . . (on this account I accede to you still to have the first. . . .)

25. Rachel Hachlili and Ann Killebrew, "The Saga of the Goliath Family—As Revealed in Their Newly Discovered 2,000-Year-Old Tomb," *BAR* 9.1 (Jan./Feb. 1983): 53.

26. William Smith, ed., *Dictionary of Greek and Roman Biography and Mythology* (Boston: Little and Brown, 1849), 1:81. She died in A.D. 60 (p. 82).

27. Theodotus is the Greek name (θεοδοτος) for the Hebrew Nathanael.

28. The fragments were published in 1905 by Emile Bourguet. An account of early publications of the inscription is given in A. Deissmann, *St. Paul: A Study in Social and Religious History* (New York: Hodder and Stoughton, 1912), 235–60. A picture of the fragments is included as the frontispiece of the volume.

29. See Colin Hemer, *BASHH,* 168–69, 251–56.

The letter from Claudius is dated to A.D. 52 by Finegan.[30] Since proconsuls normally held office for one year,[31] and these provincial governors were required to leave Rome for their posts not later than the middle of April,[32] Gallio probably began his term of office in May of A.D. 51. And since Paul arrived in Corinth eighteen months earlier than his appearance before Gallio,[33] he would have entered Corinth in the winter of 49/50—perhaps in January of A.D. 50.[34] This would coincide well with the recent arrival of Priscilla and Aquila from Claudius's expulsion in A.D. 49.

Procuratorship of Festus in Judea

The fourth pinpoint of Pauline chronology is the date when Festus succeeded Felix as procurator of Palestine (Acts 24:27). In private correspondence, Jerry Vardaman informed me that he had found a coin with micrographic writing on it that gives the date of Festus's accession and Paul's appearance before him as A.D. 56, which is about three to five years earlier than previous chronologies have allowed.[35] This would mean that Paul stood before Festus (Acts 24:27) in the spring (perhaps May) of A.D. 56, and that he had arrived in Jerusalem at the end of his third journey two years earlier.[36]

The Problem of the Deaths of James and Agrippa

An important question in Paul's chronology centers around the very difficult section of the eleventh and twelfth chapters of Acts involving the death

30. Finegan, *Handbook of Biblical Chronology,* rev. ed., 392; idem, *ANT:MW,* 13.

31. Dio Cassius, *History of Rome* 60.25.6, says that Claudius allowed some governors to hold office two years, but this is probably an indication of exceptional cases.

32. Dio Cassius, *History of Rome* 60.17.3.

33. Acts 18:11. With the above assumption that the Jews took advantage of Gallio's recent appointment to accuse Paul.

34. Some have applied the inscription to Gallio's successor and thus date it a year later. Dixon Slingerland feels that the date of Gallio's proconsulship is not certain enough to place Paul's arrival in Corinth with greater precision than between A.D. 47 and 54. However, he is unjustifiably critical of Luke's accuracy, as well as of the testimony of Orosius regarding the expulsion of Jews from Rome by Claudius ("Acts 18:1–18, the Gallio Inscription, and Absolute Pauline Chronology," *JBL* 110.3 [fall 1991]: 440 n. 3).

35. F. F. Bruce dates the accession to A.D. 59 (*Paul: Apostle of the Heart Set Free* [Grand Rapids: Eerdmans, 1977], 475); George Ogg places it at A.D. 61 (*Chronology of the Life of Paul,* 200).

36. Jack Finegan also corresponded with Vardaman about the coin and accepted the May A.D. 56 date for Festus's accession in the 1981 edition of his book on archaeology (*ANT:MW,* 14, 36, 39). However, the 1998 revised edition of Finegan's book on chronology (*Handbook of Biblical Chronology,* rev. ed., 399) reverts without explanation to the A.D. 57 date that he defended in the earlier edition of this work (*Handbook of Biblical Chronology* [Princeton, N.J.: Princeton University Press, 1964], 324).

of James, the imprisonment of Peter, and the death of Agrippa I.[37] The question has to do with whether an exact date can be given to these events. Did they occur in A.D. 44 as is commonly held, or perhaps a year earlier or later? These bear on the question of the time of the famine visit and possibly the fourteenth-year visit of Galatians 2.

Luke introduces this section with the words "in these days" (Acts 11:27). The phrases "these days" and "those days" are frequently used in the New Testament to designate an unspecified period of time. For example:

In *those days* came John the Baptist, preaching in the wilderness of Judea. (Matt. 3:1)

For as in *those days* before the flood they were eating and drinking, marrying and giving in marriage, until the day when Noah entered the ark. (Matt. 24:38)

In *those days* Jesus came from Nazareth of Galilee and was baptized by John in the Jordan. (Mark 1:9)

In *these days* he went out into the hills to pray; and all night he continued in prayer to God. (Luke 6:12)

And all the prophets who have spoken, from Samuel and those who came afterwards, also proclaimed *these days*. (Acts 3:24)

For before *these days* Theudas arose. (Acts 5:36)

Now in *these days* when the disciples were increasing in number . . . (Acts 6:1)

In *those days* a decree went out from Caesar Augustus that all the world should be enrolled. (Luke 2:1)

The days will come, when the bridegroom is taken away from them, and then they will fast in *those days*. (Luke 5:35)

In *those days* Peter stood up among the brethren. (Acts 1:15)

Yea, and on my menservants and my maidservants in *those days* I will pour out my Spirit; and they shall prophesy. (Acts 2:18)

And they made a calf in *those days,* and offered a sacrifice to the idol and rejoiced in the works of their hands. (Acts 7:41)

---

37. For a thorough discussion of the death of Agrippa, see Kirsopp Lake, "The Chronology of Acts," in *The Acts of the Apostles,* ed. F. J. Foakes-Jackson and Kirsopp Lake, The Beginnings of Christianity, part 1 (London: Macmillan, 1920–33), 5:446–52.

It is thus impossible to determine how much time Luke intends to convey by this expression—whether days, weeks, months, or years. This period of time includes the deaths of James the brother of John in Jerusalem (Acts 12:1–2) and Herod Agrippa I in Caesarea (Acts 12:19–23).[38] Also during this time Peter was imprisoned in Jerusalem (Acts 12:3–17). Luke means to say that the events in Antioch were happening simultaneously with certain events in Judea that are important to the development of his story.

The major problem in the chronology here is that Acts 12:25 seems to logically follow Acts 11:30. The passage therefore should read:

> And the disciples determined, every one according to his ability, to send relief to the brethren who lived in Judea; and they did so, sending it to the elders by the hand of Barnabas and Saul. . . . And Barnabas and Saul returned from Jerusalem when they had fulfilled their mission, bringing with them John whose other name was Mark. (Acts 11:29–30; 12:25)

Paul and Barnabas returned to Antioch from Jerusalem (Acts 12:25), but no record is given of their having gone to Jerusalem except the statement in Acts 11:30 that they took the famine relief from Antioch to the elders in Jerusalem. But what about the intervening verses? Do we have here two different trips described with *no end designated for the first visit, which began in Acts 11:30, and no beginning given for the second visit, which ended in Acts 12:25?*

Or, more likely, are the intervening verses, Acts 12:1–24, actually parenthetical, inserted to explain why Paul and Barnabas "in those days" (i.e., during the time of the events taking place in Antioch and Jerusalem) took the relief to the *elders* rather than the apostles? If this is Luke's intent, then these twenty-four verses parenthetically show how the persecution by Herod, resulting in the death of James and the imprisonment of Peter, led to the demise of the apostles' activity in the city and thus demonstrate how leadership passed from them to James the Lord's brother and to the elders.[39] If this is the case, then we have here only one visit of Paul to Jerusalem (beginning in Acts 11:30 and concluding in Acts 12:25) and not two different trips.

With explanatory interpolations in brackets, we may thus understand this difficult passage to read:

> [27]Now in these days prophets came down from Jerusalem to Antioch. [28]And one of them named Agabus stood up and foretold by the Spirit that there would be a great famine over all the world; and this took place [*two years later*] in the days of Claudius. [29]And the disciples determined [*while Agabus was*

---

38. Cf. also Josephus, *Ant.* 19.343.

39. This is suggested by David Wenham, "Acts and the Pauline Corpus: II. The Evidence of Parallels," in *The Book of Acts in Its Ancient Literary Setting,* ed. Bruce W. Winter and Andrew D. Clarke, BAFCS 1 (Grand Rapids: Eerdmans, 1993), 239.

there], every one according to his ability, to send relief to the brethren who lived in Judea; [30]and they did so [*later when the famine came*], sending it to the elders by the hand of Barnabas and Saul. . . . [25]And Barnabas and Saul returned from Jerusalem when they had fulfilled their mission, bringing with them John whose other name was Mark. (Acts 11:27–30; 12:25)

The actual sequence involved would be the following:

A.D. 43 or 44

1. The famine was prophesied   Acts 11:28
2. Antioch determined to help   Acts 11:29

A.D. 46 or 47

3. The famine occurred   Acts 11:28
4. Antioch sent help   Acts 11:30

The date of the famine is difficult to determine because famines vary in duration based on many factors, including the availability of food, inflated prices during shortages of food, the difference in time between when the countries are stricken and when the subsequent effect reaches those they supply with food (Egypt supplied most of the Mediterranean with grain).[40] A further complication in determining dates is inherent in the way a famine is reported—whether from its beginning to its end throughout the empire (which may cover years) or its duration in one particular country (which may be a shorter time).

The literary evidence supports a famine in Egypt in the fall of A.D. 45, but we cannot be sure whether the date marks the beginning or end of the famine.[41] During this famine, Helena, a Jewish proselyte from Adiabene,[42] made a trip to Jerusalem to worship in the temple. When she arrived, she found the city gripped by famine and immediately dispatched her servants to Egypt with large amounts of money to purchase grain and dried figs.[43] Her son Izates also sent large sums of money to buy food.[44] Josephus admiringly states that "she has thus left a very great name that will be famous forever among our whole people for

40. See Peter Garnsey, *Famine and Food Supply in the Graeco-Roman World: Responses to Risk and Crisis* (Cambridge: Cambridge University Press, 1988); Bradley Blue, "The House Church at Corinth and the Lord's Supper: Famine, Food Supply, and the Present Distress," *Criswell Theological Review* 5.2 (1991): 221–39; Kenneth Gapp, "The Universal Famine under Claudius," *HTR* 28.1 (1935): 258–65; Bruce Winter, "Secular and Christian Responses to Corinthian Famines," *TynBul* 40 (May 1989): 86–102.

41. Gapp, "Universal Famine," 258–59.

42. Josephus, *Ant.* 20.35.

43. Ibid., 20.51.

44. Ibid., 20.53.

her benefaction."[45] Indeed, her monumental tomb, with a rolling stone at the door, is still preserved in Jerusalem just north of the Damascus Gate.

Josephus dates Helena's visit to Jerusalem and her act of generosity within the reign of the procurator Fadus (A.D. 44–46) and/or his successor Tiberius Alexander (A.D. 46–48).[46] Thus, this famine, beginning in Egypt in A.D. 45, may have continued into A.D. 47 and may be the worldwide famine Agabus prophesied in Acts 11:28.[47] The expressions "worldwide" and "universal" in the ancient world varied in application depending on whether the author was using them in a technical geographical sense.[48] To the Romans, the area encompassed in those expressions included Africa, India, Southeast and Central Asia, and China.[49] The terms were also natural hyperbole when used of especially distressing circumstances. The use of such terms in the Book of Acts probably falls into this latter category. Bruce Winter argues that "Acts records neither the language of the geographer nor of the historian, but that of a prophet. In such discourse it is of the very essence to speak in universals when giving notice of an event with far-reaching implications and demanding action."[50]

The famine may have continued into A.D. 51, when we have evidence of a famine in Corinth for which a special curator of the famine was appointed, a man by the name of Dinippus. In inscriptions he is stated to have served in that capacity a record three times.[51] This could be the distressing situation that confronted the church in Corinth, as reflected in 1 Corinthians 7:26.[52]

In establishing the dates for these events, it should be noted that James died during the persecution conducted by Herod Agrippa I "during the days" of

45. Ibid., 20.52.

46. Ibid., 20.100. He writes: "It was in the administration of Tiberius Alexander that the great famine occurred in Judaea during which Queen Helena bought grain from Egypt for large sums and distributed it to the needy." The reading of the text is not clear here. It may read either ἐπὶ τούτου (as in the "Epitome"), referring just to the reign of Tiberius Alexander, or, as the Greek manuscripts and Eusebius (who quotes this passage in *Hist. eccl.* 2.12.1) have it, ἐπὶ τούτοις, referring to the time of both Tiberius and Fadus, whom he has just mentioned. Thus it would be translated "in their time." See *Josephus: Jewish Antiquities,* Loeb Classical Library, 13:55 n. e (*Ant.* 20.101). For the dates (44–46? and 46?–48), see A. H. M. Jones, *The Herods of Judaea* (Oxford: Clarendon, 1967), 224–25. Gapp places the famine in either 46 or 47 ("Universal Famine," 260). Lake places Fadus as procurator in 45, Tiberius Alexander in 46, and Cumanus in 47 ("Chronology of Acts," 453). See further Lake's full discussion of the problem.

47. Gapp, "Universal Famine," 263–65.

48. As does Strabo, the ancient geographer (*Geogr.* 1.1.13, 15; 2.24.2; 3.3.1).

49. For documentation see, N. H. H. Sitwell, *The World the Romans Knew* (London: Hamish Hamilton, 1984).

50. Bruce W. Winter, "Acts and Food Shortages," in *The Book of Acts in Its Graeco-Roman Setting,* ed. Gill and Gempf, BAFCS 2 (Grand Rapids: Eerdmans, 1994), 68.

51. See the discussion of this evidence in Winter, "Secular and Christian Responses to Corinthian Famines," 90. See also Blue, "The House Church at Corinth," 235–36.

52. See Blue, "House Church at Corinth."

Unleavened Bread (Acts 12:1–3). This could have been the Passover of A.D. 43[53] or, as is more generally argued, A.D. 44.[54] Eusebius gives Agrippa's death in A.D. 44 in the fourth year of the reign of the emperor Claudius (A.D. 41–54).[55] By the Roman method of inclusive reckoning, this would be A.D. 44, not A.D. 45. It was "after the completion of the third year of his [Agrippa's] reign over the whole of Judaea," according to Josephus.[56]

No month is discernable for Agrippa's death. However, in additon to the spring Passover reference in Acts, Josephus also mentions that Agrippa's death occurred in conjunction with a festival being celebrated in Caesarea.[57] Two possibilities exist for this festival of games. First, they could have been the regular games Herod the Great inaugurated, which were observed every four years. These games began in the twenty-eighth year of Herod's reign, in the 192nd Olympiad, according to Josephus.[58] This is commonly taken as the basis to calculate A.D. 44 as the year of Arippa's death during this celebration. A second possibility is the special festival of games that began in Rome in honor of Claudius's return from Britain in the spring of A.D. 44. These were celebrated in the provinces later,[59] perhaps in late summer.

The Olympiadic year is determined in relation to the date of the "founding of Rome" (the Latin abbreviation is A.U.C., *ab urbe condita*), which occurred in 753 B.C. It is calculated in four-year intervals. So the Roman year A.U.C. 1 = 753 B.C. began in Olympiad 6.3 and ended in Olympiad 6.4.[60] These dates have been used almost unanimously by scholars to set the time of Herod's founding of the games in the 192nd Olympiad as 10/9 B.C. and thus to set the date of A.D. 44 in Olympiad 205.4 for the death of Agrippa. (Four-year intervals from 9 B.C. would give A.D. 44.)[61] It has been as-

53. See Schürer, *History of the Jewish People,* 1.2:163 n. 45.

54. L. C. A. Alexander places it in early March: "Chronology of Paul," in *Dictionary of Paul and His Letters,* ed. Gerald F. Hawthorne et al. (Downers Grove, Ill.: InterVarsity, 1993), 120; S. A. Cook et al., eds., *Cambridge Ancient History,* 10:681; see also Schürer, *History of the Jewish People,* 1.2:163 n. 45; and Cary, *History of Rome,* 543.

55. See the computations of the Eusebian Chronicle in Finegan, *Handbook of Biblical Chronology,* rev. ed., 160–92, esp. 188.

56. *Ant.* 19.343.

57. Ibid.

58. Josephus mentions these: "He further instituted quinquennial games, likewise named after Caesar, and inaugurated them himself, in the hundred and ninety-second Olympiad" (*J. W.* 1.415). In the *Antiquities* (16.136), he adds "the 28th year of his [Herod the Great's, JM] reign, which fell in the hundred and ninety-second Olympiad."

59. Dio Cassius, *History of Rome* 60.23. See the discussion of both of these possibilities in Schürer, *History of the Jewish People,* 1.2:163 n. 45.

60. For an extensive list of the Olympiad years with their corresponding A.U.C. and B.C.–A.D. equivalents, see Schürer, *History of the Jewish People,* 1.2:393–98.

61. An event designated as a "quinquennial" would occur in the fifth year, following the four-year interval. This is the meaning of Josephus when he says Herod dedicated this contest to Caesar, having arranged to celebrate it every fifth year (κατὰ πενταετηρίδα) (*Ant.* 16.138).

sumed[62] that the regular games (possibility 1 above) were celebrated on March 5, because in the fourth century Eusebius wrote that this was the date on which the Martyrdom of Hadrian was celebrated,[63] and Schwartz *assumes* it to be the day Herod instituted for the games at the time of the founding of the city (Caesarea's *dies natalis*). This assumption lacks proof.[64]

Lake suggests August as a more likely date, corresponding to the celebration of the conquest of Egypt and the defeat of Antony,[65] a date also argued earlier by Wieseler.[66] Lake concludes that August of A.D. 43 is just as likely a date as May of A.D. 44. Further, Josephus states that Marcus Julius Alexander, Agrippa's son-in-law, died before Agrippa,[67] and according to an ancient inscription, Marcus was still alive in mid–A.D. 44.[68] This points to a time in the summer rather than the spring.

As to calculation of the Olympiadic year, Finegan notes, it "may be set parallel with the Roman year in the course of which it began or with the year in the course of which it ended. Thus Olympiad 6.3 began in 754 B.C. and ended in 753 B.C., and might be set parallel with either."[69] This means a date of A.D. 43 as well as A.D. 44 could be established, depending on whether one worked from the beginning or ending date of the Olympiadic year.

Those who hold to A.D. 44 argue that Acts is wrong because the Passover of that year did not occur until April 1 (Nisan 15 in the Jewish calendar), whereas the games being celebrated in Caesarea occurred in early March. However, there is "no proof that the quinquennial feast in honor of Augustus was celebrated in March," as noted above.

At any rate, the rejection of the accuracy of Acts ignores several important facts: (1) The phrase "remained there" (Acts 12:19) gives an indefinite period of time for the stay of Agrippa in Caesarea. (2) The indefiniteness of the time involved in these interim events of Acts 12:1–24 (evidenced by such phrases as "in these days," Acts 11:27, etc.—see above) makes it impossible to say dogmatically that James was killed in the final year of the reign of Agrippa. It may

---

62. Eduard Schwartz, *Zur Chronologie des Paulus,* Nachrichten von der Königlichen Gesellschaft der Wissenschaften zu Göttingen: Philologisch-historische Klasse, Jahrg. 1907 (Berlin: Weidmann, 1907).

63. See *Martyrs of Palestine* 11.30 in Eusebius, *Ecclesiastical History and the Martyrs of Palestine,* trans. H. J. Lawlor and J. E. L. Oulton (London: SPCK, 1954), 1:394 (the shorter recension).

64. See the discussion in Schürer, *History of the Jewish People,* 1.2:163 n. 45.

65. Lake, "Chronology of Acts," 452. See Dio Cassius, *History of Rome* 51.19.

66. Karl Georg Wieseler, *Chronologie des apostolischen Zeitalters* (Göttingen: Vandenhoeck & Ruprecht, 1848).

67. *Ant.* 19.276–77.

68. On Ostraca Petrie 271. The ostraca (published in G. A. Tait, *Greek Ostraca in the Bodleian,* vol. 1 [Oxford: Clarendon, 1930]) is dated Pauni 22, the fourth year of Claudius, i.e., June 16, A.D. 44, according to Dale Moody, "New Chronology," 229 n. 22.

69. Finegan, *Handbook of Biblical Chronology,* 117.

have been the preceding year. Josephus says Agrippa came to Caesarea in the third year of his four-year reign,[70] but Acts is clear that some time elapsed between James's death in Jerusalem and Agrippa's death in Caesarea, where he stayed for an unstated period of time. (3) Acts makes no claim that the events described in Acts 12:1–24 are in chronological order. They all revolved around Agrippa, and nothing is based on their need to be in chronological order. They are merely explanatory of and parenthetical to the activities of Paul and Barnabas in Antioch and Jerusalem.

Constructing a Chronology

With the above pinpoints as a basis, I submit the following detailed reconstruction of Paul's movements as a working hypothesis, with full awareness that problems exist that need refinement, but this chronology can at least provide a working framework in which to place the life of Paul and from which further study may proceed.[71]

Table 3.2 Chronology of Paul

Date	Event	Acts	Letters
5 B.C– A.D. 30	*Life of Jesus*		
c. Jan. 5 B.C.	Birth of Jesus		
c. A.D. 27–30	Ministry of Jesus		
April 6, A.D. 30	Crucifixion of Jesus		
April 9	Resurrection of Jesus		
c. May 18	Ascension of Jesus	1:3–9	
A.D. 30–43	*The Church in Palestine*	1:1–11:18	
May 28, A.D. 30	Pentecost sermon of Peter	2:1–40	
c. 33–34	Persecution over Stephen; Scattering to Judea and Samaria	8:1–3	Gal. 1:13
34	Conversion of Paul	9:1–19	Gal. 1:15–16
	Commission of Paul	26:16–18	Gal. 1:15–16
34–37	Paul in Damascus and Arabia	9:19–23	Gal. 1:17–18
	Enters Damascus	9:8; 22:10–12	

70. *Ant.* 19.343.

71. This chronology was worked out largely by my son, Rob McRay, under my direction in courses he took with me as an M.A. student at Wheaton College Graduate School in 1981 and 1982. The chronology does not fully represent either his views or mine, but a mixture of both.

Date	Event	Acts	Letters
	Is baptized and healed	9:18; 22:16	
	Several days in Damascus	9:19	
	Immediately preached in the synagogues	9:20, 27; 26:20	
	To Arabia		Gal. 1:17
March, 37	Death of Tiberius; change of frontier policy by Caligula		
Late 37	Returned to Damascus		Gal. 1:17
	Many days pass	9:23	
	Jews plot to kill Paul	9:23	
	Escapes in a basket	9:25	2 Cor. 11:32–33
	(Aretas IV dies 38–40)		
Late 37	*Paul's First Jerusalem Visit* (Third-year visit)	9:26	Gal. 1:18–19
	Preaches at Jerusalem	9:29; 26:20	
	in synagogues, not churches		Gal. 1:22
	Taken to the apostles	9:27	
	Peter and James the Lord's brother		Gal. 1:18–19
	Paul is "in and out" of the city	9:28	
	Hellenists want to kill Paul	9:29	
	Prays in temple, has vision	22:17	
	Warned to leave city	22:18	
	Sent to Tarsus	9:30	
37–43	Paul in Syria and Cilicia		Gal. 1:21
	Peter in Palestine	9:31–11:18	
c. 37–38	(Cornelius converted)		
c. 40	Paul's vision of Paradise		2 Cor. 12:2–4
c. 43	Spread of persecuted as far as Phoenicia, Cyprus, and Antioch; Greeks converted	11:19–21	
43–47	*Paul in Antioch*	11:26–13:3	
c. 43	Barnabas brings Paul to Antioch	11:25–26	
c. 43–44	Paul and Barnabas in Antioch a whole year	11:26	
44	(1) Agabus prophesies a famine	11:28	
	(2) Antioch decides to help	11:29	

Date	Event	Acts	Letters
Passover 43 or 44	James killed, Peter imprisoned	12:1–19	
43 or 44	Herod Agrippa I dies	12:20–23	
46 or 47	(3) Famine (time of Claudius)	11:28	
	(4) Antioch sends help—by Paul and Barnabas	11:30	
47	*Paul's Second Jerusalem Visit* (Famine visit)	11:30	
47	Paul and Barnabas return to Antioch, taking Mark	12:25	
47	*Paul's Third Jerusalem Visit* (Fourteenth-year visit)		Gal. 2:1–10
	Paul confronts Peter at Antioch		Gal. 2:11–14
Late 47–Mid 48	*First Missionary Journey*	13:3–14:26	
Late 47	Paul in Cyprus	13:4–13	
Fall 47–Mid 48	Paul in Galatia and Pamphylia	13:13–14:26	
Mid 48–Mid 49	*Paul in Antioch*	14:26–15:40	
Mid–Late 48	Paul writes *Galatians*		Gal. 1:1–2
Late 48–Early 49	Judaizers come to Antioch	15:1–2	
Early 49	*Paul's Fourth Jerusalem Visit* (Conference visit)	15:2–30	
Summer 49–Summer 51	*Second Missionary Journey*	15:41–18:22	
Summer 49	Paul in Syria, Cilicia, Galatia, and Phrygia	15:41–16:6	
Fall 49	Paul in Macedonia and Athens	16:6–18:1	
	Paul, Silas, leave Thessalonica and go to Beroea (Timothy comes later, Acts 17:14)	17:10	
	Paul to Athens; leaves Silas and Timothy behind at Beroea	17:14–15	
	Paul sends back word for Silas and Timothy to come as soon as possible	17:15	
	Timothy (from Thessalonica) [and Silas from Beroea?] joins Paul at Athens		
	Paul stays in Athens, sends Timothy back to Thessalonica		1 Thess. 3:1–2
49	Claudius expels Jews from Rome		
	Priscilla and Aquila to Corinth	18:2	

Date	Event	Acts	Letters
Dec. 49–June 51	Paul to Corinth; stays 18 mos.	18:1, 11	
c. Jan. 50	Timothy and Silas join Paul at Corinth	18:5	1 Thess. 3:6
c. Jan. 50	Paul, Silas, and Timothy write *1 Thessalonians;* only Timothy is mentioned as coming from Thessalonica (1 Thess. 3:1, 6); Silas may have come from Beroea		1 Thess. 1:1
Early 50	Paul, Silas, and Timothy write *2 Thessalonians*		2 Thess. 1:1
May/June 51	Gallio arrives in Corinth	18:12	
July 51	Paul before Gallio	18:12	
July 51	Paul leaves Corinth	18:18	
July 51	*Paul's Fifth Jerusalem Visit*	18:22	
Aug. 51–May 54	*Third Missionary Journey*	18:23–21:8	
Aug.–Sept. 51	Paul travels through Galatia, Phrygia, and the upper country	18:23; 19:1	
Oct.–Dec. 51	Paul in the synagogue in Ephesus	19:8	
Jan. 52–July 53	Paul in the Hall of Tyrannus in Ephesus	19:9–10	
c. Dec. 52	Paul writes the *previous letter*		1 Cor. 5:9;
or Jan. 53	to Corinth from Ephesus about the immoral person and the contribution for Jerusalem		2 Cor. 8:10; 9:1–2
c. Jan.–Mar. 53	The Corinthians write Paul in Ephesus		1 Cor. 7:1
c. Mar. 53	Paul sends Timothy and Erastus into Macedonia from Ephesus	19:22	
	Paul plans for Timothy to visit Corinth and return to him		1 Cor. 16:10–11
	Paul plans to stay in Ephesus at least till Pentecost, A.D. 53		1 Cor. 16:8
	Paul plans to then visit Macedonia and perhaps winter in Corinth	19:21	1 Cor. 16:5–6
	Paul plans to then leave Corinth for somewhere, perhaps Jerusalem or Rome	19:21	1 Cor. 16:6; cf. 16:3–4
c. Mar. 53	Paul and Sosthenes write *1 Corinthians* from Ephesus		1 Cor. 1:1
c. Apr. 53	Change of plans;		2 Cor. 1:16

Date	Event	Acts	Letters
	Paul now plans to visit Corinth first, then Macedonia, then Corinth again, then Judea		
May–Oct. 53	Paul stays awhile in Ephesus	19:22	
	(till Pentecost), then departs		(1 Cor. 16:8)
	for Macedonia (via Corinth)	20:1	(2 Cor. 1:16)
	Paul's visit to Corinth is painful		2 Cor. 2:1
	Paul goes on to Macedonia as he planned, and perhaps Illyricum	20:2	cf. Rom. 15:19
	Paul no longer plans to return to Corinth from Macedonia as it would only be painful		2 Cor. 1:23–2:1
	Paul writes a *tearful letter* to Corinth and sends it with Titus		2 Cor. 2:3–11
	Paul apparently plans to meet Titus at Troas (Titus would sail across)		
Oct.–Nov. 53	Paul does not find Titus at Troas		2 Cor. 2:12–13
Nov. 11, 53	Sailing season ends for winter		
Late Nov. 53	Paul goes into Macedonia looking for Titus, who must now come by land		2 Cor. 2:13
Dec. 53	Paul finds Titus in Macedonia and is greatly encouraged		2 Cor. 7:5–7
	Paul and Timothy wrote *2 Corinthians* from Macedonia		2 Cor. 1:1; 7:5–6; 8:1; 9:2–4
	and sent it with Titus		2 Cor. 8:16–17
	Paul plans to make a third visit to Corinth to pick up the collection		2 Cor. 12:14; 13:1; 9:3–5
Jan.–Mar. 54	Paul visits Corinth and stays 3 months in Greece	20:3?	cf. 1 Cor. 16:6
	Paul writes *Romans* from Corinth		Rom. 16:23
	Paul plans to leave Corinth for Syria and Jerusalem with the contribution, then go to Rome, then to Spain	20:3	Rom. 15:24–28
	Plot by Jews forces another change in plans; Paul sends most of his companions on to Troas; Paul and Luke return through Macedonia	20:3–6	

Date	Event	Acts	Letters
Apr. 12–19, 54	Passover and Unleavened Bread	20:6	
Apr. 23, 54	Paul and Luke sail from Philippi, arriving in Troas five days later	20:6	
May 4, 54	Paul in Troas on Sunday	20:7	
	Paul hopes to reach Jerusalem by Pentecost	20:16	
	Stops and preaches in Miletus	20:15–38	
	("3 yrs." = 2 yrs. 7 mos.)	20:31	
May 31, 54	Pentecost		
	Paul's Sixth Jerusalem Visit (Arrest visit)	21:15–23:31	
	Jews try to kill him in temple	26:21	
June 54–May 56	*Paul in Prison in Caesarea*	23:33–26:32	
	Felix leaves Paul in prison for two years	24:27	
May 56	Festus arrives in Caesarea	24:27	
Summer 56–Feb. 57	*Paul's Shipwreck Journey to Rome*	27:1—28:16	
Oct. 9, 56	Day of Atonement (the Fast)	27:9	
Nov./Dec. 56–Feb./Mar. 57	Paul on Malta for the three months of the non-sailing season	28:11	
Mar. 57–c. Feb. 59	*Paul's First Roman Imprisonment*	28:14–31	
	Under guard two whole years	28:16, 30	
c. 58	Paul writes *Philemon, Colossians, Ephesians,* and *Philippians*		
	Paul plans to send Timothy to Philippi and back		Phil. 2:19
	Paul hopes to visit Philippi soon		Phil. 2:24
	Paul plans to visit Philemon		Philem. 22
59–67	*Paul's Later Travels*		
59	Paul sails from Rome to Crete and leaves Titus		Titus 1:5
	Paul crosses to Asia and visits Philemon at Colossae		Philem. 22
	On way to Macedonia, Paul exhorts Timothy to remain in Ephesus		1 Tim. 1:3
c. 60	Paul visits Philippi		Phil. 2:24
c. 61–65	Paul goes to Spain		Rom. 15:24

Date	Event	Acts	Letters
Early–Mid 65	Paul writes *1 Timothy;* hopes to visit Timothy soon but may be delayed		1 Tim. 3:14–15
Mid 65	Paul writes *Titus;* wants Titus to join him at Nicopolis, where he will spend the winter		Titus 3:12
Winter 65–66	Paul at Nicopolis		Titus 3:12
66	Paul visits Corinth; Erastus stays		2 Tim. 4:20
	Paul visits Miletus		2 Tim. 4:20
Sept. 66–Jan. 68	Nero travels in Greece		
Late 66–Early 67	Paul arrested in Troas (leaves books and clothes)		2 Tim. 4:13
c. 67	Paul's second Roman imprisonment		2 Tim. 1:16–17
	Paul's martyrdom is imminent		2 Tim. 4:6
Mid 67	Paul writes *2 Timothy*		
	Paul wants Timothy to come soon, before winter		2 Tim. 4:9, 21
c. Winter 67–68	Paul martyred in Rome		

Recent Studies on Pauline Chronology

Virtually all studies before the publication of *Chapters in a Life of Paul* by John Knox in 1950[72] worked essentially from a framework of five Jerusalem visits by Paul in Acts as against a two-visit framework in Galatians. Materials that would permit definitive conclusions or even a consensus are still unavailable. Several years ago[73] a colloquy on Pauline chronology was conducted in Fort Worth, Texas, but rather than providing definitive conclusions, it only exacerbated the problem by further demonstrating the inevitable diversity of conclusions that eventuate from differing presuppositions.[74]

72. John Knox, *Chapters in a Life of Paul* (New York: Abingdon, 1950; rev. ed., Macon, Ga.: Mercer Press, 1987).

73. November 5–6, 1980.

74. For a compilation and discussion of various chronological hypotheses, see chapter 1 of John C. Hurd, *The Origins of I Corinthians* (New York: Seabury, 1965), 3–42; and idem, "Pauline Chronology and Pauline Theology," in *Christian History and Interpretation: Studies Presented to John Knox,* ed. W. R. Farmer et al. (Cambridge: Cambridge University Press, 1967), 225–48; J. Murphy-O'Connor, "Pauline Mission before the Jerusalem Conference," *Revue Biblique* 89.1 (January 1982): 72–91; and idem, "The Chronological Framework," in *Paul: A Critical Life* (Oxford: Oxford University Press, 1996), 1–31.

Several important studies of the subject that confirm this observation have appeared since the work of Knox. His work is built on a presupposed framework of only *three* Jerusalem visits by Paul and is characterized by an acute skepticism of the historical credibility of Acts,[75] an almost total dependence on a few selected writings of Paul as primary material, and a rejection of the Gallio inscription, which will be discussed below. His reconstruction is as follows:

Visit One: Acquaintance Visit—Gal. 1; Acts 9
Visit Two: Conference Visit—Gal. 2; Acts 18:22 (15:2)
Visit Three: Offering Visit—Acts 21 (11:29)

George Caird published an article on the "Chronology of the New Testament" in 1962[76] that provided good material on the chronological pinpoints but omitted material on Aretas IV and worked from a date of A.D. 59 for the accession of Festus, a date Jerry Vardaman has now argued to be too late, on the basis of a recently analyzed ancient coin. This late date for the accession of Festus was also assumed by F. F. Bruce at the time he wrote his masterful work on Paul.[77]

Gerd Luedemann published a book on the subject in 1980,[78] in which he accepted the skepticism of Knox about Acts and gave strict priority of evidence to the letters of Paul. Luedemann disregards the Aretas IV datum, which would put Paul's escape from Damascus (Acts 9:25; 2 Cor. 11:32–33) no later than A.D. 40. He puts Claudius's expulsion of the Jews too early (A.D. 41) and places Paul in Corinth in that year. He applies the Gallio inscription data to Paul's Corinth visit on his third rather than second journey, and he has Paul's final visit to Jerusalem in A.D. 52, which is at least two years too early for the new date on Festus in Caesarea (A.D. 56). His chronology closes in 52 with Paul in Jerusalem, and he does not discuss the coin Vardaman found mentioning Festus.

---

75. Recently Knox wrote: "And I have found in the years since no reason to revise that judgment" ("On the Pauline Chronology: Buck-Taylor-Hurd Revisited," in *The Conversation Continues: Studies in Paul and John,* ed. Robert T. Fortna and Beverly Gaventa [Nashville: Abingdon, 1990], 258). He was followed in this skepticism of Acts by C. H. Buck, "The Collection for the Saints," *HTR* 43 (1950): 1–29; C. H. Buck and Greer Taylor, *St. Paul: A Study in the Development of His Thought* (New York: Scribners, 1969); and John C. Hurd, "Pauline Chronology and Pauline Theology," 225–48; idem, "The Sequence of Paul's Letters," *Canadian Journal of Theology* 14 (1968): 188–200; idem, "Chronology: Pauline," in *IDB Supplement,* 166–67.

76. *IDB,* 1:599–607.

77. *Paul,* 475.

78. *Paulus, der Heidenapostel I: Studien zur Chronologie* (Göttingen: Vandenhoeck and Ruprecht, 1980). The English translation is *Paul, Apostle to the Gentiles: Studies in Chronology,* trans. F. Stanley Jones (Philadelphia: Fortress, 1984).

A more reasoned approach to Pauline chronology was made by Robert Jewett in 1979 in his book *A Chronology of Paul's Life*,[79] in which he accepts Knox's approach but unlike Knox allows a cautious use of Acts based on redaction criticism, a relatively recent method of New Testament study.[80] He finds the last part of Acts, containing accounts of Paul's journeys, to be especially valuable:

> The travel accounts in Acts 15:36ff. are more important than earlier sections for the immediate task, entering the realm of verifiable history with the references to Gallio (Acts 18:12), Felix (Acts 23:24ff.), and Festus (Acts 24:27ff.).[81]

Jewett's more cautious approach is probably reflective of his use of redaction criticism in evaluating the material in Acts and of the work of A. N. Sherwin-White,[82] which has given considerable support to the historical accuracy of Acts without being an apologetic for the book.[83]

The major problem in dealing with Pauline chronology is the attempt to correlate Acts with Paul's letters. This is only compounded when the letters are viewed as the primary source and Acts is viewed as a secondary source that in virtually any apparent conflict of perspective is assumed to be wrong until proven right, that is, wrong if not harmonized with a preconceived understanding of Paul's work. Most studies of the problem give little credence to the historical view of Scripture that accepts Luke and Paul as equally inspired. And those who do respect this historical posture are often viewed as compulsive harmonizers.

Apart from this issue, however, on a purely logical basis, one has to wonder why Luke would not possess reliable information about Paul's activities since he was Paul's constant traveling companion[84] and on occasion spent long periods of time with Paul while Paul was in prison.[85] During this time Luke surely did some of his research and writing, based on Paul's personal recollection. It would be unreasonable to assume otherwise.

79. Philadelphia: Fortress, 1979.

80. See Norman Perrin, *What Is Redaction Criticism?* (Philadelphia: Fortress, 1974).

81. Jewett, *Chronology of Paul's Life*, 12.

82. *Roman Society and Roman Law in the New Testament* (Oxford: Clarendon, 1963).

83. See Jewett, *Chronology of Paul's Life*, 21.

84. When Luke was with Paul, he included himself in the narrative by using the first-person pronoun "we," and when he was not present, he appropriately used the third-person "they." The "we sections" show that Luke joined Paul in Troas and accompanied him during parts of Paul's second journey (Acts 16:10–17), his third journey (Acts 20:5–15; 21:1–18), and his voyage to Rome (Acts 27:1–28:16).

85. The use of the pronoun "we" in Acts 27:1 implies that Luke was closely associated with Paul during the time of the Caesarean imprisonment and during some, if not all, of his first imprisonment in Rome. During his final imprisonment in Rome, Paul wrote that "Luke alone is with me" (2 Tim. 4:11).

It should be noted in this regard that the recent work of Martin Hengel has been rather supportive of the credibility of Acts,[86] a point made even more significant by the fact that Hengel teaches at the University of Tübingen, a school long noted for its skeptical views on the historical reliability of many New Testament writings.

It is also significant that the most important book on the historicity of Acts to be published in this generation, from the masterful pen of the late Colin Hemer,[87] convincingly demonstrates from enormous quantities of inscriptional and literary evidence the essential trustworthiness of the Book of Acts. His chapter on "Acts and the Epistles" contains a section that deals cogently with most of the available evidence bearing on the question of Pauline chronology.

Hemer's reconstruction of Paul's movements is careful, reasoned, and convincing until he reaches the date of the accession of Festus as procurator of Judea. At this point,[88] Hemer accepts the older date of A.D. 59 and, surprisingly, makes no mention of either the work of Jack Finegan, one of the leading chronologists of our time, or the recent discoveries by Jerry Vardaman. These omissions, also made in his later paper on chronology,[89] are out of harmony with the rest of his monumental study.

One of the most up-to-date treatments of Pauline chronology is Finegan's 1998 revision of his *Handbook of Biblical Chronology*.[90] For unexplained reasons, however, his revision makes no reference to Vardaman's coin mentioning Festus, which Finegan had accepted in his 1981 volume on archaeology.[91] In this revision Finegan reaffirms his first-edition (1964) date of the summer of A.D. 57 for Paul's appearance before Festus.[92]

A careful chronology has recently been published by Rainer Riesner that reasonably synthesizes the data of both history and the New Testament on Pauline chronology, but like Finegan's revised edition on the subject, it does not refer to Vardaman's work when discussing the reign of Festus.[93]

Disappointingly, Finegan makes no reference to the Acts 11 famine visit and no attempt to relate Paul's letters to his chronology. The results of Fine-

86. Martin Hengel, *Acts and the History of Earliest Christianity* (Philadelphia: Fortress, 1980).

87. Hemer, *BASHH.*

88. Ibid., 171.

89. Colin J. Hemer, "Observations on Pauline Chronology," in *Pauline Studies,* ed. Donald Hagner and Murray Harris (Grand Rapids: Eerdmans, 1990), 3–18.

90. Peabody, Mass.: Hendrickson.

91. Jack Finegan, *ANT:MW.* Chapter 2 of that volume contains forty pages on chronology, including the Aretas IV dates.

92. See the further discussion below on chronological pinpoints under Festus.

93. Riesner, *Paul's Early Period: Chronology.*

gan's recent research, like those of George Ogg in his older book, *The Chronology of the Life of Paul*,[94] basically support the historical consensus.

A thoughtful but unconvincing variation on the usual method of treating the chronology of Acts was recently published by Dale Moody. He takes the six summary statements about the growth of the church given in Acts (6:7; 9:31; 12:24; 16:5; 19:20; 28:30–31) and argues that each represents a five-year period. He uses this quinquennial method as a foundation for developing his understanding of the chronology of Acts, but he resorts to postulating page displacements in the original manuscripts, for which there is no textual support.[95]

Perhaps a better understanding of these six summary statements is to take them as topical rather than durational. Accordingly, Luke would be summarizing the important events that took place in the fulfillment of Jesus' charge in Acts 1:8: "But you shall receive power when the Holy Spirit has come upon you; and you shall be my witnesses in Jerusalem and in all Judea and Samaria and to the end of the earth." Luke arranged Acts according to this topical format showing how the commission was implemented among the different ethnic segments in progressive geographical sequence.[96]

Acts 1:1–6:7	*Period One:* evangelism among Jews in Jerusalem and Judea	A.D. 30–33
Acts 6:8–9:31	*Period Two:* Hellenistic and Samaritan outreach; conversion of Paul	A.D. 33–37
Acts 9:32–12:24	*Period Three:* Gentile outreach in Cilicia, Caesarea, and Antioch	A.D. 37–47
Acts 12:25–16:5	*Period Four:* Paul and Barnabas's work in Syria and Galatia	A.D. 47–48
Acts 16:6–19:20	*Period Five:* Paul's ministry in Western Asia and Europe	A.D. 49–53
Acts 19:21–28:31	*Period Six:* events that led Paul to Rome	A.D. 53–59

94. London: Epworth, 1968.

95. Dale Moody, "New Chronology," 223–40. Though I agree with many of his dates, his work is flawed in the assumption that a papyrus sheet of the ancient manuscript of Acts 11:19–30 was lost and later inadvertently placed after 12:25 (p. 229). There is a better way to account for the chronological problems in this section than to resort to postulating displacements in the text unsupported by any extant text-critical evidence. A similar effort to establish five-year intervals for these passages in Acts was made earlier by C. J. Cadoux, "A Tentative Synthetic Chronology of the Apostolic Age," *JBL* 56 (1937): 177–91. Colin Hemer's appraisal of the work of Cadoux, on which Moody acknowledges that he initially based his own work, is that "Cadoux . . . is driven to strain the limits of probability by an unncessary and unwarranted attempt to force the events of Acts into an artificial annalistic pattern in five-year sequences" ("Observations on Pauline Chronology," 18).

96. See the discussion of this format in chapter 4, under "The Structure of the Book of Acts."

At this stage in the scholarly development of Pauline chronology, I see no compelling reasons to abandon the traditional consensus.[97] Without attempting to offer a solution for all the complex problems inherent in Pauline chronology, and allowing for individual variations within that consensus, I suggest a six-visit framework as follows:

1. Third-Year Visit, A.D. 37 (Gal. 1:18; Acts 9:26)
2. Famine Visit, A.D. 47 (Acts 11:29–30)
3. Fourteenth-Year Visit, A.D. 47 (Gal. 2:1–10)
4. Conference Visit, A.D. 49 (Acts 15:1–29)
5. Greeting Visit, A.D. 51 (Acts 18:22)
6. Arrest Visit, A.D. 54 (Acts 21:15ff.)

In this framework, several points should be noted:

1. The third-year and fourteenth-year visits are each reckoned from Paul's conversion, so that fourteen and not seventeen years are included in the latter visit.
2. The omission of the Acts 11 famine visit in Galatians 1 and 2 can be explained on the basis that Paul and Barnabas took the money to the elders (Acts 11:30) and did not engage the apostles in a discussion of Paul's Gentile mission at that time. Therefore, the issue in Galatians of whether Paul got his authority for his mission from the apostles rather than from a divine source (the heavenly vision) did not require mention of that visit.
3. The occasion mentioned in Acts 18:22 is taken on geographical grounds to refer to Jerusalem: "When he had landed at Caesarea, he *went up* and greeted the church." One would not "go up" to greet the church anywhere in the city of Caesarea, which lies at sea level. On the contrary, one always "goes up" (ἀναβαίνω, *anabainō*) to Jerusalem (Matt. 20:18; Mark 10:33; Luke 18:31; John 7:8; Acts 15:2; 21:12; 25:9), which is twenty-six hundred feet above sea level. However, even a metaphorical use of the term "go up," reflecting the importance of the Jerusalem church, would still argue that Paul went outside the city of Caesarea for this visit.

97. Nor does Martin Hengel, *The Pre-Christian Paul* (London: SCM Press; Philadelphia: Trinity Press International, 1991), 63. The general consensus is defended by Rainer Riesner with what Hengel feels are "new and better arguments," in "Die Frühzeit des Paulus: Studien zur Chronologie, Missionsstrategie und Theologie des Apostels Paulus bis zum ersten Thessalonicherbrief" (Habilitationsschrift, University of Tübingen, 1990), published as Rainer Riesner, *Die Frühzeit des Apostels Paulus: Studien zur Chronologie, Missionsstrategie und Theologie,* Wissenschaftliche Untersuchungen zum Neuen Testament 71/1 (Tübingen: Mohr, 1994). See also idem, *Paul's Early Period.*

FOUR

In Syria, Arabia, and Cilicia before the First Journey

Since the apostle Paul's life and letters are best understood against the background of their own cultural context, it is instructive to travel with him through the various stages of his ministry, noting the historical situations that motivated the composition of his letters to both individuals and churches. For this purpose my suggested chronology in chapter 3 will serve as a guide, and frequent reference should be made to details in that chapter so that they need not be repeated. In this chapter we continue the itinerary of Paul from the time of his conversion, which was discussed in chapter 2.

The Structure of the Book of Acts

Before attempting to delineate the development of the life and letters of Paul in chronological context, with all the difficulties inherent in such an undertaking, it will be helpful to set forth the structure of Acts presupposed in this effort. In chapter 3 a topical format containing six sections was suggested for Acts. Each section concludes with a summary statement of the progress and growth of the church during the period just discussed.

These six periods are arranged in sequence by Luke in Acts 1:8, which serves as a "table of contents" for his book. This sequence forms an introduction to Acts, according to which Luke narrates the progressive carrying of the message of Jesus to Jerusalem, Judea, Samaria, and "to the end of the earth." This statement of Jesus becomes an outline for the story of how the apostles took the gospel "to the Jew first and also to the Greek" (Rom. 1:16).

Table 4.1 Sixfold Structure of Acts

Acts 1:1–6:7	*Period One:* evangelism among Jews in Jerusalem and Judea	A.D. 30–33
Acts 6:8–9:31	*Period Two:* Hellenistic and Samaritan outreach; conversion of Paul	A.D. 33–37
Acts 9:32–12:24	*Period Three:* Gentile outreach in Cilicia, Caesarea, and Antioch	A.D. 37–47
Acts 12:25–16:5	*Period Four:* Paul and Barnabas's work in Syria and Galatia	A.D. 47–48
Acts 16:6–19:20	*Period Five:* Paul's ministry in Western Asia and Europe	A.D. 49–53
Acts 19:21–28:31	*Period Six:* events that led Paul to Rome	A.D. 53–59

In the *first period* of activity, the church begins in the city of Jerusalem among the mainline Jews, both those of Judea and those who have come from fifteen other nations (Acts 2:5–11) to celebrate the Feast of Pentecost (Acts 2:1). The following chapters in this section tell of the growth of the church among mainline, ethnically unmixed Jews in Jerusalem, concluding with a summary statement: *"The word of God increased; and the number of the disciples multiplied greatly in Jerusalem, and a great many of the priests were obedient to the faith"* (Acts 6:7).

The *second period* of activity involves the progress of the church among Jews who are progressively less conventional, both ethnically and culturally, than those in the first period. In Acts 6 and 7, the Hellenists (Jews practicing Greek culture) in Jerusalem are evangelized. In chapter 8, Philip, a Hellenist, converts multitudes of Samaritans (Acts 8:6), who are Jews of mixed descent from Old Testament times.[1] Later in chapter 8, Philip converts an Ethiopian nobleman who has undergone full conversion into the Jewish religion as a proselyte (Acts 8:27). The Ethiopian represents a fourth category of Jew, proselytes. The last conversion in this section is that of a member of an especially important category of Judeans. Paul of Tarsus is a rabbi, and the account of his conversion forms a bridge between the previous varieties of Jewish converts and the conversion of the Gentiles, which is described in Acts 10. Paul's

---

1. The Samaritans themselves claim to derive from the northern tribes of Ephraim and Manasseh, some members of which survived the destruction of the northern ten tribes of Israel by the Assyrians in 722 B.C. They are probably the descendants of those Israelites who intermarried with foreigners imported by the Assyrians into the cities of Samaria (2 Kings 17:24–29). See the extensive discussion of Samaritans by Robert Anderson, *ABD,* 5:940–47.

conversion is a transition point in the story because he receives a specific commission to incorporate the Gentiles into the church (Acts 22:21; 26:17). At this point, Luke summarizes the second period: *"So the church throughout all Judea and Galilee and Samaria had peace and was built up; and walking in the fear of the Lord and in the comfort of the Holy Spirit it was multiplied"* (Acts 9:31). Interestingly, this is the only reference in the New Testament to the church in Galilee.

Luke begins *period three* by recording the conversion of Cornelius, a Roman centurion in Caesarea (Acts 10:1) and the first convert who does not have some Jewish affiliation.[2] Up to this point, Luke has recorded the progress of the gospel through Jerusalem, Judea, and Samaria (Acts 1:8). All those discussed were affiliated in some way with Judaism and were converted while Peter, James, and John were directing the evangelistic effort. Luke selected their conversions to illustrate how, from its inception, the church progressively incorporated every variety of Jew—mainline, Hellenist, Samaritan, proselyte, and rabbinic. Then he summarizes: *"But the word of God grew and multiplied"* (Acts 12:24).

In this section and the three to follow, Luke takes up the fourth and last item of his "table of contents" in Acts 1:8 (i.e., Jerusalem, Judea, Samaria, and the end of the earth) and narrates how Paul traveled to "the end of the earth" to include the Gentiles. The discussion of this period is concentrated on Caesarea and Antioch, the former as the place where the first Gentile was converted (Acts 9:36–11:18) and the latter as the place where Gentile Christianity was subsequently headquartered under the leadership of Paul and Barnabas, among others (Acts 11:19–30). Verses 1 through 24 of chapter 12 explain what was happening in the leadership in Judea while this Gentile base was being established. The elders in Jerusalem replaced the leading apostles, who were persecuted, killed, and run out of the city (Acts 12:2–3, 17). But, Luke summarizes, *"The word of God grew and multiplied"* (Acts 12:24).

Period four rehearses the launching (Acts 12:25–13:3) of Paul and Barnabas's first missionary journey to the Gentiles in Syria and Galatia, gives an account of that first journey (Acts 13:4–15:28), records the Jerusalem Conference (Acts 15:1–35), and narrates the second journey down to the time of the decision to move toward Europe (Acts 15:36–16:5). Luke concludes his discussion of this period with the summation: *"So the churches were strengthened in the faith, and they increased in numbers daily"* (Acts 16:5).

Period five records the extension of Paul's Gentile ministry to western Asia and Europe. It includes an account of that portion of his second journey that included Macedonia and Achaia (modern Greece, Acts 16:6–18:17), as well as a brief visit to Ephesus (Acts 18:18–19). Surprisingly, he was asked to stay

---

2. The story of Peter at Joppa in 9:32–43 is included to explain how he was involved in the conversion of the Gentile Cornelius.

a longer time there by the Jews with whom he argued in the synagogue, but he declined (Acts 18:20). In addition, this section contains a portion of the beginning of his third journey in Ephesus (Acts 18:23–19:20), down to the time of the decision to take the contribution to Jerusalem for the poor of that city (Acts 19:21; Rom. 15:25). After Jerusalem, he would then go on to Rome (Acts 19:21) and, with help from the saints there, continue on to Spain (Rom. 15:24). Luke concludes this section by saying: *"So the word of the Lord grew and prevailed mightily"* (Acts 19:20).

The *sixth and final period* records Paul's return to Jerusalem by way of Miletus (Acts 19:21–21:16) and his meeting with James and the elders of Jerusalem (Acts 21:17–26), where he undoubtedly presented the contribution to them (though Luke makes no mention of it!). It also contains an account of Paul's arrest in the temple and related events (Acts 21:27–23:10), his subsequent two-year imprisonment at Caesarea (Acts 23:11–26:32), and his voyage to Rome, where he was imprisoned for another two years (Acts 27:1–28:31). Luke closes this period with a summary statement: *"And he lived there two whole years at his own expense, and welcomed all who came to him, preaching the kingdom of God and teaching about the Lord Jesus Christ quite openly and unhindered"* (Acts 28:30–31).

The conversions recounted in Acts are selected to show this progressive expansion of the kingdom from Jews to Gentiles by demonstrating that all of these diverse groups came to Christ in exactly the same way and, therefore, no one of them could claim preeminence over or reject the others. Paul's view, stated in Galatians 3:27–28 ("As many of you as were baptized into Christ have put on Christ. There is neither Jew nor Greek, there is neither slave nor free, there is neither male nor female; for you are all one in Christ Jesus") is also shown in Luke's account of conversions. There are no back doors to the kingdom for Gentiles, women, or slaves. They all come to Christ in exactly the same way and on the same basis: through faith, confession, repentance, and baptism. This can be effectively demonstrated by the following table:

Table 4.2 Conversions in Acts

Types	Authority	Relationship	Change	Confession	Expression
	Name of Jesus	*Faith*	*Repentance*	*Confession*	*Baptism*
Jews					
Pentecost 2:37–38	2:38		2:38		2:38
Many 4:4	3:16; 4:7–12, 17–18	4:4			
Multitudes 5:14		5:14			

Types	Authority	Relationship	Change	Confession	Expression
	Name of Jesus	*Faith*	*Repentance*	*Confession*	*Baptism*
Samaritans					
People 8:12	8:12, 16	8:12			8:12
Simon 8:13		8:13			8:13
Proselytes					
Ethiopian 8:27				8:37(?)	8:36, 38
Gentiles (and some Jews)					
Paul (Apostle to Gentiles) 9:15; 22:21; 26:17					9:18; 22:16
God-fearer (Cornelius) 10:1	10:43, 48				10:47
Greeks 11:20, 21					
	"added" 11:24				
	"believed" 14:1				
	"joined" 17:4				
	"persuaded" 18:4				
Proconsul Sergius Paulus 13:7	13:12	13:12			
Devout proselytes 13:43; God-fearers too? 13:26			13:43		
God-fearer Lydia 16:14					16:15
Jailer 16:27–34	16:31	16:31			16:33
Athenians 17:34		17:34			
Corinthians 18:8		18:8			18:8
Crispus 18:8		18:8			?
Apollos 18:24	18:25?				
Twelve at Ephesus 19:1, 7	19:5	19:2?			19:5

The gradual progression of these conversions may be observed in the following illustration, which shows how these various ethnic categories were progressively evangelized under Peter's (1–12) and Paul's (13–28) leadership and how Paul, Barnabas, and John Mark came to be in Anti-

Figure 4.1 Conversion Sequence in Acts
(Based on Acts 1:8: To Jerusalem, Judea, Samaria, and the Ends of the Earth)

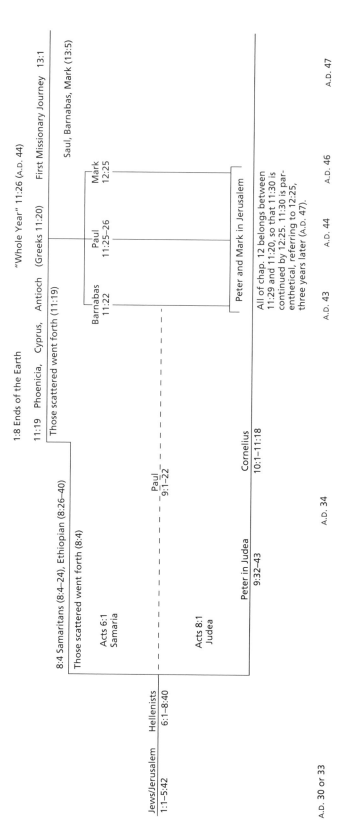

och for the beginning of the Gentile missionary outreach recorded in chapter 13.

Such, then, is the sequence of events as Luke proposed to discuss them in Acts 1:8 and as he developed that sequence throughout the book. Into this sequence, we must now attempt to fit the activity of Paul recorded in his letters.

Paul in Syria and Arabia

Following his conversion in A.D. 34, Paul spent a period of time in Syria and Arabia. He wrote: "I did not confer with flesh and blood, nor did I go up to Jerusalem to those who were apostles before me, but I went away into Arabia; and again I returned to Damascus. Then after three years I went up to Jerusalem to visit Cephas, and remained with him fifteen days" (Gal. 1:16–18).

It is impossible to determine how much of that time was distributed between Arabia and Damascus or how many months were involved. It could have been three full years or one year and parts of two others. During his time in Arabia, or Arabia Petraea (which we would normally take in this political context to mean the Nabatean kingdom of Aretas IV, most probably the northern extension of it near Syria),[3] Paul may have spent his time in contemplative soul-searching, as many argue, or, as others suggest, he may have gone there specifically to preach. If the latter was the case, the reason he refers to the Arabian experience in the first chapter of Galatians is to prove that he was preaching under his commission before he ever contacted any human authority such as the apostles.[4]

But if Paul did preach in Arabia during this time, there is no indication that he did so among Gentiles.[5] The dramatic, if not traumatic, events involved in his conversion experience, which included being blinded for three days, must have required a period of reevaluation of his life and how he would now relate to the Jewish nation and his Jewish Christian brothers, like Ananias who had baptized him. We may properly assume that Paul, the eminent religious leader in Jerusalem and relentless persecutor of Christians, would require a period of contemplation to put into perspective his revolutionary, life-changing experience. The heavenly vision of Christ would have been incredibly upsetting to Paul's thought processes, even if it had sent him only to undo what he had done in Jerusalem among the Jewish believers he had ravaged.[6] Shame, repen-

3. So also F. F. Bruce, *Paul: Apostle of the Heart Set Free* (Grand Rapids: Eerdmans, 1977), 81.

4. Ibid.

5. As F. F. Bruce implies.

6. The LB paraphrases Acts 8:3: "Paul was like a wild man, going everywhere to devastate the believers."

tance, swallowing of pride, questioning of his previous understanding of Torah, and a legitimate uncertainty of his acceptance when he returned to Jerusalem are all feelings that must have captivated Paul's mind in those weeks and
months after his revelation.

It is doubtful that Paul was ready to go immediately to the Gentiles. He
first had to determine the intent of that Gentile commission, the time frame
involved, the methodology to be employed (directly to Gentiles or to the Jews
first?), and the pragmatic and ecclesiastical result of that commission (What
would he do with the Gentiles once they had been converted? How would he
provide for their religious guidance? How would they be regarded by the Jewish "men of repute" or "pillars" in the Jerusalem church?).

It might be argued that Christ expected Paul to respond immediately to the
commission to go to the Gentiles merely because Paul had been given the
commission. However, an almost exact parallel may challenge that assumption. Jesus, during his public ministry, commissioned his twelve apostles to go
only to Jews (Matt. 10:5). After his resurrection, he extended that commission
to include the Gentiles: "Go therefore and make disciples of all nations, baptizing them in the name of the Father and of the Son and of the Holy Spirit,
teaching them to observe all that I have commanded you; and lo, I am with
you always, to the close of the age" (Matt. 28:19–20). But either Jesus did not
intend that commission to be immediately executed, or it was not so understood by the Twelve, because it was several years before Simon Peter, like Paul,
received a heavenly vision that initiated his preaching among Gentiles and resulted in the conversion of Cornelius (Acts 10:9–48). Like the Twelve, Paul
may well have prolonged his implementation of that commission until its
ramifications were clear to him. Furthermore, if Paul had preached to Gentiles in Arabia, this would have been before the conversion of Cornelius,
which is treated in Acts 11:18 as the first Gentile conversion.

After his return from Arabia, Paul spent an unstipulated period of time in
Damascus[7] ("many days," Acts 9:23). No reference is made to his contacting
Gentiles during this time in Damascus, but his teaching so angered the Jews
that they tried to kill him (Acts 9:23).

It should be remembered that Paul's commission, when first given on the
Damascus road, included the Jews as well as the Gentiles: "But the Lord said
to him, 'Go, for he is a chosen instrument of mine to carry my name before
the Gentiles and kings and the sons of Israel'" (Acts 9:15).[8] He was never sent
exclusively to the Gentiles.[9] Even though his subsequent vision in the Jerusalem temple three years after his conversion (Acts 22:21) told him he was being
sent "far away to the Gentiles," Paul carried out his missionary journeys "to

---

7. See John McRay, "Damascus: Greco-Roman Period," *ABD*, 2:7–8.
8. Cf. Acts 26:17: "delivering you from the *people* and from the Gentiles" (italics added).
9. As Bruce implies in *Paul,* 144 n. 37.

the Jew first and also to the Greek" (Rom. 1:16) and implemented this by always beginning his preaching in the synagogues (Acts 13:5, 14, 42–44; 14:1; 16:12–14, 16; 17:1; 18:1–4). He went to Gentiles only after he was rejected by the Jews, who were given first refusal.

The Jews were joined in their attempt to kill Paul by the ethnarch (governor) of Aretas IV, a Nabatean king of Arabia Petraea.[10] After the death of Tiberius, in A.D. 37,[11] Aretas had been given control of the area by the emperor Caligula and was now ruling Syria. Why, it might be asked, would a governor of Aretas (2 Cor. 11:32) want to arrest Paul? Possibly it was for personal reasons. The ethnarch knew that another eminent Jewish leader, Herod Antipas,[12] who was earlier married to Aretas's daughter, had ousted her and married another woman, thus disgracing her.[13] When she returned to her father in Arabia, he took his army and destroyed the entire army of Antipas.[14]

Another possibility is that since Aretas had just been granted control over Damascus by the Roman emperor, he would be expected to maintain Roman order and felt that he had to put a stop to the disturbances created by Paul. It should be remembered that just such a threat of disorder in Jerusalem had led Pilate to crucify Jesus. One might further speculate that Paul, during these three years, had argued with Jews and caused disruptions[15] in Arabia, where Aretas was ruling, and that Aretas was already aware of Paul's disruptive activities. At any rate, both the Jews (Acts 9:23) and the governor of Aretas (2 Cor. 11:32) wanted Paul silenced and acted separately or in concert to accomplish this. We are left to guess, but there is no inherent discrepancy in attributing the attempted capture of Paul to both the Jews and Aretas.[16] On the contrary, it is what might be expected under the circumstances. Did not both the Judeans and the Romans kill Jesus?

10. The "ethnarch of King Aretas" was probably the representative of Aretas's subjects who lived in Damascus. According to Strabo, *Geogr.* 17.1.13, ethnarchs in Egypt "were thought worthy to superintend affairs of no great importance." Josephus writes, quoting Strabo, that "in Alexandria a great part of the city has been allocated to this nation [Jews, JM]. And an ethnarch of their own has been installed, who governs the people and adjudicates suits and supervises contracts and ordinances, just as if he were the head of a sovereign state" (*Ant.* 14.117).

11. See my discussion in chapter 3 of the events involved in this change of power.

12. The ruler of Galilee who beheaded John the Baptist (Matt. 14:1–12).

13. He married Herodias, the wife of his own half-brother Philip. The entire incident is recorded by Josephus, *Ant.* 18.109–15.

14. *Ant.* 18.114.

15. Bruce, *Paul,* 81.

16. This is affirmed by Alfred Plummer in two of his commentaries: *The Second Epistle of Paul the Apostle to the Corinthians,* Cambridge Greek Testament (Cambridge: Cambridge University Press, 1903), 187–88; and idem, *The Second Epistle of St. Paul to the Corinthians,* International Critical Commentary (New York: Scribners, 1915), 334: "There is no discrepancy here between the statement(s). . . ."

Paul in Jerusalem

Paul returned to Jerusalem in A.D. 37, three years (either full or partial years) after his conversion in A.D. 34 (Acts 9:26–30). He came to discuss matters with Peter (Gal. 1:18), who was the leader of the twelve apostles. Peter seemed to be closely related to a group that met in the house of Mary, the mother of John Mark (Acts 12:12). James, the brother of Jesus, led another group in Jerusalem, perhaps more traditionally Hebrew and less Hellenistic. After his miraculous release from prison, Peter visited the group in Mary's house and upon leaving told them, "Tell this to James and to the brethren" (Acts 12:17). That Paul had not launched his mission among the Gentiles at this time is implied in Jesus' statement, "I will send you far away to the Gentiles" (Acts 22:21), made to Paul during his trance in the temple, as Paul related it during a later visit to Jerusalem.

Therefore, Paul had not come to Jerusalem to persuade Peter and the others to accept his work or to derive authority from them for what he was called to do. This was apparently yet to be determined for Paul. He had come to "visit" with Peter (Gal. 1:18), the leader of Jesus' movement, and to determine how he might fit into this movement he had formerly persecuted. The verb translated "visit" in this verse (ἱστορῆσαι, *historēsai*) means "to visit for the purpose of coming to know someone or something."[17] The only other apostle he visited was James, the Lord's brother, who was a prominent leader of the Jerusalem church.[18]

Paul and Peter had much to discuss. Undoubtedly, Paul would have wanted Peter to take him to the places where Jesus had spoken and worked—places such as the Garden of Gethsemane, the upper room, the home of Lazarus, the pools of Siloam and Bethesda, and especially Calvary. He would have wanted an explanation of all Peter knew of the life and ministry of Jesus, about which Paul knew little. Paul surely would have shown Peter where he had participated in the death of Stephen, the first Christian martyr (Acts 7:58), and Peter would have shown Paul where he three times had denied that he even knew Jesus (Matt. 26:34, 69–75). Yes, they would have had many things to discuss, some of which they were ashamed of. They spent fifteen days together (Gal. 1:18) recounting joys and sorrows.

While in Jerusalem, Paul unsuccessfully "attempted to join the disciples," but, understandably, they were afraid of him (Acts 9:26). He later wrote that at this time he was "still not known by sight to the churches of Christ in Judea" (Gal. 1:22). His reference to the district of Judea included, of course, the church in Jerusalem. Some have found a problem with this reference, because Paul had lived in Jerusalem and persecuted the church there. How could he then say that he was unknown by sight

---

17. See ἱστορέω in BAGD, 383; see also the brief article by G. D. Kilpatrick ("Galatians 1:18 ἱστορῆσαι Κηφᾶν," in *New Testament Essays: Studies in Memory of T. W. Manson*, ed. A. J. B. Higgins [Manchester: Manchester University Press, 1959]), who concludes that the meaning is "to get information from Cephas" (p. 149). See also W. D. Davies, *The Setting of the Sermon on the Mount* (Cambridge: Cambridge University Press, 1964), 453ff.

18. See the discussion in chapter 5 on James as an apostle.

Photo 4.1. Jerusalem's Temple Mount Seen from Olivet

to them? The reason he was unknown to these churches is that his earlier persecution in this area had been directed against the Hellenist Christians (Christian Jews who lived by Greek cultural standards),[19] most of whom had, by this time, been scattered beyond Judea by that persecution. The church in Jerusalem thus had become progressively less Hellenistic and more Hebrew.[20] But Paul did preach boldly to the non-Christian Hellenists, and they responded by plotting to kill him. In the temple vision, Jesus warned Paul of this plot and told him to depart from Jerusalem (Acts 22:17–21).[21] When the brothers in Jerusalem learned about the plot, they sent Paul back home to Tarsus for his own safety (Acts 9:30).

Paul in Tarsus

There is no information on Paul's activities during this time in Tarsus, a period that has been called "Paul's silent years."[22] Two writers have speculated

19. The word *Hellenist* is the English transliteration of the Greek term Ἑλληνιστής, which is derived from the root word Ἕλλην, "Greek."
20. Bruce, *Paul,* 127.
21. The reference in Acts 26:21 to an attempt to kill Paul in the temple would therefore not refer to this first visit, since Jesus warned Paul in the temple at this time to leave so that such an attempt could not be made. Acts 26:21 refers rather to the later attempt made on Paul's life in the temple at the end of his third journey. This confrontation with the Judeans in the temple (Acts 21:28; 22:22) resulted in his being taken into custody by the Roman guard and removed to Caesarea, where he later told Agrippa why he was in prison (Acts 26:19–23).
22. Robert Osborne, "St. Paul's Silent Years," *JBL* 84.1 (March 1965): 59–65.

on these years in a recent book,[23] in which one of them[24] impressively criticizes the radical rejections of the essential trustworthiness of the New Testament record. It may logically be assumed that Paul spent his time in Tarsus speaking about Jesus to Jews in the synagogue and in the marketplace where he worked. If the conversion of Cornelius in Caesarea occurred shortly after Paul's departure from that city (Acts 9:30), then Paul conceivably spent the next several years working among Gentiles in Cilicia, as well as among Jews.[25] Jesus had told him in two heavenly visions (one at his conversion, as related in his speech before Agrippa—Acts 26:17, and one at the temple, as related to the crowd in Jerusalem—Acts 22:21) that he was to go to the Gentiles, but how soon Paul was directed to implement this charge is not clear. The statement of Paul to Agrippa that he "declared first to those at Damascus, then at Jerusalem and throughout all the country of Judea, and also to the Gentiles" (Acts 26:20) gives no chronological time frame. The reference to Gentiles here probably refers to his later work in Antioch and on his journeys. But there is no compelling reason to deny that Paul would have worked among Gentiles as well as among Jews during this time in Tarsus. He would have contacted them in the marketplaces, as well as occasionally in the synagogues where God-fearers were welcomed.[26]

During this period of perhaps seven years that Paul was in Tarsus and Cilicia, Peter was working among Jews in Judea and Samaria (Acts 9:31–11:18).

23. Martin Hengel and Anna Maria Schwemer, *Paul between Damascus and Antioch: The Unknown Years* (Louisville: Westminster John Knox, 1997).

24. Martin Hengel.

25. This is suggested by Bruce, *Paul,* 133, 155.

26. On God-fearers, see the following: Adolf Deissmann, *Light from the Ancient East* (New York and London: Hodder and Stoughton, 1910), appendix 4: "A Jewish Inscription in the Theatre at Miletus," pp. 446ff. (the inscription reads Τόπος Εἰουδέων τῶν καὶ Θεοσεβίον, "Place of the Jews, who are also called God-fearing"); Louis Feldman, "The Omnipresence of the God-Fearers," *BAR* 12.5 (Sept.–Oct. 1986): 58–63; Thomas Finn, "The God-Fearers Reconsidered," *CBQ* 47 (1985): 81; John Gager, "Jews, Gentiles, and Synagogues in the Book of Acts," *HTR* 79.1–3 (Jan., Apr., July 1986): 91–99; Colin Hemer, *BASHH* (the second appendix, by Conrad Gempf, discusses the new inscription about God-fearers in Aphrodisias); M. Mellink, "An Article on an Inscription in the Synagogue at Aphrodisias," *American Journal of Archaeology* 81, 2d series (1977): 281–321; Robert Tannenbaum, "Jews and God-Fearers in the Holy City of Aphrodite," *BAR* 12.5 (Sept.–Oct. 1986): 55–57; Max Wilcox, "The 'God Fearers' in Acts—A Reconsideration," *JSNT* 13 (1981): 109; Kirsopp Lake, "Proselytes and God Fearers," in *The Acts of the Apostles,* ed. F. J. Foakes-Jackson and Kirsopp Lake, The Beginnings of Christianity, part 1 (London: Macmillan, 1920–33), 5:74–96; Irina A. Levinskaya, "A Jewish or Gentile Prayer House? The Meaning of ΠΡΟΣΕΥΧΗ," *TynBul* 41.1 (May 1990): 154–59; idem, "The Inscription from Aphrodisias and the Problem of God-Fearers," *TynBul* 41.2 (Nov. 1990): 312–18; Robert MacLennan and Thomas Kraabel, "The God-Fearers—A Literary and Theological Invention," *BAR* 12.5 (Sept.–Oct. 1986): 45–54; Ralph Marcus, "The *Sebomenoi* in Josephus," *Jewish Social Studies* 14 (1952): 247–50; Shlomo Pines, "The Iranian Name for Christians and the God-Fearers," *Proceedings of the Israel Academy of Sciences and Humanities* 2.7 (1968): 151.

Like Paul, he had received a vision; Peter's came in Joppa, a city on the coast of Israel. This vision sent him to the house of Cornelius, a Roman centurion on duty in Caesarea Maritima (Acts 10:1–48). When told to eat non-kosher (ritually unclean) food, Peter resisted the heavenly vision, but while reflecting on its meaning, he was made to understand that what God had cleansed, no one should call unclean (Acts 10:15); that is, Gentiles were to be accepted into the kingdom. The outcome was that several years after the death of Jesus, Cornelius became the first Gentile convert to Christ. The Jews already had been given the priority of acceptance, and Paul would later argue that the gospel was for the Jew first and then the Greek (Rom. 1:16).

The possibility that Cornelius was not the first Gentile convert might be argued if Acts contains parallel rather than continuous chronology. This might be inferred by the identical terminology used in Acts 8:4 and Acts 11:19 to describe the scattering of the disciples after the death of Stephen ("those who were scattered went forth," διασπαρέντες διῆλθον, *diasparentes diēlthon*). It might be concluded that Acts 11:19 is a restatement of Acts 8:4 and returns to that point in time in order to relate parallel activities. Thus, events from Acts 8:4 to Acts 11:18 would have been transpiring simultaneously with events from Acts 11:19 to Acts 15:1. If so, this could mean that Paul had been preaching in Tarsus and conducting his first missionary journey among Gentiles during the period *prior* to Cornelius's conversion. Thus, Cornelius would not have been the first Gentile convert to Christ, only the first in Judea and Samaria.

There are two reasons for rejecting this hypothesis. The first is geographical. Acts 8:4 describes the scattering of disciples only in Judea and Samaria, whereas Acts 11:19 picks up at that point and describes, not a parallel activity, but a continuation of the current dispersion into more distant geographical areas, "as far as Phoenicia and Cyprus and Antioch."

The second reason is theological. If Gentiles had already been accepted into the church elsewhere, the church leaders in Jerusalem would not have been informed on the basis of what had just happened in Caesarea that "the Gentiles also had received the word of God" (Acts 11:1). The fact that these conservative Judeans in Jerusalem called Peter into account for preaching to a Gentile (Acts 11:2–3) indicates that this was the first occurrence. They had responded similarly when Philip had first preached to Samaritans (who were partially Jewish) and had sent Peter himself, along with John, to authenticate those conversions (Acts 8:14).

On the other hand, if Cornelius was converted shortly after Paul's departure for Tarsus, then the chronology would still be continuous, and Paul could have spent the next several years in Cilicia working among Gentiles as well as Jews.

In any case, Paul undoubtedly anxiously looked for news from the leaders in Jerusalem about what place he was to fill in their evangelistic itinerary. But no word came, and the months passed into years. It is not difficult to imagine Paul feeling that he had been marginalized by his Jewish brothers in Judea, who did not yet understand that it was time for the Gentiles to be enthusiastically evangelized, and that they were to be accepted without conversion to Judaism as a prerequisite (Acts 15:1).

Paul knew he had been commissioned to extend the gospel to the Gentiles. The heavenly vision had twice said to him "I will send you . . . to the Gentiles" (Acts 22:21; cf. 26:17), and yet the years passed with no word from the principal leaders in Jerusalem. Where were Peter, James, and John? Why had they not contacted him? When was the mission to the Gentiles to be given its proper emphasis? Why was the commission of Jesus to teach all nations (Matt. 28:18–20) not being given priority, and why was Paul not being sought out for participation in a major effort?

Paul undoubtedly knew that Jesus had previously limited the twelve apostles to a ministry among Jews. When Jesus called the apostles, he had said: "Go nowhere among the Gentiles, and enter no town of the Samaritans, but go rather to the lost sheep of the house of Israel" (Matt. 10:5–6). Jesus had restricted his own earthly ministry to the Jews and had told a Gentile woman from Syro-Phoenicia that: "I was sent only to the lost sheep of the house of Israel" (Matt. 15:24).

But all of that was now in the past. The apostles had been subsequently recommissioned, after Jesus' resurrection from the dead, to expand their mission to include the Gentiles. Paul had received a similar commission at his conversion/call. And yet to Paul's knowledge no significant movement toward their conversion had yet happened in Judea and Samaria. No word had come from Jerusalem, and Paul was undoubtedly feeling perplexed and somewhat discouraged as the years went by.

We can well imagine that Paul suffered some of his hardships during this time, such as being beaten with the thirty-nine lashes in Jewish synagogues.[27] Our chronology suggests that it was at this very time of isolation and discouragement that God gave Paul his encouraging vision of paradise, which he later described in 2 Corinthians 12:1–10. He was "caught up to the third heaven," where he saw things he was not permitted to discuss. He was "elated by the abundance of revelations" and was assured that the power of Christ still rested on him.[28]

The chronological basis for placing this revelatory experience at this time in Paul's life is his statement that it came to him fourteen years prior to the time of his writing the second Corinthian letter (2 Cor. 12:2), which we have

27. 2 Cor. 11:24. He received these at the "hands of the Jews." When Jesus selected his apostles, he told them that the Jewish leaders would "flog you in their synagogues" (Matt. 10:17). See also chapter 2 on Paul's conversion.

28. See chapter 10 on apocalyptic.

dated to A.D. 53, during his third missionary journey.[29] Fourteen years prior to that would be about A.D. 40, and thus during the several years he was in Tarsus (c. A.D. 37–43).

The greatness of this revelation was accompanied by an affliction that prevented Paul from losing his human perspective and, as he said, "to keep me from being too elated" (2 Cor. 12:7). In addition to being forbidden to share the details of his revelation, he was also given a "thorn in the flesh" to keep him close to Jesus and remind him that God was the source of Paul's success in ministry. This was probably the very physical infirmity that initiated his first preaching venture into Galatia (Gal. 4:13).

Given the reaction of the Jerusalem authorities when the Samaritans (Acts 8) and the Gentiles at Caesarea (Acts 10) accepted the gospel, it is not surprising that a third and similar reaction occurred when news reached them of the conversion of large numbers of Gentiles in Antioch. The disciples who had been scattered farther north and west by the death of Stephen eventually reached Syria and "on coming to Antioch spoke to the Greeks," converting "a great number" (Acts 11:20–21). Luke records the predictable reaction in Jerusalem: "News of this came to the ears of the church in Jerusalem, and they sent Barnabas to Antioch" (Acts 11:22). His purpose was to see that these non-Jewish conversions met the standards required by Judean leaders in Jerusalem.

When Barnabas examined the circumstances, he rejoiced in what he saw, and he determined that this massive Gentile response needed a guiding hand. At this point he remembered that years ago Paul had told him about the heavenly commission given him at his conversion, to preach to Gentiles. Barnabas felt that Paul was the person this situation required, but for almost a decade Paul had been marginalized by the church in Judea, and nothing more had been heard from him. So Barnabas went to Tarsus to "look for" Paul (Acts 11:25). Luke's words perhaps suggest that Barnabas did not know precisely where Paul was living and thus that no correspondence had passed between them. Then, "when he had found him" (Acts 11:26), Barnabas brought Paul to Antioch, where the two of them worked together with the rapidly growing Gentile church.

29. See chapter 3 on chronology.

FIVE

Paul's First Journey

Paul in Antioch of Syria

Antioch of Syria was bustling with activity and excitement during a time of rebuilding when Paul first arrived about A.D. 43, the year when the city established its Olympic Games. It was a huge, cosmopolitan city, the third largest behind Rome and Alexandria,[1] with a population in the first century A.D. of about 300,000.

Paul subsequently headquartered his work here in Antioch, a city where barriers of religion, race, and nationality were easily crossed, a perfect base of operations for a new understanding of the religion of ancient Israel, which had been internationalized by Jesus of Nazareth.

A large Jewish population had existed in Antioch since the second century B.C. when three thousand Jewish soldiers from the army of Jonathan the Hasmonean helped Demetrius II secure the Seleucid throne.[2] Josephus wrote that in the first century A.D. "the Jewish colony grew in numbers, and their richly designed and costly offerings formed a splendid ornament to the temple.[3] Moreover, they were constantly attracting to their religious ceremonies multitudes of Greeks, and these they had in some measure incorporated with

---

1. F. F. Bruce, *Paul: Apostle of the Heart Set Free* (Grand Rapids: Eerdmans, 1977), 130.
2. First Maccabees 11:41–59.
3. The word *temple* here may refer to the Jerusalem temple, since Jews recognized only one temple. Others render the passage "their temple" and think it refers to the synagogue previously mentioned by Josephus (*Josephus: The Jewish War,* trans. H. St. J. Thackeray, Loeb Classical Library [Cambridge, Mass.: Harvard University Press, 1928], 4:519 n. b).

Photo 5.1. Antioch of Syria

themselves."[4] Thus, Antioch was replete with proselytes to Judaism at this time. It has been suggested that before his conversion Paul may have been active in the widespread Jewish efforts to make proselytes out of Gentiles.[5]

The Jews who lived in Antioch were thoroughly hellenized from their close association with the Seleucid dynasty there. We cannot be certain from Luke's statement in Acts 11:20 whether the initial reception of the gospel in the city was by Greeks ("Ελληνας) or Hellenists ('Ελληνιστάς). Both readings are well attested in the ancient manuscripts of Acts. The distinctiveness of these two terms in Acts, along with other related ones, is not always apparent. For example, the term Gentiles (ἔθνη), which translates the Hebrew word *goyim* (nations) in Old Testament quotations, is used twenty-nine times in Acts and almost always refers to pagans.[6] The term *Greek* is used twelve times and seems to refer to those Gentiles who were Greek either by nationality or culture as opposed to Babylonians, Persians, and others (Acts 11:20; 14:1; 16:1, 3; 17:4, 12; 18:4; 19:10, 17; 20:21; 21:28, 37). The three uses of the term *Hellenist* in Acts (Acts 6:1; 9:29; 11:20) seem to refer

4. Josephus, *J. W.* 7.45.

5. See the discussion in Bruce, *Paul*, 129 n. 16. Paul was a disciple of Gamaliel I, a Jewish rabbi and leader of the Hillelite school of diaspora Judaism in Jerualem who was very concerned with the progress and extension of Judaism in the Gentile world, especially Babylonia.

6. But "brethren who are of the Gentiles" (Acts 15:23) seems to carry no perjorative connotation in the letter sent by the Jerusalem leaders to the non-Jewish members of the church in Antioch of Syria. For selective examples of the use of *Gentile* in Acts, see 4:25, 27; 9:15; 10:45; 11:1, 18; 13:18–48; 14:2, 5; 15:3–23; 18:6; 21:11–25; 22:21; 26:17–23; 28:28.

to Jews living in harmony with Greek culture.[7] Luke uses the word *God-fearer* in its various grammatical forms[8] for those Gentiles who have rejected paganism and accepted the one true God, the God of Israel, and who often attend synagogue, but are not proselytes.[9] The word *proselyte* is used three times[10] and connotes people who have converted to a religion.

Special nuances of these words occur in several places, making it difficult for us to know exactly what the ancients must have understood clearly. For example, in the first seven verses of Acts 14, Luke refers to both Jews and Greeks in the synagogue. He says in verse 2 that the unbelieving Jews stirred up the Gentiles and poisoned their minds against the brethren. Then in verse 5 he states that both Gentiles and Jews with their rulers tried to stone Paul. Does this mean the unbelieving Jews stirred up the Gentiles in the synagogue (i.e., the God-fearing Greeks of verse 2) or the Gentiles in the city (verse 4) who were not God-fearers?

Luke can refer to some individuals as God-fearers and to others as proselytes; he can also label someone a God-fearing proselyte (Acts 13:43) or a God-fearing Greek (Acts 17:4). And so we wonder, are the God-fearing women in Iconium (Acts 13:50) who were stirred up against Paul, members of the synagogue community or just "devout women" of the city? If the latter, what is meant by devout? In any case, Antioch quickly became the headquarters for the non-Jewish branch of the early Christian movement.

Indeed, it was here among a plethora of diverse religions—Jewish, Roman, and Hellenistic—that the burgeoning group of Gentile disciples of Jesus were first called "Christians" (Acts 11:26). This comment by Luke is particularly interesting in view of the assertions by Eusebius and Jerome that Luke was from Antioch.[11]

7. The last reference (11:20) has the textual variant *Greek* rather than *Hellenist,* but the latter term is preferred on transcriptional grounds by the editorial committee of the United Bible Societies. See the brief but important discussion of the term *Hellenist* by Bruce Metzger, *A Textual Commentary on the Greek New Testament,* 2d ed. (Stuttgart: German Bible Society, 1994), 340–42.

8. Participles are generally used (predicative, 10:2, 22; 13:16, 26; adjectival, 17:4; or substantival, 17:17) and are translated at times simply "devout" (13:43, 50; 17:4) or "a worshiper" of God (16:14; 18:7). The term *God-fearer* is an English equivalent of "one who fears God," or "one who worships God" (σεβομένου τὸν θεόν, 18:7; σεβομένη τὸν θεόν, 16:14).

9. Φοβούμενος and σεβόμενος are both used to mean *God-fearer.* The former term appears in 10:2, 22; 13:16, 26. The latter term occurs in 13:43, 50; 16:14; 17:4, 17; 18:7. See the discussion of these terms by Colin Hemer, *BASHH,* 444–47.

10. Acts 2:10; 6:5; 13:43.

11. Eusebius, *Hist. eccl.* 3.4.6; Jerome, *Vir. ill.* 7. F. F. Bruce found the earliest reference to Luke as a native of Antioch in the beginning of the anti-Marcionite prologue to the Gospel of Luke, which he dated to the late second century (*Paul,* 133 n. 33). However, Bruce Metzger feels that recent study demands a date no earlier than the fourth century for these prologues (*The Canon of the New Testament: Its Origin, Development, and Significance* [Oxford: Clarendon, 1987], 94 n. 34). It is interesting that of the seven Hellenist men chosen to care for the Jerusalem Hellenist widows, the only one whose place of origin is stated is "Nicolaus, a proselyte of Antioch" (Acts 6:1–5). See the discussion on Luke and Antioch in Bruce, *Paul,* 149.

For a full year, Paul and Barnabas worked together here in the initial efforts to establish this growing Gentile church on a solid foundation (Acts 11:26). After this, the chronology is difficult to piece together because Luke continues his discussion rather imprecisely in the next verse with the introductory expression "Now in these days. . . ."

The earlier chapter on chronology[12] points out that after this full year of work in Antioch, Agabus, a prophet from Jerusalem, came and prophesied a famine in Jerusalem, which caused the church in Antioch to decide to send help (Acts 11:29). The chronological problem here is not the prediction of the famine by Agabus but how the subsequent events fit in with the prophecy, because Acts states in the past tense that the church sent Paul and Barnabas with relief. However, Luke is saying only that when the famine did occur later, the church responded as it had decided to do when it first heard the prophecy. Thus the sequence of events is as follows:

A.D. 43 or 44
    1. The famine was prophesied (11:28)
    2. Antioch determined to help (11:29)

A.D. 46 or 47
    3. The famine occurred (11:28)
    4. Antioch sent help (11:30)

In the time between the prophecy and the famine, Luke parenthetically inserts the story of three events that happened in Jerusalem. These events, the deaths of James and Agrippa I and the imprisonment of Peter, are given in the first twenty-four verses of chapter 12. Then Luke continues, after this parenthetical insertion, to state that Paul and Barnabas, having taken the relief later when it was needed (Acts 11:30), returned to Antioch (Acts 12:25). Luke probably inserted the events in chapter 12 to show what happened in Jerusalem during this time; namely, that James was killed and Peter was imprisoned and that when Peter was released, he "went to another place" (presumably other than Jerusalem—Acts 12:17). Thus the leadership in Jerusalem passed from the apostles, particularly Peter, James, and John, to the elders. And this, in turn, explains why the famine relief was taken by Paul and Barnabas to the elders rather than to the apostles (Acts 11:30).

Sometime later, Peter returned to Jerusalem, where he appears with John and James the Lord's brother, who perhaps had replaced James the martyred brother of John as one of the three special leaders of the church in Jerusa-

---

12. See chapter 3 for a discussion of this complex section of Acts involving the death of James and Agrippa and the imprisonment of Peter.

lem.[13] It is possible, if not probable, that he had been a significant leader in the Jerusalem church from its beginning. This assumption is based on the strong probability,[14] though not certainty,[15] that he is the James to whom Paul refers in 1 Corinthians 15:7, where he says that the Lord, among his special postresurrection manifestations, "appeared to James, then to all the apostles."

If this James was the oldest[16] of the four physical brothers of Jesus (Matt. 13:55) who did not believe on him (John 7:5), his subsequent conversion and place of prominence, like that of Paul, is explained on the basis of his having received a special resurrection appearance of Jesus. Although the other brothers of Jesus believed in him shortly after his resurrection and are with the disciples in Jerusalem less than fifty days after the death of Jesus (Acts 1:14), there is no indication that they received a special appearance of Jesus like that of James. During those thirty days between his resurrection and ascension, Jesus evidently appeared only to his apostles[17] and, on a special occasion, to more than five hundred brothers at one time (1 Cor. 15:6). One author notes that in Paul's list of Jesus' postresurrection appearances to individuals, only two are named, Peter and James: "It is no mere coincidence that these should be the only two apostles whom Paul claims to have seen during his first visit to Jerusalem,"[18] which came three years after his conversion (Gal. 1:18). We refer to this visit as "the third-year visit." Thus, James became one of the three "pillars" (Gal. 2:9) of the Jerusalem church[19] and is designated in some sense as being among the apostles.[20]

13. David Wenham and A. D. A. Moses argue that there is special significance in the replacement of James the brother of John by James the brother of Jesus, thus keeping three pillars of the church together as a symbol of the three—Peter, James, and John—who shared the transfiguration experience with Jesus ("'There Are Some Standing Here': Did They Become the Reputed Pillars of the Jerusalem Church? Some Reflections on Mark 9:1, Galatians 2:9, and the Transfiguration," *Novum Testamentum* 36.2 (1994): 146ff.

14. Archibald Robertson and Alfred Plummer, *A Critical and Exegetical Commentary on the First Epistle of St. Paul to the Corinthians*, International Critical Commentary (Edinburgh: Clark, 1911), 337–38.

15. Gordon Fee states unequivocally, with no attempt to substantiate the assertion, that "this James is the Lord's brother" (*The First Epistle to the Corinthians*, NICNT [Grand Rapids: Eerdmans, 1987], 731).

16. This may possibly be assumed because he is mentioned first: "James and Joseph and Simon and Judas."

17. Acts 1:2–3: ". . . until the day when he was taken up, after he had given commandment through the Holy Spirit to the apostles whom he had chosen. To them he presented himself alive after his passion by many proofs, appearing to them during forty days, and speaking of the kingdom of God."

18. Bruce, *Paul*, 85.

19. This is based on the following: (1) James the brother of John is dead by this time (Acts 12:1–2); (2) James the brother of the Lord is mentioned in context earlier (Gal. 1:19); and (3) James the Less (Son of Alphaeus) is never given a position of prominence in the New Testament. This leaves only the brother of Jesus as a candidate for this James.

20. This may be the meaning of the statement in 1 Cor. 15:7 that Jesus "appeared to James, then to *all* the apostles." It seems indisputable that James is listed by Paul as being among the

The Fourteenth-Year Visit

In his letter to the Galatians, Paul refers to a visit to Jerusalem that he says occurred "after fourteen years" (Gal. 2:1), which probably means fourteen years after his conversion, though some take it to mean fourteen years after his "third-year visit." This fourteenth-year visit was in some way prompted by a revelation. He wrote, "I went up by revelation" (κατὰ ἀποκάλυψιν, *kata apokalypsin,* Gal. 2:2). In addition to his revelatory experience of Christ at his conversion (Acts 9:3–4), Paul also had revelations on other occasions (Acts 16:9; 22:17–21; 23:11; 2 Cor. 12:1–2). Thus, it could have been a recent revelation of Christ that sent Paul to Jerusalem at this time.

On the other hand, it has been argued that the reference is to the previous revelation that Paul had been given to go to the Gentiles, and "according to that revelation," that is, because of the commission to preach to Gentiles, he has himself decided to come to Jerusalem.[21] This argument states that Paul told the Jerusalem apostles "absolutely nothing" in the first three years after his conversion. During his third-year visit, he interviewed only Peter and James and said nothing of his special revelation. The point of his discussion in the first two chapters of Galatians, therefore, was "to inform the Galatians that he did not tell the Jerusalem apostles of the uniqueness of his apostolic call until his fourteenth-year visit." In doing so, he tells them that "the trip was made in order to pass on the revelation to the apostolic authorities."[22] Up to the time of the fourteeenth-year visit, it is argued, the Jerusalem apostles had never heard from Paul's lips a detailed account of this revelation he had received to go to the Gentiles.[23]

He makes the trip now, after fourteen years, because circumstances dictate that it is time for the Jerusalem leaders to be aware of his independent authority for his work and, hopefully, to give him and Barnabas the right hand of fellowship to continue that work with the blessings of the mother church in Jerusalem. Without this confirmation, Paul would indeed "be running . . . in vain" (Gal. 2:2). This expression probably means that his work among Gentiles would not be effectively rendered without the fellowship of its Jewish base, including the blessings of the Jerusalem apostles and elders.

---

apostles in Gal. 1:19: "I saw none of the *other* apostles except James the Lord's brother." Barnabas was called an apostle (Acts 14:14). Andronicus and Junias, who were Paul's relatives, are said to be "men of note among the apostles" in Rom. 16:7. Jesus is even called an "apostle and high priest" in Heb. 3:1. So the word does not always have particular reference to the Twelve.

21. George Howard, *Paul: Crisis in Galatia* (Cambridge: Cambridge University Press, 1979), 21.

22. Ibid., 37.

23. Ibid., 39.

Paul had been working for perhaps seven to ten years in Tarsus, Cilicia, and Antioch without direct support and involvement from the Jerusalem leaders. He finally felt that the time had come to explain his revelation to them in detail, including the Gentile commission. Perhaps his brief visit to Jerusalem with the famine relief had impressed upon him the need to return later and engage the "leaders of repute" privately in a discussion of his ministry (Gal. 2:2).

Luke makes no mention of another visit (the fourteenth-year visit) of Paul between the famine visit (Acts 12:25) and the beginning of his first missionary journey (Acts 13:1–3). We can only conjecture as to the reason. Some would identify this fourteenth-year visit with the famine visit. But the purposes of the visits seem to be totally different. Others would identify the fourteenth-year visit with the Jerusalem Conference visit in chapter 15. However, Paul came to Jerusalem on his fourteenth-year visit to inform the Jerusalem leaders about his ministry (Gal. 2:1–10) and obtained their approval. In Acts 15 the approval of Paul's ministry to the Gentiles has not yet been agreed upon by the Jerusalem leaders. Thus, it is impossible to equate the two visits.

But even more significantly, if the two visits are identical, we cannot account for the conduct of Peter (and Barnabas) in Antioch, when they acted hypocritically (ὑποκρίσει, *hypokrisei,* Gal. 2:13) by breaking table fellowship with the Gentiles. This issue of imposing Jewish kosher laws on the Gentiles was decisively and negatively settled in that Jerusalem Conference with the approval of Paul, Peter, James, and Barnabas (Acts 15:6, 12, 13, 25). After that conference decision, brothers could not have come "from James" (Gal. 2:12) trying to enforce kosher laws, as they are said to have done, nor would Peter and Barnabas have yielded to their views.[24]

It seems better, therefore, to assume that Luke omitted mention of the visit for the same reason that he omitted any reference to the composition of Paul's letters; their inclusion was not essential to his presentation. Admittedly, Luke's inclusion of all Paul's visits, the place and circumstances of the composition of his letters, and the itinerary involved in the hardships he enumerates in 2 Corinthians 11 would have made our task of reconstructing Paul's life much easier. But perhaps this ultimately amounts to little more than a scholastic inconvenience. Our task is not to rewrite Acts and the Pauline letters but to read and respond to their theological intent. We do this not by lamenting what is omitted but by utilizing what is included. Arguments from silence are at best precarious and at worse irrelevant. Both Luke and Paul in-

---

24. For a recent discussion of the relation of this visit in Gal. 2 to the context of Acts 11 and 15, see David Wenham, "Acts and the Pauline Corpus: II. The Evidence of Parallels," in *The Book of Acts in Its Ancient Literary Setting,* ed. Bruce W. Winter and Andrew D. Clarke, BAFCS 1 (Grand Rapids: Eerdmans, 1993), 215–58.

cluded what they considered to be essential in painting their portraits of these events. We have no choice but to view the portraits as they were painted.

Admittedly, these observations do not enable us to determine whether the fourteenth-year visit of Galatians 2 was the famine visit of Acts 11 or the conference visit of Acts 15 or a separate visit. But they do suggest that we cannot be long deterred by the fact that Luke does not include every activity of Paul. He omits much more material from this period than he includes. Extreme selectivity was mandatory in writing the story of this period. John states about the composition of his Gospel, "Now Jesus did many other signs in the presence of the disciples, which are not written in this book; but these are written that you may believe that Jesus is the Christ, the Son of God, and that believing you may have life in his name" (John 20:30–31). Luke could have said the same thing about his account of Paul in Acts.

The Acts of the Apostles does not contain all of the acts of all of the apostles or all of the acts of some of the apostles or even some of the acts of all of the apostles, but rather some of the acts of some of the apostles. Because Luke does not include a saying or an event certainly does not mean either that he did not know about it or that it did not happen.

The context of Galatians 2 suggests that Paul's fourteenth-year visit consisted of two separate segments. On the one hand, he presented his message, "the gospel which I preach among the Gentiles" (Gal. 2:2), to the larger group of disciples in Jerusalem. This group included many who intensely opposed Paul and who secretly brought in false brothers to spy on Paul in an attempt to negate his work. Paul made no concessions to this group (Gal. 2:4–5).

The other segment of his visit, the most important one, took place privately with those leaders "of repute" (Gal. 2:2) who were considered to be "pillars" (Gal. 2:9) in the Jewish church. These were James, Cephas, and John.[25] Paul wrote that when these leaders "perceived the grace that was given to me" (Gal. 2:9), namely, that he "had been entrusted with the gospel to the uncircumcised, just as Peter had been entrusted with the gospel to the circumcised" (Gal. 2:7), they gave Paul and Barnabas their full approval.

Therefore, the best reconstruction of the visits seems to be that three years after his conversion, Paul went to Jerusalem for a brief and rather frantic visit, during which he tried to establish rapport with Jewish brothers, but they were afraid of him. No record is given about any work with Gentiles at this time (Acts 9:26–29). He apparently did not find it feasible at this time, for whatever reason, to raise the issue with the Jerusalem leaders about his Gentile

25. Galatians 2:7 and 8 contain the only two times in Paul's writings in which he uses the name Peter. All other references to him by Paul employ his Aramaic name, Cephas (1 Cor. 1:12; 3:22; 9:5; 15:5; Gal. 1:18; 2:9, 11, 14). On the use of the names Cephas and Peter in verses 7 and 9, see F. F. Bruce, *The Epistle to the Galatians: A Commentary on the Greek Text*, New International Greek Testament Commentary (Grand Rapids: Eerdmans, 1982), 100–101. Bruce thinks the use of the name Peter may reflect a reference to an underlying official statement issued at the meeting and later used by Paul.

commission. When the Hellenist Jews with whom he argued planned to kill him, he was sent by the brothers to Tarsus (Acts 9:30).

Paul spent a number of years in Cilicia after his conversion (A.D. 37–43), and because Cornelius was seemingly converted shortly after Paul left Judea (cf. Acts 9:30 with Acts 10:1), Paul may very well have worked among Gentiles as well as Jews in those years. But his activities were either unknown or ignored by the leaders in Jerusalem. Barnabas came to Paul's home city of Tarsus in Cilicia and brought Paul with him to Antioch, where they worked together for several years (A.D. 43–47) in the Gentile ministry there (Acts 11:25–26).

During this time, Barnabas was the Jerusalem representative of the work in Antioch and was the more prominent of the two men. The references through this section are to Barnabas and Paul (in that order), not to Paul and Barnabas, perhaps indicating the more prominent role of Barnabas (Acts 11:30; 12:25; 13:2, 7). This probably means that Barnabas was accepted by the Jerusalem church as a reliable monitor of the Jewish interests in this new Gentile outreach. He had been sent there by Jerusalem for this very purpose (Acts 11:22). There was, then, no reason at this early date for contact between Paul and the Jerusalem church. The prominence of Barnabas during these years in Antioch is emphasized by the fact that when the Holy Spirit called these two men to make the first missionary journey, Barnabas was addressed before Paul: "Set apart for me Barnabas and Saul for the work to which I have called them" (Acts 13:2). But after they begin preaching on the island of Cyprus, Paul is listed first (Acts 13:43, 46, 50). Then, after the first journey is completed, and they attend the Jerusalem Conference, they alternately receive first reference (Acts 15:12 B&P; 15:22 P&B; 15:25 B&P; 15:35 P&B), perhaps because of the prominence of Barnabas within the Jerusalem church.

When the famine occurred and Barnabas and Paul took the offering to Jerusalem (the famine visit), Barnabas was still in the lead and there was no reason at this point for any conflict between Paul and the Jerusalem leaders. Luke passes over the visit with only the remark that Barnabas and Paul brought the offering (Acts 11:30) and then returned to Antioch (Acts 12:25).

However, shortly thereafter and for reasons not stated by Paul or Luke, Paul felt the need to inform the Jerusalem leaders about his call to preach to Gentiles. He wanted to obtain the support, though not the permission, of those leaders. He obviously felt that not only he, during his years in Tarsus, but also he and Barnabas, during their years in Antioch, had been largely marginalized by the mainstream in Jerusalem, many of whom evidently still questioned Paul's conversion. So Paul went back to Jerusalem to get a clarification of the Jerusalem leaders' attitude toward the Gentile ministry. He went specifically for this purpose and met with the two segments of the church there, the group led by Peter and that led by James (see under "Paul in Jerusalem" in chapter 4).

It should be noted here that the prominence was beginning to pass from Barnabas to Paul. Even though Paul recounts the story by saying "I went up again to Jerusalem with Barnabas" (Gal. 2:1), he then says in verse 2 "I went up by revelation." He further refers to the gospel which "I [not we] preach among Gentiles," and points out in verse 3 that "even Titus, who was with me [not us], was not compelled to be circumcised." Note particularly that in verses 6 through 10, Paul is emphatic in his assertion that "I" (not we) had been entrusted with the gospel to the Gentiles and that the leaders perceived the grace that was given to "me" (not us) to preach to Gentiles. Interestingly, in verse 9 Paul includes Barnabas: "And when they perceived the grace that was given to *me*, James and Cephas and John, who were reputed to be pillars, gave to *me and Barnabas* the right hand of fellowship, that *we* should go to the Gentiles and they to the circumcised" (italics added). This can only mean that Paul initiated the visit and took Barnabas and Titus with him. When he says "I went up . . . with Barnabas," he means "I went up, and Barnabas with me," not that he accompanied Barnabas. The entire perspective of Galatians 2:1–10 is that of Paul demanding and receiving recognition (not permission) of his (not Barnabas's) ministry.

So the result of this fourteenth-year visit was that the authority of Paul to carry on the Gentile mission by direct revelation and commission from God was validated by the Jerusalem leaders (Gal. 2:7). Barnabas's presence at this point was only marginal. The pragmatic social issue of how the Jewish and Gentile brothers would relate to one another in terms of table fellowship, ritual purity, and so on was evidently not discussed. This explains why, shortly after the meeting, Peter visited Paul in Antioch and had a problem with the issue of table fellowship and why, surprisingly, "even Barnabas was carried away by their insincerity" (Gal. 2:13).[26] This could not have happened after the Jerusalem Conference in Acts 15, when this very issue was decisively determined and agreed on by all three of these men.

We must, therefore, follow the sequence of Acts and place the Jerusalem Conference of chapter 15 after the first missionary journey of chapters 13 and 14, rather than equate it with the fourteenth-year visit prior to the journey (thus before chapter 13).

The events may be briefly charted as follows. Note especially the locations of Jerusalem and Antioch in the table.

Table 5.1 Fourteenth-Year Visit and Subsequent Events

Gal. 2:1–3	(Met with "men of repute") In *Jerusalem*
Gal. 2:4–5	Events in *Antioch*, which occurred at a later time than the third-year visit but *before* the Conference in Acts 15:6.

26. See discussion below.

	So the verses in Galatians 2:4–5 are a parenthetical reference to events at the time of the dispute in Antioch, which are referred to in Acts 15:1–3 *before* the Conference of verse 6.[a]
Gal. 2:6–10	(Met with "men of repute") In *Jerusalem*. These verses continue those of 1 through 3 before the parenthetical verses 4 and 5 were injected, and Paul simply continues recounting his meeting with the "men of repute." This meeting validated Paul's ministry to the Gentiles without their having to become Jews. The "men of repute" did not demand that Titus be circumcised in order to have fellowship with them in that meeting.
Gal. 2:11–14	(Conflict with one of the "men of repute," Peter) In *Antioch*. The issue this time was table fellowship and the pragmatic implications of fellowship.
First Journey	To *Galatia*
	Judaizers (from *Jerusalem* or elsewhere) came to *Galatia* soon after Paul left there and created problems over the law and Paul's authority.
	Paul wrote *Galatians* to deal with these problems. He emphasized to the Galatians that he had authority and recognition from the "men of repute" in Jerusalem. So those Judaizers who challenged his acceptance in Jerusalem were wrong.
	No decision, however, had been reached on the ultimate question of how the members of the entire movement would relate to one another and to the law, and so no position had yet been officially declared as a principle of operation. Thus, some in Jerusalem were still arguing that circumcision was required, and they went to Antioch trying to enforce their views on the Gentiles there (Acts 15:1).
	Controversy in *Antioch* introduced by these men from Jerusalem. Acts 15:1 and the parenthetical verses, Galatians 2:4–5, refer to this controversy.
	Conference in *Jerusalem* to deal with this controversy (Acts 15:6). The circumcision issue is settled for the Antioch church (Acts 15:30) and, in principle, for all Gentile churches.
Second Journey	Paul delivers the decisions of the Conference to the *Galatians* (Acts 16:4).

a. Bernard Orchard argues that these verses are a parenthesis that begins with an ellipsis. His analysis merits close attention ("The Ellipsis between Galatians 2,3 and 2,4," *Biblica* 54 [1973]: 469–81). See also the unconvincing reply by A. C. M. Blommerde, "Is There an Ellipsis between Galatians 2,3 and 2,4?" *Biblica* 57 (1976): 100–102; and Orchard's response to it, "Once Again the Ellipsis between Gal. 2,3 and 2,4," *Biblica* 57 (1976): 254–55.

Peter in Antioch of Syria

Shortly after Paul's fourteenth-year visit to Jerusalem, Peter paid a visit to Antioch, where he and Paul had a serious confrontation. Peter had agreed to

Paul's independent commission to work among Gentiles, but Peter himself was still an eminent leader in the conservative Jewish Christian circles in Jerusalem, where he was fulfilling his own commission to work among Jews (Gal. 2:7–8). Therefore, Peter was in the habit of living by strict Jewish kosher standards, which forbade eating with Gentiles because they did not drain the blood from their meat before cooking it and they ate meat that was sacrificed to idols (cf. 1 Cor. 8:1; 10:19). The question of how the Jewish and Gentile Christians should deal with this practical fellowship problem had not been dealt with in the previous Jerusalem meeting with the "men of repute."

Therefore, when Peter came to Antioch, acknowledging Paul's right to eat with Gentiles, he decided to do the same (Gal. 2:12), something he would not be able to do in Jerusalem without destroying his influence. It has been argued that not all Jews opposed eating with Gentiles, since there was no law against it and it may have been viewed differently among the diverse perspectives of Judaism in the first century.[27] Another author argues that "Jews integrated extensively and said 'yes' to pagan society, although probably without renouncing Judaism."[28] A passage from the Talmud may suggest that some Jews in Caesarea Maritima participated in pagan rituals involving the sprinkling of blood from animals slaughtered for idolatrous purposes and the offering of the animals' fat parts in idolatrous contexts.[29] How long Peter stayed in Antioch is not stated, but perhaps it was a long visit.[30] During that visit, a conservative group of men who followed James came from Jerusalem and challenged Peter on what they considered compromising and even apostate behavior. At this point, Peter gave in and withdrew from table fellowship with Gentiles.

His behavior can be evaluated from two points of view. From Peter's point of view, he was not willing to compromise his commission among Jews in Jerusalem and Judea in order to eat with Gentiles. Paul then makes a statement that is nothing short of astonishing to Bible students who know Peter as the rock on which Christ built the church (Matt. 16:18), the leader of the twelve apostles, the one who opened the door of the church to both Jews (Acts

---

27. Alan F. Segal says, "We do not know how ordinary Jews, as opposed to strict Pharisees, observed the dietary laws in the first century. Since there was no explicit law forbidding Jews and Gentiles from eating together, we must assume that some, possibly many, ate with Gentiles despite qualms. There was obviously a range of practice that we cannot precisely reconstruct" (*Paul the Convert* [New Haven, Conn.: Yale University Press, 1990], 231).

28. Peter Borgen, "'Yes,' 'No,' 'How Far?': The Participaton of Jews and Christians in Pagan Cults," in *Paul in His Hellenistic Context,* ed. Troels Engberg-Pedersen (Minneapolis: Fortress, 1995), 36.

29. For an English translation of the passage, see L. I. Levine, *Caesarea under Roman Rule* (Leiden: Brill, 1975), 45.

30. Bruce suggests that it was long enough for word to reach Jerusalem about what Peter was doing and to precipitate the sending of a delegation of leaders to Antioch to confront him about it (*Paul,* 176).

2:1–42) and Gentiles (Acts 10:1–48; cf. 15:8). Paul said Peter feared those of the "circumcision party" (Gal. 2:12)!

How this could be so is almost impossible to conceive unless we remember that Peter and the other apostles from Galilee were a separate group in Jerusalem and seemingly operated somewhat independently of James and the local conservative Jewish Christian church. What Peter feared was that, even though he was the well-known leader of the Twelve and the one on whose work Christ built the church, his continuing influence in Jerusalem could easily be compromised or destroyed by these men who felt that Peter was departing from Jesus' intention to found a Jewish church. And Peter was not willing at this point to give foundation to that belief. "If the interests of the gospel in Judaea were being prejudiced by his way of life in Antioch, he was prepared to alter that way of life."[31] So Peter decided, as Paul later taught, "not to eat meat or drink wine or do anything that makes your brother stumble" (Rom. 14:21). The problem was that while he did not want to make the Jewish Christians in Jerusalem stumble, he was causing the Gentile Christians in Antioch to stumble. Therefore, Paul withstood him to his face "because he stood condemned" (Gal. 2:11).

That must have been a sight to remember! The two giants of the Jewish and Gentile missions, in the presence of the entire congregation ("before them all," Gal. 2:14), engaged in heated argument. From Paul's point of view, Peter "stood condemned" for his "insincere," or "hypocritical"[32] conduct (Gal. 2:13). The magnitude of this dispute can be measured in two ways: (1) the other Jewish Christians who were members of that church ("the rest of the Jews," Gal. 2:13) were influenced to join Peter in this action; and (2) "even Barnabas" (Gal. 2:13), the very man who had brought Paul to this Gentile mission in Antioch (Acts 11:25) and endorsed him before the apostles in Jerusalem (Acts 9:27), deserted Paul on this issue and joined Peter.

In Paul's view, it was sheer hypocrisy to eat with the Gentiles at one moment and then refuse to do so the next. But this was more than a matter of inconsistent behavior about a social issue; Peter's action was, for Paul, a Jewish rejection of the right of the Gentiles to be accepted into the church on equal footing with the Jews. He would write in the next chapter of Galatians: "For as many of you as were baptized into Christ have put on Christ. There is neither Jew nor Greek, there is neither slave nor free, there is neither male nor female; for you are all one in Christ Jesus" (Gal. 3:27–28).

Anything less than this was not only a compromise of the truth of the gospel and the validity of the Gentile mission, but also a denial of the fundamental tenet of both Jewish and Gentile Christian faith, the monotheism of God. Paul asks, "Is God the God of Jews only? Is he not the God of Gentiles also?

---

31. Ibid., 177.
32. He uses the word ὑπόκρισις, which in English transliteration is *hypocrisy*.

Yes, of Gentiles also" (Rom. 3:29). Therefore, there can be no religious difference between the two groups; both are equally justified by their faith in
Christ, by their trust in the faithfulness of Jesus to bring "the blessing of Abraham . . . upon the Gentiles" (Gal. 3:14). For Paul, if the Gentiles had to accept the kosher laws of Jews (and even be circumcised, as some in Jerusalem
required, Acts 15:1), they were in essence becoming Jews. If Jews did not need
to give up their Jewishness to be Christians, neither did Gentiles need to become Jews (i.e., practice Judaism), because God was not a God of Jews only.[33]

Thus it is clear that, although on the fourteenth-year visit Peter and the Jerusalem church had accepted Paul's commission to work among the Gentiles, the
issue of table fellowship and social (if not ethical) conduct between Jewish and
Gentile Christians had not yet been settled. If the later Jerusalem Conference of
Acts 15 had already occurred and settled this issue (Acts 15:19–29),[34] the por-
tentous confrontation between Paul and Peter over this very fellowship issue
would never have occurred. Before that conference convened, more than a year
later, however, this issue arose again after Paul and Barnabas returned from their
first journey in Galatia. Brothers from Jerusalem came again to Antioch and this
time insisted on circumcision even for Gentiles (Acts 15:1–2).

First Journey

After the return of Paul and Barnabas to Antioch following the fourteenth-
year visit, they continued to work as teachers in that church (Acts 13:1). As
noted above, the mantle was passing from Barnabas to Paul in Jerusalem with
regard to the Gentile commission, but Barnabas was still the dominant figure
in the Antioch church. This is seen in the fact that when the time came for the
missionary journeys to begin, Barnabas is mentioned first. Luke writes:
"While they were worshiping the Lord and fasting, the Holy Spirit said, 'Set
apart for me Barnabas and Saul for the work to which I have called them'"
(Acts 13:2).

Cyprus

Luke does not include the destination as a part of the heavenly announcement though it may have been part of it. He does not claim to be giving all
that was stated in any revelation, speech, or document he recorded. If the destination was left to the church or the missionaries to decide, it would seem
that Barnabas was again in the influential position because they sailed for the

---

33. This will be discussed fully in later chapters.
34. That conference is identified by some with the fourteenth-year visit we have just described.

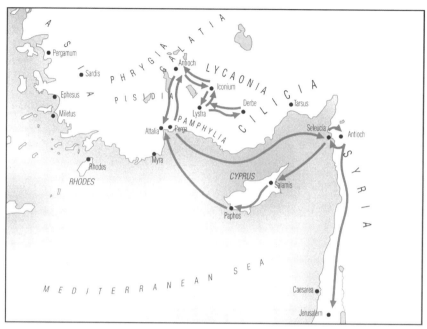

Map 5.1. Paul's First Missionary Journey

island of Cyprus[35] (Acts 13:4), which was the home of Barnabas and was an imperial Roman province.[36] Luke introduces him earlier in Acts as a man recognized by the apostles as being of special character: "Thus Joseph who was surnamed by the apostles Barnabas (which means, Son of encouragement), a Levite, a native of Cyprus, sold a field which belonged to him, and brought the money and laid it at the apostles' feet" (Acts 4:36–37).

However, the mantle of authority gradually began to shift to Paul as they arrived on the island, and Luke hints that Saul of Tarsus began to use the name Paul henceforth among the Gentiles (Acts 13:9).[37] This is the first time in Acts that the name Paul occurs; prior to this he is called Saul. Then, when Luke continues the story, he refers to "Paul and his company," not "Barnabas and his company" (Acts 13:13). From this point on, Luke refers to Paul and Barnabas (Acts 13:43, 46, 50; 15:2, 22, 35) as often as to Barnabas and Paul (Acts 14:12, 14; 15:12, 25).

35. See John McRay, "Cyprus," *ABD*, 1:1228–30.
36. On travel in this period, see L. Casson, *Travel in the Ancient World* (London: Allen and Unwin, 1974); M. P. Charlesworth, *Trade-Routes and Commerce in the Roman Empire* (Cambridge: Cambridge University Press, 1924); Steve Vinson, "Ships in the Ancient Mediterranean," *BA* 53 (1990): 13–18. For further discussion and a bibliography on Paul's sea voyages, see chapter 8 on Paul's voyage to Rome.
37. F. C. Synge, "Acts 13:9: 'Saul Who Is Also Paul,'" *Theology* 63 (1960): 199–200.

Photo 5.2. Salamis Forum in Cyprus

Luke does not state that Paul changed his name here but simply that Saul was "also called Paul" (Acts 13:9). Since, however, this is the first time the name Paul appears, and it continues to be used from this point forward, it is to be assumed that Paul himself used his Roman name as he worked among Gentiles. His Jewish name would have "suited the circumstances of his life until this point."[38] Now that he was preaching predominantly to non-Jews, his Hebrew name "has become unimportant to him."[39] It has been erroneously argued that Paul took his new name as a result of his encounter with the Roman proconsul Sergius Paulus on Cyprus, doing so with the proconsul's permission as a sign of good will.[40] I discuss this point fully in chapter 1.

On Cyprus, Paul and Barnabas worked at Salamis and Paphos (Acts 13:5–6), chief cities in two of the four districts into which the island was divided.[41] An Augustan milestone located on the road that runs along the southeast coast

38. Alanna Nobbs, "Cyprus," in *The Book of Acts in Its Graeco-Roman Setting,* ed. David W. Gill and Conrad Gempf, BAFCS 2 (Grand Rapids: Eerdmans, 1994), 288.

39. Martin Hengel, *The Pre-Christian Paul* (London: SCM Press; Philadelphia: Trinity Press International, 1991), 10.

40. H. Dessau, "Der Name des Apostels Paulus," *Hermes* 45 (1910): 347–68; G. A. Harrer, "Saul Who Is Also Called Paul," *HTR* 33 (1940): 19–33.

41. Cyprus became a Roman province in 30 B.C., the year following the defeat of Antony and Cleopatra. In 22 B.C. it was made an imperial province. "By the Roman imperial period it was divided into four districts, Paphos, Salamis, Amathus and Lapethos, though this division may have existed earlier" (Nobbs, "Cyprus," 280).

Photo 5.3. Paphos in Cyprus

of Cyprus indicates that this would have been a major Roman road and was probably the one used by Paul and Barnabas as they traveled "through the whole island" (Acts 13:6).[42] At Paphos, the proconsul Sergius Paulus believed after seeing Paul temporarily blind Elymas, a sorcerer who tried to prevent the proconsul's conversion. Inscriptional evidence possibly identifies this proconsul with one who had relatives in Pisidian Antioch, Lycia, and Pamphylia—areas Paul visited immediately after leaving Cyprus. Perhaps this proconsul's family "became Christianized" too and continued their public work, which is mentioned in the inscriptions. It is possible that he was influential in some way in Paul's decision to immediately visit these regions.[43]

Perga and Attalia (Antalya)

Luke gives no reason for the decision to leave Cyprus and go north and does not indicate who was responsible for it. He merely states that "Paul and his company set sail from Paphos, and came to Perga in Pamphylia" (Acts 13:13). When the journey began, there is no indication that they intended to

42. David Gill, "Paul's Travels through Cyprus (Acts 13:4–12)," *TynBul* 46.2 (November 1995): 219–28.

43. Stephen Mitchell states that "it is overwhelmingly likely that Paul . . . was directed to Antioch by his recent convert [Sergius Paulus, JM] ("Antioch," *ABD*, 1:264). This view is shared by Nobbs, "Cyprus," 287.

Photo 5.4. Perga

limit it to Cyprus (Acts 13:2–4). Going to Pamphylia may have been suggested by the proconsul, as mentioned above, or it may have been a natural choice because it was the next closest point. Furthermore, Phrygia and Pamphylia had a significant Jewish population,[44] and Jews from there had been present on the Day of Pentecost when the church was started in Jerusalem (Acts 2:10).

Paul, Barnabas, and Mark sailed north to Pamphylia, part of the southern coast of modern Turkey (Acts 13:13). Pamphylia had been a part of Paul's home province of Cilicia from 102 B.C. to 44 B.C., when it became part of the province of Asia. It was subsequently attached to Galatia, and eventually in A.D. 43, about five years before Paul arrived, the emperor Claudius joined it with Lycia to the west to form Lycia-Pamphylia.[45] Pamphylia is a lovely coastal plain, eighty miles wide, that stretches northward about thirty miles to the mountains of Pisidia.

However, Perga is not on the coast. It lies a considerable distance north of the sea. Extensive alluvial deposits exist along the entire coast of Turkey today, placing one-time coastal cities like Ephesus and Miletus miles from the shore. But even in Paul's time, according to the first-century geographer

44. Philo, *Legat.* 281–82.
45. Scott Carroll, "Pamphylia," *ABD*, 5:138–39. The reference to Cilicia and Pamphylia (joined by a common article—κατὰ τὴν Κιλικίαν καὶ Παμφυλίαν) in Acts 27:5 is a geographical rather than a political one. They lay together along a common coast.

Strabo, Perga was about seven miles from the coast: "Then one comes to the Cestrus River [modern Aksu, JM]; and sailing sixty stadia up this river, one comes to Perga."[46] This clearly shows that sailing up the river was not unusual and implies that there was a landing facility near the city.[47] Whether Paul went to Perga directly without landing first at the harbor of Attalia is unclear.

One would assume that a normal commercial vessel taken from Cyprus to Pamphylia would put in at Attalia.[48] Then a traveler might choose either to go by land or take a small riverboat on to Perga. Luke makes no mention of Attalia, except when discussing the return portion of this trip, when Paul and Barnabas embarked from there after first preaching in Perga (Acts 14:25–26). Perhaps this implies that Paul and Barnabas did not tarry in Perga at first but went on north after the departure of John Mark and only preached in Perga on the return portion of their journey. Purely on the basis of what Luke states, one might conclude that they did not sail from Perga, where they preached, and that they did not preach in Attalia, from which they sailed.

Although most of the cities visited by Paul on his first missionary journey remain unexcavated, Perga is an exception.[49] It is a 151-acre site with impressive archaeological remains. Recent work there has identified a large Roman marketplace.

The city walls and towers, built in the third century B.C., were standing at the time of Paul's visit and are well preserved today. In the south wall there is a pair of gates shaped like a horseshoe. This is the most impressive ruin in Perga. Paul would have entered the city from the south through these twin circular Hellenistic gates opening onto a colonnaded street running north to an exercise ground that was built and dedicated to the Roman emperor Claudius just before Paul's arrival. A Greco-Roman type of theater that would have seated about fourteen thousand spectators has been partially excavated.

For reasons unstated,[50] John Mark, the cousin of Barnabas (Col. 4:10),[51] left them at this time and went to Jerusalem, where his mother lived (Acts 12:12). Interestingly, he did not return to Antioch, from which they had

---

46. *Geogr.* 14.4.2.

47. G. E. Bean, *Turkey's Southern Shore* (London: Ernest Benn, 1979), 31–32.

48. David French assumes Paul sailed to Attalia, even though Luke does not record it ("Acts and the Roman Roads of Asia Minor," in *The Book of Acts in Its Graeco-Roman Setting,* ed. Gill and Gempf, 52).

49. For a discussion of the archaeological remains, see John McRay, *Archaeology and the New Testament* (Grand Rapids: Baker, 1991), 240.

50. Ramsay believes John Mark left because of a change in plans regarding itinerary that took them farther into Gentile territory than previously agreed upon (Sir William Ramsay, *St. Paul the Traveller and the Roman Citizen* [London: Hodder and Stoughton, 1908], 90).

51. Not "nephew" as some of the older translations have it.

begun their journey and to which Paul and Barnabas later returned (Acts 14:26). Perhaps this is an indication that Mark felt his leaving would not be viewed favorably by the Antioch church, which had commissioned their journey. Clearly, Paul considered this such a significant lapse in dedication that he later refused Barnabas's request to take Mark with him on a second journey (Acts 15:36–41). This precipiated a heated argument[52] between him and Barnabas, resulting in their parting company.

Perhaps in theology Mark was closer to Peter and his mission to the Jews (Gal. 2:7) than he was to Paul's Gentile agenda. Peter was closely associated with the group that met in the home of Mark's mother in Jerusalem (Acts 12:12). One might conjecture that while Barnabas was in charge of the mission to Cyprus, it was more oriented toward Jewish than Gentile evangelism, and his cousin Mark was in agreement with this agenda. Mark may have become dissatisfied when Paul took the lead and projected a dangerous and unplanned extension of their mission among the Gentiles of southern Galatia.

Mark's connection with Peter is well documented. He was later with Peter in Babylon (1 Pet. 5:13) and probably compiled his Gospel essentially from material obtained from Peter. Papias wrote in the second century that "Mark became Peter's interpreter and wrote accurately all that he remembered, not, indeed, in order, of the things said or done by the Lord."[53] Mark's connection with Peter is also mentioned by Justin Martyr,[54] Tertullian,[55] and Clement of Alexandria.[56]

Mark's decision to return to Jerusalem may have been further motivated by the fear of robbers in these mountains. Augustus Caesar had been prompted by this problem to establish military outposts in the region, including those at Antioch (Acts 13:13–40; 14:21) and Lystra (Acts 14:8–21), both of which Paul visited. Paul later spoke of the "danger from robbers" he encountered on his journeys (2 Cor. 11:26).

From Perga, Paul and Barnabas went on alone into the dangerous mountain country of Pisidia. What prompted this decision to leave the coast and go into the rugged mountainous terrain of Pisidia is not stated. It may have been, as I mentioned earlier, the intention from the beginning, perhaps prompted by the encounter with Sergius Paulus at Paphos. Or it may be that Paul contracted malaria in this mosquito-infested area,[57] which required that he move

---

52. Acts 15:39. Παροξυσμός is defined as a "sharp disagreement" (BAGD, 629) or "irritation, exasperation" (LSJ, 1343). It can have a milder meaning, as in Heb. 10:24, but the context in Acts 15:39 makes it clear that the former connotation is intended.

53. Eusebius, *Hist. eccl.* 3.39.15.

54. *Dial.* 106.3.

55. *Marc.* 4.5.

56. Eusebius, *Hist. eccl.* 6.14.6f.

57. As Jack Finegan suggests (*ANT:MW*, 89–90).

to higher, healthier ground for a period of recuperation. Sir William Ramsay, a scholar on the Mediterranean world of the first century, felt that the problem was a "species of chronic malaria" but that Paul had been afflicted with it for a long time. He thinks this was Paul's "thorn in the flesh" (2 Cor. 12:7) and notes that Paul later referred to this decision to go into southern Galatia (Pisidia and Phrygia) as being motivated by a "bodily ailment" (Gal. 4:13).[58] Jack Finegan, another authority on the Mediterranean world at this time, assumes the illness was "contracted in the lowlands,"[59] but Ramsay correctly points out that there is nothing in this text that suggests that this ailment began in Galatia.

Whatever the reason, Paul and Barnabas journeyed northward from Perga to Pisidia. Three routes were possible,[60] not just two:[61]

1. The far western route, a rather long one, went from Attalia northwestward to Comama, then arched in a northeasterly direction until it turned east above Lake Egridir to Antioch.[62] This road, called the Via Sebaste and built by Augustus Caesar in 6 B.C., is known from seven Roman milestones discovered along the route[63] to have run from Antioch southward to Comama. Recent discoveries have demonstrated that it continued on down to Perga and possibly to Attalia.[64] It was more than ten feet wide and, following the valley route, would have allowed an easy but lengthy journey.

2. A second route ran almost due north along the valley of the Cestrus (modern Aksu) River to the southern end of Lake Limnaei (modern Egridir) and then to Antioch. Some of this was rugged terrain and probably a rather uninviting road.

3. A third route, overlooked or ignored by some geographers[65] but plotted on a classical map by others,[66] ran from Perga eastward to Side and then north to Lake Caralis (modern Beysehir). From here it continued northward along the eastern side of the lake to Antioch. This would be a steep climb across high mountains for about eighty miles and take approximately a week, but it would probably be faster than

58. Ramsay, *St. Paul,* 92–97.

59. Finegan, *ANT:MW,* 90.

60. Ibid.; W. Ward Gasque, "Pisidia," *ABD,* 5:375.

61. As suggested by G. Walter Hansen, "Galatia," in *The Book of Acts in Its Graeco-Roman Setting,* ed. Gill and Gempf, 384; and French, "Acts and the Roman Roads," 51.

62. This is the choice of French, "Acts and the Roman Roads," 52.

63. David French, "The Road System of Asia Minor," in *ANRW,* 2.7.2:707.

64. French, "Acts and the Roman Roads," 52.

65. E.g., French, "Acts and the Roman Roads," and Hansen, "Galatia."

66. W. M. Calder and G. E. Bean, *A Classical Map of Asia Minor* (London: British Institute of Archaeology at Ankara, 1958).

Photo 5.5. Aqueduct in Antioch of Pisidia

the western route. All things considered, this seems to be the best choice of the available options.[67]

The Via Sebaste connected Antioch with Iconium, Lystra, and Derbe, the cities Paul and Barnabas visited in southern Galatia. They would have traveled easily and freely from city to city on this road. There is no evidence that Paul went into northern Galatia at this time. It lay 120 miles due north, and Luke makes no mention of it. Efforts to place Paul in northern Galatia on his second journey are unconvincing.[68] His itinerary under the guidance of the Holy Spirit took him through Phrygia and Galatia and did not even allow him time to preach in Asia, Mysia, or Bithynia (Acts 16:6–10). The terms *Phrygia* and *Galatia* here (Acts 16:6), as well as *Galatia* and *Phrygia* in Acts 18:23, refer to the ethnic Phrygian section of southern provincial Galatia.[69]

67. Finegan, *ANT:MW,* and Gasque, "Pisidia," opt for this route, and I include it in my *Archaeology and the New Testament* (see the diagram on page 245 of selected Roman roads in Asia Minor).

68. Robert Jewett agonizes over the time required for such a trip, necessitating that he lengthen his estimate of the years involved in Paul's journey (*A Chronology of Paul's Life* [Philadelphia: Fortress, 1979], 58–62).

69. Hemer, *BASHH,* 112 n. 28; and idem, "The Adjective 'Phrygia,'" *JTS,* n.s., 27 (1976): 122–26. See also a brief but good analysis of the linguistic and geographical implications of these terms in Hansen, "Galatia," 378–79. On the nature of Galatia as a Roman province, see Robert Sherk, "Roman Galatia," in *ANRW,* 2.7.2:954ff.

Antioch of Pisidia

When Paul entered Antioch, it was in its period of greatest prosperity after having been refounded as a Roman colony by Augustus.[70] It was one of the most important and influential colonies in the eastern Mediterranean. The tremendous building project for the city center was nearing completion, and the triple-arched gateway was completed only two or three years later, in A.D. 50.

As was his custom (Acts 17:2), Paul began his work in Antioch in the synagogues,[71] where there were both Jews and God-fearers (Acts 13:16, 43). In the first century, synagogues, like churches, met in homes, some of which were altered to suit the needs of a congregation at worship.[72] It has been suggested that the word *synagogue* at this time may have referred only to the community of people and not to a structure. However, while it is true that there is little archaeological evidence of first-century synagogue buildings in any part of the empire, it should be noted that (1) a few first-century synagogue buildings have been excavated in the Mediterranean area;[73] (2) by this time, Judaism, unlike Christianity, had long been a legal religion and would have been allowed to construct buildings;[74] (3) Paul encountered wealthy Jews on his journeys who were part of a social class in the empire that could afford to construct buildings;[75] and (4) a separate structure is alluded to in Acts 18:7, where Luke writes that Paul "left there and went to the house of a man named

70. On archaeological remains here, see McRay, *Archaeology and the New Testament*, 237–39. See also the article on Antioch by Stephen Mitchell, *ABD*, 1:264–65.

71. See the discussion of synagogues in chapter 1, under "Paul Went to the Synagogue As Was His Custom."

72. A synagogue and a church have been found in close proximity at Dura Europas, a city in eastern Syria. They were both domestic structures that had been altered. See Jack Finegan, *Light from the Ancient Past* (Princeton, N.J.: Princeton University Press, 1959), 497–500; Clark Hopkins, *The Discovery of Dura Europos* (New Haven, Conn.: Yale University Press, 1979), 89–177.

73. At Masada, Herodium, and Gamla, as well as at Delos in the south Aegean Sea. See McRay, *Archaeology and the New Testament*, 72, for documentation. L. M. White says the buildings in Palestine were not used exclusively as synagogues, but there is no way to prove this (*Building God's House in the Roman World: Architectural Adaptation among Pagans, Jews, and Christians* (Baltimore: Johns Hopkins University Press, 1990).

74. Emperors did not officially declare Christianity an empire-wide *religio illicita* until the time of the Flavian period, when Domitian reigned. It operated, as far as official imperial recognition was concerned, under the umbrella of its relation to Judaism. On the provincial level, the proconsul Gallio, the emperor Claudius's official representative in Greece, had in effect declared Christianity to be a part of Judaism by his decision in Corinth in A.D. 51, when Paul was brought before him by the Jews of the synagogue (Acts 18:12–17). See Bruce Winter's interesting analysis of the Jews' subsequent attack on their synagogue ruler, Sosthenes (*Seek the Welfare of the City: Christians as Benefactors and Citizens* [Grand Rapids: Eerdmans, 1994], 142).

75. See further David W. J. Gill, "Acts and the Urban Elites," in *The Book of Acts in Its Graeco-Roman Setting*, ed. Gill and Gempf, 105–18.

Titius Justus, a worshiper of God; his house was next door to the synagogue." This Gentile God-fearer lived "next door to the synagogue," which he probably attended.

In Antioch, Paul preached the resurrection of Jesus as prophesied in Psalm 2. His intitial efforts were enthusiastically received by the people, who "begged that these things might be told them the next sabbath" (Acts 13:42). There was no problem with the teaching on the resurrection or with the assertion that Jesus was the Messiah. It had been so with Jesus when he spoke in Nazareth. After Jesus identified himself with the Messiah prophesied by Isaiah, Luke wrote, "all spoke well of him, and wondered at the gracious words which proceeded out of his mouth" (Luke 4:22). The rejection came when Jesus spoke of going to the Gentiles (Luke 4:25–30).

The next Sabbath day, when "almost the whole city" (Acts 13:44) turned out to hear Paul and Barnabas, jealousy over their popularity led to their rejection by "the Jews." By this expression we are to understand the Jewish synagogue leaders other than those "Jews and devout converts" (Acts 13:43) who followed Paul and Barnabas. Paul then turned to the Gentiles (Acts 13:47–48).

A period of preaching to Gentiles followed, during which the "word of the Lord spread throughout all the region" (Acts 13:49). Remains of the pagan temple of Augustus still exist in Antioch, giving mute testimony to the emperor worship that prevailed there among Gentiles.[76]

Eventually, the two missionaries were run out of Antioch when Jewish leaders recruited men and women of political importance to oppose Paul. This suggests that Judaism was influential among the elite of the city at this time.[77] Shaking the dust off their feet (Acts 13:51) "as a testimony against them" in the symbolic manner that Jesus had instructed (Luke 9:5; 10:11; Mark 6:11; Matt. 10:14), they moved on to Iconium, Lystra, and Derbe.[78]

Iconium (Konya)

Iconium (modern Konya) was a large and wealthy city at this time, some ninety miles from Antioch. As usual, Paul initiated his work here in the synagogues, and the reception was identical to that in Antioch. When Gentiles, Jews, and their rulers attempted to have Paul and Barnabas stoned, they fled

76. See S. R. F. Price, *Rituals and Power: The Roman Imperial Cult in Asia Minor* (Cambridge: Cambridge University Press, 1983).

77. See French, "Acts and the Roman Roads," 264.

78. For a discussion of these as-yet unexcavated sites, see McRay, *Archaeology and the New Testament,* 239.

to Lystra. Inscriptions in Iconium indicate a continuing and signficant Christian influence here during the first century.[79]

It is of interest that the earliest description of Paul, which some scholars consider historically reliable,[80] comes from this city. Paul was seen traveling along the "royal road to Lystra" and is described by a man named Onesiphorus.[81]

Lystra

After their rejection in Iconium, Paul and Barnabas traveled this very royal road, the Via Sebaste, to Lystra, where they performed a miracle (Acts 14:8–18), just as they had done on numerous occasions in Iconium (Acts 14:3). Luke gives some insight into the previously discussed question of the comparative roles of Paul and Barnabas as the mission progresses by noting that Paul "was the chief speaker" (Acts 14:12).

Lystra was the southernmost of a number of colonies Augustus had established in the area as bases for Roman military campaigns against the tribes of the Taurus. It was located approximately twenty miles south of Konya.[82] Unlike Iconium, which was a Phrygian city, Lystra and Derbe were cities of the south Galatian district of Lycaonia (Acts 14:6), and Lycaonian was spoken there (Acts 14:11). Lystra was probably little more than a frontier town that retained its local cultural religion and way of life.

Interestingly, the people here identified Barnabas and Paul with Zeus and Hermes, respectively (Acts 14:12–13). Paul was called Hermes because he was the "chief speaker," but no reason is given for their calling Barnabas Zeus. One suggestion is that the people syncretized their local gods with these Greek deities. The local Zeus, Zeus Ampelites, was sometimes portrayed on reliefs as an elderly, bearded figure accompanied by a young male assistant.[83] According to this view, they thought Barnabas and Paul were acting out the roles they envisioned for their gods, Barnabas (like Zeus) initiating and Paul (like Hermes, the assistant) expediting the action.[84] Whether this analogy holds or not, Paul was viewed as the lead figure, the main speaker, and was the one who was stoned—not Barnabas.

Two significant events in Paul's ministry were associated with the city of Lystra; one on the first journey and the other on his second journey. Antagonistic Jews from Antioch and Iconium followed Paul and Barnabas to Lystra,

---

79. W. Ward Gasque, "Iconium," *ABD*, 3:357.
80. Ibid.
81. See the description and discussion in chapter 1, under "In Person He Is Unimpressive."
82. The site was identified by J. R. S. Sterrett in 1885 at Zoldera, near Khatyn Serai.
83. D. S. Potter, "Lystra," *ABD*, 4:427.
84. Such is the opinion of Potter, ibid.

where they stoned Paul and left him for dead (Acts 14:19).[85] Why Barnabas was not stoned is not stated, but perhaps it was because of the more visibly prominent role of Paul, "the chief speaker." Luke seems to imply some kind of miraculous recovery for Paul, who, though so severely injured that he appeared to be dead, "rose up and entered the city" (Acts 14:20) when the disciples gathered about him. The other event at Lystra was the enlisting of Timothy as a traveling companion (Acts 16:1–3), which will be discussed in the next chapter.

Derbe

Luke's account of Paul and Barnabas in Derbe[86] is exceedingly brief: "But when the disciples gathered about him, he rose up and entered the city; and on the next day he went on with Barnabas to Derbe. When they had preached the gospel to that city and had made many disciples, they returned to Lystra and to Iconium and to Antioch" (Acts 14:20–21). One of Paul's later traveling companions, Gaius, was from Derbe (Acts 19:29; 20:4). This city was important only because it was on the Via Sebaste and was a station for customs and frontier dues. It was the easternmost city visited by Paul and Barnabas on their journey.[87]

After preaching in Derbe, Paul and Barnabas could have continued on the road eastward to Tarsus, about 150 miles away. This road ran through the Cilician Gates, a pass through the Taurus Mountains, and then south to Tarsus and Antioch. However, they chose to return by retracing their journey in reverse order through the cities where they had preached, in spite of the hostility they had encountered. Luke writes:

85. Stoning is described in *m. Sanhedrin* 6.1–6.

86. Derbe was identified with Gudelisin by Sir William Ramsay. Michael Ballance identifies it with Devri Sehri ("The Site of Derbe: A New Inscription," *Anatolian Studies* 7 [1957]: 147–51; "Derbe and Faustinopolis," *Anatolian Studies* 14 [1964]: 139–40). Finegan accepts this identification (*ANT:MW,* 92). However a number of other suggestions have been promulgated on the basis of the inscriptions, including Kerti Hüyük (Bastiaan Van Elderen, "Some Archaeological Observations on Paul's First Missionary Journey," in *Apostolic History and the Gospel: Biblical and Historical Essays Presented to F. F. Bruce on His 60th Birthday,* ed. W. Ward Gasque and R. P. Martin [Grand Rapids: Eerdmans, 1970], 151–61). F. F. Bruce initially accepted Devri Sehri as the site (*New Testament History* [London: Nelson, 1969], 259) but later agreed with Van Elderen (idem, *Paul,* 171). For further discussion about Derbe and the inscriptions found that contain the name of the city, see McRay, *Archaeology and the New Testament,* 239–40. See William Ramsay's discussion of Derbe in *The Cities of St. Paul* (London: Hodder and Stoughton, 1907), 395.

87. Ramsay described it as "one of the rudest of the Pauline cities, education had made no great progress in it, and therefore it was not fitted to produce a strong impression on the history of the Church or of Asia Minor. Its inscriptions are late in date, and show little trace of contact with the Roman world" (*Cities of St. Paul,* 399).

Photo 5.6. Antalya Harbor

When they had preached the gospel to that city [Derbe] and had made many disciples, they returned to Lystra and to Iconium and to Antioch, strengthening the souls of the disciples, exhorting them to continue in the faith, and saying that through many tribulations we must enter the kingdom of God. And when they had appointed elders for them in every church, with prayer and fasting, they committed them to the Lord in whom they believed. (Acts 14:21–23)

The phrase "every church" refers to the disciples as a whole in every town. They were divided into small groups that met in various members' homes at this time. A parallel statement is made later by Paul to Titus: "This is why I left you in Crete, that you might amend what was defective, and appoint elders in every town as I directed you" (Titus 1:5). Churches, like the synagogues discussed above, met in homes in the first century.[88] Unlike Judaism, Christianity was not a legal religion until the time of Constantine, in the

88. Bradley Blue, "Acts and the House Church," in *The Book of Acts in Its Graeco-Roman Setting,* ed. Gill and Gempf, 119–222; idem, "In Public and in Private: The Role of the House Church in Early Christianity" (Ph.D. diss., University of Aberdeen, 1989); Robert Jewett, "Tenement Churches and Communal Meals in the Early Church: The Implications of a Form-Critical Analysis of 2 Thessalonians 3:10," *BR* 38 (1993): 23–43; Richard Krautheimer, *Early Christian and Byzantine Architecture,* 3d ed., Pelican History of Art (Harmondsworth, Eng., and Baltimore: Penguin, 1979); Vincent Branick, *The House Church in the Writings of Paul* (Wilmington, Del.: Glazier, 1989); G. Hermansen "The Roman Apartment," in *Ostia: Aspects of Roman City Life* (Edmonton: University of Alberta Press, 1982), chap. 1; McRay, *Archaeology and the New Testament,* 72–73.

early fourth century, and churches could not own property or maintain bank accounts.

After preaching in Perga, Paul left Asia Minor from Attalia (Acts 14:25), a major harbor that provided excellent shelter from the prevailing westerly winds. As noted above, he had probably entered Pamphylia through this harbor. From here Roman roads led in every direction: northwestward to Asia and Galatia, westward along the coast of Lycia, and eastward through Pamphylia to Tarsus and Antioch of Syria, as well as northeastward to Lycaonia. From such a major intersection, Paul and Barnabas could find a coast-hopping vessel to Antioch without difficulty.

From here they sailed to Antioch (Acts 14:26), where they gathered the church together and reported on their work, declaring how God had "opened a door of faith to the Gentiles" (Acts 14:27).

The Jerusalem Conference

Following their report, Paul and Barnabas stayed a "long time" (Acts 14:28 NIV) in Antioch with the disciples. During this time some men came from Jerusalem and tried to lay upon the Gentiles an even more stringent requirement than the earlier Jerusalem emissaries had done (Gal. 2:12). It was no longer simply a matter of requiring the Gentiles to observe Jewish food laws in order to maintain fellowship with Jewish Christians. They were now demanding that Gentile males be circumcised in order to be saved (Acts 15:1).

After a period of considerable debate, the church appointed Paul, Barnabas, and some of the other members to "go up to Jerusalem to the apostles and the elders about this question" (Acts 15:2). We note that Paul is now listed first by Luke. They traveled by land, through Phoenicia and Samaria, reporting the conversion of the Gentiles to churches along the way. These churches in Samaria and Phoenicia had been established by disciples who had been run out of Jerusalem by the persecution of Christians conducted earlier by Paul himself (Acts 8:1–4; 11:19). It must have been quite an experience for Paul to now share with these very churches not only his new faith but also the success of his ministry. Indeed, Luke writes that the news Paul and these Antioch delegates brought to the churches "gave great joy to all the brethren" (Acts 15:3).

Arriving in Jerusalem, Paul and the others met with the apostles and elders (Acts 15:6) to whom they were sent (Acts 15:2). As mentioned before, Peter, in his earlier visit to Antioch, represented the apostles in Jerusalem and feared the circumcision group that purportedly came from James (Gal. 2:12). This indicates a dual element of power and influence in the Jerusalem community—Peter and the Galilean apostles on the one hand, and James, the Lord's brother, with the Judean elders on the other hand.

The deliberations began with what Luke calls "a long debate" or "much discussion" (Acts 15:7), after which Peter rose and reminded them that some time ago God had chosen him to open the door to the Gentiles (Acts 15:8) and had confirmed Peter's understanding of this decision by giving the Gentiles the Holy Spirit in exactly the same way he had given it to the Jews when Peter preached at Pentecost (cf. Acts 11:17). Peter then said that the Jews should not put a yoke (i.e., the law of Moses) on the Gentiles and that the Jews would be saved by the grace of the Lord Jesus, just like the Gentiles (Acts 15:10–11). The impact was evidently poignant because after he finished "all the assembly kept silence" (Acts 15:12).

Then Barnabas and Paul spoke, relating the "signs and wonders" that God had performed through them among the Gentiles (Acts 15:12). "Signs and wonders" refer to the miracles that accompanied and confirmed the message of Paul and Barnabas to the Gentiles (Acts 13:8; 14:3, 8–10) exactly as God had confirmed by "signs and wonders" the message to the Jews through Peter and John (Acts 3:1–10; 4:29–30) and the other apostles (Acts 5:12), to the Hellenists by Stephen (Acts 6:8), and to the Samaritans by Philip (Acts 8:6, 13). Thus, Paul and Barnabas were able to validate their Gentile mission with precisely the same authenticity as the other ethnic missions.[89]

After these presentations by Peter, who represented the Galilean apostles in Jerusalem, and by Paul and Barnabas, who represented the Gentiles in Antioch, James addressed the assembly on behalf of the elders and Jewish Christians in Jerusalem. He agreed with what had been presented by these brothers. (His use of "my judgment" in Acts 15:19 indicates he was speaking as the unchallenged leader of the Jerusalem elders.) James said that they should send word to Antioch and to the Gentile converts in general, requiring only that they observe four[90] ethical prohibitions. These were prohibitions (Acts 15:20, 29) against idolatry (including the eating of meat offered to idols), blood (i.e., bloodshed), things strangled (i.e., not draining the blood according to kosher law before eating the flesh of an animal, Lev. 17:10–14), and immorality.

Three of these four were a part of God's requirements for all humankind; namely, the forbidding of idolatry (Rom. 1:18–24), immorality (Rom. 1:26–28), and murder (Rom. 1:29). Thus, they did not originate in the law of Moses and were not "Jewish" requirements. Paul's accusation of the Gentiles in his letter to the Romans is that they disobeyed the "creation" laws, not the laws of Moses.

---

89. See my outline of Acts based on ethnic divisions in chapter 4, under "The Structure of the Book of Acts."

90. The Western text of Acts 15:20, 29 (cf. 21:25) combines strangulated animals and blood into one, thus making three prohibitions—idolatry, bloodshed, and immorality (see Bruce, *Paul,* 185 n. 28).

The fourth prohibition, that of eating the meat of animals that had been strangled, was given to Noah and his descendants in Genesis 9:4: "Only you shall not eat flesh with its life, that is, its blood." Jewish rabbis taught that the laws of Genesis 9:1–7 were binding upon all Noah's descendants, which included both Jews and Gentiles. They argued that six of the seven "Noachian decrees" or "laws of Noah," which were binding upon Gentiles, had been previously given to Adam. The seventh, the prohibition of eating flesh with the blood in it, was given first to Noah.[91]

So, the decision of the Jerusalem Conference was that in addition to the ethical demands God had always made upon all people, the Gentile Christians should observe one more, the one that lay at the heart of their division. They must not eat blood. But there were other ramifications of the decrees. The prohibition of idolatry also had table connotations. It prohibited the eating of meat offered to idols, which was viewed by the Jews as a form of idolatrous worship.

Paul knew that an idol was nothing, and therefore meat offered to idols by pagans could not be contaminated by gods that do not exist. He later wrote to Gentile Christians in Corinth: "Hence, as to the eating of food offered to idols, we know that 'an idol has no real existence,' and that 'there is no God but one'" (1 Cor. 8:4). However, Paul's advice to them parallels the decision of the Jerusalem leaders at the conference. In Corinth, table fellowship between those who knew the meat was not defiled and those whose consciences would not allow them to eat would be impossible unless, in the interest of fellowship, the knowledgeable ones loved the "weaker brothers" enough to voluntarily deny themselves their right to eat the meat. In Antioch, table fellowship between the Gentile Christians, who were not bound by kosher law, and the "rest of the Jews" in the Antioch church (Gal. 2:13) would be impossible unless the Gentiles loved the Jews enough to make this accommodation. Paul's teaching to those who did not feel bound by these rules was this: "Only take care lest this liberty of yours somehow become a stumbling block to the weak. . . . Therefore, if food is a cause of my brother's falling, I will never eat meat, lest I cause my brother to fall" (1 Cor. 8:9, 13).

My impression, then, is that the rules of the conference were intended, not for salvation, but for maintaining fellowship between Jewish and Gentile Christians. They were intended to deal with the very problem Peter had encountered earlier in Antioch (Gal. 2:11–14). The meaning is that Jews will not be able to share a fellowship meal (a love feast, *agape,* Jude 12) with Gentiles unless the Gentiles are willing to respect the Jews' conscience on these matters. It should also be remembered that these meals were most often eaten in the home, where the early church also ate the Lord's Supper (cf. 1 Cor.

91. *Deuteronomy Rabbah* 2.25 on Deuteronomy 4:41; *b. Sanhedrin* 59b.

11).[92] Paul would find no problem with this, as long as the Gentile acceptance of the rules was voluntary (determined individually by conscience and Christian love) and not mandatory (a matter of salvation or a question of law rather than expedience).[93]

Under Paul's heavenly commission, the Gentile Christians did not have to acquiesce to any regulations from Jerusalem in order to be saved or to operate as independent churches. This was not the issue. Jerusalem had already acknowledged Paul's authority during the fourteenth-year visit, but even if they had not, Paul would have continued his work. The issue now being discussed was whether there would be a close fellowship between the Jewish and Christian elements of the church, not only between Jerusalem and Antioch, but also between the Jewish and Gentile Christians in Antioch and elsewhere. Paul's gospel "envisioned a continued ethnic and cultural distinction between the Jewish and Gentile wings of the church."[94]

Paul taught that the Gentiles were wild olive branches that had been grafted into the natural Jewish tree and that the Jewish root supported the branches; the branches did not support the root (Rom. 11:18, 24). He very much wanted a close relationship to exist between his churches and those in Judea. The long-range success of his work depended on it. He later brought a contribution from these poor Gentile churches to the needy Jerusalem churches to bolster this relationship (Rom. 15:16, 25–27; 2 Cor. 8:1–5).

The letter formulated by the Jerusalem leaders is recorded by Luke (Acts 15:23–29). It was taken to Antioch by Paul and Barnabas. They were accompanied by Judas and Silas, who were selected for the mission by the "apostles and elders, with the whole church" (Acts 15:22) to add a sense of authority and importance to the letter.

92. John McRay, "House Churches and the Lord's Supper," *Leaven* 3.3 (1995): 13–16; Jewett, "Tenement Churches," 23–43; Bradley Blue, "The House Church at Corinth and the Lord's Supper: Famine, Food Supply, and the Present Distress," *Criswell Theological Review* 5.2 (1991): 221–39.

93. Bruce, *Paul,* 187.

94. See Howard's discussion of this point in *Crisis in Galatia,* 40–41.

SIX

Paul's Second Journey

To Troas

After Paul and Barnabas returned to Antioch from the Jerusalem Conference, bringing Silas and Judas with them (Acts 15:22), they remained in Antioch for an unspecified period of time "teaching and preaching the word of the Lord." They were assisted in this by "many others also" (Acts 15:35). "After some days" (Acts 15:36), which could mean days, weeks, or even months, Paul initiated the second missionary journey. Barnabas wanted to take his cousin John Mark with them, but Paul refused because Mark had deserted them on the first journey.[1] After a heated argument, Barnabas and Paul parted company (Acts 15:39). Barnabas took Mark with him and returned to Cyprus, where they had begun the first journey.

Paul selected Silas as his traveling companion (Acts 15:40). He and Judas (also called Barsabbas, Acts 15:22) had been sent along with Paul and Barnabas by the Jerusalem church to Antioch. They carried the letter containing the decision of the Jerusalem Conference regarding Gentile fellowship. After they delivered the letter, verse 33 says "they" (i.e., Silas and Judas) were sent back to "those who had sent them" (i.e., Jerusalem, Acts 15:22).

However, Silas either stayed on in Antioch after delivering the letter or returned to Jerusalem and then came back to Antioch later to accompany Paul on this second journey. The text of the New Testament is uncertain on this point. Almost every English translation since the King James Version omits

1. See the discussion of this occasion in chapter 5, under "Perga and Attalia (Antalya)."

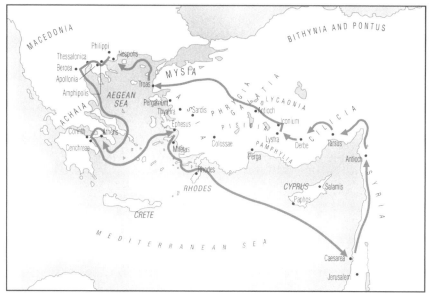

Map 6.1. Paul's Second Missionary Journey

Acts 15:34, which says "But it pleased Silas to remain there."[2] The verse was apparently added to the text by later copyists to explain the presence of Silas in Antioch in verse 40, when Paul selects him as a traveling companion.[3] The problems with accepting 15:34 are that it appears only in late Greek manuscripts and that verse 33 has a plural verb,[4] which requires the departure of both men. Silas must have gone back to Jerusalem and then subsequently returned on his own or been summoned by Paul, after his separation from Barnabas, to travel with him.

It is three hundred miles from Jerusalem to Antioch, which would require about fifteen days of normal land travel to make the trip.[5] However, the trip

2. The King James Version and Today's English Version include it.

3. According to Bruce Metzger, *A Textual Commentary on the Greek New Testament,* 2d ed. (Stuttgart: German Bible Society, 1994), 388.

4. Ἀπελύθησαν.

5. Barry Beitzel calculates, from a sizeable body of archaeological and literary evidence all over the Mediterranean world, that a normal day's journey on land by foot covered between fourteen and twenty-three miles on average ("How to Draw Ancient Highways on Biblical Maps," *Bible Review* 4 [October 1988]: 37). This suggests an average of about twenty miles a day, which is indicated in Acts 10:23–30, where Peter's trip from Joppa to Caesarea, a distance of about forty miles, took two days one way and four days round trip. See the estimates of other scholars, which essentially agree with Beitzel's figures, in Brian M. Rapske, "Acts, Travel and Shipwreck," in *The Book of Acts in Its Graeco-Roman Setting,* ed. David W. J. Gill and Conrad Gempf, BAFCS 2 (Grand Rapids: Eerdmans, 1994), 6 n. 20. See further chapter 7 on Paul's travel from Troas to Assos.

Photo 6.1. Cilician Gates

by sea from Caesarea to Seleucia, the port for Antioch, would be faster.[6] The selection of Silas by Paul was no doubt carefully considered. A respected leader in the Jerusalem church, Silas would provide a definite advantage to Paul as he delivered the Jerusalem Conference letter to the churches (Acts 16:4). If anyone questioned Paul's credibility, as some did in Galatia, Silas could vouch for his accurate representation of Jerusalem's position. The two were commended by the church in Antioch to make the trip (Acts 15:40). Interestingly, nothing is said about Barnabas and Mark having received such commendation. Paul and Silas went through Syria and Cilicia, strengthening the churches (Acts 15:41).

Paul's second journey was undertaken with the stated intention of revisiting the churches in the same cities he had visited on his first journey in order to check on their welfare (Acts 15:36). The journey took Paul and Silas on the main road from Antioch to Tarsus of Cilicia, Paul's hometown. From here, they traveled north through the Cilician Gates, a pass through the Taurus Mountains, and then in a westward direction about 150 miles to Derbe and then to Lystra, where Paul asked Timothy to join them (Acts 16:1).

Did Paul convert Timothy? It is possible, but not necessarily so. Timothy was already a "disciple." Luke wrote that when Paul returned to Lystra, "a disciple was there, named Timothy, the son of Jewish woman who was a believer" (Acts 16:1). Thus, it might be argued from Acts that Paul did not convert him. And when Paul later refers to Timothy as "my true child in the faith"

6. See Rapske, "Acts, Travel and Shipwreck," 22ff.

(1 Tim. 1:2) and "my beloved child" (2 Tim. 1:2), he may have been referring to the subsequent nuturing he had given Timothy, rather than to his giving him spiritual birth through conversion.

The implication of the term *son* is probably best seen in Philippians 2:22, where Paul wrote: "But Timothy's worth you know, how as a son with a father he has served with me in the gospel." This may mean that their relationship in service was like that of a father and a son. It does not necessarily mean that Paul had converted him. The enormous affection that Paul had for Timothy and his trust in him is evident in his further comment to Philippi: "I have no one like him, who will be genuinely anxious for your welfare" (Phil. 2:20). However, Paul does not say of Timothy as he does of Onesimus that he *became* his father (Philem. 10).

The "prophetic utterances which pointed to you" (1 Tim. 1:18) may refer to Paul's being led to Timothy as a potential traveling companion as much as to his conversion. This may have begun with the impartation of a gift to Timothy by the laying on of Paul's hands (2 Tim. 1:6).

A recently discovered inscription in Beroea, Greece, provides a reasonable basis to conjecture that Timothy may have been between the ages of eighteen and twenty-two at this time. The inscription was found in a gymnasium and categorized participants into three groups by age.[7] The oldest group listed comprised ages eighteen to twenty-two and was designated with the root form of the word Paul used when he told Timothy "Let no one despise your youth" (νεότης, *neotēs,* 1 Tim. 4:12).[8]

Timothy's faith had dwelt first in the Jewish heritage of his grandmother Lois and his mother, Eunice (2 Tim. 1:5), who had taught him the Scripture since he was a child (2 Tim. 3:15). His father was a Greek (Acts 16:1), which, from the way Luke uses this term in Acts,[9] may mean he was a God-fearer who attended synagogue with the family but had not become a Jewish proselyte. Timothy had evidently followed his father in this matter. Although he had a Jewish mother and grandmother and had been taught the Scripture, he, like his father, had not been circumcised. So, Paul circumcised him "because of the Jews that were in those places, for they all knew that his father was a Greek" (Acts 16:3). Since Paul always began his work among the Jews first, Timothy would be a stumbling block without circumcision.

---

7. (1) Παῖδες (*Paides*), up to age 15; (2) Ἔφεβοι (*Epheboi*), ages 15–17; and (3) Νέοι (*Neoi*) or Νεανίσκοι (*Neaniskoi*), ages 18–22.

8. The inscription was published in 1951 by C. I. Makaronas, *Makedonika* 2 (1951): 629–30, no. 71. For more recent study of it, see J. M. R. Cormack, "The Gymnasiarchal Law of Beroea," in *Ancient Macedonia II: Papers Read at the Second International Symposium Held in Thessaloniki,* Institute for Balkan Studies 155 (n.p.: Institute for Balkan Studies, 1977), 139–49; Jeanne and Louis Robert, *Bulletin Epigraphique* 9 (1978): 430ff.

9. See the discussion of the use of the terms *Gentile, Greek, God-fearer,* and *proselyte* in chapter 5.

It should be emphasized that this situation was quite different from that of Titus, who earlier had not been compelled to be circumcised in Jerusalem (Gal. 2:3) because he was not Jewish. Like Timothy's father, Titus was "a Greek" (Gal. 2:3). Paul would not have allowed Titus or any Gentile to be compelled to become a Jew, but he found no problem with a Jew keeping Jewish customs.[10] Indeed, Paul made a better Jew out of Timothy after he had become a Christian than he was before! After his conversion/call, Paul himself remained a Jew in culture (Acts 21:39; 23:6) and religion (Acts 21:20–26).[11] Paul insisted that a Jew may be Jewish and keep the law, but he may not impose the law on the Gentiles. It may be kept as a cultural and religious heritage but not as a means of salvation. In this matter, Christ had become the "goal" or "end" of the law (Rom. 10:4).[12]

We learn later that Timothy, like Paul, had problems with his health. His "frequent ailments" referred to in 1 Timothy 5:23 necessitated that Timothy drink wine rather than just water. After Timothy was enlisted to join Paul, who had his own severe physical ailments,[13] it is perhaps a matter of providence that they were joined a short time later on this same journey by a physician, Luke, who could attend to their needs (Acts 16:10–11; Colossians 4:14).[14]

The original plan of the second journey—to visit and strengthen the churches established on the first journey—was altered. Why Paul's plans changed to include a trek into western Asia Minor is not revealed, but at least two explanations immediately come to mind.

First, Paul might have been operating under a mandate from the Holy Spirit given to him at Antioch, where his original travel plans had been completed. The Spirit of God is manifestly active in this next part of his journey. Luke writes that when they left Antioch of Pisidia they were "forbidden by the Holy Spirit to speak the word in Asia" (Acts 16:6); the "Spirit of Jesus did not allow them" to preach in Bithynia (Acts 16:7); and in Troas Paul had "a vision" that sent them to the continent of Europe (Acts 16:9).

The second possible explanation supplements rather than supersedes the first one. At the conclusion of his visit to Antioch of Pisidia, Paul might have decided that rather than return the way he had come on the long and tiring

10. See chapter 15 on Paul and the law.

11. See the discussion of this in chapter 2, under "I Am a Jew."

12. See the discussion of this verse in chapter 15.

13. On Paul's ailment, see chapter 1, under "In Person He Is Unimpressive."

14. The narrative in Acts 16:11 continues in the first person after shifting from the third person in verse 10. As we noted earlier, in chapter 3, the author of Acts joins the travelers at this time in Troas. When Luke is with Paul, he includes himself in the narrative by using the first-person pronoun "we," and when he is not present, he appropriately uses the third-person "they." The "we sections" show Luke joined Paul in Troas and accompanied him during parts of his second journey (Acts 16:10–17), his third journey (20:5–15; 21:1–17), and on his voyage to Rome (27:1–28:16).

land route, which would serve no purpose now that he had already strengthened the churches, he would instead go on west and catch a coastal ship back to Syrian Antioch, preaching in new territory along the way. Accordingly, three possible routes presented themselves:

1. If Paul were simply looking for the fastest route home, he could have gone south to Attalia, as he did on his first journey (Acts 14:25–26).
2. He could even have chosen to go due west from Antioch on the postal route through Laodicea to Ephesus or Smyrna and sail from there.
3. On the other hand, if time was not a factor, he may simply have decided to take the northern route to Troas, a large and active port city where a vessel could be found going in almost any direction. Troas was certainly not the fastest of the options available to Paul, but for reasons unstated this is the alternative he chose.[15]

The actual route on which Paul traveled westward from Antioch to Troas is not recorded.[16] However, it is evident from the activity of the Holy Spirit that more was involved in divine providence on this occasion than the mere choice of routes. It is not revealed whether the prohibitions on entering these districts took the form of a direct divine communication to Paul by the Holy Spirit or was implemented by political policies of local authorities who refused to allow him into their jurisdiction. We only know that having been forbidden to preach in these areas, he and his companions went directly to Troas (Acts 16:8).

Since there was no direct route from Antioch northwestward to Troas, Paul would have had to journey directly westward to Ephesus or in a northern di-

15. Previous commitments prevented my accepting an invitation to join an international team of scholars, led by Robert Jewett, which is trying to map a section of the Roman road north of Antioch. The first study trip was made in the summer of 1997. See Robert Jewett, "Mapping the Route of Paul's 'Second Missionary Journey' from Dorylaeum to Troas," *Tyn-Bul* 48.1 (May 1997): 1–22.

16. For the best map of this area in this period, see W. M. Calder and G. E. Bean, *A Classical Map of Asia Minor* (London: British Institute of Archaeology at Ankara, 1958). See also the map by William Ramsay, "Roads and Travel in the New Testament," *A Dictionary of the Bible,* ed. James Hastings (New York: Scribners, 1909), vol. 5 (extra vol.), after page 400. See also Ramsay's map inside the split back jacket of *St. Paul the Traveller and Roman Citizen* (London: Hodder and Stoughton, 1908). Some of Ramsay's century-old identifications are being confirmed and some corrected through ongoing surveys conducted by D. H. French. The results of his surveys are published annually in *Anatolian Studies* in the section on "The Year's Work" and entitled "Roman Roads and Milestones of Asia Minor." He recently noted that "South of Suhut (ancient Synnada), Ramsay's road through the mountains towards Tatarli proved to be a 'ghost' and the true course of the Roman road from Suhut to Dinar was established along a quite different route." He then traces the correct route by using modern Turkish towns. It runs west of Ramsay's projected route (*Anatolian Studies* 40 [1990]: 10).

rection toward Dorylaeum or Cotiaeum.[17] Acts indicates clearly that Paul chose the latter road system because he is next found in the northern regions of Mysia and Bithynia, rather than in the southern region of Asia around Ephesus. He was forbidden to speak in all three of these areas (Acts 16:6–8). The only place Paul could have been traveling through the boundaries of these three districts was in the north. He ended up in Troas, not Ephesus.

From Dorylaeum or Cotiaeum, Paul could not travel directly west to Troas on a major road, because no such road existed. (Such a road has been postulated but never proven.)[18] Thus we would expect him either to have traveled north to the coast and then followed it southward to Troas or to have skirted Mysia on the south, taking a long, circuitous route to Pergamum and then to the coast, where he would have turned north to Troas. However, Luke seems to suggest that Paul and his companions went rather directly to Troas from this area: "So, passing by Mysia, they went down to Troas" (Acts 16:8).

A prominent geographer suggests that Paul traveled such a direct route on a "less important road" running from just west of Dorylaeum, through the Rhyndakos River valley to Artemeia, and then down to Troas.[19] On a main road, Paul would have had to travel around the south side of the district of Mysia and north along the coast to Troas or north to the coast of the Black Sea and then south to Troas. But if he followed a less important road, he might have gone more directly to Troas. We cannot be sure which route he traveled.[20]

More significant, perhaps, than which route he traveled is the question of why Paul chose Troas as a destination, when Ephesus, Miletus, Adramyttium, and ports on the north coast of Bithynia and on the southern coast of Pamphylia were more readily available and provided access to every harbor from Spain to Egypt. As I noted above, it has been suggested that Paul, perhaps by earlier supernatural intervention, had been told that he was to go to Macedonia.[21] This would explain why he did not take the more circuitous southern and northern main roads, which required more time, and why Luke seems to

17. See these roads on the maps in Ramsay ("Roads and Travel," after p. 400) and in Calder and Bean (*Classical Map of Asia Minor*).

18. J. A. R. Munro and H. M. Anthony, "Explorations in Mysia," *The Geographical Journal* 9 (1897): 150–69, 256–76 (see esp. pp. 256ff. and the map opposite p. 248). There is evidence for only a small portion of road from the coast east to Scepsis. A fragmentary milestone was discovered in the Scamander Valley between Scepsis and Troas (J. M. Cook, *The Troad: An Archaeological and Topographical Study* [Oxford: Clarendon, 1973], 396–97).

19. Ramsay, "Roads and Travel," map after p. 400. W. P. Bowers concurs that such a route is conceivable ("Paul's Route through Mysia: A Note on Acts 16:8," *JTS*, n.s., 30 [1979]: 507–11). He calls them "minor trails" (509 n. 3).

20. Colin Hemer concurs: "It must be considered an open question whether Paul's haste to Troas brought him over some rugged path which linked with this [Scepsis-to-Troas road, JM] or whether they came around the northern or southern coastal roads of the Troad" ("Alexandria Troas," *TynBul* 26 [1975]: 102).

21. So Bowers, "Paul's Route," 511.

suggest that he went directly to Troas. If he already knew that his destination was Macedonia, then Troas would have provided the best harbor for going there, and the vision at Troas would only have confirmed that understanding and given it an even stronger sense of urgency (Acts 16:9–10).

On the other hand, Luke says that after Paul received the vision, they concluded (Acts 16:10) that they should go into Macedonia. The text here reads as though this is the first revelation of their destination and that they had to "conclude" that this was the intent of the vision. Questions of this kind must remain enigmatic. What is clearly stated, however, is that the Holy Spirit was involved in a prophetic way in the selection of Timothy (1 Tim. 1:18) and was actively guiding Paul away from preaching in Bithynia, Mysia, and Asia as he traveled westward. Whether Paul knew it or not when he started his journey, God intended for him to enter Europe. He was being sent "far away to the Gentiles" (Acts 22:21), and the launching point was Troas. Furthermore, had Paul sailed from any other port, he would not have found Luke, who joined him here. Perhaps the same prophecies that led Paul to Timothy (1 Tim. 1:18) also led him to Luke.

Troas

Troas was one of the great harbors along the eastern Aegean Sea; from here two major routes led to Rome. One was the sea route, which ran from Troas southward through the Aegean and then westward to Rome and Spain or eastward to Egypt and Syro-Palestina, and the second was a land route. Troas was the "jumping-off point" of the fastest, all-season land route of the Roman imperial postal system from Asia Minor to Rome. This route included a short trip across the Aegean Sea to Neapolis, the port city of Philippi. From there the Egnatian Way ran across Macedonia to the Adriatic Coast at Dyrrachium and from there to Brundisium in Italy and thence to Rome.[22] When the winds were favorable, the 150-mile trip from Troas to Neapolis could be made in two days (Acts 16:11), and when they were unfavorable it could take five days (Acts 20:5).[23] Paul opted for the land route.

---

22. On the Egnatian Way (the Via Egnatia), see John McRay, *Archaeology and the New Testament* (Grand Rapids: Baker, 1991), 282–83.

23. Comparatively, the voyage eastward from Rome to Rhodes took from seven to eleven days in the summer season when the northwesterlies were persistently blowing, but the reverse journey took from forty-five to sixty-three days (L. Casson, "Speed under Sail of Ancient Ships," *Transactions of the American Philological Association* 82 [1951]: 136–48). Cf. also idem, "The Isis and Her Voyage," *Transactions of the American Philological Association* 81 (1950): 43–56.

Photo 6.2. Troas

Troas has little in the way of archaeological remains. Extensive fields and orchards cover the site of ancient Troas, with only occasional scattered pieces of architecture protruding from the ground. We know comparatively little about the city.[24] There are a few, largely unimportant, ancient literary references to it, and epigraphic evidence is scant. Strabo's *Geography,* our chief source, has little information about the city, its author being more interested in nearby Troy. The best evidence available for the city is from coins.

In Troas, Paul had the heavenly vision at night in which Luke says he saw a man of Macedonia saying, "Come over to Macedonia and help us" (Acts 16:9). Luke joined Paul, Timothy, and Silas here, and the four travelers launched the European segment of the mission from the now-silted ancient harbor of Troas. Paul and his companions caught a ship following this well-traveled route from Troas to Neapolis, sailing first to the island of Samothrace off the coast of Macedonia, where they spent the night.

Samothrace

The voyage from Troas to Neapolis was about 150 miles, arching north-ward around the island of Samothrace, which lay about halfway between

24. For a thorough discussion of what is known about Troas, see Colin Hemer, "Alexandria Troas." See also Edwin Yamauchi, "Troas," *ABD,* 6:666–67; and Ramsay, *St. Paul the Traveller,* 198–205.

Photo 6.3. Samothrace

them. Paul's boat reached the island of Samothrace[25] in one day and probably dropped anchor on the north coast, where the remains of an old harbor mole (pier or breakwater) may still be seen. This port, only twenty miles south of the Thracian coast, was widely used in ancient times because its mile-high summit, the highest of any in the Aegean islands, provided a safe haven and was visible to ships from a great distance.

Near the port were the ruins of the pagan Sanctuary of the Great Gods, built in honor of the idol Demeter, as well as other divinities, including the twin attendant demons known as the Kabeiroi. In Paul's time, the mystery religion that developed around the Kabeiroi attracted many people to the island and strongly opposed Christianity. Whether he visited this famous shrine is not stated in Acts, but he could have done so since his boat anchored here for the night. The sanctuary's mysterious rites were held at night and were open to everyone.

The sixty-nine-square-mile island contained a number of impressive buildings in a captivatingly beautiful geographical context. A picturesque terrace view northward to the sea overlooked the Rotunda of Queen Arsinoe, the largest circular building presently known in Greek architecture (sixty-five feet across) and the largest circular classical building constructed prior to

25. For a description of the island and its archaeological remains, see McRay, *Archaeology and the New Testament*, 279–81.

Photo 6.4. Neapolis Harbor

Hadrian's Pantheon in Rome.[26] The sacred area contained several buildings used in the initiation ceremonies of the mystery religion.

We cannot help wondering why Paul's travel plans did not include a period of preaching at this major pagan sanctuary. Samothrace, though granted political autonomy by Rome in 19 B.C., was geographically closer to Thrace than Macedonia, and it might be argued that Paul was responding to the vision that called him to Macedonia. I think, however, the answer lies in the fact that Samothrace had no Jewish population, and Paul's consistent mode of operation was to begin in the synagogues. Accordingly, he sought out cities with synagogues and bypassed major sites that could not provide a Jewish springboard for his ministry. We will notice this as the journey continues and Paul bypasses such important cities as Neapolis, Amphipolis, and Apollonia.

Neapolis

From Samothrace, Paul sailed the next day, probably in the same boat, which was undoubtedly a commercial vessel, to Neapolis (modern Kavalla). Neapolis lay on the coast of Thrace, just inside the border of the Roman province of Macedonia.[27] The city, which has one of the most beautiful harbors in

26. Donald Thorsen, "Samothrace," *ABD*, 5:949.
27. See John McRay, "Greece," *ABD*, 2:1092–98.

the Aegean, was built in a natural amphitheater through which passed the international east-west road, the Egnatian Way, which connected Europe with Asia.

There is almost nothing to be seen in Kavalla today that bears on the time of Paul.[28] He passed through this important harbor city without preaching, evidently because there was no Jewish population in the city. He left immediately for Philippi, which was situated ten miles northwest of Neapolis along the Egnatian Way. This international highway traversed the entire province of Macedonia. It ran from Kypsela on the east coast, which was north of Samothrace, to Apollonia on the west coast—the distance between these two cities given by Roman milestones in the area is 535 Roman miles (493 English miles). Paul would undoubtedly have traveled these excellent roads on his journey through Macedonia.

Philippi

Paul and his companions traveled on to Philippi,[29] which like Corinth was a Roman colony (Acts 16:12). After the death of Julius Caesar, his assassins were defeated here in 42 B.C. by Mark Antony and Octavian, Caesar's great-nephew.[30] The city was then refounded as a colony by Octavian and veterans of the battle and named Colonia Julia Augusta Philippensis. The name appears on inscriptions found in the city.[31] A Greek theater, which was standing when Paul was there, is still preserved at Philippi in its remodeled Roman form.

Acts 16:12 in most translations reads "Philippi . . . is the leading city of the district of Macedonia," but this is not the best translation of the sentence. It could also read "Philippi was a city of the first district of Macedonia," or possibly "Philippi was a leading city of the district of Macedonia."[32] Macedonia had been divided into four districts for administrative purposes in 168 B.C.; Philippi was located in the "first" of these districts but was not its leading city. According to the ancient author Pliny, that honor belonged to Amphipolis.[33] A better translation, based on historical

---

28. McRay, *Archaeology and the New Testament,* 281–82.

29. See further John McRay, "Philippi," *EEC,* 725–26.

30. M. Cary, *A History of Rome down to the Reign of Constantine,* 2d ed. (London: Macmillan, 1962), 424.

31. See documentation in McRay, *Archaeology and the New Testament,* 283 nn. 25 and 26.

32. See the discussion in McRay, *Archaeology and the New Testament,* 284. Cf. Metzger, *Textual Commentary,* 393–95, who prefers to render it "a leading city of the district of Macedonia" (p. 395). There is no article before *city* in Greek.

33. *Nat.* 4.38. Thessalonica was the capital of the second district, Pella of the third, and Pelagonia of the fourth.

Photo 6.5. Forum in Philippi

and geographical considerations, would probably be "a city of the first district of Macedonia," which is the New Revised Standard Version's marginal reading. However, some prefer to sacrifice the factual accuracy of the passage in preference to the better-attested textual support for the city as the first or leading city, based on the "social context of civic pride in Greco-Roman antiquity."[34]

On the Sabbath day, Paul and his companions went outside the gate to the riverside, where they "supposed there was a place of prayer," that is, a place where Jews would be assembled for worship (Acts 16:13, 16). Luke uses the identical Greek phrase in verse 16 that Josephus uses to refer to a synagogue (εἰς τὴν προσευχήν, *eis tēn proseuchēn*).[35] The phrase does not contain the word *place*, which has to be supplied when the word *prayer* means place of prayer. It simply reads "unto the prayer [place]." Thackeray translates the phrase in Josephus as "prayer house."[36]

34. Richard Ascough, "Civic Pride at Philippi: The Text-Critical Problem of Acts 16:12," *NTS* 44 (1998): 93–103. He argues that "the first way of reading the text [i.e., first city, JM] presents a case of civic pride on the part of the author, but at the expense of factual accuracy. The second reading [i.e., city of the first district, JM] preserves the factual accuracy of the account, but has negligible textual support" (p. 93).

35. *Life* 277, 280, 293.

36. "The Life," in *Josephus,* trans. H. St. J. Thackeray (Cambridge: Harvard University Press, 1976), 1:103, 105, 109.

However, in the ancient world the term *synagogue,* like the word *church,* was used to refer to a community of people as well as a building. Evidently there was no synagogue building in Philippi. A minyan, a minimum of ten males, was required for the constitution of a synagogue,[37] but Paul found only "the women who had come together" (Acts 16:13).

Lydia, a God-fearing[38] Gentile, was worshiping "outside the gate" at the riverside" (Acts 16:13). The exact location is not known, but it might have been any one of three locations.[39] Lydia was a seller of purple goods (Acts 16:14), the color of royalty,[40] and was evidently a wealthy business-woman from Thyatira, a city that had prosperous trade guilds.[41] When Paul presented the gospel to her, "the Lord opened her heart to give heed to what was said by Paul" and she was "baptized, with her household" (Acts 16:14–15).

Presumably, either Lydia was now resident in Philippi or she traveled with her household. In either case it is unclear whether this is a "nuclear" family or her *familia,* consisting of servants and other dependents and any animals.[42] It is assumed that only those who were capable of believing were baptized, or immersed in water. This would exclude animals as well as infant children. The natural meaning of the text is that her household came to faith in Christ and

37. This tradition, which probably prevailed in Paul's time, was recorded later in the Mishnah. See *Sanhedrin* 1.6; *Avot* 3.6 (Herbert Danby, trans., *The Mishnah* [Oxford: Oxford University Press, 1933], 383, 450). David H. Stern translates this as "where we understood a minyan met." In his explanatory footnotes of special Jewish terms, he defines a minyan as "a quorum of 10 or more men gathered for Jewish worship" (*Jewish New Testament* [Jerusalem: Jewish New Testament Publications, 1989], 179).

38. See the discussion of this term in chapter 5.

39. Options: (1) Paul Collart, one of Philippi's excavators, thinks it was beside the Gangites River, west of the city. (2) Paul Lemerle, another excavator of Philippi, suggests that it was outside the Krenides Gate, the western gate in the city wall near the Krenides River. He thinks this gate might be the one mentioned in 16:13. It is about a half mile from the forum in the center of the city. Local tradition calls the Krenides stream the "River of Lydia"! (3) The third possiblity is the eastern gate of the city, the Neapolis Gate. A portion of it has been excavated on the south side of the modern road, next to the theater. A streambed may still be seen immediately outside the gate. The Greek archaeologist Pelekanides excavated a fourth-century church beside this stream in 1956 and recently discovered another one, an octagonal church with mosaic floors, just inside the Neapolis Gate on the south side of the road. The church, which was dedicated to Paul, was reached through a gate from the nearby Egnatian Way, on which Paul was traveling when he initially entered the city. It is possible that the location of these churches near the eastern gate suggests an early recollection that Lydia was converted near here. For further discussion of the archaeological data and documentation, see McRay, *Archaeology and the New Testament,* 286–87.

40. Luke 16:19; Rev. 17:4; 18:12, 16. Cf. Mark 15:17, 20; John 19:2, 5. See further, I. Irving Ziderman, "Seashells and Ancient Purple Dyeing," *BA* 53.2 (June 1990): 98–101.

41. See the documentation in McRay, *Archaeology and the New Testament,* 244–46 nn. 8–9.

42. F. F. Bruce, *Paul: Apostle of the Heart Set Free* (Grand Rapids: Eerdmans, 1977), 220. It is not stated whether she was married.

Photo 6.6. Philippi Jail

responded voluntarily to baptism. There is no reason to assume that Lydia forced her household to join her.

Paul and Silas were arrested and imprisoned in Philippi after an encounter with a slave girl who followed them for many days and "annoyed" Paul (Acts 16:18). She was possessed by an evil spirit,[43] and when Paul cast the spirit out of her, her owners, who used her fortune-telling for monetary gain, had Paul imprisoned for proselytizing in this Roman colony. There was no "positive veto" of such activity during the reign of Claudius, but it was discouraged.[44] This is the first recorded clash between the apostles and non-Jewish interests involving the ordinary citizens of a colony.[45]

Vitruvius, a first-century Roman architect, wrote that prisons were normally built near the forum,[46] which was a marketplace in an ancient city. The one in Philippi is delineated by columns and has some paving still in place in its center.

43. Luke literally calls it a "pythonic spirit," identifying it perhaps with the spirit that possessed the Pythian prophetess (the oracle) at Delphi, so that she was acting as a mouthpiece for Apollo. Perhaps ventriloquisim was involved. See Bruce, *Paul*, 221 n. 37.

44. See the discussion of the issue in A. N. Sherwin-White, *Roman Society and Roman Law in the New Testament* (Oxford: Oxford University Press, 1963; reprint, Grand Rapids: Baker, 1992), 78–81; A. Momigliano, *Claudius the Emperor and His Achievement* (Oxford: Oxford University Press, 1934), 29ff.

45. Sherwin-White, *Roman Society and Roman Law*, 78.

46. *On Architecture* 5.2.1.

On the north side of the modern road, above the northwest corner of the forum, stands a small crypt that may have been the place where Paul and Silas were imprisoned. Since the fifth century it has been considered Paul's prison.[47]

Roman Prisons

As much as 25 percent of Paul's time as an itinerant missionary may have been spent in prison. This includes the two years he was incarcerated in Caesarea, two years in a first imprisonment in Rome, an undisclosed duration of time in his last confinement in Rome, and a brief lockup in Philippi. But these recorded confinements do not tell the whole story. Paul wrote that he experienced "far more imprisonments" than his opponents (2 Cor. 11:23), a phrase that implies more than a few, but no account of these is given in the New Testament.

In addition to the shame associated with imprisonment in Roman culture, Paul endured "countless beatings" and was "often near death" (2 Cor. 11:23). Roman imprisonment was preceded by inquisitorial flogging, a painful and bloody ordeal[48] that involved the further humiliation of public nakedness, since the clothing was stripped away for the flogging.[49]

Inside the prison, the bleeding wounds went untreated as the prisoners sat in leg and/or wrist chains,[50] which inflicted additional pain. The mutilated clothing was not replaced, and prisoners were cold in winter. During his final imprisonment in Rome, Paul asked Timothy to bring him his cloak, which he had left at Troas. The cloak was used as a cover at night.[51] Presumably, his sudden arrest in Troas had prevented the packing of his clothing and books (2 Tim. 4:13).

Natural light was poor in most prisons, even in the best of cells, and would have been nonexistent in the dungeons or inner cell where Paul and Silas were placed in Philippi (Acts 16:24). The pain, immobility, and utter darkness sometimes led to suicide attempts by prisoners who were incarcerated over long periods of time. Such attempts were difficult in custody, and guards were

47. Robin Barber, *Greece,* 5th ed., Blue Guide (New York: Norton, 1987), 637. The structure is discussed in McRay, *Archaeology and the New Testament,* 289, along with several other structures in the city noted on pp. 282–89. Some have identified the cell as a "pagan Hellenistic crypt" and called the identification as Paul's prison "demonstrably wrong" (Eric Meyers and L. Michael White, "Jews and Christians in a Roman World," *Archaeology* 42.2 [March–April 1989]: 31).

48. Brian Rapske, *The Book of Acts and Paul in Roman Custody,* BAFCS 3 (Grand Rapids: Eerdmans, 1994), 219, 124.

49. Ibid., 125, 219.

50. Ibid., 206.

51. Ibid., 199.

forbidden by threat of severe punishment to assist in suicides.[52] Prisoners sometimes begged for a speedy death.

There was normally no access to bathing facilities or barbers in Roman prisons. Male and female prisoners were incarcerated together until the time of Constantine, when a law was enacted forbidding it. This led to occasional, if not frequent, acts of immorality.[53]

Prisons designed for maximum security were structures of misery. Unbearable heat in summer and cold in winter, dehydration for lack of water, suffocating closeness in cramped quarters, constant noise, sickening stench from lack of access to toilets on request, and the soreness associated with leg and wrist chains made sleep difficult.[54]

Prison food, when available, was restricted in quantity and poor in quality. Observance of religious strictures on eating, such as keeping kosher, was almost impossible, unless such food was supplied by friends or family from the outside. Most prisons expected the prisoners to provide their own food from outside sources. Those who were fortunate enough to have an outside source of food had a better chance of maintaining a reasonable degree of health.[55] It will be remembered that when Paul was in prison in Caesarea, Felix, the procurator, gave orders to the centurion that "none of his friends should be prevented from attending to his needs" (Acts 24:23).[56] Conditions could be mitigated to some extent if the prisoner was eminent or willing to pay a bribe, as Felix hoped to receive from Paul in Caesarea (Acts 24:26).

Not all prisons were alike. Military and provincial prisons like those at Caesarea and Philippi were harsh. On the other hand, a prominent individual or one expected to be released might be kept under house arrest if he or she could afford the rent. In Rome, where housing was excessively expensive, Paul was given the privilege of house arrest. He paid the rent himself (Acts 28:30). The source of his income is not revealed.

The facility Paul rented was large enough to accommodate "great numbers" of visitors, whom he taught from morning till evening (Acts 28:23), but it was undoubtedly not a private house. Luke's word "lodging" (Acts 28:23) probably refers to an apartment. Houses were prohibitive in price and virtually nonexistent in big cities except for homes owned by the wealthy and powerful. In cities like Rome, Ostia, Ephesus, and Corinth, the populace lived in high-rise apartment complexes, some of which have been found in excavations. Paul probably rented a third floor of one of these, since the first floor was normally used for shops and the second floor was extremely expensive. Of

52. Ibid., 223.
53. Ibid., 279.
54. Ibid., 198.
55. Ibid., 426.
56. See B. M. Rapske, "The Importance of Helpers to the Imprisoned Paul in the Book of Acts," *TynBul* 42.1 (1991): 7–13.

course, his final imprisonment in Rome, perhaps in the Mammertine Prison, was under the adverse conditions of normal incarceration mentioned above.

Paul and Silas were released from the prison in Philippi by an earthquake, after which their jailor believed in Jesus and was baptized, like Lydia, with all his house (Acts 16:33).[57] Paul and Silas then informed the magistrates that they were both Roman citizens (Acts 16:37) and had been beaten illegally. Why they allowed themselves to be beaten in the first place is a mystery. Perhaps they felt that their suffering would be a more effective witness to the community than using their Roman privilege to avoid hardships. The Lord had told Ananias that he would show Paul "how much he must suffer for the sake of my name" (Acts 9:16), and Ananias must have told Paul about it when he baptized him. It is also possible that the police who arrested Paul were told that he was a citizen but did not believe what they heard. On two other occasions, Paul was beaten with rods, a Roman form of punishment (2 Cor. 11:25). The magistrates in Philippi, perhaps, were forced to take him more seriously.

Because Paul would not compromise the integrity of his mission by being viewed as a common criminal, the magistrates were forced to come to the prison, take out Paul and Silas, and release them publicly (Acts 16:38–39). Then, after a visit with Lydia (Acts 16:40), with whom they apparently had been staying, they departed from the city, leaving Luke behind.[58]

When Paul was traveling in the ancient world, he did not have the option of staying in clean, convenient, and relatively inexpensive motels with good food available, as is customary in our modern Western society. There was comparatively little travel in the ancient world by the average individual.

Ancient travelers had basically four options open to them for lodging.[59] (1) The wealthy might own villas along a frequently traveled route. (2) Important people—such as imperial officials, municipal officials, and soldiers— had the power to requisition facilities of local citizens if the need required it. (3) The ordinary traveler would have to stay in a boardinghouse or wayside inn, which according to the available archaeological and literary sources had "dilapidated and unclean facilities, virtually nonexistent furnishings, bed bugs, poor quality food and drink, untrustworthy proprietors and staff, shady clientele, and generally loose morals."[60] (4) A traveler might seek hospitality in the private homes of family or friends. This last option was the one most often used by Paul and his traveling companions, who sought out Christians in each city and were happily hosted by them. As our story continues, we will note how often Paul relied on this resource. Since the earliest

---

57. The Greek text simply states that he "and all of his" (καὶ οἱ αὐτοῦ πάντες) were immersed, but family or household is implied, as the RSV and NIV translate.

58. This is indicated by a change in pronoun from "we" (16:16) to "they" (16:40). The author of Acts remained behind. See the discussion of the "we" sections earlier in this chapter.

59. Rapske, "Acts, Travel and Shipwreck," 14–15.

60. Ibid., 15.

Photo 6.7. Amphipolis

churches also met in these homes, Paul was able not only to receive lodging by his hosts but also to share his preaching and teaching in these domestic/ecclesiastical contexts.

Given these four alternatives for travel in the ancient world, it is understandable that there are frequent admonitions in the New Testament for Christians to show hospitality.[61] One requirement of a bishop (elder) is that he be "hospitable" (1 Tim. 3:2; Titus 1:8), and a Christian widow must not be put on the church roll in an official position unless she has "shown hospitality" (1 Tim. 5:10).

Amphipolis and Apollonia

Paul and Silas evidently planned to go directly to Thessalonica, because they bypassed Amphipolis on the way. If Paul had been merely seeking the large, metropolitan areas of Macedonia, which was essentially a rural area, he certainly would have stopped here.

Amphipolis was a very large city and one of the most beautiful sites along the eastern seaboard of Greece, overlooking the Aegean three miles to the south. Recent investigations at sixty-four places around Amphipolis have re-

61. For example, Rom. 12:13; Heb. 13:2; 1 Pet. 4:9.

vealed sections of a wall with a circuit of almost four and one-half miles. As noted earlier, it was the chief city of the first district of Macedonia.[62] Excavators have uncovered a gymnasium, located in the eastern part of the city, that was still standing when Paul passed through the area but was destroyed by fire only a few years later

A lengthy inscription from 21 B.C. found here contains references to the city's road system, factories, a theater, and a marketplace, confirming the impression of Amphipolis as a major city.[63] However, there is no archaeological or literary evidence, to my knowledge, of a Jewish population here, and this may be why Paul bypassed this major capital city.

Paul also bypassed Apollonia, which was just off the Egnatian Way. Although the site has not yet been dug, a chance discovery of an inscription that may have come from Apollonia indicates that it was a town of significant size and importance in the late Hellenistic and early Roman periods. It refers to the "Boule (Council), the Ekklesia (Assembly), to Roman provincial officials called Politarchs, to Superintendents of the athletic games called Agonothetai, to the Agora and to tribal divisions."[64] But once again, Paul bypassed a city of considerable size and continued his journey to Thessalonica, which was ninety miles from Philippi. Why? Probably because there was no Jewish synagogue in Apollonia.

Thessalonica

It is significant that Luke introduces the arrival of Paul and his companions in Thessalonica as follows: "Now when they had passed through Amphipolis and Apollonia, they came to Thessalonica, where there was a synagogue of the Jews" (Acts 17:1). This seems to imply that there was no synagogue in Amphipolis and Apollonia. In Thessalonica, the largest city in Macedonia, Paul preached "as was his custom" in the synagogue for a period of three successive Sabbaths (Acts 17:2). During that time some of the Jews were persuaded to become believers and joined Paul and Silas along with "a great many of the devout Greeks [i.e., God-fearers] and not a few of the leading women" (Acts 17:4).[65] For some reason, Timothy is not mentioned, though he was with Paul and Silas (Acts 17:14). Perhaps it is because only Paul and Silas were preaching. Timothy was acting as their young assistant (1 Tim. 4:12).

62. Pliny, *Nat.* 4.38.
63. For pictures of the site and a description, see McRay, *Archaeology and the New Testament,* 289–92.
64. K. Sismanides, in *Archaiologikon Deltion* 38 (1983): 75–84.
65. See the discussion of the term *God-fearer* in chapter 5, under "Paul in Antioch of Syria."

Photo 6.8. Politarch Inscription at Thessalonica

Several men who later became connected with Paul's work became disciples of Jesus in Thessalonica, perhaps at this time. Aristarchus and Secundus were among them (Acts 20:4; 19:29). Aristarchus, who later accompanied Paul on his voyage to Rome is called "a Macedonian from Thessalonica" (Acts 27:2). Another of the men who responded to Paul's teaching and apparently hosted him during this time was named Jason (Acts 17:5–7). This Greek name was often taken by Jews whose Hebrew name was Joshua or Jeshua.[66]

Once again, predictably, jealous Jews in the synagogue who rejected Paul's message stirred up some rabble-rousers whom Luke called "men who hung around the marketplace."[67] They looked for Paul and his companions in Jason's house and, failing to find them, dragged Jason and some of the other believers before the local Roman authorities (Acts 17:6). After a period of interrogation, Jason and the others were released upon posting bail (Acts 17:9).

At this point, archaeology has made a positive contribution to a problem that has centered around Thessalonica for many years. Critics of the New Testament have insisted that Luke was mistaken in his use of the term πολιτάρχαι (politarchs) for the officials before whom Jason and the others were taken for interrogation (Acts 17:6, 8). However, it is now well known that an inscription containing the term Luke uses was found on an

66. Bruce, *Paul*, 224.

67. Ἀγοραῖος (*agoraios*) is the adjective used here with an article as a substantive for "the marketplace crowd" (τῶν ἀγοραίων ἄνδρας, *tōn agoraiōn andras*). The term *market* in Greek is ἀγορά (*agora*), which corresponds to the Latin word *forum*.

arch at the end of modern Egnatia Street.[68] Also, thirty-two additional examples have now been found, nineteen of which come from Thessalonica. Three of these nineteen date to the first century A.D.[69] Another one of the thirty-two—found in Beroea, Paul's next stop on his journey—also dates to the first century A.D. Therefore, it is now incontrovertible that, as Luke states, politarchs existed in Macedonia both before and during the time of the apostle Paul.

How long Paul and his companions stayed in Thessalonica is not stated. It would appear that after preaching for three Sabbaths in the synagogue and making converts there of God-fearing Greeks as well as some Jews, the missionaries were turned out and went to work among pagans. This, as we have noticed, appears to be a pattern for Paul. He begins in the synagogue among Jews and God-fearers. When he is accepted by some but rejected by most, he then turns to the pagan Gentiles. This may be assumed at Thessalonica from what Paul later wrote in his first letter to this church: "For they themselves report concerning us what a welcome we had among you, and how you turned to God from idols, to serve a living and true God" (1 Thess. 1:9). Since no pagan converts are cited in Acts, Paul must have stayed a longer time in the city than might appear on first reading.[70]

The charge that Paul and the others were acting against the decrees of Caesar by saying that there is another king, Jesus, does not seem to have been officially investigated at this time, as it was later in Corinth by the proconsul Gallio, who found no violation of Roman interests (Acts 18:12–16). In fact, it does not appear that Paul or any of his traveling companions were brought before the officials in Thessalonica, but the brothers who had been interrogated felt it advisable to send them away immediately by night to Beroea (Acts 17:10).

Some of the problems that Paul dealt with in the Thessalonian letters probably developed soon after his departure. He had not been able to stay there long enough to put the church on a sound basis (1 Thess. 3:2). Some of his teaching about the return of Jesus was misunderstood, and perhaps this mis-

68. The first-century A.D. arch was torn down in 1867 to be used in the repair of the city's walls, but a piece of inscription from the arch that contains the disputed word was subsequently found and is now displayed in the British Museum.

69. Numbers 8, 9, and 10. Carl Schuler published the list in 1960 ("The Macedonian Politarchs," *Classical Philology* 55 [1960]: 90–100). I observed one on a stele in the backyard of the museum in Thessalonica. One of the thirty-two is in the museum in Beroea. It also dates to the first century A.D. The word *politarch* appears in line 110. Three more may be added to Schuler's list of thirty-two. One is inside the Thessalonica Museum. The other two I have documented in my book, *Archaeology and the New Testament*, 295. See further discussion on the inscriptions there. A list of sixty-four was published by G. H. R. Horsley (1992), which lists twenty-nine from Thessalonica, twenty-seven of which are dated before the third century A.D., and ten from the first century A.D. or earlier ("Politarchs," *ABD*, 5:384–89).

70. Bruce takes this for granted (*Paul*, 224).

Photo 6.9. Thessalonica Forum

understanding was exacerbated by the persecutions they had experienced.[71] Paul said they had "received the word in much affliction" and had become an example "to all the believers in Macedonia and in Achaia" (i.e., northern and southern Greece, 1 Thess. 1:6–7). A short time later, Paul sent Timothy back to them from Athens to strengthen them "that no one be moved by these afflictions" (1 Thess. 3:1–3; cf. Acts 18:5). Word of what they were enduring was circulated through the churches. Just as the Jewish antagonists followed Paul from city to city (Acts 14:19; 17:13; etc.), some of the disciples also must have gone from church to church carrying the latest news. At least enough time lapses between Paul's initial preaching and his writing of 1 Thessalonians for the church there to have people who labored among them and were appointed over them "in the Lord" (1 Thess. 5:12).

Thessalonica is beautifully situated at the head of the Thermaic Gulf, in a natural amphitheatre. Little is to be seen here from the time of Paul because the city, the second largest in Greece, still functions busily over the buried remains of Roman Thessalonica. However, a typical rectangular Roman forum with a paved, open court and small odeum have been excavated.[72]

71. On problems in Thessalonica that precipitated the Thessalonian letters, see the discussion below on Athens and Corinth.

72. See further description of the city and its remains in McRay, *Archaeology and the New Testament*, 292–95.

Beroea

From Thessalonica, Paul and Silas (Acts 17:10) and presumably Timothy (Acts 17:14) journeyed a short distance westward on the Egnatian Way and then turned southward to Beroea, modern Verroia. It may have been Paul's original intention when he arrived in Neapolis to travel the Via Egnatia west through Philippi, across Macedonia to Dyrrachium, and then—taking a boat across the Adriatic to Brundisium (modern Brindisi), Italy—to continue by land to Rome. He had been asked in his vision only to come to Macedonia and help (Acts 16:9), but Paul may have planned to continue on to Rome after preaching all the way across Macedonia. He twice told the Romans he had often intended to visit them but had been hindered (Rom. 1:13; 15:22–23).

A hindrance this time might have been the edict of Claudius expelling Jews from Rome at precisely this point, A.D. 49. If the edict was directed against all Jews and not just those involved in the tumult caused by Jewish conversions to Christianity,[73] it would thus be impossible for Paul to use the synagogues as a beginning point of his work in Rome at this time. A few weeks later in Corinth, he would meet Priscilla and Aquila, who had been expelled from Rome by this very edict (Acts 18:1–2).

At a later time, perhaps on his third journey, Paul probably traveled this road across Macedonia and entered Illyricum (Rom. 15:19), where he preached the gospel to Greek-speaking people in its southern sector.[74] But on this occasion, Paul was sent by the Thessalonian believers to Beroea, which lay twenty miles south of the Via Egnatia. Cicero described Beroea as "an out-of-the-way town."[75]

The museum in Verroia is literally full of high-quality Roman-period statues, inscriptions, and funerary altars that overflow into a congested and cluttered courtyard. One of these inscriptions contains the name Beroea in the center of the top line. The politarch inscription mentioned previously is also in this museum.

As we would expect, upon their arrival Paul and the others went into the Jewish synagogue (Acts 17:10). Here they found a more dedicated group of Jewish worshipers than they had previously encountered, eliciting the remark by Luke that "these Jews were more noble than those in Thessalonica, for they received the word with all eagerness, examining the scriptures daily to see if these things were so" (Acts 17:11).

---

73. The reference to this edict in Suetonius mentions that the expulsion was based on a tumult instigated by a person called Christ (or Chrestus, in the Latin form of his letter; *Claud.* 25.4).

74. Hemer thinks Paul would have limited his ministry to those cities that used Greek as the first language (C. J. Hemer, *The Book of Acts in the Setting of Hellenistic History,* ed. C. H. Gempf [Tübingen: Mohr, 1989], 261 n. 34).

75. *Pis.* 36.89.

The pattern of acceptance here is consistent with Paul's former experience, however, in that many Greek women of high standing, as well as men, believed. In addition, "many" of the Jews in the synagogue believed (Acts 17:12). Sopater, the son of Pyrrhus (Acts 20:4), who later accompanied Paul as a traveling companion, may have been converted at this time. If he is identical with Sosipater,[76] mentioned in Romans 16:21, he may have been a Jewish convert, because Paul calls him in that verse one of his "kinsmen."

Predictably, when Jews in Thessalonica heard about Paul's success in Beroea, they came there and stirred up the crowds against him (Acts 17:13). The brethren immediately sent Paul off on his way to the sea, but Silas and Timothy stayed behind for reasons unstated (Acts 17:14). When Paul got to Athens, however, he sent back with the brothers who had accompanied him a command for Silas and Timothy to come to him as soon as possible (Acts 17:15).

From Beroea to Athens

Paul's route out of Beroea is not clear. Luke simply states that he went from the city "to the sea" (Acts 17:14). This most naturally implies that he continued his journey to Athens by boat,[77] but his point of departure is uncertain.[78] Hammond's *Atlas of the Greek and Roman World* provides two possibilities.[79] One is a road going from Beroea thirty miles southeast to Dion, near the coast, from which Paul might have sailed. The other road proceeds from Beroea northeastward, circles the northern end of Mount Pieria, and then continues southward to Dion, covering a distance of fifty miles. However, the existence of the first road from Beroea to Dion is now called into question by a Greek cartographer who omits it on his map of the Central Macedonian Plain.[80]

If such a road existed, providing a direct route to Dion, Paul undoubtedly would have traveled it and put to sea from this point. The city was accessible to the sea, four miles away, down the Baphyras, a stream made navigable in

---

76. Bruce so identifies him (*Paul,* 236).

77. Jack Finegan, *ANT:MW,* 125.

78. Codex Bezae, a fifth-century Greek manuscript of the Gospels and Acts, adds a phrase to Acts 17:15 stating that "he passed through Thessaly, because he was forbidden to preach the word to them." The Greek construction of the sentence is like that of Acts 16:6 and 16:8, where the same words are used for "forbid"(κωλύω) and "pass through" (παρέρχομαι). The Western text of 17:15 may have been influenced at this point by this passage in chapter 16.

79. H. L. Hammond, *Atlas of the Greek and Roman World in Antiquity* (Park Ridge, N.J.: Noyes, 1981), map 12.

80. M. B. Hatzopoulos, "Strepa: A Reconsideration of New Evidence on the Road System of Lower Macedonia," in *Two Studies in Ancient Macedonian Topography,* ed. M. B. Hatzopoulos and L. D. Loukopoulou (Athens: American School and National Hellenic Research Foundation, 1987), 18–60.

Photo 6.10. Piraeus Harbor

the Hellenistic period to serve Dion. If this road did not exist, it is difficult to imagine why he would not have sailed from ports north of Dion, which he would have encountered much sooner on the northern road. In the region north of Dion, there are three possible harbors from which Paul might have sailed, Methone, Pydna, and Aliki.[81]

The Harbors of Athens

Whether from Dion or some point to the north, Paul evidently departed by sea for Athens, which, like Philippi, is not situated on the sea. His boat

81. The road eastward from Beroea met the sea at *Methone,* which the ancient Athenians used as a base against the Macedonians. Three miles south of this is Makrigialos, where Hammond's atlas locates ancient *Pydna.* Almost four miles further south is *Aliki,* which was probably the harbor of Pydna in Paul's time, though the city itself was moved five miles northwest to Alonia. If Hatzopoulos is right and there was no southern road out of Beroea to Dion, then Paul would have been traveling this northern road and would likely have put to sea at one of these harbors rather than traveling another twenty miles (another full day) to Dion. In the unlikely event that he chose to go to Dion, he would have found an important city that was reestablished as a Roman colony (Colonia Julia Diensis) after the decisive battle of Pydna in 168 B.C. Excavations here from 1928 to the present time have revealed a large and beautiful city. For further details and photos of these sites, see McRay, *Archaeology and the New Testament,* 297–99.

could have docked at any one of three harbors, Phaleron, Glyfada, or Piraeus.[82] However, Paul would undoubtedly have landed at Piraeus, which is now, and has been since classical times, the harbor of Athens. Although it was destroyed in 86 B.C., it was restored and functioning when Paul was in Athens. Apollonias of Tyana,[83] a contemporary of Paul, and Pausanias,[84] an author in the second century, both seem to have entered Athens from this harbor.

When Paul entered the harbor, he could see the Acropolis rising majestically above Athens about five miles to the west, with the huge statue of the pagan goddess Athena close by the Parthenon. When a Jewish Christian traveler such as Paul arrived in Athens, he must have felt admiration mixed with revulsion at the sight of the Acropolis—admiration for the splendor of the architectural achievements but revulsion for the polytheism and pagan idolatry it had represented for a half millennium.[85]

Athens

Athens was one of the most interesting and well-known cities of the ancient world. The combination of extensive archaeological excavation and numerous ancient literary sources has made it possible to understand much about the Athens of the New Testament period.[86] Athens, unlike the great cities of Paul's time such as Antioch of Syria, Ephesus, Alexandria, Rome, and even Corinth, could only be described as a "provincial backwater,"[87] a small university town of about 25,000 people, more concerned with ideas than commerce, and living in the memories of its glorious history. However, Paul's visit here during the reign of Claudius came during a brief resurgence of building activity such as the city had not seen since the reign of Augustus and would not see again until the extensive construction program of the emperor Hadrian in the second century.[88]

We can only assume that Paul and his companions went to the top of the Acropolis, and if so, they would have gazed upon several pagan temples. The

82. Glyfada, a modern resort city, stands on a lovely bay with a good harbor.

83. Philostratus, *Vit. Apoll.* 4.17.

84. He also mentions Mounikhias and Phaleron (*Descr.* 1.2.2).

85. See further, McRay, *Archaeology and the New Testament,* 301.

86. Approximately 7,500 inscriptions have been found in the Agora (civic center) of the city in addition to the usual information that is gained through stratigraphical excavation of structures (John Camp, *The Athenian Agora* [London: Thames and Hudson, 1986], 17).

87. T. Leslie Shear Jr., "Athens: From City State to Provincial Town," *Hesperia* 50 (1981): 372.

88. See especially D. J. Geagan, "Roman Athens, Some Aspects of Life and Culture, I. 86 B.C.–A.D. 267," in *ANRW,* 2.7.1:371–437; Camp, *Athenian Agora,* 181–214.

Photo 6.11. Athens Acropolis

Parthenon (temple of Athena) stood imposingly on the southern side of the Acropolis. With its Porch of Maidens, the Erechtheion, another temple of Athena, stood opposite the Parthenon on the northern side.

Less well known but more significant for Paul and his "new religion" was the temple of Roma and Augustus, only a few yards east of the Parthenon. It was built very soon after 27 B.C.[89] and is identified through a dedicatory inscription on the structure.[90] This temple, dedicated to the goddess Roma and the emperor Augustus, emphasizes the importance of emperor worship in the New Testament period, which is reflected especially in the Book of Revelation.

Although we must assume that Paul visited the Acropolis, it is explicitly recorded that he carried on discussions daily in the *agora* (Acts 17:17), a Greek word for marketplace. There were both a Greek agora and a Roman forum in Athens when Paul visited the city.

The western Greek market lay due north of the Areopagus and contained the prominent temple of Hephaestus and the reconstructed Stoa (colonnaded porch) of Attalos, where poet and philosopher would meet to promenade and

89. Shear, "Athens," 363; John Travlos, *Pictorial Dictionary of Ancient Athens* (New York: Praeger, 1971), 494. Judith Binder suggested to me a date of 18 B.C. Geagan says "sometime between 27/26 and 18/17 B.C." ("Roman Athens," 382).

90. See *Inscriptiones graecae* II² 3173. See further McRay, *Archaeology and the New Testament*, 301–2.

Photo 6.12. Eastern Agora in Athens

talk. The square was kept free of public and private buildings alike for almost five hundred years, being reserved for political purposes. But beginning with the arrival of the Romans in the reign of Augustus (under whom Christ was born), the entire public square had begun to be filled with buildings and monuments. There was almost no political activity in the Greek market after the death of Augustus, so Paul probably spent most of his time in the commercial Roman market to the east.

The western market had "assumed something of the aspect of a museum"[91] by the mid–first century A.D. when Paul strolled its walkways. It contained such a repository of altars, statues, and temples that Petronius, the Roman satirist, remarked, "It was easier to find a god than a man in Athens"![92] Paul was impressed that among so many objects of pagan superstition, there should actually be an altar dedicated to an "unknown god" (Acts 17:23). Although this altar no longer exists, Pausanias, who visited Athens between A.D. 143 and 159, saw such altars.[93] Apollonius of Tyana, a contemporary of Paul, spoke of Athens as the place where there

91. Shear, "Athens," 362.
92. *Satiricon* 17.
93. Describing his trip from the harbor to Athens, he wrote "The Temple of Athene Skiras is also here, and one of Zeus further off, and *altars of the 'Unknown gods.'* . . ." (*Descr.* 1.2.4, italics added). See Peter Levi, trans., *Guide to Greece,* 2 vols., Penguin Classics (Harmondsworth and New York: Penguin, 1979), 1:12.

are "altars of unknown gods."[94] Diogenes Laertius[95] and Oecumenius[96] both wrote of altars dedicated to unknown gods.

By contrast, the other sector of the agora, named for Julius Caesar and Augustus Caesar, would have been alive with everyday commercial activity. Paul would more likely have found the ear of the ordinary citizen of Athens in this eastern market, which is 360 feet square, about the same size as the Forum of Julius Caesar in Rome.

This area contains one of the best-preserved ancient monuments in Greece, a tall octagonal marble tower containing sculptured images of the eight winds around the top of its eight sides and popularly called "The Tower of the Winds." It was a huge water clock, sundial, and weather vane[97] and served as a public timepiece for the city. We can well imagine Paul checking the time of day by this clock while he carried on his teaching in this forum.

While preaching to God-fearers in this agora, Paul was arrested and taken before the Areopagus (Acts 17:17–19), which in the decades preceding his arrival in Athens had seemingly begun to act as a municipal senate.[98] By the time of Paul's visit, the council of the Areopagus had become prominent among the three corporations of Athenian government.[99] Since Paul had been speaking about "foreign divinities" (Acts 17:18), he fell under the jurisdiction of the Areopagus, which had "surveillance over the introduction of foreign divinities."[100]

The location of the meeting place of the Areopagus at this time is not certain. It met in various locations in the classical period, but Mars Hill, on the west side of the Acropolis, was the traditional location for its meetings,[101] and the evidence from Lucian, a contemporary of Paul, seems to indicate that jury panels were assigned to hear trials from this point.[102] While there is no certainty that the council was meeting here when Paul stood before it, neither is there any compelling reason to deny that it was.[103] The eastern part of Mars

94. In Greek, ἀγνώστων δαιμόνων βωμοί, recorded by his biographer, Flavius Philostratus (A.D. c. 170—c. 245) (*Vit. Apoll.* 6.3). See F. C. Conybeare, trans., *The Life of Apollonius of Tyana,* 2 vols., Loeb Classical Library (Cambridge, Mass.: Harvard University Press, 1969), 2:13.

95. Diogenes Laertius, *Lives of Eminent Philosophers* 1.110.

96. Comments on Acts 17:23 (PG 118:238).

97. Built by Andronikos of Kyrrhos in the last half of the first century B.C.

98. Geagan, "Roman Athens," 388.

99. Daniel Geagan, "The Athenian Constitution after Sulla," *Hesperia,* supplement 12 (1967): 32, 48ff.

100. Ibid., 50.

101. Ibid., 53; Oscar Broneer, "Athens, City of Idol Worship," *BA* 21.1 (1958): 27 n. 4.

102. *Bis. acc.* 4.12.

103. This was the conclusion of a research paper on the history and function of the Areopagus Council presented by a student at the American School of Classical Studies in Athens to a group of doctoral students on the top of the Areopagus Hill in the spring of 1988.

Photo 6.13. Mars Hill near the Acropolis in Athens

Hill, now a barren limestone hilltop, was undoubtedly covered in marble in Paul's day and was thus suitable for such meetings.

Paul left Athens after a surprisingly brief stay, perhaps because he had limited success with the Greek intellectuals and correspondingly little success with the Jews and God-fearers in the synagogue (Acts 17:17). It is surprising that Luke records no adverse reaction to Paul in the synagogue similar to what he experienced in Macedonia. If there was such a reaction, it was simply preempted in significance by what happened among the Greeks, who reacted in three ways to his preaching on the Areopagus.

The first reaction was by some Athenians who mocked his teaching on the resurrection (Acts 17:32). It should be remembered that Paul was in the cultural center of a civilization that believed in the immortality of the soul but not the resurrection of the body. The body was a prison house of the soul, which after death would ascend to the Elysian Fields of the unseen world and enjoy immortality, unencumbered by physical restraints. Any talk of possessing a resurrected body after death was considered repugnant and primitive. Greek philosophers regarded Jewish culture, like all other cultures, as a curiosity in comparison to their own glorious history.

The Athenians called Paul a "babbler" or "seedpicker" (σπερμολόγος, *spermologos*, Acts 17:18). The word was used by Greeks of a guttersnipe, a little bird that followed peddlers' carts, picking up scraps and seeds that fell from them as they bumped along Athens's rough, stone streets. The Athenian philosophers viewed Paul the Jew as representing a culture that could only pick up scraps from the glorious history of Greece. What could he tell them? "What would this babbler say" that they did not already know? When he spoke of the resurrection of the body, this only confirmed their judgment, and his reception on Mars Hill was meager at best.[104]

The second reaction was one of procrastination: "We will hear you again about this" (Acts 17:32). They never did. The third reaction was positive, but the results were meager: "Some men joined him and believed" (Acts 17:34). Among those who believed was Dionysius, a member of the court of the Areopagus (Acts 17:34).[105]

Paul does not seem to have been as successful in Athens as he was in some other cities. He wrote no letters to a church in this major cultural center—at least none have been preserved. This might suggest that no church of historical importance was founded here among the few who believed him. Perhaps this experience only confirmed Paul's view that the gospel is seldom appealing to the arrogant and intellectually elite. In some ways his later words to Corinth, which he would visit next, were apropos to, and perhaps intentionally reminiscent of, his Athenian experience. Here in a city that for centuries had been the intellectual and cultural capital of the known world, his message was viewed as babbling. The Corinthian Christians, some of whom were noble born (1 Cor. 1:26), were told:

> Where is the wise man? Where is the scribe? Where is the debater of this age? Has not God made foolish the wisdom of the world? For since, in the wisdom of God, the world did not know God through wisdom, it pleased God through the folly of what we preach to save those who believe. For Jews demand signs and Greeks seek wisdom, but we preach Christ crucified, a stumbling block to Jews and folly to Gentiles, but to those who are called, both Jews and Greeks, Christ the power of God and the wisdom of God. For the foolishness of God is wiser than men, and the weakness of God is stronger than men. For consider your call, brethren; not many of you were wise according to worldly standards, not many were powerful, not many were of noble birth; but God chose what is foolish in the world to shame the wise, God chose what is weak in the world to shame the strong, God chose what is low and despised in the world, even things that are not, to bring to nothing things that are, so that no human being might boast in the presence of God. He is the source of your life in Christ Jesus, whom God made our wisdom, our righteousness and sanctification and re-

104. See Bruce's discussion of charges that the Areopagus sermon was not actually preached by Paul (*Paul,* 243).

105. Dionysius became the first bishop of Athens, was martyred under Domitian, was canonized by the Orthodox Church, and became, and still is, the patron saint of Athens. Paul's success in Athens was so modest that it is ironically appropriate, but equally perplexing, that one of his few converts, rather than Paul himself, became the patron saint of the city. For archaeological evidence about the Church of Dionysius on the Areopagus, see McRay, *Archaeology and the New Testament,* 309–10.

demption; therefore, as it is written, "Let him who boasts, boast of the Lord." (1 Cor. 1:20–31)

It would appear that Timothy and Silas joined Paul in Athens, as he had commanded them (Acts 17:15), and then Paul sent Timothy back to Thessalonica (1 Thess. 3:1–2), and perhaps Silas to Beroea.[106] Timothy returned to Paul in Athens and gave him a report on Thessalonica (1 Thess. 3:6—and if Silas went to Beroea, he would have returned with a report on the church there), after which Paul apparently sent Timothy and Silas back to Thessalonica with one of the Thessalonian letters (1 Thess. 1:1 or 2 Thess. 1:1).

We cannot be certain which of the two letters was written first. They carry no designation of sequence in their texts and were arranged in the Pauline corpus according to length, not time of writing.[107] Second Thessalonians may have been written first,[108] an assumption based on the fact that it speaks of the church there currently enduring persecution for their faith (2 Thess. 1:4), whereas their persecution is mentioned as being in the past in 1 Thessalonians 1:6 and 2:14. This may suggest a later time of writing for 1 Thessalonians. If 2 Thessalonians was written first and taken by Timothy to Thessalonica, 1 Thessalonians was written to respond to the report Timothy brought back to Paul in Corinth.[109]

The letters deal with the problem of the church's misunderstanding of Paul's teaching on the immediacy of the return of Christ. He evidently had not been there long enough to clarify this teaching, so he wrote to emphasize that Christ will indeed return and their dead loved ones who had only recently died will not be left behind but will rise first. Then those who are alive and remain will together with them be caught up to meet the Lord in the air (1 Thess. 4:13–18). Nothing is said here of a reign of Christ on the earth.

Paul further reminded them of what he had taught them about future events while he was in Thessalonica. The time would come when a "man of lawlessness," a "son of perdition," would set himself up in the very temple of God, proclaiming himself to be God (2 Thess. 2:3–12). Only a decade earlier (in A.D. 40), the emperor Caligula (A.D. 37–41) had issued orders for a statue of himself to be placed in the Jerusalem temple. Fortunately, he died before the order could be carried out. Nevertheless, this extremely frightening event lingered in the mind of every Jew.

Now this new "mystery of lawlessness" was already at work but was being temporarily restrained by an unnamed individual (2 Thess. 2:7). Everyone from Paul

---

106. Though we have no letter to the Beroeans to tell us, as we have for Timothy in 1 Thess. 3:1–2.

107. The letters were arranged in descending order of length. See my discussion of the order of Paul's letters in chapter 9, under "The Letters of Paul and the Canon."

108. T. W. Manson, *Studies in the Gospels and Epistles* (Philadelphia: Westminster, 1962), 268–78; Johannes Weiss, *Earliest Christianity* (New York: Harper, 1959), 1:289ff.

109. This seems to be the preference of Bruce (*Paul,* 229, 231).

himself[110] to the Roman emperor[111] has been identified with this person, but confirmation is impossible. What was important to Paul, however, was that the Thessalonians continue working and living exemplary lives before those who were not Christians (1 Thess. 4:9–12; 2 Thess. 3:6–12). Paul's letters also deal with sexual purity and the need to regard one's mate with holiness and honor (1 Thess. 4:3–8).

It has been suggested that 1 Thessalonians was written to the Gentile Christians in Thessalonica and 2 Thessalonians was written to Jewish Christians.[112] But I do not think Paul would encourage ethnic separation in his churches, although he did encourage them to respect their ethnic distinctions. Ephesians, for example, is written specifically to Gentile Christians (Eph. 2:11; 3:1) but emphasizes their equality with Jewish Christians and encourages them to respect the Jewish minority that spawned their faith, a point also strongly emphasized in Romans 9–11.

Corinth

Paul left Athens, evidently being unable or unwilling to wait for the return of Timothy and Silas, and went on to Corinth, which was situated on the Gulf of Corinth, about fifty miles away. Timothy and Silas later joined Paul in Corinth (Acts 18:5). The city was one of the largest and most important commercial cities in the empire.[113] Strabo wrote that "the city of the Corinthians was always great and wealthy."[114] Much like the modern Olympic Games, the Isthmian Games,[115] according to Strabo,[116] Plutarch,[117] and Pausanias,[118] must have provided enormous income for the city. Its first-century B.C. population far exceeded that of Athens, numbering perhaps above 145,000.[119] The walls are now known to have extended for six miles around the city.

110. Johannes Munck, *Paul and the Salvation of Mankind,* trans. Frank Clarke (Atlanta: John Knox, 1977), 36ff., following the original suggestion in an article by Oscar Cullmann, which Munck elucidates.

111. See Bruce, *Paul,* 233.

112. Kirsopp Lake, *The Earlier Epistles of St. Paul: Their Nature and Origin,* 2d ed. (London: Rivingtons, 1914), 83ff.

113. Gordon Fee states that "after Rome and Alexandria, it would certainly have vied for distinction as the third city of the Empire" (*The First Epistle to the Corinthians,* NICNT [Grand Rapids: Eerdmans, 1987], 2 n. 5).

114. *Geogr.* 8.6.23.

115. Isthmia, near Corinth, was one of four permanent sites for the Panhellenic games. The superintendent of these games had his office in the forum at Corinth. See McRay, *Archaeology and the New Testament,* 317–19.

116. *Geogr.* 8.6.20.

117. *Quaest. conv.* 5.3.1–3; 8.4.1.

118. *Descr.* 2.2.

119. James Wiseman, *The Land of the Ancient Corinthians,* Studies in Mediterranean Archaeology 50 (Goteborg: Astrom, 1978), 12. No scientific estimate has been made of the population in Paul's time (J. Murphy-O'Connor, *St. Paul's Corinth: Texts and Archaeology* [Wilmington, Del.: Glazier, 1983], 32).

Photo 6.14. Temple of Athena in Corinth with Acrocorinth Behind

Paul probably first entered the city from the north on the then-graveled Lechaion Road. The architecture he saw everywhere reflected the transition from a half millennium of Greek culture to the culture of a Roman colony— religious, commercial, civic, and athletic—just as he had recently seen in the Roman colony of Philippi. What impressions he must have had as he walked along the street! After a disappointing experience in Athens, his cultural sensitivities must have been heightened and his religious perspectives challenged.

Undoubtedly, the religious impressions were the first and most intense to be felt by this monotheistic, Jewish Christian apostle. Pagan sanctuaries abounded everywhere he looked. Just inside the northern city wall, on the west side of the road, was the Sanctuary of Asclepius, where medicine was practiced in the context of pagan idolatry. Nearer the forum was the temple of Athena.[120] It is one of the oldest in Greece and had been restored by the time Paul arrived. Nearby on the west end of the forum was the huge "Temple E," which was probably built under the emperor Tiberius (A.D. 14–37) or possibly earlier to house the imperial cult. It testifies to the shift in empha-

120. See the discussion in C. K. Williams, "The Refounding of Corinth: Some Roman Religious Attitudes," in *Roman Architecture in the Greek World,* ed. S. Macready and F. H. Thompson (London: Society of Antiquaries, 1987), 26–37. Its earlier identification as the temple of Apollo is derived almost entirely from the imprecise account of Pausanius (*Descr.* 2.3.6). Fragments of an inscription found on Temple Hill suggest Athena as a better possibility. See the discussion in James Wiseman, "Corinth and Rome I:228–A.D. 267," in *ANRW,* 2.7.1:475, 530, and footnotes.

sis in the first century A.D. from worship of the Olympian gods to worship of the emperor.[121]

According to Strabo, another temple contributed to Corinth's earlier wealth.[122] Describing its earlier history, he says that the temple of Aphrodite, located on the Acrocorinth,[123] "owned a thousand temple-slaves, prostitutes, whom both men and women had dedicated to the goddess." Because of these women, he maintains, "the city was crowded with people and grew rich."[124] Because of its size, moral reputation, and other reasons, Corinth has been called "the New York, Los Angeles, and Las Vegas of the ancient world."[125]

Totally independent of Strabo's disputed comment about the thousand prostitutes in the earlier temple, archaeological and literary evidence shows that a temple stood here in Roman times,[126] and regardless of its size,[127] it could have owned a large number of prostitutes. This possibility is made probable, in my judgment, based on (1) the size of Corinth at the time, (2) the wealth of the city,[128] (3) the international traffic that daily passed through it on the *diolkos* (the road across the isthmus), (4) its involvement with the Isthmian Games, and (5) the traditional association of Aphrodite with immorality. We are certainly not dependent on Strabo for our impression of the city's moral condition. The temple prostitutes probably functioned in the city below. There can be little question that Corinth had a history of being an exceptionally immoral city and that it was still filled with immorality in Paul's day. Paul writes of the prevalent immorality (τὰς πορνείας, *tas porneias*) in the city (1 Cor. 7:2).[129]

121. Williams, "Refounding of Corinth," 29ff.

122. *Geogr.* 8.6.20.

123. Carl Blegen did some meager excavation on the Acrocorinth, found evidence of the temple's foundations, and estimated its size to have been no larger than thirty-three feet by fifty-two feet ("Excavations at the Summit," in *Acrocorinth: Excavations in 1926,* Corinth, vol. 3, part 1 [Cambridge, Mass.: Harvard University Press, 1930], 20). Strabo called it "small" (*Geogr.* 8.6.21).

124. *Geogr.* 8.6.20. This statement has been rejected as "completely false" by Jerome Murphy-O'Connor in "The Corinth That Paul Saw," *BA* 47.3 (Sept. 1984): 152; and as "pure fabrication" in idem, "Corinth," *ABD,* 1:1136; and by Hans Conzelmann, *Korinth und die Mädchen der Aphrodite: Zur Religionsgeschichte der Stadt Korinth,* Nachrichten der Akademie der Wissenschaften in Göttingen: Philologisch-Historische Klasse, Jahrg. 1967, Nr. 8 (Göttingen: Vandenhoeck & Ruprecht, 1967), 8:247–61.

125. Fee, *First Epistle to the Corinthians, 3.*

126. "Corinthian coins show the temple of Aphrodite as restored on Akrokorinthos" (Williams, "Refounding of Corinth," 32, and see plates 4a and b). See also Blegen, "Excavations."

127. Strabo uses the present tense when he says, "Now the summit [of the Acrocorinth, JM] *has* a *small* temple of Aphrodite" (*Geogr.* 8.6.21, italics added).

128. Strabo, who visited the city in the first century B.C., described it as "wealthy because of its commerce" (*Geogr.* 8.6.20).

129. I take the use of the Greek article with "fornications" (τὰς πορνείας) to indicate prevalence.

Photo 6.15. Erastus Inscription in Corinth

Evidently a man named Erastus was converted during the eighteen months Paul was in Corinth (Acts 18:11). He provides an interesting cross-cultural link in the Corinthian church. One of the paving stones excavated beside the city's theater[130] contains part of an abbreviated Latin inscription that reads "Erastus in return for his aedileship laid [the pavement] at his own expense."[131] The excavators identify the Erastus of this inscription with the Erastus mentioned by Paul in a letter later written from Corinth, in which he sends greetings from "Erastus, the city treasurer" (Rom. 16:23).[132] This

130. One of the most imposing structures in Corinth was the 14,000-seat theater located northwest of the forum. It was used not only for theatrical performances but also for large civic meetings and was in use in Paul's time. It had been renovated about five years before he arrived. About this time the large stone plaza was also laid at the northeast corner of the theater area where the inscription was found.

131. There are 104 inscriptions found in Corinth that date from 44 B.C. to the early second century A.D. Of these, 101 are in Latin; only three are in Greek.

132. John Harvey Kent, *The Inscriptions, 1926–1950,* Corinth vol. 8, part 3 (Princeton, N.J.: American School of Classical Studies at Athens, 1966), nos. 232, 99, and plate 21. See also the recent discussion of Erastus as both *aedile* (Latin) and *oikonomos* (Greek, οἰκονόμος) at Corinth by David Gill, "Erastus the Aedile," *TynBul* 40.2 (November 1989): 293–302. The identification is also shared by Bruce Winter, *Seek the Welfare of the City: Christians as Benefactors and Citizens* (Grand Rapids: Eerdmans, 1994), 195; and by Gerd Theissen, "Social Stratification in the Corinthian Community: A Contribution to the Sociology of Early Hellenistic Christianity," in *The Social Setting of Pauline Christianity: Essays on Corinth,* ed. and trans. John H. Schutz (Philadelpia: Fortress, 1982), 83.

is undoubtedly the same Erastus who later remained in Corinth when Paul was taken to Rome (2 Tim. 4:20).[133] He was also with Paul in Ephesus on his third journey (Acts 19:22).

The conversion of Erastus, a high official who was subject to public election, is significant for understanding the sociological level of the Corinthian church. The impression that one occasionally gets from reading Paul's polemic against the misuse of wealth might lead to the idea that his churches were established only among the poor. A more careful reading, however, corrects this view. Erastus is a case in point. People who held his position were somewhat wealthy,[134] and the inscription states that he laid the pavement at his own expense.[135] These officials, who held office by the permission of Roman authority, found it expedient to express appreciation by donating a work of art or architecture to the city.

Another example of the sociological level of Paul's churches is a couple who were also somewhat prosperous. In Corinth, Paul met Priscilla and her husband, Aquila (Acts 18:2), who had recently arrived from Rome as a result of the expulsion of Jews in A.D. 49 by the emperor Claudius.[136] Like Paul, they were tentmakers or leather workers (Acts 18:2–3) and apparently had done well in their business. They were prosperous enough to have a home in which Christians could meet—presumably in Corinth but certainly later in Ephesus (1 Cor. 16:19) and even later in Rome (Rom. 16:3–5)—or possibly they rented a vaulted shop with a high ceiling. In the latter case, it was customary to build a wooden platform halfway to the top to divide the room into two levels. The upper rooms were often used as living quarters for the shopkeepers. These rooms were usually eight to fourteen feet wide and twelve to twenty-four feet deep. Such a room could accommodate ten to twenty persons.[137]

In large cities of the empire, only very prosperous people could afford a domus or villa, some of which have been found in Corinth just northwest of

133. The name is an uncommon one in Corinth and is not otherwise found in the literature and inscriptions of the city. The pavement on which the name occurs was laid near A.D. 50, the time when Paul arrived in Corinth. See further McRay, *Archaeology and the New Testament,* 331–33. However, Colin Hemer notes that the cognomen *Erastus* was not uncommon among prominent people in Ephesus (*Book of Acts,* 235).

134. Kent, who published the inscriptions of Corinth, comments, "Erastus was probably a Corinthian freedman who had acquired considerable wealth in commercial activities" (*Inscriptions,* 100) since there was no room on the broken inscription for a patronymic before his Greek name. Wayne Meeks concludes that he was "a person of both wealth and high civic status" (*The First Urban Christians: The Social World of the Apostle Paul* [New Haven, Conn.: Yale University Press, 1983], 59).

135. Another inscription was found there on a monument erected earlier by Cnaeus Babbius Philinus, who was a city treasurer in the reign of Augustus. It too says that the treasurer erected the monument at his own expense. Erastus was treasurer later, in the reign of Nero.

136. See chapter 3 on chronology for further data. See also Jerome Murphy-O'Connor, "Priscilla and Aquila," *Bible Review* 8.6 (December 1992): 40–51.

137. Murphy-O'Connor, "Priscilla and Aquila," 48.

the forum.[138] The poorer classes lived in high-rise apartment houses.[139] The fact that Priscilla's name[140] is mentioned before that of her husband, once by Paul (in Rom. 16:3, but not in 1 Cor. 16:19) and two out of three times by Luke (in Acts 18:18, 26, but not in 18:2), may suggest that she had a higher status than he.[141] And the fact that she, as well as her husband, was involved in teaching the eloquent and learned Apollos (Acts 18:24–26), her name even being mentioned first, underscores her stature.

Eventually Silas and Timothy arrived from Macedonia and reported on the status of the churches there (Acts 18:5), informing Paul of further problems. This prompted Paul to write the next Thessalonian letter and send it back by these same two men.[142] In the letter designated 2 Thessalonians, Paul found it expedient to verify that the letter was actually dictated by him: "I, Paul, write this greeting with my own hand. This is the mark in every letter of mine; it is the way I write" (2 Thess. 3:17). Perhaps this suggests that among the problems in Thessalonica was the issue of whether Paul's teaching was being accurately conveyed to them.

In Corinth, Paul "argued in the synagogue every sabbath, and persuaded Jews and Greeks" (Acts 18:4). The typical reaction of Jewish opposition and reviling of his message caused Paul to "shake out his garments" and "go to the Gentiles" (Acts 18:6). He was subsequently hosted by a God-fearer, Titius Justus, who lived "next door to the synagogue" (Acts 18:7). As suggested earlier, the use of the word *synagogue* in this context indicates a building and not just a group of people. The ruler of this next-door synagogue, Crispus, also believed, together with all his house (Acts 18:8). Titius Justus was among Paul's "first converts in Achaia" (cf. 1 Cor. 16:15 with 1:15–16), and he was Paul's host in Corinth. He may have been otherwise known as Gaius, whom Paul also says was host to him and to all the church in Corinth (Rom. 16:23). If so, his Roman name would have been Gaius Titius Justus.[143] Paul specifi-

---

138. See Wiseman, "Corinth and Rome I," 528; and Murphy-O'Connor, *St. Paul's Corinth,* 153ff.

139. See John McRay, "House Churches and the Lord's Supper," *Leaven* 3.3 (1995): 13–16; Bradley Blue, "Acts and the House Church," in *The Book of Acts in Its Graeco-Roman Setting,* ed. Gill and Gempf, 119–222; idem, "In Public and in Private: The Role of the House Church in Early Christianity" (Ph.D. diss., University of Aberdeen, 1989); Robert Jewett, "Tenement Churches and Communal Meals in the Early Church," *BR* 38 (1993): 23–43; Richard Krautheimer, *Early Christian and Byzantine Architecture,* 3d ed., Pelican History of Art (Harmondsworth, Eng., and Baltimore: Penguin, 1979); G. Hermansen, "The Roman Apartment," in *Ostia: Aspects of Roman City Life* (Edmonton: University of Alberta Press, 1982), chap. 1; McRay, *Archaeology and the New Testament,* 72–73.

140. Priscilla is the diminuitive form of Prisca. Cf. Silvanus and Silas.

141. Meeks, *First Urban Christians,* 59.

142. Either 1 or 2 Thessalonians, as I mentioned above. Note both Silvanus, or Silas, and Timothy are mentioned in verse 1 of each letter.

143. See E. J. Goodspeed, "Gaius Titius Justus," *JBL* 69 (1950): 382f.

cally remembered baptizing Gaius, as well as Crispus and the house of Stephanus. "Beyond that, I do not know whether I baptized any one else," he writes (1 Cor. 1:16). Timothy and Silas probably did most of the baptizing for Paul, since they arrived from Athens soon after Paul got to Corinth.[144]

Corinth was different from anywhere Paul had been. Unlike Athens, it was an international crossroads of commerce and travel. Corinth lay on the northern side of the Peloponnesus, southwest of the Corinthian Gulf and northwest of the Saronic Gulf. It was served by harbors on these two gulfs.[145] Ships sailed from Asia and Egypt into the eastern Saronic harbor at Cenchreae and from Europe into the western Corinthian harbor at Lechaion. Corinth was thus a gateway between Asia and Europe. All the vices and crimes characteristic of such a melting pot must have characterized this city. It would undoubtedly have been the last city of all those through which Paul traveled that he might have expected to be receptive to the gospel.

And yet Paul did not become discouraged and leave Corinth as he had left Athens (Acts 17:33–18:1) or feel the need to flee the city as he had fled Iconium (Acts 14:6). Neither was he driven out by irate synagogue members and civic leaders as he had been from some cities of Galatia and Macedonia (Acts 13:50; 14:19; 16:39). Nor did the new converts send him away for his own safety as they had previously done in Thessalonica (Acts 17:10) and Beroea (Acts 17:14). Why? Luke writes that in Corinth "the Lord said to Paul one night in a vision, 'Do not be afraid, but speak and do not be silent; for I am with you, and no man shall attack you to harm you; for I have many people in this city'" (Acts 18:9–10).

After Paul had been in Corinth a year and a half, the Jews made a united attack on him, presumably because of the inauguration of a new proconsul named Gallio in May or June of 51 (Acts 18:12).[146] This man was the brother of Seneca, a Greek Stoic philosopher who would become an adviser to the emperor Nero and perhaps influence the favorable outcome of Paul's first arrest in Rome, as we will see later. Gallio found no violation of Roman law or custom by Paul, no "wrongdoing or vicious crime" (Acts 18:14), and refusing to be a judge of Jewish law, he drove Paul's accusers from the "tribunal" (Acts 18:15–16).

One of the most important discoveries at Corinth relating to the New Testament is this very tribunal (Greek βῆμα, *bēma*), or speaker's platform, from which official proclamations might be read and citizens might appear before appropriate officials. It was here that Paul stood before Gallio. The structure was identified by several pieces of an inscription found nearby and dated to the period between A.D. 25 and 50, just prior to Paul's arrival in the city.[147]

---

144. So Bruce, *Paul,* 252.
145. Strabo, *Geogr.* 8.6.22.
146. See chapter 3 on chronology.
147. Robert Scranton, *Monuments in the Lower Agora and North of the Archaic Temple, Corinth,* vol. 1, part 3 (Princeton, N.J.: American School of Classical Studies at Athens, 1951).

Photo 6.16. Bema at Corinth with Acrocorinth Behind

The occasion for Gallio's visit to Corinth at this time may have been the Panhellenic Games. Since Gallio became proconsul in A.D. 51, the year in which these games were being held at Isthmia, near Corinth,[148] he may have been en route to the games and have stopped by Corinth where the office of the superintendent of the games was located in the forum.[149] Paul was in Corinth in A.D. 51,[150] and there is evidence that the festival of games was held in that year.

Oscar Broneer, who excavated sites at both Isthmia and Corinth, thought that these games were the motivating reason Paul chose to "settle down" in Corinth and make it the "chief base" or "pilot plant for his work on Greek soil."[151] I have argued against this view for the following reasons. First, Paul's primary concern was to reach Jews first with his message and then from them

148. Oscar Broneer, "The Apostle Paul and the Isthmian Games," *BA* 25.1 (1962): 20. L. Rutilius was ἀγωνοθέτης (president of the games) in A.D. 51. See Kent, *Inscriptions,* 31; Allen West, ed., *Latin Inscriptions, 1896–1936,* Corinth, vol. 8, part 2 (Cambridge, Mass.: Harvard University Press, 1931), 66–69, no. 82. See also Daniel Geagan, "Notes of the Agonistic Institutions of Roman Corinth," *Greek, Roman, and Byzantine Studies* 9 (1968): 71–75; Oscar Broneer, "Paul and the Pagan Cults at Isthmia," *HTR* 64 (1971): 185 and n. 42. Isthmia was one of four permanent sites for these Panhellenic games. Others included Olympia, Delphi, and Nemea. See McRay, *Archaeology and the New Testament,* 317–19.

149. McRay, *Archaeology and the New Testament,* 330.

150. See my discussion on Pauline chronology in chapter 3.

151. Broneer, "Paul and the Isthmian Games," 20ff.; idem, "Paul and the Pagan Cults," 169.

to branch out to Gentiles. The existence or extent of a Jewish presence in Isthmia is unknown, but Paul worked *immediately* among Jews in Corinth. One of Corinth's excavators writes: "Paul must have been attracted to Corinth for a number of reasons: the large size of its Jewish community, swollen by the edict of Claudius. . . ."[152] Second, the games did not occur until more than a year *after* Paul arrived in Corinth. Third, there was little in Isthmia itself that would attract Paul, outside the games.[153]

Contrariwise, the games may actually have been involved in Paul's leaving the city. The Jews may have taken advantage of the opportunity to accuse Paul of improperly worshiping God at a time when loyalty to Poseidon was running high among Romans who were into the spirit of the Isthmian Games, which had just been completed or were about to begin. "Greek national consciousness was one of the by-products of the Panhellenic Games."[154]

The extent to which the rebuilt Greek city of Corinth had become Roman after the commissioning of the colony in 44 B.C. is seen in the fact that after this date Latin predominated in its inscriptions. Of 104 inscriptions prior to Hadrian in the early second century, 101 are in Latin and only 3 in Greek.[155] The structure and administration of Corinth was Roman, but Paul wrote to the church there in Greek, which indicates that the unofficial language was still Greek. By the time of Hadrian and the visit of Pausanias, Greek had established itself once again as the official language. But Corinth was a Roman colony, like Philippi, and exhibited evidence of its Roman base through these Latin inscriptions. In fact, eight of the surviving seventeen names of Corinthian Christians are Latin.[156] The other names are Greek.[157]

Two of those disciples who bore Roman names were Priscilla and Aquila. After his encounter with Gallio, Paul remained at Corinth "many days longer" and then sailed with these two for Syria (Acts 18:18). During eighteen months in the cultural melting pot of Corinth, a Roman colony situated in the midst of Greek culture on an international crossroads, Paul had found hearts that opened to the message of Jesus and had established a church to which he later wrote at least four letters. In addition to 1 and 2 Corinthians,

152. Wiseman, "Corinth and Rome I," 504.

153. McRay, *Archaeology and the New Testament,* 318. See also the evidence for the structures still standing in Paul's day (ibid.).

154. Jerome Murphy-O'Connor, *St. Paul's Corinth,* 15.

155. Kent, *Inscriptions,* 19.

156. Aquila (Acts 18:2), Fortunatus (1 Cor. 16:17), Gaius (Rom. 16:23), Lucius (Rom. 16:21), Priscilla (Acts 18:2; or Prisca, Rom. 16:3), Quartus (Rom. 16:23), Tertius (Rom. 16:22), Titius Justus (Acts 18:7).

157. Achaicus (1 Cor. 16:17), Erastus (Acts 19:22; Rom. 16:23; 2 Tim. 4:20), Jason (Acts 17:5, 6, 7, 9; Rom. 16:21), Crispus (Acts 18:8; 1 Cor. 1:14), Phoebe (Rom. 16:1), Sosipater (Rom. 16:21), Sosthenes (Acts 18:17; 1 Cor. 1:1), Stephanas (1 Cor. 1:16; 16:15, 17), Chloe's people (1 Cor. 1:11).

Photo 6.17. Cenchreae Harbor

he wrote a "former letter" (1 Cor. 5:9) and a "severe or tearful letter" (2 Cor. 2:4).[158]

Cenchreae

Paul and the others disembarked from the eastern port of Cenchreae, which was built into a lovely natural cove south of the Isthmus, about two and one-half miles south of Isthmia (Acts 18:18).[159] A church was founded here either at this time or not long thereafter. Less than three years later (early in A.D. 54), at the end of his third journey, Paul wrote to the church in Rome from Corinth commending Phoebe, "a deaconess [διάκονον, *diakonon*] of the church at Cenchreae" (Rom. 16:1). It would appear from verse 2 that she carried the letter from Corinth to Rome.

Here in Cenchreae Paul cut his hair short because he had taken a vow that was now fulfilled. The regular Nazirite vow could not be taken outside of Israel because of defilement in Gentile lands.[160] This may have been a "private

158. See chapter 3 for their probable time of writing, as indicated in table 3.2. See chapter 7 for a discussion of the composition of these letters.

159. For a description of Cenchreae and its remains, see McRay, *Archaeology and the New Testament,* 336–38; and Robert Hohlfelder, "Cenchreae," *ABD,* 1:881–82.

160. *m. Nazir* 7.3. See Danby, *Mishnah,* 290, 284 n. 3.

religious exercise" of thanksgiving by Paul for the fulfillment of the promise of protection given him in the heavenly vision (Acts 18:10).[161] Unless a longer time was specified, the duration of a Nazirite vow was thirty days.[162] The vow was concluded by cutting off the hair, which remained uncut throughout the duration of the vow (Num. 6:5).[163] In Israel, the head would be shaved at the door of the temple (or tabernacle earlier) and the hair burned on the fire under the peace offering (Num. 6:18).

Ephesus

Paul and his companions stopped in Ephesus, where he probably had to change ships for the journey on to Antioch. During his brief time there, he argued with the Jews in the synagogue (Acts 18:19). A remarkable thing occurred at this point—one that was exceedingly rare in Paul's experience up to this time—the synagogue members asked him to stay longer, and he declined. Perhaps the reason was that he needed to get on to Jerusalem to complete his vow by offering his severed hair in the temple. Some of the late ancient Greek manuscripts add the comment in verse 21 that Paul "had to keep the feast that was coming up in Jerusalem," a comment that appears in the King James Version of the Bible,[164] among others.[165] Perhaps this was the Feast of Pentecost, and Paul wanted to make his offering at this special feast, which along with Passover and Tabernacles comprised the three major festivals.

Leaving Priscilla and Aquila in Ephesus (Acts 18:18–19), Paul and his companions departed with the promise that, God willing, Paul would return to those in the synagogue who wanted him to stay longer (Acts 18:21). Soon after he left, these eager listeners in the synagogue were treated to the preaching of an eloquent native of Alexandria named Apollos (Acts 18:24–26).

Apollos was not only eloquent but also well versed in the Scriptures (Acts 18:24). He had been taught accurately many things about Jesus and his movement, but apparently he knew nothing about what had happened at Pentecost (Acts 2) under the great postresurrection commission. He "knew only the baptism of John" (Acts 18:25). Presumably, he had been taught about Jesus before Jesus initiated immersion in his own name for remission of sins (Matt. 28:19; Acts 2:38; 22:16) and therefore before John's baptism had been super-

161. F. F. Bruce, *The Acts of the Apostles: The Greek Text with Introduction and Commentary*, 3d rev. ed. (Grand Rapids: Eerdmans, 1990), 398; idem, *Paul*, 255.

162. *m. Nazir* 1.3; 5.3.

163. *m. Nazir* 6.5.

164. The Western text (Codex Bezae) has this reading, as does the Majority text (Byzantine manuscripts), and thus it appears in the King James Version, which is based on the Majority text, or Textus Receptus.

165. The LB and perhaps others.

seded by the baptism of Jesus. When Priscilla and Aquila heard him in the synagogue, they took him aside and "expounded to him the way of God more accurately" (Acts 18:26). It should be noted that these two Jewish converts from Corinth were still attending synagogue in Ephesus while perhaps hosting a church in their home (1 Cor. 16:19).[166]

We have no explicit information on the origin of the church in Ephesus. It is obvious that Paul did not found it because this is his first visit to Ephesus and nothing is recorded about his making converts there among either Jews or Gentiles. Furthermore, it was a very brief visit (Acts 18:20). Priscilla and Aquila may have founded the church here, because they stayed behind when Paul left (Acts 18:18–19) and presumably hosted a church in their home.[167] Luke mentions that, not long after Paul left, "the brethren" assisted Apollos, who had just been taught by Priscilla and Aquila, in going from Ephesus to Corinth (Acts 18:27). These must have been Christian believers, and when Paul returned a short time later, he found "some disciples" in Ephesus (Acts 19:1) who knew only the baptism of John the Baptist (Acts 19:3), probably indicating that they had been taught by Apollos or someone else like him who had not yet heard the story of Jesus beyond the death of John. Furthermore, we note Paul's later comment to the Ephesian elders that while he was in Ephesus on his third journey he had taught them both "in public and from house to house" (Acts 20:20), probably alluding to already established churches like the one in the home of Priscilla and Aquila.

After Paul's brief stay in Ephesus, he sailed for Caesarea (Acts 18:21). He did not prolong his visit in Caesarea but apparently immediately "went up" to Jerusalem (Acts 21:22).[168] The road he traveled is not revealed. No inscribed Roman milestones have been discovered in Judea from before the reign of Vespasian in A.D. 69.[169] It appears that the only stretch of paved road in the country was not completed until A.D. 56, during the reign of Nero, and it only went from Antioch of Syria to Ptolemais.

Paul therefore would have traveled one of the local roads south from Caesarea.[170] One of these would have gone south along the coast to Joppa (a part

166. On house churches, see the discussion of Derbe in chapter 5.

167. See further Murphy-O'Connor, "Priscilla and Aquila," 40–51.

168. The expression "go up" is customarily used of simply journeying to a particular place, but in Palestine it also has geographical connotations. Jerusalem is 2,600 feet above sea level, and one always goes up to Jerusalem and down to everywhere else from Jerusalem.

169. David Graf, review of *Roman Roads in Judaea II: The Jaffa-Jerusalem Roads,* by Moshe Fischer, Benjamin Isaac, and Israel Roll, *BA* 59.4 (Dec. 1996): 244. Graf states elsewhere that "no milestones dated before the reign of Claudius have been found anywhere in the E. provinces beyond Anatolia. This is also true for Judea" (David Graf, Benjamin Isaac, and Israel Roll, "Roman Roads," *ABD,* 5:785).

170. David French thinks that Paul at times deliberately rejected major public roads and places in Asia Minor for security reasons ("Acts and the Roman Roads of Asia Minor," in *The Book of Acts in Its Graeco-Roman Setting,* ed. Gill and Gempf, 57).

of the old international highway) and then east to Jerusalem via Lydda (Diospolis, modern Lod) and Nikopolis (Emmaus).[171] The other would have taken him south to Antipatris (east of Joppa) and then either farther south to Diospolis and Jerusalem or east to Gophna and then south to Jerusalem. This latter route seems to be the one on which he was later taken by the Roman guard at the end of his third journey, when he was arrested in Jerusalem and taken via Antipatris to Caesarea (Acts 23:31–33).[172]

After greeting the church in Jerusalem (Acts 18:22) and offering his hair, thus ending his vow (Acts 18:18), Paul "went down" to Antioch. He stayed an unspecified period of time (Acts 18:23), which Luke passes over in silence.

171. On this section of road, see Moshe Fischer, Benjamin Isaac, and Israel Roll, *Roman Roads in Judaea II: The Jaffa-Jerusalem Roads,* BAR International Series 628 (Oxford: Tempus Reparatum, 1996).

172. This opinion is shared by Israel Roll and Etan Ayalon, "Roman Roads in Western Samaria," *PEQ* (1986): 121: "We may assume they travelled along the Gophna-Antipatris road." The Mishnah, *Gittin* 7.7, speaks of traveling to Antipatris on a road that ran from Judea to Galilee. A section of this route has recently been unearthed (S. Dar and S. Applebaum, "The Road from Antipatris to Caesarea," *PEQ* 105 [1973]: 91–99). See also the map of the road in Michael Avi-Yonah, "The Development of the Roman Road System in Palestine," *IEJ* 1 (1950–51): 57.

SEVEN

Paul's Third Journey

Ephesus

After spending "some time" in Antioch, Paul left for Ephesus again (Acts 18:23), probably in the late summer or fall of A.D. 51. His journey took him through the same regions of Phrygia and Galatia (Acts 18:23) as his second journey (Acts 16:6).[1] We may conclude that it was essentially the same route as his second journey because he went "from place to place . . . strengthening the disciples" (Acts 18:23). These disciples were undoubtedly those in the churches established in southern Galatia on his first journey. On this trip he was not prohibited by the Holy Spirit from speaking along the way but seems to have been intent on returning directly to those eager listeners in Ephesus, as he had promised them (Acts 18:21).

The statement that Paul passed through "the upper country" (Acts 19:1) refers not to northern Galatia but to the area west of where he had previously established the churches he now strengthened, that is, southern Galatia.[2] A southern route went from Antioch through the Lycus Valley, past Colossae, Hierapolis, and Laodicea to Ephesus. Having traveled this valley route on several occasions, I would describe it

---

1. For a discussion of the expression "Phrygia and Galatia" in these two passages, see Kirsopp Lake, "Paul's Route in Asia Minor," in *The Acts of the Apostles,* ed. F. J. Foakes-Jackson and Kirsopp Lake, The Beginnings of Christianity, part 1 (London: Macmillan, 1920–33), 5:231–39.

2. See Colin Hemer's extensive and conclusive discussion of the north Galatian versus south Galatian theory of Paul's ministry in his *BASHH,* 277–307, which rejects the northern hypothesis as founded on a flawed critical analysis of the biblical and nonbiblical literary texts.

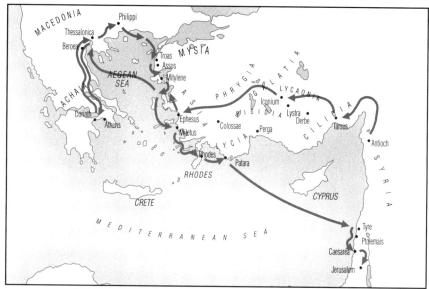

Map 7.1. Paul's Third Missionary Journey

as a lower route. Paul instead must have left Antioch of Pisidia along the route that ran through the eastern Meander Valley and then taken the more direct northern or upper route that passed along the north side of Mount Messogis east of Ephesus,[3] a route Ramsay accurately calls "higher-lying and more direct."[4]

Ephesus was a city of approximately 200,000 people in Paul's time,[5] picturesquely situated on the Aegean seaboard between Mount Pion and Mount Koressos.[6] Ephesus was uniquely laid out to relate to these two hills.

When Paul was in the city, it had two centers of activity—a civic forum up the hill to the east and a commercial marketplace near the harbor. The city's commerce, trade guilds, and banking capacities made it preeminently impor-

3. For the best map of this area in this period, see W. M. Calder and G. E. Bean, *A Classical Map of Asia Minor* (London: British Institute of Archaeology at Ankara, 1958). See also the map by William Ramsay, "Roads and Travel in the New Testament," *A Dictionary of the Bible,* ed. James Hastings (New York: Scribners, 1909), vol. 5 (extra vol.), after p. 400; also Ramsay's map inside the split back jacket of *St. Paul the Traveller and Roman Citizen* (London: Hodder and Stoughton, 1908).

4. Ramsay, *St. Paul the Traveller,* 265.

5. Bernard McDonagh puts it above 250,000 in *Turkey: The Aegean and Mediterranean Coasts,* Blue Guide (New York: Norton, 1989), 270; as does C. E. Arnold, "Ephesus," *A Dictionary of Paul and His Letters,* ed. G. F. Hawthorne et al. (Downers Grove, Ill.: InterVarsity, 1993), 249.

6. For a description of the city during the time of Paul, see John McRay, *Archaeology and the New Testament* (Grand Rapids: Baker, 1991), 250–61; Richard Oster, "Ephesus," *ABD,* 2:542–49.

Photo 7.1. Theater and Harbor at Ephesus

tant. Strabo wrote in the first century that it was the largest commercial center in Asia Minor west of the Taurus Mountains.[7]

Shops have been found in the commercial market that were used by people like Paul who worked at small businesses in such market areas. There was opportunity to speak to people who came to the market area. It was the hub of social activity in a Roman town.

When Paul arrived in Ephesus, he found some Christian disciples, presumably Jewish, who had accepted the baptism of John the Baptist but knew nothing about the Holy Spirit (Acts 19:1–7). These men could have been baptized elsewhere, perhaps even in Palestine, but since Luke placed this story immediately following the account of Apollos (Acts 18:24–28), one is led to think that they were baptized by Apollos when he "knew only the baptism of John" (Acts 18:25).

Nothing is said of Apollos being rebaptized when he was taught the way more perfectly, but these men were rebaptized by Paul. It is a natural inference that Apollos was baptized under John's baptism when it was still effective (i.e., before Pentecost in Acts 2), but they were baptized after that time, when it was no longer in force. Thus they needed to be baptized in the name of Jesus in order to receive the Holy Spirit promised at Pentecost (Acts 2:38). John the Baptist did not make such an offer (Matt. 3:11; Mark 1:8). Upon their baptism, Paul laid his hands on them, the Holy Spirit came upon them, and they spoke with tongues and prophesied (Acts 19:6).

7. *Geogr.* 14.1.24.

Photo 7.2. Lecture Hall of Tyrannus in Ephesus

For three months, Paul spoke in the synagogue to those who had been eager to hear him as he passed through the city earlier (Acts 18:19–20). However, some of them, perhaps not the leaders, now became stubborn and disbelieved (Acts 19:9), causing Paul to turn from them to the Gentiles. He took the disciples with him and began arguing daily in the lecture hall of Tyrannus. "This continued for two years, so that all the residents of Asia heard the word of the Lord, both Jews and Greeks" (Acts 19:8–10). But if Paul was personally involved in taking the gospel to "all the residents of Asia" during these two years, he could not, of course, simultaneously have spent "every day" (καθ᾽ ἡμέραν, *kath' hēmeran,* Acts 19:9) teaching in the lecture hall.

One possible explanation is that Paul literally taught "every day" in the hall for two years, and during these years his students, not Paul himself, went into all Asia and preached. Acts 19:10 does not expressly say Paul did the evangelizing of Asia.

Another possiblity is that Paul himself evangelized Asia, and though he periodically went to various cities from his base in Ephesus, when he was back there he taught in the lecture hall daily, rather than on Sabbath days in the synagogue. This dual ministry lasted for two years.

Archaeological evidence of the probable location of this hall has been found adjacent to the southern gates of the market.[8] It is referred to in a first-century

8. Other than the inscription, little, if any, of the actual structure has yet been found. However, portions of a circular platform that was destroyed when the auditorium was constructed have been found. Ekrem Akurgal, *Ancient Civilizations and Ruins of Turkey* (Istanbul: Mobil Oil, 1970), 161.

A.D. inscription.[9] According to some of the ancient texts of the Book of Acts,[10] Paul used the hall "from the fifth hour to the tenth" (i.e., from 11 A.M. to 4 P.M.), when most people in the Mediterranean world then, as now, closed their businesses, ate lunch, and rested. The students of Tyrannus may also have gone home during these hours, giving Paul free use of the building.

Opposition to Paul's monotheism was rooted in the polytheistic history of the city. Gentile paganism was replete in Ephesus, as might be expected in a city of this size and location. When Paul turned to the Gentiles, he immediately had to deal with their pagan temples. One of the largest in the world was located here, the temple of Artemis (Roman Diana), which was four times larger than the Parthenon in Athens. It was the first monumental structure ever constructed of marble and the largest building in the Greek world.[11] The temple was considered one of the "seven wonders" of the ancient world.[12]

Ephesus prided itself in being "temple keeper of the great Artemis" (Acts 19:35). In Paul's time the expression "temple keeper" probably meant only that the Ephesians worshiped Artemis in her greatest temple here.[13] But it soon came to refer to a special distinction given a Roman city housing a temple built to a Roman emperor. Worship of the Roman emperor through an imperial cult had been authorized for the provinces of Asia and Bithynia in 29 B.C. under Augustus, whose temple in Pergamum was the first built to an emperor in Asia.[14] A second was built in honor of Tiberus at Smyrna.[15] The third temple was built in Ephesus, probably during the reign of Claudius.[16]

9. J. Keil, *Ephesos: Ein Führer durch die Ruinenstätte und ihre Geschichte,* 5th ed. (Vienna: Osterreichisches Archäologisches Institut, 1964), 109.

10. Principally Codex Bezae (D) of the Western Text and the Harclean Syriac.

11. Akurgal, *Ancient Civilizations,* 148. For recent measurements based on excavation, see "Recent Archaeological Research in Turkey," *Anatolian Studies* 37 (1987): 189.

12. There is virtually nothing left of the famed structure, which was destroyed and then later rebuilt, except portions of the original foundations, recently discovered sections of the north and south faces of the original building (Akurgal, *Ancient Civilizations,* 148), and some of the great altar on the west side of the temple (*Archaeological Reports* 31 [1984–85]: 84; 25 [1978–79]: 72). A detailed report of recent excavations is given in *Anatolian Studies* 32 (1982): 61–87.

13. David Magie, *Roman Rule in Asia Minor, to the End of the Third Century after Christ* (Princeton, N.J.: Princeton University Press, 1950), 2:1433.

14. M. Cary, *A History of Rome,* 2d ed. (London: Macmillan, 1962), 510.

15. Magie, *Roman Rule in Asia Minor,* 1:501. Tiberius, unlike Augustus, resisted emperor worship, but in his desire to maintain the general policies of his predecessor, acquiesced to a request by Asia in A.D. 23 and authorized a second temple to be built for him, his wife, and the Roman senate. It was built in Smyrna in 26, after three years of squabbling by the Roman senate (ibid.). See Tacitus, *Ann.* 4.37–55.

16. Magie, *Roman Rule in Asia Minor,* 1:572; 2:1432. Cf. 1:448. Sometime in the late first century, probably in the reign of Domitian, these three cities that were seats of emperor worship became officially designated "Temple Wardens" (νεωκόροι, *neōkoroi*), a term used by the clerk of the city of Ephesus in Acts 19:35 (ibid., 1:637; 2:1433, 1451).

Some cities, such as Pergamum, Smyrna, and Ephesus,[17] built two such temples and were designated by the second century as "Twice Temple Wardens," that is, places where there was "a temple founded for the worship of the emperors."[18] A few of the more important ones even became "Thrice Temple Wardens."[19] An inscription still standing at the top of the theater declares that Ephesus was given this distinction.[20]

Ephesus was also a well-known center for the practice of magical arts, as the abundance of "magical papyri" found there indicates.[21] While in Ephesus, Paul was confronted by some Jewish exorcists who tried to imitate his miracles (Acts 19:11) by using the name of Jesus in a magical way. They had seen Paul perform his miracles in the name of Jesus and thought there was something magical in the name itself. When they attempted to use it to cast out evil spirits from the demon possessed, a spirit assaulted them, saying, "Jesus I know, and Paul I know; but who are you?"(Acts 19:15–16). The message was clear; it was dangerous for those who were not properly related to Jesus as disciples to use his name.[22] The result of this incident was that many people who had practiced magic burned their books in a public demonstration, and some became disciples (Acts 19:18–19).

Opposition to Paul's teaching in Ephesus became acute when he began to affect the financial stability of the craftsmen. Statues of Artemis, such as those found in the town hall and preserved in the museum at Seljuk (modern Ephesus), were reproduced by the guild of silversmiths and placed in miniature shrines or altars (ναούς, naous, Acts 19:24) for sale to worshipers who visited her temple. This was a major source of income for these craftsmen, and Paul's success in converting people from idolatry was affecting their business. Demetrius, who was probably the president of the guild,[23] gathered his fellow craftsmen together in the theater, where public meetings of this kind were normally held, and incited them against Paul.

This theater, the most impressive structure in the city, is still standing. It was enlarged under Claudius near the time when Paul was in the city. The cavea would seat twenty-four thousand on three levels of twenty-two rows each, reaching a height of almost one hundred feet. The stage wall was three stories high. It stood adjacent to the lower commercial market near the harbor. The noise in the theater was easily heard by the town clerk (γραμματεύς,

---

17. Ibid., 1:594, 615, and 619 respectively.

18. Ibid., 2:1432.

19. Ibid., 1:637.

20. Richard Oster mentions a fourth such temple at Ephesus ("Ephesus," 544).

21. For the publication of the collections of these documents, see F. F. Bruce, *The Book of the Acts*, rev. ed., NICNT (Grand Rapids: Eerdmans, 1988), 369 n. 38.

22. See further F. F. Bruce, *Paul: Apostle of the Heart Set Free* (Grand Rapids: Eerdmans, 1977), 291–93.

23. Bruce, *Paul*, 293.

grammateus, Acts 19:35), a city official whose office was in the town hall, which has been found in excavation. It was located on the south side of Mount Pion in close proximity to the theater, which had been built on Pion's north side. This official, who may have been the most important individual in the city,[24] went to the theater to quiet the mob. Roman rule was impatient with disturbances.

The town clerk found both Jews and Gentiles involved in the demonstration. A man named Alexander tried to speak but was shouted down when it was discovered that he was a Jew. He may have been trying to disclaim any connection between Paul's disciples and the Jewish population of the city, but he never got the chance. This could have been Alexander the coppersmith, who Paul said did "great harm" to him (2 Tim. 4:14).[25] Second Timothy was probably written to Timothy in Ephesus, where Priscilla and Aquila were living (2 Tim. 4:19; cf. Acts 18:18, 26).

Paul spoke of having "many adversaries" in Ephesus (1 Cor. 16:9), some of whom were undoubtedly Jews. He later reminded the elders from Ephesus of the trials he endured through "the plots of the Jews" (Acts 20:19). At a later point in Jerusalem, some of these Asian Jews would recognize Trophimus the Ephesian (Acts 21:29) and accuse Paul of taking him (a Gentile) inside the forbidden area of the temple.

Although the town clerk, whose job required maintaining order, tried to quiet the mob for personal and political reasons rather than out of any regard for Paul, it is significant that Paul did have "friends" in Ephesus who were Roman political officials of wealth and power, called Asiarchs (Ἀσιάρχαι, *Asiarchai*) by Luke. These men sent to Paul and begged him for his own good not to go into the theater (Acts 19:31). Asiarchs were the "foremost men of the province of Asia, chosen from the wealthiest and the most aristocratic inhabitants of the province,"[26] and were elected by the various cities to their posts with the expectation that they would personally finance public games and festivals.

The fact that such men were friends of Paul may suggest that the wealthy and educated people of Ephesus were not as opposed to Paul as the superstitious crowd in the theater and that Paul's ministry was not as exclusively oriented to the poor and uneducated as is sometimes assumed. It probably also suggests that the policy of the Roman Empire at this time was not hostile to Christianity.[27]

24. William Ramsay, "Ephesus," *A Dictionary of the Bible,* ed. James Hastings, 5 vols. (New York: Scribners, 1908), 1:723.

25. I see no reason to connect him with the Alexander in 1 Tim. 1:20, who appears to have been a nominal Christian who had little regard for his own conscience (1 Tim. 1:19).

26. Other provinces—Bithyniarch, Galatarch, Lyciarch, and so on—had theirs (Lily Taylor, "The Asiarchs," in *The Acts of the Apostles,* ed. Foakes-Jackson and Lake, 4:256).

27. Bruce, *Book of the Acts,* 376–77.

Ephesus was not without its symbol of pagan lust for human suffering. An inscription indicates that the stadium in the northern part of the city was rebuilt in the reign of the emperor Nero. It was used to conduct festivals, athletic contests, and the racing of horses and chariots.

A circular area at the eastern end of the stadium in Ephesus was designated for gladiatorial fights and the baiting of animals. This is of interest in the study of the life of Paul because he states in 1 Corinthians 15:32 that "humanly speaking" he "fought with beasts at Ephesus." It is unlikely that Paul would have literally fought beasts in this arena because he was a Roman citizen and could not be forced to engage in such activity reserved for criminals, prisoners of war, or hired fighters who, like gladiators, were trained in special schools.[28] Also, if he had been inadvertently put into an arena, he would surely have mentioned his miraculous delivery from death in his list of personal hardships in 2 Corinthians 11. And Luke would surely have referred to it in Acts. If my date of A.D. 53 is correct for Paul's departure from Ephesus (see chapter 3, table 3.2), the stadium would not yet have been built, since it was constructed during the reign of Nero (A.D. 54–68). But even if my dates are wrong, Paul would not literally have fought beasts in this stadium. It is more likely that Paul would have appealed to his citizenship to prevent his engaging in such combat. Perhaps Paul meant by his comment that the "beasts" against whom he "fought" in Ephesus were of a human nature. Perhaps the "beasts" of 1 Corinthians 15:32 were the "many adversaries" of 16:9.[29]

It has been suggested that Paul not only was imprisoned in Ephesus but also wrote the Philippian letter from that imprisonment (Phil. 1:13–14; 2:23).[30] However, "the fatal flaw in the Ephesian imprisonment hypothesis is that it is totally built on conjecture."[31] This is accentuated by the absence of

28. "Venationes," *Harper's Dictionary of Classical Literature and Antiquities,* ed. Harry Thurston Peck, 2d ed. (New York: American Book, 1897), 1640. Bruce Winter writes: "Wildbeast fighters (venatores) were often freedmen from good families who were connected with the provincial imperial cult." However, the imperial cult with which these wild beast shows were connected was not celebrated in Ephesus at this time (*Seek the Welfare of the City: Christians as Benefactors and Citizens* [Grand Rapids: Eerdmans, 1994], 143 n. 95). See further, C. Roueche, "Gladiators and Wild-Beast Fighters," in *Performers and Partisans at Aphrodisias in the Roman and Late Roman Periods,* Journal of Roman Studies Monograph 6 (London: Society for the Promotion of Roman Studies, 1993), chap. 5.

29. This is argued by Abraham Malherbe, who also suggests a literary background for considering human passions as beasts ("The Beasts at Ephesus," *JBL* 87.1 [1968]: 71–80).

30. Advocates of an Ephesian origin for Philippians include Adolf Deissmann, "Zur ephesinischen Gefangenschaft des Apostels Paulus," in *Anatolian Studies Presented to Sir William Ramsay,* ed. W. H. Buckler and W. M. Calder (Manchester: Manchester University Press, 1923), 121–27; G. S. Duncan, "A New Setting for Paul's Epistle to the Philippians," *ET* 43 (1931–32): 7–11; idem, "St. Paul's Ministry in Asia—the Last Phase," *NTS* 3 (1956–57): 211–18; and D. T. Rowlingson, "Paul's Ephesian Imprisonment," *Anglican Theological Review* 32 (1950): 1–7.

31. Gerald Hawthorne, *Philippians,* Word Biblical Commentary 43 (Waco: Word, 1983), xxxix. See his analysis of the Ephesian origin of Philippians on pp. xxxviii–xl.

any mention of an Ephesian imprisonment in Acts. Paul's horrifying experience here transcended mere imprisonment. Although a case has also been made for Corinth[32] and Caeasarea[33] as the place from which Philippians was written, the evidence is still most weighty for Rome.[34]

Recent discoveries in Ephesus have revealed a housing complex on the south side of the main street. The interiors of some of these houses, which testify to the considerable wealth in the city, could have provided space enough for Christians to assemble in house churches for study and worship.[35]

Luke emphasizes the dual outreach of Paul in Ephesus to both Jews and Gentiles (Acts 19:10, 17). Part of the impact of Paul's ministry lay in the "extraordinary miracles" (Acts 19:11) God performed through him. Even handkerchiefs or aprons, presumably the sweat-rags and aprons Paul used in his tentmaking work,[36] were carried away to the sick, who were healed by the power of Jesus upon contact with them (Acts 19:12). Evil spirits were cast out in this same way.

1 Corinthians

During the period of Paul's Ephesian ministry, he wrote at least four letters to the church in Corinth.[37] The first of these, his "former letter," is referred to in 1 Corinthians 5:9. We will designate it as "Corinthians A." It was a letter telling them not to associate with members who are guilty of immorality, greed, idolatry, reviling, drunkenness, and robbery. These problems no doubt arose out of their pagan background and required Paul's admonition. Later, he received word from Corinth that a member of the church was committing sexual immorality with his step-mother, a sin that went even beyond the bounds of paganism (1 Cor. 5:1).

Paul apparently heard about the situation in Corinth through a visit by Stephanus, Fortunatus, Achaicus, and Chloe's people (1 Cor. 16:15–17; 1:11) and through a letter sent to him from Corinth (1 Cor. 7:1). He then responded by writing "Corinthians B" (our 1 Corinthians). A man named Sosthenes joined Paul in writing the letter (1 Cor. 1:1). If he is the same Sosthenes who was the ruler of the synagogue in Corinth (Acts 18:17), he had

32. S. Dockx, "Lieu et date de l'épître aux Philippiens," *Revue biblique* 80 (1973): 230–46. See further, Ralph Martin, *The Epistle of Paul to the Philippians,* Tyndale New Testament Commentary (Grand Rapids: Eerdmans, 1959), 44.

33. See the discussion by Hawthorne, who leans toward Caesarea (*Philippians,* xliii).

34. See Donald Guthrie, *New Testament Introduction,* 4th rev. ed. (Downers Grove, Ill.: InterVarsity, 1990), 547–50, who prefers Rome (p. 555).

35. See chapter 16, under "The Composition of Paul's Churches and the Lord's Supper."

36. Bruce, *Book of the Acts,* 367.

37. Bruce suggests possibly five (*Paul,* 318).

become a Christian and was beaten by the Jews in the presence of the proconsul Gallio. Subsequently, he came to Ephesus where he was with Paul. Crispus, another ruler of a synagogue in Corinth (Acts 18:8; 1 Cor. 1:14), had also believed in the Lord and was baptized together with all his household (Acts 18:8).

A variety of issues were pressing the church, and Paul responded from Ephesus (1 Cor. 16:8), perhaps in the spring of 53. The issues are categorically discussed beginning with the basic question of whether the gospel was to be properly proclaimed in unambiguous and straightforward teaching rather than in the tradition of worldly wisdom inherited from their Greco-Roman cultural background.[38]

One issue of particular importance is the relation of the Corinthian Christians to Roman government and religion, since Corinth, although situated in Greece, had been refounded as a Roman colony. The recent redating of a letter formerly thought to belong to the time of the emperor Julian in the fourth century has provided a "new" document for scholars relative to the study of Corinth. The letter is now dated to A.D. 80–120 by Anthony Spawforth[39] and identified as a petition from the city of Argos, near Corinth, to the Roman governor of Achaia. Winter points out that this is the "only major, non-Christian literary source we possess that refers to first century developments" in the city of Corinth.[40] Spawforth concludes that the document proves the establishment of a quasi-provincial imperial cult in Corinth in about A.D. 54, during the very period (A.D. 51–54) when Paul was corresponding with the church there. And Winter argues that this provides the appropriate background for Paul's discussion in 1 Corinthians 8 of Corinthian Christians exercising their "right" to participate in banquets conducted in Roman temples.

1 Corinthians Outline

I. Response to Oral Reports from Corinth, 1:11 (1:1–6:20)
  A. Divisiveness (1:1–4:21)
  B. Immorality (5:1–13; 6:12–20)
  C. Litigation (6:1–11)

38. Duane Litfin, rather than interpreting wisdom in the light of first-century Greco-Roman mystery religions, sees this issue of the wisdom of man versus the gospel of Christ at Corinth as involving a cultural tradition that dates back to the fifth century B.C. (*St. Paul's Theology of Proclamation: I Corinthians 1–4 and Greco-Roman Rhetoric,* Society for New Testament Studies Monograph Series 79 [Cambridge: Cambridge University Press, 1994]).

39. "Corinth, Argos, and the Imperial Cult: Pseudo-Julian, Letters 198," *Hesperia: Journal of the American School of Classical Studies in Athens* 63.2 (1994): 211–32. See also the condensed version of it: "The Achaean Federal Cult Part I: Pseudo-Julian, Letters 198," *TynBul* 46.1 (May 1995): 151–68; and the related essay by Bruce Winter, "The Achaean Federal Imperial Cult II: The Corinthian Church," *TynBul* 46.1 (May 1995): 169–78.

40. Winter, "Achaean Federal Imperial Cult II," 169.

II. Response to a Letter from Corinth, 7:1 (7:1–16:24)
    A. Marriage and Divorce (7:1–40)
    B. Christian Conscience and Idolatry (8:1–11:1)
    C. Respect for Authority (11:2–16)
    D. Abuses of the Lord's Supper (11:17–34)
    E. Spiritual Gifts (12:1–14:40)
    F. The Resurrection of the Body (15:1–58)
    G. The Collection for Jewish Christians in Jerusalem (16:1–24)

In Ephesus during this period of time (A.D. 51–53), Paul was especially involved with gathering a collection for the needy Jewish Christians in Jerusalem, as he had been admonished to do by Peter and other leaders of the Jerusalem church (Gal. 2:10). The collection lay very much on Paul's heart, and the divisive and immoral situation in Corinth was presenting a potential hindrance to its successful completion. Throughout the time of his evangelization of the provinces on either side of the Aegean, this was a major concern of Paul. He reminded the Corinthians in this letter, "Corinthians B" (1 Cor. 16:1–4), that they should continue to do as he had directed the churches in Galatia (undoubtedly when he had passed through the region of Galatia and Phrygia, Acts 18:23) and put something aside each Lord's Day for this purpose.

They had made the commitment a year earlier (2 Cor. 8:10; 9:2), but the divisions in Corinth were probably affecting that pledge. Tensions were developing between Paul and many of the Christians in Corinth, prompted by unnamed opponents who were charging Paul with being a false apostle (1 Cor. 9:1–18). Among other things, Paul wrote this letter to defend himself against these charges.

The reference to giving on the first day of the week so that "contributions need not be made when I come" (1 Cor. 16:2) may refer to the fear Paul had of arriving in Corinth to pick up the contribution and finding they had not collected it (2 Cor. 9:4), which would be humiliating to them as well as Paul. This contribution was especially important in Paul's ministry since it was a gift from Gentiles for Jews and was regarded as a sacrificial offering and an expression of appreciation for the initial role the Jews had played in providing the gospel for them (Rom. 15:16, 25–27). The Gentiles were in debt to the Jews and needed to acknowledge it.

Paul addressed the Jewish Corinthian Christians as "saints" and included the Gentile Christians along with them as "those who in every place call on the name of our Lord Jesus Christ" (1 Cor. 1:2).[41] F. F. Bruce reminds us that "the members of the Jerusalem church are the 'saints' *par excellence,* being at

41. See the discussion of the distinction between Jewish Christians and Gentile Christians in chapter 13.

once the faithful remnant of Israel and the nucleus of the people of God in the new age. If Gentile believers can also be called 'saints,' it is because they have become 'fellow citizens with the saints' of Jewish stock and with them 'members of the household of God' (Ephesians 2:19)."[42]

At this point Paul felt the need to make some plans to deal with the Corinthian situation. He sent two of his coworkers, Timothy and Erastus, to Macedonia from Ephesus (Acts 19:22), planning for Timothy to go on to Corinth and bring a report back to him (1 Cor. 16:10–11). Paul planned to visit Macedonia later and then go on to Achaia (Acts 19:21), where he would perhaps spend the winter in Corinth (1 Cor. 16:5–6), but in the meantime he felt it necessary to remain in Ephesus until Pentecost (late spring/early summer) because God had opened a door for effective work, even though there were many adversaries (1 Cor. 16:8–9). After this period of time, he planned to go to Corinth and from there to Jerusalem and then Rome (Acts 19:21).

However, when Timothy returned from Macedonia, he must have given a report that caused Paul to change his travel plans and go to Corinth first, then visit Macedonia, and return again to Corinth so that the church would have the pleasure of a double visit by Paul. When he later wrote "Corinthians D" (2 Corinthians), he mentioned this change of plans and the subsequent charge that some made against him, accusing him of vacillating (2 Cor. 1:15–17). Timothy's report had also prompted Paul (and Sosthenes) to write 1 Corinthians ("Corinthians B"), informing the Corinthians that Timothy was coming and urging them to "put him at ease" because he was doing the Lord's work (1 Cor. 16:10; 4:17).

At this point the reconstruction of Paul's activity is especially difficult because Luke omits the next several months in Acts 20:1–3. Several possibilities exist for reconstructing this period by correlating the events mentioned in 1 and 2 Corinthians. The following is one possibility.

Timothy returned and reported to Paul, prompting Paul to pay an unplanned visit to Corinth, where he had a difficult time. He referred to it as a "painful" visit (2 Cor. 2:1). The difficulty apparently had something to do with the brother who was denied fellowship with the church, perhaps the one who was living with his step-mother (1 Cor. 5:1–7). In his first letter, Paul had commanded the church to disfellowship the brother ("turn him over to Satan") until he repented of his sin (1 Cor. 5:5). This had caused some problems. Whatever the cause, Paul had a difficult time on this visit and determined not to return until the situation could be corrected.

In Acts 20 Luke does not mention this visit, possibly because it was such a bitter experience. Paul went on to Macedonia (Acts 20:3) as planned (2 Cor. 1:16) and then returned to Ephesus and wrote the church at Corinth a severe letter ("Corinthians C," 2 Cor. 2:3, 9) to test their willingness to obey him.

42. Bruce, *Paul*, 321.

He admonished the church to grant forgiveness where repentance had occurred and to comfort the individual lest he be "overwhelmed by excessive sorrow" (2 Cor. 2:7). Paul did not want to be pained over this matter on a return visit, he said, and this is why he sent Titus instead of coming himself (2 Cor. 2:3–11).

While he was back in Asia, Paul had a difficult time, which he described as being so "unbearably crushed that we despaired of life itself" (2 Cor. 1:8). This seems to be the one occasion in Paul's experience when he saw no way out. Death seemed inevitable. Paul had faced death often. He had only recently written to the Corinthians telling them "I die every day" (1 Cor. 15:31). But this was different; this time, for the first time, Paul saw no escape. This experience seems to have modified his thinking about death and resurrection; from now on Paul speaks of his death before the coming of Christ as probable.[43] Subsequently, he would write, "We speak knowing that he who raised the Lord Jesus will raise us also with Jesus and bring us with you into his presence" (2 Cor. 4:13–14). So although we cannot know precisely what the terrifying danger was from which God delivered Paul in Ephesus, it was clearly a landmark experience for him, one that was formative in his thinking.

Paul anxiously waited to hear the response to the severe letter to Corinth that he evidently sent by Titus (2 Cor. 2:13), who may have been an older and stronger person than Timothy.[44] It thus seems to have been written during a time of personal suffering and hardship. In the meantime, Paul planned to continue to take advantage of the "open doors" God had provided in Ephesus, in spite of the "many adversaries" (1 Cor. 16:9).

Troas

Evidently, when Paul sent Titus to Corinth with the severe letter, the two had made plans to meet in Troas. Titus would sail from the Corinthian harbor at Cenchreae to Troas and meet him there. So Paul left Ephesus after Pentecost and went to Troas, where God opened further doors of opportunity for preaching (2 Cor. 2:12). However, Paul was unable to take advantage of these opportunities because of his concern for Titus, who did not meet him there (2 Cor. 2:13). Titus had been forced to travel by land through Macedonia toward Troas[45] because he evidently missed the last ship out of Cenchreae before the sailing season closed due

43. So Bruce, *Paul,* 310. See also A. E. Harvey, *Renewal through Suffering: A Study of 2 Corinthians* (Edinburgh: Clark, 1996). Harvey believes the way Paul faced death had a profound impact on his theology and is the key to understanding the letter, especially chapters 4 and 5.

44. So Bruce, *Paul,* 274.

45. See further J. Murphy-O'Connor, "Traveling Conditions in the First Century: On the Road and on the Sea with St. Paul," *Bible Review* 1 (1985): 41.

to bad weather, which usually occurred from November 11 to March 10.[46] It should be noted that even the great apostle was sometimes unable to walk through open doors because of human anxiety over a situation.

Macedonia

So Paul left Troas by land and crossed the Dardanelles by ferry to Macedonia, anxiously looking for Titus in each city along the way. Titus would be checking with Christian homes in each city, as would Paul.[47] They undoubtedly both traveled the route of Paul's second journey and eventually met somewhere in Macedonia. Even in Macedonia, Paul was "afflicted at every turn—fighting without and fear within" (2 Cor. 7:5).[48] But God comforted Paul with the coming of Titus (2 Cor. 7:6).

Titus brought news that Paul's severe letter ("Corinthians C") had produced repentance among the Corinthian Christians, and so Paul felt that even though he had made them sorry by writing so severe a letter and initially regretted that he had written it, he now rejoiced in its results (2 Cor. 7:8). He had written them not only because of the one who had done the wrong or on account of the one who had suffered the wrong but also to enhance their zeal for Paul and his work (2 Cor. 7:12).

At this point, somewhere in Macedonia, Paul and Timothy wrote "Corinthians D" (2 Corinthians) as a follow-up to the severe letter "C" and sent it back to Corinth by Titus (2 Cor. 8:16–17). Timothy apparently had traveled with Paul from Ephesus to Troas and on into Macedonia and shared in the writing of the letter (2 Cor. 1:1). The fact that Paul was concerned over the status of the collection for the saints throughout all this trouble is made clear at this time in 2 Corinthians (8:10–15).

Illyricum

Consideration must also be given here to another comment made by Paul that "from Jerusalem and as far round as Illyricum I have fully preached the

---

46. In the Roman Empire at this time, "winter shipping was forbidden by custom and in the case of imperial transports, by law." The normal sailing season was May 27 to September 14, while the two interim periods, in the spring (March 10–May 26) and the fall (Sept. 14–Nov. 11), were considered risky (Brian M. Rapske, "Acts, Travel and Shipwreck," in *The Book of Acts in Its Graeco-Roman Setting,* ed. David W. J. Gill and Conrad Gempf, BAFCS 2 [Grand Rapids: Eerdmans, 1994], 22–23).

47. Cf. Paul's practice of visiting the homes of Christians when he passed through a town: Acts 21:4, 7, 8, 16.

48. Bruce calls his fear within "severe depression" (*Paul,* 274).

gospel of Christ" (Rom. 15:19). Three questions arise from this enigmatic verse: (1) Where was Illyricum? (2) Did Paul actually preach in Illyricum? (3) If so, when did it occur? I have discussed this more fully elsewhere,[49] but the following observations are pertinent here.

First, how far north did Paul actually go? Illyricum was a Roman province in the northwestern part of the Balkan peninsula along the east coast of the Adriatic Sea. It was one of four large provinces established by the Romans across the north part of the peninsula. The territory included in these provinces, Illyricum, Moesia, Dacia, and Pannonia, covered the area from Vienna to the Black Sea and from Macedonia to the Carpathian Mountains. Illyricum was the westernmost of these provinces and, in the early first century A.D., was divided into two sections: Pannonia in the north, and Dalmatia in the south.[50] The term Illyricum refers at times to Dalmatia and at other times to a larger area which includes Dalmatia. What is meant by Dalmatia in 2 Timothy 4:10 is not clear, but it probably designates the southern sector of Illyricum.[51]

Had Paul used the Greek name of the territory, Illyria, rather than the Latin name Illyricum, he might have been thinking of the area in western Macedonia around Dyrrachium, the coastal city at the western end of the Egnatian Way.[52] In Greek usage the territory of Illyria extended farther south than the Roman province of Illyricum.[53] Therefore, if Paul had used the term Illyria, it might have meant only the northwestern sector of Macedonia. The use of Illyricum, on the other hand, designates an area farther north in the region of what was once Yugoslavia and Albania. So he may have meant the province as a whole, just the southern portion of it (Dalmatia, 2 Tim 4:10), or perhaps just the border of it near the city of Dyrrachium.

Second, it is quite possible that Paul himself did not actually preach in Illyricum. Contrary to most modern translations, the word "preach" does not occur in the text of Romans 15:19. Rather, it states that he "fulfilled" or "completed" (πεπληρωκέναι, *peplērōkenai*) the gospel of Christ in a geographical

---

49. John McRay, "Illyricum," *ABD*, 3:388–89. See also Cary, *History of Rome;* Bruce Metzger, "Romans 15:14–33 and Paul's Conception of His Apostolic Mission," *JBL* 83.1 (March 1964): 1–11; M. I. Finley, *Atlas of Classical Archaeology* (New York: McGraw-Hill, 1977).

50. See map 19 in F. van der Meer and Christine Mohrmann, eds., *Atlas of the Early Christian World,* trans. and ed. Mary Hedlund and H. H. Rowley (New York: Nelson, 1958).

51. McRay, "Illyricum," 388.

52. This international highway ran from Kypsela on the east coast, which was north of Samothrace, to Dyrrachium and Apollonia on the west coast. It thus traversed the entire province of Macedonia. The distance between these two cities given by Roman milestones in the area is 535 Roman miles (493 English miles). See N. G. L. Hammond, "The Western Part of the Via Egnatia," *JRS* 64 (1974): 185–94. On the Egnatian Way (Via Egnatia), see McRay, *Archaeology and the New Testament,* 282–83.

53. Bruce, *Paul,* 316–17.

circle that stretched from Jerusalem to Illyricum. He may have viewed his ministry among Gentiles as a completion of the work begun among Jews in Jerusalem by the Apostles before him, a work that reached all the way west to Illyricum, where some of his companions labored (e.g., Titus in Dalmatia, 2 Tim. 4:10).[54]

The word *preach* (εὐαγγελίζεται, *euangelizetai*) is used in the next verse (Rom. 15:20), where Paul continues: "thus making it my ambition to preach the gospel, not where Christ has already been named, lest I build on another man's foundation." However, Paul may be saying only that his associates like Titus had taken the gospel to Dalmatia/Illyricum under Paul's oversight, and thus he considered it to be a part of his own ministry. Yet, the natural and most evident meaning of the two verses taken together is that Paul himself did the "fulfilling" or "completing" of his gospel commission by preaching in this area.

Third, if Paul himself preached in Illyricum, when did it occur? Since Romans was written at the end of his third journey, the Illyricum ministry mentioned in Romans 15:19 cannot be assigned to a later time, such as the period after his first imprisonment. What, then, are the possibilities? He never left Asia on his first journey. There was no time for a trip to this region on the second journey; Luke says he spent only "some days" in Philippi (Acts 16:12) and then turned southwest to Thessalonica, where he spent a few weeks (Acts 17:2), and then continued southward to Beroea, after which he left Macedonia. There is no time here for a trip northwest to Illyricum.

This leaves only the third journey. The earlier portion of that journey was spent in Asia (Acts 19:10), so it must have been in the *latter part* of the third journey, while Paul was in Macedonia dealing with problems at Corinth, that he went to Illyricum.[55] As elsewhere in Acts, Luke abbreviates the record of Paul's travels in Macedonia at this time, merely stating that Paul was in "these parts" (Acts 20:2) without specifying a time frame. It may have been as much as eighteen months.[56] After going through "these parts," he spent three months in Greece, that is, Achaia, the southern part of Greece, from where he left for Jerusalem (Acts 20:3).

It has been argued that during this time in Macedonia Paul went to Nicopolis in the western part of Greece to spend the winter (Titus 3:12),[57] but this predicates Paul's having left Titus on Crete at some earlier time (Titus 1:5), which is difficult if not impossible to fit into the chronology up to this point.[58] There is no record of Paul's contact with Crete before his voyage to

---

54. McRay, "Illyricum," 388–89.

55. Bruce, *Paul,* 318.

56. "Eighteen months, indeed, would not be an excessive estimate" (ibid., 317).

57. George S. Duncan, *St. Paul's Ephesian Ministry* (London: Hodder and Stoughton, 1929), 217ff.

58. Bruce, *Paul,* 318.

Rome more than two years later. I will deal further with Paul in Crete in the next chapter.

2 Corinthians

It has also been argued that 2 Corinthians consists of two letters joined together. According to this view, the first of these letters, "Corinthians D," includes chapters 1 through 9, and the second, "Corinthians E," consists of chapters 10 through 13.[59] Some even suggest that there is evidence of six or more fragmentary letters in 2 Corinthians.[60] One of the primary reasons for this is the optimistic and joyful tone of the first nine chapters, based on Paul's positive news from Titus, in contrast to the severe and harsh response to opponents in chapters 10 through 13,[61] which tempts the identification of these latter chapters as the "severe letter" Paul mentions in 2 Corinthians 2:3–11.

Those who hold the two-document theory on the letter are divided about which was written first,[62] but if the two-document view is correct, it seems most likely that the severity of the second document was caused by a rejection of Titus and the letter he brought from Paul (i.e., the first nine chapters) and that it was therefore written last. By this scenario, certain Hebrew leaders (2 Cor. 11:22) had come from the "superlative apostles" (2 Cor. 11:5; 12:11), presumably in Jerusalem, and were claiming apostolic authority themselves (2 Cor. 11:13). They had rejected the Gentile ministry of Paul and Titus and were pressing for Jerusalem's preeminence in their leadership.[63]

Since no existing manuscripts of 2 Corinthians give any indication of a division in the book, the case for a divided letter has to be made entirely from internal literary analysis.[64] The unity of the letter is maintained by seeing two moods of Paul expressed in the separate parts relative to different segments of the Corinthian church. In the first, he is happy with the reception given Titus by the majority and optimistic over the anticipated

---

59. Among those supporting the view that 2 Corinthians consists of two letters are Bruce, *Paul,* 276f.; Richard Batey, "Paul's Interaction with the Corinthians," *JBL* 84.2 (June 1965): 139–46; and Ralph Martin, *2 Corinthians,* Word Biblical Commentary (Waco: Word, 1986), 298–99. See the discussion in H. D. Betz, *2 Corinthians 8 and 9: A Commentary on Two Administrative Letters of the Apostle Paul,* ed. George W. MacRae, Hermeneia (Philadelphia: Fortress, 1985). See further the bibliography in Donald Guthrie, *New Testament Introduction,* 444 n. 2.

60. See the discussion by H. D. Betz in "Corinthians, Second Epistle to The," *ABD,* 1:1149ff.

61. See Roy B. Ward, "The Opponents of Paul," *Restoration Quarterly* 10.4 (1967): 185–95.

62. See the discussion in Guthrie, *New Testament Introduction,* 444.

63. Such is the analysis of Bruce, *Paul,* 276–77.

64. So Betz admits ("Corinthians," *ABD,* 1:1149).

visit to pick up their contribution for the saints in Jerusalem. In the second part, he is critical of those Hebrew leaders who represent a minority at Corinth and who have come from Jersualem to attack Paul's authority and ministry.[65]

2 Corinthians Outline

I. Paul's Defense of His Ministry (1:1–7:16)
II. The Collection for the Jewish Christians in Jerusalem (8:1–9:15)
III. Paul's Vindication of His Character (10:1–13:14)

Paul writes that he sent with Titus a brother (perhaps Luke),[66] who was "famous among all the churches for his preaching of the gospel" (2 Cor. 8:18) so that "no one should blame us about this liberal gift which we are administering, for we aim at what is honourable not only in the Lord's sight but also in the sight of men" (2 Cor. 8:20–21). Along with these two, another unnamed brother who had great confidence in the church in Corinth was sent to bolster their reliance on the validity of the contribution (2 Cor. 8:22).

Paul now hoped that he would return for a third visit to Corinth to pick up this contribution (2 Cor. 9:5; 12:14; 13:1–2). These plans evidently materialized, and Paul subsequently spent three months in Greece and went back to Corinth (Acts 20:3; cf. 1 Cor. 16:6). During this time in Corinth, he wrote the letter to the church in Rome, in which he says he was hosted by Gaius (Rom. 16:23), who lived in Corinth (1 Cor. 1:14). I see no reason to doubt that these two references in Romans and 1 Corinthians are to the same individual. Erastus, the city treasurer and brother in Christ in Corinth, also sent greetings in Romans 16:23.[67]

Romans

In his letter to the Romans, Paul speaks of the contribution he was collecting among the Gentile churches for the Jewish brothers and sisters in Jerusalem (Rom. 15:25–29). He refers to Jesus as a "servant" (διάκονον, *diakonon*) among the Jews (Rom. 15:8), while describing himself as a "priestly" minister (λειτουργόν, *leitourgon*) of Christ to the Gentiles, and he calls the contribution a priestly "offering of the Gentiles" (Rom. 15:16). After he delivered the contribution to Jerusalem, he planned to go to Rome and wanted the church

---

65. So argues Guthrie, *New Testament Introduction,* 445–46.
66. Bruce, *Book of the Acts,* 383.
67. See the discussion of Erastus and the inscription found in Corinth bearing this name in chapter 6.

there, which he did not establish and had never visited,[68] to assist him in going on to Spain (Rom. 15:24, 28).

It is important to note that at this very time Paul's sensitivity about the relationship between Jews and Gentiles was at a peak, and for more than a year he had been gathering this large and theologically pivotal offering from poor Gentiles to famine-stricken Jews. At this time, then, he dictated a letter to Tertius for the Roman believers (Rom. 16:22), in which he gives his fullest expression of the Jew-Gentile relationship (especially chapters 9 through 11). Romans is generally regarded as Paul's greatest letter and his most systematic treatment of his theology.[69]

Paul begins this letter by pointing out that he was given his apostleship to bring about all nations' obedience to the faith, Gentiles as well as Jews (Rom. 1:5–6), and that the gospel is the power of God for all who believe, whether Jew or Gentile (Rom. 1:16). Whoever is righteous through faith (whether Jew or Gentile) shall live (Rom. 1:17). Gentiles disobeyed the revelation of God given to them in nature (chapter 1), but Jews also disobeyed their additional revelation in the law of Moses (chapter 2). The result is that both Jews and Gentiles are under sin (chapter 3). Abraham is set forth as a father of Gentiles as well as Jews, because he is a spiritual father by faith and not by physical ancestry (chapter 4). In chapters 5 to 8, Paul tells the Romans how those who through faith are righteous, Jew or Gentile, shall live; they shall live free from the wrath of God, the dominion of the law of Moses, the dominion of sin, and the dominion of death.

Then he shows in chapters 9 through 11 that this righteousness is not against the promise of God that declared that the Jews will have an important and continuing place in the purposes of God. God has not cast off his people whom he foreknew (Rom. 11:1–2). There is a role for believing Jews in the future plans of God. The Gentiles have been grafted as wild olive branches into the trunk of the Jewish tree and must never forget that it is the Jewish root and trunk that sustains them, and not the Gentile branches that support the root (Rom. 11:18). Paul tells them that he is on his way to Jerusalem with a gift from Gentiles that will make this clear to everyone (Rom. 15:25).

In the last five chapters of the letter, Paul describes the life of the individual, Jew or Gentile, who through faith is righteous. This life includes living sacri-

68. Raymond Brown postulates that the church in Rome was established in the 40s, probably from Jerusalem, and that the members there were "more attached to Jewish law and customs than were his [Paul's] own converts." They were Jewish Christians who made some Gentile converts, and though they did not insist on circumcision, they did require some Jewish observances ("Further Reflections on the Origins of the Church of Rome," in *The Conversation Continues: Studies in Paul and John,* ed. Robert T. Fortna and Beverly Gaventa [Nashville: Abingdon, 1990], 98–99).

69. For a fuller discussion of the letter, see John McRay, "Romans," *Baker Encyclopedia of the Bible,* ed. Walter A. Elwell (Grand Rapids: Baker, 1988), 2:1863–68.

ficially before God with love and respect for everyone (chapter 12), recognizing and obeying civil authority (even in Nero's Rome, chapter 13), and being patient and loving with those who have a weak conscience and are not yet mature in their knowledge of God's expectations (chapter 14). The fifteenth chapter expresses Paul's travel plans, and the sixteenth contains salutations by name to almost thirty people in Rome and sends greetings by name from four in Corinth.

The letter may thus be outlined as follows:

Romans Outline

Theme: The Righteousness of God Revealed in Jesus Christ
Theme Verse: "He who through faith is righteous shall live" (1:17)

I. He Who through Faith Is Righteous . . . (1:1–4:25)
    A. Under the Wrath of God (1:1–3:20)
        1. The Wrath of God Revealed against Unrighteous Gentiles (1:1–32)
        2. The Wrath of God Revealed against the Righteousness of the Law—Unfaithful Jews (2:1–3:20)
    B. The Righteousness of God Revealed (3:21–4:25)
        1. The Righteousness of God Extended to All by Christ (3:21–31)
        2. Abraham Is the Father of Gentiles as well as Jews (4:1–25)
II. Shall Live (5:1–8:39)
    A. Free from God's Wrath (5:1–21)
    B. Free from Sin (6:1–23)
    C. Free from the Law (7:1–25)
    D. Free from Death (8:1–39)
III. The Righteousness of Faith Not against the Promise of God (9:1–11:36)
    A. The Problem: Jewish Resistance to the Gospel (9:1–5)
    B. Five-Part Answer (9:6–11:36)
        1. Israel's Rejection Is God's Purpose by Election (9:6–29)
        2. Israel's Rejection Is Its Own Fault as History Shows (9:30–10:21)
        3. Israel's Rejection Is Not Final—a Remnant Exists (11:1–10)
        4. Israel's Rejection Is the Way of Gentiles' Salvation (11:11–24)
        5. Israel's Rejection Is God's Means of Saving Israel (11:25–36)
IV. The Life of Him Who through Faith Is Righteous (12:1–15:13)
    A. Conduct in the New Age (12:1–13:14)

Back through Macedonia

Paul's plan was to leave Corinth and sail directly to Syria and Jerusalem with the contribution, but this plan had to be altered because of a plot on his life by the Jews (Acts 20:3). This evidently involved an attempt to kill him at the harbor in Cenchreae, so he sent his traveling companions on by sea while he and Luke took the slower land route through Macedonia, planning to meet the others in Troas (Acts 20:3–5). It is clear that Luke was with Paul, because Luke uses the first-person pronoun "we" in referring to their later departure from Philippi (Acts 20:6).

Paul, Luke, and perhaps some others left Corinth and traveled north through Macedonia to Philippi. Just after the Feast of Passover or Unleavened Bread, which occurs in the spring about the time of the Christian observance of Easter, they sailed from Philippi (i.e., from its harbor at Neapolis) for Troas (Acts 20:6). In our chronology, this was the year 54, and Passover was April 12–19 of that year. Because of unfavorable winds,[70] it took them five days to sail the 150 miles to Troas (rather than the two days it had taken a few years earlier when they were traveling in the opposite direction, Acts 16:11). It was Paul's desire to reach Jerusalem with the contribution by Pentecost on May 31 (Acts 20:16). This is one of the three major annual festivals in Israel, along with Passover and Tabernacles, and the presentation of such a contribution from his Gentile churches would be far more impressive on this occasion.

Return to Troas

Paul was traveling by commercial vessels and had to accommodate their schedules. This was probably the reason he stayed seven more days in Troas when he was in hurry to reach Jerusalem (Acts 20:6). On the other hand, if there were more frequent departures available to him or if he had hired the boat himself (which is highly unlikely), then he deliberately chose to delay his urgent journey by another seven days even though he had already unexpectedly lost several days coming from Philippi. If he deliberately delayed his departure, then perhaps that delay could be accounted for by his desire to be with the church at their Lord's Day assembly, when they all gathered together in one place to eat the Lord's Supper (Acts 20:7). He obviously had arrived seven days earlier on Monday and had missed this service. If this is what hap-

70. Otto Meinardus, *St. Paul's Last Journey* (New Rochelle, N.Y.: Caratzas, 1979), 4.

pened, it sheds some light on the importance Paul attached to the Sunday observance of the Supper by the united body. However, it is probably more likely that Paul was simply tied to the sailing schedule of his ship and was forced to stay longer in Troas than he intended.

Further light is shed on this question by his subsequent travel from Troas to Miletus. Luke writes that Paul "had decided to sail past Ephesus, so that he might not have to spend time in Asia" (Acts 20:16). He did not want to return to Ephesus because of the risk of spending excessive time there with both friends and enemies.[71] Another confrontation with enemies there would cause him to miss Pentecost in Jerusalem. Thus two scenarios present themselves: (1) he chose a boat (either at Philippi's harbor of Neapolis or at Troas) that was not stopping at Ephesus,[72] or (2) he hired the vessel himself and personally made the decision not to stop at Ephesus. However, it is doubtful that Paul would or could have hired such a vessel because of the extreme cost. It would be comparable to chartering a commercial airplane today. But even more compelling against this latter position is the fact that it is clearly stated later (Acts 21:1–2) that when Paul's group got to Patara on the southwest coast, they "found a ship crossing to Phoenicia." They were obviously, then, not sailing in the same (rented) vessel they had boarded at Philippi (Neapolis).

In any case, Paul made arrangements to be picked up at Assos by the boat that sailed around the promontory of Lectum to Assos (Acts 20:13). He decided, for reasons unrevealed, either to walk the thirty or more miles of road[73] or to travel by horseback from Troas to Assos.[74] A normal day's journey at this time was about twenty miles on foot or thirty on horseback.[75] It would take the boat longer to travel round Cape Lectum (modern Bababurun) and arrive at the Assos harbor.

Perhaps Paul needed more time in Troas to establish and instruct the infant church there,[76] or he wished to instruct the believers further during the land journey to Assos,[77] or he just wanted to be by himself as he contemplated the

---

71. Meinardus, *St. Paul's Last Journey,* 8. See other options in Rapske, "Acts, Travel and Shipwreck," 16.

72. Colin J. Hemer, *The Book of Acts in the Setting of Hellenistic History,* ed. C. H. Gempf (Tübingen: Mohr, 1989), 125.

73. Meinardus, *St. Paul's Last Journey,* 5.

74. Colin J. Hemer, "Alexandria Troas," *TynBul* 26 (1975): 105.

75. Edwin Yamauchi gives the average rate of travel for a pedestrian as three miles per hour; for soldiers, four miles per hour. The distance covered would be fifteen to twenty miles per day for a pedestrian, twenty miles for a donkey caravan, and from twenty-five to fifty miles for a carriage. He notes that Julius Caesar once traveled eight hundred miles from the Rhone River to Rome in eight days, and Tiberius traveled two hundred miles in twenty-five hours (*Harper's World of the New Testament* [San Francisco: Harper and Row, 1981], 116f.). See also Yamauchi's popular article "On the Road with Paul," *Christian History* 14.3, issue 47 (1995): 17. See further the discussion in chapter 6, under "To Troas."

76. Hemer, "Alexandria Troas," 105.

77. D. W. Burdick, "With Paul in the Troad," *Near East Archaeological Society Bulletin,* n.s., 12 (1978): 31–65.

Photo 7.3. Assos Harbor

implications of leaving his friends in Asia, perhaps permanently (Acts 20:38).[78] Perhaps the raising of Eutychus from the dead when he fell from the window during Paul's lengthy sermon in Troas (Acts 20:9–12) opened more doors for evangelism and required that Paul spend more time there.[79] Paul had been in Troas only briefly on his first visit when he got the Macedonian call to go to Philippi (Acts 16:8–10), and his next visit was cut short by his anxiety over Titus, which did not allow him to take advantage of the "open door" God had provided for him in the city (2 Cor. 2:12). He now had much he wanted to say to this small group of believers during his week with them.

Assos

As Paul drew near Assos on the coast, he approached a mountain on the south of the road that stood high above the harbor below and had on its summit a pagan temple of Athena, the ruins of which still stand majestically on the cliff above the sea. The city (modern Behramkale) stands on a volcanic cone 750 feet above the sea, directly north of the island of Lesbos. It was encompassed by almost two miles of walls, which still stand today in a good state of preservation. They have been described as "the most complete fortifications

78. Edwin Yamauchi, "Assos," *ABD*, 1:503.
79. Bruce, *Paul*, 341.

in the Greek world."[80] Remains of a theater, an agora (marketplace) with two rows of shops, a small agora temple, a senate house, a gymnasium, and a cemetery are still partially preserved.

Assos was not without its claim to fame. Aristotle began work on his treatise *Politics* during a stay here from 347 to 343 B.C. Cleanthes, the Stoic philosopher Paul probably quoted on Mars Hill (Acts 17:28), was born in Assos about 331 B.C.[81]

From the vantage point of the upper city, Paul could see his companions' ship in the picturesque harbor below. Making his way down the narrow southern cliffside road, Paul would have quickly reached the harbor. The modern harbor is in the same location as the one of Paul's day, which probably was not much larger than the present harbor, though it was busier. Only a few hotels, restaurants, and small businesses relating to tourism now stand beside the harbor.

Mitylene

Luke writes that "when he met us in Assos, we took him on board and came to Mitylene," on the east coast of the island of Lesbos (Acts 20:14). At this point, mention should be made of these men with whom Paul was traveling, the men who left Corinth with him and traveled ahead to Troas to await him (Acts 20:4–5). Because of the strained relations Paul had with the church in Corinth, several men from various churches had been with him to pick up the contribution there. They would have been able to help carry the money and also to vouch for its proper use. Paul had been concerned about whether he would be humiliated in their presence by Corinth's response (2 Cor. 9:4).

When he had written to the church in Rome from Corinth, Paul had told the Romans that "all the churches of Christ salute you" (Rom. 16:16). Indeed, representatives from churches in Macedonia and Asia Minor were with him (Acts 20:4–5). The churches in Macedonia were represented by Sopater from Beroea (probably the Sosipater of Romans 16:21)[82] and Aristarchus (cf. Acts 19:29; 27:2; Col. 4:10) and Secundus, both from Thes-

---

80. Ekrem Akurgal, *Ancient Civilizations and Ruins of Turkey,* 7th ed. (Istanbul: Net Turistik Yayinlar A.S., 1990), 64.

81. Paul cited the line "for we are indeed his offspring," which appears in Aratus's *Phaenomena* 1–5, and also in Cleanthes's *Hymn to Zeus* 4, in modified form: "for from thee we are born and above of living things that move on earth are we created in God's image." Thus Paul introduced the quote with a reference to more than one poet: "as even some of your poets have said" (Acts 17:28). See Miltos Anghelatos, *Paul in Athens* (Athens: Hellenic Scripture Union, 1990), 62.

82. Bruce, *Paul,* 382 n. 16.

salonica (Acts 20:4). Churches in Asia were represented by Tychicus (perhaps from Colossae; cf. Eph. 6:21–22; Col. 4:7–8; 2 Tim. 4:12; Titus 3:12) and Trophimus from Ephesus (cf. Acts 21:29; 2 Tim. 4:20). Galatian churches were represented by Gaius of Derbe, who had possibly become a convert of Barnabas and Paul when they first visited Derbe (Acts 14:20–21). Timothy, from the city of Lystra in Galatia, was also in the group (Acts 16:1) but probably not as a representative. He was Paul's longtime colleague in travel.

Luke does not mention a delegate from Corinth, which may reflect the strained relations Paul had with that church.[83] Or it is possible that Corinth had entrusted its contribution to Titus (2 Cor. 8:6–23; 12:18). If so, it is peculiar that Titus is not mentioned in the list of Acts 20:4, which only exacerbates the puzzling nature of the fact that Titus is not mentioned anywhere in Acts. Another possiblity is that Luke himself, who wrote this account, had been entrusted with the contribution and was listing only the other representatives.

Miletus

Leaving Mitylene, the boat sailed south and the next day passed through the channel between the island of Chios and the mainland. Continuing southeastward, Paul and his company sailed beside the mile-long strait of Trogilium[84] and put in briefly on the western shore of Samos, an island just off the coast from Ephesus. The next day they came to Miletus (Acts 20:14–15), a city located thirty miles due south of Ephesus, on the south side of the Gulf of Latmia[85] near the mouth of the Meander River. This entire gulf is now silted up.

Paul had to wait a few days for the ship to sail again from the city, so he took advantage of the opportunity to summon the elders from Ephesus to meet him there. It was a day's journey from Ephesus to Miletus by land, a bit shorter by boat.

As Paul and his companions approached Miletus,[86] they could see a huge theater standing on the coast. This was before the silting process left it standing in the midst of a huge plain, as it does today. Today this theater contains some of the best-preserved hallways among excavated theaters. An inscription

---

83. Bruce, *Book of the Acts,* 382.

84. The Western text (Codex Bezae) and the Byzantine text (Majority texts) of the New Testament mention this promontory at Acts 20:15. Its geographical presence is obvious.

85. Latmia is used in the English translation of Strabo in the Loeb Classical series, but it is called Latmicus (Λατμικός) in the Greek text (*Geogr.* 14.8).

86. See further, John McRay, "Miletus," *ABD,* 4:825–26.

Photo 7.4. Miletus Theater

allocating a section of seats to Jews and "God-fearers" was found here,[87] testifying to a significant Jewish presence in the city.

Strabo, a first-century geographer, says there were four harbors in Miletus during his time, "one of which is large enough for a fleet."[88] Paul undoubtedly would have sailed into the Bay of Lions Harbor,[89] which is named for the lion monuments on either side of the entrance to the harbor. The outline of the bay can still be seen, though it is now silted up for several miles inland, and the two stone-carved lions that guarded it are partially buried in the sediment. The harbor provides a dock adjacent to the marketplace.

87. Adolf Deissmann, "A Jewish Inscription in the Theatre at Miletus," in *Light from the Ancient East* (New York and London: Hodder and Stoughton, 1910), 446ff. The inscription reads ΤΟΠΟΣΕΙΟΥΔΕΩΝΤΩΝΚΑΙΘΕΟΣΕΒΙΟΝ = Τόπος Εἰουδέων τῶν καὶ Θεοσέβιον. B. Schwank corrected Deissmann by pointing out that the inscription was found in the eastern, not western, section of the theater ("Theaterplatze für gottesfürchtigen Milet," *Biblische Zeitschrift* 13.2 [1969]: 262–63); Louis Feldman, "The Omnipresence of the God-Fearers," *BAR* 12.5 (Sept.–Oct. 1986): 58–63; Thomas Finn, "The God-Fearers Reconsidered" *CBQ* 47 (1985): 81; Colin J. Hemer, *BASHH* (the second appendix, by Conrad Gempf, discusses the new inscription of God-fearers in Aphrodisias). In *BAR* 12.2 (March–April 1987): 52f., there is a report on a session on the subject at the 1986 national Society of Biblical Literature meeting, specifically dealing with Thomas Kraabel's position, which advocates that there were not as many God-fearers as commonly thought and that they did not constitute a distinct social class.

88. *Geogr.* 14.6.

89. Richard Stillwell, ed., *Princeton Encyclopedia of Classical Sites* (Princeton, N.J.: Princeton University Press, 1976), 578.

This huge marketplace contains some of the most impressive remains of ancient Miletus. It was divided into several sections, including north, west, and south market areas. Paul would have disembarked from the ship through the sixteen-columned harbor gateway. On his left was the Delphinion, the chief religious center of the city, where Apollo was worshiped. From there he would have entered the processional road that ran through the lovely Ionic stoa (or porch), which was completed around the time Paul was here (in the reign of Claudius, A.D. 41–54). This lovely colonnaded walkway led to the large south market, which was about 150 yards south of the dock.[90]

Paul's meeting with the elders of the church of Ephesus, one of the most touching scenes in the recorded journeys of Paul, occurred somewhere here in Miletus.[91] If there was no church here, and significantly Luke mentions none, Paul would not have had a home in which to meet. But somewhere in this city, perhaps on the beach, Paul spoke to these Ephesian elders about his three-year ministry with them (Acts 20:31).

This is the only speech in the Book of Acts that is addressed to Christians. In it, Paul described the nature of his ministry at Ephesus, in which he served the church with tears, and recalled the plots of the Jews against him. He spoke of working with his own hands to support himself and those with him (Acts 20:34) and of the importance of helping the weak. He reminded them of the words of Jesus (which had been remembered and handed down by tradition outside the New Testament) that "it is more blessed to give than to receive" (Acts 20:35).

Three important aspects of the elders' leadership position are indicated by Luke's use of carefully chosen terminology. He spoke of their age and maturity by calling them "elders" (Acts 20:17), of their supervisory role by calling them "guardians" or "overseers" (ἐπίσκοποι, episkopoi, bishops, Acts 20:28), and of their teaching and nuturing function by charging them to "feed" the church of the Lord (Acts 20:28). The word *feed* is the verb form (ποιμαίνειν, poimainein) of the noun *shepherd* (ποιμήν, poimēn, a word translated *pastor* in Eph. 4:11). He reminded them that they had been given this position of responsibility by the Holy Spirit (Acts 20:28).

At one point, Paul said that the Holy Spirit had testified to him "in every city" that imprisonment and afflictions awaited him (Acts 20:23). Perhaps this was an indication to him that since he had been treated this way in so many cities, he could expect the same in Jerusalem. Later, at Tyre (Acts 21:4), the disciples would tell Paul and the others "through the Spirit" that they should not go to Jerusalem, merely confirming what Paul already knew. And

90. A monumental gate entering the south forum from the north and dating to the second century A.D. was found well preserved by German excavators who disassembled it and transported it to the Pergamon Museum in Berlin, where it has been beautifully reassembled.

91. For a description of the city, see McRay, "Miletus," 825–26.

in Caesarea "the Holy Spirit" would say through Agabus, the prophet who had foretold the famine in Judea (Acts 11:27–28), that in Jerusalem Paul would be bound and delivered over to the Gentiles (Acts 21:10–11). Once more, both the disciples there and Luke's traveling companions as well (Acts 21:12) begged Paul not to go. Again, the prophecy only confirmed what had been testified to Paul in every city (Acts 21:13–14). This was nothing new to him. Seeing Paul's determination to go on to Jerusalem, Luke and the others responded: "The will of the Lord be done."

In this farewell address, Paul told the Ephesian elders that he *knew* all those among whom he had gone "preaching the kingdom" would not see his face again (Acts 20:25). This caused them the most sorrow of anything he had said (Acts 20:38), because he had already predicted his own imprisonment and afflictions in Jerusalem (Acts 20:23). It seems clear that Paul assumed he would not see them again because of these prophecies of imprisonment and perhaps death. He said: "I do not account my life of any value nor as precious to myself, if only I may accomplish my course and the ministry which I received from the Lord Jesus, to testify to the gospel of the grace of God" (Acts 20:24).

But to whom was Paul referring when he spoke of all those among whom he had gone (Acts 20:25)? Was he referring in general to Christians in Asia, to Christians in Ephesus, or just to the elders of Ephesus? Luke and Paul's traveling companions were also present, and perhaps other disciples as well, though this is not stated.

Whomever he was referring to, this verse need not be pressed as a divinely inspired mandate by the Spirit of God that Paul would never be in the eastern part of the empire again. At least two reasons suggest this. First, in the context Paul is *assuming* that he will not see again those to whom he refers because the prophecies "in every city" testified to his afflictions (Acts 20:23). Second, when Paul said "I know" you will not see me again (Acts 20:25), he used the Greek word οἶδα (*oida*) in the perfect tense rather than γινώσκω (*ginōskō*) in the present. The former word strictly means "I have acquired the knowledge of"[92] and probably reflects the conclusion he had reached because of these prophecies. The meaning of his statement is "I am confident (on the basis of what I perceive) that you will not see me again."

But Paul's assumption was not God's mandate. God's mandate was that he would suffer affliction and imprisonment. This came to pass. Paul's assumption was that he would never see them again. This did not come to pass. On the contrary, after his first imprisonment in Rome, Paul would be released and come back into this area again. Whether he saw these particular elders again is impossible to say, but he certainly was with Luke and Tychicus again (2 Tim. 4:11–12), both of whom were with him in Miletus, and he again vis-

---

92. C. F. D. Moule, *An Idiom Book of New Testament Greek* (Cambridge: Cambridge University Press, 1953), 16.

Photo 7.5. Cos Harbor

ited many Christians of Asia (Phil. 1:26–27; 2:24; 1 Tim. 1:3; Titus 1:5; 2 Tim. 4:9–16). Therefore, this verse (Acts 20:25) cannot be used to prove that Paul never returned to the eastern Mediterranean again.

Cos, Rhodes, and Patara

Leaving Miletus, Paul and his party sailed south to the city of Cos, on the northeastern shore of the island of the same name. Cos lies west of Halicarnassus (modern Bodrum). Here they spent the night (Acts 21:1), probably putting in at the lovely harbor of the city of Cos, which faced the northeast. Cos was famous for its Asklepium, where healing was practiced in the context of pagan worship, as it was in the Asklepium in Corinth and Epidarus. Hippocrates, the father of medicine, who lived in the early fourth century B.C., founded a medical school here and died here at the age of 104. Luke, the beloved physician (Col. 4:14), probably appreciated this stop more than the others. Physicians today still take the Hippocratic oath when receiving their medical degrees.

The next morning they sailed to the city of Rhodes, on the northern promontory of the island of Rhodes. Upon entering the harbor, they would have seen the remains of the Colossus of Helius, which Strabo, in the first century, called "one of the Seven Wonders" of the ancient world.[93] It was a huge bronze moument that had stood more than a hundred feet in height when it was built between 304 and 284 B.C. but had been broken down at the knees

93. *Geogr.* 14.2.5.

Photo 7.6. Rhodes Harbor

by an earthquake in 225 B.C. Strabo said of Rhodes that "it is so far superior to all others in harbors and roads and walls and improvements in general that I am unable to speak of any other city as equal to it, or even as almost equal to it, much less superior to it."[94] There is a tradition in Rhodes that Paul went ashore here and converted many people, but Acts gives no indication that the boat spent the night here.

From Rhodes the ship sailed east to the port at Patara, which lay on the west side of the Lycian peninsula jutting out of the southwest coast of Asia Minor (Turkey). Here Paul and his company had to change boats. The boat on which they were sailing was evidently a coast hopper that was scheduled to continue eastward along the Turkish coast to Attalia or Antioch.

Paul would later have to make the same changes in reverse when he traveled back along this coast on the way to Rome from Caesarea in a boat headed for Adramyttium on the northwestern coast of Asia (near Assos). Luke says the boat on this later voyage was "about to sail to the ports along the coast of Asia" (Acts 27:1–2). When they got to Myra, they changed ships and boarded a vessel from Alexandria that was sailing to Italy (Acts 27:5–6). The ports at Patara and Myra were both used by the Alexandrian corn fleet, which fed much of the Mediterranean world at that time.

This is pertinent to Luke's continuing story of Paul's journey to Jerusalem in Acts 21, because some Greek texts of Acts say that Paul's group did not change ships at Patara but went on another fifty miles east, changing at Myra, on the other side of the same Lycian peninsula.[95] These later Greek texts probably added Myra in Acts 21:1 because of Acts 27:5.

94. Ibid.
95. The Western text of Codex Bezae supports this reading, as probably does an eighth-century manuscript, $\mathfrak{P}^{41}$. According to some ancient manuscripts, the text reads "Patara and Myra." See Bruce Metzger, *A Textual Commentary on the Greek New Testament*, 2d ed. (Stuttgart: German Bible Society, 1994), 427.

Photo 7.7. Patara Coastline

Patara was the port for the city of Xanthus, which lay twelve miles north on the east bank of the Xanthus River. From the ruins of its unexcavated theater, I observed the familiar pattern of a harbor now completely silted in, with remains of a Roman bath and a monumental triple-arched gate leading into the city. Current excavations are revealing huge decorated stone coffins (sarcophagi) lining the road near the gate. A famous temple and oracle of the Lycian god Apollo once stood here. From the top of the theater, one can gaze across miles of abandonded beaches and desolate alluvial plains where nothing suggests that the great Christian apostle ever passed through.

Tyre

Paul's party boarded a vessel headed for Phoenicia and sailed for the city of Tyre. In contrast to the smaller coast hoppers, this would probably have been a large merchant ship. It took advantage of the strong winds from the west at this time of year (Pentecost—spring and summer) and sailed south of the island of Cyprus directly for Tyre. Luke gives no indication of the time involved, but it was a voyage of two days with favorable winds[96] or from five[97] to seven days in the opposite direction with con-

96. Meinardus, *St. Paul's Last Journey,* 15.
97. So Chrysostom reckoned it (*Hom. Act.* 45).

trary winds.[98] On Paul's later journey in the opposite direction, Luke says his ship sailed "under the lee of Cyprus [i.e., on the north side of the island], because the winds were against us" (Acts 27:4).

Luke gives the destination of the vessel as both Phoenicia (Acts 21:2) and Syria (Acts 21:3). Phoenicia is the name of a geographical region that extends north from Acco (modern Haifa) along the coast of Palestine. It was not a country or nation.[99] Syria was a large country to the east of Phoenicia that became a Roman province in 64 B.C. In Paul's time Phoenicia was administratively a part of Syria. Syria and Palestine were actually administered as separate provinces, the exact relationship of the one to the other being a matter of current scholarly dispute.[100]

The vessel docked at Tyre to unload its cargo (Acts 21:3). In the time of Paul, this city was a commercial center from which Phoenician glass and purple goods were exported. The name *Phoenicia* means purple or crimson;[101] this region was famous for dyes produced here.[102] Imports included grain from Egypt but also from the Black Sea region. This may have been the cargo on Paul's vessel coming from the north. Wine was also imported from the Greek islands.

Roman remains have been found beneath the impressive ruins from the Byzantine period. Although none of these date to the period of the New Testament itself, there are remains from the second century A.D., including a monumental arch, which has been partially restored. Beyond the arch, the excavators found a Roman road beneath the Byzantine pavement. Just outside Tyre, as was typical at other Roman cities, the road was lined with tombs. This was also the case at Patara and is true of the Appian Way at Rome. Excavation of the necropolis has produced scores of beautiful marble sarcophagi with carved inscriptions.

Paul and his party sought out "the disciples" in Tyre and spent seven days with them before boarding the ship again (Acts 21:4, 6). The church in Tyre was probably founded by the early disciples from Jerusalem whom Paul himself had previously scattered "as far as Phoenicia" during the persecution that arose over Stephen (Acts 11:19). Paul and Barnabas had probably visited the Christians here earlier, when they traveled through Phoenicia and Samaria on their way from Antioch to the Jerusalem Conference (Acts 15:3).

98. Lucian, in the second century, gives seven days for the voyage from Sidon (near Tyre) to the Lycian Coast (*Nav.* 7).

99. See the extensive article on Phoenicia in *ABD,* 5:349–57.

100. Robyn Tracey finds it diffcult to show "any formal, legal relationship between the two" ("Syria," in *The Book of Acts in Its Graeco-Roman Setting,* ed. Gill and Gempf, 257). See chapter 1 for a discussion of the relation of Cilicia to Syria after 25 B.C.

101. M. C. Astour, "The Origin of the Terms Canaan, Phoenician and Purple," *JNES* 24 (1965): 346–50.

102. J. B. Jensen, "Royal Purple of Tyre," *JNES* 22 (1963): 104–18. See the bibliography in I. Irving Ziderman, "Seashells and Ancient Purple Dyeing," *BA* 53.2 (June 1990): 98–101.

Photo 7.8. Tyre Harbor

The apocryphal *Acts of Paul* records a visit of Paul to Tyre during which Jews came out to meet him and heard him preach. He cast out demons, and when "the crowd saw these things, in the power of God they praised him. . . ."[103] This work dates before the third century but is fragmentary at this point, and which particular visit of Paul to Tyre is described cannot be determined.[104]

While Paul was in Tyre, prophets among the disciples told him not to go to Jerusalem, as we discussed above. But Paul was determined to complete his ministry by taking the contribution to Jerusalem. When the week was ended, the disciples accompanied him and his companions to the beach, where they knelt, prayed, and said goodbye (Acts 21:5). Then the ship sailed for Ptolemais (Acts 21:7).

Ptolemais

Ptolemais lies on the northern end of the Bay of Haifa and is known today as Acco, as it was in its only Old Testament occurrence (Judg. 1:31).[105] The

103. *Acts of Paul* 6 in J. K. Elliott, *The Apocryphal New Testament* (Oxford: Clarendon, 1993), 376.
104. The *Acts of Paul* is first cited by name in the writings of Origen, *Princ.* 1.2.3. Eusebius discusses its relation to the New Testament canon (*Hist. eccl.* 3.3.5), and Jerome rejects its orthodoxy (*Vir. ill.* 7).
105. In Crusader times, the eleventh and twelfth centuries A.D., it was called Acre.

Photo 7.9. Acco Harbor at Ptolemais

city's importance was due in large measure to its location. It was on a bay at the juncture of the coastal highway and the road leading northeast through Galilee to Damascus and on northward to Antioch of Syria. Paul and his companions spent one day with the church here, but we know nothing of the church's origin or composition; this is the only place Ptolemais is mentioned in the New Testament.

Caesarea Maritima

The journey continued the next day to Caesarea Maritima (Acts 21:8), but we are not told whether they went by land or sea. Caesarea served for three centuries as the base of Roman political activity in Palestine. At least two of the Roman legions, the Tenth Fretensis and the Sixth Ferrata, were stationed here. An inscription on the high-level aqueduct still bears witness to the Tenth Legion's presence. The procurators Felix and Festus (Acts 23:26; 24:27) had their headquarters in this city. Pontius Pilate, who delivered Jesus for crucifixion, had lived here earlier. An inscription bearing his name was found in the theater. Cornelius, the Roman centurion and first Gentile convert in Palestine, was stationed here (Acts 10:1) as well.

My decade of excavation here (1972–83) was personally rewarding in many ways. Because of the ongoing excavations, we are able to provide a partial description of the expansive ancient city, which covered about 165 acres

Photo 7.10. Caesarea Harbor Seen from the Temple of Augustus

in Paul's time.[106] Whether Paul arrived here from Ptolemais by sea or by land, he would have been impressed almost immediately by the Herodian harbor. He could see the lovely theater south of the harbor, standing adjacent to the palace of Herod the Great. Roman temples stood to the east of the harbor, an aqueduct stretched to the north, and warehouses lay to the east and south.

Herod's harbor, which Josephus says was larger than the harbor of Athens at Piraeus,[107] was the first artificial harbor in the ancient world and was built with the latest technology available at the time. This was the first extensive use of newly developed hydraulic concrete in the eastern Mediterranean.[108]

Underwater excavation has shown that Josephus's description of the design and size of Caesarea Maritima's harbor is substantially accurate.[109] Beneath the currently visible small Crusader harbor lie the underwater remains of the much larger Herodian harbor. It was formed by two breakwaters extending 1,500 feet into the water, the northern one being 150 feet wide and the south-

106. For a fuller description of the archaeological excavations, see McRay, *Archaeology and the New Testament,* 139–45.

107. *J. W.* 1.410.

108. This cement, the first-century architect Vitruvius says, was made from pozzolana, a volcanic sand that hardens under water (*On Architecture* 2.6.1). A major quarry for it can be seen on the Greek island of Santorini.

109. Described in *J. W.* 1.408–15. For a beautiful color presentation of the site, including the harbor, see Kenneth Holum et al., *King Herod's Dream: Caesarea on the Sea* (New York: Norton, 1988).

Photo 7.11. Caesarea Harbor Seen from the Sea

ern one 200 feet wide. At the northwest area where the two met, there was a 60-foot-wide entrance. An inner quay not mentioned by Josephus has been found extending 500 feet into the vaulted warehouse section inside the modern Crusader fort. Portions of two loading docks have been located. There can be no doubt that this harbor was the center of extensive trade between the east and the west and that Herod was able to finance his building projects partially through this business.

Clear evidence of the extensive shipping tonnage passing through the city came to light in 1973 with the discovery of many huge vaults stretching along the coast from inside the present Crusader fort south to the theater. These are warehouses rebuilt in later times on Herodian foundations.

To meet the needs of his new city, Herod built an aqueduct, partially on the ground and partially on arches above the ground, to bring water to the city from beyond Mount Carmel to the east. The aqueduct reaches an elevation of around twenty feet along the coast. Portions of it may still be seen with its clay pipe set in concrete.

Josephus mentioned a theater Herod built at Caesarea,[110] which is the one standing on the southern coast. The reconstructed cavea (seating area), measuring about three hundred feet in diameter, seats approximately four thousand people.

110. *J.W.* 1.415.

By excavating beneath the circular towers in the north wall around Caesarea, we have determined that the wall dates to Herod's city. A major street passed through these gates on the way to the heart of the city, and we are now able to reconstruct the street system of Caesarea, having found evidence of several other streets in the excavations. Herodian foundations were found beneath the eastern extensions of these walls.

Paul and his companions had been successful enough in their efforts to reach Jerusalem by Pentecost that they still had a few days to spare. They spent this time with the church in Caesarea, hosted by Philip the evangelist and his four unmarried daughters, who were prophetesses (Acts 21:8). There were other disciples in Caesarea as well (Acts 21:16), the church having been founded there earlier by Peter (Acts 10:44–48).

Paul and Philip would have had much in common, because Philip had also been extensively involved in taking the gospel beyond the borders of mainline Judaism. He had served as one of seven leaders in the Hellenist church in Jerusalem (Acts 6:5), broken new ground in converting Samaritans (Acts 8:5; half-Jews whose access to the gospel Jesus had forbidden prior to his resurrection, Matt. 10:5), converted the Ethiopian nobleman (a proselyte to Judaism, Acts 8:26–39), and now lived and worked in Caesarea, where the first Gentile convert had been made (Acts 10:1–48). Indeed, Paul and Philip had much to discuss.

Paul was now among brothers and sisters who were very much at the heart of a ministry like his own. The leaders of the Jerusalem church had sent Peter and John to investigate Philip's activities in Samaria and had approved his work among the Samaritans (Acts 8:14–25), as they had later approved Peter's work among the Gentiles of Cornelius's house here in Caesarea (Acts 11:1–18).

Eventually Philip and his daughters left Caesarea and moved to Hierapolis in Phrygia, where they finished their ministries, died, and were buried.[111] But while Paul was in Caesarea, he had a visit from a Jerusalem prophet named Agabus, who dramatically foretold Paul's arrest in Jerusalem (Acts 21:10–11), just as in Antioch he had earlier prophesied the famine in Jerusalem (Acts 11:27–28). When Luke (note the use of "we" in Acts 21:12) and the other disciples heard it, they begged Paul not to go, but he replied, "What are you doing, weeping and breaking my heart? For I am ready not only to be impris-

111. Eusebius (*Hist. eccl.* 3.31.2–5) records this using excerpts from Polycrates of Ephesus and Proclus in his dialogue of Gaius. There is a bit of confusion in the two stories as to which Philip is intended, but Proclus's mention of the four daughters as prophetesses leaves no doubt that it is this Philip and not one of the twelve apostles, though Polycrates's comment is unclear. In this passage, Eusebius says Polycrates, in Ephesus, wrote to Victor, bishop of Rome about A.D. 195: "Philip, one of the 12 apostles, who has fallen asleep in Hierapolis, as have also his two daughters who grew old in virginity, and his other daughter who lived in the Holy Spirit and rests at Ephesus. . . ."

Photo 7.12. Temple Mount in Jerusalem

oned but even to die at Jerusalem for the name of the Lord Jesus" (Acts 21:13). No one who traveled with Paul doubted that he meant what he said. He did not serve God for the loaves and fish but rather, as he later wrote, because of the "surpassing worth of knowing Christ Jesus my Lord. For his sake I have suffered the loss of all things, and count them as refuse, in order that I may gain Christ" (Phil. 3:8).

Jerusalem

Paul traveled on to Jerusalem, a distance of about sixty miles, accompanied by some of the disciples from Caesarea (Acts 21:16).[112] The trip on foot would normally take a minimum of three days, since twenty miles a day was customary on good roads. It would be easier and faster by horseback, perhaps requiring two days.[113]

In Jerusalem, Paul was hosted by Mnason of Cyprus. His name is Greek, perhaps a hellenized form of the Hebrew Manasseh. Luke's identifying him as a disciple "from the beginning" (ἀρχαίῳ μαθητῇ, *archaiō*

112. He traveled on one of the roads discussed near the end of chapter 6.

113. William Ramsay argues, somewhat questionably on unclear grammatical grounds, that Paul traveled on horseback (*St. Paul the Traveller,* 302). See the analysis of this argument by F. F. Bruce, *The Acts of the Apostles: The Greek Text with Introduction and Commentary,* 3d rev. ed. (Grand Rapids: Eerdmans, 1990), 443. Bruce thinks on other grounds that the use of mules was likely.

mathētē, Acts 21:16) may mean he was one of the very early converts in Jerusalem more than twenty years earlier. It is unlikely that he had been converted on Cyprus during Paul and Barnabas's first journey, which was only about seven years earlier. The housing arrangements[114] had been made in advance (Acts 21:16), since it was important to find someone in the Jerusalem area who would be willing to house such a large number of Gentile Christians. Counting Luke and Paul, there were at least nine of them (Acts 20:4–5).

In order to appreciate what happened next, it is necessary to remember that Paul and his eight or more traveling companions were carrying a sizeable contribution from Gentile churches all over Macedonia, Greece, and Asia Minor. They were bringing this gift to help Jewish Christian brothers and sisters in Jerusalem who were in desperate need. Paul, as we previously noted, considered this contribution to be a sacrifice of priestly service he was offering on behalf of his Gentile churches. The validity of his entire ministry was at stake. Paul felt it extremely important for the Gentiles to give this offering, even though they were in need themselves (2 Cor. 8:3), and the Gentiles had indeed "begged" Paul to let them share in it, even at such a cost (2 Cor. 8:4). He felt it equally important that the Jewish Christian leaders in Jerusalem accept the gift, even though it was humbling to do so, in order to publicly acknowledge their endorsement of his Gentile mission.

Paul had been working on the collection for more than a year (2 Cor. 8:10; 9:2). He had been hurrying to Jerusalem to be there by Pentecost so that the gift could be presented in an appropriate, festive setting when the city was crowded with Jewish Christians who had come for the holidays. With this in mind and with arrangements made in advance for the meeting (all the elders were present with James, Acts 21:18), we can only imagine the state of anticipation that must have existed in Paul's group.

A reflection of this must be seen in the way Luke records their entrance into the meeting. He says "Paul went in with us" rather than "we went in with Paul" (Acts 21:18). What excitement, what joy, and what tension! Paul was earlier apprehensive about how this might turn out. He had written the Roman Christians from Corinth before leaving on this momentous trip, asking them to pray "that my service for Jerusalem may be acceptable to the saints" (Rom. 15:31).

But incredibly, after all this preparation and concern over the contribution, there is not one word in Acts about its presentation by Paul or its reception by the Jerusalem leaders. Luke's account passes over it in total silence. We can only conjecture as to the reasons. It has been argued that Luke omitted it because it was refused by the Jewish brothers and proved to be the embarassment

114. See H. J. Cadbury, "Lexical Notes on Luke-Acts, III. Luke's Interest in Lodging," *JBL* 45 (1926): 305–22.

Paul had feared.[115] According to this view, Paul had earlier told Luke what he wrote to the Romans, that the rejection of his ministry by the Jewish Christians in the east had prevented his doing any further work there, and so he was going to move west toward Rome and Spain. This is based on Paul's comment in Romans 15:23, where he said "I no longer have any room for work in these regions."[116]

However, Paul was referring not to Jewish opposition in this statement but to the method of his ministry enunciated in Romans 15:20: "to preach the gospel, not where Christ has already been named, lest I build on another man's foundation." Since he had already preached throughout the east, from Jerusalem to Illyricum (Rom. 15:19), he had planned to go on to Rome and Spain before he ever got to Jerusalem with the contribution.

It seems more likely that Luke omitted the story because, though the contribution was accepted with gratitude,[117] the greater concern at the time was not whether the Jerusalem church approved Paul's work among Gentiles (which it had already done at the conference years earlier, Acts 15) but whether Paul approved the Jerusalem church's work among Jews who became Christians but continued to keep the law of Moses.

This is evident in the fact that after Paul related one by one the things he had done among the Gentiles through his ministry, the Jerusalem leaders "glorified God" (Acts 21:20). Their reaction to Paul's report of his ministry was clearly favorable. The issue that was most pressing at this point was raised by a report the Jerusalem church had received that Paul was requiring Jewish converts to Christ to forsake the law of Moses, telling them not to circumcize their children or keep the Jewish customs (Acts 21:21). Many of these Jewish Christians,[118] indeed thousands of them (Acts 21:20), were "zealots for the law." Paul's attitude toward the law was a critical issue for them.

I will discuss the issue further in chapter 15 on Paul's view of the law, but suffice it here to say that Paul emphatically denied the truthfulness of that report and willingly acquiesced to James's request that he prove the point by pu-

115. "The biggest shock to Luke was the refusal of the Jerusalem church to accept Paul's collection, thereby symbolizing their break with the Pauline mission" (A. J. Mattill, "The Purpose of Acts Reconsidered: Schneckenburger Reconsidered," in *Apostolic History and the Gospel: Biblical and Historical Essays Presented to F. F. Bruce on His 60th Birthday,* ed. W. Ward Gasque and R. P. Martin [Grand Rapids: Eerdmans, 1970], 116).

116. Mattill, "Purpose of Acts Reconsidered."

117. Keith Nickle feels that "it may be confidently conjectured that the collection was well received" (*The Collection: A Study in Paul's Strategy,* Studies in Biblical Theology 48 [Naperville, Ill.: Allenson, 1966], 70).

118. It has been argued that the phrase "of those who have believed" (Acts 21:20) is Luke's added comment to James's actual words and that James was actually speaking of Jews in Jerusalem who had not accepted Christianity but were affiliated with the church for political reasons (Johannes Munck, *Paul and the Salvation of Mankind,* trans. Frank Clarke [Atlanta: John Knox, 1977], 240ff.).

rifying himself in the temple and paying for the sacrifices of four Jews in the temple who were completing a vow. If these were regular Nazirite vows, they lasted thirty days if no other time was specified, according to the Talmud.[119] At the end of that time, the participant went through a process of purification; cut his hair, which he had left uncut along with abstaining from wine; and offered a sacrifice in the temple, which included the burning of his severed hair. Years earlier Paul had cut his hair in Cenchreae at the close of a personal vow and had probably brought it to Jerusalem as an offering (Acts 18:18).[120] He had no objection to taking Jewish vows.

The offerings required were expensive (Num. 6:14), and it was especially difficult for a poor person to take such a vow. It was not uncommon for a wealthy person to help the poor in such cases, making it possible for them to perform their religious duty. Josephus tells of Herod Agrippa I financing the expenses of Nazirites on occasion in order to win popularity.[121] But where would Paul get the money to finance four such vows? He was just returning from a three-year ministry in Ephesus in which he worked to support himself and his coworkers. "These hands ministered to my necessities, and to those who were with me," he reminded the Ephesian elders at Miletus (Acts 20:34). Perhaps the Jerusalem leaders felt the matter important enough to use some of the contribution Paul had brought them for this purpose, or maybe Paul himself suggested it.

Another possibility is that the four men had experienced some kind of defilement during the period of the vow and, according to the law, had to purify themselves and delay their sacrifice for a week (Num. 6:9–11)[122] before they shaved their heads and made their offering. In this case the week delay involved only the further offering of "two turtledoves or two young pigeons to the priest" and would not be too expensive. Perhaps Paul involved himself only in this requirement ("when the seven days were almost completed," Acts 21:27) and incurred a correspondingly lesser expense. The result would have been the same, that is, his public approval of and sharing in the performance of Jewish vows.

Paul satisfied the Jewish Christian leadership in Jerusalem by his acquiescence to their request, but while he was in the temple for this purification ceremony, he ran afoul of Asian Jews who were in the city for Pentecost and as a result experienced the fulfillment of the prophecies about his affliction and imprisonment (Acts 20:23). These Jews had apparently seen Paul in Asia and knew of his work there among Gentiles. They accused Paul of taking Trophi-

119. See *m. Nazir* 1.3; 5.3; 6.3.
120. See the discussion of that vow at the end of chapter 6.
121. *Ant.* 19.294.
122. See *m. Nazir* 6.6.

Photo 7.13. Model of Herod's Temple in Jerusalem

mus the Ephesian, who was also from Asia, into the area of the temple forbidden to non-Jews and immediately tried to kill Paul (Acts 21:28, 31).

The temple building, which contained the Holy Place and the Most Holy Place, was situated within the inner Court of Israel and was accessible only to Jewish men. In front of it, and separated by the Nicanor Gate, was the Court of the Women. This entire complex was in turn situated within the parameters of a small partition wall called the balustrade. Outside this, the rest of the temple mount area consisted of a huge stone platform, called the Court of the Gentiles, into which Gentiles could come and worship the God of Israel. This is the area Jesus had cleansed during his last week in Jerusalem, impressing on those present the words of the prophets: "These I will bring to my holy mountain, and make them joyful in my house of prayer; their burnt offerings and their sacrifices will be accepted on my altar; for my house shall be called a house of prayer for all peoples" (Isa. 56:7; Mark 11:17).

Josephus described the little wall separating the Gentiles from the Jews. The Jewish portion was "surrounded by a stone balustrade with an inscription prohibiting the entrance of a foreigner under threat of the penalty of death."[123] The Jews were allowed by the Romans to put to death anyone who crossed this boundary wall, even Roman citizens.[124] Josephus further said the

123. *Ant.* 15.417.
124. *J.W.* 6.125–26.

wall was three cubits (four and one-half feet) high,[125] and at "regular intervals stood slabs giving warning, some in Greek and others in Latin characters,[126] of the law of purification, to wit that no foreigner was permitted to enter the holy place. . . ."[127]

Two of these stone slabs containing the inscriptions described by Josephus have been found and published.[128] The text was republished with further analysis and current bibliography.[129]

> μηθένα ἀλλογενῆ εἰσπορεύεσθαι
> ἐντὸς τοῦ περὶ τὸ ἱερὸν
> τρυφάκτου καὶ περιβόλου. ὃς
> δ᾿ ἂν ληφθῇ ἑαυτῷ αἴτιος ἔσται
> διὰ τὸ ἐξακολουθεῖν θάνατον

> No foreigner is to enter within
> the forecourt and the balustrade
> around the sanctuary. Whoever is
> caught will have himself to blame
> for his subsequent death.

Paul was rescued by Roman guards from the Antonia Fortress, which was a large four-towered garrison[130] standing adjacent to the northwest corner of the Court of the Gentiles. The southeast tower "commanded a view of the whole Temple area,"[131] and from it the guards had observed Paul's predicament. He was allowed to address his Jewish assailants from one of the two stairways that Josephus says led down to the north and west colonnaded porches surrounding the court (Acts 21:35, 40).

The Roman tribune was surprised to learn that Paul spoke Greek, for he had assumed him to be an Egyptian radical (Acts 21:37–38) who had recently led four thousand assassins (Josephus says "about thirty thousand")[132] out of the desert to the Mount of Olives, where they had prepared to attack Jerusalem. They were defeated by the procurator Felix with the Roman heavy infantry. In a matter of days, Paul himself would stand before Felix in Caesarea (Acts 24:1–2).

125. The Mishnah says it was ten handbreadths high, i.e., 2 1/2 feet (*Middot* 2.3).
126. "Engraved in Greek characters and in our own" (*J.W.* 6.125).
127. *J.W.* 5.194.
128. See Jack Finegan, *ANT:LJ*, 197.
129. Peretz Segal, "The Penalty of the Warning Inscription from the Temple in Jerusalem," *IEJ* 39.1–2 (1989): 79–84.
130. *J.W.* 5.242. See the description of the Antonia in Brian Rapske, *The Book of Acts and Paul in Roman Custody*, BAFCS 3 (Grand Rapids: Eerdmans, 1994), 137f.
131. *J.W.* 5.242–43.
132. Ibid., 2.261–63.

The Egyptian, with a few of his followers, had escaped Felix, and under-standably, the tribune, Claudius Lysias, initially assumed Paul was this very Egyptian. But when Paul corrected this mistake, informing the tribune that he was in fact "a Jew, from Tarsus in Cilicia, a citizen of no ordinary city" (Acts 21:39 NIV), the tribune allowed him to speak to the mob. Paul's speech on this occasion contains the second of three accounts (Acts 9, 22, 26) of his conversion experience and call and is the most Jewish oriented of them all.

Paul spoke to the people in their Aramaic vernacular (Acts 22:2), normally called Hebrew in the New Testament. This caused them to listen more atten-tively, and Luke preserved highlights of the speech that emphasized to this Jewish audience the important elements in Paul's Jewish background: his education in Jerusalem under the great rabbi Gamaliel according to the strict manner of the law of their fathers (Acts 22:3); his initial persecution of the church (Acts 22:5); his baptism by Ananias, whom Paul called "a devout man according to the law" (Acts 22:12, 16); and the appearance of Christ to him later in the temple itself, confirm-ing his conversion/call and sending him to the Gentiles (Acts 22:17–21).

The Jews listened intently to Paul "up to this word" (Acts 22:22), the word *Gentile.* Then they became highly agitated, crying out, waving their garments, and throwing dust into the air (Acts 22:23). This was the word that had triggered the mob frenzy to begin with. Paul, they thought, had taken a Gentile into the forbid-den zone. In his Gospel, Luke had previously recorded an identical reaction to Jesus that parallels Paul's experience here in Acts. It happened when Jesus spoke in the synagogue in Nazareth and so impressed the congregation that "all spoke well of him, and wondered at the gracious words which proceeded out of his mouth" (Luke 4:22), even when he implied that the Scripture of Isaiah was being fulfilled by him that very day (Luke 4:21). It seems that no one had a problem with that, but when Jesus continued speaking and applied the Scripture to the Gentiles, they were "filled with wrath" and tried to kill him (Luke 4:28–29).

The truth is that Paul had not taken Trophimus into the Jewish courts. If this had actually happened, it was a capital offense, and priests and Levites were authorized by Roman authority to carry out the punishment. The tri-bune was not concerned with this but rather commanded that Paul be "exam-ined by scourging, to find out why they shouted thus against him" (Acts 22:24). When Paul revealed that he was a Roman citizen by birth (Acts 22:28), not just a citizen of Tarsus, which he had already made known to the tribune (Acts 21:39), he was immediately exempted from the whipping, and the trembling officials realized that they had already committed a crime them-selves by binding an untried and uncondemned citizen of Rome. For this they could be severely punished.[133]

---

133. On the importance of citizenship in such matters, see P. Garnsey, "Legal Privilege in the Roman Empire," in *Studies in Ancient Society,* ed. M. I. Finley, Past and Present Series 2 (London and Boston: Routledge and Kegan Paul, 1974). Also Rapske, *Paul in Roman Custody,* 47ff.

The tribune still needed to determine Paul's identity and the nature of his crime (as he had earlier inquired, Acts 21:33). It may be asked why Paul did not reveal his citizenship earlier. The answer is that Paul was making every effort, at the request of the Jerusalem leaders, to align himself with them as a zealous Jew. In this temple conflict, where the terms *Jewish* and *Roman* were viewed as antithetical, publicly identifying himself as a Roman citizen would have been counterproductive. It was the last thing Paul would have wanted to do. He told the crowd publicly in Aramaic that he was a zealous Jew, but only in Greek did he privately inform the tribune that he was a citizen of Tarsus, and only in the exclusively Roman context of the Antonia Fortress did Paul mention his Roman citizenship.

The next day Lysias took Paul before the Jewish supreme court, the Sanhedrin, which had jurisdiction in cases involving the violation of the sanctity of the temple. Paul considered himself to be on trial by the Jews (Acts 23:3, 6; cf. 24:21) although Lysias did not consider the meeting to be a trial (Acts 22:30; 23:28).[134] Standing before the high priest Ananias, a man of questionable reputation,[135] Paul declared himself to be at that time, long after his conversion, "a Pharisee, a son of Pharisees" (Acts 23:6), and insisted that he had "lived before God in all good conscience up to this day" (Acts 23:1). Paul had not been living with a guilty conscience prior to his conversion! He had told the Corinthians, "I am not aware of anything against myself, but I am not thereby acquitted. It is the Lord who judges me" (1 Cor. 4:4).

Ananias responded by having Paul slapped, perhaps because he was incensed by Paul's claim,[136] whereupon Paul rebuked him, probably assuming that no true high priest would have had him slapped contrary to the law (Acts 23:3). The law protected the innocent until proven guilty. Why Paul did not recognize Ananias as the high priest is not stated. Some have suggested it may have been because of a problem with his vision,[137] but this is purely conjectural. Others have wondered whether Paul actually saw who had commanded the action because there were many present and Paul may not have been looking at Ananias. Or it may rather have been that Paul had been in Jerusalem so infrequently since his conversion that he would not have known Ananias by sight,[138] since Ananias was not appointed high priest until A.D. 47 or 48, the years of Paul's first missionary journey. He served in that office till A.D. 58.

134. For the intricacies of Paul's custody in the Antonia, see Rapske's excellent discussion in *Paul in Roman Custody,* 135–49.

135. Josephus tells of Ananias's having commandeered tithes that belonged to the priests (*Ant.* 20.205–7). He was murdered by Zealots in A.D. 66 in the first revolt against Rome, while hiding out in the palace (*J.W.* 2.441).

136. So Bruce, *Book of the Acts,* 425.

137. Supported by his comment to the Galatians that "if possible, you would have plucked out your eyes and given them to me" (Gal. 4:15).

138. Such is Bruce's opinion (*Book of the Acts,* 427).

Paul used his affiliation with the Pharisees to further advantage by crying out in the council that he was being tried for his belief in the resurrection of the dead (Acts 23:6–7). This immediately pitted the Pharisees against the Sadducees and created violent dissension in the council. It was a brilliant strategy on Paul's part. When this happened, the tribune, who had kept his soldiers out of the council proceedings, sent them down to rescue Paul for fear he would be torn in pieces by the violence (Acts 23:10). He was taken back to the Antonia, where he enjoyed relatively pleasant confinement as a Roman citizen, having been immediately released from his chains earlier when he declared his Roman citizenship (Acts 22:29). The soldiers' fear over having bound a citizen would have precipitated the immediate removal of chains.[139]

That night the Lord appeared to Paul, probably in a dream or vision, and reassured him that all the prophecies about his affliction and imprisonment were not yet fulfilled. He must bear witness also in Rome (Acts 23:11). The very next day, God providentially began to bring this about with the visit of Paul's nephew to the fortress. Paul's sister was possibly a resident of Jerusalem, or perhaps her son had been sent to Jerusalem, like Paul in his youth, for further education.

Paul's nephew had somehow learned of a plot on Paul's life by more than forty Jews who had the approval of the chief priests and elders (Acts 23:12–15), and came to warn him about it. His access to Paul in confinement can be explained by Paul's status as an untried Roman citizen and by the boy's youth, which posed no threat to prison security. Luke calls him a "young man" (νεανίας, *neanias,* Acts 23:17), a term that normally refers to one between the ages twenty-four and forty.[140] However, Luke also twice used the diminutive form of this word (νεανίσκος, *neaniskos,* Acts 23:18, 22) in referring to him, and this coupled with the fact that the guard "took him by the hand" (Acts 23:19) and led him to Paul makes it clear that he was just a child. When his nephew informed Paul of the plot, Paul gave the information to the centurion guarding him, who then took the young man to the commander of the barracks in the Antonia Fortress. When the commander heard of the planned assassination, he immediately arranged to have Paul taken under heavy guard to Caesarea Maritima, where as a Roman citizen he would fall under the authority and protection of the Roman governor.

---

139. See further Rapske, *Paul in Roman Custody,* 146ff.
140. BAGD, 534.

EIGHT

The Voyage to Rome, Later Travels, and Death

Paul before Felix

The tribune, Claudius Lysias, having already illegally bound Paul in Jerusalem, could not afford to have the responsibility for the assassination of a Roman citizen under his charge, so he immediately dispatched almost five hundred soldiers to take Paul to Caesarea, where he would be the responsibility of the procurator Felix (Acts 23:23–24). Lysias sent a letter with Paul, pointing out that he had committed no crime against Roman law and had done nothing deserving imprisonment or death. He said Paul was in danger only because he was accused of questions about Jewish law.

Under cover of night (after 9 P.M., Acts 23:23), the soldiers took Paul via Antipatris to Caesarea, sixty miles away.[1] The hasty departure was implemented by the provision of mounts for Paul,[2] to make the trip faster. They spent the rest of the night in Antipatris,[3] which was about halfway to Caesarea (twenty-six miles south of the city). From there all the soldiers except the sev-

---

1. See the discussion of this route at the end of chapter 6.
2. The plural, κτήνη, is used for animals, whether donkeys or horses. Perhaps more than one was provided because it was a long trip, normally requiring two days.
3. Antipatris was constructed on the site of Aphek in Sharon, one of five Old Testament sites named Aphek. Herod the Great renamed it in honor of his father Antipater. See the articles on Antipatris and Aphek in *ABD,* 1:272–74, 275–77.

Map 8.1. Paul's Journey to Rome

enty horsemen returned to Jerusalem (Acts 23:23, 32). Then Paul and his
company continued to Caesarea the next day.[4]

Lysias had required Paul's accusers, including the high priest Ananias, to
come to Caesarea (Acts 23:30–35; 24:1) and not wait to be summoned, which
would delay the proceedings. This was probably a concession to Paul.[5] They
arrived within five days, and in the meantime Paul was kept in Herod's praetorium.[6] Excavations in Caesarea have demonstrated the probablility that
Herod's palace was the Promontory Palace, the remains of which lie south of
the harbor and west of the theater. According to the excavators, "the palace
had become the *praetorium,* or official residence of the Roman governor."[7]
Paul probably stayed here.

When the accusers arrived from Jerusalem, Felix gave them a formal hearing. Ananias and some of the elders brought with them a representative

4. On Caesarea, see John McRay, "Caesarea," *EEC,* 165–67.

5. Brian Rapske finds several concessions to Paul in the letter from Lysias, probably because
he was concerned about how Paul initially had been unlawfully and incompetently handled
and the way it could reflect upon him (*The Book of Acts and Paul in Roman Custody,* BAFCS 3
[Grand Rapids: Eerdmans, 1994], 153).

6. Rapske thinks Paul received no exceptional treatment at this time and was given the concessions he had experienced under Lysias only later, after he had presented his case to Felix. At
that point Felix gave orders that Paul should be kept in custody but "should have some liberty,
and . . . none of his friends should be prevented from attending to his needs" (Acts 24:23)
(*Paul in Roman Custody,* 157). See my chapter 6, on Paul's second journey, for a description
of prison life in Paul's world.

7. Barbara Burrell, Kathryn Gleason, and Ehud Netzer, "Uncovering Herod's Seaside Palace," *BAR* 19.3 (May–June 1993): 56.

Photo 8.1. Caesarea Harbor Seen from Promontory Palace

spokesman, an orator named Tertullus, who called Paul a "ringleader of the sect of Nazarenes" (a reference to Christians who followed Jesus of Nazareth) and accused him of being an agitator of Jews and attempting to profane the temple (Acts 24:1–9). Paul then replied by pointing out that he had arrived in Jerusalem only twelve days before and had created no problems. Even when he went into the temple for purification, he had created no problem, and no such charge had been leveled against him by the Sanhedrin in Jerusalem. He pointed out that no witnesses had come forward in Jerusalem as now in Caesarea to bear witness to any improper conduct. He said his only "wrongdoing" was that he preached the resurrection from the dead (Acts 24:10–21).

The response of Felix to Paul was influenced by contemporary cultural conditions. Josephus wrote: "In Judaea matters were constantly going from bad to worse. For the country was again infested with bands of brigands and impostors who deceived the mob. Not a day passed, however, but that Felix captured and put to death many of these impostors and brigands."[8]

The Jews and Syrians in Caesarea were quarreling and killing each other over the issue of equal civic rights,[9] and the situation had deteriorated to the point that Felix hired assassins to kill Jonathan, the former high priest of the Jews, who had initially urged the appointment of Felix as procurator.[10]

So when Paul stood before Felix, the procurator was clearly confronted with a serious problem. He had no desire to agitate the already volatile Jewish

8. *Ant.* 20.160–61.
9. See further Irving Levey, "Caesarea and the Jews," in *The Joint Expedition to Caesarea Maritima,* vol. 1, *Studies in the History of Caesarea Maritima,* ed. D. N. Freedman, BASOR Supplemental Studies 19 (Missoula, Mont.: Scholars Press, 1975), 43–78.
10. *Ant.* 20.162–63.

situation with which he continually wrestled (as would his successor, Festus, Acts 25:9). Ten years later, these hostilities would reach a climax when the Syrians in A.D. 66 massacred about twenty thousand Jews in Caesarea and sent the remainder to the galleys. Josephus says the city was thus "completely emptied of its Jewish population" at that time.[11] This precipitated the war with Rome that resulted in the destruction of the Jerusalem temple in A.D. 70.

Felix himself was a freed slave from the family of the emperor Claudius[12] and was married to a Jewish woman, Drusilla (Acts 24:24), the youngest daughter of King Herod Agrippa I.[13] He wanted to please the Jews whenever he could (Acts 24:27), not out of love but in order to decrease the hostilities they were promulgating. With this Jewish connection, he was rather well informed (Acts 24:22) about the Jewish Christian movement in Judea and correctly analyzed the problem with Paul. He saw that the issue really was a conflict among Jews about whether Jesus was the Christ.

While on the one hand, Felix did not want to unncessarily agitate the Jews, on the other hand, since Paul was a Jewish Roman citizen who had not broken either Jewish or Roman law, Felix could not condemn him. His solution was to procrastinate. He said he would decide the case after the tribune Lysias came to Caesarea and he had a chance to talk to this Roman officer who had arrested Paul (Acts 24:22).

Felix also saw an opportunity to exact a bribe from Paul and wanted to keep him in prison until it was offered (Acts 24:26). According to Luke, Paul had not revealed the fact that the gifts he had brought to Jerusalem were donations from churches outside Judea, and when Paul said "I came to bring to my nation alms and offerings" (Acts 24:17), Felix may have thought that Paul himself had made the donation and was wealthy. This is the only reference to the contribution in Acts. Felix sensed, either because of Paul's reference to the contribution or because of his prominence in the movement (called "the Way" in Acts 9:2; 19:9, 23; 24:14, 22), that Paul had money or could obtain it.[14]

This reaction was consistent with what we know from Josephus of the character of Felix. Furthermore, Tacitus, the first-century Roman historian, described him as "the governor of Judaea who thought that he could do any evil act with impunity"[15] and "indulging in every kind of barbarity and lust, exercised the power of a king in the spirit of a slave."[16] During the next two years, he had frequent conversations with Paul, hoping that a bribe would be of-

---

11. *Ant.* 2.457.

12. David Braund, "Felix," *ABD,* 2:783.

13. *Ant.* 18.132; *J.W.* 2.220; cf. *Ant.* 19.354.

14. Rapske argues strongly but not conclusively that Paul was in a "financially privileged position" (*Paul in Roman Custody,* 106). He thinks Paul had money throughout most of his ministry but cannot account for its source.

15. *Ann.* 12.54.

16. *Hist.* 5.9.

fered,[17] but being such a moral reprobate, Felix was terrified when Paul spoke to him about "justice and self-control and future judgment" (Acts 24:25).

Paul before Festus

Two years later, in A.D. 56, Felix was succeeded by Porcius Festus. The accession of Festus is a pivotal date in the chronology of Paul. If this newer date of A.D. 56 (rather than the older one of A.D. 59) is accurate,[18] then Paul was in prison in Caesarea from A.D. 54 to 56.

Within three days Festus went to Jerusalem to pay respects to the high priest and was informed of the Jewish leaders' grievance against Paul. They hoped that the new procurator would send Paul back to Jerusalem, and they would have him killed on the way (Acts 25:1–3). They had been involved in a similar plot on Paul's life earlier (Acts 23:12–15). Festus refused but invited representative authorities from the temple to go to Caesarea and together with him determine the truth of the accusations against Paul.

Eight to ten days later, Festus returned to Caesarea and set up a hearing for Paul. Presumably Paul's traveling companions from Asia and Macedonia, who had accompanied him to Jerusalem with the contribution, had returned home. Perhaps they were discouraged by the events that had transpired, none of which they had wanted but which they had heard prophesied in every city (Acts 20:23). Only two of them, Luke and Aristarchus, seem to have stayed in Jerusalem and eventually to have come to Caesarea, because they later accompanied Paul on his journey from Caesarea to Rome (Acts 27:1–2).

An inscription discovered in excavations at Caesarea in 1997 has been tentatively identified by the excavator, Joseph Porat, as belonging to the official Roman bureau for internal security, where Paul appeared before Felix and Festus (Acts 24:27).[19] The building complex where it was found is fifteen thousand square meters in size and includes a large palace, administrative offices, a bathhouse, and a courtyard, according to Joseph Porat, who is in charge of Israel Antiquities Authority excavations in Caesarea. It is located between the Palace of Herod on the coast and the hippodrome to the east.

According to Porat, the governmental complex is the only seat of Roman government unearthed in Israel and one of the few ever excavated in the ancient Roman world. Further exploration will provide clarification of its purpose. Since Roman rule over Palestine was centered in Caesarea, the praeto-

17. See the extended discussion of Paul's experience in Caesarea in Rapske's excellent work, *Paul in Roman Custody,* 151–72.

18. See the discussion of this in chapter 3, under "Procuratorship of Festus in Judea."

19. Abraham Rabinovich, "Archaeological Site Linked to Paul," *Jerusalem Post,* 10 September 1997.

rium complex there functioned as the seat of Roman government from the first century to the middle of the third century. A mosaic inscription on one of the floors reads, "I came to this office—I shall be secure."

Festus, being a new governor of a Jewish province and having just returned from a three-day visit with its leaders in Jerusalem, understandably wanted to "do the Jews a favor" (Acts 25:9). At the same time, he wanted to avoid having to deal with Paul himself. So he proposed that Paul go to Jerusalem to answer charges there. However, Paul had already been before the Sanhedrin, and there was nothing more to be said there since he had not been convicted by witnesses of any wrongdoing (Acts 25:10).

On the other hand, Paul knew the Jews were plotting to kill him in Jerusalem (Acts 23:12–15), so he exercised his right as a Roman citizen and "appealed to Caesar" (Acts 25:11). This right, known as *lex Julia de vi publica,* had only been in force since 23 B.C.,[20] but it was available to Paul, and he did not hesitate to use it. This law would not allow any official to kill, scourge, chain, or torture a Roman citizen, or even to sentence him ("in the face of an appeal") or prevent him from going to Rome to make his appeal there within a specified period of time. So Felix had no choice but to grant Paul's appeal, and it was probably what he preferred since it removed this difficult situation from his responsibility.

How Paul could prove he was a Roman citizen is not known, but it was a capital offense to falsely claim citizenship, and few would dare risk it.[21] The registration of citizens at birth seems to have been a fairly recent innovation,[22] and whether Paul had a birth certificate cannot be determined.[23] Citizens living in the provinces, as Paul once did in Cilicia, could confirm citizenship through the local census archives, which existed for the purposes of taxation. Even if Paul had a certificate, it is not known whether travelers carried the certificates with them. The nature and extent of travel so familiar in the modern world was unknown in the Roman Empire. Families stayed in one place from generation to generation, and citizenship was easily determined in local contexts. Special arrangements were made for soldiers and merchants, who were given metal certificates of citizenship known as *diplomata.*[24] It is doubtful,

20. See my discussion of the law in chapter 1, under "I Was Born a Citizen."

21. F. F. Bruce, *Paul: Apostle of the Heart Set Free* (Grand Rapids: Eerdmans, 1977), 39.

22. Enacted by the *lex Aelia Sentia* of A.D. 4 and the *lex Papia Poppaea* of A.D. 9. If Paul was born prior to these decrees, and he may have been, he would not have a certificate (Bruce, *Paul,* 40).

23. See F. Schulz, "Roman Registers and Birth Certificates I," *JRS* (1942): 78f.; "Roman Registers and Birth Certificates II," *JRS* (1943): 55f.

24. See further A. N. Sherwin-White, "The Roman Citizenship and Acts," in *Roman Society and Roman Law in the New Testament* (Oxford: Oxford University Press, 1963; reprint, Grand Rapids: Baker, 1992), 148–49.

however, that Paul carried either a paper or metal certificate, since it was not really necessary.

Neither was there any way to look at Paul and determine whether he was a citizen. Claudius Lysias in Jerusalem was surprised to learn from Paul that he was a citizen (Acts 22:27–28). Paul was trying to emphasize his Jewish identity in Jerusalem and certainly would not have been wearing a Roman toga, the large piece of cloth that was worn outside the tunic and wrapped around the body, over one shoulder, and sometimes over the head.[25] No one but a Roman citizen was supposed to wear a toga, but in the provinces it was seldom worn because it was cumbersome, and even in Rome at this time it was an unpopular garment.

Paul before Agrippa II

A few days after Paul appealed to Caesar, Agrippa II, a Jewish king, visited Caesarea. He was the son of Agrippa I and brother of Drusilla, the wife of Felix, whom Festus had replaced. Agrippa governed the territory northeast of Festus's province, including Ituraea, Trachonitis, and Abilene, and had come down to Caesarea to welcome the new procurator (Acts 25:13). Since Agrippa was regarded as an expert in Jewish religious matters, Festus told him about Paul's situation, and Agrippa asked to hear Paul.

Paul's address to Agrippa recounts his conversion/call for the third time in Acts. He began by emphasizing his Jewish credentials, noting that he had lived a strict life as a Pharisee (Acts 26:5).[26] He said he was now on trial for his hope in the promise of God made to the Jews (i.e., the resurrection of the dead), and he asked why any of those present should find it incredible that God raises the dead (Acts 26:6–7).

This account contains Paul's emphasis on his commission to preach to the Gentiles (Acts 26:16–18), a commission Christ himself had been given for his postresurrection ministry (Acts 26:23). Paul refers to the Jewish Christians as "saints" (the antecedent of the recurring "they" and "them" in Acts 26:10–11) whom he persecuted. The term *saints* was the special designation of Jews. Christians shared in that special designation when they were grafted into the Jewish tree (Rom. 11). The profound implications of this fact are discussed in chapter 13.

Paul then asked Agrippa if he believed the prophets and, by implication, the fulfillment of their prophecies in Christ. This put Agrippa in a difficult situation. If he said yes, he would appear as a fool in the eyes of Festus, who had just yelled at Paul, "Your great learning is turning you mad" (Acts 26:24).

25. Sherwin-White, *Roman Society and Roman Law,* 149–50.
26. See chapter 1 and the discussion of Paul's Jewish background in Bruce, *Paul,* 41–52.

And if he said no, he would destroy his influence with the Jews, who believed in the prophets and considered Agrippa to be an expert in such matters. So Agrippa responded by saying to Paul, "Do you think that with such little persuasion you can make me a Christian?"[27] or, less likely, given the difficult position Agrippa was in, "With a little more persuasion you might make me a Christian."[28] Bruce thinks Agrippa meant "you are trying to make me play the Christian."[29]

Upon this, Agrippa arose and left, accompanied by the others who had been listening to Paul. He commented to Festus in private that if Paul had not appealed to Caesar, he might have been set free, because he had not violated any Jewish law (Acts 26:32). Luke means for this to confirm the fact that neither in Jerusalem nor in Caesarea had the Jews been able to show that Paul had violated Jewish law. How Luke learned of this private comment to Festus by Agrippa is not revealed. Evidently it was later related to Paul or Luke by Agrippa or someone else who had heard it.

Paul's Voyage to Rome

Paul was sent to Italy, along with some other prisoners, under the supervision of Julius, a centurion of the Augustan Cohort. He was accompanied by Luke and Aristarchus. They boarded a small coast-hopping vessel that was bound for Adramyttium, on the northern coast of Turkey opposite the island of Lesbos. It was therefore scheduled to "sail to the ports along the coast of Asia" (Acts 27:2), one of which was Sidon, where they landed the next day and where Paul was permitted to visit friends and "be cared for" (Acts 27:3). This indicates some measure of trust and respect for Paul by Julius but also testifies to the difficulty of finding suitable lodging while traveling in the ancient world. The centurion was no more anxious than Paul to stay in the unclean and uncomfortable facilities available to travelers.[30]

From Sidon, the boat would normally have sailed northwest, skirting the southwestern coast of Cyprus, and made directly for Myra, on the Lycian peninsula of Asia Minor. However, it was now late in the sailing season, and the winds from the west prevented this. The fast, or Day of Atonement, which occurred on October 9 of A.D. 56, had already passed (Acts 27:9). The small coast-hopping vessels could push the normal closing date for sailing (November 11) because they were not on the open sea and could sail

27. LB, RSV, TEV, NIV, NEB.

28. This seems to be the meaning intended in the KJV, ASV, and NASB. This may also be the intended meaning in the translations of the JB and PHILLIPS, though it is not clear.

29. F. F. Bruce, *The Book of the Acts,* rev. ed., NICNT (Grand Rapids: Eerdmans, 1988), 471.

30. See my discussion of these facilities in chapter 6, under "Roman Prisons."

Photo 8.2. Myra

under the protection of the coast.[31] So the boat sailed north instead, under the lee of Cyprus (Acts 27:4; i.e., along the eastern and northern sides of the island, where the southwestern winds blowing against them were blocked by the island). Maps that plot Paul's voyage usually draw straight lines from one harbor to the next, but in reality sailing against the wind required the vessel to zigzag.[32]

At Myra, on the eastern side of the Lycian Peninsula, the boat docked, Paul and his company disembarked, and the ship sailed on up the coast toward Adramyttium. The coastline at Myra is rugged but beautiful. A natural inlet opens deep into the heart of the peninsula, extending to a harbor that is still used today but is now silted up at its northern extremity, as we have noted about most ancient harbors along the coast of Turkey. The best-preserved remains in Myra today are those of the Roman theater.

Here in Myra "the centurion found an Alexandrian ship sailing for Italy and put us on board," Luke writes (Acts 27:4–6 NIV). This was a much larger vessel than the one on which they had been sailing. No doubt it was a typical grain ship from Alexandria, which brought huge cargoes of grain from Egypt to Rome. It was probably a three-masted ship, though most vessels had only

31. See Brian Rapske on seasonal travel and pushing the limits in "Acts, Travel and Shipwreck," in *The Book of Acts in Its Graeco-Roman Setting,* ed. David W. J. Gill and Conrad Gempf, BAFCS 2 (Grand Rapids: Eerdmans, 1994), 22ff.

32. See the map in James Smith, *The Voyage and Shipwreck of St. Paul* (London: Longmans, Green, and Co., 1866; reprint, Grand Rapids: Baker, 1978), 60. This excellent work is updated in Günter Kettenbach, *Das Logbuch des Lukas,* European University Studies Series 23: Theology 276 (Frankfurt am Main and New York: Lang, 1986).

two masts.[33] No Alexandrian grain ship has yet been excavated[34] among the numerous shipwrecks that have been found.[35] Lucian, a second-century A.D. Greek writer and traveler, describes an Alexandrian grain ship named the *Isis,* which followed a route similar to that of Paul's ship. It was also pressing the lateness of the season and was blown off course, finally docking in the harbor of Athens at Piraeus.[36] Lucian says the *Isis* was 174 feet in length (180 Roman feet) and 45 feet wide and had a "crew like an army."[37] A ship almost this large (147 1/2 feet long) was found in excavations off the coast of Caesarea. It has a frame larger than that of any known wreck of a Roman vessel.[38] Josephus tells of sailing for Rome from Judea in a huge boat that carried about 600 people. It, like Paul's vessel, foundered in the midst of the Sea of Adria, and the passengers had to swim all night in the open sea (as Paul once did, 2 Cor. 11:25). About 80 of them were rescued by a vessel from Cyrene, which took them to Puteoli, on the western coast of Italy.[39] The total number of people on board Paul's new vessel was 276 (Acts 27:37).[40]

Sailing was difficult for the next few days (Acts 27:7–8) because the contrary winds did not allow them to sail on west from Cnidus but forced a southward turn under the lee of the island of Crete, taking them past Salmone, the eastern promontory of Crete (Acts 27:7).[41] The ship sailed along the southern side of Crete, where the boat docked at Fair Havens (Acts 27:8, 12), near the city of Lasea. Crete and Cyrene in Libya had been a combined Roman province since 67 B.C.[42] The crew persuaded the centurion not to winter here but

33. We have only one pictorial representation of a large three-masted "superfreighter" from the Roman period: Michael Fitzgerald, "The Ship of Saint Paul: Comparative Archaeology (Part II)," *BA* 53.1 (March 1990): 31. See the mosaic photograph on p. 38. See further on the subject of ships at this time, Lionel Casson, *Ships and Seamanship in the Ancient World,* rev. ed. (Baltimore and London: Johns Hopkins University Press, 1995).

34. Nicolle Hirschfeld, "The Ship of Saint Paul: Historical Background (Part I)," *BA* 53.1 (March 1990): 29.

35. For a map of some of the locations of shipwrecks in the eastern Mediterranean, see George Bass, "Nautical Archaeology and Biblical Archaeology," *BA* 53.1 (March 1990): 8.

36. *Nav.* 5.

37. See further L. Casson, "The *Isis* and Her Voyage," *Transactions of the American Philological Association* 81 (1950): 51–56.

38. Fitzgerald, "Ship of Saint Paul," 36.

39. *Life* 3.

40. According to the best textual evidence. Some manuscripts, including Codex Vaticanus and the Sahidic Coptic, give seventy-six as the number (Bruce Metzger, *A Textual Commentary on the New Testament,* 2d ed. [Stuttgart: German Bible Society, 1994], 442).

41. See further Greg Horsley, "Sailing in Stormy Weather," in *New Documents Illustrating Early Christianity* (North Ryde, N.S.W., Australia: Ancient History Documentary Research Centre, Macquarie University, 1982), 74; and idem, "Travel Risks," in *New Documents Illustrating Early Christianity* (North Ryde, N.S.W., Australia: Ancient History Documentary Research Centre, Macquarie University, 1983), 58–59.

42. Jerry Pattengale, "Crete," *ABD,* 1:1206.

to sail a bit farther to Phoenix, a more desirable harbor for the winter on the west side of the island (27:11–12).[43]

Some people may have been converted here during Paul's brief contact with the island, though Luke makes no mention of it. If so, Titus's later work here would have been to put that brief beginning on a firmer foundation by amending "what was defective" and appointing "elders in every town" (Titus 1:5). This verse implies that a long enough period had transpired for the planting of churches in several towns. This could certainly have been done during the two years Paul spent in prison in Rome, following his brief visit to Crete. On the other hand, Crete may have been evangelized under other circumstances.

Against Paul's warning of injury and loss if they sailed, the passengers and crew boarded the boat, left the harbor at Fair Havens, and started for Phoenix. But soon after leaving and before the ship reached Phoenix, probably as it rounded Cape Lithinon and lost the protection of the shore, they suddenly encountered the "tempetuous," or typhoon-like,[44] winds of a "northeaster" (Acts 27:14), called in Greek *Euraquilo* (εὑρακύλων, *eurakylōn*). It is produced when a low-pressure system develops in the autumn over Libya, in North Africa, pulling the air violently in a southwesterly direction.[45]

For the third time, Luke mentions that the boat sailed under the lee of an island, this time the island of Cauda or Clauda,[46] which lay a short distance south of Phoenix (Acts 27:16). In the heart of the storm, the boat was being driven southwestward with no possibility of navigation, and the crew did not know where they were. After several days they began to fear they had been blown all the way to the coast of North Africa and were in danger of wrecking on the Syrtis (Acts 27:17). This is the "name of two gulfs along the Libyan coast which, because of their shallowness and shifting sandbanks, were greatly feared by mariners."[47]

When they had gone without food for a long time and all hope was abandoned, Paul encouraged them by revealing that an angel of God had appeared

---

43. For a detailed discussion of the geographical complexities of the harbors at Phoenix, see Jack Finegan, *ANT:MW*, 196f. Warnecke tried to identify Phoenix with Phoinikas on the Peloponnesus of Greece, but his position was rebutted by J. Wehnert. See the bibliography in Rapske, "Acts, Travel and Shipwreck," 36–37.

44. The Greek word *typhoon* (τυφωνικός) is used in Acts 27:14 by Luke to describe the wind.

45. For discussion of the terms and geographic conditions involved, see further, C. J. Hemer, "Euraquilo and Melita," *JTS* 26 (1975): 100–111; and Rapske, "Acts, Travel and Shipwreck," 38.

46. J. Rendel Harris, "Clauda or Cauda?" *ET* 21 (1909–10): 17–19. See Metzger's discussion of the variant chosen for the Greek text in *Textual Commentary*, 40–41.

47. BAGD, Σύρτις, *Syrtis*, 794. Finegan notes that the larger one, Syrtis Major, is now the Gulf of Sidra, west of Cyrenaica (which is probably the one meant here). The smaller one, Syrtis Minor, now called the Gulf of Gabes, is much further west (*ANT:MW*, 198).

to him that very night and assured him that none on the ship would be lost, although the ship would eventually run on some island (Acts 27:21–26). On the fourteenth night, they had reached the Adriatic Sea (or Sea of Adria, Acts 27:27),[48] and when daylight broke on the fourteenth day (Acts 27:33), Paul encouraged them, all 276, to eat and gain strength since none was going to perish. When the ship ran aground on an island and the stern broke apart, everyone swam or floated ashore on driftwood (Acts 27:43–44).[49]

They did not know it at the time, but the shore on which they had wrecked belonged to the little island of Malta[50] (Melita in Greek).[51] Malta is located sixty miles south of Cape Passero at the southeastern tip of Sicily. Sicily is a much larger island off the toe of the boot of Italy. Unsuccessful attempts have been made to identify the island with two other sites. The first is Mljet (Meleda, called Melitene, Μελιτήνη, by Ptolemy)[52] in the Adriatic Sea off the coast of Dalmatia. This view is based partially on the assumption that the textual variant "southeast"[53] wind is to be preferred over the one reading "northeast" wind (Acts 27:14), and thus describes a northwestern rather than southwestern destination for the boat.[54] But the site is simply too far north to be a viable candidate, and the northeaster winds in the best manuscripts of Acts make it an impossible candidate.

In addition to the two reasons just mentioned for locating Malta at Mljet—namely, limiting the Sea of Adria exclusively to a northern prove-

48. For the dispute over the southern limits of the Adriatic, see Rapske, "Acts, Travel and Shipwreck," 40; and F. F. Bruce, *The Acts of the Apostles: The Greek Text with Introduction and Commentary,* 3d rev. ed. (Grand Rapids: Eerdmans, 1990), 522. Strabo (*Geogr.* 2.5.20), Pausanias (*Periegesis of Greece* 5.25.3), and Ptolemy (*Geography* 3.4.1; 15.1) all indicate that the Adriatic sea reached south to Sicily and even Crete.

49. On details of the shipwreck, see "Shipwrecks and St Paul," in *The Sea Remembers: Shipwrecks and Archaeology from Homer's Greece to the Rediscovery of the Titanic,* ed. Peter Throckmorton (New York: Weidenfeld & Nicolson, 1987), 78–80.

50. Μελίτη (Μελιτήνη, by dittography in some manuscripts). It is translated Malta in the RSV, NIV, NEB, JB, TEV, and LB. The word is from the Semitic word *melita,* meaning "refuge," and was probably used of the island because of its safe harbors. W. Gasque, "Malta," *ABD,* 4:489–90; S. Gaul, *Malta, Gozo and Comino* (London: Cadogan, 1993).

51. KJV, PHILLIPS.

52. Ptolemy, *Geography* 2.16.9.

53. This is predicated on accepting the Textus Receptus variant εὐροκλύδων over the better attested εὐρακύλων. See the discussion in Rapske, "Acts, Travel and Shipwreck," 38–39.

54. A. Acworth, "Where Was St. Paul Shipwrecked? A Re-examination of the Evidence," *JTS,* n.s., 24 (1973): 190–92; and Otto Meinardus, "Melita Illyrica or Africana? An Examination of the Site of St. Paul's Shipwreck," *Ostkirchliche Studien* 23 (1974): 21–36; idem, "St. Paul Shipwrecked in Dalmatia," *BA* 39 (1976): 145–47; idem, "Dalmatian and Catalonian Traditions about St. Paul's Journeys," *Ekklesiastikos Pharos* 61 (1979): 221–30; and idem, *St. Paul's Last Journey* (New Rochelle, N.Y.: Caratzas, 1979), 79–85. In this last reference, Meinardus has collected many of the subsequent local traditions about Paul's supposed presence in Mljet. However, the arguments of these authors are convincingly rebutted by Hemer, "Euraquilo and Melita."

nance and choosing the variant reading in the Greek text that allows a south-west wind to blow the vessel northward—Meinardus lists a third: the fact that there are presently no poisonous snakes (Acts 28:3–6) on Malta.[55] As noted, the first two reasons have been refuted. The third is a precarious argument from silence, lacking proof. "The present lack of poisonous snakes on Malta does not foreclose their existence there in Paul's day."[56]

The other even less likely suggestion is that Paul's boat landed at Cephallenia (or Kefallinia), a large island at the entrance to the Corinthian Gulf on the western side of the Peloponnesus of Greece.[57] But there is no evidence that the island was ever called Melita, and the northeaster in this case, as for the case of Mljet, would have blown the boat away from the island.

Some have argued that the story is a fabrication and the shipwreck never actually happened. An archaeological team led by Margaret Rule is searching for the shipwreck, whose discovery would silence such agnostic rumor.[58]

Paul and his company spent the three months of the non-sailing season on the island (Acts 28:11), probably from sometime in November of A.D. 56 until sometime in February or early March.[59] During this time they were treated with "unusual kindness" (Acts 28:2) by the local people, whom Luke calls barbarian (βάρβαρος, barbaros), meaning only that they did not speak Greek.[60] The word carries no connotation that the people were heathen or primitive. The island had a history of advanced cultural civilization as a Phoenician trading colony and had been part of the Roman province of Sicily before Augustus put it under its own procurator.[61] Under the procurator, the leading local official of the island was designated "the chief man" (ὁ πρῶτος, ho prōtos), a title found in Greek and Latin inscriptions[62] and accurately used in Acts of the Roman official on Malta who was named Publius. Luke calls

---

55. *St. Paul's Last Journey,* 81–85.

56. Rapske, "Acts, Travel and Shipwreck," 41. There are snakes on Malta today but none that are poisonous.

57. H. Warnecke, *Die tatsächliche Romfahrt des Apostels Paulus,* Stuttgarter Bibelstudien 127 (Stuttgart: Katholisches Bibelwerk, 1987). His position ignited considerable debate and is refuted by Jürgen Wehnert in *Lutherische Monatshefte* 21 (1989): 98–100. See also Wehnert's "Shipwrecked—A Commentary on a New Thesis about the Shipwreck of Paul on His Way to Rome," in *St. Paul in Malta: A Compendium of Pauline Studies,* ed. Michael Galea and Canon John Ciarlò (Zabbar, Malta: Veritas, 1992), 5–38. For bibliography on the debate, see Rapske, "Acts, Travel and Shipwreck," 37 n. 170.

58. J. M. Gilchrist, "The Historicity of Paul's Shipwreck," *JSNT* 61 (1996): 29–51; P. Guillaumier, "New Perspective on the Historicity of St. Paul's Shipwreck on Melite," in Galea and Ciarlò, *St. Paul in Malta,* 53–114.

59. We noted earlier that the Day of Atonement had already passed before they started the journey (Acts 27:9), but we are not told how long before the journey that was, whether days or weeks.

60. Cf. Rom. 1:14 where Paul says he is debtor "to Greeks and barbarians."

61. Gasque, "Malta," 489.

62. *CIG* 14.60; *CIL* 10.7495.

Photo 8.3. Smith's Bay and Island of Paul at Malta

him "the chief man of the island" (τῷ πρώτῳ τῆς νήσου, *tō prōtō tēs nēsou*, Acts 28:7). Greek and Latin inscriptions even refer to "the first man of the Maltese."[63]

The language spoken on Malta was a Phoenician dialect[64] of the Semitic family.[65] Semitic inscriptions have been found on the island, one of them in Hebrew.[66] Paul may have conversed with the inhabitants in Aramaic. The culture was Punic, and Punic inscriptions are preserved from the island.

There are three bays on the northern coast of Malta, Salina Bay, Saint Paul's Bay, and Mellieha Bay. Saint Paul's Bay has been the traditional site for the landing of Paul's ship, and the geographical features there fit the circumstances described in Acts.[67]

The residents of the island not only welcomed the 276 survivors (Acts 27:37) but also built them a fire to provide warmth amid the cold winds that had caused their wreck. When Paul was also gathering sticks for the fire, he

63. Greek in *CIG* 5754; Latin in *CIL* 10.7495.

64. Bruce, *Acts of the Apostles: The Greek Text*, 531.

65. Gasque, "Malta," 489.

66. A. M. Honeyman, "Two Semitic Inscriptions from Malta," *PEQ* 93 (1961): 151–53. See further bibliography in Colin Hemer, *BASHH*, 152 n. 149. The Semitic texts have been published in G. A. Cooke, *A Text-Book of North-Semitic Inscriptions* (Oxford: Clarendon, 1903), 102–7.

67. Finegan notes that "the approaches to St. Paul's Bay fit generally well with the soundings reported in Acts 27:28" (*ANT:MW*, 202).

Photo 8.4. Church of St. Paul at Malta

was bitten by a poisonous serpent, which caused the islanders to assume he was a murderer being punished by their gods (Acts 28:4). But when Paul did not die, they quickly changed their opinion, believing now that he was a god. Assumptions by critics that the snake was not poisonous leaves the reaction of the local people without explanation.[68] They certainly would have known the difference between a poisonous and a nonpoisonous snake on their island.

Then Publius, the chief man of the island, who had property near the site of the wreck, shared the same spirit of hospitality as the other residents of Malta (Acts 28:2) by entertaining the survivors for three days (Acts 28:7). While there, Paul visited the father of Publius and healed him from his fever and dysentery. This, coupled with the fact that Paul did not die from the snake bite (Acts 28:3–6), provoked a mass reaction, and people with diseases came from all over the island to be healed by God through Paul (Acts 28:9). The grateful residents gave Paul and his company gifts and provided their necessities when the voyagers left the island three months later (Acts 28:10). It is likely, though unrecorded in Acts, that some of the inhabitants of the island

68. W. M. Ramsay suggests that the snake was the nonpoisonous *Coronella austriaca,* which resembles a viper (*Luke the Physician* [1908; reprint, Grand Rapids: Baker, 1956], 63ff.).

became Christians at this time.[69] The presence of Paul was remembered for centuries in the Church of St. Paul at Milqui on Malta.

There were others like Paul's company who were stuck on Malta for the non-sailing period. A ship, undoubtedly a grain ship from Alexandria, had gotten this far north and had to winter on the island. When the sailing season opened again in February or early March, Paul's company boarded this vessel, which must have been rather large to accommodate this many extra passengers, and sailed north for Rome. They stopped for three days at the port in Syracuse, on the southeastern tip of Sicily, and then continued north to Rhegium on the southwestern toe of the boot of Italy. Waiting one day until a south wind began to blow, they sailed on north, passing Messina on the west and arriving a day later at Puteoli (modern Pozzuoli), which had a small harbor on the northwestern end of the huge Bay of Naples (Acts 28:11–13).

Paul's Arrival in Rome

As the boat entered the bay from the west, Paul would have gazed upon majestic Mount Vesuvius directly to the east, dominating the bay. He could not know, of course, that this volcanic mountain would erupt about twenty years later (A.D. 79), destroying Pompeii, Herculaneum, and Stabiae, all located on the bay. His ship would have sailed past the island of Ischia on the north and the surpassingly beautiful island of Capri on the south. The emperor Caesar Augustus visited Capri in 29 B.C., and his successor, Tiberius, lived there in retirement from A.D. 26 or 27 until he died in A.D. 37. Tacitus said Tiberius had "filled the island with twelve country houses, each with a grand name and a vast structure of its own."[70]

The Bay of Naples served as the major seaport for Rome until Claudius built the harbor at Ostia and Trajan further developed it. Until the first century A.D., the normal means of approaching Rome by sea was to sail into Puteoli, as Paul did. The most important area in the Bay of Naples when Paul landed here was that which extended to the west of Naples, around the gulf to Cumae. This region, with its beautiful panoramic views of the bay, was called the Phlegraean Fields.[71] Puteoli was the bay's important commercial port, Cumae its political

---

69. John Chrysostom, in the fourth century, asserted this in his fifty-fourth homily. Arator, in the fifth century, believed that Paul had consecrated Publius as bishop of the island. Many ancient traditions, of course, have arisen about Paul all over the Mediterranean. These at Malta are unsupported by evidence. The earliest undisputed Maltese bishop, Meinardus says, is Julianus, mentioned in the council lists of the Three Chapters Council in Constantinople, A.D. 553 (*St. Paul's Last Journey*, 85). This little volume discusses many of the traditional spots on Malta that have been associated with Paul's visit, as does Finegan, *ANT:MW*, 200–204.

70. *Ann.* 67.

71. Pliny, *Nat.* 3.5.61.

Photo 8.5. Puteoli

center, Misenum the Roman naval base, and Baiae the pleasure resort. The area of the harbor into which Paul sailed is discernable today.

Before the time of Claudius, both passengers and cargo were unloaded in Puteoli.[72] Now passengers disembarked in Puteoli, and then the cargo of grain was taken up to Portus, the new harbor built by Claudius at Ostia, near the mouth of the Tiber River.[73] In Puteoli, Paul and his smaller group of traveling companions found Christian brothers and spent seven days with them (Acts 28:14).[74] The Roman centurion and his guards were undoubtedly ready for a bit of shore leave by this time. It is doubtful that the centurion had sufficient business here to require a week of his time, as Bruce suggests,[75] or that he would have become involved in the commercial affairs of the Alexandrian grain ship that had given them unexpected passage from Malta.

From Puteoli, Paul and the others would have traveled north on suburban roads to Capua,[76] where they would intersect the Via Appia (Appian Way), a major national highway that ran from Rome south to Capua and then southeast to Brundisium (Brindisi) on the eastern coast.[77] Roman highways were normally

72. Hemer, *BASHH,* 155 n. 155.

73. Ibid., 154f.

74. On the evidence for the possible presence of Christians in Herculaneum and Pompeii at this time, see ibid., 155 n. 155.

75. *Paul,* 374.

76. The slave revolt under Spartacus broke out in the amphitheater still preserved here.

77. See map 53 in A. A. M. Van der Heyden and H. H. Scullard, eds., *Atlas of the Classical World* (New York: Nelson, 1959), 128.

thirteen to fifteen feet wide and covered with large polygonal blocks of hard stone.[78] Near Rome the road was covered with basalt stones (formed from volcanic lava), as were the streets in Pompeii and Herculaneum. There is no essential difference in their construction in these various places. Running along either side of the Appian Way were slightly raised footpaths, covered with gravel.[79]

The distance from Capua to Rome was about 120 miles and would have been covered in five to six days. The road ran from Capua to the coast at Tarracina and then north to Rome, part of the distance being through the wetlands of the Pomptine Marshes,[80] which impeded communication between Rome and the Bay of Naples.[81] At Tarracina the Appian Way first touched the sea, and two rivers formed a great marsh nearby.[82] Canals allowed travel by barge at night, thus saving time, but Horace (65–8 B.C.) wrote about the discomforts of traveling on these canals, including lazy boatmen, insects, and frogs.[83] Strabo, the first-century geographer, wrote about this area as well:

> Near Tarracina, as you go toward Rome, there is a canal which runs alongside the Appian Way, and is fed at numerous places by waters from the marshes and the rivers. People navigate the canal, preferably by night (so that if they embark in the evening they can disembark early in the morning and go the rest of their journey by the [Appian] Way), but they also navigate it by day. The boat is towed by a mule.[84]

The Forum of Appius (Acts 28:15), forty miles south of Rome,[85] was located near this canal. Horace wrote that the forum was "crammed with boatmen and stingy tavern-keepers."[86] When Paul arrived there, he was met by Christians from Rome who had heard he was coming (Acts 28:15). Word had probably been sent ahead while Paul spent the week in Puteoli (Acts 28:14). Their presence was a comfort to Paul and gave him courage (Acts 28:15).

From the Forum of Appius, Paul's company traveled another ten miles north to Three Taverns,[87] which was six miles from Tripontium, the point at

78. Edwin Yamauchi gives fourteen to twenty feet for the width of the Appian Way (*Harper's World of the New Testament* [San Francisco: Harper and Row, 1981], 116).

79. For discussion of the materials and method of construction, see "Viae," *A Dictionary of Greek and Roman Antiquities,* ed. William Smith (London: John Murray, 1878), 1191–95.

80. Strabo refers to this plain (*Geogr.* 5.3.6).

81. M. Cary, *A History of Rome down to the Reign of Constantine,* 2d ed. (London: Macmillan, 1962), 30. Julius Caesar planned to drain the marshes and a large lake in central Italy. Cary notes that these projects were not carried out in his lifetime, but "most of them were brought to fruition under the early emperors" (409).

82. Strabo, *Geogr.* 5.3.6.

83. *Sat.* 1.5.3–6.

84. Strabo, *Geogr.* 5.3.6. For an amusing account of this canal trip, see Horace, *Sat.* 1.5.

85. *CIL* 10.6824.

86. *Sat.* 1.5.3–6.

87. It was located thirty miles south of Rome (*CIL* 10.685).

which the Appian Way entered the Pontine marshes. The exact location of Three Taverns is not known but is near the modern town of Cisterna.[88] From the way Luke records Paul's arrival, it seems that Christians from Rome met him at Three Taverns as they had at the Forum of Appius (Acts 28:15). The term *taverns* in the Latin name *Tres Tabernae,* which is transliterated into Greek in Acts, also designates inns, and this stopping place at the intersection of the Appian Way and the road from Antium to Norba was probably a major rest stop for travelers like Paul.

From here the expanding flock that clustered around Paul traveled to Rome. It must have provided an impressive sight to the onlookers. In addition to Paul, Luke,[89] and their seven companions (Acts 20:3–4), there were the centurion and the soldiers necessary to guard the other prisoners (Acts 27:1), along with the Christians who had met them in the two places just mentioned (Acts 28:15).

And so, finally, they came to Rome, the city Paul had been trying to visit for over two years (Acts 19:21; 23:11; 27:24; Rom. 1:15). Here Paul was allowed to stay by himself with the soldier who guarded him (Acts 28:16). This clearly indicates that Paul had been and continued to be treated with respect as a Roman citizen of some stature who had not been formally accused of any crime. He was here by his own appeal to Caesar to await such accusations. During his time in Rome, he stayed in his own dwelling (Acts 28:23) at his own expense (Acts 28:30) and was lightly chained to the soldier who guarded him (Acts 28:16, 20).[90] Paul spoke of being "bound with this chain" (Acts 28:20), as he had been earlier in Caesarea (Acts 26:29).

It is interesting that only two years earlier, Paul had written a letter from Corinth to the church in Rome in which he stated, "Let every person be subject to the governing authorities. For there is no authority except from God, and those that exist have been instituted by God. . . . Would you have no fear of him who is in authority? Then do what is good, and you will receive his approval . . ." (Rom. 13:1, 3). Now he is in Rome awaiting a hearing before that authority. In our excavations of Caesarea Maritima in 1972, we found a mosaic inscription on the floor of a late-fifth- or early-sixth-century building that preserves the exact wording of the Greek text of Romans 13:3.[91]

After Paul had been there for three days, he invited the local Jewish leaders to his dwelling to explain his situation to them and inform them that he was bound "be-

---

88. John Wineland, "Three Taverns," *ABD,* 6:544.

89. V. K. Robbins, "By Land and by Sea: The We-Passages and Ancient Sea Voyages," in *Perspectives on Luke-Acts,* ed. Charles Talbert (Edinburgh: Clark, 1978), 215–42; Colin Hemer, "First Person Narrative in Acts 27–28," *TynBul* 36 (1985): 79–109.

90. Bruce, *Acts of the Apostles: The Greek Text,* 537.

91. See John McRay, *Archaeology and the New Testament* (Grand Rapids: Baker, 1991), 373; Robert Bull, "Caesarea Maritima—the Search for Herod's City," *BAR* 8.2 (May–June 1982): 24–40, esp. 38.

Photo 8.6. Romans 13:3 Inscription at Caesarea

cause of the hope of Israel" (Acts 28:20). Paul invited them to return for an extended discussion, and they came in "great numbers" (Acts 28:23).[92] We do not know how large the Jewish population of Rome was at this time, but under Augustus it had probably passed the million mark.[93] Josephus spoke of "more than eight thousand Jewish residents" there in the first century.[94] During the reign of Tiberius (in A.D. 19), the whole Jewish population had been banished from Rome, and four thousand of them were drafted into military service and sent to the island of Sardinia.[95]

92. Inscriptions found thus far testify to eleven synagogues in Rome, four of which definitely date to the time of Paul (Rapske, *Paul in Roman Custody,* 180).

93. Cary, *History of Rome,* 569. George Foot Moore simply calls the number of Jews "considerable" (*Judaism in the First Centuries of the Christian Era: The Age of the Tannaim* [Cambridge: Harvard University Press, 1962], 1:106). However, Michael Grant estimates only 100,000 Jews in all of Italy in the time of Julius Caesar (*The Jews in the Roman World* [New York: Dorset, by arrangement with Scribners, 1984], 60).

94. *Ant.* 17.300; *J.W.* 2.80.

95. Josephus, *Ant.* 18.83–84. This expulsion is mentioned also by Suetonius, *Tib.* 36; Dio Cassius, *History of Rome* 57.18.5a; and Tacitus, *Ann.* 2.85. On the banishment, see W. A. Heidel, "Why Were the Jews Banished from Italy in 19 A.D.," *American Journal of Philology* 41 (1920): 38–47; E. T. Merrill, "The Expulsion of the Jews from Rome under Tiberius," *Classical Philology* 14 (1919): 365–72; H. R. Moehring, "The Persecution of the Jews and the Adherents of the Isis Cult at Rome, A.D. 19," *Novum Testamentum* 3 (1959): 293–304; G. Volkmar, "Die Religionsverfolgung unter Kaiser Tiberius und die Chronologie des Flavius Josephus in der Pilatus-Periode," *Jahrbuch für Protestant Theologie* 11 (1885): 136–43; Max Radin, *The Jews among the Greeks and Romans* (Philadelphia: Jewish Publication Society of America, 1915), 306–13.

They had been allowed to return under a subsequent emperor, but in A.D. 49 they were expelled again under Claudius, shortly before Paul visited Corinth (Acts 18:1–2).[96] Now, when Paul arrived in Rome in A.D. 57, a new emperor was on the throne (Nero, since A.D. 54), and Jews were again being allowed to return to Rome.

The fact that these Jewish leaders knew nothing about Paul clearly shows that the Jerusalem leaders had not contacted them about him. But this is not surprising since Paul had appealed to Caesar just before he left Caesarea and had been delayed in reaching Rome only by the closed sailing season. The Jews would have had no way to reach Rome any sooner than Paul. But they must have come eventually. Two bits of evidence support this position. First, Rome dealt severely with false or even unsuccessful accusations, and accusers were required to present their case or suffer consequences.[97] Second, Paul had specifically been told by an angel of God, "You must stand before Caesar" (Acts 27:24).

The nature of Paul's two-year custody in Rome is most fully and carefully discussed in Brian Rapske's excellent volume *The Book of Acts and Paul in Roman Custody*.[98] The book, and especially his chapter on "Paul's Custody in Rome," gives a picture of a man of some financial means,[99] providing his own hired dwelling,[100] with complete freedom to preach quite "openly and unhindered" (Acts 28:31), and conducting what amounts to a house church during this time. In a later chapter Rapske comments, "We contend that Luke wanted to show to his readers that *the prisoner Paul's entire two year ministry in Rome was house church-like*."[101]

Rapske finds no reason to assume that the treatment given Paul was exceptional. He was now in Rome, where his citizenship and rank were no longer exceptional. He was placed under the guard of a regular soldier instead of the centurion who had brought him to Rome (Acts 28:16). So matters unrelated to status account for Paul's comparative freedom—matters like money. Paul was given unusually lenient custody, but his wealth and status did not require it, Rapske argues.[102]

The fact that Luke concludes his account without relating Paul's hearing before Nero is disappointing to modern readers but not inconsistent with similar decisions elsewhere, such as his determination not to record the recep-

96. See the discussion in chapter 6.

97. See the discussion of this point in Sherwin-White, *Roman Society and Roman Law*, 112ff. He shows that Cadbury's assumptions of the existence of a statute of limitations which released the accused in a specified period of time if the accusers did not present themselves were never proven. Such a law cannot be shown to have existed. Hemer was also convinced that Paul stood before Caesar (*BASHH*, 157 n. 159).

98. Rapske, *Paul in Roman Custody*, 227–42.

99. "Felix would have been right to assume that Paul was materially well off" (ibid., 167).

100. See ibid., 178ff.

101. Ibid., 365.

102. Ibid., 181.

tion of the extremely important contribution Paul brought to Jerusalem. Luke leaves his readers to assume that since Paul had been found guiltless before three previous Roman officials, Gallio, Felix, and Festus, he was not convicted by Nero.

The City of Rome

Rome was built on seven hills along the east bank of the Tiber River, twenty miles from its mouth.[103] The heart of the city was the area between the Palatine and Esquiline Hills, occupied by the Roman Forum and the Imperial Fora. Here people gathered to conduct commercial, political, and religious affairs. By the first century B.C., the Palatine had become the choicest residential area in Rome, where notables such as Cicero, Mark Antony, and Augustus Caesar lived.

Adjacent to this area on the south was the Colosseum, and to the west between the Palatine and Aventine Hills stood the Circus Maximus, where many Christians lost their lives before the eyes of the morally depraved spectators. Many impressive buildings, such as temples and bathhouses, were built surrounding this central area, including the Pantheon (a temple to the Roman gods) and the Baths of Agrippa in the northwest sector of the city. In A.D. 52, only five years prior to Paul's arrival, Caligula completed a new aqueduct.

Associated with the Roman Forum, which Julius Caesar had reconstructed in the heart of the city, were two buildings that would figure prominently in Paul's final imprisonment (2 Tim. 4:6–8). One of these was the Basilica Julia, built by Julius Caesar on the western side of the forum. Paul probably heard his death sentence in this building.[104] The other was the Mammertine Prison, located nearby at the foot of the Capitoline Hill and near the Temple of Concord. It was a two-level structure in which both Paul and Peter may have been incarcerated before their martyrdoms.[105]

At the west end of this forum, Paul the traveler would have seen the Milliarium Aureum (the Golden Milestone), from which were measured the distances to the main cities of the empire. He would have seen many inscribed milestones along the road marking the distance from Rome. North of the Golden Milestone stood the Umbilicus Romae, which marked the center not only of Rome but also of the Roman world.

103. See a fuller description of Rome in McRay, *Archaeology and the New Testament*, 341–50.

104. Finegan, *ANT:MW*, 223. Cf. the unconvincing article by Arthur Droge, "Did Paul Commit Suicide?" *Bible Review* 5.6 (December 1989): 14–21. Cf. also Reader's Reply in *Bible Review* 6.2 (April 1990): 6, 8; and 6.3 (June 1990): 7.

105. Finegan, *ANT:MW*, 224. See Finegan's rather full discussion of Paul and Peter's death in Rome (ibid., 222ff.).

Paul Writing from Rome

During the "two whole years" (Acts 28:30) that Paul spent in house arrest during this first imprisonment in Rome, he probably wrote the four "prison letters," Philemon, Colossians, Ephesians, and Philippians, all of which mention his incarceration. The second letter to Timothy was also written from prison (2 Tim. 4:6–8), but unlike these four, which anticipate Paul's release, that letter anticipates his death and thus requires a different historical context. For this reason it is appropriate to refer to the four Prison Letters as a group.

It is clearly stated in the letters of Philemon, Colossians, and Ephesians that Paul is in confinement at the time of their composition (Philem. 1, 9; Col. 4:18; Eph. 3:1; 4:1; 6:20). Philippians is also to be classed in this group of Prison Letters, since Paul was imprisoned at the time of its composition (Phil. 1:7, 13–14), but there is evidence that the first three were composed independently as a group.

The probable context for the composition of these Prison Letters is as follows. During his imprisonment in Rome, Paul came into contact with Onesimus, a runaway slave who belonged to Philemon, a citizen of Colossae. That Philemon was a member of the church in Colossae is indicated in the chart below, which shows that the Philemon letter was written to Colossae because seven of the same individuals are referred to in both letters and Onesimus is called "one of you" in the Colossian letter (Col. 4:9). Whether Onesimus was converted by Paul is not certain but is probable, since Paul speaks of having become his father during Paul's imprisonment (Philem. 10).

Now that Onesimus had either become a Christian through Paul or, already having been a problematical Christian in Colossae, had been changed by his contact with Paul, the problem of his servitude prompted Paul to write Philemon, admonishing him to receive Onesimus back as a brother (Philem. 16–17). At the same time, Paul also was motivated by the opportunity to send another letter with Tychicus and Onesimus to the Colossian church to deal with the subject of slavery more generally as well as other theological problems confronting the church. Paul did not want the forgiveness of Onesimus, which he requested from Philemon, to be interpreted as an endorsement of irresponsible behavior on the part of any Christian, slave or free.

So in the letter to Colossae, he said of slaves (Col. 3:22), "The wrongdoer will be paid back for the wrong he has done, and there is no partiality" (Col. 3:25). These words seem out of place in reference to a slave but are to be expected in reference to a master, as they appear in the expanded Ephesian letter (Eph. 6:9). Therefore, the probability is that the application of these words to slaves in Colossians was with Onesimus specifically in mind.[106]

---

106. He may be the Onesimus who became a bishop in the church in Ephesus (Ign. *Eph.* 1.3; 2.1; 6.2; Eusebius, *Hist. eccl.* 3.36.5).

In the more general letter to Ephesus, written immediately following the composition of Colossians, Paul did not need to deal with the specific situation of Onesimus, so he used the words more appropriately of a master's responsibility to his slaves. There is nothing here that necessitates attributing the letters to two different authors.[107]

As the following comparative chart shows, several facts tie these three letters together in an unusual way. Onesimus, about whom the letter of Philemon was written, accompanied Tychicus when he delivered the Colossian letter (Col. 4:7–9). Tychicus also carried with him at that time the letter to the Ephesians (Eph. 6:21). It seems clear, therefore, that Tychicus and Onesimus carried these three letters to their destinations. Furthermore, a close connection between the Philemon letter and Colossians is seen in the fact that Archippus, who is addressed by Paul in Philemon (Philem. 2), received a message from Paul in Colossians (Col. 4:17). Both letters carry Timothy's name along with that of Paul in the greetings (Col. 1:1; Philem. 1). In both letters greetings are sent from Aristarchus, Mark, Epaphras, Luke, and Demas, all of whom were with Paul at the time the letters were written (Col. 4:10–14; Philem. 23–24).

Table 8.1 Persons Mentioned in the Prison Epistles

Person	Colossians	Philemon	Ephesians	Philippians
Timothy	1:1	1		1:1
Tychicus	4:7		6:21	
Epaphras	1:7; 4:12	23		
Onesimus	4:9	10		
Archippus	4:17	2		
Aristarchus	4:10	24		
Mark	4:10	24		
Jesus Justus	4:11			
Luke	4:14	24		
Demas	4:14	24		
Epaphroditus				2:25; 4:18
Clement				4:3
Imprisonment	4:3, 10, 18	1, 9, 10, 13, 23	3:1; 4:1; 6:20	1:7, 13, 14, 17

The doctrinal content of Ephesians and Colossians is so obviously similar, not only in general outline but also in parallel phraseology, that one immediately thinks of the close relation between the first three Gospels as a similar

---

107. As does John Knox, *Philemon among the Letters of Paul* (London: Collins, 1960), 37.

literary parallel. It is generally held that Ephesians is an expansion of Colossians for a wider audience, in which the author generalized some of the particular issues facing the church in Colossae for a broader application to the churches in Asia. Ephesians contains a summary of God's scheme of redemption. The close parallels between these two letters can be seen in the following table.

Table 8.2. Ephesians and Colossians Compared

		Ephesians	Colossians
I.	Greeting	1:1–2	1:1–2
II.	Christ's Work and Reconciling of Gentiles	1:3–2:22	1:3–23a
III.	Paul's Commission to and Concern for the Gentiles	3:1–21	1:23b–2:5
IV.	The Gentile Christians Should Walk Worthily of Their Conversion	4:1–5:20	2:6–3:17 (heresy, 2:8–23; cf. Eph. 4:14, 16)
V.	Subjection in Christ to Each Other	5:21–6:9	3:18–4:1
VI.	Final Exhortations		
	A. Arm Selves against Spiritual Hosts	6:10–17	—
	B. Pray, Especially for Paul	6:18–20	4:2–4
	C. Walk in Wisdom	—	4:5–6 (related to heresy)
VII.	Conclusion		
	A. Tychicus Sent	6:21–22	4:7–9
	B. Greeting Sent	—	4:10–17
	C. Benediction	6:23–24	4:18

Since Tychicus and Onesimus, who would be carrying the letters to Philemon and Colossae, would be sailing into the harbor at Ephesus or nearby Miletus in order to travel to Colossae on the main road through the Lycus Valley,[108] Paul took advantage of the opportunity to also send a letter to Ephesus, which Tychicus could drop off for him. In the ancient world, mail had to be sent when the opportunity presented itself. During Paul's two years with the Ephesians, this church had spread the gospel to "all Asia" (Acts 19:10) and would be able to circulate Paul's letter among those churches. There is evidence in Ephesians that it was intended to be a general letter to several churches.

First, unlike Colossians with its local references, the Ephesian letter contains no specific reference to people or circumstances in Ephesus. Second,

108. See John McRay, "Colossae," *EEC,* 220–21.

three of the oldest and best Greek manuscripts of Ephesians omit the phrase "in Ephesus" from 1:1,[109] thereby making the letter an encyclical, addressed generally "to the saints and faithful."[110] Examples of this type of letter in the New Testament include Hebrews, James, 1 Peter, 1 John, and the Book of Revelation, which is addressed to the seven churches of Asia (Rev. 1:4).

The generalizing of the particular themes of Colossians[111] for Ephesians[112] was, therefore, especially appropriate for a letter intended for a larger audience. However, the same conditions are satisfied if Paul wrote the letter as an encyclical for all the churches in Asia but sent it to Ephesus with the expectation that the Ephesian church would circulate it among the others. He had just written Colossae, telling them to have their letter read at Laodicea and to be sure that the Colossians read the letter he had written to Laodicea (Col. 4:16). Whether that Laodicean letter was written at the same time as these other Prison Letters is not known. An apocryphal letter to the Laodiceans circulated in the early church. Tertullian, writing in the second century, said a heretic named Marcion considered Ephesians to be the Laodicean letter.[113] A copy of this Laodicean letter still exists in Latin.[114]

The churches in Colossae, Hierapolis, and Laodicea were apparently having problems (Col. 2:1; 4:13–17) because of a heresy that had developed among Christians who had become entangled with some kind of Jewish Hellenistic philosophy (Col. 2:8) and were promoting the necessity of observing Sabbaths, festivals, and new moons (Col. 2:16); the worship of angels (Col. 2:18); aescetic regulations regarding food and sex (Col. 2:20–23); circumci-

---

109. These are $\mathfrak{P}^{46}$ (the Chester Beatty Papyrus) and the original hands of Codex Sinaiticus and Vaticanus. $\mathfrak{P}^{46}$ also omits the subscript πρὸς Ἐφεσίους (to Ephesus) at the end of the letter.

110. Richard Batey ("The Destination of Ephesians," *JBL* 82 [1963]: 101) suggests a possible conjectural emendation. Accepting the manuscripts that do not contain the words "at Ephesus" as containing the original reading, he thinks a scribe might have mistaken ACIAC (Asia) for OYCAIC (the feminine participle meaning "who are") and written in the masculine form of the participle, OYCIN, as a correction of the gender. The construction τοῖς ἁγίοις τοῖς Ἀσίας καὶ πιστοῖς ("to the saints and faithful in Asia") thus became τοῖς ἁγίοις τοῖς οὖσιν καὶ πιστοῖς ("to the saints who are also faithful") as it now reads in extant manuscripts. This emendation solves several problems, Batey says: (1) inept syntax is removed; (2) it accounts for the encyclical character of the letter; (3) it explains Marcion's attribution of the letter to the Laodiceans (he saw a copy in Laodicea, or knew of one, that was simply addressed to the Asians); and (4) the similarity between a general letter to Asia and a specific one to Colossae is elucidated.

111. See below for the theology of Colossians. See also John McRay, "Colossians," in *Evangelical Commentary on the Bible,* ed. Walter Elwell (Grand Rapids: Baker, 1989), 1049–63.

112. See chapter 13 on the theology of Ephesians.

113. *Marc.* 5.17; 5.11.

114. The oldest text is contained in the Codex Fuldensis (A.D. 546). It is mentioned by Gregory the Great, and its widespread occurrence in English medieval Bibles may be due to Gregory's influence. See the discussion in J. K. Elliott, *The Apocryphal New Testament* (Oxford: Clarendon, 1993), 543–46.

sion (Col. 2:11–13; 3:11); improper teaching on the intermediary role of Christ and other angelic powers between God and man (Col. 1:15–20; 2:8, 20); and a resultant immorality (Col. 3:5–10).[115] These issues are reflected in the following outline of Colossians.

Colossians Outline

I. Salutation (1:1–2)
   A. Sender (1:1)
   B. Addressee (1:2a)
   C. Greeting (1:2b)
II. Thanksgiving (1:3–14)
   A. Thanksgiving for the Gentile Colossians' Love for the (Jewish) Saints (1:3–8)
   B. Thanksgiving for the Knowledge That the Gentile Colossians Share in the Inheritance of the (Jewish) Saints (1:9–14)
III. Body (1:15–3:4)
   A. Christ's Work and the Reconciling of the Gentiles (1:15–23)
   B. Paul's Ministry to the Gentiles (1:24–2:5)
   C. Gentile Christians Should Walk Worthily of Their Conversion (2:6–19)
   D. The Colossians Have Been Freed from the Elemental Spirits to Live a New Life in Christ (2:20–3:4)
IV. Ethical Exhortations and Instructions (3:5–4:6)
   A. Put to Death What Is Earthly (3:5–11)
   B. Put on Christian Virtues (3:12–17)
   C. Wives and Husbands (3:18–19)
   D. Children and Parents (3:20–21)
   E. Slaves and Masters (3:22–4:1)
   F. Continue in Prayer (4:2–4)
   G. Conduct Yourself Wisely toward Outsiders (4:5–6)
V. Closing (4:7–18)
   A. Greeting (4:7–17)
   B. Benediction (4:18)

The themes of Ephesians and Colossians are not as different as some would seem to make them. The emphasis in Colossians on Christ as the head of the church but in Ephesians on the church as a body of Christ is not as different as it may first appear. The problem at issue in both books is the salvation of all people, Jew and Gentile, in one body—the church. The point to be seen is that God, in fulfilling the promise to Abraham that *all nations* would be blessed in him and his seed (Christ, Gen. 12:3; Gal. 3:16), had to destroy the

115. See also McRay, "Colossians," 1049–63.

satanic power that caused the existing religious division between Jew and Gentile. The Jews under the old law had come under the control of "elemental spirits of the universe" (Gal. 4:3, 9), and Christ had to destroy those spirits' power to blind the minds of people (2 Cor. 4:4) to the truth of monotheism. The Jews were affirming the existence of more than one God when they insisted that a Gentile had to become a Jew in order to have access to Jehovah, the God of the Jews (Rom. 3:29–30). They expected God to save Gentiles in a separate body, if at all (Acts 11:18; Gal. 2:12).

The theme of Ephesians and Colossians, however, is that God's "mystery," the salvation of Jew and Gentile in the same body (Col. 3:11, 15; Eph. 2:16; 3:1–6), has been revealed through the death of Jesus on the cross. There he not only removed the partitioning effects of the law (separating Jew and Gentile) but also "disarmed the principalities and powers" (Col. 2:14–15). However, although Satan has lost, his power is still felt in the Christian struggle to live for God (Eph. 6:12). Any attempt to reject the unification of all people in one body to God through the cross (which is the argument of Ephesians; cf. 2:15–19; 3:6) is tantamount to denying the unity of the divine Godhead in the person of Jesus when he suffered on the cross (the argument of Col. 2:8–9, 14–15; 1:16). The fatherhood of God necessarily demands the brotherhood of humanity.

It is only when this basic theme is ignored that Ephesians and Colossians can be viewed as dealing with different issues. The "philosophy" troubling the Colossian church (Col. 2:8), which exhibited certain Jewish ascetic tendencies (Col. 2:16–23) as well as pagan denials of the one Creator (Col. 1:15–17), was probably an embryo of a second-century heresy that, when fully developed, was known as Gnosticism. Because of its dualistic emphasis, this philosophy later denied the reality of the flesh and blood of Jesus. Paul was aware of such tendencies and insisted that God's redemptive work took place only through the "body of flesh" (Col. 1:22) that hung on the cross.

In Ephesians also, Paul stated that redemption and reconciliation took place "in his flesh" (Eph. 2:15). So the themes of Ephesians and Colossians are not actually different. The emphasis in Colossians simply falls more heavily on one aspect of the major theme (the unity of the divine Godhead and its representative fullness in the flesh of Jesus), while the emphasis in Ephesians falls more heavily on another aspect of the major theme (the unity of the spiritual body and its representative fullness in the fleshly unification of Jew and Gentile). The theological content of Ephesians will be discussed more fully in chapter 13.

Paul's Last Years

In the closing two verses of Acts (28:30–31), Luke states that Paul "lived there [in Rome] two whole years at his own expense, and welcomed all who came to him, preaching the kingdom of God and teaching about the Lord Jesus Christ quite openly and unhindered." The question naturally arises as to whether Paul died at this time.

Paul had already appeared before the Roman procurators Felix (Acts 24:24–27) and Festus (Acts 25:7, 25) in Caesarea Maritima, Israel, and they had found no sufficient grounds to accuse him of disloyalty to the Roman Empire. Paul later said, "When they had examined me, they wished to set me at liberty, because there was no reason for the death penalty in my case" (Acts 28:18). He had previously been taken before Gallio, the Roman proconsul in Corinth (Acts 18:12–17), who also did not find Paul guilty of "wrongdoing or vicious crime" (Acts 18:14) and refused to condemn him.[116] By the close of the Book of Acts, Paul has been in Rome for two years under house arrest and has not been condemned by Nero. It is likely that Nero was waiting for Paul's accusers to come from Israel and charge him, but evidently they had not yet come because Jews in Rome told Paul, "We have received no letters from Judea about you, and none of the brethren coming here has reported or spoken any evil about you" (Acts 28:21).

It is probable that Nero had already heard about his own proconsul Gallio's trying Paul and finding no guilt in him, because Nero's court adviser was Seneca, Gallio's brother, and he undoubtedly would have given Nero the information favorable to Paul derived from his brother.

The most likely scenario, then, is that Luke records nothing further about Paul because this is as far as the story had progressed when he composed Acts. The fourth-century church historian Eusebius of Caesarea wrote, "Luke probably wrote the Acts of the Apostles at that time, carrying down his narrative until the time when he was with Paul. We have said this to show that Paul's martyrdom was not accomplished during the sojourn in Rome which Luke describes."[117] Hence, there is nothing in Acts that in any way demonstrates a termination of the life and ministry of this great apostle with whom Luke traveled.[118] On the contrary, the Prison Epistles—Colossians (4:3, 10, 18), Philemon (1, 9, 10, 13, 23), Ephesians (3:1; 4:1), and Philippians (1:7, 13, 17, 22)—all mention Paul's imprisonment but with no anticipation of anything but release and a visit to Colossae and Philippi. It is thus most likely that Paul was released from his house arrest in Rome after two years, with no accusers coming to speak against him, and that he subsequently continued his journeys in the Mediterranean world.

116. See chapter 3, under "Gallio's Proconsulship in Achaia."

117. Eusebius, *Hist. eccl.* 2.22.6 (trans. Kirsopp Lake and J. E. L. Oulton, Loeb Classical Library [Cambridge, Mass.: Harvard University Press, 1953], 1:169).

118. John Mauck (*Paul on Trial: The Book of Acts as a Defense of Christianity* [Nashville: Nelson, 2001]) argues that Luke wrote Acts specifically as a defense of Paul's loyalty to Rome that Paul could present in court at Rome.

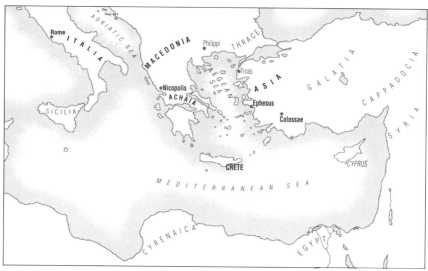

Map 8.2. Paul's Post-Captivity Visits (Bold indicates places Paul probably visited. Arrows are omitted because Paul's exact route is unknown.)

It is possible that Paul went on to Spain with the help of the church in Rome, a desire he had expressed earlier when writing to the Romans from Corinth (Rom. 15:24). However, the strongest traditions from Spain relate to James and not Paul. Based on information gleaned from three of the Prison Epistles, I suggest, rather, that Paul went on to visit Philemon in Colossae as he had planned (Philem. 22). The evidence is as follows: Tychicus carried letters from Paul in Rome to Ephesus (Eph. 6:21–22) and Colossae (Col. 4:7–8), and Onesimus, the slave of Philemon, accompanied Tychicus on this trip (Col. 4:7–9). In the letter Paul wrote to Philemon, he says that he is sending Onesimus back to him (Philem. 10–12), and Paul asks Philemon to prepare a guest room for Paul's anticipated visit (Philem. 22). That Paul sends Onesimus with Tychicus to the church in Colossae (Col. 4:7–9) suggests that Philemon lived in Colossae.

Since Paul would have traveled from Rome (or Spain) through the Mediterranean Sea eastward to Colossae in Asia Minor, he would have passed by the island of Crete and probably stopped there for a while. From a later letter, we learn that Paul left Titus in Crete to appoint elders and set in order the things that were lacking (Titus 1:5). There is no other time in Paul's recorded journeys when this could have taken place.[119] It seems likely, then, that Paul left Titus on Crete, traveled on to Colossae and visited Philemon as planned, and then eventually made his way to Macedonia, leaving Timothy at Ephesus

119. See chapter 3 on chronology for further discussion.

Photo 8.7. Nicopolis

(1 Tim. 1:3). He then traveled to Achaia and chose to spend the winter on the west coast of this southern sector of modern Greece. When Paul wrote to Titus, he was spending the winter in Nicopolis, a city on the western shore of Greece (Titus 3:12). From here, then, Paul would have written 1 Timothy and Titus, following his release from his first Roman imprisonment. This setting for the composition of these two Pastoral Epistles seems to fit the historical and geographical data best.

1 Timothy

First Timothy was written to a young man (4:12) who was in poor health (5:23) and was probably overwhelmed by the responsibilities placed on his shoulders (4:15–16). Paul's prophecy to the Ephesian elders (Acts 20:29–30) was already coming to pass (1 Tim. 5:15), and Timothy was in the midst of grave problems (1:6–7, 18–20; 4:6–7).

Apparently Timothy had been converted to Christianity on Paul's first journey (1 Tim. 1:2, 18; Acts 14:6–23) and had joined him on the second journey (Acts 16:1–3). He was dedicated to the ministry (1 Tim. 4:14; 2 Tim. 1:6) and worked with Paul in Troas, Philippi, Beroea, and Athens. About five years after Timothy's mission to Thessalonica on behalf of Paul (Acts 18:5), he reappears in Ephesus on Paul's third journey and is sent to Macedonia with Erastus (Acts 19:22). When Paul wrote 2 Corinthians from Macedonia, Timothy was with him (2 Cor. 1:1, 19) and probably accompanied Paul to Corinth, since he sends greetings to Rome in the letter Paul wrote from Corinth (Rom. 16:21). Later, he accompanied Paul again into Macedonia and then into Asia as far as Troas (Acts 20:1–3). Timothy disappears from the pages of the New Testament for the next two years while Paul is imprisoned in Caesarea, but his name appears again in the letters sent from Rome, indicating that he must have been with Paul during his first imprisonment (Phil. 1:1; Col. 1:1; Philem. 1). From Rome, Timothy went to Philippi (Phil. 2:19–23) and then disappears again from the record. He probably went to Ephesus to work, where he received the first of the two New Testament letters bearing his name. Writing in the fourth century, Eusebius says that the tradition is strong in support of Timothy's having been prominent in the church in Ephesus.[120]

The three letters of Paul to Timothy and Titus are usually classified together as the "Pastoral Epistles" because they have to do with the work of preaching. For convenience, the early evidence for their existence and Pauline authorship will be cited together.

Clement of Rome, in the first century, is among the first to use phraseology from these letters in his writing.[121] Irenaeus, Eusebius, Athenagoras, Marcion, and others of the Western division of the church in the Roman Empire allude to the letters in one way or another. Among the Eastern writers, Ignatius, Polycarp, Justin Martyr, Hegesippus, and Theophilus all refer to these three letters to such an extent that there is a "continuous testimony to the circulation of the Pastoral Epistles in the East as far back as the year 116."[122]

The internal evidence is quite strong for Paul's authorship, because in all three letters the author claims to be Paul (1 Tim. 1:1; 2 Tim. 1:1; Titus 1:1). The relationship between writer and recipients reflected in these letters mirrors that known to exist between Paul and the two young men Timothy and Titus, both of whom Paul had converted (1 Tim. 1:2; Titus 1:4). The letters are obviously written from an older man who possessed the authority and the assumed right to direct the younger men addressed in the letters (Titus 1:5; 2 Tim. 1:5; 1 Tim. 1:18; 4:12). From the Book of Acts it is clear that such a relationship existed between Paul and these two young men.

The three letters are usually thought to have been written at about the same time, because their content is so much alike in language, thought, doctrines combated, and so on. This homogeneity is characteristic of other groupings of Paul's letters. For example, those written to Thessalonica form the first group and are very much alike in content. The letters to Corinth, Galatia, and Rome were written not too far apart, and the two to Corinth are so much alike as to

---

120. *Hist. eccl.* 3.4.5.

121. *First Clement* 2.7 refers to Titus 3:1; *1 Clem.* 29.1 refers to 1 Tim. 2:8; *1 Clem.* 45.1 refers to 2 Tim. 1:3.

122. J. H. Bernard, *The Pastoral Epistles*, Cambridge Greek Testament (Cambridge: Cambridge University Press, 1906), xvi.

be supplementary to each other. The third group of Paul's letters, the Prison Epistles, written from Rome, are very similar in style and content (compare especially Ephesians with Colossians). In light of this pattern, the argument for a mutual date based on similarities in style and content among the three Pastoral Epistles is quite strong. Assuming Paul's death under Nero in A.D. 67 or 68,[123] it is feasible to date 1 Timothy a few years earlier, perhaps 65, to allow for the events that transpire between its writing and the writing of 2 Timothy.

1 Timothy Outline

I. Instruction for the Church (1–3)
   A. Warning against False Teachers (1)
   B. Instructions about Worship (2)
   C. Instructions about Church Officials (3)
II. Instruction to Timothy of a Personal Nature (4–6)
   A. Doctrine and Practical Matters (4)
   B. Elders, Widows, and Slaves (5)
   C. Dangerous Attitudes and Activities in the Church (6)

Titus

As noted above, Titus was on the island of Crete, off the western coast of Palestine, when he received his letter from Paul (1:5). There is no evidence, however, that Paul founded the church there, although he stopped there briefly on his journey to Rome (Acts 27:7–13, 21). It may be that some of those from Crete who were present in Jerusalem on Pentecost (Acts 2:11) came back to the island and founded the church. Apparently Apollos and Zenas the lawyer were going in the direction of Crete, and Paul took advantage of the opportunity for messenger service and wrote this letter (Titus 3:13). The church in Crete was plagued with false teachers advocating adherence to Jewish law and customs. Paul wrote to correct this. Titus was in a more difficult field than Timothy since the work in Crete was new, whereas the work in Ephesus was well established. Paul's instructions to Titus reflect the needs of this challenging situation.

Titus appears by name in only four books in the New Testament (2 Corinthians, Galatians, 2 Timothy, Titus). His name does not appear in the Book of Acts, although he was involved in events connected with the progress of the early church that are discussed in the book. From what is recorded elsewhere, it is clear that Titus was a Greek (Gal. 2:3) and a companion of Barnabas and Paul (Gal. 2:1). He was evidently converted by Paul (Titus 1:4) and either worked with the church in Antioch of Syria or was from that general vicinity,

---

123. The time of Paul's death is generally agreed to have been during the reign of Nero. Clement's reasons for Paul's death seem to fit Nero's persecution best (*1 Clem.* 5.2, 5).

because it was from there that he accompanied Paul and Barnabas to Jerusalem on Paul's fourteenth-year visit (Gal. 2:1–10). He may have worked as far away as the province of Galatia, since his name is mentioned in the Galatian letter written to the churches of that area. After a few years of silence, he is seen again, carrying the first letter of Paul to the church of Corinth along with an unnamed brother (2 Cor. 12:18). He also seems to have carried the "severe letter" of Paul to Corinth that was written between 1 and 2 Corinthians (2 Cor. 7:6–12; 2:3–4, 9). Paul went to meet Titus in Macedonia, unable to wait for him in Troas because of his strong desire to hear from him about the welfare of the church in Corinth (2 Cor. 2:12–13; 7:5–16). Titus later carried 2 Corinthians to the church in Corinth (2 Cor. 8:16–24).

We lose sight of Titus for another several years until Paul wrote him in Crete where he had left him to "straighten out what was left unfinished and appoint elders in every town" (Titus 1:5). He was to meet Paul at Nicopolis after Tychicus and Artemas arrived in Crete, apparently to relieve him (Titus 3:12). The last reference to Titus is from the pen of Paul in a list of several of his traveling companions. During his last imprisonment in Rome before his death, Paul states that Titus had gone to Dalmatia (2 Tim. 4:10). He was probably not a deserter like Demas but had been sent out by Paul.

Paul is named as the author of the letter to Titus (Titus 1:1), and from the historical allusions in the book, there is no reason to doubt this. Who else in the church of this period could so amply fill the position that the author of this letter must have occupied? The relation he sustained to Titus is exactly that which he sustained to Timothy. Both were Paul's converts. The letter to Titus is so much like 1 Timothy that they must have been written at about the same time. A probable date of A.D. 65 is reasonable for the letter,[124] thus placing it less than three years before 2 Timothy. It may have been written from Corinth, Ephesus, or some other city where Paul would have had opportunity to see Apollos (Titus 3:13). Paul asks Titus to meet him in Nicopolis, but it is apparent that Paul is not there at the time of the composition of the letter, because he tells Titus that he has decided to spend the winter "there" rather than the place from which he was then writing.

Titus Outline

   I. Instruction for Appointing Elders and Reproving False Teachers (1:1–16)
   II. Domestic Relations (2:1–10)
   III. Instruction for Christian Living (2:11–15)
   IV. Christian Citizenship (3:1–2)
   V. The Meaning of Regeneration (3:3–8)
   VI. Procedure for Dealing with Troublemakers (3:9–15)

124. See chapter 3 on chronology.

2 Timothy

The second letter to Timothy is without question the last of Paul's preserved literary correspondence. His journeys had led him to Nicopolis after his release from prison in Rome (Titus 3:12) and then to Troas in Asia Minor. He must have been forced to leave Troas hurriedly, because he did not take his cloak, books, or parchments with him (2 Tim. 4:13). His arrest must have come soon after this, and we next hear of him in Rome as he writes this second letter, asking Timothy to bring these things to him. Evidently Paul was prompted to write the letter by his desire for these belongings as well as by his genuine concern over the problems Timothy was facing and a desire to see him again soon.

Although Timothy was in Ephesus when Paul wrote him the first letter (1 Tim. 1:3–4), he does not seem to be there at the time of the writing of the second letter. Paul states in the second letter that he has sent Tychicus to Ephesus (2 Tim. 4:12), but he makes no mention of Timothy's presence there. Paul assumes that Timothy would pass through Troas on his way to Rome (2 Tim. 4:13), and Paul's urging him to come before winter (2 Tim. 4:21) suggests that Timothy's route would require travel by sea. Also, Paul warns Timothy about Alexander the coppersmith (2 Tim. 4:14–15) and tells him to greet Onesiphorus (2 Tim. 4:19); both of these persons lived in Ephesus (1 Tim. 1:20; 2 Tim. 1:16–18). It is therefore probable that Timothy was somewhere in the Roman province of Asia and that he would pass through both Troas and Ephesus on his way to Paul in Rome.

Paul is stated to be the author of this letter (2 Tim. 1:1) as well as of the four earlier Prison Epistles, but his situation has changed considerably from what it was during his first imprisonment in Rome. He is now accused by Roman authority and treated as a prisoner. During Paul's first imprisonment, he was accused by the Jews and allowed to stay by himself (Acts 28:16, 30). Now he is able to acknowledge friends only with difficulty (2 Tim. 4:16). Formerly, he was free to have guests in his own hired dwelling and preach the gospel without restraint (Acts 28:30–31), and he even anticipated freedom (Philem. 22). Now he anticipates death (2 Tim. 4:6). The personal references in the letter and the position of authority assumed by the writer are consistent with what we find in Paul's other letters and with what we would expect from Paul. From Rome, then, near the end of his life, Paul pens his final words of advice. Since Paul's death seems imminent and there is little doubt that he died under Nero's reign in A.D. 67 or 68, the letter is best dated to this time.[125]

2 Timothy Outline

I. An Appeal to Faithfulness (1:1–2:13)
II. Personal Instruction to Timothy (2:14–26)

125. For further discussion of Paul's last years, see Bruce, *Paul,* 441–55.

Photo 8.8. Mammertine Prison in Rome

III. Warning against False Teaching (3:1–17)
IV. A Charge to a Young Preacher (4:1–8)
V. Personal Matters (4:9–22)

The context of the composition of Paul's last letter is undoubtedly the worst of any of his many imprisonments. Paul may have spent as much as 25 percent of his years as an itinerant missionary in prison. This included two years incarceration in Caesarea, two years in a first imprisonment in Rome, an undisclosed duration of time during his last confinement in Rome, and a brief lockup in Philippi. But these recorded confinements do not tell the whole story. Paul wrote that he experienced "far more imprisonments" than his opponents (2 Cor. 11:13, 23), a phrase that implies more than a few, but no account of these is given in the New Testament.

Clothing was not replaced in Roman prisons, and prisoners were cold in winter. During his final imprisonment in Rome, Paul asked that his cloak, used as a cover at night, be brought to him (2 Tim. 4:13). He had left it at Troas, his sudden arrest apparently preventing him from packing his clothing.[126]

Paul probably spent his last days in the Mammertine Prison near the Roman Forum and then was beheaded, tradition says, at Aquae Salviae (modern Tre Fontane) near the third milestone on the Ostian Way. A memorial

126. See further on Roman prisons in chapter 2. See also my "Life in a Roman Prison," *Christian History* 14.3, issue 47 (1995).

Photo 8.9. Church of St. Paul Outside the Walls near Rome

chapel was built here in the fifth century, above which stands the present church of St. Paul at Tre Fontane.[127] It has been *San Pietro in Carcere* since the sixteenth century, preserving a tradition that Peter was imprisoned there. It is possible that both Peter and Paul were incarcerated in this two-level prison.[128] It is located at the foot of the Capitoline Hill, near the Temple of Concord.

The largest church in Rome after St. Peter's is the Church of St. Paul Outside the Walls, located about a mile from the Gate of St. Paul, on the Via Ostiense. No significant excavation has been done there, but the site is thought to be the location of the church built by Constantine in the fourth century to replace an oratory (prayer chapel) that had been built over the place where Lucina, a Roman matron, had buried Paul in her vineyard.[129] When the present church was being built, a marble slab was seen under the altar that contained the words PAULO APOSTOLO MART[YRI] in letters of the time of Constantine.[130] Finegan appropriately points out that there was little reason for a church to be built in this particular location unless some special situation ne-

127. See the brief discussion by Bruce, *Paul,* 450–51.
128. Finegan, *ANT:MW,* 224. See Finegan's rather full discussion of Paul and Peter's death in Rome (ibid., 222ff.).
129. See the "Blue Guide" on *Rome and Central Italy,* 2d ed. (London: Ernest Benn, 1964), 61.
130. Finegan, *ANT:MW,* 30.

cessitated it, for (1) the site was in a pagan cemetery, (2) it was in a constricted space between two roads, and (3) it was in an swampy area often flooded by the Tiber River.[131]

And so here we close our journeys with this great apostle as he sits in squalid conditions with the expectation of imminent death. "For I am already on the point of being sacrificed; the time of my departure has come. I have fought the good fight, I have finished the race, I have kept the faith. Henceforth there is laid up for me the crown of righteousness, which the Lord, the righteous judge, will award to me on that Day, and not only to me but also to all who have loved his appearing" (2 Tim. 4:6–8). This prompted the respectful and admiring words of Clement of Rome, written near the end of the first century: "Through jealousy and strife Paul showed the way to the prize of endurance; seven times he was in bonds, he was exiled, he was stoned, he was a herald both in the East and in the West, he gained the noble fame of his faith, he taught righteousness to all the world, and when he had reached the limits of the West he gave his testimony before the rulers, and thus passed from the world and was taken up into the Holy Place—the greatest example of endurance" (*1 Clem.* 5.5–7).[132]

---

131. Ibid.
132. For further information on Paul's imprisonment, see Rapske, *Paul in Roman Custody.*

Part 2

PAUL'S TEACHING

NINE

The Form, Function, and Canonicity of Pauline Letters

The New Testament is not a book but a collection of twenty-seven documents of various kinds written over a period of perhaps fifty years by several different authors. New Testament literature, unlike that of the Old Testament, contains no books of law, prophecy, poetry, or wisdom. The genres of New Testament books differ from those of the Old Testament. The New Testament consists of:

Gospels—Evangelistic adaptations of portions of the life of Jesus

Acts—A theological presentation of a selected portion of the history of the church's beginnings among Jews and Gentiles in a selected portion of the known world

Letters—Formal or informal correspondence between two or three parties

Apocalypse (Revelation)—a representation of a kind of literature widely disseminated in the Jewish world of the period between the Old and New Testaments and characterized by the use of bizarre imagery, esoteric numerology, and an emphasis on eschatology

Of these, we are concerned only with the letters, because the only extant Pauline literature is in this format.

Letters in the ancient world have both similarities and dissimilarities with modern letters. It is important to understand these comparisons in order to comprehend the nature of the New Testament as a source of authority for Christian faith, since most of the documents in the New Testament are letters. In addition to the fact that twenty-one of the twenty-seven "books" of the New Testament are epistles, it is significant that seven more letters are contained in the Book of Revelation, which is addressed to the seven churches of Asia (Rev. 1:4). The Book of Acts also contains several letters, such as the communication from the Jerusalem church to the church in Antioch (Acts 15:23–29) and the correspondence about Paul from Claudius Lysias in Jerusalem to the Roman procurator Felix in Caesarea (Acts 23:25–30).

For those who believe that the New Testament contains the inspired revelation of God's truth to his church,[1] it is important to understand that this revelation is given, by divine choice, not in the genre of law but in other genres, one of which is the letter. Therefore, just as Jewish methods of interpreting the Law necessarily vary from those used in interpreting the Psalms, so also Christian interpretation of the letters differs from that of the Gospels or Revelation. One intrinsically interprets law differently from history, and poetry differently from prose.

How then are we to understand these letters of Paul? Are they merely personal notes prompted by historical circumstances? Are they to be considered "literature"? Should one try to interpret them according to modern literary standards? Were they consciously written to be Scripture? Is it significant if they were not? What may we learn from letter writing in Paul's day that would help in understanding some of the enigmatic passages in his writings? Even Peter wrote about the difficulty of dealing with Paul's letters: "So also our beloved brother Paul wrote to you according to the wisdom given him, speaking of this as he does in all his letters. There are some things in them hard to understand" (2 Peter 3:15–16).

Since divine providence chose this method of communication for so much of the New Testament, it is important to understand both the form and the function of ancient letters in order to interpret them properly. Fortunately, ancient letter writing has been the subject of considerable study in recent years,[2] and we are now in a position to understand the genre more fully than

1. See the discussion by Roger Nicole of seven criteria historically used for determining the canon of the New Testament: "The Canon of the New Testament," *JETS* 40.2 (June 1997): 199–206.

2. Stanley Stowers, *Letter Writing in Greco-Roman Antiquity* (Philadelphia: Westminster, 1986); John White, "New Testament Epistolary Literature in the Framework of Ancient Epistolography," *ANRW*, 2.25.2:1730–56; idem, *The Form and Function of the Body of the Greek Letter: A Study of the Letter-Body in the Non-Literary Papyri and in Paul the Apostle*, SBL Dissertation Series 2 (Missoula, Mont.: Scholars Press, 1972); idem, *Light from Ancient Letters* (Philadelphia: Fortress, 1986); idem, "New Testament Epistolary Literature in the Framework of Ancient Epistolography" (paper presented at the annual meeting of the Society of Biblical Literature, November 1979); C. J. Roetzel, *The Letters of Paul: Conversations in Context*, 2d ed. (Atlanta: John Knox, 1982); George Bahr, "Paul and Letter Writing in the First Century," *CBQ* 28 (1966): 465–77; idem, "The Subscriptions in the Pauline Letters," *JBL* 87.1 (March 1968): 27–41; W. Doty, *Letters in Primitive Christianity* (Philadelphia: Fortress, 1973).

we have in the past. The study actually began in 1895, when Adolf Deissmann published a comparative study of the Greek papyri letters and those of the New Testament.[3] He tried to distinguish between "letters" and "epistles," arguing that the papyrus letters were produced by families and businesses as ordinary correspondence. In his view, these letters were written conversations, occasional letters without literary intent or merit, and were written merely to convey information in the way letters do today. Epistles, by contrast, were literary in nature and were intended for publication or at least for public reading. Examples of such epistles are to be found in the correspondence of Pliny and Seneca.[4]

Deissmann concluded that the New Testament writings were letters rather than epistles. They were informal, nonliterary correspondence, written for ordinary people in churches that were composed primarily of the lower classes of society. He argued wrongly that Paul wrote the letters spontaneously as private correspondence.[5] Clearly, most of Paul's letters were written to be shared with the churches, as Colossians 4:16 shows: "And when this letter has been read among you, have it read also in the church of the Laodiceans; and see that you read also the letter from Laodicea."

It has recently been argued that Paul employed the format of the nonliterary papyrus letters in the body of his own letters.[6] This format is as follows:

Salutation—sender, addressee, greeting

Thanksgiving

Body—composed of formal opening, connective and transitional formulae, concluding "eschatological climax," apostolic parousia

Ethical Exhortations and Instructions—paraenesis

Closing—greetings, doxology, benediction

Another contemporary writer finds this same format in 1 Thessalonians, 1 Corinthians, 2 Corinthians, Galatians, Philippians, and Romans.[7]

The similarities between Paul's letters and those of the papyri may be seen by comparing two of them side by side. The following papyrus letter, from the second or third century A.D., was written by a person named Irenaeus to his brother Apollinarius.[8] For comparative purposes, the entire text of the papy-

---

3. See Adolf Deissmann, *Bible Studies* (Edinburgh: Clark, 1909), 3–59. This is the English translation of his *Bibelstudien,* which he wrote in 1900.

4. Available in the Loeb Classical Library Series.

5. Leander E. Keck, *Paul and His Letters* (Philadelphia: Fortress, 1988), 21.

6. John White, "Comparison of the Body of the Letter in Paul and the Papyri," in *The Form and Function of the Body of the Greek Letter,* 93–100.

7. C. J. Roetzel, "The Anatomy of the Letters," in *Letters of Paul,* 29–40.

8. *Agyptische Urkunden aus den königlichen Museen zu Berlin: Griechische Urkunden* I, I–VII (Berlin: 1895–1926), #27 (H.E. 113).

rus letter is included here, followed by the comparison with Paul's brief letter to Philemon about the latter's slave Onesimus.[9]

> Irenaeus to Apollinarius his dearest brother many greetings. I pray continually for your health, and I myself am well. I wish you to know that I reached land on the sixth of the month Epeiph and we unloaded our cargo on the eighteenth of the same month. I went up to Rome, on the twenty fifth of the same month and the place welcomed us as the god willed, and we are daily expecting our discharge, it so being that up till today nobody in the corn fleet has been released. Many salutations to your wife and to Serenus and to all who love you, each by name. Goodbye. Mesore 9. (Addressed) To Apollinarius from his brother Irenaeus.[10]

Table 9.1 Philemon and Ancient Letter Compared

Structure	Papyrus Letter	Letter to Philemon
I. Salutation		
A. Sender	Irenaeus	Paul, a prisoner for Christ Jesus, and Timothy our brother
B. Recipient	To Apollinarius his dearest brother	To Philemon our beloved fellow worker and Apphia our sister and Archippus our fellow soldier, and the church in your house
C. Greeting	many greetings	Grace to you and peace from God our Father and the Lord Jesus Christ
II. Thanksgiving		
(Prayer)	I pray continually for your health, and I myself am well	I thank my God always when I remember you in my prayers
III. Body	(Information about his arrival on the grain boat from Egypt to Rome)	(Discussion of the return of Onesimus the slave)
IV. Ethical Exhortations and Instructions	(Absent here, but present elsewhere)	Receive him. . . . Charge that to my account. . . . Refresh my heart in Christ. . . . Prepare a guest room for me. . . .
V. Closing		
A. Peace Wish	(Absent)	(Absent here, but present elsewhere)

---

9. The comparison is taken from Roetzel, *Letters of Paul,* 30–31.
10. As translated in C. K. Barrett, ed., *The New Testament Background: Selected Documents,* rev. ed. (San Francisco: Harper & Row, 1989), 30.

Structure	Papyrus Letter	Letter to Philemon
B. Greetings	Many salutations to your wife and to Serenus and to all who love you, each by name	Epaphras, my fellow prisoner in Christ Jesus, sends greetings to you, and so do Mark, Aristarchus, Demas, and Luke, my fellow workers
C. Kiss	(Absent)	(Absent here, but present elsewhere)
D. Close (Grace and Benediction)	Goodbye	The grace of the Lord Jesus Christ be with your spirit

This comparison shows that both letters were written in the same basic format. The five-category letter structure delineated here has been found in six other letters of Paul, which are presented by Roetzel as follows:[11]

Table 9.2 Structure of Paul's Letters

	1 Thessalonians	1 Corinthians	2 Corinthians	Galatians	Philippians	Romans
1. Salutation						
Sender	1:1a	1:1	1:1a	1:1–2a	1:1	1:1–6
Recipient	1:1b	1:2	1:1b	1:2b	1:1	1:7a
Greeting	1:1c	1:3	1:2	1:3–5	1:2	1:7b
2. Thanksgiving	1:2–10; 2:13; 3:9–10	1:4–9	1:3–7	None	1:3–11	1:8–17
3. Body	2:1–3:8; (possibly 3:11–13)	1:10–4:21	1:8–9:15 (letter incomplete); 10:1–13:10 (letter fragment)	1:6–4:31	1:12–2:11; 3:1–4:1; 4:10–20	1:18–11:36
4. Ethical Exhortations and Instructions	4:1–5:22	5:1–16:12; 16:13–18 (closing paraenesis)	13:11a (summary)	5:1–6:10; 6:11–15 (letter summary)	2:12–29; 4:2–6	12:1–15:13; 15:14–32 (travel plans and closing paraenesis)
5. Closing						
Peace Wish	5:23f.	—	13:11b	6:16	4:7–9	15:33

11. Roetzel, *Letters of Paul,* 40.

	1 Thessalonians	1 Corinthians	2 Corinthians	Galatians	Philippians	Romans
Greetings	—	16:19–20a	13:13	—	4:21–22	16:1–15?
Kiss	5:26	16:20b	13:12	—	—	16:16?
Apostolic Command	5:27	16:22	—	6:17	—	—
Benediction	5:28	16:23–24	13:14	6:18	4:23	16:20?

It is becoming increasingly clear through these studies that Paul employed something of a hybrid arrangement in his correspondence, combining and modifying aspects of both formal and informal correspondence. His adaptations of ancient letter writing to his own individual needs may be seen in all the various sections of the letters delineated by Roetzel.

1. The *salutation* becomes more elaborate in Paul's letters, with the names of his traveling companions occasionally included. The simple "greetings" (χαίρειν, *chairein*) becomes "Grace to you and peace," the word *grace* (χάρις, *charis*) reflecting and deepening the meaning of the customary greeting, and the term *peace* probably representing the Jewish greeting *shalom*. Perhaps this is Paul's way of speaking to both Jews and Gentiles in his churches.

2. The *thanksgiving* follows the salutation and is addressed to the one true God as opposed to pagan deities and includes Jesus Christ as well. Paul thanks God in this section of his letters for the faith, hope, and love (Col. 1:4; 1 Thess. 1:3; cf. 1 Cor. 13:13) of his fellow Christians and for their steadfast service to God. He also sometimes includes themes that will be developed in the body of the letter. For example, Romans 1:16–17 employs a quotation from Habakkuk 2:4, "He who through faith is righteous shall live," which is then developed in the following chapters: "He who through faith is righteous" (Gentile and Jew, Rom. 1–4) "shall live" (free from wrath, sin, the law, and death, Rom. 5–8).

3. The *body* of the letter deals with the purposes for which Paul wrote it, and these vary considerably from occasion to occasion. It is a mistake for scholars to assume that Paul wrote all his letters from virtually the same motivation, using virtually the same vocabulary, and almost always dealing with the same "Pauline" themes. One cannot come to the Pauline corpus with a preconception that Romans, Corinthians, and Galatians are "Pauline" and then proceed to argue that the issues discussed in these books must be present in every letter that he wrote. This would be as illogical as beginning with the assumption of Pauline authorship of Ephesians and Colossians and then denying "Paulinity" to Romans, Corinthians, and Galatians.

And yet, in spite of the considerable theological diversity that exists in the body of his letters, a unity of structure is discernable. Three features have been found to be commonly employed in the body and exhortation sections of

Paul's letters: (1) A tendency to build toward an eschatological comment; (2) the inclusion of travel plans; and (3) the inclusion of exhortations and advice for his audiences.[12]

4. The *closing* in Paul's letters also reflects changes from the norm. The usual closing containing the words "I pray for your health," (ἐρρῶσθαί σε εὔχομαι, *errōsthai se euchomai*)[13] or simply "goodbye" (ἔρρωσο, *errōso*)[14] is expanded by the inclusion of benedictions and doxologies. Some of his letters also close with an exhortation to greet one another with a "holy kiss" (Rom. 16:16; 1 Cor. 16:20; 2 Cor. 13:12; 1 Thess. 5:26).

The closing segments of these letters have been the focus of recent study related to questions of authorship. They bear directly on the question of whether Paul wrote all the letters that bear his name, and if so, how much of each letter is actually from Paul's own hand and how much may have been written by a secretary, such as Tertius, who wrote Paul's letter to Rome (Rom. 16:22). They also raise the question of how much freedom was given to a secretary in the composition of a letter.[15]

Since we have no autographs of Paul (i.e., the original documents themselves), we are limited in our study to manuscripts that have been copied by various scribes. These, of course, do not contain the signature of Paul on them, as at least some of the originals did. It is clear from some of Paul's letters that he put his signature or "mark" (σημεῖον, *sēmeion*) at the close of the documents, indicating thereby that he personally wrote at least the last part of the letters "with his own hand." This clearly implies that he did not personally write down the rest of each letter, and indeed, as noted above, Tertius says he wrote the Roman letter: "I Tertius, the writer of this letter, greet you in the Lord" (Rom. 16:22). Five of Paul's letters make this indisputably clear:

Gal. 6:11	"See with what large letters I am writing to you with my own hand."	Ἴδετε πηλίκοις ὑμῖν γράμμασιν ἔγραψα τῇ ἐμῇ χειρί.
1 Cor. 16:21	"I, Paul, write this greeting with my own hand"; or, more literally, "the salutation of Paul, by my own hand."	Ὁ ἀσπασμὸς τῇ ἐμῇ χειρὶ Παύλου.

12. Keck, *Paul and His Letters*, 22.

13. See, for example, letters 42 and 44 in George Milligan, *Selections from the Greek Papyri* (Cambridge: Cambridge University Press, 1910), 102, 107. Ἔρρωσο is a form of ῥώννυμι, a verb that was obsolete in New Testament times. The forms used in letter closings during this period, ἔρρωσο and ἔρρωσθε, are perfect passive imperatives. The verb means "to be strong or healthy."

14. See letter 41 (ibid., 102). The word (Ἔρρωσθε) appears in the New Testament letter sent by the church in Jerusalem to the one in Antioch (Acts 15:29).

15. E. Randolph Richards, "The Role of the Secretary in Greco-Roman Antiquity and Its Implications for the Letters of Paul" (Ph.D. diss., Southwestern Baptist Theological Seminary, 1988).

Col. 4:18	(Same as 1 Corinthians)	
2 Thess. 3:17	(Same as 1 Corinthians, with an added phrase, "This is the mark in every letter of mine.")	Ὁ ἀσπασμὸς τῇ ἐμῇ χειρὶ Παύλου, ὅ ἐστιν σημεῖον ἐν πάσῃ ἐπιστολῇ.
Philem. 19	"I, Paul, write this with my own hand."	ἐγὼ Παῦλος ἔγραψα τῇ ἐμῇ χειρί.

We know from ancient writings outside the New Testament that it was common practice for authors to dictate their letters to an amanuensis or secretary.[16] These five letters of Paul demonstrate rather clearly that he did the same. His letters were written to be read in public worship services of the early church and with the full understanding and expression of his apostolic authority behind them. "If anyone refuses to obey what we say in this letter, note that man, and have nothing to do with him" (2 Thess. 3:14; cf. 1 Thess. 2:6, 13; 1 Cor. 2:13; 4:21; 2 Cor. 10:8; 13:3; Gal. 1:8, 11–14; 2:6). None of his preserved letters were impromptu personal correspondence; they were carefully produced documents for public hearing: "Have this letter read to all the brothers" (1 Thess. 5:27 NIV). Even his letters to Philemon, Timothy, and Titus[17] were doubtless intended for reading to the churches, containing as they do instructions for church organization and worship. He clearly states his expectation that at least some of his letters will be read by more than one church. Writing to the church in Colossae, he says, "And when this letter has been read among you, have it read also in the church of the Laodiceans; and see that you read also the letter from Laodicea" (Col. 4:16).

It is self-evident that a document written to be read in public would be more formal in style and less personal in content than a letter written to an individual for private reading. The differences between formal and informal writings, which Adolf Deissmann explored in his study of "epistles" versus "letters," is being further explored in recent studies that demonstrate differences also between ancient "records" and "letters."[18] One of these studies argues that

> a *letter* is any communication in writing between two parties (individuals or groups) who are separated from each other; a letter is a substitute for conversation. A *record*, on the other hand, is not essentially an instrument of communication between separated parties, but a recounting or report by a third person of the oral agreement reached by two parties; a record has only secondary importance in that it is a fixed form of the original oral agreement. In the Greek

16. See the citations in Bahr, "Paul and Letter Writing in the First Century," 465ff.

17. I am of the opinion that Paul wrote these letters. See my article, "The Authorship of the Pastoral Epistles," *Restoration Quarterly* 7 (1963): 2–18.

18. John White, "A Discussion of Light from Ancient Letters," *BR* 32 (1987): 42–53; Bahr, "Subscriptions in the Pauline Letters," 27f.

sources, a letter may be called χειρόγραφον, *cheirographon* (something written by hand), and a record is appropriately named ὑπόμνημα, *hypomnēma* (a reminder).[19]

Using this distinction, George Bahr argues the exact opposite of Deissmann, that the Pauline epistles are records rather than letters, and believes that "we can determine with a high degree of probability what comes from the hand of Paul himself and what comes from the hand of Paul's secretary."[20] Ancient authors, he argues, as a rule gave considerable freedom to their secretaries to compose records that contained the essence of what the authors wanted said and then wrote their own signatures at the end.

But unlike modern convention, an ancient signature was much more than a name; it was the finalizing of a record with the author's own handwriting and his personal affirmation of its contents. This fuller signature, called a "subscription" by Bahr, contained the *author's* summary of what the *secretary* had written in the body. In this way the author affirmed that the contents of the body were approved by him and enabled the recipients to differentiate his writings from fraudulent ones written in his name (2 Thess. 2:2).

Disagreeing with those scholars who limit the subscriptions of Paul to little more than a signature and brief comment at the very end of his letters,[21] Bahr identifies a greater percentage of each of Paul's letters as "subscriptions" and categorizes Paul's correspondence as "records" rather than "letters." He begins the subscription in each letter, where Paul himself seems to be taking pen in hand, at an earlier point than scholars have generally suggested. These beginning points are as follows (I am placing in brackets suggestions previous to Bahr):

Table 9.3 Paul's Letter Subscriptions

Gal. 5:2	Now I, Paul	ἴδε ἐγὼ Παῦλος
[6:11]	See with what large letters I am writing to you with my own hand	Ἴδετε πηλίκοις ὑμῖν γράμμασιν ἔγραψα τῇ ἐμῇ χειρί
Philem. 17	So if	εἰ οὖν
[19]	I, Paul, write this with my own hand	ἐγὼ Παῦλος ἔγραψα τῇ ἐμῇ χειρί
Col. 2:8	See to it	βλέπετε
[4:18]	I, Paul, write this greeting with my own hand	ὁ ἀσπασμὸς τῇ ἐμῇ χειρὶ Παύλου

19. Bahr, "Subscriptions in the Pauline Letters," 27.
20. Ibid.
21. Such as the five Pauline books listed above: Galatians, 1 Corinthians, Colossians, 2 Thessalonians, and Philemon.

1 Thess. 4:1	Finally	λοιπὸν οὖν
[none]		
2 Thess. 3:1	Finally	τὸ λοιπὸν
[3:17]	I, Paul, write this greeting with my own hand. This is the mark in every letter of mine	ὁ ἀσπασμὸς τῇ ἐμῇ χειρὶ Παύλου, ὅ ἐστιν σημεῖον ἐν πάσῃ ἐπιστολῇ
1 Cor. 16:15–16	Now, . . . I urge you	παρακαλῶ δὲ ὑμᾶς
[16:21]	I, Paul, write this greeting with my own hand	Ὁ ἀσπασμὸς τῇ ἐμῇ χειρὶ Παύλου
2 Cor. 10:1	I, Paul, myself entreat you	αὐτὸς δὲ ἐγὼ Παῦλος παρακαλῶ ὑμᾶς
[same]		
Phil. 3:1	Finally	τὸ λοιπόν
[none]		
Rom. 12:1	I appeal to you therefore	παρακαλῶ οὖν ὑμᾶς
[none]		
Eph. 4:1	I therefore, . . . beg you	παρακαλῶ οὖν ὑμᾶς ἐγὼ
[none]		

It was characteristic of "records" to include these lengthy summaries from the pens of the authors themselves. This leads Bahr to conclude that "the Pauline letters would represent the mind of Paul only in part," and that "it may be that we cannot even write a theology of Paul, unless it is based on the subscriptions alone."[22]

This view seems extreme and does not necessarily follow from the data presented by Bahr. Although his insights are valuable and the material he brings together is important in expanding our understanding of the nature of Paul's correspondence, he has not proven that the Pauline correspondence is written *exclusively* in the "record" format of ancient literature. Some of his conclusions are forced, and he fails to deal seriously enough with instances in which the data do not fit his conclusions.

Perhaps a better solution at present is to suggest that Paul's letters reflect his own creative amalgamation of both formal and informal conventions of ancient letter writing. There can be no doubt that Paul did not personally write all of his letters. This much he acknowledges himself. How much of his letters represent his own composition, however, is highly speculative at this point, and further study is necessary, although it will probably never produce the certainty that Bahr seems to feel.

One thing does seem rather clear, however: we may not proceed as confidently as some have done in denying the Pauline authorship of some letters

22. Bahr, "Subscriptions in the Pauline Letters," 27, 41.

and parts of others on the basis of "Pauline literary style."[23] Even though the *literary style* of the bodies of his letters may be that of his various secretaries, there is no compelling reason that the *content* of these letters should not accurately represent his own thinking, which was probably dictated, however freely, to these secretaries. His own personal compositions would then be limited to the subscriptions, regardless of their length. We see no reason why Paul's theology cannot, therefore, be clearly and accurately discerned in the body of his letters, even though his literary style remains enigmatic. There is simply not enough of Paul's own composition in the subscriptions to determine his style.[24] One writer on the subject requires a sample of about ten thousand words in order to determine an author's style,[25] and many of the letters attributed to Paul do not qualify.

The Letters of Paul and the Canon

There are two important questions relative to the Pauline corpus in the New Testament. The first has to do with its content: How many books were in the early lists of Paul's letters? The second has to do with its arrangement: What was the order of the books in these early lists? The two questions are inseparably connected, and answering the second helps to answer the first. These questions are especially significant in view of the prevailing rejection of Pauline authorship of several books in the New Testament. A number of important books on the canon of the New Testament have appeared recently.[26]

23. Nils Dahl has dealt with the questions of when, where, how, and why Paul's letters were first collected and circulated and under what conditions, with what presuppositions, for what purposes, and to what extent they may have been edited ("The Particularity of the Pauline Epistles as a Problem in the Ancient Church," in *Neotestamentica et Patristica: Eine Freundesgabe, Herrn Prof. Dr. Oscar Cullmann zu seinem 60. Geburtstag,* Novum Testamentum Supplement 6 [Leiden: Brill, 1962], 261–71).

24. See the questions raised by P. F. Johnson about how applicable the statistical method is to linguistic analysis of these letters: "The Use of Statistics in the Analysis of the Characteristics of Pauline Writing," *NTS* 20 (1973): 92–100.

25. G. Udney Yule, former reader in statistics at Cambridge University, *The Statistical Study of Literary Vocabulary* (Cambridge: Cambridge University Press, 1944), 281. See further McRay, "Authorship of the Pastoral Epistles," 5.

26. Lee Martin McDonald, *The Formation of the Christian Biblical Canon,* rev. and expanded ed. (Peabody, Mass.: Hendrickson, 1995); F. F. Bruce, *The Canon of Scripture* (Downers Grove, Ill.: InterVarsity, 1988); Bruce Metzger, *The Canon of the New Testament: Its Origin, Development, and Significance* (Oxford: Clarendon, 1987); Harry Y. Gamble, *The New Testament Canon: Its Making and Meaning* (Philadelphia: Fortress, 1985); W. R. Farmer and Denis M. Farkasfalvy, *The Formation of the New Testament Canon: An Ecumenical Approach* (New York: Paulist Press, 1983); Brevard Childs, *The New Testament as Canon: An Introduction* (Philadelphia: Fortress, 1984); James Barr, *Holy Scripture: Canon, Authority, Criticism* (Philadelphia: Westminster, 1983).

These should be consulted along with some of the older standards[27] in the study of the Pauline corpus.[28]

There are several extant collections of Paul's letters that date between the second and seventh centuries A.D. In these manuscripts his letters are grouped together as a corpus and placed in various locations. For example, they are found *following Acts* in most of these early sources just as they are in modern English translations. These include the Muratorian Canon (probably second century),[29] the Sinaitic Syriac, Amphilocius, and others in the fourth century. They are found *following the General Epistles* in Codex Vaticanus, Athanasius, and the Council of Laodicea's list, in the fourth century, and in the Peshitta Syriac, Codex Ephraemi, and Codex Alexandrinus, among others, in the fifth. They even appear *after the Gospels* in the fourth-century lists of Cheltenham, the Apostolic Canons, Epiphanius, Jerome, and Augustine. Chrysostom lists them first in his New Testament collection in the fourth century. The list could easily be expanded:

Table 9.4 Position of Pauline Corpus in the New Testament

After Acts

Muratorian Canon
Amphilocius (c. 380 in Iconium)
Philastrius (died 387 in Italy)
Gregory of Nazianzus (329–389 in Cappadocia)
Council of Carthage (397 in Africa)
Sinaitic Syriac (c. 400)
Rufinus (345–410 in Cyprus)
Ethiopic Versions (c. 500 in Abyssinia)
Gelasius Decree (6th century in Italy)

27. Some of the older classics are B. F. Westcott, *A General Survey of the History of the Canon of the New Testament* (London: Macmillan, 1896); C. R. Gregory, *Canon and Text of the New Testament* (Edinburgh: Clark, 1907); A. Souter, *The Text and Canon of the New Testament* (London: Duckworth, 1954); E. J. Goodspeed, *The Formation of the New Testament* (Chicago: University of Chicago Press, 1926); A. E. Barnett, *Paul Becomes a Literary Influence* (Chicago: University of Chicago Press, 1941). Some of the later studies include Robert Grant, *The Formation of the New Testament* (New York: Harper and Row, 1965); F. V. Filson, *Which Books Belong in the Canon?* (Philadelphia: Westminster, 1957); Eduard Lohse, *The Formation of the New Testament,* trans. M. Eugene Boring (Nashville: Abingdon, 1972, 1981); Hans von Campenhausen, *The Formation of the Christian Bible* (Philadelphia: Fortress, 1972).

28. For a thorough list of publications on the canon, see Metzger, *Canon of the New Testament,* 11–36.

29. Albert Sundberg's attempt to date this document to the fourth century is tenuous at best and has been "sufficiently refuted (not to say demolished!) by Ferguson" (Metzger, *Canon of the New Testament,* 193). See A. C. Sundberg, "Canon Muratori: A Fourth-Century List," *HTR* 66 (1973): 1–41; Everett Ferguson, "Canon Muratori: Date and Provenance," in *Studia Patristica: Papers Presented to the International Conference on Patristic Studies,* Texte und Untersuchungen zur Geschichte der altchristlichen Literatur, vol. 18, part 2 (Berlin: Akademie-Verlag, 1989), 677–83.

Stichometry of Nicephorus (806–814 in Byzantium)
Hugo of St. Victory (1046–1141 in France)
Martin Luther (1522 in Germany)
William Tyndale (1525 in England)
Council of Trent (1546 in Germany)
Bishop's Bible (1563–64 in England)
Thirty-Nine Articles of the Church of England (1571)
Geneva Bible (1599 edition)
King James Version (1611)

After the General Epistles

Codex Vaticanus (4th century)
Council of Laodicea (c. 343–81)
Athanasius of Alexandria (367)
Cyril of Jerusalem (died 386)
Peshitto Syriac (c. 412 in Syria)
Codex Ephraemi Rescriptus (c. 450 in Egypt)
Codex Alexandrinus (c. 450 in Egypt)
Cassiodorus (c. 560 in Italy)
Leontius (c. 590 in Byzantium)
List of the sixty canonical books (7th century in Asia Minor)

After the Gospels

Codex Sinaiticus (4th century in the Sinai)
Cheltenham List (c. 360 in North Africa)
Apostolic Canons (c. 380 in Syria or Constantinople)
Epiphanius (died c. 403 on Cyprus)
Jerome (c. 394 in Rome)
Augustine (c. 400 in North Africa)
Codex Bezae (5th century in Egypt)
Isidore of Spain (died 636)
John Wycliffe (c. 1388 in England)

Listed First

John Chrysostom (c. 380 in Constantinople)—Paulines,
Gospels, Acts, three General Epistles

There are also many variations of the books within the Pauline corpus it-self. Seventeen different arrangements of Paul's letters have been found in Greek, Latin, and Coptic manuscripts.[30] In the traditional order of the letters, those written to churches were placed first, followed by those written to individuals. Thus, Romans to 2 Thessalonians was followed by Timothy, Titus, and Philemon. These two groups, in turn, were generally, though not always, arranged in order of decreasing length. This method of arranging books ac-

---

30. Metzger, *Canon of the New Testament*, 298 n. 8. See H. J. Frede, *Epistula ad Colossenses, Vetus Latina* 24.2 (Freiburg, 1969), 290–303. Interestingly, more than 284 different sequences of scriptural books appear in Latin manuscripts alone.

cording to decreasing length seems to have been used also in placing the trac-
tates in the six orders (Sedarim) of the Jewish Mishnah, with the exception of
the first tractate.[31] It was also used in arranging the sections (suras) of the
Qur'an, with the exception of the first sura. The 1,628 hymns of the Hindu
scriptures, the Rig-Veda, are arranged this way, as also are the texts of the Sut-
tapitaka of the second part of the Buddhist Pali canon.[32]

Ancient scribes often produced lists of New Testament books giving the
number of lines (stichoi) in each.[33] They are not uniform in the way they
count the lines, and the lines indicated do not always match the actual lines
in the document,[34] but the general pattern of decreasing length may be discerned in them. For example, one list reads as follows:[35]

Table 9.5 Ancient Line Counts for Paul's Letters

Letter	Lines
To Churches	
Romans	979
1 Corinthians	908
2 Corinthians	607
[Galatians	311]
Ephesians	331
Philippians	221
Colossians	215
1 Thessalonians	207
2 Thessalonians	111
To Individuals	
1 Timothy	238
2 Timothy	182
Titus	100
Philemon	44

31. Hermann Strack finds another reason for the arrangement: the location of the laws in
question in the Pentateuch (*Introduction to the Talmud and Midrash* [Philadelphia: Jewish Publication Society, Meridian, 1963], 27).

32. Metzger, *Canon of the New Testament*, 298 n. 5.

33. A stichos (στίχος) consists of sixteen syllables of about thirty-six letters. For various uses
of these in antiquity, see Bruce Metzger, *Manuscripts of the Greek Bible* (New York: Oxford
University Press, 1981), 38–40.

34. For the Chester Beatty Papyri in this respect, see Frederick Kenyon, *The Chester Beatty
Biblical Papyri: Descriptions and Texts of the Twelve Manuscripts on Papyrus of the Greek Bible*,
fasciculus 3 supplement, *Pauline Epistles* (London: Emery Walker, 1936), xiii.

35. See Metzger, *Canon of the New Testament*, 298.

The earliest collection of Pauline letters extant is the Chester Beatty Papy-rus ($\mathfrak{P}$46), which dates to about A.D. 200. It is also the earliest manuscript that contains stichoi, although only the stichoi for Romans, Hebrews, Ephesians, Galatians, and Philippians have survived in condition to be read. They are ba-sically *but not strictly* arranged in order of decreasing length, as are the books in the Latin list inserted into Codex Claromontanus.[36] (It should be remem-bered that the stichoi, as noted above, do not always represent the actual length of the book.)

Table 9.6 Line Counts in the Chester Beatty Papyrus

Letter	Lines
Romans	1000
Hebrews	700
1 Corinthians	(lost)
2 Corinthians	(uncertain)
[Ephesians	316]
Galatians	375
Philippians	225 (or 222)
Colossians	1(..)

Table 9.7 Line Counts in Codex Claromontanus

Letter	Lines
Romans	1040
1 Corinthians	1060
2 Corinthians	(.)70
Galatians	350
Ephesians	365[a]
Philippians	omitted
Colossians	251

a. The number is given as 365 by Metzger, *Canon of the New Testa-ment,* 310; and by Westcott, *General Survey,* 575; but it is given as 375 by Kenyon, *Chester Beatty Biblical Pa-pyri,* fasc. 3 (Text), xi; and by Bruce, *Canon of Scripture,* 218.

36. Frederick Kenyon, *Chester Beatty Biblical Papyri,* xii–xiii. See also Metzger, *Canon of the New Testament,* 310. On the Chester Beatty Papyri in general, see discussion in John McRay, *Archaeology and the New Testament* (Grand Rapids: Baker, 1991), 356–57.

One of the more interesting contributions this study makes to our understanding of the canonicity of Pauline letters is the light it sheds on the position of Hebrews in early collections of Paul's letters.[37] In the first of these—the Chester Beatty Papyrus, our earliest list of Pauline letters—not only is Hebrews included among Paul's writings, but it also appears in second position, immediately following Romans! It is clear that the editors of this manuscript regarded the book as Pauline. Sir Frederick Kenyon, who published the Beatty Papyri wrote: "Its present position is a proof of the high importance assigned to it, and of the unquestioning acceptance of its Pauline authorship."[38]

Codex Vaticanus, our second oldest copy of Paul's letters, clearly indicates that Hebrews stood between Galatians and Ephesians in the manuscript from which Vaticanus was copied. Although Vaticanus itself places Hebrews after 2 Thessalonians, at the end of Paul's letters to the churches, an ancient paragraph numbering system used in Vaticanus shows that it originally stood after Galatians (i.e., the sequence ran—Romans, 1 Corinthians, 2 Corinthians, Galatians, Hebrews, Ephesians, etc.). The pertinent part of the numbering system is as follows:

Table 9.8 Paragraph Numbering in Codex Vaticanus

Bible Book	Paragraph Number	Verse	Ending or Beginning
Galatians	νζ	4:11	
	νη	5:17	Ends at #58
Ephesians/Philippians, Colossians, 1 Thessalonians	οα	2:8	Begins at #71
	οβ	4:1	
	ογ	4:17	
	οδ	5:15	
	οε	6:10	
2 Thessalonians			Begins at #93
Hebrews	ξ	2:18(?)	Begins at #59
	ξ		
	ξβ	6:8 or 9	
	ξγ	7:19	
	ξδ	9:11	Ends at #64

37. W. H. P. Hatch, "The Position of Hebrews in the Canon of the New Testament," *HTR* 29 (1936): 133–51.

38. Kenyon, *Chester Beatty Biblical Papyri,* fasc. 3 (Text), xi.

"Obviously an ancestor of B [Vaticanus] contained the Epistle to the Hebrews between Galatians and Ephesians."[39] One of the exemplars rearranged the books, taking Hebrews out of its sequentially numbered position after Galatians and placing it at the end of the church letters, after 2 Thessalonians, which begins with #93. It is also interesting that all the manuscripts in the Sahidic dialect of Coptic (used in Egypt) put Hebrews between 2 Corinthians and Galatians.[40]

This, of course, does not prove that Paul wrote Hebrews,[41] but it does indicate that the letter had a significant position in the Pauline corpus in the early centuries. The diversity of order in the Pauline corpus may be demonstrated in the following collection of early documents.

The position of the Pastoral Epistles (Timothy and Titus) in these early documents is also interesting because of the frequent denial of their Pauline authorship.[42] While it is true that the Chester Beatty Papyrus does not include these letters, it should be noted that Philemon is also missing, and it is universally acknowledged as Paul's. The problem is that some folios (groups of pages) are missing from the manuscript in several places, including its beginning and end, resulting in the loss of Romans 1:1–5:17 and 6:14–8:15; 1 Thessalonians 2:3–5:5; and whatever followed 1 Thessalonians 5:28. Based on the number of lines per page in the rest of the manuscript, nineteen more pages would be required to complete the Pauline corpus with 2 Thessalonians, 1 and 2 Timothy, Titus, and Philemon. Only half that amount would be available if the missing sheets of the document in its present state could be restored. However, Kenyon points to the possibility that "some additional leaves may have been attached at the end so as to take the Pastoral Epistles."[43]

Similarly, leaves are missing in Codex Vaticanus from Hebrews 9:14 onward, and it does not contain the Pastoral Epistles or Philemon. However, there is no good reason to doubt that it originally contained the Pastorals. The New Testament portion of the Latin list inserted into Codex Claromontanus between Philemon and Hebrews has the Pastorals between Ephesians and Colossians (as seen in table 9.9), and Philippians, 1 and 2 Thessalonians, and He-

---

39. Metzger, *Manuscripts of the Greek Bible,* 41.

40. Bruce Metzger, *The Early Versions of the New Testament: Their Origin, Transmission, and Limitations* (Oxford: Clarendon, 1977), 114.

41. On the most recent literature dealing with Hebrews, see P. E. Hughes, "The Epistle to the Hebrews," in *The New Testament and Its Modern Interpreters,* ed. Eldon J. Epp and George W. MacRae (Philadelphia: Fortress; Atlanta: Scholars Press, 1989), 351–70.

42. Most recently, see Stanley E. Porter, "Pauline Authorship and the Pastoral Epistles: The Implications for Canon," *BBR* 5 (1995): 105–23; Robert Wall, "Pauline Authorship and the Pastoral Epistles: A Response to S. E. Porter," *BBR* 5 (1995): 125–28; Stanley E. Porter, "Pauline Authorship and the Pastoral Epistles: A Response to R. W. Wall's Response," *BBR* 6 (1996): 133–38.

43. Kenyon, *Chester Beatty Biblical Papyri,* fasc. 3 (Text), xi. Kenyon does not prefer this assumption, however.

Table 9.9 Position of Hebrews in the Pauline Corpus

	1	2	3	4	5	6	7	8	9	10	11	12	13	14
MC	1Cor	2Cor	Eph	Phil	Col	Gal	1Thess	2Thess	Rom	Philem	Titus	1Tim	2Tim	
𝔓46	Rom	Heb	1Cor	2Cor	Eph	Gal	Phil	Col	1Thess	…	…	…		
Exp	Rom	1Cor	2Cor	Gal	Heb	Eph	Phil	Col	1Thess	2Thess	unknown	…	…	
Vat	Rom	1Cor	2Cor	Gal	Eph	Phil	Col	1Thess	2Thess	Heb	…	…	…	
Sin	Rom	1Cor	2Cor	Gal	Eph	Phil	Col	1Thess	2Thess	Heb	1Tim	2Tim	Titus	Philem
Lao	Rom	1Cor	2Cor	Gal	Eph	Phil	Col	1Thess	2Thess	Heb	1Tim	2Tim	Titus	Philem
Ath	Rom	1Cor	2Cor	Gal	Eph	Phil	Col	1Thess	2Thess	Heb	1Tim	2Tim	Titus	Philem
Amp	Rom	1Cor	2Cor	Gal	Eph	Phil	Col	1Thess	2Thess	1Tim	2Tim	Titus	Philem	Heb
Sah	Rom	1Cor	2Cor	Heb	Gal	Eph	Phil	Col	1Thess	2Thess	1Tim	2Tim	Titus	Philem
Aug	Rom	1Cor	2Cor	Gal	Eph	Phil	Col	1Thess	2Thess	1Tim	2Tim	Titus	Philem	Heb
Eph	Rom	1Cor	2Cor	Gal	Eph	Phil	Col	1Thess	2Thess	Heb	1Tim	2Tim	Titus	Philem
Eth	Rom	1Cor	2Cor	Gal	Eph	Col	Phil	1Thess	2Thess	Heb	1Tim	2Tim	Titus	Philem
Cla	Rom	1Cor	2Cor	Gal	Eph	Col	Phil	1Thess	2Thess	Heb	1Tim	2Tim	Titus	Philem
Cas	Rom	1Cor	2Cor	Gal	Eph	Phil	Col	1Thess	2Thess	Heb	1Tim	2Tim	Titus	Philem
Isi	Rom	1Cor	2Cor	Gal	Eph	Phil	Col	1Thess	2Thess	1Tim	2Tim	Titus	Philem	Heb
Six	Rom	1Cor	2Cor	Gal	Eph	Phil	Col	1Thess	2Thess	1Tim	2Tim	Titus	Philem	Heb
Sti	No list of the letters; says only "14 letters of Paul"													

Abbreviation Key

MC	Muratorian Canon (2d cent.)
𝔓46	Chester Beatty Papyrus (c. 200)
Exp	Exemplar of Vaticanus (4th cent. or earlier)
Vat	Codex Vaticanus (4th cent.)
Sin	Codex Sinaiticus (4th cent.)
Lao	Council of Laodicea (4th cent.)
Ath	Athanasius of Alexandria (4th cent.)
Amp	Amphilocius of Antioch (4th cent.)
Sah	All Sahidic (Coptic) versions (before 600)
Aug	Augustine (4th cent.)
Eph	Codex Ephraemi (5th cent.)
Eth	Ethiopic Version (6th cent.)
Cla	Codex Claromontanus (6th cent.)
Cas	Cassiodorus (6th cent.)
Isi	Isidore of Spain (7th cent.)
Six	List of the Sixty Books (7th cent.)
Sti	Stichometry of Nicephorus (9th cent.)
…	indicates missing portions of the manuscript

brews are omitted from the list. Bruce Metzger attributes this to an error made either by a scribe or a translator. He thinks the error may have occurred when the copyist looked back at the text and mistakenly continued copying after Hebrews (Ἑβραίους, *hebraious*) rather than after Ephesians (Ἐφεσίους, *Ephesious*), due to the similiarity of the words in Greek.[44] Thus, 1 Timothy would have followed Ephesians rather than Hebrews. However, it is diffcult to account for the position of Colossians under this hypothesis, unless it was originally joined to Philemon, with which it is closely associated in content. In general, we might observe that the Pastoral Epistles are a part of the Pauline corpus in most of the ancient manuscripts.

Finally, a word should be said about the division of the Pauline letters into chapters and verses. All ancient manuscripts of the New Testament were written without these divisions in the text. The paragraph divisions in Vaticanus are the oldest known in Greek texts of the New Testament, but they do not correspond to our modern chapter divisions, which were introduced into the Latin Vulgate (New and Old Testaments) by Stephen Langton at the beginning of the thirteenth century. The further division of the text into verses was done by Robert Stephanus, who published a Latin edition of the New Testament in 1551 in Geneva with the text of the chapters divided into verses. Chapter and verse divisions make Paul's letters easier to handle but tend to obscure the fact that they were produced by Paul as letters, not legal documents, and should be studied from that perspective.

In recent studies on Paul, one notices that there is almost no consensus among scholars on these or *any other aspects* of Paul's life and teaching, a point that a current exhaustive assessment of these studies makes repeatedly, not only about Paul, but about virtually every aspect of New Testament scholarship.[45]

---

44. *Canon of the New Testament*, 230.

45. Epp and MacRae, eds., *The New Testament and Its Modern Interpreters*. On Pauline studies, see chap. 12, "Pauline Studies," by V. P. Furnish, 321–50.

TEN

Paul's World of Apocalyptic and Demonology

The world in which Paul lived and wrote was quite different from the highly sophisticated and scientifically oriented world culture of the twenty-first century. In comparison it might be said that modern culture is dominated by paganistic scientism, hedonistic materialism, and religious skepticism, while the Greco-Roman culture of Paul's day was dominated by religious superstition and polytheistic idolatry.

Jewish culture had long since been fragmented into a fanatic sectarianism,[1] with the effect of virtually negating its impact as a monotheistic society. For Jews it was an especially frustrating time, living in the aftermath of the unsuccessful Maccabean Revolt against Syria and in the clutches of the might of Rome. For about two hundred years, they had tried to throw off outside domination and establish their independence but to no avail. Inevitably, they com-

---

1. Jacob Neusner, ed. *History of the Jews in the Second and First Centuries B.C.* (New York: Garland, 1990); Jacob Neusner and W. S. Green, eds., *History of the Jews in the First Century of the Common Era* (New York: Garland, 1990); Shemaryahu Talmon, ed., *Jewish Civilization in the Hellenistic–Roman Period* (Philadelphia: Trinity Press International, 1991); Elias J. Bickerman, *The Jews in the Greek Age* (Cambridge, Mass.: Harvard University Press, 1988); R. H. Charles, *Religious Development between the Old and New Testaments* (1914; reprint, Folcroft, Pa.: Folcroft Library Editions, 1977); Michael Stone, *Scriptures, Sects, and Visions: A Profile of Judaism from Ezra to the Jewish Revolts* (Philadelphia: Fortress, 1980); Donald E. Gowan, *Bridge between the Testments: A Reappraisal of Judaism from the Exile to the Birth of Christianity* (Pittsburgh: Pickwick, 1976).

pensated for their external frustrations by turning inward, looking to their religious beliefs for consolation and endurance under these distressing circumstances.

Fresh understandings of God had been set forth by Jewish writers in their literature during the two or three centuries preceding the birth of Christ, as they tried to come to grips with the problem of theodicy.[2] How could they defend the goodness and justice of God in a situation in which Israel was thought to be suffering because of her sin? This is a problem Paul later dealt with in Romans 9–11.

Jewish culture had been significantly and permanently altered by the experience of Jerusalem's destruction by the Babylonians in the sixth century B.C. and the time spent in Babylonian and Persian exile. When the remnant returned from Persia under Cyrus and rebuilt the temple in Jerusalem, they brought with them the ingredients of a whole new way of thinking. They now viewed themselves as having been severely punished by God for their idolatrous inclinations, a punishment that included even the destruction of his holy temple.

From this experience Jewish authors had concluded that God no longer dwelt in their midst as he once had. They felt that his holiness was so incompatible with their sinfulness that he had withdrawn from them. This transcendentalizing of God left a terrible void in their lives. There could no longer be inspired prophets and thus no more inspired Scripture. No books were allowed into the Jewish canon during this intertestamental period—inspiration had ceased![3]

Jewish culture splintered and a sectarianism evolved out of this frame of mind. Sects emerged such as the Pharisees, Sadducees, Essenes, and eventually Herodians, Zealots, and others, each with its own solution to Judaism's spiritual and political problems.

One of the most significant aspects of the theology that developed during this period of intellectual and religious depression was an "apocalyptic" approach to their problems.[4] This approach is represented in a large

2. That is, the apparent contradiction between belief in God's power and goodness and the presence of evil and suffering in the world.

3. Some scholars, however, date Daniel to the second century.

4. On the definition and meaning of apocalyptic literature, see Martha Himmelfarb, *Ascent to Heaven in Jewish and Christian Apocalypses* (New York: Oxford University Press, 1993); idem, *Tours of Hell: An Apocalyptic Form in Jewish Christian Literature* (Philadelphia: Fortress, 1985); John J. Collins, *The Apocalyptic Imagination: An Introduction to the Jewish Matrix of Christianity* (New York: Crossroad, 1984); D. S. Russell, *Apocalyptic: Ancient and Modern* (Philadelphia: Fortress, 1978); idem, *The Method and Message of Jewish Apocalyptic* (Philadelphia: Westminster, 1964); Jean Danielou, *The Theology of Jewish Christianity,* A History of Early Christian Doctrine 1, trans. J. A. Baker (London: Darton, Longman and Todd, 1964), 7–54, 173–204; Walter Schmithals, *The Apocalyptic Movement: Introduction and Interpretation,* trans. John Steely (Nashville: Abingdon, 1975); W. G. Lambert, *The Background of Jewish Apocalyptic* (London: Athlone, University of London, 1978).

number of documents categorized as "Apocalyptic Literature."[5] Apocalyptic thought exercised a significant influence on Jewish literary works until the birth of Christ and the fall of the temple in Jerusalem, after which it continued in Jewish Christian literature.[6] Jewish Christian theology "provided the characters and scenes in terms of which the Christian drama was unfolded."[7]

The Revelation of John is the best-known example of Christian apocalyptic literature (the Greek word ἀποκάλυψις is normally translated "Revelation" or transliterated "Apocalypse"), but the *Revelation of Peter* was also widely circulated in the early church,[8] and several more apocalyptic books were written during these later years,[9] including the Apocalypses of Paul (two of them),[10] Thomas, Stephen,[11] James, and Adam.[12]

Although details differ in individual apocalyptic books, there are themes that are integral to the genre, one of which is the ascension motif.

The temporary exaltation of a man so that he may contemplate heavenly realities, is the central theme of all Jewish apocalyptic. . . . It was made up of infor-

5. R. H. Charles, *The Apocrypha and Pseudepigrapha of the Old Testament in English*, 2 vols. (Oxford: Clarendon, 1963); James Charlesworth, *Old Testament Pseudepigrapha*, 2 vols. (Garden City, N.Y.: Doubleday, 1983–85); idem, *Old Testament Pseudepigrapha and the New Testament* (Cambridge: Cambridge University Press, 1985); idem, *The Pseudepigrapha and Modern Study* (Missoula, Mont.: Scholars Press, 1976); H. F. D. Sparks, ed., *The Apocryphal Old Testament: A Translation of the Pseudepigrapha* (New York: Oxford University Press, 1984).

6. M. R. James, *New Testament Apocrypha* (Philadelphia: Westminster, 1964), 2:579–803; W. Barnstone, *The Other Bible* (San Francisco: Harper and Row, 1984), 485–602; Adela Y. Collins, "Early Christian Apocalyptic Literature," in *ANRW*, 2.25.4.

7. Danielou, *Theology of Jewish Christianity*, 173.

8. It dates to about A.D. 125–50 (Metzger, *Canon of the New Testament*, 184). It is included in the Muratorian Canon, standing after the Apocalypse of John, with the warning that "some of our people do not wish it to be read in church." Clement of Alexandria accepted it as genuine (*Ecl.* 41.2 and 47.1), but both Jerome (*Vir. ill.* 1) and Eusebius (*Hist. eccl.* 3.25.4) rejected it. However, even until the fifth century it was read in some churches on Good Friday (Sozomen, *Historia ecclesiastica* 7.19).

9. See F. C. Burkitt, *Jewish and Christian Apocalypses* (London: Milford, for the British Academy, 1914); Collins, "Early Christian Apocalyptic Literature."

10. See the previously known book in Barnstone, *The Other Bible,* 538ff. The new and much shorter one, recently found at Nag Hammadi among the Gnostic texts, has nothing to do with the older one. It may be seen in J. M. Robinson, ed., *The Nag Hammadi Library in English* (San Francisco: Harper and Row, 1977), 239–41. The previous one, widely known in the early church, was written probably c. A.D. 250 (Metzger, *Canon of the New Testament,* 186) and is extant in Greek, with Syriac, Coptic, Ethiopic, Slavic, and Latin versions. On these sources, see R. P. Casey, "The Apocalypse of Paul," *JTS* 34 (1933): 1–32.

11. See these two in the collections by James (*New Testament Apocrypha*); Barnstone (*The Other Bible*); and Wilhelm Schneemelcher, ed., *New Testament Apocrypha,* rev. ed., 2 vols. (Cambridge: Clarke; Louisville: Westminster/John Knox, 1991–92).

12. These may be seen in Robinson, *Nag Hammadi Library,* 242–64.

mation about the hidden realities of the heavenly world and the ultimate secrets of the future.[13]

It was this kind of theological and philosophical ideology, widely known in the ancient world, that provided the cosomological format Paul utilized in his discussions of the atonement. The major dogmas of Jewish Christianity were developed along cosmological lines, although ancient authors were concerned with Christology rather than cosmology and used cosmological data simply as a medium of expression. Jewish Christian theology has been summarized as follows:

> The incarnation was presented as a descent of the Word through the angelic spheres; the Passion as Christ's combat with the angels of the air, followed by the descent into Hell; the Resurrection as an exaltation of Christ's humanity above all the angelic spheres; and after death the soul would pass through the various spheres, on its way encountering their guardians, to whom it would have to render an account. All these conceptions are based on a vision of the heavenly spheres which is part of the framework of Jewish Christianity.[14]

Within this framework, the word *apocalypse* designates an "unveiling" by which any particular individual who is selected to "ascend through the heavens," may contemplate the secrets of the cosmos and history, and, if permitted, reveal them to others. It is represented in Jewish literature two hundred years before Christ and continues on into Jewish Christian literature until around A.D. 100.

In this view, the celestial world was highly structured, containing multiple heavens, sometimes called the "Cosmic Ladder," which included angels and demons. The "Cosmic Ladder" has been defined as the "mythological geography of Jewish Apocalyptic."[15]

Paul described his revelatory experience in terms of this cosmological geography when he wrote that he was "caught up to the third heaven . . . into paradise . . . and . . . heard things that cannot be told, which man may not utter" (2 Cor. 12:2–4). He often speaks of the multiple heavens in his letters, including a divergent array of beings within them. For example, consider the following variety of occupants of the "heavenly places," realms that are designated in Paul's letters by two different but related words for heavens (ἐπουράνιοι, and οὐρανοί, *epouranioi* and *ouranoi*—the former is always plural in Ephesians and is not used in Colossians).

13. Danielou, *Theology of Jewish Christianity,* 25–26.
14. Ibid., 179.
15. Ibid., 173.

Table 10.1 Paul's Words for Heavens

Ephesians	Context	Greek Word
1:3	"Us" (probably Jewish Christians)	ἐπουράνιος
1:10	"All things"	οὐρανοῖς (contrasted with earth, γῆ)
1:20	"Christ, at God's right hand"	ἐπουρανίοις
2:6	"Us" (Jewish and Gentile Christians)	ἐπουρανίοις
		Col. 1:5 τοῖς οὐρανοῖς
		Phil. 3:20 οὐρανοῖς
3:10	"Principalities and Powers"	ἐπουρανίοις
3:15	"Every family"	οὐρανοῖς (contrasted with earth, γῆ)
		Col. 1:16 τοῖς οὐρανοῖς
		Col. 1:20 τοῖς οὐρανοῖς
		Col. 1:23 ὑπὸ τὸν οὐρανόν
		1 Cor. 15:40 ἐπουράνια (contrasted with earthly bodies, ἐπίγεια)
		1 Cor. 15:48–49 ἐπουράνιος (contrasted with earthy, χοϊκός)
		Phil. 2:10 ἐπουρανίων (contrasted with earthly, ἐπιγείων, and with subterranean, καταχθονίων)
4:10	"Christ" (ascended far above all heavens)	οὐρανῶν
6:9	"The Lord" (Christ or God)	οὐρανοῖς (plural)
		Col. 4:1 ἐν οὐρανῷ (singular)
6:12	"World rulers of this present darkness, spiritual hosts of wickedness" (the devil)	ἐπουρανίοις

It is thus clear that Paul categorizes this sphere more broadly as the "heavenly places" because the spiritual hosts of wickedness (Eph. 6:12) cannot be in the "heaven" where God dwells, nor can Christ, seated at the right hand of God (Eph. 1:20), be in the abode of the demons.

Ascensions through the heavenly places are typical in this literature. To "be caught up into a (third) heaven" or to "see the heavens opened" is apocalyptic terminology meaning that one "had a revelation."

Thus, when Jesus was baptized by John, the message of God was preceded by the *opening of the heavens:* "And when Jesus had been baptized, just as he came up from the water, suddenly the heavens were opened to him and he saw the Spirit of God descending like a dove and alighting on him. And a voice from heaven said, "This is my Son, the Beloved, with whom I am well pleased" (Matt. 3:16–17 NRSV).

Stephen, at the time of his martyrdom, said, "I see the heavens opened, and the Son of man standing at the right hand of God!" (Acts 7:56).

Paul describes his revelation similarly: "I know a person in Christ who fourteen years ago was caught up to the third heaven—whether in the body or out of the body I do not know; God knows. And I know that such a person—whether in the body or out of the body I do not know; God knows—was caught up into Paradise and heard things that are not to be told, that no mortal is permitted to repeat" (2 Cor. 12:2–4 NRSV).

Similarly, John writes in Revelation 4:1–2: "After this I looked, and there in heaven a door stood open! And the first voice, which I had heard speaking to me like a trumpet, said, 'Come up here, and I will show you what must take place after this.' At once I was in the spirit, and there in heaven stood a throne, with one seated on the throne!" (NRSV).

The *Shepherd of Hermas,* written in the second century A.D., is divided into three parts, one of which is the *Visions.* In chapter 1, Hermas states, "Now while I was praying the Heaven was opened, and I saw that woman whom I had desired greeting me out of the Heaven" (ἐκ τοῦ οὐρανοῦ, *ek tou ouranou,* 1.1.4).

One author argues that in the earliest stratum of traditional Judaism, there were only three heavens—the place of the meteors, the place of the stars, and the realm of the heavens—but by the New Testament period the three had become seven in Jewish Christian literature (though not in traditional Jewish writings). He notes that the idea of seven heavens is not found in contemporary *Jewish* documents such as 2 Esdras or Apocalypse of Baruch but derives instead from Iranian-Babylonian influences becoming characteristic of Syriac *Jewish Christianity.*[16]

Whatever its origin, however, "the doctrine of the seven heavens was prevalent in Judaism before and after the time of Christ."[17] It is found in Jewish literature of the second or first century B.C. that was edited in the first century A.D. (*Testament of Levi*), in Jewish Christian literature (as we

16. Danielou, *Theology of Jewish Christianity,* 174–75. Adela Yarbro Collins argues that the seven planetary spheres of Greek cosmology are not the source of this view of the heavens, but that it originated in the prominence of the number seven in Sumerian and Babylonian magic, which became influential after Paul in the rise of Mithraism ("The Seven Heavens in Jewish and Christian Apocalypses," in *Death, Ecstasy, and Other Worldly Journeys,* ed. John J. Collins and Michael Fishbane (Albany: SUNY Press, 1995). Reinhold Merkelbach argues that the evidence for Mithraism's existence dates to about A.D. 80 and becomes abundant after 140 ("Mithraism," *ABD,* 4:877).

17. Charles, *Apocrypha and Pseudepigrapha,* 2:304 (footnote comment on verse 5).

shall see below), and in Gentile Christian writers from the second century A.D., such as Irenaeus. Some hold that the references to the seven heavens in *Testament of Levi* are later Jewish Christian interpolations.[18] Seven heavens are also to be found in Greek Stoic thought as well as centuries later in the Qur'an of Islam. A look at the concept in some of these sources indicates its prevalence at the time.

1. *Testament of Levi.* This document was initially composed in the late second century B.C. (during the reign of John Hyrcanus, 135–104 B.C.) but edited in the first century A.D.[19] In chapters 2 and 3 it portrays the seven heavens as "opened to" Levi, who then ascends through them to the third, from which he sees into the seventh. Then the seventh, sixth, fifth, and fourth are revealed in descending order to Levi. God dwells in the seventh, and in the sixth are angels who "make propitiation to the Lord for all the sins of ignorance of the righteous" (3.5).

2.5Then there fell upon me a sleep, and I saw a high mountain, and I was upon it. 6And behold *the heavens were opened* and an angel of God said to me, Levi, enter. 7And I entered from the *first heaven,* and I saw there a great sea hanging. 8And further I saw a second heaven far brighter and more brilliant, for there was a boundless height also therein. 9And I said to the angel, Why is this so? And the angel said to me, Marvel not at this, for you shall see *another heaven* [*third,* JM] more brilliant and incomparable. 10And when you have ascended there, you shall stand near the Lord, and shall be his minister, and shall declare His mysteries to men. . . .

3.1Hear, therefore, regarding the heavens which have been shown to you. The *lowest* is for this cause gloomy unto you, in that it beholds all the unrighteous deeds of men. 2And it has fire, snow, and ice made ready for the day of judgment, in the righteous judgment of God; for in it are all the spirits of the retribution for vengeance on men. 3And in the *second* are the hosts of the armies which are ordained for the day of judgment, to work vengeance on the spirits of deceit and of Beliar. And *above them* [*third?,* JM] are the holy ones. 4And in the *highest* [*seventh,* JM] of all dwells the Great Glory, far above all holiness. 5In [*the heaven next to*] it [*sixth,* JM] are the archangels who minister and make propitiation to the *Lord* for all the *sins of ignorance of the righteous;* 6Offering to the Lord a sweet smelling savor, a reasonable and a bloodless offering. 7And [in the *heaven below this*] [*fifth,* JM] are the angels who bear answers to the angels of the presence of the Lord. 8And in the heaven next to this are thrones and dominions, in which always they offer praise to God. 9When, therefore, the Lord looks upon us, all of us are

18. Danielou, *Theology of Jewish Christianity,* 14. On the view that three heavens were replaced at this time by seven, see Himmelfarb, *Ascent to Heaven,* 32ff. R. H. Charles believes that the original text of *Levi* had three heavens but was edited to seven in the first century A.D. (*Apocrypha and Pseudepigrapha,* 2:304 note).

19. R. H. Charles, *The Testaments of the Twelve Patriarchs,* Translations of Early Documents, Series 1: Palestinian Jewish Texts (London: SPCK, 1917), xvii.

shaken; yea, the heavens, and the earth, and the abysses are shaken at the presence of His majesty. [10]But the sons of men, having no perception of these things, sin and provoke the Most High.[20]

2. *2 Enoch* 3–20. This work has been dated in its present form to the period between 30 B.C. and A.D. 70.[21] The angels who fell are in the second heaven in this scheme. Nothing is said of what is below the firmament. It deals more with the dwelling place of the souls of men, however, than with angels.[22]

3. *Apocalypse of Paul* [shorter one]. This probably dates to the second century A.D. The Greek text was translated into Coptic later, perhaps in the fourth century.[23] Paul ascends to the third heaven (the work is obviously based on 2 Cor. 12) and then goes on into the fourth, fifth, and so on until he reaches the tenth. Thus there are seven heavens above the third. The text does not deal with the first three. Angels are in the fourth and fifth; a "toll collector" is in the sixth; an old man is in the seventh; the twelve apostles are in the eighth; the ninth mentions no people by name; the tenth has "fellow spirits" in it.

4. *Ascension of Isaiah*. This work is dated by the translator to the second half of the second century A.D. at the earliest.[24] In this apocalypse, Isaiah ascends through the heavens when an angel appears to him while he is prophesying. He goes first to the firmament, where he sees Satan and his angels. Then he ascends through the other heavens, which are filled with various kinds of angels. God dwells in the seventh, surrounded by "angels without number" (9.6). Also there are Enoch and those with him, "stripped of their garment of the flesh, and . . . in their higher garments," and they are like the angels. Christ's descent to earth is then predicted and described as a descent that is "hidden from the heavens" (9.15). Satan is called "the God of that world" (9.14).

The document gives this scheme three times: (1) the connection with Isaiah, (2) the incarnation of Christ, and (3) the ascension of Christ. Beneath the lowest heaven is the firmament, where apostate angels are imprisoned till consigned to hell (gehenna) at the judgment of Christ. Beneath that is the lower

---

20. R. H. Charles, *The Greek Versions of the Testaments of the Twelve Patriarchs* (London: Oxford University Press, 1908; reprint, Hildesheim: Olms, 1966), italics added; M. De Jonge, *Testamenta XII Patriarchum* (Leiden: Brill, 1964) [paperback, Greek text]. English translation in Charles, *Apocrypha and Pseudepigrapha of the Old Testament,* vol. 2, *Pseudepigrapha,* 282ff.; and idem, *Testaments of the Twelve Patriarchs,* 36–37.
21. This is the date given by R. H. Charles.
22. Charles, *Apocrypha and Pseudepigrapha,* 2:425–69.
23. Robinson, *Nag Hammadi Library,* 239ff.
24. Schneemelcher, ed., *New Testament Apocrypha,* 2:604.

air (ἀήρ, *aēr*) where demons live. This may be reflected in Paul's letter to the Ephesians (2:2; 6:12).[25] The system would appear schematically thus:

Figure 10.1 Seven-Heaven Cosmology

7th Heaven (God)

6th Heaven
5th Heaven
4th Heaven
3d Heaven (Revelations)
2d Heaven
1st Heaven

Firmament (Apostate Angels, Prison)
ἀήρ, *aēr* (Demons)

Earth

5. *Tertullian* (c. A.D. 140). Tertullian describes the Gnostic Valentinian system. "He (the Demiurge) then completes the *sevenfold stages of heaven* itself, with his own throne above all."[26]

6. *Irenaeus* (c. A.D. 180). Irenaeus, like Tertullian, describes the Gnostic Valentinian system and compares the heavens to a menorah (Jewish seven-branched lampstand). But he conceives of angels, not God, in the seventh heaven, so perhaps he thinks of a threefold tradition, including God, seven heavens, and the lower air.

> The Earth is encompassed by seven heavens in which dwell Powers and Angels and Archangels giving homage to the almighty God, who created all things.[27]

> He created also seven heavens, above which they say that he, the Demiurge, exists. And on this account they term him Hebdomas. . . . They affirm, moreover, that these seven heavens are intelligent and speak of them as being angels, while they refer to the Demiurge himself as being an angel bearing a likeness to

25. G. Abbott-Smith defines ἀήρ in Homer and Hesiod (ninth century B.C.) as used of "the lower air which surrounds the earth, as opposed to the purer αἰθήρ of the higher regions" and in the New Testament "of the air as the realm of demons" (*A Manual Greek Lexicon of the New Testament,* 11). BAGD, 20, says ἀήρ is used "of the kingdom of the air, in which spirit beings live." G. W. H. Lampe cites it as "distinguished from αἰθήρ" by Hippolytus in the third century A.D. (*A Patristic Greek Lexicon* [Oxford: Clarendon, 1961], 41); but Liddell and Scott cite the terms as "wrongly distinguished" by Aristarchus in the third to second century B.C. (LSJ, 37, 30).

26. *Against the Valentinians* 20, in *Ante-Nicene Fathers,* ed. A. Roberts and J. Donaldson (Grand Rapids: Eerdmans, n.d.), 3:514, italics added.

27. *Demonstratio* 9, in *Patrologia orientalis,* ed. R. Graffin and F. Nau (Paris: Firmin-Didot, 1903–), 12:761.

God; and in the same strain, they declare that Paradise, situated above the third heaven, is a fourth angel. . . .[28]

The Gnostic system he describes is similar to the Greek Stoic system of seven heavens as shown below.

Table 10.2 Stoic and Gnostic Cosmologies Compared

Stoic	Gnostic
αἰθήρ (aithēr, Ethereal Realm)	πλήρωμα (plērōma, Fullness)
Stars	8 Throne of Demiurge
7	7
6	6
5 Planetary	5
4 Heavens	4
3	3
2	2
1	1
ἀήρ (aēr, Air)	ἀήρ (aēr, Air)
Earth	Earth

7. *Clement of Alexandria* (c. A.D. 190–210). Clement, a "mainline" Christian of the period, also speaks of "the seven heavens which some reckon as being one on top of another."[29]

8. *Origen* (A.D. 185—254). Origen knows of some who appeal to the Book of Baruch in support of the idea of seven heavens, although he is not clear on his own views.

Finally, they summon the book of Baruch the prophet to bear witness to this assertion, because in it the seven worlds or heavens are more clearly pointed out.[30]

The Scriptures which are current in the Churches of God do not speak of "seven" heavens, or of any definite number at all, but they do appear to teach the existence of "heavens" whether that means the "spheres" of those bodies which the Greeks call "planets," or something more mysterious. Celsus, too, agreeable to the opinion of Plato, asserts that souls can make their way to and from the earth through the planets; while Moses, our most ancient prophet,

28. *Against Heresies* 1.5.2, in *Ante-Nicene Fathers,* ed. Roberts and Donaldson, 1:322. See also *Against Heresies* 1.17.1.
29. *Miscellanies* 4.25, in ibid., 2:438.
30. *De Principiis* 2.3.6, in ibid., 4:274.

says that a divine vision was presented to the view of our prophet Jacob,—a ladder stretching to heaven, and the angels of God ascending and descending upon it, and the Lord supported upon its top,—obscurely pointing, by this matter of the ladder, either to the same truths which Plato had in view, or to something greater than these. On this subject Philo has composed a treatise which deserves the thoughtful and intelligent investigation of all lovers of truth.[31]

9. *Apocalypse of Paul* [longer one]. This document, which was widely circulated in the early church, probably was written around A.D. 250.[32] It is much longer than the other one mentioned above (item 3) and merely states in the beginning that Paul "looked into the height and saw other angels." A lengthy description of what Paul saw follows, but it is not divided into multiple heavens.[33]

Although little is said about angels or demons in the Old Testament, the New Testament is full of allusions to them, taking their existence for granted as a well-known and well-established belief. This is due to the fact that the intertestamental literature, just prior to the composition of the New Testament, is filled with references to angels, expanding Old Testament rudiments of these beliefs in many directions.[34]

This literature describes a celestial liturgy that angels performed in these multiple heavens. The *Testament of Levi,* as noted above, describes some of this liturgy, where the archangels in the sixth heaven "minister and make propitiation to the Lord for all the sins of ignorance of the righteous; offering to the Lord a sweet smelling savor, a reasonable and a bloodless offering." In the fifth heaven, there are "angels who bear answers to the angels of the presence of the Lord," while in the fourth heaven are "thrones and dominions, in which always they offer praise to God."

The Book of Tobit, written between 190 and 170 B.C.,[35] has an angel telling Tobit and his son, "I brought a reminder of your prayer before the Holy One. . . . I am Raphael, one of the seven holy angels who present the prayers of the saints and enter into the presence of the glory of the Holy One" (Tob. 12:12–15).

The Dead Sea Scrolls community seems to have held a view of a heavenly temple in which angels performed a liturgy. A document has been published from the Qumran literature called *The Songs of the Sabbath Sacrifices,* dating

---

31. *Cels.* 6.21.
32. Metzger, *Canon of the New Testament,* 186. It is extant in Greek, with Syriac, Coptic, Ethiopic, Slavic, and Latin versions. On these sources see, Casey, "The Apocalypse of Paul," 1–32.
33. Barnstone, *The Other Bible,* 538ff.
34. Bruce Metzger, *An Introduction to the Apocrypha* (New York: Oxford University Press, 1957), 38.
35. Metzger, *Introduction to the Apocrypha,* 31.

to the first or second centuries B.C., in which angels are said to serve as priests at the temple in heaven. A rite of sacrifice was performed on the Sabbath by the community, which was thought to be shared by the angels in heaven.[36]

Thus, Paul lived and wrote in a religious culture that recognized the existence of intermediary beings between God and humanity and that believed these beings interacted with humanity, some positively and some negatively. Paul presents his teaching against this background because he was divinely inspired to do so and because the gospel could best be understood and dealt with by his contempories in this context with which they were at least partially familiar.

36. This is the understanding of John Strugnell, who published the document ("The Angelic Liturgy at Qumran—4Q Serek Sirot Olat Hassabbat," in *Congress Volume: Oxford, 1959,* Supplements to Vetus Testamentum 7 [Leiden: Brill, 1960], 318–45).

ELEVEN

Paul and the Incarnation
of Jesus Christ

The Gospel of Matthew quotes Isaiah 7:14, which prophesies that "a virgin shall conceive and bear a son, and his name shall be called Emmanuel (which means, God with us)" (Matt. 1:23). Jesus of Nazareth was a man, the son of Mary, but he was more than a mere man; he was Emmanuel, God incarnate, or God in the flesh. The word *Emmanuel* occurs only here in the New Testament, but Jesus is unquestionably called God in 1 John 5:20 in every major translation: for example, "He is the true God" (NIV) and "This is the true God" (KJV, RSV, NEB).

A comparison of eight passages (John 1:1, 18; Acts 20:28; Rom. 9:5; 2 Thess. 1:12; Titus 2:13; Heb. 1:8; 2 Peter 1:1) in ten versions of the New Testament that directly bear on the question of whether Jesus is called God reveals that "all versions except (inevitably) the New World Translation[1] contain at least one verse which teaches the deity of Christ."[2] Three of the eight are from the pen of Paul (Rom. 9:5; 2 Thess. 1:12; Titus 2:13), and one is from Hebrews 1:8, which may be Pauline.

In Romans 9:5, Paul writes of the Jewish people that "to them belong the patriarchs, and of their race, according to the flesh, is the Christ. God who is over all be blessed for ever." But the variant translation in the footnotes of the

---

1. Made by Jehovah's Witnesses, who emphatically deny the deity of Jesus.
2. Victor Perry, "Problem Passages of the New Testament in Some Modern Translations," *ET* 87 (1975–76): 215.

294

RSV renders it "or Christ, who is God over all, blessed for ever." This rendering, which declares the deity of Jesus, is also made by three other versions.[3]

In 2 Thessalonians 1:12, Paul uses the phrase "according to the grace of our God and the Lord Jesus Christ." Here the Greek article *the* is used before *God* (τοῦ θεοῦ) but not before *Lord*. However, all ten versions uniformly translate it as referring to two persons, Jehovah God and Christ Jesus.

Titus 2:13 is rendered "our great God and Savior Jesus Christ" by six of the translations[4] in the *Eight Translation New Testament,*[5] thus declaring his deity, while the other two render it "of the great God and our Savior Jesus Christ,"[6] thereby separating Jesus from God.

The passage in Hebrews 1:8, whose authorship is uncertain but possibly Pauline, is rendered in all eight of the versions as God saying of his Son Jesus, "Your throne, O God, is for ever."[7]

The incarnation of Jesus is one of the most difficult concepts for the human mind to grasp. When the New Testament speaks of "the Son of God," it does not mean to convey all the connotations of that phrase in everyday terminology. For example, it does not mean that Jesus had an earthly mother and father or a heavenly mother and father. He, unlike anyone else who ever lived, had a heavenly father and an earthly mother. Nor is the phrase meant to convey the idea that Jesus is the Son of God in the same way that a human son is a product of the union of a male sperm and a female egg.

The phrase *Son of Jehovah* or *Son of the Lord* is never used in the New Testament. The expression *Son of God* conveys the thought that Jesus is divine, just as *Son of Man* identifies him with humanity. In this phrase, the word *God* does not refer to Jehovah, just as the word *man* does not refer to Joseph, the husband of Mary. *God,* which is plural in Hebrew, sometimes merely means that which is divine, just as *man* sometimes merely means that which is human. And in this sense, Son of God is a title affirming the deity of Jesus.

On one occasion Jesus accepted both the titles Son of Man and Son of God (Matt. 26:63–64). He used the title Son of God in reference to himself (John 10:36; cf. 3:18; 5:25; 11:4, 27) and frequently referred to himself in all four Gospels as the Son of Man.[8] Significantly, however, no one in the New Testament ever called him Son of Man, perhaps because those who knew him and

3. KJV, NIV, and the Modern Language Bible.

4. LB, RSV, TEV, NIV, JB, NEB.

5. Wheaton, Ill.: Tyndale House, 1974.

6. KJV and PHILLIPS.

7. MOFFATT translates this verse as he does all eight of the passages studied by Perry ("Problem Passages") in a way that does not affirm the deity of Jesus. Goodspeed (*The Complete Bible: An American Translation*) does the same with this verse and with four others, affirming the deity of Jesus in his translation of only three verses (Acts 20:28; Titus 2:13; and 2 Peter 1:1).

8. A partial list includes: Matt. 8:20; 11:19; 12:40; 16:13; Mark 2:10; 8:38; 13:26; 14:21, 62; Luke 6:5; 7:34; 9:22, 26, 44, 58; 11:30; 17:24–30; 22:22, 48, 69; 24:7; John 3:14; 5:27; 6:27, 53, 62; 12:34; 13:31.

wrote about him wanted to emphasize his deity rather than his humanity. The only place in the New Testament outside the Gospels where "son of man" is used is in Hebrews 2:6, where six of the eight translations mentioned above do not regard it as a title, and therefore do not capitalize the word *son*.[9] In Hebrews the author is not using the phrase to address Jesus but is quoting Psalm 8:4–6, where the meaning of *son of man* in context is clearly expressed by the Today's English Version: "What is man, that you think of him; *mere man, that you care for him?*" The parallelism in Hebrew poetry makes it clear in this quotation from Psalms that "man" and "son of man" symbolically depict Jesus as the embodiment of humanity. To say that he was the Son of Man was to say that he was fully human. And to say that he was the Son of God was to say that he was fully divine. Such is the meaning of Emmanuel, God with us.

The apostle Paul calls Jesus "Son of God" in Romans 1:4, where he says Jesus was "designated Son of God in power according to the Spirit of holiness by his resurrection from the dead." In Galatians 2:20, Paul writes, "I have been crucified with Christ; it is no longer I who live, but Christ who lives in me; and the life I now live in the flesh I live by faith in the Son of God, who loved me and gave himself for me." Paul's only other reference to Jesus by this title is in Ephesians 4:13, where he speaks of the need of the ethnically diverse church in Ephesus to "attain to the unity of the faith and of the knowledge of the Son of God."

But the title is used four times by the author of Hebrews (Heb. 4:14; 6:6; 7:3; 10:29), who writes to show the supremacy of Jesus as the Son of God over angels, the law of Moses, Moses himself, the Aaronic priesthood, Melchizedek, and the old covenant. In one dramatic statement, this author says of Jesus, quoting Psalm 45:6–7, "But of the Son he says, 'Thy throne, O God, is for ever and ever,'" clearly identifying Jesus as God (Heb. 1:8). Jesus is referred to as Son several other times in Hebrews (Heb. 1:2, 5 [twice]; 3:6; 5:5; 6:6; 7:28).

Paul's perspective on Jesus' incarnate state as the Son of God is seen in his use of the phrase "his Son," that is, God's Son (Rom. 5:10; 8:29; 1 Cor. 1:9; Gal. 1:16; 4:4, 6; 1 Thess. 1:10). He calls him God's "own Son" in Romans 8:3 and 8:32 and his "beloved Son" in Colossians 1:13.

Paul's unequivocal acceptance of Jesus as both divine and human, both God and man, leads to the question of how Paul viewed Jesus' incarnation in relation to his preexistence. The most frequently discussed passage from Paul's pen on this issue is Philippians 2:5–11:

> Have this mind among yourselves,
> which you have in Christ Jesus,
> who, though he was in the form of God,

9. The LB is the only one to capitalize *Son.*

did not count equality with God
a thing to be grasped,
but emptied himself,
taking the form of a servant,
being born in the likeness of men.
And being found in human form
he humbled himself
and became obedient unto death,
even death on a cross.
Therefore God has highly exalted him
and bestowed on him the name
which is above every name,
that at the name of Jesus
every knee should bow,
in heaven and on earth and under the earth,
and every tongue confess that Jesus Christ is Lord,
to the glory of God the Father.

This passage has long been interpreted as a narrative expression by Paul of the incarnation of Jesus, which states that Jesus existed preincarnately with God the Father, left that place in heaven, came to the earth in his incarnation as a human being, obediently died for the sins of humanity on the cross, was resurrected from the dead, and ascended back to the throne of God, where he was highly exalted and is henceforth worshiped by those who believe in him.

Jewish scholarship has generally rejected the idea of a divinely incarnate Messiah. However, the pseudepigraphical book of *1 Enoch* (48.6) states that the Son of Man had been "chosen and hidden before Him [i.e., God] before the creation of the world and for evermore."[10] Phillip Segal says,

This might simply mean his identity was kept secret, or that the person and not only his name was pre-existent. Should the latter be the case, it becomes necessary for those who believe this to also have a belief in an incarnation of this pre-existent celestial messianic figure in an earthly being in order to fulfill his mission on earth. . . . The originators of Christianity were Jews, and they found their notion of a divine messiah in their own heritage."[11]

After discussing pre-Christian writings including the Dead Sea Scrolls and the Pseudepigrapha, Segal concludes:

10. *The Book of Enoch*, in *The Apocrypha and Pseudepigrapha of the Old Testament in English*, ed. R. H. Charles (Oxford: Clarendon, 1963), 2:216.
11. Phillip Segal, "Further Reflections on the 'Begotten' Messiah," *Hebrew Annual Review* 7 (1983): 221–22 [the Robert Gordis volume].

When one takes into consideration the lengthy tradition of pre-existent Messiah which requires incarnation at the appropriate time and the various pre-Christian strands that point to an idea of divine conception and the Isaac allusions it might be considered reasonable to hypothecate that this, as in other facets of Christology expressed in the New Testament, we are dealing with elements of Judaic theology and not with original post-separation Christian concepts or hellenistic philosophical encrustations.[12]

Christian scholars have long been divided over whether Philippians 2:5–11 is referring to a preexistent Messiah. The issue is not whether Christ was preexistent but whether this is taught in this passage. Several scholars have in recent decades argued that it is not.[13] Their arguments are rooted in the view that these verses are actually an ancient hymn that spoke only of Christ's activities as a man.[14] It is appropriate to caution, however, that "one hymn need not be thought to represent the entirety of an author's christology."[15] Christ's preincarnation is not denied by viewing this hymn as a composition about aspects of Christ's incarnate ministry.

The passage has been arranged poetically into three strophes, which allows the presumed parallel thoughts to appear in their proper places:[16]

I

who, though he was in the form of God,
did not count equality with God
a thing to be grasped,
but emptied himself,
taking the form of a servant,

---

12. Ibid., 231.

13. Charles Talbert, "The Problem of Pre-Existence in Philippians 2:6–11," *JBL* 8 (1967): 141–53; Jerome Murphy-O'Connor, "Christological Anthropology in Philippians 2:6–11," *Revue biblique* 83 (1976): 25–50; George Howard, "Philippians 2:6–11 and the Human Christ," *CBQ* 40 (July 1978): 368–87. See also H. W. Bartsch, *Die konkrete Wahrheit und die Lüge der Spekulation* (Frankfurt-Main and Bern: Lang, 1974). Bartsch denies the preexistence motif and interprets the passage to refer to Christ's humanity.

14. The confessional structure of the passage is argued by Adolf Deissmann, who contends that "these lines are not written in the hard tone of a theological thesis, they are not calculated for discussion by modern western Kenoticists . . . they are a confession of the primitive apostolic cult, made by Paul" (*Paul: A Study in Social and Religious History* [1912; reprint, New York: Harper and Row, 1957], 193). E. Lohmeyer saw the passage as a hymn and arranged it into six strophes in an essay written in 1928 and reprinted in *Kyrios Jesus: Eine Untersuchung zu Philippians 2:5–11,* 2d ed. (Heidelberg: Winter, 1961).

15. Howard, "Philippians 2:6–11 and the Human Christ," 369.

16. Joachim Jeremias, "Zur Gedankenführung in den paulinischen Briefen," in *Studia Paulina: In Honorem Johannis de Zwaan Septuagenarii,* ed. J. N. Sevenster and W. C. van Unnik (Haarlem: De Erven F. Bohn, 1953), 152–54; idem, "Zu Phil. 2:7; EAYTON EKENΩ-ΣEN," *Novum Testamentum* 6 (1963): 182–88.

II

being born in the likeness of men.
And being found in human form
he humbled himself
and became obedient unto death,
(*even death on a cross*).

III

Therefore God has highly exalted him
and bestowed on him the name
which is above every name,
that at the name of Jesus
every knee should bow,
(*in heaven and on earth and under the earth*),
and every tongue confess that Jesus Christ is Lord,
(*to the glory of God the Father*).

It has been argued that the first half of the passage consists of two parallel strophes.

Strophe 1		Strophe 2
who, though he was in the form of God,	=	being born in the likeness of men
did not count equality with God a thing to be grasped,	=	and being found in human form
but emptied himself,	=	he humbled himself
taking the form of a servant,	=	and became obedient unto death

This postulated poetical division of the passage[17] provides a basis for the argument that only the earthly, incarnate life of Jesus is reflected in these words.[18]

Based on this postulation, lines three and four of strophe 2 speak of Jesus' "humbling himself and becoming obedient unto death." This is clearly a reference to the crucifixion. Accordingly, it is argued that in strophe 1, the "emptying of himself" is parallel to humbling himself in strophe 2, and the "taking the form of a servant" is parallel to "becoming obedient unto death" in strophe 2. By this analogy there is, therefore, no implication of preexistence in strophe 1.

Furthermore, this parallelism between the two strophes breaks the link between the phrases "taking the form of a servant" and "being born in the likeness of men." This is most important because "this link has formed the crucial point in any argument for the preexistence of Christ in this hymn."[19] Without this link, there is nothing requiring the interpretation of these words as a ref-

17. Talbert divides the last half also into two strophes, making a total of four.
18. This view is held by Jeremias, Talbert, and Howard.
19. Talbert, "Problem of Pre-Existence," 148.

erence to Christ's preexistence. Does the phrase "taking the form of a servant" in the last line of strophe 1 refer to the death of the obedient Son at Calvary (last line of strophe 2) or to the birth of the preincarnate Son at Bethlehem (first line of strophe 2)? The traditional narrative reading of the passage has argued the latter, while the more recent hymnic parallelism has advocated the former.

As to the rest of the passage, critics of its preincarnate application also argue that the expression "God has highly exalted him," which begins strophe 3, "does not involve anything other than a post-resurrection exaltation of Christ which took place while he was still on earth."[20] In support of this view, it is pointed out that in Matthew 28:18, before his ascension, Jesus says, "All authority in heaven and on earth has been given to me." The third Gospel also pictures in dramatic terms the glorified, resurrected Lord prior to his ascension (Luke 24). One author writes: "We may conclude from this that while the early church believed in the heavenly coronation of Christ (Eph. 1:20–23; Heb. 1:3) it preserved a tradition that the exaltation of Christ to supreme lordship and to glorious magnification took place during his post-resurrection pre-ascension period."[21] The entire passage of Philippians 2:6–11 is thus interpreted as referring only to the early life of Jesus, with no reference to his preincarnate state or his postincarnate glorification. It should be repeated, however, that this does not imply a denial of his preexistence by these critics but only that they believe his preexistence is not referred to in this passage.

A final point to notice in the argument against the traditional understanding of these verses is the assumption that the phrase "and bestowed on him the name which is above every name" means that God *named* Christ his own name *Yahweh,* or *Jehovah.*[22] Two objections have been raised to the argument that Jesus was actually named *Yahweh.* First, the Greek phrase Paul uses here (ἐχαρίσατο αὐτῷ τὸ ὄνομα, *echarisato autō to onoma*) does not mean "to name him the name"[23] ("the name" standing here for the word *Yahweh,* which pious Jews would not pronounce). This Greek verb (χαρί-ζομαι, *charizomai*) is not used with this meaning anywhere else in the New Testament or in the Greek Old Testament (Septuagint).[24] Its meaning is, quite literally, "he gave to him the name." The idea seems to be that God

20. Howard, "Philippians 2:6–11 and the Human Christ," 379.

21. Ibid., 381.

22. F. Hahn, *The Titles of Jesus in Christology: Their History in Early Christianity* (New York: World, 1969), 110. No vowels were written in Hebrew manuscripts of the Old Testament until the ninth century A.D. The two forms *Yahweh* and *Jehovah* are transliterations of the same Hebrew name, differing in transliteration only on the basis of whether two vowels are used with the Hebrew consonants YHWH (producing the word *Yahweh*), or three vowels (producing the word *Jehovah*).

23. This is ordinarily expressed by ἐπονομάζειν τὸ ὄνομα αὐτοῦ (cf. Gen. 5:2, 3, Septuagint) or ἐκάλουν αὐτὸ ἐπὶ τῷ ὀνόματι (Luke 1:59; cf. Matt. 1:25).

24. The definitive classical Greek dictionary LSJ refers to no such usage in its literature.

gave his name to Christ, not to be worn, but *to be used* as an instrument of divine power over the universe.[25]

The second objection is that Jesus never used the Hebrew name *Yahweh* of himself, nor did anyone recorded in the New Testment ever use it of him. Of course, since the name *Yahweh* is a Hebrew name, it could be recorded in the Greek language of the New Testament only by transliteration (i.e., spelling it out letter by letter), and this is never done. The name is neither transliterated nor translated in the Greek Old Testament used by the early church. The reason for this is that Jewish people had come to regard the name as so sacred that they refused to pronounce it, and when scribes later made copies of the Hebrew text and encountered the name, they wrote a different name in the margin, which was to be pronounced by those reading the text aloud. This alternate name in Hebrew is *adonai,* which means "Lord."

When the translators of the Septuagint came across the name *Yahweh* in the Hebrew text, they made no attempt to translate it but rather used the marginal word *adonai,* translating it with the Greek term κύριος (*kyrios*), which also means Lord.

While it is true that Jesus was called Lord by his disciples, who used the Greek term *kyrios,* there is no evidence that he ever used the name *Yahweh* in Hebrew or allowed his disciples to refer to him by that name. The word *Lord* was used most often with the normal meaning of "master," the antithesis of "slave." Jesus was being acknowledged by his followers as their master. They were not equating him with his heavenly Father.

The Jewish attitude on this issue is illustrated in the Gospel of John, which records that a number of Jewish officers and soldiers (John 18:3) were brought to the Garden of Gethsemane by Judas Iscariot to capture Jesus. When they arrived in the night and said they were seeking Jesus of Nazareth, he said, "I am he" (John 18:5). Instead of seizing him and binding him, as they had planned to do, John says "they drew back and fell to the ground" (John 18:6). What accounts for this opposite reaction to what was anticipated? Perhaps it was the very issue at point here—how did a first-century Jew react to the pronunciation of the sacred name of *Yahweh?* If, as it may legitimately be assumed, these guards and Jesus' disciples were speaking either Hebrew or Aramaic, they might have thought that when Jesus said "I am he," he had pronounced the sacred and unpronounceable name of God—*Yahweh.* In these languages the noun *Yahweh* is probably derived from the verb *yihyeh,* which means "to be." In the Greek text of the Gospel of John, Jesus is recorded as having said ἐγώ εἰμι (*egō eimi*), "I am." The word *he* (αὐτός, *autos*) is not in the text but is legitimately supplied by translators. If then Jesus said *yihyeh* ("I am"), and they thought he had pronounced the similar sounding, unpronounceable word *yahweh,* it would have produced this radical effect upon them. Thus, it is not likely that Jesus' disciples would ever have used this word of him or that he would have used it of himself in that cultural context.

---

25. Howard, "Philippians 2:6–11 and the Human Christ," 381.

TWELVE

Atonement in Pauline Literature

Why was the incarnation of Jesus necessary? Did he have to die? Was it necessary for him to die in such a way as to cause the shedding of his blood? Did atonement require the death of a divine being? Was his resurrection from the dead a necessary aspect of atonement, or was death alone sufficient? How did his death relate to the sacrificial system of the Old Testament? How could he, as a Jew, function as a high priest and make atonement for sin when he was not from the priestly tribe of Levi? Did atonement occur entirely at Calvary or did it also include postresurrection activity by Jesus? These are some of the questions that lie at the heart of the Christian view of atonement, and they are questions with which Paul dealt to a greater or lesser extent in his writings. I will try to provide some insight into these questions in the pages that follow.

Paul's view of atonement is the substructure of his theology. He writes that he knew nothing among the Corinthians except "Jesus Christ and him crucified" (1 Cor. 2:2). This, of course, includes Jesus' burial and resurrection. Paul defines "the gospel" as the death, burial, and resurrection of Christ in 1 Corinthians 15:1–4. For Paul the one central, surpassing truth is the incarnation of Jesus for the purpose of making atonement for all nations, Gentiles as well as Jews. It was to proclaim this fact that Paul was converted, called, and commissioned. Jesus said to him:

> Rise and stand upon your feet; for I have appeared to you for this purpose, to appoint you to serve and bear witness to the things in which you have seen me and to those in which I will appear to you, delivering you from the people and from the Gentiles—to whom I send you to open their eyes, that they may turn

from darkness to light and from the power of Satan to God, that they may receive forgiveness of sins and a place among those who are sanctified by faith in me. (Acts 26:16–18)

As a rabbi, Paul understood the life and death of Jesus in the context of Israel, the Old Testament people of God who had been created and prepared for the purpose of bringing the messianic redeemer into the world. Thus, it is necessary to begin a study of the atonement in Paul's thought in the context of Israel's history.

What Is Sin in the Old Testament?

Sin necessitates atonement. The Book of Hebrews is based on the concept of the conditional nature of atonement in the Old Testament. The fact that Jesus' death redeemed people from transgressions committed under the first covenant (Heb. 9:15) emphasizes the point that "it is impossible for the blood of bulls and goats to take away sins" (Heb. 10:4 NRSV). The old system that was only a "copy and shadow of the heavenly sanctuary" (Heb. 8:5) could not actually remove sins. The "law made nothing perfect" (Heb. 7:19). The priests in the old covenant system of sacrifice offered "repeatedly the same sacrifices which can never take away sins" (Heb. 10:11); they could not "perfect the conscience of the worshiper" (Heb. 9:9). For the author of Hebrews, this system was temporary from its inception, "imposed until the time of reformation" (Heb. 9:10).

Atonement in the sacrificial system of the Old Testament was primarily for the day-by-day violations of ritual and religious precepts described in Leviticus 1–5 and not for violations of conscience, sins of the heart and mind as delineated by Jesus and the New Testament. These kinds of sins had no daily sacrificial offering for atonement. One author observes that "ensuring the *holiness of the institution* is of paramount importance, and this is the purpose, explicitly or implicitly, of all the special expiatory rites given in the texts."[1]

Another writer notes that "the specific purifications and expiations of the Law apply almost solely to cases which have intrinsically no *moral* quality . . . to accidental or unwitting infringement of such rules"; "sin offerings are brought for unwitting sins, not for presumptuous sins." "Sin offering is not made for what we call sin."[2]

This raises the question, What is sin? Many modern theories of atonement, "even among the most recent, rest upon profound misunderstandings of the

1. John Dunnill, *Sacrifice and Covenant in the Old Testament,* Society for New Testament Studies Monograph Series 75 (Cambridge: Cambridge University Press, 1992), 97.

2. George Foot Moore, *Judaism in the First Centuries of the Christian Era: The Age of the Tannaim* (Cambridge, Mass.: Harvard University Press, 1962), 1:497, 497 n. 1; 3:141 n. 188.

nature of the Old Testament sacrifices, and entirely ignore Jewish conceptions of the effect and operation of sacrifice."[3]

A recent study states that

> the Old Testament has no main general word for sin, like the New Testament. Its theological reflection on sin is not so fully developed as, for example, in Paul. Yet sin, over and above the guilt of the individual, was clearly recognized as reality separating man and nation from God. . . . Sin, guilt and punishment were frequently not separated because sin is an estrangement from him, and thus brings harm and punishment upon itself. . . . Sin is both a falling away from a relationship of faithfulness towards God and also disobedience to the commandments and the Law. The former is described as unfaithfulness to God's covenant (Hos. 2; Jer. 3:10), the latter is a violation of God's word and command (1 Sam. 15:23ff.; Ps. 78). In both cases man shuts himself off from fellowship with God and becomes God-less (cf. Jer. 2:29). . . . The sin of the individual cannot be separated from that of the nation.[4]

Another writer concludes that sin

> is fundamentally any departure from the divinely revealed rule of life, whether in the sphere of *morals or of religious* observance, whether deliberate or unwitting. . . . Although, in the Jewish use of the word, a man may "sin" without meaning to and even without knowing it, the "sinner" in our sense of the word is only the man who knowingly and wilfully transgresses or ignores the revealed will of God, and that persistently or habitually.[5]

Commenting on the Old Testament idea of sin, one author writes:

> Interest in the *moral* aspect of sin is hard to document, but sin as "impurity" is fundamental to these rites: ritual uncleanness of a material even contagious character. Similarly the *moral and personal* overtones of the English word "atone" are misleading in this context, and translation of *kipper* by "expiation" is to be preferred, not least in having likewise a restricted, technical sense which resists reduction to other concepts.[6]

In the Old Testament sacrificial system, intentional sins were not atoned for by the regular sacrifices (Num. 15:30). Thus it has been argued that for such sins committed "'with a high hand' . . . , *wilfully and defiantly,* or arrogantly, insolently . . . no expiation is provided." These sins caused a person to

    3. G. F. Moore, "Sacrifice," *Encyclopedia Biblica* (London: Adam & Charles Black, 1903), 4:4232.

    4. Wolfgang Günther, "Sin," *NIDNTT* 3:577–78.

    5. Moore, *Judaism,* 1:493 (italics added).

    6. Dunnill, *Sacrifice and Covenant,* 93.

be "utterly cut off, his guilt is upon him."[7] The reference here is to violations of the laws in Numbers 15:1–21, which this writer says "are purely ritual."[8] These laws apparently refer to the regular offerings rather than to the Day of Atonement.

The Day of Atonement seems to be different: One writer states that "the term *pasha* ('act of rebellion') stands for any acts that were *intentional violations* of God's Law."[9] It is used in Leviticus only in the discussion of the Day of Atonement in 16:16. "Its usage," this writer asserts, "certainly communicates that *willful sins* were expiated by this rite."[10] These intentional violations were evidently religious and not moral.

The nature of sin in the Old Testament can be further clarified by the observation that "the name 'sin offering' suggests to the modern reader a sacrifice for the expiation of sin in our sense of the word, and it is often imagined that the Jewish sacrificial system provides and requires such expiation for *every* sin. Both these notions are erroneous."[11]

Moore observes that the "sin offering" (*hattath* in Hebrew) is prescribed for two classes of sin:[12]

1. Ignorant or inadvertent transgression of certain prohibitions ("taboos"—including *some* in which we see a moral character—e.g., incest), but not all moral wrongs. This category *"does not include the commonest offenses against morals."*

2. Purifications of various kinds. "The special *piacula* (*Latin term for expiatory sacrifices*) called sin offerings have a very limited range of employment. They are prescribed chiefly for unintentional ceremonial faults or as purifications; the trespass offering is even more narrowly restricted. *The great expiation for the whole people, at least in later times, was the scape-goat; not any form of sacrifice."*

What Is Sin in the New Testament?

When we look at the concept of sin in the New Testament, a different perspective emerges. "Paul does not define sin, but clearly he does not see it as primarily an offense against other people; for him sin is primarily an offense against God (cf. Rom. 8:7; 1 Cor. 8:12). The disruption of a right relation-

7. Moore, *Judaism,* 1:463, italics added.
8. Ibid., 1:463 n. 7.
9. John E. Hartley, *Leviticus,* Word Biblical Commentary 4 (Dallas: Word, 1992), 240.
10. Ibid.
11. Moore, "Sacrifice," 4204–5.
12. Ibid., 4219.

ship with God has its results in hindering right relationships with people, but it is the offense against God that is primary."[13]

Another author expresses it this way: "The predominant conception of the nature of sin in the Bible is that of personal alienation from God. . . . The intensely personalistic, or, better, theological conception of sin is the most characteristic view of the O[ld] T[estament] and the exclusive conception of the N[ew] T[estament]." A difference between the Old Testament and the New Testament, he says, is that Jesus "provides something which the saints of the Old Testament yearned for but could never find: real and certain victory over sin."[14]

This is further clarified by another writer, who says, "It is sin which has created the need for atonement, because sin, besides corrupting the heart and deadening the conscience and making man increasingly prone to sin again, causes man to be estranged from God, separated from God by an unseen barrier, a 'dividing wall of hostility' (Eph. 2:14)."[15]

Further clarification is added by still another writer, who believes that the generic term *sin* is pervasive for the various concepts of sin: "Following the prominent use of *hamartanō* and its cognates in the LXX [Greek translation of the Old Testament], the N[ew] T[estament] uses them as the comprehensive expression of everything opposed to God. The Christian concept of sin finds its fullest expression and its deepest theological development in Paul and John. . . . All the other concepts and synonyms are overshadowed by *hamartia* and are to be understood in the light of this concept. . . . *hamartia* is always used in the N[ew] T[estament] of man's sin which is ultimately directed against God."[16] This author argues that "in the LXX two words, *hamartia* [sin] and *adikia* [unrighteousness], represent between them almost the whole range of Heb[rew] words for guilt and sin."[17]

This generic concept of sin, unrelated to the specific violation of a revealed law, is enunciated forcefully in Paul's letter to the Romans. "For Paul it is the rejection of the light of nature and the Law implanted by God in human intelligence and conscience; Romans 1:18–32; 2:8–16."[18]

Words for Sin in the New Testament

Sin is a multifaceted concept expressed by many different terms in the New Testament. "There are more than thirty words in the New Testament that

13. Leon Morris, "Sin, Guilt," *Dictionary of Paul and His Letters,* ed. Gerald F. Hawthorne et al. (Downers Grove, Ill.: InterVarsity, 1993), 877.

14. S. J. De Vries, "Sin, Sinners," *IDB,* 4:362, 371.

15. C. L. Mitton, "Atonement," *IDB,* 1:313.

16. Günther, "Sin," 579.

17. Ibid., 577.

18. Moore, *Judaism,* 1:462 n. 1.

convey some notion of sin, and Paul employs at least twenty-four of them."[19] A representative list of these words would include the following, grouped according to their basic semantic orientation.

Formal Terms Indicating Deviation from the Good

1. *Miss a mark* (ἁμαρτία, *hamartia*), miss one's aim, a mistake; the idea of sin in the abstract (Rom. 3:23; 5:12). It is the most frequent word in the New Testament for sin.
   Results of missing the mark (ἁμάρτημα, *hamartēma*), referring to individual actions. The word is from the same root as the one above (Rom. 3:25; 1 Cor. 6:18; Chrysostom argued in the fourth century that infants were free from these but not from "sin" as represented in the above word). Both words appear in a variant reading of 2 Peter 1:9 in Greek manuscripts, however.
   Guilty or wicked person (ἁμαρτωλός, *harmartōlos*, 1 Tim. 1:9; Gal. 2:17; Rom. 5:8; Heb. 7:26).
2. *Transgression* (of a line—παράβασις, *parabasis*), passing the bounds God sets on human action (Rom. 4:15; 5:14; Gal. 3:19; 1 Tim. 2:14; Heb. 2:2 [with παρακοή]; 9:15); going beyond the norm. The Jews used it for violations of the law, but Gentiles do not transgress the law. "Only in Rom. 4:14–20 is sin as a universal fact referred to as a transgression . . . because Adam is a type of sin as the transgressing of God's commandment."[20]
3. *Trespass* (παράπτωμα, *paraptōma*), "falling away" from the divinely ordered course of duty, a false step (Rom. 4:25; 5:15–18, 20; 11:11–12; 2 Cor. 5:19; Gal. 6:1; Eph. 1:7; 2:1, 5; Col. 2:13). It can also be committed against other humans (Matt. 6:14–15). In Classical Greek literature, it is a blunder or an error in measurement.
4. *Ignorance* (ἀγνόημα, *agnoēma*) of what one should have known (Heb. 9:7). Also ἄγνοια (*agnoia*).

Terms with Theological Orientation

5. *Lawlessness* (ἀνομία, *anomia*), nonobservance of a law (1 John 3:4). It appears opposite of righteousness (δικαιοσύνη, *dikaiosynē*, 2 Cor. 6:14; Heb. 1:9) and is coupled with scandal (σκάνδαλα, *skandala*, Matt. 13:41), with hypocrisy (ὑπόκρισις, *hypokrisis*, Matt. 23:28),

19. Leon Morris, "Sin, Guilt," 877. For a list of many of these, see J. Murray and B. A. Milne, "Sin," *New Bible Dictionary,* ed. J. D. Douglas and N. Hillyer, 2d ed. (Leicester, Eng.: Inter-Varsity, 1982), 1116–17; and De Vries, "Sin, Sinners," 371.
20. Günther, "Sin," 585.

with uncleanness (ἀκαθαρσία, *akatharsia,* Rom. 6:19), and with missing a mark (ἁμαρτία, *hamartia,* Rom. 4:7; Heb. 10:17; cf. Ps. 32:1 [31:1 LXX]).

Breach of law (παρανομία, *paranomia;* noun, 2 Peter 2:16; verb, Acts 23:3).

6. *Disobedience* (παρακοή, *parakoē*) to a voice, namely, the voice of God (Rom. 5:19; 2 Cor. 10:6; Heb. 2:2).

7. *Ungodliness* (ἀσέβεια, *asebeia*), impiety, active irreligion, withholding prayer and service that is due God (Rom. 1:18; 11:26; 2 Tim. 2:16; Titus 2:12; Jude 15, 18). This has been considered by some the "most profoundly theological word for 'sin.' . . . It indicates offense against God in distinction from ἀδικία [*adikia*], which refers to wrongdoing against mankind."[21] One writer says it is "perhaps the profoundest New Testament term. . . . It implies active ungodliness or impiety."[22]

Terms Indicating Spiritual Badness

8. *Active evil* (πονηρία, *ponēria*), qualitative moral evil, wickedness, baseness, maliciousness. In the New Testament and early Christian literature, it is used only in the ethical sense (Rom. 1:29; 1 Cor. 5:8). Satan is the evil one (ὁ πονηρός, *ho ponēros,* Matt. 13:19; Eph. 6:16; 2 Thess. 3:3; 1 John 3:12).

9. *Viciousness* (κακία, *kakia*), qualitative moral evil, malice, evil disposition (Rom. 1:29; 1 Cor. 5:8).

10. *Unholy* (ἀνόσιος, *anosios*), wicked (1 Tim. 1:9; 2 Tim. 3:2).

11. *Defect* (ἥττημα, *hēttēma*), defeat, failure (Rom. 11:12; 1 Cor. 6:7).

12. *Scandal* (σκάνδαλον, *skandalon*). The RSV translates it "causes of sin" in Matthew 13:41; 18:7, 9 (cf. "hindrance," Matt. 16:23; "temptations to sin, stumbling blocks," Luke 17:1; Rom. 9:33; 11:9; 14:13; 16:17; 1 Cor. 1:23; Gal. 5:11; 1 Peter 2:8; 1 John 2:10).

Ethical and Juridical Terms

13. *Unrighteousness* (ἀδικία, *adikia*), injustice (Rom. 1:18; with ungodliness [ἀσέβεια, *asebeia*], Rom. 2:8; 3:5; 6:13; 9:14; 1 Cor. 13:6; 2 Cor. 12:13; 2 Thess. 2:10; 2 Tim. 2:19). Jeremiah 31:34 (= LXX 38:34) is quoted in Hebrews 8:12, which uses the word ἀδικία, but in 10:17 ἀνομία (*anomia*) is used when quoting the same verse. Ἀδικία "is the main classical term for wrong done to one's neigh-

---

21. De Vries, "Sin, Sinners," 371.
22. Murray and Milne, "Sin," 1117.

bour."[23] The term is translated variously in different contexts as injustice (Rom. 9:14), unrighteousness (Luke 18:6), falsehood (John 7:18), wickedness (Rom. 2:8), and iniquity (2 Tim. 2:19) and is equated with ἁμαρτία (*hamartia,* sin) in 1 John 5:17.

14. *Guilty or liable* (ἔνοχος, *enochos*), a legal term in courts of law used for a particular wrong (1 Cor. 11:27; Heb. 2:15) or to declare one liable to judgment (Matt. 5:21).

15. *Debt* (ὀφείλημα, *opheilēma,* Rom. 4:4). In Matthew 6:12 (cf. Luke 11:4) it indicates the burden of guilt that the sinner bears in the sight of God.

In addition to these general terms, there are many more terms that designate particular sins, such as those found in the following lists: Mark 7:21–22; Romans 1:29–31; Galatians 5:19–21; Ephesians 4:31; 5:3–5; Colossians 3:5–9.

However, as has been observed, "the definition of sin . . . is not to be derived simply from the terms used in Scripture to denote it. The most characteristic feature of sin in all its aspects is that it is directed against God (Ps. 51:4; Rom. 8:7). . . . Essentially, sin is directed against God, and this perspective alone accounts for the diversity of its form and activities. It is a violation of that which God's glory demands and is, therefore, in its essence the contradiction of God."[24]

Atonement Theories

In the past four hundred years, various theories have been constructed to explain Christ's atonement for sin. Before the historically pivotal work of Martin Luther in the sixteenth-century Reformation movement, most Christian writers held that Jesus mediated to humans the righteousness of the cross by means of the Mass. The *sacramental system* of the Roman Catholic Church was the agent through which God's grace and blessing were mediated to humans. The church, with its sacramental system, thus stood in a position between God and humanity, controlling the access that humans have to God, and consequently the forgiveness that God mediates to humanity through that system.

However, German theologians subsequently argued for a different view of atonement, asserting that Jesus merely had a unique association with God and set an example for the world by dying on the cross. They said that when we follow Christ's example, we are thereby transformed into better people. This view was called the *martyr theory.* The idea was that nothing objective and su-

23. Ibid.
24. Ibid.

pernatural happened at the cross. Something good happens in our lives only as we follow Jesus, who was a great martyr for his cause. He inspires us to be like him by virtue of what he did. So if there is no response on our part, then nothing actually took place at Calvary.

Early in the twentieth century, Karl Barth, an eminent German theologian who had initially held this martyr view, reacted to it on the basis of 2 Corinthians 5:19, which states that "God was in Christ reconciling the world to himself." Barth understood this statement to mean that something did indeed happen at the cross, in and of itself, regardless of any human response. Something objective actually occurred at Calvary!

Barth said phrases like "be baptized for the remission of your sins" imply that Christ did not bear all of our sins at Calvary, because if he had, no further response would be required on our part. If Christ totally removed the sins of humanity at Calvary, there would be no need to be baptized for "remission of sins" (Acts 2:38 KJV) or to "wash away . . . sins" (Acts 22:16).

On the other hand, if nothing objective happened at Calvary, we have to complete that potentiality ourselves. That, however, was a position Barth had already rejected. If remission of sins is entirely potential, then nothing in and of itself happened at the cross, he said. Thus, Barth sought to find the truth somewhere between these two positions—something did happen at Calvary, but something also happens to us—and the result of his study became the theological basis for incipient *neoorthodoxy.* These views he set forth in his monumental work *Church Dogmatics* (1936–69).

Rudolf Bultmann, another prominent German theologian, wrote an influential two-volume work entitled *New Testament Theology* (1952–55), in which he rejected Barth's conclusions and continued to defend the position that nothing objective and supernatural happened at Calvary. However, unlike old-line liberals who had held this view, he argued that something could happen through Jesus' death on the cross if combined with a human response. Bultmann asserted that Christ becomes Redeemer only when he is preached and accepted, only when one makes a decision to respond to the gospel.

This view has been appropriately designated *existentialism* because it deals with what happens inside a person when that person makes a decision through faith. According to this view, when one takes what eminent theologian Søren Kierkegaard called a "leap of faith" and accepts Christ through faith, then something really happens. A conscious decision has to be made to become existentially involved with one's faith. It is not enough to understand abstract truth intellectually. To be changed internally, one must make a decision and commit oneself to Christ.

Bultmann did not view Scripture the way Barth did. Bultmann believed that the Bible is full of fabrications, which he called mythology. The miracles of Jesus did not actually occur as they were reported in the text. The stories had been filtered and modified by the faith of the early church, and we have to discount that mythological aspect of the New Testament in order to really understand who Jesus was. But once we commit ourselves to him, then things happen to us that would not have happened otherwise.

Therefore, if Bultmann were asked whether anything actually happened at Calvary if no one ever believed it, he would say no. What took place was only a potentiality. If no one believes in him, then Christ died in vain.

More recently, a school of thought emerged in Europe called the *Lundensian school,* centered in the University of Lund in Sweden. Gustaf Aulén, in his book *Christus Victor* (Christ the Conqueror),[25] advocated a more objective view of atonement, arguing that something *actually happened* at Calvary. What happened, he argued, was that Christ conquered Satan and the forces of evil through his death and resurrection.

He argues that Luther did not hold the Latin view of atonement, the traditional Protestant view, but that Luther was really a proponent of the classical approach to the Dramatic view, which was accepted by the early church for centuries after Christ, as it continues to be in the Orthodox Churches. Aulén argues that although there are three major views of atonement widely discussed by contemporary theologians (which may be designated Dramatic, Latin, and Moral), the early church held to the Dramatic view.

As the following table shows, prevalent atonement theories may be separated into two categories, objective and subjective. The objective category comprises the Dramatic and the Latin views, while the subjective category includes only the Moral view.

Table 12.1 Atonement Theories

Objective				Subjective
Dramatic		Latin		
Ransom	Classical	Satisfaction	Governmental	Moral
God	*God	*God*	*Law*	*Jesus
*Jesus	Jesus	Jesus	Jesus	*Humanity*
Humanity	Humanity	*Humanity	*Humanity	
Devil	*Devil*			

In table 12.1, the asterisk designates the one who does the atoning, and the italicized word designates the being or thing affected by the atonement. The unique characteristic of the objective category is that the various views it embraces all assert that something objective happened at Calvary, regardless of any human response. In this category, the Dramatic view embraces the ransom and classical views, which are essentially the same, except that in the ran-

25. New York: Macmillan, 1967.

som view, Jesus does the atoning, and in the classical view, God atones for sin. In both concepts, the devil is the object of atonement.

Objective Views

Dramatic: Ransom View

Atonement, in the ransom approach to the Dramatic view, involves two basic elements. First, God is reconciling the world to himself. It is God who does the reconciling, not humanity. And, second, God is himself reconciled. The idea is that since humanity is guilty of sin, there is enmity between it and God, and the atonement reconciles both to each other. So, when God reconciles man, he of necessity reconciles himself by removing the cause of his wrath, the devil. This is achieved by a *ransom* in the ransom view and by *conquest* in the classical view.

The ransom view asserts that the devil is a robber, a tyrant, a usurper who is unjustly trying to take hold of that which does not belong to him, to steal humanity away from God; and it is right that he should be defeated and driven out. But at the same time, humanity is also guilty, having sold itself to the devil. Therefore, God does not use brute force but acts according to justice. Even with the devil, God deals in an appropriate way; he acts justly.

So God redeems humanity from this demonic tyrant by sending Christ as a ransom to the devil. The price was paid to the devil himself. However, although God sent Jesus, it is Jesus who, by his life and his death at Calvary and the shedding of his blood, pays the ransom to Satan. Humanity is thus redeemed from Satan by the blood of Christ. Words like *ransom, redeem,* and *purchase* appear with some frequency in the discussion of this perception of atonement. In this view, the blood of Christ is the price paid.

This approach was argued in the second century by Irenaeus, who "is the first writer in early church history to provide us with a clear and comprehensive doctrine of the atonement and redemption."[26] It seems to have been the prevailing view in the church until the time of Augustine in the fourth century.[27]

Dramatic: Classical View

The classical approach is that God himself makes atonement; forgiveness is granted through grace because of Christ's sacrifice, but it is God who makes the initial step. God does the atoning by forcibly conquering Satan through the work of Christ.

26. Aulén, *Christus Victor,* 17.
27. Ibid.

The point of emphasis in both the ransom and classical views is that Christ's work is seen as complete. Atonement is not merely a potential but has already occurred in history. It was objective, and it cannot be repeated. God conquered Satan, shackled him, and placed limitations upon him. Death was conquered (Heb. 2:14) by the resurrection of Jesus, and irrespective of any human response, it remains a fact of history. Therefore, there can be no blood-less repetition of the sacrificial act of Christ in the Mass. The finality of Christ's heavenly sacrifice precludes the effectiveness of any such repetitive act.

In the classical approach, atonement is performed not to satisfy the wrath of God but to conquer the power of Satan. The idea of ransom is viewed *met-aphorically* of the *effect* of what happened. God did not actually make a bar-gain with Satan in order to "buy him off" with the blood of Jesus.

Latin: Satisfaction View

In the Latin view, there are two approaches to the atonement—satisfaction and governmental. The Latin view, as the name suggests, has been held in the Roman Catholic, Latin-speaking part of the church for centuries. Contrary to the Dramatic view, the Latin view holds that atonement has its *origin* in God's will, but its *implementation* is by Christ as a human being on behalf of God.

In the satisfaction approach, the emphasis is on the necessity of the human-ity of Christ. It is Christ incarnate, Christ as a human, who atones; atonement has to be made by human beings because they are the ones who sinned. Whereas in the classical approach, God conquered Satan, in the Latin view, the problem is preeminently a human dilemma. Humanity has provoked the problem by violating its relationship to God, and God's wrath is expressed against it. *Satisfaction* must be made by humans, but they are sinful and inca-pable of providing atonement.

Tertullian, a Christian lawyer in Rome in the second century, used the word *satisfaction* for the compensation a person makes for the lack of personal righteousness.[28] Penance is satisfaction: the performance of a temporal penalty to escape eternal loss. For example, one does penance by paying something or making a pilgrimage. This view lies at the heart of the medieval sale of indul-gences, which finally triggered Luther's reaction and sparked the Reformation.

After Tertullian, Gregory the Great (Gregory I, A.D. 590–604) argued that human guilt necessitates a sacrifice, but animal sacrifice is not sufficient. Christ, therefore, becomes a human being in order that, as a sinless human being, he may make an offering to God on behalf of human beings.

Anselm, the Archbishop of Canterbury, England, in the late eleventh cen-tury, took these rather disorganized views and arranged them into a system in

28. *Paen.* 6.

his Latin work *Cur Deus Homo* [Why God man?—i.e., Why did God become human?].[29] Answering the question, he argued that humans are not able to make the necessary satisfaction for our transgressions because we are all guilty of sin, so God became human and did it for us in the person of Jesus Christ.

Luther, who lived in this theological ambience in the sixteenth century, was grounded in the Latin view of atonement while also embracing much of the Dramatic view. However, his followers propagated the Latin view because that tradition was established long before the period of Lutheran orthodoxy. Consequently, most Protestant theology today is rooted in the Latin view of atonement.

Latin: Governmental View

A second approach to the Latin view emphasizes that justice as well as wrath was a factor. God had told Adam that if he ate the fruit, he would die (Gen. 2:17). Adam and Eve ate and eventually died. To be just, God had to punish them. His justice was at stake. God had made a law, and that law had been broken. A just ruler must see that his law is kept. This is at the heart of the governmental view. Hugo Grotius, a Dutch lawyer (1583–1645), developed this view in reaction to Socinianism, the forerunner of modern-day Unitarianism.[30]

According to this view, Christ does the atoning as a human, but the object of atonement is the necessity of upholding divine law, not God's wrath or anger. This raises the question of whether God himself becomes subject to a law that he makes or has the power to supersede it. This further provokes the question debated in early Christian literature about whether God does a thing because it is right, or whether it is right because God does it.[31]

Abraham once asked, "Shall not the Judge of all the earth do right?" (Gen. 18:25). The response might be, "Whatever the Judge of all the earth does *is* right." But some argue that the will of God is subject to the nature of God, and the nature of God is such that he will always do what is right. God, by nature, will not do evil.

According to the governmental view, then, the act of atonement must be performed by a human being, but the effect of atonement is upon law. Christ had to take the place of Adam and suffer the penalty prescribed by the law.

This has been illustrated by the story of a king who made a law that anyone in his kingdom who committed theft would be blinded. As it unexpectedly

29. See Robert Ferm, *Readings in the History of Christian Thought* (New York: Holt Rinehart and Winston, 1964), no. 35, pp. 214–39. For a brief discussion of Anselm's satisfaction view, see Otto Heick, *A History of Christian Thought* (Philadelphia: Fortress, 1965), 1:275ff.

30. See Ferm, *Readings*, no. 38, p. 253.

31. In early church history, the controversy between the supralapsarians and the infralapsarians dealt with a similar, though not identical, issue.

turned out, the first person who broke his command was his son. The king faced a dilemma. The law had to be respected, but his parental love cried out for extending mercy. So, he decided to satisfy his law that two eyes had to be taken by taking one of his own eyes and one of the eyes of his son. Thereby, justice was met while mercy was granted.

Subjective View: Moral View

The emergence of the movement called Pietism marked the decline of the Latin view within Protestantism. It moved the understanding of the atonement in the subjective direction, the essence of which is the idea that nothing objective in atonement happened when Jesus died. The unique element in this view is that although Jesus made atonement, its subjective effect is upon mankind. According to this view, a person looks at Jesus' life, tries to emulate that life, and by his example becomes a better person. There is nothing objectively supernatural in this view, nothing of God's forgiveness based on an act of Christ's atonement. From this perspective, forgiveness occurs only after one has become a better person, at which time God grants forgiveness and acceptance.

Pietism shows a preference for imagery such as "Christ the physician of the soul" over the legal language of the orthodox doctrines. And with the emergence of Pietism in the Renaissance and Reformation, the notion of being involved in one's own atonement became more and more popular. The watchword of pietism was *new birth* rather than *justification.*

This view of atonement places emphasis on the benevolence and goodwill of God rather than upon wrath. Instead of appeasing the wrath of God, the individual repents and amends his or her life, whereupon God responds by rewarding that change with increased blessing. The view is anthropocentric and essentially moralistic.

The foremost exponent of this view was Peter Abelard in the early twelfth century,[32] who argued that Christ demonstrated humanity's need to respond to divine grace, a viewpoint that Luther soundly rejected, arguing that one only needed to believe.

Summation

In summation, the *objective view* emphasizes the actuality of atonement as a fact of history. Something objective happened at Calvary, whether anyone responds or not. In the Dramatic categories of this view (ransom and classical), the emphasis is on the deity and power of God as the divine, primary

---

32. Abelard's views are expressed in his *Exposition of the Epistle to the Romans.* An excerpt of it can be found in section 36 of Robert Ferm, *Readings,* 239–43.

agent in atonement. In the Latin approaches (satisfaction and governmental), the emphasis is upon the humanity and obedience of Christ as the human, primary agent whose incarnation is dominant. In the *subjective view,* by contrast, atonement is purely potential. It never occurs until someone believes and is responsive to the gospel message.

One of the primary problems with the theories of atonement outlined above is their tendency toward exclusiveness. Each theory acquired an exclusive position in its particular religious tradition, and advocates of each theory tend to defend one particular view exclusively, as though either sin, guilt, slavery, enmity, or ignorance were the only issue Jesus came to address. But there are, in reality, many ramifications of the life and death of Jesus, none exclusively valid.[33] He came to deal with many issues; thus atonement has many aspects.

Modern scholarship is progressively "warning against confining the atonement to a single act."[34] "No precise explanation . . . is offered in the New Testament, nor has the church officially sponsored any one of the theories of the atonement which have been propounded."[35] "It is abundantly apparent that the atonement is vast and deep. The New Testament writers strive with the inadequacy of language as they seek to present us with what this great divine act means. There is more to it by far than we have been able to indicate."[36]

One writer emphasizes that God's atoning work is not completely transparent to human thinking and that the reality of atonement is complex.[37] A century ago, another author wrote: "The subject is too vast, it runs up into mysteries too remote or impenetrable to encourage the hope that any teacher, however great, any age of the Church, however ripe, will be able to express it in a single form of words."[38] And more recently yet another writer has meaningfully stated that

> it is one thing to try to show that the atonement does not contradict what we know to be true; quite another to understand fully how God works. . . . The reality of the atonement may be complex and multi-dimensional. The problem of guilt is complex and multi-dimensional, and so it is reasonable that the solution to the problem will have the same qualities. . . . It is not surprising or embarrassing then that the universal witness of the Christian Church is that Christ's life, death, and resurrection is the story of how atonement was made

33. See the helpful summation of views in C. M. Tuckett, "Atonement in the New Testament," *ABD,* 1:518–22.

34. R. J. Thompson, "Sacrifice and Offering: I. In the Old Testament," *New Bible Dictionary,* 1052.

35. Mitton, "Atonement," 313.

36. Leon Morris, "Atonement," *New Bible Dictionary,* 106.

37. Colin Gunton, *The Actuality of Atonement: A Study of Metaphor, Rationality, and the Christian Tradition* (Grand Rapids: Eerdmans, 1989).

38. H. B. Swete, *The Forgiveness of Sins* (London: Macmillan, 1916), 159.

possible, *rather than to a particular theory of how this was accomplished.* . . . The fact that no single theory of the atonement has won universal acceptance does not show that the story is one that lacks power and relevance today. It is rather confirmation of the fact that the work the Church claims God accomplished in Christ is both complex and mysterious. [39]

With the church's long history of discussion and debate on the theories of how the atonement occurred, it is significant that "Judaism had no motive for discussing the *modus operandi* of sacrificial atonement, and never even raised the question."[40]

Pauline Perspectives on Atonement

Paul used the metaphor of "redemption" in describing what Jesus did. He spoke of "redemption through his blood" (Eph. 1:7) and said we were "bought with a price" (1 Cor. 6:20; 7:23). It is not stated whether this merely means that a price was paid (the blood of Jesus) or whether it implies some kind of purchase from Satan. Paul spoke of redemption when he wrote that Jesus "gave himself as a ransom for all, the testimony to which was borne at the proper time" (1 Tim. 2:6; cf. Matt. 20:28; Mark 10:45). It is not clear whether he refers to a purchase when he says "Christ redeemed us from the curse of the law, having become a curse for us" (Gal. 3:13) and "came to redeem those who were under the Law, so that we might receive adoption as sons" (Gal. 4:5). Paul may have been using the redemptive language of the exodus. But in just two verses of the sixth chapter of Exodus, God says he will *redeem* Israel from Egypt, *bring them out, deliver them,* and *take them* for his people (Exod. 6:6–7). Are these synonymous terms? To whom did God pay a price for Israel, and what was that price? In the context, do the communal or covenantal overtones of the language supersede any literal idea of a ransom price being paid?[41]

Another aspect of Paul's view of atonement involves Christ's conquest of the power of Satan, as expressed in the classical view (1 Cor. 15:24–26; Eph. 2:1–10; Col. 2:14–15). In Romans 7:7–12, sin is personified as an evil power, which, of course, is Satan. Christ conquered "him who has the power of death, that is, the devil" (Heb. 2:14). This was done by the resurrection of Christ from the dead.[42]

39. C. Stephen Evans, *The Historical Christ and the Jesus of Faith* (Oxford: Clarendon, 1996), 91, 96.
40. Moore, *Judaism,* 1:500.
41. Tuckett, "Atonement," 521; Morna Hooker, *Jesus and the Servant* (London: S.P.C.K., 1959), 77–78.
42. See the next chapter (13), on Ephesians, for a fuller discussion of this.

The classical view is not really a view of atonement in the Old Testament sense but deals with the means by which Jesus could become a high priest like Melchizedek (since he was from the tribe of Judah, not Levi) and offer his own blood on the mercy seat in heaven (Heb. 9:12). Therefore, destroying Satan's power over death (Heb. 2:14) is not atonement per se but provides the means by which he became a high priest (i.e., by resurrection, Acts 13:33; Heb. 5:5–10) in order to offer his blood for atonement.

Thus, the atonement in the Latin view (involving substitution, blood, etc.) is the counterpart of the Old Testament system and is made possible in the analogy in Hebrews only by the previous ordination of Jesus as high priest by his resurrection. Consequently, the classical view stresses only a partial, though vital, part of the atonement, which is a *process* not a single *act*. In the analogy in Hebrews, God accepted us and forgave us, not just when Christ died or conquered death by resurrection, but also when the resurrected Christ presented to God his life's blood as an offering on the mercy seat (ἱλα-στήριον, *hilastērion*) in the highest heaven (Heb. 9:12; cf. Lev. 16:17; Eph. 4:10; Heb. 4:14; 7:26).

In Hebrews, Jesus' role as high priest is in the heavens, not on earth. His death as the sacrificial lamb, however, takes place, of necessity, on earth, and unlike the Old Testament priesthood, it does not require him to be from the tribe of Levi. "There is no doctrine of the sacrifice of Christ in the New Testament as there may be said to be doctrines of redemption or justification."[43] "It is true that we can but dimly see why such sacrifice as the death of Christ should have been necessary and guess in the light of partial human analogies at the secret of its power. But it is enough for our present guidance to know that the sacrifice itself has been offered, and that there have been men in every age who, from their own experience, have borne witness that it is effectual."[44]

The Meaning of *Atonement*

The archaic meaning of *atonement* in English is "reconciliation."[45] Thus, the etymology of the word is "at-one-ment."[46] It is now commonly defined as "satisfaction or reparation for a wrong or injury; amends," and theologically as "the doctrine concerning the reconciliation of God and man, especially as

43. Moore, "Sacrifice," 4233.

44. J. O. F. Murray, "Atonement," *A Dictionary of the Bible,* ed. James Hastings (New York: Scribners, 1908), 1:199.

45. *Webster's New Collegiate Dictionary* (Springfield, Mass.: Merriam, 1977), 72. Webster regards that meaning as now "obsolete." So also Jess Stein, ed., *The Random House Dictionary of the English Language: The Unabridged Edition* (New York: Random House, 1967), 95: "*Archaic.* reconciliation; agreement. [from phrase *at-onement* at unity . . . now obsolete."

46. Stein, *Random House Dictionary,* 95.

accomplished through the life, suffering, and death of Christ."[47] Paul speaks of Christ's work as "reconciliation" (Rom. 5:8–11; 11:15; 2 Cor. 5:18–19; Eph. 2:16; Col. 1:20). The King James Version translates the Greek word καταλλαγή (*katallagē*) in Romans 5:11 as "atonement," but the Revised Standard Version translates it "reconciliation." Both reconciliation and justification precede salvation in Romans 5:8–10. While Romans 5:10 states that humans are reconciled to God, Ephesians speaks of the reconciliation of Jews with Gentiles. This is achieved by the removing of the middle wall of hostility (the law of Moses) that divides them, subsequent to which they are reconciled in the one new body *to God* (Eph. 2:14–16). Reconciliation is the removal of hostilities, or enmity, between two parties, resulting in peace: "For in him all the fullness of God was pleased to dwell, and through him to reconcile to himself all things, whether on earth or in heaven, making peace by the blood of his cross" (Col. 1:19–20). Hostility between God and humanity is removed by reconciliation.

The word *atonement* usually translates the Hebrew term *kippur,* as in *Yom Kippur,* "the Day of Atonement" (e.g., Lev. 23:27; 25:9). *Kippur* means a cover, pardon, and hence expiation (Exod. 29:36).[48] The Greek Old Testament (Septuagint), which was used extensively by the New Testament authors, used two forms of the same word in these passages: *hilasmos* (ἱλασμός, Lev. 23:27) and *exhilasmos* (ἐξιλασμός, Lev. 25:9). Another form of this same root word, *hilastērion* (ἱλαστήριον), was used in the Old Testament exclusively for the mercy seat, the lid on the ark of the covenant, which stood in the Holy of Holies in the tabernacle and temple. This lid was the place where the high priest sprinkled blood on the Day of Atonement and thus where expiation occurred (Lev. 16:13–15; Exod. 25:16–22). The author of Hebrews also used the word to refer to the mercy seat (Heb. 9:5), which the NIV (1978) first translated "place of atonement" and then "atonement cover" (1984). Paul used this same Greek word to refer to Jesus as an "expiation" ("propitiation," KJV; "atonement," NRSV, NIV) "whom God put forward . . . to be received by faith" (Rom. 3:25).

The Book of Hebrews and Atonement

Since all of the historically developed ideas discussed above find some measure of expression in Pauline literature, we cannot limit our understanding of atonement exclusively to any one of these views. And we must hasten to warn against the tendency to restrict New Testament views about the atonement of

47. Ibid.
48. William Gesenius, *Gesenius' Hebrew and Chaldee Lexicon to the Old Testament,* trans. S. P. Tregelles (Grand Rapids: Eerdmans, 1954), 411.

Christ to the meaning of his death alone. It also involves his resurrection, ascension, and coronation at the right hand of God. While Hebrews may not have been written by Paul, the early church considered it sufficiently "Pauline" in its content to include it in the two oldest and best-known lists of the Pauline canon—the Chester Beatty Papyrus of the early second century and Codex Vaticanus of the mid–fourth century.[49] Many of the presuppositions of Hebrews are parallel to those of Ephesians and Romans. Among these is a cosmic framework of angelic activity, which is typologically depicted in the structure and liturgy of the tabernacle/temple.[50]

Typology of the Tabernacle/Temple

Hebrews speaks typologically of the tabernacle system as a "symbol" (παραβολή, *parabolē*, parable) for the present age (Heb. 9:9) and refers to its furniture as only "copies of the heavenly things" (Heb. 9:23). Jesus, being from the tribe of Judah, never entered into the sanctuary (tabernacle/temple) made with hands. But the earthly tabernacle was only a "copy of the true one" in heaven (Heb. 9:24), which was a "greater and more perfect tent" (Heb. 9:11). As our high priest, Jesus has "passed through the heavens" (Heb. 4:14), been "exalted above the heavens" (Heb. 7:26), entered "into heaven itself" (Heb. 9:24), and "sat down at the right hand of God" (Heb. 10:12).

Typology provides the basis for understanding the purpose and function of the tabernacle system and thus for the eventual atoning work of Jesus as high priest. When Moses was given the instruction to build the tabernacle in the wilderness of Sinai, he was shown a "pattern" to be used in its construction (Exod. 25:40). In this verse, the Hebrew word for "pattern" (*tabnith*) implies "that Moses was shown something like a scale model of the sanctuary which was to be erected."[51] The word *pattern* here was translated "type" (τύπον, *typon*) in the Greek Old Testament (Septuagint) and is quoted in Hebrews 8:5, whose author considers the earthly tabernacle to be an "antitype" (ἀντίτυπος, *antitypos*, Heb. 9:24) of a heavenly "type." The pattern shown Moses was that of a structure that would allow the priestly liturgy to function as an antitype of the real activity transpiring in the heavenly places (the type). The tabernacle service symbolically represented the reality of heavenly activity. Thus, the tabernacle system is considered typologically to be only a "copy" (ὑπόδειγμα, *hypodeigma*, Heb. 8:5; 9:23) of the true one in heaven.

49. See chapter 9 on the canonicity of Paul's letters.

50. On the cosmic framework of the heavens, see D. S. Russell, *The Method and Message of Jewish Apocalyptic* (Philadelphia: Westminster, 1964); and Jean Danielou, *The Theology of Jewish Christianity,* History of Early Christian Doctrine 1, trans. J. A. Baker (London: Darton, Longman and Todd, 1964).

51. F. F. Bruce, *The Epistle to the Hebrews,* NICNT (Grand Rapids, Eerdmans, 1964), 165 n. 27.

Continuing the typology, the law of Moses itself is viewed as only a "shadow" of the reality in heaven, rather than being "the true form" or "image" (εἰκών, *eikōn,* Heb. 10:1) of these realities. It was never able, therefore, to make perfect the people who offered sacrifices year after year (Heb. 10:1). Since it was "impossible for the blood of bulls and goats to take away sins" (Heb. 10:4 NRSV), Christ's death "redeems them from the transgressions under the first covenant" (Heb. 9:15). So Christ came to abolish this imperfect shadow and do the will of God in establishing the reality of atonement "through the offering of the body of Jesus Christ once for all" (Heb. 10:10).

Typology of the High Priesthood

The problem discussed in Hebrews relative to the atonement performed by Christ was especially difficult for a Jewish audience to accept. How could Jesus function as a high priest and make atonement when he was from the tribe of Judah? The author wrote, "In connection with that tribe Moses said nothing about priests" (Heb. 7:14) and "if he were on earth, he would not be a priest at all" (Heb. 8:4). Thus, in the typology, Christ's role as high priest in making atonement had to take place after his crucifixion, resurrection, and ascension.

Before Jesus' death, the law of Moses was still binding, and under it priests could be appointed only from the tribe of Levi. Therefore, Jesus, being from the tribe of Judah (Heb. 7:14), could become a priest only after that law was no longer in force. He removed this barrier by "nailing it to the cross" (Col. 2:14) and making the first covenant "obsolete" (Heb. 8:13). He was appointed high priest "by him (i.e., God) who said to him, 'Thou art my Son, today I have begotten thee. . . . Thou art a priest for ever, after the order of Melchizedek'" (Heb. 5:5–6, quoting Ps. 2:7 and Ps. 110:4). Paul used the same passage, Psalm 2:7, to argue that this appointment as high priest occurred on the basis of Christ's resurrection from the dead (Acts 13:33).

Since through his death Christ's blood established a new covenant (Heb. 8:6; 9:15) validated by his resurrection and conquest of death (Heb. 2:14), the old covenant stipulation that priests must come from the tribe of Levi was no longer binding, and he could become a priest forever after a different order, the order of Melchizedek (Heb. 6:20). Abraham had recognized the validity of Melchizedek's priesthood four hundred years before the law of Moses was given (Gen. 14:17–20; Heb. 7:1–10).[52] Now that the law was fulfilled and made obsolete (Heb. 8:13), the Melchizedek type of priesthood, which was prophesied by David (Ps. 110:4), was reestablished and utilized by Christ. If perfection had been attainable under the Levitical system, there would have been no need for another priest to be appointed after the order of Melchizedek (Heb. 7:11).

---

52. Paul says the law was given 430 years after the promise to Abraham (Gal. 3:17).

The Typological Ritual of Christ's High Priesthood

At this point Leviticus 16 must be considered, for it gives an account of the ritual performed in the tabernacle/temple each year at *Yom Kippur* (The Day of Atonement) by the high priest. Although details of the ritual are greatly multiplied in the Mishnah,[53] which represents the period of the New Testament and later, the ritual is rather concisely presented in Leviticus.[54] Even though the efficacy of the ritual was dependent upon the genuineness of repentance,[55] the ritual of the high priest is most relevant to the typology of the Book of Hebrews.

Generically, it is stated that the high priest presented the bull and killed it as a sin offering for himself and his house (Lev. 16:11). But his specific actions are detailed in following verses and also include taking the blood of the bull and the goat into the Most Holy Place to make atonement there: "There shall be no man in the tent of meeting when he enters to make atonement in the holy place until he comes out and has made atonement for himself and for his house and for all the assembly of Israel" (Lev. 16:17). He first makes atonement "for" the Most Holy Place (Lev. 16:16) and then for himself and others "in" the Most Holy Place (Lev. 16:17). Next, after once more changing his clothing, he comes forth and again makes "atonement for himself and for the people" (Lev. 16:24). *Several activities* are thus involved in which he makes "atonement for the sanctuary, and . . . atonement for the tent of meeting and for the altar, and . . . atonement for the priests and for all the people of the assembly" (Lev. 16:33). No particular one of these acts constitutes atonement; it is a process involving all of them.

What this suggests is that *atonement was a process* rather than a single act. One author warns "against confining the atonement to a single act, as if it were the death alone, or the presentation of the blood, or the disposal of the victim, which atoned."[56] Another observes that one should "accept a rich variety in Paul's interpretation of the atonement."[57]

Many of the ideas that have been separated and historically individualized in the various views of atonement discussed above are found in Paul. He

---

53. See the tractate *Yoma* in Herbert Danby, trans., *The Mishnah* (Oxford: Oxford University Press, 1933), 162–72.

54. See the discussion by C. F. Keil and F. Delitzsch, *Commentary on the Old Testament* (reprint, Grand Rapids: Eerdmans, 1980), 1:394ff.

55. See *m. Yoma* 8.9. George Foot Moore notes that in the Mishnah "the effect of the piacula [expiatory sacrifice, JM] is not *ex opere operato:* Sin offering and prescribed trespass offering expiate; death and the Day of Atonement expiate when conjoined with repentance; repentance alone expiates for venial sins of omission and (some) sins of commission. For grave offenses, repentance suspends the sentence till the Day of Atonement comes and expiates. Repentance is thus the *conditio sine qua non* of the remission of sins" (*Judaism,* 1:498).

56. Thompson, "Sacrifice and Offering: I. In the Old Testament," 1052.

57. Tuckett, "Atonement," 520.

speaks of *redemption* (1 Cor. 6:20; 7:23; Eph. 1:7; 4:30), *reconciliation* (2 Cor. 5:18–20; Eph. 2:12–17), *propitiation* (appeasing God's wrath, Rom. 5:9), *expiation* (nullifying the effects of sin,[58] Rom. 3:25; cf. Heb. 2:17), and *the conquest of evil powers* (1 Cor. 15:24–25; Phil. 2:10; Rom. 8:35–39; Eph. 1:20–23; cf. Heb. 2:14). This leads one author to suggest: "Perhaps the very variety itself is indicative of the fact that theories about the atonement were probably of second order importance. What was primary was the experience of forgiveness and new life which the first Christians claimed to enjoy."[59]

The distinctive contribution made to this understanding of Christ's atonement by the Book of Hebrews is the typological explanation to a Jewish audience of how one from the tribe of Judah could be a high priest and what constituted his sacrificial liturgy. Here what I discussed in chapter 10 should be remembered: In Paul's time the cosmos was viewed in both Jewish and pagan cultures as consisting of multiple heavens. God dwells in the highest heaven, and the earth is beneath the lowest. Christ's work as high priest is explained in Hebrews 4:14 as passing "through the heavens and in Hebrews 7:26 as being "exalted above the heavens." In Ephesians, Paul says Christ "ascended far above all the heavens" (Eph. 4:10). It was in the realm of the "heavenly things" (Heb. 9:23), the "true" things that functioned as a pattern from which the tabernacle was constructed as a "copy" (Heb. 9:24), that Christ entered into the "presence of God on our behalf" with "better sacrifices than" the copies (Heb. 9:23).

This can be seen in comparative analogy by the following diagrams, which depict the heavens as sevenfold. R. H. Charles, the editor of a major collection of apocryphal and pseudepigraphical documents, affirms that "the doctrine of the seven heavens was prevalent in Judaism before and after the time of Christ."[60] The *Testament of Levi* and *2 Enoch,* edited in the first century A.D. and reflective of an already existing Jewish tradition, speak of the seven heavens, with the third heaven designated as a place of revelation. Paul described his revelation as "being caught up to the third heaven" in 2 Corinthians 12:2–3. Satan and other demonic powers live in the heavenly places (Eph. 6:12), in particular the lower air (ἀήρ, *aēr,* Eph. 2:2), which, in this literature, is the firmament around the earth, beneath the first heaven.[61] The author of Hebrews affirms that when Christ, our high priest, was resurrected and ascended to God, he "passed through the heavens" (Heb. 4:14) unhindered by these powers. He thereby destroyed "him who has the power of death, that is, the

58. On the difference in the translation of ἱλαστήριον (*hilastērion*) as propitiation or expiation, see Tuckett, "Atonement," 519f.; and Thompson, "Sacrifice and Offering: I. In the Old Testament," 1052.

59. Tuckett, "Atonement," 522.

60. R. H. Charles, *The Apocrypha and Pseudepigrapha of the Old Testament in English* (Oxford: Clarendon, 1963), 2:304 (note on *Testament of Levi* 2.7).

61. See the discussion in chapter 10.

devil" (Heb. 2:14). The author means that Christ, by his resurrection and ascension, destroyed Satan's power over death.

Figure 12.1 Tabernacle Typologies

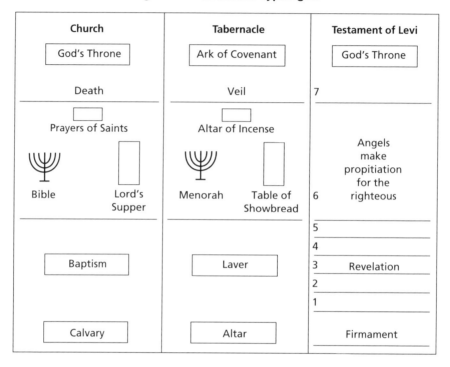

Hebrews describes the tabernacle as "symbolic" for the present age (Heb. 9:9) and our high priest, Christ, as going into "the greater and more perfect tent (not made with hands, that is, not of this creation)" (Heb. 9:11), "taking . . . his own blood" and thus securing our "eternal redemption" (Heb. 9:12). In this typology, Jesus is portrayed as reenacting the movements of the high priest on the Day of Atonement by taking the sacrificial blood (his own) into the Holy of Holies (the seventh heaven) and there making atonement. This means, of course, that atonement had not been completely made when Jesus died as a sacrifice on the cross. It is a process that finds analogous completion in the subsequent activity of Jesus in becoming a high priest and functioning as such. In addition to his crucifixion, that process includes his resurrection, ascension, and coronation as Son of God and high priest "after the order of Melchizedek" (Heb. 5:5–6).

The heavenly role of Christ as high priest may be typologically understood in the following figure (12.2). In this analogy, God gave to Israel both the law, which was but a *shadow* of reality, and the tabernacle, which was only a *copy* of the true one in heaven. Since the law and the sacrificial system of the tab-

Figure 12.2 Typology of Christ's High Priestly Work

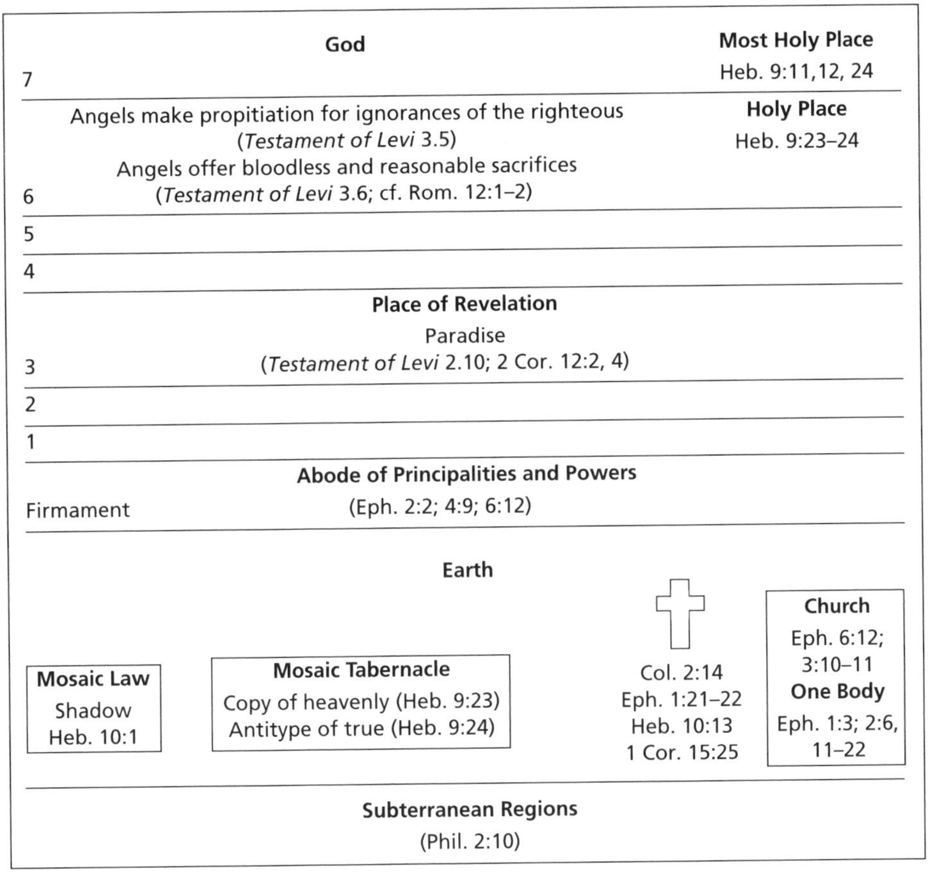

	God	**Most Holy Place** Heb. 9:11,12, 24
7		
6	Angels make propitiation for ignorances of the righteous (*Testament of Levi* 3.5) Angels offer bloodless and reasonable sacrifices (*Testament of Levi* 3.6; cf. Rom. 12:1–2)	**Holy Place** Heb. 9:23–24
5		
4		
3	**Place of Revelation** Paradise (*Testament of Levi* 2.10; 2 Cor. 12:2, 4)	
2		
1		
Firmament	**Abode of Principalities and Powers** (Eph. 2:2; 4:9; 6:12)	

Earth

Mosaic Law Shadow Heb. 10:1	**Mosaic Tabernacle** Copy of heavenly (Heb. 9:23) Antitype of true (Heb. 9:24)	Col. 2:14 Eph. 1:21–22 Heb. 10:13 1 Cor. 15:25	**Church** Eph. 6:12; 3:10–11 **One Body** Eph. 1:3; 2:6, 11–22

Subterranean Regions
(Phil. 2:10)

ernacle were not able to remove sin, as Hebrews states several times, Christ came to put away sin's penalty permanently. He descended through the heavens, lived incarnately, and died on the cross, thus providing the ultimate, effective sacrifice for sin. He was raised from the dead and ascended through the heavens to the throne of God, taking his blood with him, as Hebrews affirms. After being designated high priest after the order of Melchizedek, he presented his blood to God in the highest heaven.

Atonement, Unity, and Monotheism

One aspect of atonement, a major one in the thought of Paul, is that Christ, by his resurrection and ascension through the heavenly domain of the cosmic powers, conquered death and removed Satan's power to deceive mortals about the monotheistic nature of God. The means employed by Satan to create this disbelief in God's oneness was to use the law as a dividing wedge between Jews and Gentiles. Paul argues that Jesus destroyed this power by his resurrection and removed this barrier between them.

> For he is our peace, who has made us both one, and has broken down the dividing wall of hostility, by abolishing in his flesh the law of commandments and ordinances, that he might create in himself one new man in place of the two, so making peace, and might reconcile us both to God in one body through the cross, thereby bringing the hostility to an end. (Eph. 2:14–16)

The "dividing wall of hostility" erected on the basis of the law is probably an allusion to the low wall that surrounded the temple structure, separating it from the Court of the Gentiles, with appropriate warning signs every few feet. Paul was erroneously accused of taking Trophimus the Ephesian beyond this wall, and the Jewish crowd consequently tried to kill him (Acts 21:31). One of these signs found in Jerusalem was recently published. It reads as follows:

> No foreigner is to enter within
> the forecourt and the balustrade
> around the sanctuary. Whoever is
> caught will have himself to blame
> for his subsequent death.[62]

Jesus had prayed for unity among his disciples, saying that their disunity would cause the world to disbelieve that he came from God (John 17:21). For Paul, the attempt by Jewish Christians to force the Gentiles to keep the law of Moses was exactly what Jesus had feared. In his discussion of the atonement in Romans 3:21–31, Paul argues that justification by faith means, not the antithesis of works righteousness as subsequently construed in the Protestant Reformation, but rather that Gentiles have direct access to God without having to go through the law and thus become Jews.[63]

He argued that if we are justified by works, meaning works of the law (i.e., by becoming Jews), then God would be a god of Jews only and not a god of monotheistic Gentiles as well (Rom. 3:29). If God is one, he is the God of

---

62. μηθένα ἀλλογενῆ εἰσπορεύεσθαι
    ἐντὸς τοῦ περὶ τὸ ἱερὸν
    τρυφάκτου καὶ περιβόλου. ὃς
    δ᾽ ἂν ληφθῇ ἑαυτῷ αἴτιος ἔσται
    διὰ τὸ ἐξακολουθεῖν θάνατον

(Peretz Segal, "The Penalty of the Warning Inscription from the Temple in Jerusalem," *IEJ* 39.1–2 [1989]: 79–84). See my discussion in chapter 7 about Paul and Trophimus in the temple.
  63. See further chapter 13 on Ephesians.

both Jews and Gentiles. Gentiles do not have to become Jews, and Jews do not have to become Gentiles. Rather, Ephesians states that Christ "is our peace, who has made us both one. . . . Through him we both [Jew and Gentile] have access in one spirit to the Father. So then you [Gentiles] are no longer strangers and sojourners, but you are fellow citizens with the saints [Jewish Christians] and members of the household of God. . . . The Gentiles are fellow heirs, members of the same body, and partakers of the promise in Christ Jesus through the gospel" (Eph. 2:14, 18–19; 3:6).

Since atonement means "at-one-ment," the use of the law to separate Jewish Christians from Gentile Christians is the antithesis of the reconciliation implied by this concept. Forcing the law upon Gentiles, thus making God a god of Jews only, is nothing less than henotheism, the belief that each nation has its own god or set of gods. Thus, Jewish Christians were in reality rejecting the very monotheistic basis of their religion by forcing Gentiles to become Jews.

The Atonement of Christ: A Solution to Religious Division

Relationship between Polytheism and Demons

Polytheism, the belief in many gods, postulates the idea of local gods over each nation. In the ancient world, polytheism involved the worship of demons. Deuteronomy states: "They stirred him to jealousy with strange gods; with abominable practices they provoked him to anger. They sacrificed to demons which were no gods, to gods they had never known, to new gods that had come in of late, whom your fathers had never dreaded" (Deut. 32:16–17; cf. Bar. 4:7; Rev. 9:20). Psalm 106:36–37 declares: "They served their idols, which became a snare to them. They sacrificed their sons and their daughters to the demons."

The book of *Jubilees* (written between 135 and 105 B.C.)[64] makes this same identification, saying the worship of "graven images" includes "sacrifice to demons" (*Jubilees* 1.11–12).

Paul affirmed this truth to be operative in his own time when he wrote to the Corinthians: "Consider the practice of Israel; are not those who eat the sacrifices partners in the altar? What do I imply then? That food offered to idols is anything, or that an idol is anything? No, I imply that what pagans sacrifice they offer to demons and not to God. I do not want you to be partners with demons" (1 Cor. 10:18–20).

64. According to Charles, *Apocrypha and Pseudepigrapha*, 2:1.

The idea of local gods over each nation creates division within humanity. As the following figure illustrates, each nation's territorial boundaries marked the jurisdiction of its particular deity or dieties.

Ahura-Mazda	Marduk	El, Baal	Ra	Zeus	Jupiter
Persia	Babylon	Canaan	Egypt	Greece	Rome

Daniel wrote: "Then he [the angel] said, 'Do you know why I have come to you? But now I will return to fight against the prince of Persia; and when I am through with him, lo, the prince of Greece will come. But I will tell you what is inscribed in the book of truth: there is none who contends by my side against these except Michael your prince'" (Dan. 10:20–21). The princes in chapter 10 of Daniel are angelic beings, in contrast to the human rulers designated as kings.

This henotheistic view that a god controlled a particular territory also required that the god be worshiped on that turf. For example, when Naaman the leper from Syria visited Elisha and was healed by Jehovah God in Israel, he wanted to take some of Jehovah's dirt back to Syria with him because he had to worship Jehovah on his own soil. Naaman said, "Let there be given to your servant two mules' burden of earth; for henceforth your servant will not offer burnt offering or sacrifice to any god but the LORD [Jehovah in Hebrew]" (2 Kings 5:17).

The problem Paul confronted with the Judaism of his day was that rather than bringing other nations to God, their misuse of the law of Moses as a dividing wedge between the Jews and the Gentiles only created further division. Paul said his Jewish countrymen had hindered him "from speaking to the Gentiles that they may be saved" (1 Thess. 2:15). He was emphatic in his declaration that this Mosaic law, represented by the balustrade wall around the temple in Jerusalem that separated Gentiles from Jews, was "broken down" by Christ so that he might "create in himself one new man in place of the two, so making peace" (Eph. 2:14–15). The law, then, rather than bringing unity, only fostered division by keeping the Jews at a distance from the other nations, as this figure depicts.

gods	gods	gods	gods	gods	gods	L a w	God
							Jews

The Concept of Monotheism Destroys Religious Division

This leads to the second important point, which is that *monotheism destroys religious division*. As the following figure illustrates, a belief in one God over all of necessity means that local gods have been superseded and that there is one body (the church) for all people. When the law was removed as a barrier between the Jews and the other nations, it meant God was over all and that all nations had equal access to him (Eph. 2:14–22; Col. 2:14).

God						
Ahura-Mazda	Marduk	El-Baal	Ra	Zeus	Jupiter	Jehovah
Persia	Babylon	Canaan	Egypt	Greece	Rome	Jews

Paul wrote, "For we maintain that a man is justified by faith apart from observing the law. Is God the God of Jews only? Is he not the God of Gentiles too? Yes, of Gentiles too, since there is only one God, who will justify the circumcised by faith and the uncircumcised through that same faith" (Rom. 3:28–30 NIV). Justification by faith rather than by the law for Gentiles as well as Jews meant for Paul that God was necessarily the God of Gentiles as well as Jews. In Paul's words this meant "there is no distinction between Jew and Greek; the same Lord is Lord of all" (Rom. 10:12), and "there is one God, and there is one mediator between God and men, the man Christ Jesus" (1 Tim. 2:5).

Christ Revealed God and Thereby Destroyed Polytheism and the Worship of Demons

The third point is that *Christ, by his atonement, revealed the reality of one true God over all, and this inherently obliterated polytheism with its worship of demons through idolatry.* The following figure shows that this implied removal of local gods.

God						
Christ						
Persia	Babylon	Canaan	Egypt	Greece	Rome	Jews

Christ's life and death provided a revelation of the one true God. John writes, "For the law was given through Moses; grace and truth came through Jesus Christ. No one has ever seen God; the only Son, who is in the bosom of the Father, he has made him known" (John 1:17–18). Paul writes that this revelation of God through the life and death of Jesus was the means God provided for the destruction of demons (2 Tim. 2:25–26). The author of Hebrews affirms that Christ came "that through death he might destroy him who has the power of death, that is, the devil" (Heb. 2:14). John adds that "the reason the Son of God appeared was to destroy the works of the devil" (1 John 3:8). Jesus entered the strong man's house in order to plunder his goods (Mark 3:27). This conquest and destruction of the power of Satan and his demons removed the presence of local gods in the thought of the worshiper and thus destroyed the practice of idolatry among those who now came to believe in God through Jesus.

This Brought Unity to All Nations

One major result of this atoning work of Jesus was that he provided the basis for potential unity of the cosmos. The removal of the demons and local gods from the minds of worshipers resulted in the removal of the territorial boundaries, thus bringing peace and unity. In place of the many nations ruled by many gods, there was now one body in Christ, a unified body consisting of both Jews and Gentiles. Paul writes that when Christ was nailed to the cross, "he disarmed the principalities and powers and made a public example of them, triumphing over them in him" (Col. 2:15). These "principalities and powers" are demonic powers—the devil, "the world rulers of this present darkness," and the "spiritual hosts of wickedness in the heavenly places" (Eph. 6:11–12). The following figure shows the lines of territorial division removed on the basis of monotheism.

God						
Persia	Babylon	Canaan	Egypt	Greece	Rome	Jews

The Mystery of the Gospel Is Unity

Paul refers to this plan of monotheistic unity as the "mystery" that was revealed to him when he was given his stewardship to preach to Gentiles (Eph. 3:2–5). This is the gospel of which he "was made a minister" (Eph. 3:7). A mystery is the heart of a thing, and Paul defines this mystery as the fact that "the Gentiles are fellow heirs, members of the same body, and partakers of the promise in Christ Jesus through the gospel" (Eph. 3:6; cf. Col. 1:26–27). In Romans 11:25–32, Paul ties this "mystery" to the inclusion of the Gentiles along with the Jews in the plan of God. It is further emphasized in what was probably part of a hymn in the early church:

Great indeed, we confess, is the mystery of our religion: He was manifested in the flesh, vindicated in the Spirit, seen by angels, preached among the nations, believed on in the world, taken up in glory. (1 Tim. 3:16)

Unity Is the Fulfillment of the Promise to Abraham

Paul emphasizes that *"the gospel" was preached to Abraham and defined that gospel as the equal blessing of Gentiles and Jews through Christ* (Gal. 3:8). He says that "in Christ Jesus the blessing of Abraham might come upon the Gentiles, that we might receive the promise of the Spirit through faith. . . . For in Christ Jesus you are all sons of God, through faith" (Gal. 3:14, 26). He writes in Romans 4:16, "That is why it depends on faith, in order that the promise may rest on grace and be guaranteed to all his descendants—not only to the adherents of the law but also to those who share the faith of Abraham, for he is the father of us all."

Ultimate Goal—Unity of All Things

The ultimate goal of the atonement was not just unity among Jews and Gentiles but unity in the cosmos as well. Even in the heavens, things had not gone well. Angels had sinned and were cast into hell (literally, Tartarus;[65] 2 Pet. 2:4) there to await judgment. Satan and his demons are continuing to produce sin and disunity in the world (Eph. 6:12). But Paul says God's plan for the "fullness of time," is "to unite all things in him, things in heaven and things on earth" (Eph. 1:10), "for in him all the fullness of God was pleased to dwell, and through him to reconcile to himself all things, whether on earth or in heaven, making peace by the blood of his cross" (Col. 1:19–20).

This exalted concept prompts Paul's majestic words in Philippians 2:9–11, "Therefore God has highly exalted him and bestowed on him the name which is above every name, that at the name of Jesus every knee should bow, in heaven and on earth and under the earth, and every tongue confess that Jesus Christ is Lord, to the glory of God the Father."

Concluding Summary

In summation, the consequences of the atonement include the following:

1. Jesus fulfilled the typology—gave essence to the Old Testament system.
2. Jesus invalidated the ritual—removed ritual sin.

65. The word in Greek is a participle ταρταρώσας (*tartarōsas*) meaning "tartarized"; BAGD, 805.

3. Jesus conquered the cosmic powers—and provided hope through resurrection.
4. Jesus functioned as a scapegoat to take away personal sin.

Paul asserts the finality of Christ's work in atonement when he writes that Christ "ascended far above all the heavens, that he might fill all things" (Eph. 4:10). Similarly, the author of Hebrews emphasizes finality when he states that Christ, having ascended above the heavens, "*sat down* at the right hand of God" (Heb. 10:12; 1:3). Priests were never allowed to sit down while performing the sacrificial ritual in the tabernacle/temple. This showed symbolically that the offering was never finalized. Hebrews states typologically that when Christ "offered for all time a single sacrifice for sins, he sat down at the right hand of God, then to wait until his enemies should be made a stool for his feet" (Heb. 10:12).

The focus here is on the triumphant aspects of Christ's work and the possibility of a victorious daily walk for the Christian, not by virtue of what one believes and does, but by virtue of what Christ has done. This work of Christ in the atonement may be intended in seven passages where Paul probably uses the expression πίστις Χριστοῦ (*pistis Christou,* faith of Christ) as a subjective genitive meaning "faithfulness of Christ" rather than as an objective genitive meaning "faith in Christ" (Rom. 3:22; Gal. 2:16 [twice]; 3:22; Eph. 3:12 [pronoun "his" instead of "Christ"]; Phil. 3:9).[66] From this perspective, it was through Christ's faithfulness to the Abrahamic promise that he died on Calvary and conquered the power of Satan. Whether anyone believes it or not, atonement nevertheless occurred.

In Romans 5:9 Paul differentiates justification and salvation: "Since, therefore, we are now justified by his blood, much more shall we be saved." Salvation is here predicated on justification. What happened at Calvary was an *objective* act of history upon which the *potentiality* of salvation is based, predicated upon the response of faith and obedience. This verse declares that salvation is not justification but is predicated upon it.

There is no disputing the fact that Satan has power in the world. The encounter of Jesus with Satan immediately after his baptism clearly shows that Satan had the world in his control and was capable of giving it to Jesus. His statement "All these [kingdoms] I will give you, if you will fall down and worship me" (Matt. 4:9) is no temptation to Jesus unless Satan has the kingdoms and can deliver them. This suggests that the world has been sold under sin to Satan and has to be purchased with the blood of Christ (Acts 20:28). His blood is indeed a ransom for our sins (Mark 10:45). But in the classical view of atonement, verbs such as *ransom, purchase,* and *redeem* are used only in a metaphorical way. They simply mean that a price was paid when Christ con-

66. See chapter 14.

quered the devil. Ransom is not an expression of an actual bargain, transaction, or sale.

Some of the early church fathers expanded on this metaphorical language. Augustine developed the mousetrap theory, arguing that God tricked Satan by using Jesus as the bait. When Satan came to take the bait, the mousetrap caught him. A bargain was made by which Jesus said to Satan, "I will trade my life for the world." Satan agreed to this, thinking it would be worth surrendering the world just to get rid of Christ. But there was a catch. Satan thought he would destroy Christ, but he was caught in a trap by the resurrection. Others explain it as a fishhook that God offered to Satan with the death of Christ as the bait. Satan took the bait, not knowing there was a hook in it—the resurrection.

In the satisfaction view of atonement, God pays half and Jesus pays half. God performs atonement as a divine being, but he does it through Jesus as a human who is also divine. Therefore, two basic requirements of the satisfaction view are met in the person of Christ: (1) a human being who is under condemnation for the effect of sin, but not its guilt, came in the likeness of sinful flesh and died for sin in the flesh (Rom. 8:3); and (2) someone who is sinless suffered in a body that experienced the *consequence* of Adamic transgression (death) but not its *guilt*. The essence of this view is that atonement is accomplished by a human, but the effect of the atonement is not upon humanity but upon God. It satisfies God.

In the classical view, the conquest of Satan required the power of deity. In the Latin view, the satisfaction of God's just wrath necessitated the sinlessness of deity.

Furthermore, there is an element of potentiality in the Latin view that says there is no effect of the atonement apart from human faith. Christ takes our place on the cross, and we experience substitutionary atonement through him. So, for those who do not believe that Jesus took their place, God's wrath has not been satisfied and nothing actually happened at Calvary to benefit them. Contrariwise, as explained above, the Dramatic view holds that Christ destroyed the power of Satan to deceive and control human beings (Heb. 2:14; 1 John 5:18). That conquest of Satan through the resurrection of Christ from the dead occurred as a fact of history, whether anyone believes it or not.

In the Latin view, there is a concentration on humanity's *continuing* guilt and unworthiness that is not prevalent in the Dramatic view. Martin Luther felt a perpetual sense of pervasive guilt and constant unworthiness that drove him to despair. Since God's wrath is ever present, one has to make constant appeal to the atonement of Jesus in order to remove it. So even after conversion, Luther felt a constant need for application of the atonement to assuage the wrath of God. In the medieval church, this was the purpose of the system of penance.

THIRTEEN

The Heart of Paul:
The Theology of Ephesians

Since the Ephesian letter contains the name of the apostle Paul as its author, comparisons between it and other Pauline letters are unavoidable. However, there are some well-known difficulties with the Pauline authorship of this letter. One is that, unlike his other correspondence with churches, this letter does not contain the name of the church to which it is addressed in the three oldest and best collections of Paul's letters (Chester Beatty Papyrus, Codex Vaticanus, and Codex Sinaiticus).

Also, unlike Paul's usual correspondence with churches, Ephesians was not written to address specific problems. Instead, it addressed a wider need for deeper theological understanding of the nature of the church.

The case against Pauline authorship of Ephesians has centered around subjective evaluations of and assumptions about the content of the letter itself, since the external evidence of the early centuries is devastating to arguments against the authenticity of this letter. Space permits us to look only at the most significant challenge to Pauline authorship in the past century.

That challenge has been made by Edgar J. Goodspeed in a number of significant publications.[1] His arguments center around the fact that a number of

1. "The Place of Ephesians in the First Pauline Collection," *Anglican Theological Review* 12 (1930): 189–212; *An Introduction to the New Testament* (Chicago: University of Chicago Press, 1937); *The Key to Ephesians* (Chicago: University of Chicago Press, 1956); *The Meaning of Ephesians* (Chicago: University of Chicago Press, 1933); *New Solutions of New Testament Problems* (Chicago: University of Chicago Press, 1927).

words occur in Ephesians that do not occur in other Pauline letters. For example, the word *devil* is used in Ephesians but nowhere else in Paul's letters. The phrase "in the heavenlies" occurs in Paul's letters only in Ephesians 1:3; 2:6; 3:10; and 6:12.

Goodspeed believed that these different words and phrases in Ephesians indicate that the epistle was written sometime after the writing of Luke-Acts, whose publicaton created an interest in collecting Paul's letters. The man who collected the letters, he argued, was Onesimus, who twenty years later was likely a major motivator in the collection of the letters of Ignatius by Polycarp.[2] Goodspeed states that "there is no evidence of the circulation of Paul's letters before the publication of Luke-Acts (ca. A.D. 90) but the author of Ephesians knows them all." [3] He thinks Onesimus wrote Ephesians as an introduction to the Pauline corpus, which was collected and published shortly after the appearance of Luke-Acts. Detrimental to this view, however, are the facts that the letter has never been found at the beginning of any early list of Paul's letters and that an introduction ought to introduce.

An argument was also made from the similarity of Ephesians to Colossians. Goodspeed asserted that a great number of the words in Ephesians have been borrowed from Colossians and rejected the possibility of explaining this by common authorship.[4] The reason for this rejection was that the same terms and phrases in Colossians are used in entirely different ways in Ephesians. Rejecting common authorship on the assumption that one man could not use, or would not use, the same words with completely different meanings, he assigns a date of about A.D. 90 for the composition of Ephesians.

Goodspeed, as well as others who reject the authenticity of Ephesians, erroneously argue that Christians of the first century approved of pseudepigraphy.[5] It is also urged strongly by opponents of Pauline authorship that the Jew-Gentile controversy seems settled in Ephesians, but in their view it could not have been settled in Paul's own lifetime. This is a supposition based upon an incorrect assumption. The erroneous nature of the assumption is evident in the above discussion (chap. 8) of the common theme running through

---

2. Goodspeed, *Key to Ephesians*, xv.

3. Goodspeed, *Meaning of Ephesians*, 6; idem, *Key to Ephesians*, xiii, x.

4. Goodspeed, *Key to Ephesians*, 2–75. A. E. Barnett says essentially the same thing and also gives full documentation in *Paul Becomes a Literary Influence* (Chicago: University of Chicago Press, 1941), 2–40.

5. See Donald Guthrie, "Epistolary Pseudepigraphy," appendix C in *New Testament Introduction*, 4th rev. ed. (Downers Grove, Ill.: InterVarsity, 1990), 1011–29. John McRay, "The Authorship of the Pastoral Epistles," *Restoration Quarterly* 7 (1963). Kurt Aland, "The Problem of Anonymity and Pseudonymity in Christian Literature of the First Two Centuries," *JTS*, n.s., 12 (April 1961): 39ff. This article is also in paperback in *The Authorship and Integrity of the New Testament* (London: S.P.C.K., 1965), 1–13. The last book also contains a valuable article by Donald Guthrie on the subject: "The Development of the Idea of Canonical Pseudepigrapha in New Testament Criticism," 14–40.

Ephesians and Colossians, which has been inadequately appreciated by many who write on the letters.

In reply to these rejections of the authenticity of Ephesians, we can make the following observations. The weight of subjective evidence presented by critics is not sufficient to meet the tremendous external attestation to Pauline authorship, as well as the letter's own claims. While the overall approach by Goodspeed seems to have some weight when considered as a whole, it breaks down when investigated point by point.[6] It has not been shown conclusively why Paul, who wrote Colossians, could not have expanded that letter immediately after it was written into the form of Ephesians and have applied some of the same terms and phrases differently from the way he did in the former letter, which dealt with more specific matters. Furthermore, Goodspeed has not dealt with the real issue of the letters at all—the unity of the Jews and Gentiles—in such a way as to see the relation of many of the words and phrases to the central theme of Christ's conquest of demonic forces through his death and the consequent unity that this conquest must bring both to the body (the church) and the head (Christ, in whom the fullness of the Godhead dwells—a concept involving a cosmic as well as an earthly approach to the subject). Such an understanding accounts for many of the "different" usages of terms, which are not really different usages at all but different applications of the same terms to a common problem. It also accounts for the letters' presenting seemingly different approaches to the church, universal and local.

It is far more reasonable, in my judgment, to account for differences in the letters by acknowledging the varying purposes for the production of the letters than by rejecting common authorship. It is more difficult to explain the extreme similarity the letters if they were written by different authors, which Goodspeed is at great pains to do, than to accept Pauline authorship for both and account for the differences in the manner I have described. The cosmological approach to the writings of Paul has not been adequately appreciated by those who see two radically different approaches in the letters. No scissors-and-paste method that accepts the ethic of pseudepigraphy and denies the overwhelming evidence of ancient history can seriously be considered as a solution to supposed internal difficulties in these letters until that method displays a real understanding of what the internal argument really is. This, I believe, Goodspeed has not done. His treatment of the theology of the letters is superficial.[7]

The style of Ephesians is thought by some to be un-Pauline because it contains extremely long sentences (Eph. 1:3–10, 15–23) and many relative clauses coupled with consecutive dependent and final clauses. There are explanatory

6. See Guthrie's further discussion in his *New Testament Introduction,* 509–28.

7. For a detailed discussion of the problems involved in Pauline authorship, both pro and con, Donald Guthrie's *New Testament Introduction* is excellent.

appositions and attributes, parallel phrases whose sequences are not entirely clear (e.g., Eph. 4:12), many abstract nouns, and synonyms connected by genitive constructions that are almost redundant (e.g., Eph. 1:19). It is argued that none of these is characteristic of Paul's other letters.

The validity of this argument, however, is predicated on the assumption that an author may write in only one style, regardless of the nature of his correspondence, and it makes no allowance for the use of a secretary like Tertius (the scribe Paul used to write the letter to Rome [Rom. 16:22]), whose use of shorthand in taking dictation might affect the style of a letter. The diversity and uniqueness of vocabulary exhibited in this letter may only testify to the originality and literary acumen of its author (and perhaps his secretary) rather than to its being written by a different author.

There is no disharmony between the assertion of Paul that he built only on the foundation of Christ (1 Cor. 3:11) rather than of mere men (1 Cor. 3:4) and the statement in Ephesians 2:20 that the foundation is the apostles with Christ as chief cornerstone. In the latter passage, Paul is asserting that Gentiles are the superstructure "built upon" (i.e., added to) the Jewish foundation.

The exclusive use of the word *church* (ἐκκλησία, *ekklēsia*) for the church universal in Ephesians (1:22; 3:10, 21; 5:23–25, 27, 29, 32) is not inconsistent with Paul's use of it for the local congregation in his other letters, since Ephesians is written as an encyclical and is not limited to the problems peculiar to any one church.

Whereas elsewhere in Paul (Rom. 16:25; 1 Cor. 2:1, see NRSV) the word *mystery* has a general meaning of God's ancient and hidden purposes, its use in this letter (Eph. 3:4–6 and in Col. 1:26; 2:2; 4:3) is appropriately particularized to refer to God's ancient and hidden plan to include the Gentiles fully into his redemptive plan.

The argument has been frequently expressed that Ephesians cannot be by Paul because it accentuates the cosmological nature of redemption rather than concentrating on justification by faith as the "be-all and end-all of Paul's teaching." This view has been rightly criticized as "lop-sided and defective" by one author, who adds that "it is a pity when Paulinism is identified so exclusively with the emphasis of Galatians and Romans that the corporate and cosmic insights of Colossians and Ephesians are overlooked, or felt to be un-Pauline."[8] With the cosmological nature of the church being the central emphasis of the theological section of the letter (Eph. 1–4), the author found no occasion to argue for the resurrection of the body of either Jesus or believers, which is of eschatological but not cosmological import.

In Ephesians we find carefully reasoned and precisely worded theology presented in a systematic way. There is no letter in the Pauline corpus that more precisely and succinctly presents the rudimentary elements of his understand-

---

8. F. F. Bruce, *The Epistle to the Ephesians* (London: Pickering and Inglis, 1961), 15.

ing of salvation history than this one. Although some scholars have argued that "Paul probably never thought out 'the center of his theology,'"[9] this letter, combined with Romans, provides the clearest and fullest explication of Pauline theology in the New Testament.

To fully grasp the theological core of this letter, it is important to remember the nature of Paul's conversion/call on the road to Damascus. He was told at that time by the divine voice: "Get up and stand on your feet; for I have appeared to you for this purpose, to appoint you to serve and testify to the things in which you have seen me and to those in which I will appear to you. I will rescue you from your people and from the Gentiles—to whom I am sending you to open their eyes so that they may turn from darkness to light and from the power of Satan to God, so that they may receive forgiveness of sins and a place among those who are sanctified by faith in me" (Acts 26:16–18 NRSV).

Paul's entire life after this experience was guided by this commission he had received to take the gospel as a Jew to the Gentiles (Gal. 1:15–16). He functioned somewhat as a priestly servant sent "to be a minister of Christ Jesus to the Gentiles in the priestly service of the gospel of God, so that the offering of the Gentiles may be acceptable, sanctified by the Holy Spirit" (Rom. 15:16).

The gospel Jesus commissioned Paul to preach was nothing less than the very promise God had made to Abraham: "The scripture, foreseeing that God would justify the Gentiles by faith, preached the gospel beforehand to Abraham, saying, 'In you shall all the nations [i.e., Gentiles] be blessed.' So then, those who are men of faith are blessed with Abraham who had faith" (Gal. 3:8–9).

The key to the theology of Ephesians is in the second chapter, where Paul sets forth the implications of the equal union of Jews and Gentiles in the one body, the church. Both Gentiles (Eph. 2:1) and Jews (Eph. 2:3–5) were once dead in their trespasses and sins. Nevertheless, the Jews had prepared the way for the Messiah and were the first to be called into the church. The Gentiles had since been included, largely by Paul's own work, in keeping with divine forethought and predestination. They must now be accepted fully as equal partners in the kingdom.

It is of fundamental importance that *both* Gentiles and Jews are made alive *together* with Christ, have been raised up *together,* and made to sit *together* with Christ in the heavenly places (Eph. 2:5–6). Thus, the Gentile disciples are *fellow* citizens with the Jewish disciples and members *together* with them of the household of God (Eph. 2:19).

---

9. Raymond Brown, *An Introduction to the New Testament* (New York: Anchor Doubleday, 1997), 440. Brown lists six attempts by various scholars to identify the "theological center of Paul's theology" and concludes that "christocentrism" is the closest to being true.

The church was built upon the Jewish foundation of apostles and prophets (Eph. 2:20; 3:5), with Christ Jesus as the chief (Jewish) cornerstone (Eph. 2:20). The Gentiles have now been included and, "joined together" with the Jewish foundation, they grow together into a holy temple in the Lord (Eph. 2:20–21). Their conduct should be guided by this truth (Eph. 4:17–6:24).

This is the central theme, not only of this letter, but of Paul's entire ministry—his role as a Jewish minister to Gentiles (Rom. 15:16). A number of key theological terms and concepts in Ephesians revolve around this Pauline understanding of the place of the Jews in God's redemptive history from the time of Abraham and of Paul's own place in that process, that of bringing the Gentiles into Christ's body (cf. Gal. 1:15–16). These key theological terms and concepts include the following:

1. The affirmation of Israel as God's elect, chosen to bring the Messiah into the world (Eph. 1:1–14).
2. The special, restrictive use in Ephesians of first- and second-person plural pronouns to distinguish Jewish from Gentile Christians for precision and clarity of argument. Second-person plural pronouns refer to Gentiles throughout the letter; first-person plural pronouns fall into four categories of use.
3. The special and restrictive use in Ephesians (and probably Colossians) of the word *saints* to distinguish Jewish Christians from Gentile Christians.
4. The role of cosmic, demonic powers in attempting to prevent and/or destroy the unity of Jews and Gentiles in the one body. This includes the use of apocalyptic ideas and thought patterns prevalent in Paul's world.
5. The fact that access to God is equally available to Jew and Gentile through faith rather than through the law of Moses. Otherwise, God is a God of Jews only.

Israel as God's Elect

The first of these key concepts is Paul's teaching on election or predestination in chapter 1. It is in the context of the role of Israel as the elect—chosen to provide the Messiah—rather than in the context of individual predestination to salvation, that Paul speaks of election. Both Augustine and Calvin seem to have missed this context. Paul asserts in this chapter that the Jews, God's saints or holy ones, were "chosen" to bring the blessing of redemption to all nations in fulfillment of the promise to Abraham. It was the Jews who were foreordained unto adoption for this purpose (Eph. 1:5), chosen in the beloved (i.e., Messiah) for God's glory (i.e., to declare the sovereignty of monotheism, Eph. 1:6) before the foundation of the world to be "holy and blameless" (i.e., saints, Eph. 1:4) and to be the first to hope in the Messiah (Eph. 1:12).

The Specialized Application of Pronouns

Most studies on Ephesians approach the letter by investigating its major theological terms and comparing them to their use in Paul's generally acknowledged letters. Although that methodology has its value, it is more likely that the real thinking of an author (or redactor) will be found in those more commonly used parts of speech that he employs at times almost subconsciously. These parts of speech may reflect the biases and theological perspectives out of which an author or redactor formulates his doctrine and from which he expresses that doctrine. In this respect the pronouns in Ephesians provide a key to the theology of the book. If studied on the assumption of consistency in use, they reveal the thinking of the author in a way that allows important conclusions to be drawn about the point of view from which he writes and therefore about his theology.

The Book of Ephesians especially exemplifies this use of pronouns,[10] although it has been noted as well in the generally acknowledged Pauline books.[11] Krister Stendahl has emphasized his concern for the proper understanding of the pronouns in Galatians: "Many of Paul's uses of we and our," he writes, "are that stylistic plural by which he really means only himself, but in many cases, much more serious and difficult to detect, the uses of 'we'— 'we Jews'—stand in direct contrast to 'you Gentiles.' Romans 3:9 is a case in point: here the RSV translates the Greek 'we' by 'we Jews.' It is important to develop a sensitivity to these distinctions."[12]

The importance of the pronouns in Ephesians has not gone unnoticed in the Anchor Bible Commentary.[13] The author sees the necessity of formulating some kind of careful distinction in the various uses made of the first-person and second-person plural pronouns.[14] He even makes an initial attempt at suggesting categories into which they might be divided.[15] But like a number of other authors, this commentator does not treat the subject consistently by

10. See Markus Barth, *Ephesians,* 2 vols., Anchor Bible 34 and 34A (Garden City, N.Y.: Doubleday, 1974), 1:131.

11. Krister Stendahl, *Paul among Jews and Gentiles* (Philadelphia: Fortress, 1976), 12, 18, 23.

12. Ibid., 23.

13. Barth, *Ephesians,* 1:130ff.

14. Like Stendahl, Munck, and others.

15. Barth, *Ephesians,* 1:130ff.

trying to discern a pattern of pronoun use by which predictability of occurrence might be indicated.

A discernable pattern of pronoun use would have at least three benefits for the study of Ephesians and other Pauline literature: (1) it would help readers to detect apparently subconscious modes of thought that run like a thread throughout the works; (2) it would provide fresh insights into the theology of the author by revealing more clearly the background of social and religious concern that he brings to his use of special terminology; and (3) it would make an important contribution toward understanding the "seemingly inexplicable" confusion caused by the similarity in Greek of the variant readings "we" (ἡμᾶς, *hēmas*) and "us" (ὑμᾶς, *hymas*).[16]

There can be no doubt that the second-person pronoun refers to the audience of the letter. It is equally clear from two passages that an exclusively Gentile Christian audience is intended by the term. In Ephesians 2:11 the author says, "Remember that . . . you Gentiles in the flesh, called the uncircumcision," and in Ephesians 3:1, "I, Paul, a prisoner for Christ Jesus on behalf of you Gentiles." In one verse (Eph. 4:17) the term *Gentile* is used of pagans as opposed to Gentile Christians.

The use of first-person plural pronouns may be categorized as follows.

Category 1: Stylistic Use in Letter Writing

Sometimes first-person plural pronouns naturally appear in a context of personal communication. For example, when Paul says, "I have sent him [Tychicus] to you . . . that you may know how we are" (Eph. 6:22), the pronouns refer to Paul and his associates (probably including Timothy, as in Col. 1:1 and Philem. 1, both likely written at the same time).

Category 2: Supplemental Material Quoted in Ephesians

Sometimes first-person plural pronouns in the New Testament, as in ancient literature generally, are used in hymnic and liturgical material and confessional formulae.[17] An example in Ephesians is the standard greeting "Grace to you and peace from God *our* father" (Eph. 1:2). Conventional formulae like this throughout the New Testament raise the question as to whether the antecedent of the pronoun should be determined by the original context of the formulaic statement or by the author's own situation and use. Such formulae must be isolated and studied independently to determine their original contexts versus their current applications.

16. Ibid.,1:131.
17. The passages that seem to Barth to reflect such hymnic material are Eph. 1:3–14, 20–23; 2:4–7, 10, 14–18, 20–22; 3:5, 20–21; 4:4–6(8), 11–13; 5:2, 14, 25–27.

Category 3: Differentiating Jews from Gentiles

The theology of Ephesians is discernable in Paul's distinctive application of first- and second-person plural pronouns. As a Jew, he distinguishes himself from his Gentile audience (Eph. 2:11; 3:1) by referring to himself and his kinsmen with the first-person plural pronouns, *we, us,* and *our* ("my own people, my kindred according to the flesh," Rom. 9:3 NRSV), while specifically designating those to whom he writes as "you Gentiles" (Eph. 2:11; 3:1).

The perspective of Ephesians is that of a Jewish author writing to a Gentile audience. It is this perspective that dominates the use of the majority of the first-person plural pronouns in the letter. And this same perspective provides a workable hypothesis for reconstructing the priority reading of a number of textual variants in the letter. There is probably no letter in the Pauline corpus that more effectively uses the pronouns in developing its central theme than Ephesians, though only slightly more so than Colossians.[18]

The significance of this perspective can be seen in the following example. After the epistolary greeting in the first two verses of chapter 1, the Gentiles are not referred to until verse 13, where they are said to have been added to God's redemptive work among the Jews, who thus far have been designated by first-person plural pronouns (Eph. 1:3–12). Paul then addresses the Gentile readers in verse 13 by saying "*you also,* who have heard the word of truth, the gospel of *your* salvation, . . . were sealed with the promised Holy Spirit, which is the guarantee of *our* [Jewish] inheritance."

It is thus clear that the two first-person plural pronoun variant readings in verse 13 ("in him *we* also . . . the gospel of *our* salvation") could not have been in the original letter. Even without the pronouns, the transition from Jews to Gentiles is evident in the second-person plural ending of the verb ἐσφραγίσθητε, *esphragisthēte* (corresponding to the second-person plural pronoun ὑμεῖς [*hymeis,* you] in Eph. 2:11).

This approach can also be seen in Paul's use of liturgical and confessional material (category 2 above), which is often presented from his own perspective rather than that of the original authors. Thus, while the statement in Ephesians 1:2, "Grace to you and peace from God our Father," customarily refers to the God of all believers, it might have the restrictive meaning "God of the Jews" in this particular letter (especially here in Eph. 1:1–12). If so, Paul

---

18. In addition to Johannes Munck's well-known work (*Paul and the Salvation of Mankind* [Atlanta: John Knox, 1977]) and that of Stendahl (*Paul among Jews and Gentiles*), which argue that Paul's self-conception was formulated more by his sense of commission to preach to Gentiles than by a conversion arising from an introspective conscience, there has also appeared in the Cambridge series a monograph by George Howard, *Paul: Crisis in Galatia* (Cambridge: Cambridge University Press, 1979), that accentuates the surpassing importance of this socio-theological focal point of Pauline thought. What Howard and Stendahl see in Galatians and Munck sees in Romans may also be observed in Ephesians.

would be saying "Grace and peace to you Gentile believers from the God of us Jewish believers."

Furthermore, the greeting as a whole is rather unique in early literature. *Grace* (χάρις, *charis*) is a Gentile Christian variation of *greeting* (χαίρειν, *chairein*), the customary word used in papyrus letters at the time. *Peace* (εἰρήνη, *eirēnē*) is Greek for *shalom,* the common Jewish greeting. For his special purposes, then, Paul probably adapts the two secular greeting formulae of everyday correspondence and modifies them to produce a uniquely spiritual greeting for his racially mixed churches. He uses this formula in the greetings of his letters to the churches in Rome, Corinth, and Galatia as well.

Category 4: Referring to Jews and Gentiles Together

This brings us to the fourth and final use of these pronouns in Ephesians—that of mutual inclusion. After the statements in Ephesians 2:1 and 5, declaring that the Gentiles now have been brought together with the Jews into the body of Christ, the first-person plural no longer refers exclusively to Jews or Jewish Christians, as it does down to this point in the letter, but to Jews and Gentiles *together.* The transition point is verse 3, where Paul first introduces the encompassing phrase "we all" (Jew and Gentile) for those who once lived among the sons of disobedience.

Thus, the first eight verses of chapter 2 may be paraphrased as follows: "*You* Gentiles were dead in your trespasses and sins (v. 1) just as we Jews were (v. 5), so *we all* shared the same guilt of sin (v. 3). But God has now forgiven us (Jew and Gentile alike) by his grace (vv. 6, 8), made us alive together with Christ, raised us up *together,* and made us sit *together* with Christ in the heavenly places" (vv. 5–8).

Therefore, from Ephesians 2:3 on, the first-person plural pronouns include the Gentiles as well, those who have been grafted as wild olive branches into the Jewish tree (Rom. 11:17–24). They are now, like the Jews, included among the descendants of Abraham "in order that in Christ Jesus the blessing of Abraham might come to the Gentiles, so that we [Jew and Gentile] might receive the promise of the Spirit through faith"(Gal. 3:14 NRSV).

Paul wrote similarly of Gentile inclusion in his letter to the Romans: "For this reason it depends on faith, in order that the promise may rest on grace and be guaranteed to *all his descendants,* not only to the adherents of the law [Jews] but also to *those* [*Gentiles*] *who share* the faith of Abraham (for he is the *father of all of us,* as it is written, 'I have made you the father of *many nations*' [i.e., Gentiles as well, not just the Jewish nation])" (Rom. 4:16–17 NRSV, italics added).

In Ephesians there are a number of significant occurrences of the first-person plural pronouns used in this inclusive way after 2:3.

The first example, and perhaps the most significant, occurs in Ephesians 2:5, where Paul uses three compound verbs to describe the uniting of Jews and Gentiles together in Christ ("made alive together, raised together, and made to sit together"—συνεζωοποίησεν, *sunezōopoiēsen,* συνήγειρεν, *sunēgeiren,* and συνεκάθισεν, *sunekathisen*). Paul then states in verse 7 that God's rich grace is manifested toward "us," the pronoun now meaning Jews and Gentiles together, who are declared to be his workmanship by the first-person plural (v. 10).

Special attention must be called to these compound verbs.[19] They furnish a key point in the theology of Ephesians. It is almost universally argued in commentaries on the Greek text that chapter 1 essentially deals with what God has done for Christ and chapter 2 with what God has therefore subsequently done for all believers. These three compound verbs in Ephesians 2:5 are thus taken to indicate the twofold union of Christ and his believers. Such is the approach of a number of important studies on Paul that express difficulty in dealing with the first five verses of chapter 2.[20] However, none of them deals with the thematic consistency of pronoun use in the passage or sees that the meanings of the three compound verbs render this interpretation implausible. I suggest that the compounds do not refer to any union with Christ, whether Christ and Jews, Christ and Gentiles, or Christ and Christians.

Two of the three compound verbs, "made to sit together" (συνεκάθισεν, *sunekathisen*) and "made alive together" (συνεζωοποίησεν, *sunezōopoiēsen*), are followed by the word *Christ* in the dative case (Χριστῷ, *Christō*). The meaning cannot be that Christians *and* Christ are made to sit together *with Christ,* nor that Christians *and Christ* are made alive together *with Christ.*[21]

Also, the preposition *in* (ἐν, *en*) appears before *Christ* (Χριστῷ, *Christō*) (Eph. 2:5, 6, 10) in the Chester Beatty Papyrus ($\mathfrak{P}^{46}$) and Codex Vaticanus, our two oldest manuscripts of Paul's letters. Who then are those who the compound verbs indicate are brought *together in Christ,* since Christ is logically excluded from being one of the two parties? Clearly God (Eph. 2:4) is the sub-

---

19. Note also συναρμολογούμενον (*synarmologoumenon,* joined together) in Eph. 2:21 and 4:16, which Barth says is the earliest known use of the compound in Greek literature and "may be Paul's creation" (*Ephesians,* 2:272–73).

20. H. A. W. Meyer, *Critical and Exegetical Handbook to the Epistle to the Ephesians* (New York: Funk & Wagnalls, 1884; reprint, Winona Lake, Ind.: Alpha, 1979), 356; Charles J. Ellicott, *A Critical and Grammatical Commentary on St. Paul's Epistle to the Ephesians* (Andover: Draper, 1868), 42; S. T. Bloomfield, Ἡ Καινὴ Διαθήκη: *The Greek Testament with English Notes* (Philadelphia: Perkins, 1848), 2:266; Barth, *Ephesians,* 1:220 (he sees a "double connotation" in the verbs: [1] Jews and Gentiles and [2] their resurrection with Christ); S. D. F. Salmond, "The Epistle to the Ephesians," in *The Expositor's Greek Testament,* ed. W. Robertson Nicoll (reprint, Grand Rapids: Eerdmans, 1983), 3:283.

21. Cf. Col. 2:13: συνεζωοποίησεν ἡμᾶς [ὑμᾶς] σὺν αὐτῷ (*synezōopoiēsen hēmas [hymas] syn autō*), which would be equally senseless with this interpretation.

ject of the verbs, and the compounds indicate that he brings two divergent groups together in Christ. Who are they? The only two groups dealt with in the immediate context are the "Gentiles in the flesh" (Eph. 2:11–12) and the Jewish Christians (*saints,* Eph. 2:19). The meaning of the passage, then, consistent with the theological argument of the letter as a whole, is that God has brought Jew and Gentile together in Christ, raising them together with him and making them alive together with him.

The second example of the inclusive use of the first-person plural pronoun is in Ephesians 2:16, where Paul asserts that God has reconciled "*both* to God in one body," and created of the *two* "one new man" (Eph. 2:15). This statement of unification is then followed by the first-person plural verb (ἔχομεν, *echomen*): "We *both* have access in [by] the spirit to the Father" (Eph. 2:18). The result is that the Gentiles (Eph. 2:11) are now "fellow citizens with the saints," that is, with Jewish Christians (Eph. 2:19).[22]

A third occurrence is in Ephesians 3:8, where Paul calls himself the "least of all the saints [Jewish Christians]," who was given the commission to "preach to the Gentiles the unsearchable riches of Christ." This statement of Gentile inclusion is then followed again by the first-person plural verb (ἔχομεν, *echomen*) in Ephesians 3:12, signifying that both Jew and Gentile now have boldness and access in confidence through the faith of Christ.

A fourth example is found in Ephesians 4:13, where it is stated that the work of the saints (Jewish Christians) in building up the body of Christ (i.e., by including the Gentiles) will continue "until we all attain to the unity of the faith." Then in verses 14 and 15, first-person plural verbs are used (ὦμεν, *ōmen,* "we may be," and αὐξήσομεν, *auxēsomen,* "we will grow up"), referring to the newly created union of Jews and Gentiles, who should no longer be babes but "grow up in every way into him who is the head, into Christ." That "growing up" or "maturity" comes by including the Gentiles.

If this analysis is correct, *Ephesians 2:3 is the transition point in the letter, and from this point on all the first-person pronouns and those implicit in first-person verbs refer to the union of Jews and Gentiles.*[23] Prior to this, the first-person pronouns refer to the Jews as a people or to Jewish Christians. The third verse is the decisive point, indicated by the phrase "we all" (ἡμεῖς πάντες, *hēmeis pantes*), which appears also in Ephesians 4:13, in both instances expanding the first-person reference to include the Gentiles as well.

Henry Alford is one of the few commentators who sees the special implications of this phrase (*we all*). He discusses its use in Ephesians and the uniqueness of the expression in other Pauline literature, where it also refers to the

---

22. See the discussion below on "Contrasting of Saints with Gentiles by Pronoun Use."
23. With the exception of uses that fall into category 1 and possibly 2.

union of Jews and Gentiles (Rom. 4:16; 8:32; 1 Cor. 12:13; 2 Cor. 3:18).[24] However, he does not see its position as the transition point in the use of the first-person pronoun in Ephesians and therefore understands the Jews in chapter 1 to be spiritual Israel.[25] Thus he misses the meaning of the word *mystery* in Ephesians 1:9, which denotes the hitherto unrevealed intention of God to include the Gentiles as fellow citizens with the saints (Eph. 2:19)—the meaning that, interestingly, he defends in his discussion of Ephesians 3:3–6. This ambivalence is characteristic of all commentators who fail to recognize the consistency of pronoun use in this beautifully thought out and well-argued letter.

It seems likely that the variant readings ἡμεῖς (*hēmeis*) and ὑμεῖς (*hymeis*), which so frequently plague the interpreter of Ephesians and Colossians,[26] were probably produced in part by scribes who operated on the same presuppositional basis as the majority of modern commentators, resulting in the confused state of the current texts. They could not understand why the author changed the pronouns as he did. Observing the distinction in these pronouns between Jews and Gentiles helps alleviate that perplexity.

Contrasting of Saints with Gentiles by Pronoun Use

A number of times in Ephesians, Paul uses the word *saints* to refer to Jewish Christians. The word means "holy ones" and was used in its various forms in the Old Testament to refer to the Jewish people who worshiped the holiness of God in the Holy Place of the temple. Paul uses the word in Ephesians to distinguish Jewish Christians from Gentile Christians.

When he differentiates Jews from Gentiles by pronoun variation in Ephesians 2:19, Paul refers to the Jews as saints: "So then you [Gentiles] are no longer strangers and aliens, but you are citizens with the saints" (NRSV). This designation of Jewish Christians as saints occasionally occurs in special contexts in other Pauline literature (e.g., Rom. 15:25–26). That the author considers himself among the saints and that the saints are Jewish Christians is clear from Ephesians 3:1 and 8. In verse 1 he says, "I, Paul, a prisoner on be-

24. See Henry Alford, *Alford's Greek Testament: An Exegetical and Critical Commentary* (1857; reprint, Grand Rapids: Guardian, 1976), 3:90 (on Eph. 2:3).

25. Alford thus vascillates: "we" in Eph. 1:1–22 refers to Jews and Gentiles, in Eph. 1:12 it refers only to Jews, and in Eph. 2:3 it refers again to Jews and Gentiles. No criteria are suggested by which to determine the interpretation of these pronouns.

26. The consistent pattern of the author of Ephesians of using first-person plural pronouns after statements of Jew-Gentile union makes it almost certain that the autograph of Col. 2:13 (parallel to Eph. 2:1–5) would have read "we" (ἡμᾶς, *hēmas*) with 𝔓[46] and B, rather than "you" (ὑμᾶς, *hymas*), preferred in both the United Bible Societies 4th edition and the Nestle-Aland 27th edition.

half of you Gentiles," and in verse 8 he continues, "to me, . . . the very least of all the saints, this grace was given to preach to the Gentiles" (cf. Col. 1:26–27).

This distinction between Gentiles and saints is seen also in Ephesians 3:18, where the text states: "in order that you [Gentiles] may be able to apprehend with all the saints" the greatness of God (author's translation).[27]

The mystery in Ephesians 1:9, which Paul says was made known to "us" (Jews), is identified in Ephesians 3:3–6 as a revelation to the *saints* (Jews, Eph. 2:19; 3:8): that the *Gentiles* are to be fellow participants in God's eternal purpose.

> The mystery was made known to me [the *least of the saints*, Eph. 3:8] by revelation, as I wrote above in a few words, a reading of which will enable you to perceive my understanding of the mystery of Christ. In former generations this mystery was not made known to humankind, as it has now been revealed to his holy apostles and prophets by the Spirit: *that is, the Gentiles* have become fellow heirs, members of the same body, and sharers in the promise in Christ Jesus through the gospel. (Eph. 3:3–6 NRSV, italics added)

This, then, is the meaning of Ephesians 2:19, that "you [Gentiles] are *fellow citizens with the [Jewish] saints.*"

A failure to recognize this special use of the term *saints* and treat it consistently as a part of the Jew-Gentile paradigm revealed in the pronouns has been responsible for the often awkward and noncohesive interpretation of the text. Commentators have trouble with what one calls "the extremely difficult" problem of understanding the variation in prepositions in Ephesians 4:12:[28] "*to* equip the saints *for* the work of ministry, *for* building up the body of Christ" (NRSV, italics added).

An awareness of the Jew-Gentile motif in the pronouns clarifies the use of these prepositions (πρός, *pros;* εἰς, *eis*) in this verse and points to an important distinction in the mind of the author. He uses πρός (for) here in referring to the Jewish Christians and εἰς (for, or unto) in referring to the Gentile Christians.

The verse would thus be understood as follows: "He gave the gifts for (πρός) the equipping of the saints (i.e., Jewish Christians) in order to do (εἰς) the work of ministry, in order to (εἰς, i.e., which is to) build up the body (i.e, bring in the Gentiles)." This ministry would last until "we all" (i.e., Jew and

27. This is also the meaning of the prayer in Eph. 1:15–19, in which the author prays that God "may give you [Gentiles] a spirit of wisdom and revelation" to experience the rich "inheritance among the saints" (i.e., Jewish Christians) (NRSV).

28. Ellicott, *Ephesians,* 42. Barth (*Ephesians,* 2:479) shares this feeling. He gives three interpretations of Eph. 4:11–13, none of which sees the meaning of *saints* as "Jews."

Gentile) attain to the oneness of the faith (Eph. 4:13), that is, accept each other as equally acceptable to God in one body.

The Role of Cosmic Powers

Paul emphatically asserts in Ephesians that "our struggle is not against enemies of blood and flesh, but against the rulers, against the authorities, against the cosmic powers of this present darkness, against the spiritual forces of evil in the heavenly places" (Eph. 6:12 NRSV).

The celestial world was highly structured in the Hellenistic Jewish thought of Paul's time, having multiple heavens, usually seven in number, and containing both angels and demons. This "cosmic ladder" has been defined as the "mythological geography of Jewish Apocalyptic."[29] Paul uses this apocalyptic background to present his theology to Ephesus and other churches in Asia, the same area to which the Book of Revelation was written, because his readers understood it.[30] Ephesus was the center of magic, astrology, and the mystery religions, and many converts to Christ in that city were once involved with these religious practices. They believed that their lives were under the influence of cosmic powers. Paul may have written, among other purposes, to alleviate their fears by showing that Christ is sovereign in the cosmos.[31]

The major dogmas of Jewish Christianity were developed along cosmological lines. Although they were more concerned with Christology than cosmology, they used cosmological data as a medium of expression. Jewish Christian theology has been summarized as follows:

> The incarnation was presented as a descent of the Word through the angelic spheres; the Passion as Christ's combat with the angels of the air, followed by the descent into Hell; the Resurrection as an exaltation of Christ's humanity above all the angelic spheres; and after death the soul would pass through the various spheres, on its way encountering their guardians, to whom it would have to render an account. All these conceptions are based on a vision of the heavenly spheres which is part of the framework of Jewish Christianity.[32]

29. See chapter 10 on apocalyptic and Jean Danielou, *The Theology of Jewish Christianity*, A History of Early Christian Doctrine 1, trans. J. A. Baker (London: Darton, Longman and Todd, 1964), 173.

30. On the definition and meaning of apocalyptic literature, see D. S. Russell, *Apocalyptic: Ancient and Modern* (Philadelphia: Fortress, 1978); idem, *The Method and Message of Jewish Apocalyptic* (Philadelphia: Westminster, 1964); Danielou, *Theology of Jewish Christianity*, 7–54, 173–204; Walter Schmithals, *The Apocalyptic Movement: Introduction and Interpretation*, trans. John Steely (Nashville: Abingdon, 1975).

31. Such is the argument of Clinton Arnold, *Power and Magic: The Concept of Power in Ephesians* (Grand Rapids: Baker, 1997).

32. Danielou, *Theology of Jewish Christianity*, 179.

Paul describes one of his revelatory experiences in the language of cosmological geography when he writes that he was "caught up to the third heaven . . . and heard things that are not to be told, that no mortal is permitted to repeat" (2 Cor. 12:2–4 NRSV). He speaks in Ephesians of multiple heavens, saying that Christ ascended "far above all the heavens" (Eph. 4:10). It is important to notice who the inhabitants of these "heavenly places" are in Ephesians. They include God, Christ, Jewish and Gentile Christians, and demonic powers.

Table 13.1 Heavenly Inhabitants in Ephesians

Ephesians	Context	Greek Word
1:3	"Us" (Jewish Christians)	ἐπουρανίοις, epouranios
1:10	"All things"	οὐρανοῖς, ouranois (contrasted with earth, γῆ, gē)
1:20	Christ, at God's right hand	ἐπουρανίοις, epouraniois
2:2	"The prince of the power of the air" (Satan)	ἀέρος, aeros
2:6	"Us" (Jewish and Gentile Christians)	ἐπουρανίοις, epouraniois
3:10	"Principalities and powers"	ἐπουρανίοις, epouraniois
3:15	"Every family"	οὐρανοῖς, ouranois (contrasted with earth)
4:10	Christ ("ascended far above all the heavens")	οὐρανῶν, ouranōn
6:9	The Lord (Christ or God)	οὐρανοῖς, ouranois
6:12	"World rulers of this present darkness, . . . spiritual hosts of wickedness" (the devil)	ἐπουρανίοις, epouraniois

Paul, thus, uses the plural term *heavenly places* rather than the singular *heaven* because the singular would be understood as designating the eternal abode of God, and the spiritual hosts of wickedness who are in these heavenly places (Eph. 6:12) are not in the seventh heaven where God dwells. So also Christ, seated now at the right hand of God in the heavenly places (Eph. 1:20), is in the seventh heaven, not in the lower heavens where the demons dwell. Satan, the "prince of the power of the *air*" (Eph. 2:2), dwells in this lower region around the earth known as the firmament in Jewish apocalyptic thought. Paul uses the word ἀήρ (*aēr*) for air in this verse, indicating thereby the lower, darker air. Greek authors used another word for air, αἰθήρ (*aithēr*), to designate the ethereal regions (the higher heavens) where their gods dwelled.

Paul's perspective, then, is that Satan, who dwells in the region around the earth (Eph. 2:2), is actively trying to destroy the unity of the church. Our warfare is with him, not with flesh and blood (Eph. 6:12). By fostering disunity in the body of Christ, he destroys its witness to the oneness of God (Eph. 4:4–6), which it constantly seeks to make known through its unity, even to these principalities and powers in the heavenly places (3:10).

Justification Is by Faith Rather Than by Law

The fifth and final theological concept in Ephesians is that access to God is equally available to Jew and Gentile alike through faith rather than through the law of Moses. Otherwise, God is a God of Jews only. This topic merits a full discussion and is dealt with in chapter 15 on Paul's view of the law.

From these considerations I suggest an additional note to the work of Goodspeed,[33] and others,[34] on the relation of the production of both Acts and Ephesians to the publication of the Pauline corpus. The Book of Acts would have been an appropriate introduction for the circulation of a corpus of letters dealing with the inclusion of the Gentiles. Ephesians too may have been written for that purpose. The omission of the name *Ephesus* in the oldest manuscripts of Ephesians may indicate that Acts and Ephesians were used in Asia as introductory letters to a Pauline corpus. In support of this, we note that in addition to Paul's own view of the importance of his work among Gentiles and the fact that the theme of Ephesians is the inclusion of the Gentiles in the body of Christ, the Book of Acts concerns itself only with the beginnings among Jews and Gentiles. Several significant studies on Acts have not considered the material omitted from Acts as an indication of the purpose of the book.[35] The fact that Acts is concerned only with the beginning of the church among Jews and Gentiles explains

1. Why most of the apostles are not discussed at all in Acts: Although their work must have been regarded as important, it was only a continuation of Peter's work among the Jews.

---

33. E. J. Goodspeed, *The Formation of the New Testament* (Chicago: University of Chicago Press, 1926); idem, *New Solutions of New Testament Problems*; idem, *The Meaning of Ephesians*; idem, *An Introduction to the New Testament*.

34. John Knox, "Acts and the Pauline Letter Corpus," in *Studies in Luke-Acts*, ed. L. Keck and J. Martyn (Nashville: Abingdon, 1966), 279–87.

35. Henry J. Cadbury, *The Making of Luke-Acts* (New York: Macmillan, 1927); idem, *The Style and Literary Method of Luke* (Cambridge, Mass.: Harvard University Press, 1919–20); Adolf Harnack, *Luke the Physician* (New York: Putnam, 1907); more recently the Festschrift edited by Keck and Martyn, *Studies in Luke-Acts*; A. Q. Morton and G. H. C. Macgregor, *The Structure of Luke and Acts* (New York: Harper and Row, 1964).

2. Why Peter is the primary figure in Acts 1 through 12 and Paul in Acts 13 through 28: Luke is concerned with the beginnings among the Jews in chapters 1 through 12 and among the Gentiles in chapters 13 through 28.

3. Why there are some problems in the chronology of Acts as compared with Paul's letters: Luke is concerned only with those activities in Paul's life that directly and briefly highlight the inclusion of the Gentiles.

4. Why the Book of Acts ends in such abruptness in Rome: Paul has brought his divinely appointed work in the east to a close, evidenced not only by the contribution that has been delivered as a seal of this work, but also by his moving out of the area of the church's beginnings and for the first time teaching in Rome, a place where he did not found a church. Any further contact by Paul with the eastern part of the empire would fall outside the scope of Luke's purpose in writing.

A second look at both Acts and Ephesians may be in order in view of this common purpose that motivated the production of both books.[36] Perhaps there is considerably more of Paul in both books than has usually been admitted.

---

36. Ernst Käsemann offers little of value in this regard ("Ephesians and Acts," in Keck and Martyn, *Studies in Luke-Acts,* 288).

FOURTEEN

The Faith(fulness) of Christ in Pauline Literature

Among the various views of atonement that have appeared in the history of Christian thought, the subjectivity of the Latin view has often overshadowed the objectivity inherent in the classical view, which emphasizes the reality of what happened at Calvary separate and apart from any human response to that event. The classical approach views the conquest of Satan as an objective event with which human faith has little, if anything, to do. While it is true that humanity must respond to that event in order to appropriate salvation, that in no way alters the reality of the justifying act itself.[1]

In atonement contexts of Paul's Roman letter, there are some instances where he uses the phrase "faith of Christ" in a way consistent with this objective perspective of the atonement. This "faith of Christ" formula (πίστις Χριστοῦ, *pistis Christou*) appears seven times in the New Testament, all in passages that refer to the faithfulness *of* Christ rather than to our faith *in* Christ. This phrase appears in the following verses: once each in Romans 3:22, 26; twice in Galatians 2:16; once in Galatians 3:22; once in Ephesians 3:12 (where Paul merely uses the pronoun *his* instead of *Christ*); and once in Philippians 3:9.[2]

---

1. See the full discussion in chapter 12.
2. For a recent discussion of the issue, see Richard B. Hays, "ΠΙΣΤΙΣ and Pauline Christology: What Is at Stake?" in *Looking Back, Pressing On,* ed. E. Elizabeth Johnson and David M. Hay, vol. 4 of *Pauline Theology,* Society of Biblical Literature Symposium Series 4 (Minneapolis: Fortress, 1991–97), 35–60; and James D. G. Dunn, "Once More, ΠΙΣΤΙΣ ΧΡΙΣΤΟΥ," in *Looking Back,* 61–81. See also Paul Achtemeier's response to these papers, in *Looking Back,* 82–92.

On the other hand, there are many places in the writings of Paul where the phrase "faith *in* Christ" occurs, expressed either by the verb *believe* followed by the preposition *into* or *on* (εἰς, *eis*) or by the preposition *in* (ἐν, *en*). This is the usual way to say one believes in Christ or in God, meaning to put one's faith in or into the inner person of Christ. But Paul does not express himself this way in these seven instances. In these, he uses "faith *of* Christ," which employs the Greek genitive case following the noun *faith*. While the Greek phrase can be taken as an objective genitive (meaning Christ is the object of the faith) and thus be translated "faith in" Christ, it can also be taken as a subjective genitive (meaning Christ is the subject of the faith) and thus be translated "faith of" Christ.

The subjective rendering has been supported by four arguments.[3] First, the Greek construction *faith* followed by a genitive case used with the name of a person or the personal pronoun *his,* occurs twenty-four times in Paul's writings, and all of them refer to the faith *of* the individual, never to faith *in* the individual. These are categorized as follows: (1) on twenty occasions the reference is to Christians individually or collectively, and therefore the "faith of" the various individual Christians would mean not "faith in them" but "their faith"; (2) one time (Rom. 3:3) it refers to the faith of God and is uniformly rendered in the various translations "faithfulness of God"; (3) two times (Rom. 4:12, 16) it refers to the faith of Abraham, clearly meaning not "faith in Abraham" but "Abraham's faith"; and (4) one time (Rom. 4:5) it refers to anyone who has faith reckoned to him for righteousness.

The second argument is from the change of idiom in Galatians 2:16, where Paul makes a distinction in grammatical construction by alternating the phrase "faith of" Christ (πίστις Χριστοῦ, *pistis Christou*—genitive case) with "faith in" Christ (ἐπιστεύσαμεν Χριστὸν Ἰησοῦν, *episteusamen Christon Iēsoun*—accusative case). Thus, Paul says that we "know that a person is not justified out of works of the law but through the faith(fulness) of Jesus Christ, and we have put our faith in Christ in order to be justified out of the faith(fulness) of Christ" (author's translation). The article does not appear before either law or faith in this verse.

The argument has been made that in these contexts Paul is almost always talking about faith in contrast to law and about some form of righteousness. According to this approach, Paul is intending to convey a legal notion expressed by the term *testament* (διαθήκη, *diathēkē*), which would be found in ordinary legal documents in the Roman juridical system, and he is using faith or trust as the means by which the benefits of a Roman legal testament are transmitted.[4]

    3. George Howard, "Notes and Observations on the Faith of Christ," *HTR* 60 (1967): 459–84.
    4. Greer Taylor, "The Function of ΠΙΣΤΙΣ ΧΡΙΣΤΟΥ in Galatians," *JBL* 85.1 (March 1966): 58–76.

Conversely, others do not see Paul referring here to the Roman idea of a legal *testament* but to the Old Testament idea of the *covenant* of faith made with Abraham, Isaac, and Jacob, which is contrasted with the legal notion of *testament* (law) given under Moses. The conditions of the covenant were based on faith, not on keeping a law. The progression of thought in Galatians 2:16, then, is from the faithfulness of Christ to faith in Christ.

The argument of Protestant reformers that Paul is here contrasting salvation by faith with salvation by meritorious works has been supported by the assumption that "works of the law" in this verse means doing good deeds from a legalistic point of view. Until recently, no use of the expression "works of law" (ἔργων νόμου, *ergōn nomou*) had been known in ancient literature outside the New Testament to help clarify its meaning. However, a recently published document from the Dead Sea Scrolls contains this phrase in Hebrew (*miqsat ma'ase ha-torah*), referring to "legal rulings of the Torah."[5] Fragmentary portions of six different copies of this scroll were found in the 1950s,[6] indicating its widespread use at Qumran, but the reconstruction of the scroll was not published until 1994. The scroll was dubbed 4QMMT.[7]

The document has been carefully studied by Martin Abegg, who reported his findings in *Biblical Archaeology Review*,[8] which also printed a copy of the original Hebrew text with an English translation.[9] Abegg writes

> *Ma'ase ha-torah* is equivalent to what we know in English from Paul's letters as "works of the law." This Dead Sea Scroll and Paul use the very same phrase. The connection is emphasized by the fact that this phrase appears *nowhere* in rabbinic literature of the first and second centuries A.D.—*only* in Paul and in MMT. The works of the law that the Qumran text refers to are obviously typified by the twenty or so religious precepts (*halakhot*) detailed in the body of the text. For the first time, we can really understand what Paul is writing about. Here is a document detailing works of the law.[10]

We now better understand Paul's argument. It is made not in the context of meritorious works but in the context of ethnic equality before God. His contrast is between being justified by faith in the faithfulness of Christ and being justified by observing religious precepts from the law of Moses.

5. According to Lawrence H. Schiffman, "The New Halakhic Letter (4QMMT) and the Origins of the Dead Sea Sect," *BA* 53 (1990): 67.

6. Elisha Qimron and John Strugnell, "For This You Waited 35 Years," *BAR* 20.6 (Nov.–Dec. 1994): 57.

7. Elisha Qimron and John Strugnell, *Qumran Cave 4-V: Miqsat Ma'ase Ha-Torah*, Discoveries in the Judaean Desert 10 (Oxford: Clarendon, 1994).

8. "Paul, 'Works of the Law,' and MMT," *BAR* 20.6 (Nov.–Dec. 1994): 52–55.

9. Qimron and Strugnell, "For This You Waited 35 Years," 56–61.

10. Abegg, "Paul, 'Works of the Law,' and MMT," 53.

Gentile Christians do not have to keep the law in order to be saved, just as Jews were never justified by performances (works) of the law but by faith in God.

We believe in Christ, not that we might be justified by that belief, but that we might be justified by his faith(fulness) to God in the atonement. We put our faith in him, which is the salvific aspect of atonement, that we might be justified out of his faith(fulness), which is the justifying aspect of atonement. Our faith in Christ is based upon the faith(fulness) of Christ. So, the "faith of Christ" should be translated in Galatians 2:16 in the same way the "faith of God" is translated in Romans 3:3 as the "faithfulness of God."

Paul makes the distinction in the Galatians passage by alternating the Greek prepositions for *through* (διά, *dia*) and *out of* (ἐκ, *ek*), which take the genitive case, with the preposition for *in* (εἰς, *eis*), which takes the accusative case. Thus, he writes: "We have put our faith *in* Christ in order to be justified *out of* his faithfulness, because *out of* works of law, no one is able to be justified" (author's translation). Paul uses these prepositions in this passage to show emphatically that there is a difference between the two concepts of "faith in" and "faith of."

The Peshitta version of the Syriac New Testament, completed sometime in the early fifth century and thus untouched by the Protestant Reformation,[11] renders this construction as "faith of" Christ. It reads: "Therefore we know that a man is not justified from the works of the law, but by the *faith of Jesus the Messiah,* and we believe *in* him, *in Jesus the Messiah,* that *from his faith, that of the Messiah,* we might be justified, and not from the works of the law" (italics added).

Antioch of Syria, which functioned as Paul's home base for his missionary journeys, was located in the country of Syria, where this version was produced. Not long after he finished his work in this city, a school was established there that emphasized the literal interpretation of Scripture in contrast to the allegorical approach of schools like the one in Alexandria, Egypt. The school in Antioch boasted such prominent teachers as Theophilus of Antioch and Ignatius of Antioch, who dedicated themselves to perpetuating literal Pauline teaching in that place. This translation clearly shows that the subsequent Syriac translators believed it was the faith of Christ, and not our faith in him, that Paul had in the mind in this passage.

This translation also renders Ephesians 3:12 as "in him we have the boldness and the access in the confidence of his faith," taking this genitive construction also to be subjective.

Martin Luther seems to be the first person in modern times to translate the construction objectively as "faith in" Christ. The following diagram shows the various passages where the expression *pistis Christou* (faith of/in) occurs in

11. S. P. Brock, "Versions, Ancient (Syriac)," *ABD,* 6:797.

Paul's writings and in James 2:1. The phrase is translated "faith of" Christ in most of the English versions prior to Luther. The point of comparison, as these translations show, is not between human faith as opposed to human work but between human faith and Christ's faith, which is a totally different point of orientation. Christ's faith would here then be understood as his faithfulness.

Table 14.1 Faith in/of Christ in Translations

Translation	Rom. 3:22	Gal. 2:16	Gal. 2:20	Gal. 3:22	Gal. 3:9	James 2:1
1380 Wycliffe	of	of	of	of	of	of
1534 Tyndale	of	of	of	of	*in*	of
1539 Cranmer	of	of	of	of	of	of
1539 Great Bible	of	of	*in*	of	of	of
1557 Geneva	of	of	*of* (facsimile 1560 in Hexapla)	of	of	of
1582 Rheims	of	of	of	of	of	of
1611 KJV	of	of	of	of	of	of

The basic meaning of the Greek word *faith* (πίστις, *pistis*) in the time of Paul was "faithfulness." This is the word used by Josephus when he says that certain cities in Palestine did not engage in the revolt against Rome but "kept faith" with Rome, that is, they remained faithful to Rome. The idea that πίστις (*pistis*) was intellectual belief as opposed to works is a much later development. The meaning of the Hebrew word for faith (*'emunah*) was well known among Jews of Paul's day as "faithfulness."[12]

In Roman juristic terms, *faith* had a meaning that was quite different from the more pietistic meaning given to it in later Christian history. It can be argued that Paul uses this word in Galatians to "explain, in juristic terms, how the inheritance of Abraham is transmitted, through Jesus Christ, both to Jews and Gentiles and upon precisely the same terms."[13]

The expression "faith of Christ" in Romans 3:22 and 26 is parallel to the expression "faith of God" in Romans 3:3, which is uniformly translated in English versions as "faithfulness of God," and not "faith in God." This sheds light upon two passages in Paul dealing with the inclusion of the Gentiles, one in Galatians 3, and the other in Romans 3. In Galatians 3:8–22, Paul is making the point that through the faithfulness of Christ, the promise

---

12. Joseph Shulam, *A Commentary on the Jewish Roots of Romans* (Baltimore, Md.: Messianic Jewish Publishers, 1997). See his discussion of Rom. 1:17–3:31.
13. Greer Taylor, "Function of ΠΙΣΤΙΣ ΧΡΙΣΤΟΥ in Galatians."

of the blessing of Abraham has been given to the Gentiles. In verse 8, he says that the Scripture, foreseeing that God would justify the Gentiles by faith, announced the gospel beforehand to Abraham, saying, "In you shall all the nations be blessed." So Paul here perceives the gospel to be the promise to Abraham.

Then he proceeds to say that those who rely on works of the law are living under a curse, because "cursed be every one who does not abide by all things written in the book of the law, and do them" (Gal. 3:10). Paul knew that Jewish history was filled with disobedience to the law. But he also knew that the promise to Abraham was given so the Gentiles could share the inheritance through the seed of Abraham (Gen. 12:3; Gal. 3:14, 16), which is Christ, and that the law, which was given later, could not annul the promise given by God. Paul wrote that "the law, which came four hundred and thirty years afterward, does not annul a covenant previously ratified by God. . . . If the inheritance is by the law, it is no longer by promise; but God gave it to Abraham by a promise" (Gal. 3:17–18). Therefore, the promise of inheritance by faith is still in effect. Christ was faithful to what God said he would do. This is the faith(fulness) of Christ.

In the second passage, Romans 3:21–30, Paul argues that the righteousness of God has been revealed through the faith of Jesus for all who believe in him, and that righteousness is the basis for their belief in him (Rom. 3:22). Paul makes the point that there is no distinction between the Jew and the Gentile in this matter, both being equal beneficiaries of this grace. Then in Romans 3:25–26 he argues that by the death of Christ, God proved that he is righteous and that he justifies individuals by the faithfulness of Jesus. The following verses (Rom. 3:27–31) put this in the context of the monotheism of God being extended to the Gentiles, not in the context of faith versus meritorious labor. The theme of the inclusion of the Gentiles is pervasive in these verses as Paul argues that through the loyalty of Christ to God's promise to Abraham, all nations are included in the atonement.[14] Divine loyalty is basic to the proper understanding of the atonement; "the ground of our justification is the faith-obedience of Jesus Christ."[15]

In Philippians 3:8–9, Paul uses this phrase again, saying that he has suffered the loss of everything that was meaningful to him in order to gain Christ and "be found in him, not having a righteousness [justification] of my own, *based on law,* but that which is through *faith of* Christ" (author's translation).

---

14. "'The gospel' is the announcement of Jesus' lordship which works with power to bring people into the family of Abraham, now defined around Jesus Christ and characterized solely by faith in him. 'Justification' is the doctrine which insists that all those who have this faith belong as full members of this family on this basis and no other" (N. T. Wright, *What Saint Paul Really Said* [Grand Rapids: Eerdmans, 1997], 133).

15. Colin G. Kruse, *Paul, the Law and Justification* (Peabody, Mass.: Hendrickson, 1996), 190.

Paul is arguing that his righteousness is based upon Christ's act at Calvary rather than upon the law of Moses. The contrast is between Moses and Christ, not between Paul's faith in Christ and his own work of merit in keeping the law. Paul still has in mind the argument he made in Ephesians and Romans for the inclusion of the Gentiles in the monotheism of God. Here too the point is that what Christ did at Calvary was to fulfill the promise God made to Abraham and that the law of Moses, which came four hundred years later, did not annul that promise. Christ remained faithful to God and fulfilled that promise. This, again, is the faith(fulness) of Christ.

The contrast, then, was between justification by the law of Moses and justification in the seed of Abraham. This was the real issue confronting Paul: Did righteousness come through the law, as the Jews argued, or through the messianic role of Christ in fulfillment of Abraham's promise, as he clearly argues in Galatians 3? The issue was not Paul's faith versus Paul's work. It was justification by the faithfulness of God through Jesus Christ versus justification by the law—the promise on the one hand, and the law on the other. It was God's faith(fulness) through Christ that was at issue.

This righteous act of God (Phil. 3:9) depended upon the "faithfulness *of* Christ" in bringing it about. And that faithfulness forms the basis, in verses 10 and 11, of Paul's "faith *in* Christ": "that I may know him and the power of his resurrection, and may share his sufferings, becoming like him in his death, that if possible, I may attain the resurrection from the dead."

Summation of the Arguments for "Faith of Christ"

A. Faith of Christ—πίστις Χριστοῦ (*pistis Christou*)—in Paul's Letters:

> Romans 3:22, 26
> Galatians 2:16 (twice); 3:22
> Ephesians 3:12 (his) [noun does not occur here]
> Philippians 3:9

B. Reasons for Subjective Genitive:

1. The construction πίστις (*pistis*) followed by the genitive of person or of a personal pronoun occurs in Paul's writings twenty-four times. All of them refer to the faith *of* the individual, never faith *in* the individual.

   a. Twenty times individually or collectively to Christians
   b. One time to faith(fulness) of God (Rom. 3:3)
   c. Two times to faith of Abraham (Rom. 4:12, 16)
   d. One time to anyone who has his faith reckoned to him for righteousness (Rom. 4:5)

2. Change of idiom occurs in Galatians 2:16.

   A distinction is made by Paul in grammatical construction

by alternating πίστις Χριστοῦ, *pistis Christou* (genitive, "faith of") with ἐπιστεύσαμεν Χριστὸν Ἰησοῦν, *episteusamen Christon Iēsoun* (accusative, "faith in")

3. Syriac (Peshitta) Version understands it as subjective.
   a. Galatians 2:16: "Therefore we know that a man is not justified from the works of the law, but by the faith of Jesus the Messiah, and we believe in him, in Jesus the Messiah, that from his faith, *that of the Messiah,* we might be justified, and not from the works of the law."
   b. Ephesians 3:12: "In him we have the boldness and the access in the confidence *of his faith.*"
4. Luther seems to be the first exegete in modern times to translate the construction as objective genitive ("faith in").

C. Meaning of "Faith of Christ" (πίστις Χριστοῦ, *pistis Christou*):
   1. Parallel meanings in Romans 3:22, 26 and Romans 3:3 indicates it describes faith(fulness) of Christ.
   2. Refers to Abrahamic promise—Christ was faithful to the promise of God in Genesis 12:3 to bless *all* nations.
   3. Sheds light on two passages in Paul about the inclusion of the Gentiles.
      a. Galatians 3:8–22. The point is that through the faithfulness of Christ to the promise to Abraham, the blessing of Abraham has been given to the Gentiles.
      b. Romans 3:21–30.
   4. Faith (πίστις, *pistis*) is best understood as "faithfulness" in Jewish Hellenistic Greek and Old Testament Hebrew much more often than as "belief." It refers to inclusion of Gentiles in the theme of monotheistic universalism in Romans 1:5, 16; 2:10–11; and 3:21–31.

FIFTEEN

Paul's View of the Law

In the *Dictionary of Paul and His Letters,* Scott Hafemann states that "Paul's understanding of the Law is currently the most debated topic among Pauline scholars."[1] The bibliography of articles and books is extensive and rapidly expanding.[2]

1. Scott J. Hafemann, "Paul and His Interpreters," in *Dictionary of Paul and His Letters,* ed. Gerald F. Hawthorne et al. (Downers Grove, Ill.: InterVarsity, 1993), 671.
2. A selective list of articles includes Martin Abegg, "Paul, 'Works of the Law,' and MMT," *BAR* 20.6 (Nov.–Dec. 1994): 52–54; Linda Belleville, "'Under Law': Structural Analysis and the Pauline Concept of Law in Galatians 3:21–4:11," *JSNT* 26 (1986): 70–71; F. F. Bruce, "Paul and the Law of Moses," *Bulletin of the John Rylands University Library of Manchester* 57 (1975): 259–79; Shaye J. D. Cohen, "Was Timothy Jewish (Acts 16:1–3)?" *JBL* 105.2 (June 1986): 251–68; C. E. B. Cranfield, "'The Works of the Law' in the Epistle to the Romans," *JSNT* 43 (1991): 89–101; idem, "Giving a Dog a Bad Name: A Note on H. Räisänen's *Paul and the Law,*" *JSNT* 38 (1990): 77–85; idem, "St. Paul and the Law," *SJT* 17 (1964): 42–68; James D. G. Dunn, "Yet Once More—'The Works of the Law': A Response," *JSNT* 46 (1992): 99–117; Eldon J. Epp, "Jewish-Gentile Continuity in Paul: Torah and/or Faith? (Rom. 9:1–5)," *HTR* 79.1 (1986): 80–90; Paula Fredriksen, "Judaism, the Circumcision of Gentiles and Apocalyptic Hope: Another Look at Galatians 1 and 2," *JTS,* n.s., 42 (1991): 532–64; R. H. Gundry, "Grace, Works, and Staying Saved in Paul," *Biblica* 66.1 (1985): 1–38; Donald Hagner, "Paul's Quarrel with Judaism," in *Anti-Semitism and Early Christianity: Issues of Polemic and Faith,* ed. Craig Evans and Donald Hagner (Minneapolis: Fortress, 1993); Morna Hooker, "Paul and Covenantal Nomism," in *Paul and Paulinism: Essays in Honour of C. K. Barrett,* ed. M. D. Hooker and S. G. Wilson (London: SPCK, 1982), 47–56; E. Larsson, "Paul: Law and Salvation," *NTS* 31.3 (July 1985): 425–36; Richard N. Longenecker, "Three Ways of Understanding Relations between the Testaments: Historically and Today," in *Tradition and Interpretation in the New Testament: Essays in Honor of E. Earle Ellis,* ed. Gerald

Because Paul was commissioned on the road to Damascus to become an apostle to the Gentiles (Acts 26:17–18), the question of the role the law of Moses would play in his ministry became immediately paramount. This is dis-

---

Hawthorne and Otto Betz (Grand Rapids: Eerdmans, 1987), 22–28; David Lull, "'The Law Was Our Pedagogue': A Study in Galatians 3:19–25," *JBL* 105.3 (Sept. 1986): 481–98; Brice Martin, "Paul on Christ and the Law," *JETS* 26.3 (Sept. 1983): 271–82; Douglas Moo, "Paul and the Law in the Last Ten Years," *SJT* 40 (1987); H. Räisänen, "Legalism and Salvation by the Law," in *Die paulinische Literatur und Theologie,* ed. S. Pederson (Aarhus: Aros, 1980), 63–83; idem, "Das 'Gezetz des Glaubens' (Rom. 3:27) und das 'Gesetz des Geistes' (Rom. 8:2)," *NTS* 26 (1979–80): 101–17; idem, "Galatians 2:16 and Paul's Break with Judaism," *NTS* 31 (1985): 543–53; idem, "Paul's Conversion and the Development of His View of the Law," *NTS* 33 (1987): 404–19; Thomas Schreiner, "'Works of Law' in Paul," *Novum Testamentum* 33 (1991): 217–44; Moisés Silva, "The Law and Christianity: Dunn's New Synthesis," *Westminster Theological Journal* 53 (1991): 349–53; Peter Stuhlmacher, "Paul's Understanding of the Law in the Letter to the Romans," *Svensk Exegetisk Årsbok* 50 (1985): 87–104; Frank Thielman, "Law," *Dictionary of Paul,* ed. Hawthorne et al., 529–42; idem, "The Coherence of Paul's View of the Law: The Evidence of I Corinthians," *NTS* 38 (1992): 235–53; Stephen Westerholm, "Letter and Spirit: The Foundation of Pauline Ethics," *NTS* 30 (1984): 229–48; Ulrich Wilckens, "Statements on the Development of Paul's View of the Law," in *Paul and Paulinism,* ed. Hooker and Wilson; Christopher Wright, "The Ethical Authority of the Old Testament: A Survey of Approaches, Part I," *TynBul* 43 (1992): 101–20; idem, "The Ethical Authority of the Old Testament: A Survey of Approaches, Part II," *TynBul* 43 (1992): 203–31.

A selective list of books includes James D. G. Dunn, *Jesus, Paul, and the Law: Studies in Mark and Galatians* (Louisville: Westminster/John Knox, 1990); idem, *The Parting of the Ways: Between Christianity and Judaism and Their Significance for the Character of Christianity* (London: SCM Press; Philadelphia: Trinity Press International, 1991); H. Hübner, *Law in Paul's Thought* (Edinburgh: Clark, 1984); Colin Kruse, *Paul, the Law, and Justification* (Peabody, Mass.: Hendrickson, 1997); John B. Polhill, *Paul and His Letters* (Nashville: Broadman & Holman, 1999), chap. 6; Heikki Räisänen, *Jesus, Paul and Torah: Collected Essays,* JSNT Supplement Series 43 (Sheffield: JSOT Press, 1992); idem, *Paul and the Law,* Wissenschaftliche Untersuchungen zum Neuen Testament 29 (Tübingen: Mohr, 1983; Philadelphia: Fortress, 1986); Eckart Reinmuth, *Geist und Gesetz: Studien zu Voraussetzungen und Inhalt der paulinischen Paränese* (Berlin: Evangelische Verlagsanstalt, 1985); E. P. Sanders, *Jewish Law from Jesus to the Mishnah: Five Studies* (London: SCM Press; Philadelphia: Trinity Press International, 1992); idem, *Paul, the Law, and the Jewish People* (Philadelphia: Fortress, 1983); Thomas Schreiner, *The Law and Its Fulfillment* (Grand Rapids: Baker, 1993); Krister Stendahl, *Paul among Jews and Gentiles, and Other Essays* (Philadelphia: Fortress, 1976); Frank Thielman, *From Plight to Solution: A Jewish Framework for Understanding Paul's View of the Law in Romans and Galatians,* Supplements to Novum Testamentum 61 (Leiden: Brill, 1989); idem, *Paul and the Law: A Contextual Approach* (Downers Grove, Ill.: InterVarsity, 1994); Peter J. Tomson, *Paul and the Jewish Law: Halakha in the Letters of the Apostle to the Gentiles,* Compendia rerum Iudaicarum ad Novum Testamentum, section 3, Jewish Traditions in Early Christian Literature, vol. 1 (Assen, Netherlands: Van Gorcum; Minneapolis: Fortress, 1990); Francis Watson, *Paul, Judaism, and the Gentiles: A Sociological Approach,* Society for New Testament Studies Monograph Series 56 (Cambridge: Cambridge University Press, 1986); Stephen Westerholm, *Israel's Law and the Church's Faith: Paul and His Recent Interpreters* (Grand Rapids: Eerdmans, 1988); Michael Winger, *By What Law? The Meaning of Νόμος in the Letters of Paul,* Society of Biblical Literature Dissertation Series 128 (Atlanta: Scholars Press, 1992); N. T. Wright, *The Climax of the Covenant: Christ and the Law in Pauline Theology* (Edinburgh: Clark, 1991).

cussed to some extent in Romans, Galatians, Corinthians, Ephesians, Colossians, and 1 Timothy. Two aspects of the question present themselves in his teaching as independent and yet vitally connected:

1. The first aspect of the question is: What place should the law have in the life of a Jewish Christian? Is a Jewish Christian obligated or allowed to keep any of the law?
2. The second aspect of the question is: What place should the law have in the life of a Gentile Christian? Is a Gentile Christian obligated or allowed to keep any of the law?

Before addressing these questions, we must put into perspective the basic presupposition on which they are formulated—that Paul maintained a distinction between Jewish and Gentile believers. Such a distinction underlies the entire argument of Romans 9–11, among other passages. He did not argue that one was better than the other. On the contrary, they are equally valued by God, both having been immersed into the one body, where there is "neither Jew nor Greek, there is neither slave nor free, there is neither male nor female" (Gal. 3:28).

But this no more means that a Jewish Christian is indistinguishable from a Gentile Christian than it means that a female Christian is indistinguishable from a male Christian. Each is equally acceptable to and loved by God, but each has a special role in God's salvific plan. The obliteration of these distinctions can only result in grave confusion about the relation of Christians to the history and purpose of Israel in God's promise to Abraham. That promise was to bless all nations (i.e., Gentiles) in Abraham's seed (i.e., his son Isaac, and particularly Christ; Gal. 3:16).

The dangers in homogenizing the gospel so that there is no longer a distinctive Jewish Christianity and Gentile Christianity have been emphasized.[3] Most of the recent treatments on Paul and the law, while discussing the relation of Jews to Gentiles, do not give sufficient importance to the distinction that persevered between them *after* they became Christians.

One author correctly sees them as amalgamated into one body but incorrectly perceives them as becoming virtually indistinguishable upon conversion. For example, he writes that "as a Christian he [the convert, JM] has been freed from an obligation which applied to Jews under the old dispensation, that of observing the demands of the Law."[4] However, such an indiscriminate use of the word *Christian* in this context is confusing, because Gentile Christians were *never* under the law. They have not, therefore, been "*freed* from an obligation" to keep a law to which they were never subject.

---

3. Stendahl, *Paul among Jews and Gentiles,* 5.
4. Westerholm, *Israel's Law,* 206.

More accurately, it could be said that Gentile Christians were exempted from the necessity of being *placed under* Mosaic law after they became Christians. This, of course, is the point at issue in Paul's letter to the Galatians. However, the question still remains as to whether Jews who become Christians *remain* under that law or are "freed from an obligation which applied" to them earlier.

Another author writes: "The gospel as Paul preached it demanded a continued ethnic distinctiveness between Jews and Gentiles in order that Yahweh, the God of the Hebrews, could be conceptualized by both Jews and Gentiles as the God of all nations."[5]

We will explore the ramifications of this later, but first we must return to the questions asked above concerning the relation of Jewish and Gentile Christians to the law. "The Christian church found it extraordinarily difficult to decide whether and how the Law continued to be valid after the coming of Jesus. It was perhaps the most contentious issue that the first Christians faced."[6]

1. First, we must inquire whether a Jewish Christian is obligated or allowed to keep any of the law. Recent discussions have provided different answers. Frank Thielman argues that Paul's discussion of sanctity and ethics is based on the law.[7] Because Jewish Christians are God's temple and God's congregation, they should maintain a sanctified separation between themselves and non-Christian Gentiles. This is done not by keeping the ethnically specific aspects of the law—circumcision and dietary restrictions—that Paul considers no longer valid but rather by keeping the moral and monotheistic aspect of the law. Binding the ceremonial laws on potential converts would only serve to limit membership in God's people to ethnic Jews and those willing to convert to Judaism after becoming Christians.

Thielman argues that God has not abolished all Mosaic legislation but rather has abolished the just sentence of condemnation for transgressing it (2 Cor. 3:1–18, esp. vv. 7, 9). The law, which was bound to a specific period of time and to a people who were under condemnation for not having kept it (Jews), has come to its appointed end (2 Cor. 3:13).[8] Some parts of the law remain valid, he argues, namely, those that are not tainted by the temporal nature of the curses and barriers. These are not only valid but are fulfilled by Christians who walk in the Spirit (Gal. 5:22–23; 6:2).[9]

5. George Howard, *Paul: Crisis in Galatia* (Cambridge: Cambridge University Press, 1979), 66.

6. David Wenham, *Paul: Follower of Jesus or Founder of Christianity? A New Look at the Question of Paul and Jesus* (Grand Rapids: Eerdmans, 1995), 225.

7. "Law," 536.

8. Ibid., 538.

9. Ibid., 539.

Many Jewish authors writing on Paul agree that Paul continued to observe the law and encouraged Jewish Christians to do so as well.[10] By this they mean that Paul upheld the moral law, which in his view everyone should keep. But they argue that Paul believed Jewish Christians were not bound by the ceremonial and purity laws, a perspective that allowed him to extend his mission into the Gentile world. Accordingly, Jews and Gentiles should not be divided by this ceremonial part of the law, which Paul would not allow to be bound upon Gentiles but could be observed as a matter of choice by Jewish converts.[11]

Paul certainly did not think that by accepting Jesus as the prophesied Jewish Messiah he had departed from his ancestral religion.[12] He did not think it wrong for a Jew to practice Judaism as long as it was not done as an attempt to establish one's standing before God.[13] The Book of Acts shows that Jewish believers in Jesus believed they had to fulfill the demands of the Torah.[14] Observing circumcision and obeying the law was a part of their Jewish identity, and it was not obliterated by accepting Jesus as the Messiah.[15] But for neither the Jewish nor the Gentile follower of Christ did the law have anything to do with salvation.[16]

This implies a careful distinction between "doing the Law" and "fulfilling the

10. Claude G. Montefiore, *Judaism and St. Paul: Two Essays* (London: Goschen, 1914; reprint, New York: Arno, 1973); idem, "Rabbinic Judaism and the Epistles of Paul," *Jewish Quarterly Review* 13 (1901): 162–217 (reprinted in *Judaism and Christianity,* ed. Jacob B. Agus [New York: Arno, 1973]); Kaufmann Kohler, "Saul of Tarsus," *Jewish Encyclopedia,* ed. I. Singer et al. (New York: Funk & Wagnalls, 1905), 11:79–87; idem, *The Origins of the Synagogue and the Church* (New York: Macmillan, 1929; reprint, New York: Arno, 1973), 260–70; Joseph Klausner, *From Jesus to Paul,* trans. William F. Stinespring (New York: Macmillan, 1943; reprint, Boston: Beacon, 1961); Martin Buber, *Two Types of Faith,* trans. N. P. Goldhawk (London: Routledge and Kegan Paul, 1951); Leo Baeck, "The Faith of Paul," *Journal of Jewish Studies* 3 (1952): 93–110 (translated into German in *Paulus, die Pharisäer und das Neue Testament* [Frankfurt am Main: Ner-Tamid, 1961], 7–37); Samuel Sandmel, *The Genius of Paul: A Study in History* (New York: Farrar, Straus & Cudahy, 1958; reprinted with new introduction, New York: Schocken, 1970); idem, *Judaism and Christian Beginnings* (New York: Oxford University Press, 1978), 308–36; Hans J. Schoeps, *Paul: The Theology of the Apostle in the Light of Jewish Religious History,* trans. Harold Knight (Philadelphia: Westminster, 1961); Schalom Ben-Chorin, *Paulus: Der Völkerapostel in jüdischer Sicht* (München: Paul List, 1970), 223–30; Richard L. Rubenstein, *My Brother Paul* (New York: Harper and Row, 1972).

11. Donald Hagner, "Paul in Modern Jewish Thought," in *Pauline Studies: Essays Presented to Professor F. F. Bruce on His 70th Birthday,* ed. Donald A. Hagner and Murray J. Harris (Exeter, Eng.: Paternoster; Grand Rapids: Eerdmans, 1980), 156.

12. See the recent commentary by Joseph Shulam, *A Commentary on the Jewish Roots of Romans* (Baltimore: Messianic Jewish Publishers, 1997).

13. Gundry, "Grace, Works," 38 n. 103.

14. Edvin Larsson, "Paul, Law and Salvation," *NTS* 31.3 (July 1985): 433.

15. Ibid., 431.

16. Ibid., 434.

Law."[17] Jewish Christians are never obligated in New Testament documents to observe the demands of the law.[18] "Only if, by submitting to the requirements of circumcision, they return to the yoke of the Law will they be 'bound to keep the whole law'" (Gal. 5:1, 3).[19] It has been argued that there is a distinction between "doing" the law (Jews had to fulfill specific demands) and "fulfilling" the law. [20] Christians do not have to "do" the law, but they do have to "fulfill" it.[21] This, it is argued, is because "the Law does not bind believers."[22]

Fundamental to this train of thought, one author argues, is Paul's presupposition of a "continued ethnic distinctiveness between Jews and Gentiles in order that Yahweh, the God of the Hebrews, could be conceptualized by both Jews and Gentiles as the God of all nations."[23] This commentator insists that "any attempt on either side to erase the ethnic and cultural nature of the other would be to destroy Paul's particular concept of unity between Jews and Gentiles."[24] Another author writes of the dangers in homogenizing the gospel so that there is no longer a distinctive Jewish Christianity and a Gentile Christianity.[25]

Others have argued that Paul's negative statements about the law were prompted by the fact that the Jews had failed to keep the heart of the law in the forefront of their teaching and were rather emphasizing the "boundary-marking ritual" as preeminent. In their focus on nationalistic zeal, the law had become too closely identified with matters of the flesh and had thus become a tool of sin. Freed from that restricted perspective, the law still has an important part to play in the obedience of faith.[26]

Are Jewish Christians, then, forbidden to keep the law? Some say yes, arguing that the law was completely replaced by the new covenant and that this new system of grace has much in it that is similar to the "moral" teachings of the old law.[27] This approach argues that Paul consistently distinguishes between the *doing* of the law's commands, required of those who are subject to it, and the *fulfilling* of the law by Christians.[28] Matthew 5:17 and Romans 13:8 are used in support of this distinction. Jesus says in the former passage,

17. Westerholm, *Israel's Law,* 204.

18. Ibid., 206–7. He says Paul believed that "as Christians, the Galatians are not obliged to keep the law" (p. 207).

19. Ibid., 207.

20. Westerholm makes such a distinction. Larsson seems not to make such a distinction.

21. Westerholm, *Israel's Law,* 204.

22. Ibid., 205.

23. Howard, *Crisis in Galatia,* 66.

24. Ibid., 79.

25. Stendahl, *Paul among Jews and Gentiles,* 5.

26. This is the argument of James D. G. Dunn in *Romans 1–8,* Word Biblical Commentary 38 (Dallas: Word, 1988), lxxii.

27. E.g., Westerholm, *Israel's Law.*

28. Westerholm, *Israel's Law,* 203.

"Think not that I have come to abolish the law and the prophets; I have come not to abolish them but to fulfil them." Christians are never described as "doing" the law, but Jews "under the law" are obligated to "do" its commands (Rom. 10:5; Gal. 3:10, 12; 5:3). On the other hand, it is argued that where Christian behavior is related positively to the Mosaic law, Paul invariably uses πληροῦν (*plēroun*, fulfill) or a cognate (Rom. 8:4; 13:8, 10; Gal. 5:14). He never uses *fulfill* when talking of what the Jews did who lived under the law.[29]

2. This brings us to the alternative question, which is whether a Gentile Christian is obligated or allowed to keep any of the law. Here again scholars are divided in their responses. Some argue that the Judaizing Christians in Galatia taught that Gentile Christians had to keep circumcision and other elements of the law in order to *remain* in God's grace, not to *enter* that grace. The Gentile believers were viewed as already Christians, but keeping some elements of the law was now necessary to remain in that relationship.[30]

Others argue for a categorization of the elements of the law, stating that "Jewish Christians keep the entire Law of Moses; the Gentile-Christians keep just four rules out of it."[31] These four are viewed as moral principles, not ritual aspects of the law, though the issue of refraining from "what is strangled" (Acts 15:20) is arguably ritualistic. But it is of fundamental importance in this approach that the law has nothing to do with salvation for either the Jewish Christian or the Gentile Christian.[32] The Gentile Christians keep this part of the law only for the purpose of maintaining fellowship with Jewish Christians.

Others define the law as consisting of both moral and ritual categories and contend that Paul has been charged with ignoring them both.[33] It is argued that according to Paul the law must be kept by all Christians, both Jewish and Gentile, who indeed are the only ones who can keep it. "It is Christians and they alone who really fulfill what the Law requires."[34]

While some divide the law of Moses into moral and ceremonial categories, others argue that it is all one and that none of it is made binding on Christians. A Christian "has been freed from an obligation which applied to Jews under the old dispensation, that of observing the demands of the Law."[35] But, again, this approach does not carefully distinguish between Jewish and Gentile Christianity. It fails to see that Gentiles were never under the law of Moses

29. Ibid., 204.
30. E.g., Gundry, "Grace, Works," 8, 9, 11.
31. Larsson, "Paul, Law and Salvation," 434.
32. Ibid.
33. Heikki Räisänen, *Paul and the Law* (1983; reprint, Philadelphia: Fortress, 1986), 199.
34. Ibid., 115.
35. Westerholm, *Israel's Law,* 206.

and are not therefore "freed from it." They are, rather, exempt from having to be placed under it when they become Christians.

According to Westerholm, Christians have a new and different relationship to the law, one of "fulfillment." He says, "Christian love inevitably meets the standards set by the Law."[36] He argues that if Paul "considered the Law or any part of it still binding for the Christian, he would have had to provide his churches with detailed instructions as to which commands they were obligated to observe and which they were not . . . but there is no evidence that he made any such distinctions. On the contrary, it is clear that, for Paul, Torah was a unit. . . . The person who is obligated to observe the Law is obligated to observe its every precept."[37] Those who hold this view cite the Mishnah (*Avot* 2.1; 4.2).

Assessment

In assessing these views, I would suggest that no consideration of Paul's teaching on the law can be deemed satisfactory if it does not recognize that he had one view of the law for a Jew and another for a Gentile. This was inherent in his commission to be a Jewish apostle to the Gentile world. His position was that a Jew could keep the law but should not impose it upon the Gentiles and that even a Jew could keep it only for cultural and ethnic reasons, not as the means of salvation. This is abundantly clear in Paul's relation to Timothy and Titus. He circumcised Timothy, who had a Jewish mother (Acts 16:1; 2 Tim. 1:5), *after* Timothy had become a Christian (Acts 16:3), thereby making him a better Jew after he became a Christian than he had been before! But he did not require the circumcision of Titus because he was not a Jew but a Greek (Gal. 2:3). Although Paul's part in that decision is not explicit in Galatians, it is certainly implicit.

After preaching for several years and establishing churches among Gentiles on three missionary journeys, Paul returned to Jerusalem, where he acquiesced to the request of James and the elders to prove to Jewish Christians in Jerusalem that he still lived "in observance of the law" (Acts 21:24). Thereby he would show that he did not "teach all the Jews who are among the Gentiles to forsake Moses, telling them not to circumcise their children or observe the customs" (Acts 21:21).

It is constantly asserted in the Book of Acts that Jewish Christians, including Paul, continued to practice Judaism and keep the law after their conversion to the messianic faith. Twenty-eight relevant statements and events confirming this are listed in chapter 2, under "I Am a Jew."

36. Ibid., 202.
37. Ibid., 208.

Legalism versus Demonology

Although much of traditional Christian theology focuses its discussion of the law on the issue of legalism, attention is increasingly being given to the role of demonology in the improper application of the law, which has contributed to the cosmic denigration and denial of monotheism.[38] It is contended that in theology Paul considered the Judaizers synonymous with pagans, because by demanding circumcision the Judaizers were making God a national God of the Jews just as the pagans nationalized their gods in their idolatry and henotheism.[39]

It does seem that Paul's view of the law in Galatians 4:3 included the influence of demonology, for he says of Jews, "We were slaves to the elemental spirits of the universe [τὰ στοιχεῖα τοῦ κόσμου, *ta stoicheia tou kosmou*]." This was when the Jews were still children under a custodian (παιδάγωγος, *paidagōgos*), which was the law (Gal. 3:24).

The expression τὰ στοιχεῖα τοῦ κόσμου (*ta stoicheia tou kosmou*) can refer to material elements of the universe, as it evidently does in 2 Peter 3:10. But the Galatians context seems to demand more than this, because it appears to include both Jews and pagans together under the servitude of the "elemental spirits" (στοιχεῖα, *stoicheia*, Gal. 4:9). Paul says in Galatians that the Gentiles, who before they became Christians were in bondage to beings that were not really gods, are going back into that bondage by accepting the law; they are returning to being enslaved to the "weak and beggarly elemental spirits" (τὰ ἀσθενῆ καὶ πτωχὰ στοιχεῖα, *ta asthenē kai ptōcha stoicheia,* Gal. 4:9).

Jews traditionally accused the Gentiles of worshiping the elements as gods.[40] And the phrase in Galatians 4:8 (μὴ οὖσιν θεοῖς, *mē ousin theois,* "are no gods") reflects standard Old Testament polemic against idolatry:

Isa. 37:19	"for they were no gods (LXX, οὐ γὰρ θεοὶ ἦσαν, *ou gar theoi ēsan*), but the work of men's hands"
Jer. 2:11	"even though they are no gods" (LXX, καὶ οὗτοι οὐκ εἰσιν θεοί, *kai houtoi ouk eisin theoi*)
Jer. 5:7	"have sworn by those who are no gods" (LXX, τοῖς οὐκ οὖσιν θεοῖς, *tois ouk ousin theois*)
Jer. 16:20	"such are no gods" (LXX, οὗτοι οὐκ εἰσιν θεοί, *houtoi ouk eisin theoi*)

38. Howard, *Crisis in Galatia;* J. Louis Martyn, "Christ, the Elements of the Cosmos, and the Law in Galatians," in *The Social World of the First Century Christians: Essays in Honor of Wayne A. Meeks,* ed. L. Michael White and O. Larry Yarbrough (Minneapolis: Fortress, 1995).
39. Howard, *Crisis in Galatia.*
40. Wisdom of Solomon 13:2; Philo, *Contempl. Life* 3.

The real difficulty in the Galatians 4 passage is the inclusion of Jews with those who "turn back" (v. 9) to the elemental spirits by accepting the law. This clearly implies that the Jews (v. 3) were under bondage to these "elemental spirits" (στοιχεῖα, *stoicheia*) just like the pagans were in their idolatry!

Various approaches to these verses have been taken, all of which struggle with the seeming equation of Judaism with paganism.[41] Therefore, we must ask, in what sense does Paul consider the Jews' attitude toward the law to be essentially the same as that of the pagan Gentiles? Most scholars consider the problem to be one of legalism (relative to the Torah for Jews and the law of nature for Gentiles). Both had failed to keep their laws. The Jews, then, who did not keep their law were no different than the pagans.

From one viewpoint Christ redeemed *both Jew and Gentile* from the bondage to law since both were enslaved to legalistic principles.[42] Another approach sees in the passage a reference to both Jew and Gentile and asserts that Jews were subject to the elemental spirits just as the Gentiles were since the angels who mediated the law (Gal. 3:19) were among the elemental spirits.[43] On the other hand, the Gentiles were under the law like the Jews in the sense that they had the law of nature, which was to some extent equivalent to the revelation the Jews received in the Torah. (In Romans 1:18 Paul argues that the basic revelation to Gentiles was enough to make them responsible to God.)

A similar, though not identical, view sees in the Greek word νόμος (*nomos*, law) a reference to law in general, not to the Torah specifically.[44] Caird argues that both Gentile and Jew are under law in some sense, and Christ came to redeem both since subservience to law is enslavement to the elemental spirits. Galatians 4:8–9 applies to Gentiles, and in astrology the stars were held to be gods and were called στοιχεῖα (*stoicheia*), or elements. The unalterable law of astrological fate enslaved men and robbed them of hope and meaning in life. From this perspective, "the demonic forces of legalism, then, both Jew and Gentile, can be called 'principalities and powers' or 'elemental spirits of the world.'"[45]

A similar perspective has been put forward that views Judaism and paganism as converging to form a disciplinary period in which mankind was prepared for the coming of Christ.[46] Judaism was a system of bondage like hea-

41. See a list of these in Howard's discussion of this passage in his *Crisis in Galatia,* 66–82.

42. E. D. Burton, *A Critical and Exegetical Commentary on the Epistle to the Galatians,* International Critical Commentary (Edinburgh: Clark, 1921), 216, 219, 518.

43. Bo Reicke, "The Law and This World according to Paul: Some Thoughts concerning Galatians 4:1–11," *JBL* 70 (1951): 259–76.

44. G. B. Caird, *Principalities and Powers: A Study in Pauline Theology* (Oxford: Clarendon, 1956), 47–50.

45. Ibid., 51.

46. J. B. Lightfoot, *The Epistle of Paul to the Galatians* (1865; reprint, Grand Rapids: Zondervan, n.d.), 173.

thenism, and heathenism had been a disciplinary training like Judaism. Both were limited in the sense that both were under law, and law only served to underscore sin and even to exaggerate it. Neither could offer hope, since both were under weak and beggarly elemental spirits (Gal. 4:9). Here, too, legalism is the issue.

In these expositions of the passage in Galatians, *two presuppositions* are evident, both of which proceed along the lines of legalism:

1. To be subject to the requirements of the law is to be under bondage. This is taken to mean subservience to legal requirements and is assumed to be an evil that enslaves.
2. Legalism leads to the sin of pride. It is self-righteous.

The problem with this is the false assumption that legalism automatically places one in bondage. On the contrary, legal requirements in the civil realm provide the assurance of freedom and fairness. Close adherence to law by every citizen enhances the freedom and privileges everyone enjoys. "The fact is, man's problem never has been his enslavement to God's requirements; often, as Scripture shows, his problem has been estrangement from them. But in Galatians the problem was not that the Galatians were struggling with a law that was too hard to keep or that they were proud of their accomplishments. It was that they were enslaved to evil spirits who darkened their mind and led them into idolatry."[47] Paul's point was that the Galatian Christians, by placing themselves under the law, were returning to idolatry (Gal. 4:8–9), not that they were being legalistic.

Paul never deprecates the law. Even in Galatians 3:19 he is only trying to show that the law is separate from, not inferior to, the promise. *Paul's problem with the idolatry of paganism was not legalism but rather polytheism.* It is in this light that we must understand Galatians. Paul's view was certainly that of the intertestamental authors, who viewed pagan gods as demons (1 Cor. 10:20) that held the Gentile world in the bondage of idolatry.[48]

These authors believed that a time was coming when this falsehood of idolatry would be destroyed and truth established.[49] All nations at that time would leave their idols and come to Jehovah in united peace (*1 Enoch* 90.28–42; cf. Isa. 2:2–3). The impact of polytheism was to divide mankind and destroy the notion of universal humanity.

It is precisely this *partitioning effect* of the law—its capacity to divide Jew and Gentile—that Paul has in mind in his letter, an effect that was fostered by

47. Howard, *Crisis in Galatia,* 76.
48. See further D. S. Russell, *The Method and Message of Jewish Apocalyptic* (Philadelphia: Westminster, 1964, 235–62.
49. See the Dead Sea Scroll 1QS 4.18–23.

demonic influence. The Galatians who return to the law actually return to the divisiveness inherent in the elemental powers and consequently to enslavement to them once again. It was as important to genuine monotheistic belief for the Jew to accept uncircumcised Gentiles as it was for the Gentiles to refuse subservience to the law. Though they did not realize it, the Judaizers were in effect turning Christianity into a local cult.

Paul would say that "observance of the Law by Jewish Christianity was important for the salvation of the Gentile world and that non-observance of the Law by the Gentile Christians was important for the salvation of the Jewish world. Only in this way could he proclaim Yahweh, the God of the Hebrews, as the God of all nations. Only in this way could Israel ever conceptualize their God as a universal God, and only in this way could the Gentiles conceptualize the one God of the world as the God of Abraham the Hebrew."[50]

50. Howard, *Crisis in Galatia,* 81.

SIXTEEN

The Composition of Paul's Churches: Organization, Lord's Supper, and Baptism

Paul's Missionary Method

The apostle Paul had a significant impact on the organization and worship of the early church as he took the message of Jesus to the vast non-Jewish world beyond the borders of the Holy Land. When he founded a church in a town, he often left rather soon after converting some of its residents and moved on to another location. The duration of his stay was sometimes determined by the hostile opposition to his preaching by Jewish opponents in the synagogue (as at Thessalonica, Acts 17:2, 5), sometimes by the meager response of the Gentile residents (as in Athens, Acts 17:32–33), and sometimes by the rejection of both Jews and Gentiles (as at Iconium, Acts 14:5). On occasion he refused to stay longer without a reason being stated (as at Ephesus, of which Luke writes: "When they asked him to stay for a longer period, he declined," Acts 18:20). Whatever the cause, Paul usually did not stay in a town more than a few weeks or months (e.g., eighteen months in Corinth, Acts 18:11); a stay of three years in Ephesus was exceptional (Acts 20:31).

Paul's deliberate method was to begin his preaching in a synagogue and then, when rejected by most of its members, to turn to the Gentiles ("to the

Jew first and also to the Greek," Rom. 1:16).[1] He vocalized this approach in Antioch of Pisidia on his first journey, where he said to the large number of Jewish people who did not accept his message: "It was necessary that the word of God should be spoken first to you. Since you thrust it from you, and judge yourselves unworthy of eternal life, behold, we turn to the Gentiles" (Acts 13:46).

When Paul left these new churches, he had no New Testament to leave them and no one to leave behind to work with them. The Jews among the converts were acquainted with the Hebrew Scriptures, and the Gentiles knew only what they had observed about God in nature (Rom. 1:20), but neither had any knowledge of this new church of Jesus Christ, except what Paul told them. How were they now to worship? What would be the composition of the church ethnically, sexually, socially? How would the church function? How would it be organized? How would the leaders function? How would they be chosen? How could all of these issues and questions be dealt with after Paul left? How could they know they were doing what God wanted?

The answer lay in Paul's appointment of leaders chosen by each congregation to shepherd the flock after Paul and his companions left. This apparently was a method Paul consistently employed in his missionary work. For example, on the first journey, after Paul and Barnabas had preached in Asia Minor in the cities of Antioch, Iconium, Lystra, and Derbe (Acts 13:14–14:20), Luke writes that "when they had appointed elders for them in every church, with prayer and fasting, they committed them to the Lord in whom they believed" (Acts 14:23).

As time passed, others who had matured in the faith were appointed to leadership positions in these congregations. This was done later on the island of Crete by Titus, another traveling companion of Paul. Paul wrote him, saying, "This is why I left you in Crete, that you might amend what was defective, and appoint elders in every town as I directed you" (Titus 1:5). And Timothy evidently appointed men to office in the church in Ephesus after Paul had worked there for three years (Acts 20:17, 31). When he was going to Macedonia, Paul wrote that he had urged Timothy to remain at Ephesus to deal with issues of church leadership (1 Tim. 1:3), one of which was the appointing of overseers (1 Tim. 3:1–13) who should "rule well" as they "labor in preaching and teaching" (1 Tim. 5:17).

It also appears that God gave the supernatural manifestation of his Holy Spirit to many of these initial converts, which enabled them to demonstrate the possession of charismatic gifts and thus carry on the work and worship of the church by God's direction when the apostles were no longer with them. Although this is scarcely mentioned in Acts, it was probably a consistent phe-

---

1. See my discussion of this aspect of Paul's missionary method in chapter 6 on his second missionary journey—e.g., at Samothrace, Amphipolis, Apollonia, and Thessalonica.

nomenon in the evangelistic ministry of Paul. Luke does record an instance of this kind in Ephesus on Paul's third journey when about twelve disciples, whose gender is not identified, "were baptized in the name of the Lord Jesus. And when Paul had laid his hands upon them, the Holy Spirit came on them; and they spoke with tongues and prophesied" (Acts 19:5–6).

Christian scholarship is divided over whether these charismatic gifts continue today since we now have the written New Testament to convey the will of God, which these early converts did not have. But there is no doubt that these gifts enabled the early church to function through the guidance of the Spirit of God. In his letter to the new converts in Corinth, Paul addressed the abuses of these gifts, which was a very early problem in the church (1 Cor. 12–14).

There is no doubt as to the importance of these gifts in the leadership of the first-century church. Paul tells Timothy at one point to "rekindle the gift of God that is within you through the laying on of my hands" (2 Tim. 1:6). Through the teaching of his mother, Eunice, and his grandmother Lois (2 Tim. 1:5), Timothy had known from infancy the Hebrew Scriptures or sacred writings (2 Tim. 3:15). This Scripture, along with Paul's laying his hands on Timothy to transmit the Holy Spirit to him, had thoroughly equipped this young evangelist to proclaim the Word of God.

This is probably what Paul is referring to when he tells Timothy that "all scripture is inspired by God and profitable for teaching, for reproof, for correction, and for training in righteousness, that the man of God may be complete, equipped for every good work" (2 Tim. 3:16–17). Perhaps the phrase "man of God" here refers not just to Timothy as a man like any man committed to serving God but rather to the fact that he had received the laying on of Paul's hands and now possessed the Holy Spirit to give him direction in his ministry. In his first letter (1 Tim. 6:11), Paul had previously addressed Timothy directly (vocative case in Greek, ὦ ἄνθρωπε, ō anthrōpe) as "man of God." Possibly, then, Paul means to say that the Hebrew Scriptures, combined with Timothy's reception of the Holy Spirit through Paul's hands, have together equipped him with all he needs to perform his ministry. That is, he has both the Old Testament and the Holy Spirit's divinely inspired understanding of the New Testament, which was still in the process of being written at that time. Once that New Testament was completed and made available to the church, it would no longer require a supernatural revelation conveyed by the laying on of the apostles' hands.

Organization of Paul's Churches

The leadership of the churches in Paul's writings and in the section of the Book of Acts dealing with Paul consists of various categories involving the questions of age, gender, and maturity, as well as diversity of function. The fullest list of leadership categories in the Pauline corpus is given in Ephesians 4:11, where he lists apostles, prophets, evangelists, pastors, and teachers. Because of the contemporary, restrictive use of the term *pastor* for one who preaches to a congregation, it is better to translate the Greek word as "shepherd" to avoid confusing the preacher with the official referred to by this term, which I will discuss later. The word ποιμήν (*poimēn*) occurs seventeen times in the New Testament (Matt. 9:36; 25:32; 26:31; Mark 6:34; 14:27; Luke 2:8, 15, 18, 20; John 10:2, 11, 12, 14, 16; Eph. 4:11; Heb. 13:20; 1 Pet. 2:25) and is consistently translated *shepherd* every place except Ephesians 4:11.

Apostles

The first group is designated simply *apostles*, which means "those who are sent with a commission." A special closed group of apostles was selected by Jesus to accompany him during his ministry and to eventually carry the news of the gospel to all nations. This group of apostles is sometimes called generically the "twelve disciples" in the Gospel of Matthew (10:1; 11:1; 20:17; 26:20); at other times they are given the exclusive title of simply "the twelve" (Mark 3:14; 6:7; Luke 8:1; 18:31; Acts 6:2). Paul uses this latter designation in 1 Corinthians 15:5 when he refers to a postresurrection appearance of Jesus to this exclusive group. Jesus had earlier told them that they would "sit on twelve thrones, judging the twelve tribes of Israel" (Matt. 19:28; Luke 22:30). It appears that the number of this special group was based on the number of the tribes that constituted Israel, and they symbolically represented the Jewish nation on the Day of Pentecost, when the church began among the Jews (Acts 2:1, 5). Paul refers to the nation of Israel in his defense before King Agrippa as "our twelve tribes" (Acts 26:7), and James addresses his letter to the Jews living outside Israel in Asia Minor as "the twelve tribes in the Dispersion" (James 1:1; cf. Rev. 21:12).

It was typologically important that the number be kept at twelve for the Pentecost event; so when Judas Iscariot, who is called "one of the twelve" (Mark 14:10; John 6:70), betrayed Jesus, he had to be replaced from among 120 disciples before Pentecost (Acts 1:21–22). Judas had been "numbered" (κατηριθμημένος, *katērithmēmenos*) among the twelve and "allotted his share" (ἔλαχεν τὸν κλῆρον, *elachen ton klēron*) in their ministry (Acts 1:17). The person who replaced Judas had to have been with Jesus from his baptism until his ascension and was to become a witness to his resurrection (Acts 1:22).

The word *apostle* came to have a broader use in the passing years after the death of Jesus, being used also of those who were commissioned by churches to specific tasks as special envoys or spiritual ambassadors. Paul and Barnabas are designated apostles in Acts 14:14. Andronicus and Junias are described by

Paul as people "of note among the apostles" in Romans 16:7. And in Hebrews 3:1, Jesus himself is called the "apostle and high priest of our confession."

So the word *apostle* was used of more than just the Twelve. Paul refers to himself as an apostle (1 Cor. 9:1), although he considers himself to be the "least of the apostles" because he had persecuted the church of God (1 Cor. 15:9). In a previous verse (1 Cor. 15:7), Paul speaks of Christ's postresurrection appearance to "all the apostles" and then to himself last of all "as to one untimely born" (1 Cor. 15:8). Here Paul uses the Greek term ἔκτρωμα (*ektrōma*), which means a "miscarriage," or one "untimely born" or "born out of the normal (nine-month) birth sequence." He is acknowledging that he is an apostle but not one of the Twelve. Yet he is emphatic that although he is not one of the original twelve, he nevertheless is an apostle who has seen the resurrected Lord (1 Cor. 9:1) and has been entrusted with the gospel to the uncircumcised (Gentiles, cf. Acts 26:17), just as Peter has been entrusted with the gospel to the circumcised (Jews, Gal. 2:7–8).

Prophets

The second group of leaders in Ephesians 4:11 is the prophets, who, along with the apostles, are spoken of by Paul as the foundation of the church in Ephesians 2:20. Since a foundation can only be laid once, these ministries belonged to the initial founding phase of the church, in essence its Jewish foundation. In Ephesians 3:5, Paul refers to apostles and prophets again when discussing the mystery of the gospel, which is the inclusion of the Gentiles in the church on an equal basis with the Jews. The mystery that has been revealed is a *present* reality, which is that "the Gentiles are fellow heirs, members of the same body, and partakers of the promise in Christ Jesus through the gospel" (Eph. 3:6). Paul says this mystery "has now been revealed to his holy apostles and prophets by the Spirit" (Eph. 3:5).

This verse clearly shows that Paul was not thinking of Old Testament prophets. They would have been listed *before* the apostles, but in all three passages in Ephesians (2:20; 3:5; 4:11), Paul places the prophets in second position.

This second gift to the church, that of prophets, is an independent office or function. The prophets functioned in the initial phases of the establishment of the church (Acts 13:1; 21:9; 1 Cor. 14:1–39), but being a part of the foundation with the apostles, their ministry was not intended to be perpetual. "The foundation has been laid once-for-all and will not go on being laid."[2] Their task may have been to relate Old Testament events and prophecies to the New Testament era. There were prophets in the church at Antioch with Hebrew, Greek, and Latin names (Acts 13:1). There were prophets in the church in Jerusalem, such as Agabus (Acts 11:27–28). Prophets were ap-

---

2. Ernest Best, *Essays on Ephesians* (Edinburgh: Clark, 1997), 159.

pointed in the church in Corinth (1 Cor. 14:29–32), who evidently included women as well as men (1 Cor. 11:4–5). Philip's four unmarried (παρθένοι, *parthenoi*) daughters prophesied in Caesarea Maritima (Acts 21:8–9). Prophecy is one of the nine charismatic gifts enumerated in 1 Corinthians 12:8–11, but not everyone who prophesied occupied the office of prophet, just as not everyone who worships in church occupies the office of worship leader. Prophecy was a gift to various church members for the building up of the body of Christ on the foundation of the offices of apostles and prophets.

Since the apostles and prophets are considered by Paul to be the foundation of the church in Ephesians 2:20, they constitute an important part of the Jewish substructure upon which the Gentile churches are built. Paul's carefully constructed argument in Ephesians 1–4 is designed to show how the gospel was brought to the vast non-Jewish world by the Jews, and although Paul considered himself to be the "least of all the [Jewish] saints," he had been given the grace "to preach to the Gentiles" (Eph. 3:8).[3] It is, therefore, significant that prophets in the church in Antioch were involved in the commissioning of Barnabas and Paul to begin their work as missionaries among the Gentiles (Acts 13:1–3) and "thus may have been more widely involved in the movement towards the Gentiles than is sometimes thought."[4]

If this analysis is correct, it may suggest that in Ephesians 4:11 the apostles and prophets formed the Jewish foundation upon which the Gentile superstructure of evangelists, shepherds, and teachers was built. Paul probably is thinking here of the exclusive twelve apostles and those Jewish prophets who were involved in the beginning of the church. Both Gentiles and Jews in the church were granted the offices or functions of evangelists, shepherds, and teachers.

Evangelists

The third group of officials is designated evangelists. The word *evangelist* (εὐαγγελίστης, *euangelistēs*), which derives from the verb εὐαγγελίζομαι (*euangelizomai*), meaning to "announce the good news," is applied to Paul's traveling companion Timothy, who is told by Paul to "do the work of an evangelist" (ἔργον ποίησον εὐαγγελιστοῦ, *ergon poiēson euangelistou*, 2 Tim. 4:5). He is also told to "preach the word" (κήρυξον τὸν λόγον, *kēruxon ton logon*, 2 Tim. 4:2) and is called a "minister" (διάκονος, *diakonos*, 1 Tim. 4:6)—probably not in its specialized sense of "deacon" as the word is used in 1 Timothy 3:8. It is significant that Timothy is referred to by the noun form *evangelist* (2 Tim. 4:5) while he is expected to "remain at Ephesus" (1 Tim. 1:3) to carry on the work Paul has begun there. Thus, he is expected not to travel

---

3. See further my discussion of "saints" as Jewish Christians in chapter 13.
4. Best, *Ephesians,* 159.

but to work in a designated city. He is not told by Paul to seek the conversion of unbelievers but to attend "to the public reading of scripture, to exhorting [παράκλησις, *paraklēsis*], to teaching" (1 Tim. 4:13 NRSV). This exhortation is further specified in the command "Do not rebuke an older man but exhort [παρακαλέω, *parakaleō*] him as you would a father" (1 Tim. 5:1).

The only other occurrence of the noun *evangelist* in the New Testament is in Acts 21:8, where Philip, one of the seven who has been appointed to relieve the apostles in Jerusalem from administrative duties (Acts 6:1–6), is later called an evangelist. At that time he is living in Caesarea Maritima with his four virgin daughters, who prophesy. It thus appears that he is no longer a "traveling missionary" when he wears this title.

The term *evangelist,* then, is not restricted to one who proclaims the good news about Jesus to unbelievers. Paul writes to the Christians in Rome, "I am eager to preach the gospel [evangelize, εὐαγγελίζομαι, *euangelizomai*] to you also who are in Rome" (Rom. 1:15). He still preaches the cross to *believers* in Corinth (1 Cor. 1–4). Thus, care needs to be exercised lest we be too rigid in our differentiation of the functions of the various ministries enumerated in Paul's writings. Often they are not exclusive ministries, and people like Paul and others in Acts functioned in multiple capacities. Paul was an apostle, an evangelist, a prophet, a teacher, and a shepherd. It should not be assumed, for example, that being a teacher excludes the role of evangelist. When Paul evangelizes Sergius Paulus on the island of Cyprus, his work is referred to as teaching (Acts 13:12). An evangelist may teach, just as a teacher may evangelize. Their titles merely designate the primary roles they were called to fill.

Shepherds and Teachers

The last two terms used by Paul in Ephesians 4:11 of the later offices in the church are *shepherds* and *teachers.* Whether Paul speaks here of two different offices or of two functions performed by the same office is debatable. The latter view can be supported by the author's use of the Greek article ("the") before each of the first three offices—apostles, prophets, and evangelists—while linking the last two together with only one article before shepherds (τοὺς δὲ ποιμένας καὶ διδασκάλους, *tous de poimenas kai didaskalous*). But the former view can be supported by the rejoinder that in Ephesians 2:20 and 3:5 Paul names apostles and prophets in the same way, using only one article though they clearly constitute two offices. If Paul means to separate shepherds (bishops) and teachers as offices in the organization of the church, it is not because shepherds or bishops do not teach. In 1 Timothy 3:2 he states that a bishop must be an apt teacher. In a broader sense of the term, all Christians are expected to teach each other in various ways (Col. 3:16; Heb. 5:12).

It should be remembered that in the language of the New Testament, shepherds were also elders (1 Peter 5:1–5). In Paul's speech to the *elders* (presbyters, πρεσβύτεροι, *presbyteroi*) of Ephesus in Miletus (Acts 20:17), he calls them *overseers* (or bishops, ἐπίσκοποι, *episkopoi*) and charges them to "tend the flock" (ποιμαίνειν ποίμνιον, *poimainein poimnion*), or be *shepherds* (Acts 20:28). Thus, all three terms are employed for the same men. These men, known as presbyters or elders, overseers or bishops, and pastors or shepherds, are referred to in these various ways to emphasize the different functions and qualifications for their offices.

The word *presbyter* connotes age. It is a transliteration of the Greek term πρεσβύτερος (*presbyteros*) and refers to an older person and hence is sometimes rendered by the rather archaic term *elder.* This is the word that gives its name to the presbyterian form of church government. In today's churches, those who hold the title of elder are often younger men who would be offended if they were called by the more contemporary translation "older." This is, however, the meaning the term is intended to convey—age. Among Jews of the New Testament period, the elders who oversaw the synagogues were never "youngers." In the Jewish culture, as well as throughout the Middle East and Asia, older people have always been highly respected, honored, and cherished for their wisdom. Contemporary Western societies would be greatly enhanced by emulating this attitude that is so pervasive in Eastern cultures.

The Greek word ἐπίσκοπος (*episkopos*) is the second term used of these officials in the New Testament. It is translated "bishop" or "overseer" and indicates *function.* The episcopal form of church government derives its name from this word. The verb form (*episkopeō*) means "to look over or oversee" and is graphically employed for the name of Mount Scopus, north of Mount Olivet, which overlooks or oversees Jerusalem.

The third word used for this office in the New Testament is *shepherd,* which also indicates function, specifically leadership. The Greek term ποιμήν (*poimēn*), the word used here in Ephesians 4:11, is translated "pastor" in this verse in most major versions even though it is consistently translated "shepherd" in the other sixteen passages where it appears in the New Testament.[5] Paul uses the word here to convey the idea that an overseer or elder of a congregation functions as a shepherd tending sheep (cf. Acts 20:17–28), not as a cowboy in the Western world, herding or driving cattle.

Elder and *bishop* are thus synonymous terms in Paul's speech in Acts 20:17 and 28, as they are in Titus 1:5, where Paul writes that he left Titus in Crete to "appoint elders in every town" and then beginning in verse 7 adds the qualifications that "a bishop" must have.[6]

---

5. For example, KJV, RSV, TEV, NIV, JB, NEB.
6. See the discussion on the two terms in William D. Mounce, *Pastoral Epistles,* Word Biblical Commentary 46 (Nashville: Nelson, 2000), 160–66, 307–9.

Elders were appointed in various cities, such as in Philippi (Phil. 1:1), in towns on the island of Crete (Titus 1:5), and in Jerusalem (Acts 11:30). This is probably the meaning of Acts 14:23, which states that Paul and Barnabas "appointed elders . . . in every church." The use of *church* here probably indicates that the church was coterminus with the city, as in Titus 1:5. Groups evidently met in small house churches in a city, and the elders oversaw them all (cf. Rom. 16:5, 14, 15, and perhaps 10 and 11; Col. 4:15). This was the norm in the three centuries prior to the reign of the Roman emperor Constantine, who first allowed the church to own property as a *religio licita,* a "legal religion," and thus to build church buildings.

There is no distinction between an elder and a bishop in *1 Clement,* which was written about A.D. 90.[7] Clement writes that the apostles preached "from district to district and from city to city where they appointed their first converts to be bishops and deacons of the future believers."[8] In *1 Clement* 44.1 he refers to a bishop as a part of the episcopate, who are called "blessed Presbyters" in verses 4 and 5.

Bishops and elders are first differentiated in Ignatius of Antioch, who died in A.D. 108. He wrote to the church in Smyrna in Asia Minor: "See that you all follow the bishop as Jesus Christ follows the Father, and the presbytery as if it were the Apostles. And reverence the deacons as the command of God" (Ign. *Smyrn.* 8.1). He goes on to say that it is not lawful to either baptize or hold an "agape" (love feast) without "the bishop." He refers to "the bishop, the presbyters, and the deacons" in his letter *To the Philadelphians* (introduction). Eusebius in his early-fourth-century church history (*Hist. eccl.* 3.22) lists Ignatius as the second bishop of Antioch, behind Euodius.

The modern division of church government into a threefold system with a bishop, a subordinate group of elders or presbyters, and another subordinate group of deacons has no parallel in Paul's writings or anywhere in the New Testament. These officers are always referred to as constituting a plurality in one church. Never is there a plurality of churches under one bishop in the New Testament (cf. Jerusalem in Acts 11:30; Asia Minor in Acts 14:23; Jerusalem in Acts 15:6; Ephesus in Acts 20:17; Philippi in Phil. 1:1). There was complete congregational autonomy (i.e., self-government), yet the churches cooperated (Acts 11:29).

In Ignatius's differentiation between elders and bishops,[9] there is no indication that his references to the bishop[10] in these letters is to an office of a monarchial bishop,[11] which developed only later, but rather to one who was a

---

7. *1 Clem.* 42.4; 44.1–4.
8. Ibid., 42.4.
9. Ign. *Magn.* 13.1; Ign. *Eph.* 2.3; 4.1; Ign. *Trall.* 3.1.
10. Ign. *Trall.* 3.1; Ign. *Smyrn.* 8.1b.
11. *Monarchial* is a term that is applied in later church history to the position occupied by one bishop who is put in an authoritative position over other bishops of a church or diocese.

preacher or minister like Timothy and Titus.[12] No evidence for such an office exists prior to his writings. Ignatius is evidently trying to establish the position of a monarchial bishop rather than representing it as already in existence. He argues that "the bishop's" voice is equal to that of Christ,[13] and he says that apart from "the bishop" there is only error.[14] There is a hint of the roots of apostolic succession in his letters, in which the apostles are represented by the eldership or presbytery.[15] He writes to the church in Tralles, "Let all respect the deacons as Jesus Christ, even as the bishop is also a type of the Father, and the presbyters as the council of God and the college of the Apostles."[16]

Deacons

The *deacons* constitute another category of church leaders discussed by Paul in 1 Timothy 3 and Titus 1, but they are not mentioned in Ephesians 4:11. The term *deacon* is a transliteration of the Greek word διάκονος (*diakonos*), which is normally translated in general contexts as "servant." The deacons are referred to as holding an independent office when Paul addresses his letter to the church in Philippi to "all the saints in Christ Jesus who are at Philippi, with the bishops and deacons" (Phil. 1:1). Qualifications for the office are set forth beginning in 1 Timothy 3:8, immediately following those of the bishops. Phoebe was possibly a deaconess of the church in Cenchreae. Paul refers to her with this term in Romans 16:1. Whether the term *deaconess* refers to a separate office for women, to the wives of the deacons, or just to servants in the church is not clear.

The origin of this group of church officials is not enunciated by Paul, but some find it in the appointment of the seven men in Acts 6 to assist the apostles in administrating the physical needs of Grecian widows in Jerusalem. However, these seven were not necessarily deacons. While it is true that the verb form (διακονέω, *diakoneō*) of the noun *deacon* (διάκονος, *diakonos*) is used in Acts 6:2 in reference to the need to "serve tables," this does not necessarily imply that those who served were deacons in the technical sense of that term, that is, holding an office by that name. This verb is commonly used in the New Testament for anyone who serves in any capacity:

Paul (Rom. 15:25)

Timothy and Erastus (Acts 19:22)

12. Cf. F. F. Bruce, *The Spreading Flame: The Rise and Progress of Christianity from Its First Beginnings to the Conversion of the English* (Grand Rapids: Eerdmans, 1961), 205, who compares this bishop to a modern church minister.
13. Ign. *Smyrn.* 8.1; Ign. *Magn.* 6.1.
14. Ign. *Eph.* 4.1–2; Ign. *Magn.* 3.2; Ign. *Trall.* 2.1–2; Ign. *Smyrn.* 8.2; 9.1.
15. Ign. *Smyrn.* 8.1.
16. Ign. *Trall.* 3.1.

Onesimus (Philem. 13)
Prophets of the Old Testament (1 Pet. 1:12)
Angels (Matt. 4:11)
Peter's mother-in-law (Matt. 8:15)
Martha (John 12:2)
Jesus (Matt. 20:28)

The noun *deacon* is also commonly used for anyone who is a servant in various capacities (a total of twenty-nine times in the New Testament):

Household servants (John 2:5)
Paul and Apollos (1 Cor. 3:5)
Timothy (1 Thess. 3:2)
Satan's servants (2 Cor. 11:15)
Phoebe (Rom. 16:1)
Jesus (Rom. 15:8)

Nowhere in the Book of Acts are the seven men of Acts 6 called by the noun form *deacon* (διάκονος, *diakonos*), which does not appear in the book. They were a special group known simply as "the seven," and later Philip the evangelist was remembered as "one of the seven" (not "one of the deacons"), when he no longer lived in Jerusalem but resided in Caesarea Maritima (Acts 21:8). Later, the church in Philippi had deacons (Phil. 1:1), but none are mentioned in Jerusalem.

So who were "the seven"? They were probably "almoners," men who distribute alms,[17] who later became elders, as the following points argue. (1) Their work is designated as caring for the needy. They were chosen for the apostles to "appoint to this duty" (χρεία, *chreia,* Acts 6:3), which was specifically to care for the neglected Grecian widows. (2) The same work of caring for the needy is done by elders in Acts 11:29–30. (3) No elders are mentioned in the Jerusalem church before Acts 11. Their appointment is probably recounted here in chapter 6. If not, there is no record of their appointment (Jewish elders appear in Acts 4:5, 8, 23, etc.). (4) Although deacons never are named in Acts, a pattern appears for the appointment of elders.

Acts 1–5	The apostles govern the church in Jerusalem, caring for their spiritual needs (Acts 6:2).
Acts 6	Elders are appointed to relieve the apostles in caring for the needy.

17. F. F. Bruce, *The Book of the Acts,* rev. ed., NICNT (Grand Rapids: Eerdmans, 1988), 122.

Acts 11	Elders care for the needy. The money brought from Antioch to help those in Jerusalem is not given to any deacons or to the apostles, evidently because of the reason stated in Acts 6:2–3, but rather is given "to the elders" (Acts 11:30).
Acts 15:2, 4	Apostles and elders appear together as a group in Acts 15:6, 22, 23; 16:4.

And thus it might be concluded that the apostles shepherded the church in Jerusalem until the influx of new Christian converts from Hellenistic Judaism, who began to be neglected by the Hebrew Christians in the daily ministration of food and other necessitites. Thus, when the apostles eventually needed help so that they could continue their work as spiritual leaders, they told the church, "It is not right that we should give up preaching the word of God to serve tables" (Acts 6:2). So men were appointed "to this duty" (Acts 6:3) and later received money from Antioch to meet some of these needs, money which was sent to Jerusalem "to the elders by the hand of Barnabas and Saul" (Acts 11:30). Then when the apostles were later sent out of Jerusalem to engage in the worldwide mission of converting non-Jews, according to the Great Commission Christ had given them (Matt. 28:18–20), they left Jerusalem in the care of these elders.

Though it is not mentioned in Acts, it is likely that these elders, like the apostles they were chosen to assist, would now need help too. They assumed the work in Jerusalem previously done by the apostles in caring for the spiritual needs of the church, and deacons would need to be appointed to take the elders' place in caring for the physical needs of the group. Churches throughout the Roman Empire were evidently organized this way, with elders (bishops or shepherds) to guide the churches spiritually and deacons to assist with material needs. Philippians 1:1 is addressed to elders and deacons in the church in Philippi, and both 1 Timothy and Titus have qualifications for these two groups of church officials in Ephesus and on the island of Crete.

These elders, known as "the seven" (Acts 21:8), thus operated alongside the Twelve (apostles) in the Jerusalem church as a special group with a special job. Josephus, writing in the New Testament period, says Jewish villages of this period were governed by groups of seven men (*Ant.* 4.8.14, 38; *J.W.* 2.20.5). Perhaps this is the reason seven men were chosen in Jerusalem.

Method of Appointing Officials

The method used by Paul in organizing the churches he founded included the appointment of elders and deacons to function as leaders after he left. His methods can be detected in the references in his letters to these appointments and by comparing them with those appointments of various officials recorded in Acts, both in Jerusalem and in the churches Paul founded outside Israel. There appears to be a basic pattern in these appointments, involving two parts:

First, the congregation or group selects the men.
Second, the appointments are then made to their specific work.

Five instances of such appointments that can be used to determine the method are contained in Acts and Paul's letters.

The first appointment relates to the replacement of an apostle, Judas Iscariot, with Matthias in Acts 1:15–26.

1. The selection of two men, Justus and Matthias, was made initially by "the brethren" (Acts 1:15), who are described as a "company of persons . . . in all about one hundred and twenty." Luke writes: "*they* put forward two" (v. 23), "*they* prayed" (v. 24), and "*they* cast lots" (v. 26). The apostles did not choose the two candidates; the disciples did. Then they cast lots for the two, and God made the final choice (v. 26).

2. The appointment of Matthias was then made when he was "enrolled with the eleven" (v. 26) after his selection by the disciples.

The second example is the selection of men to assist the apostles in Jerusalem in Acts 6:1–7. Peter said, "Pick out from among you seven men . . . whom we may appoint."

1. The selection was made by "the *body* of the disciples" (v. 2). The *brethren* chose among themselves (v. 3), and "these *they* set before the apostles" (v. 6). What the twelve apostles said "pleased the *whole multitude,* and *they* chose" (v. 4).

2. The twelve apostles did not choose the seven. They *appointed* (καταστήσομεν, *katastēsomen,* v. 3) them to office *after* their selection (v. 6). The announcement was made by the Twelve (v. 2), who "prayed and laid their hands upon" the seven chosen by the whole multitude (v. 6).

The third example of appointments is in Acts 15:22–25, where delegates are chosen to accompany Paul and Barnabas to represent the Jerusalem church in Antioch of Syria.

1. The delegates were chosen by "the apostles, and the elders, *with the whole church*" (v. 22). It was a unified selection. The church wrote in an accompanying letter that "it seemed good to us *having come to one accord* [RSV, 2d ed.], to choose men" (v. 25). The NIV translates the Greek word ὁμοθυμαδόν (*homothymadon*) as *"we all agreed."* This word is also used in Acts 1:14; 4:24; 8:6; 15:25; 19:29; and Romans 15:6. A close parallel use of this word occurs in Acts 5:12.

2. The apostles and elders shared in the process but did not arbitrarily appoint men who had not been selected by the "whole church," as is often done in churches today. Luke writes that when the process of selection was completed and the letter was written to accompany them, "they were sent off" (Acts 15:30). Presumably this was their commissioning and appointment to their duties, probably by the laying on of hands as in Acts 6:5–6.

The next instance of an appointment is the selection of someone to accompany Titus, who was taking a contribution to the church in Jerusalem. This is referred to by Paul in 2 Corinthians 8:18–19.

1. Titus's companion, who was "famous among all the churches for his preaching of the gospel," was "appointed" by those churches to accompany Titus (v. 19). Appointment here does not mean an arbitrary commission by a church leader. The Greek word for *appoint* in this passage, χειροτονέω (*cheirotoneō*), originally meant to "stretch out one's hand for the purpose of giving one's vote in the assembly,"[18] "to choose, elect by raising hands."[19] Thus it seems that the process involved the churches in selecting this person by voting.

2. This companion, having been chosen by a hand vote, was "sent" by Paul and his associates, like the delegates sent by the Jerusalem church to Antioch in Acts 15:30.

The fourth example of appointments has to do with the selection of elders in Acts 14:23.

1. Though it is not stated, the elders were probably selected by a congregational show of hands.

2. The apostles Paul and Barnabas (Acts 14:14) "appointed elders for them in every church," including Antioch, Iconium, Lystra, and

18. LSJ, 1986.
19. BAGD, 889.

Derbe (Acts 14:20–23). The Greek word for *appoint* here is the same one used in 2 Corinthians 8:18 and thus reflects the method used by Paul and Barnabas, that of having the congregation express by a show of hands the ones they want, after which the apostles commissioned them to office. The point is that the word *appoint* here does not mean choose or select but rather to acknowledge by the show of hands, which is something the congregation did, not the apostles. The meaning of this Greek word is illustrated by a mid-second-century text in which Polycarp, an elder of the church in Smyrna, is asked "to summon a godly council and elect [χειροτονέω, *cheirotoneō*] someone . . . and appoint [καταξιόω, *kataxioō*, consider worthy][20] him to go to Syria. . . ."[21]

The fifth and final example is found in Paul's letter to Titus, where Titus is told to "appoint elders in every town" (Titus 1:5). The Greek word *appoint* (καταστήσῃς, *katastēsēs*) in this verse, though different from the one in Acts 14:23, is the same as the one in Acts 6:3, where the congregation chooses (ἐκλέγω, *eklegō*) and the apostles appoint (καθίστημι, *kathistēmi*). Thus, the sequence was probably the same:

1. The congregation chose the elders.
2. Titus then appointed (not chose) the elders in every town.

Qualifications of Elders and Deacons

In the letters of Paul to Timothy and Titus, the specific qualifications of those who are to be chosen by the congregations and appointed to their offices as church leaders are precisely spelled out. Considering the involvement of the congregations, stated or implied, in the selecting of their leaders in the five instances cited above, it is not surprising to find that almost the same qualifications expected of elders and deacons are also required of every Christian. This shows that in Paul's mind one is not first appointed to the office and then expected to develop the qualities gradually. The fact that leaders are chosen from the congregation by the congregation means that they must meet the qualifications before being chosen as candidates for the office, and they must therefore already be living the kind of life outlined in this list of requirements. A careful comparison of the qualifications for leaders in 1 Timothy 3 and Titus 1 with those for all Christians elsewhere in the New Testament shows their similarity.

20. BAGD, 415.
21. Ign. *Pol.* 7.2.

Table 16.1 Qualifications of Elders, Deacons, and Christians

Quality	Elders	Deacons	Christians
1. Without reproach	a. ἀνεπίλημπτον (1 Tim. 3:2) b. ἀνέγκλητος (Titus 1:6, 7)	a. ἀνέγκλητοι (1 Tim. 3:10)	a. 1 Tim. 5:7; 6:14 b. 1 Cor. 1:8; Col. 1:22
2. Husband of one wife	μιᾶς γυναικὸς ἄνδρα (1 Tim. 3:2; Titus 1:6)	μιᾶς γυναικὸς ἄνδρες (1 Tim. 3:12)	1 Cor. 7:2
3. Ruling household well	a. children in subjection, ἐν ὑποταγῇ (1 Tim. 3:4) b. τέκνα . . . πιστά (Titus 1:6) c. προΐστημι (cf. 1 Tim. 5:17, elder's rule)	a. ruling children well, καλῶς προϊστάμενοι (1 Tim. 3:12) c. and their houses (1 Tim. 3:12)	a. 1 Pet. 5:5; Eph. 6:1–4; Col. 3:20–21 c. Eph. 5:23; 6:4
4. Temperate	a. temperate (in the use of wine) νηφάλιον (1 Tim. 3:2) b. μὴ πάροινον (1 Tim. 3:3; Titus 1:7)	a. not given to much wine (addicted to, προσέχω, 1 Tim. 3:8)	a. Titus 2:2 (older men) b. Titus 2:3, not enslaved, δουλόω (older women)
5. No brawler	μὴ πλήκτην (1 Tim. 3:3; Titus 1:7)		Titus 3:2
6. Sober-minded, prudent	a. self-controlled, σώφρονα (1 Tim. 3:2; Titus 1:8) b. self-controlled, ἐγκρατῆ (Titus 1:8)		a. Titus 2:2 (older men); Titus 2:5 (younger women); 1 Tim. 2:9, 15 (women) b. ἐγκράτεια (Gal. 5:23)
7. Orderly (respectable, honorable)	κόσμιον (1 Tim. 3:2)		1 Tim. 2:9; 1 Peter 3:5 (women)
8. Given to hospitality	φιλόξενον (1 Tim. 3:2; Titus 1:8)		1 Pet. 4:9; Rom. 12:13; Heb. 13:2 (φιλοξενία)
9. Apt to teach (skilled in teaching)	διδακτικόν (1 Tim. 3:2)		2 Tim. 2:24

Quality	Elders	Deacons	Christians
10. No bully	a. μὴ πλήκτην (1 Tim. 3:3; Titus 1:7)		a. Eph. 4:26; Titus 3:2
	b. not quick tempered, ὀργίλον (Titus 1:7)		b. Matt. 5:22; Eph. 4:26, 31 (ὀργίζω)
11. Gentle	a. ἐπιεικῆ (1 Tim. 3:3)		a. Titus 3:2
	b. not contentious, ἄμαχον (1 Tim. 3:3)		
12. No lover of money	a. ἀφιλάργυρον (1 Tim. 3:3)		a. Heb. 13:5
	b. not fond of dishonest gain, αἰσχροκερδῆ (Titus 1:7)		b. Titus 1:11 (αἰσχροῦ κέρδους)
13. Not a novice	νεόφυτον (1 Tim. 3:6)	first be proved (1 Tim. 3:10)	cf. 1 Pet. 2:2; 1 Cor. 3:2 with Heb. 5:12–14
14. Good testimony from without	μαρτυρίαν (1 Tim. 3:7)	gain good standing (1 Tim. 3:13)	Col. 4:5; 1 Thess. 4:12
15. Not self-willed	αὐθάδης (Titus 1:7)		2 Pet. 2:10
16. Lover of good	φιλάγαθον (Titus 1:8)		Heb. 13:16; 1 Tim. 6:18; Gal. 5:22; 1 Thess. 5:15; Titus 3:2
17. Just, upright	δίκαιον (Titus 1:8)		1 Pet. 4:18; 1 Tim. 1:9
18. Holy	ὅσιον (Titus 1:8)		1 Tim. 2:8
19. Holding to the faithful word	ἀντεχόμενον (Titus 1:8)	holding to the mystery of the faith (1 Tim. 3:9)	Col. 3:16–17
20. Grave		serious, σέμνους (1 Tim. 3:8); dignified, worthy of respect	Titus 2:2 (older men)
21. Not double-tongued		διλόγους (1 Tim. 3:8)	Eph. 4:25

These qualifications fall into two categories, *absolute* and *relative*. The absolute qualifications are expected of elders but are not required of every church member. There are two qualifications in the absolute category.

The first is that he not be a novice, or a neophyte (νεόφυτον, *neophyton*). He must have been a Christian long enough to be mature in the faith and for the church to respect him and be willing to follow him as a shepherd. On the other hand, Christians are inherently novices when they first come to the faith (1 Pet. 2:2; 1 Cor. 3:2), and so some time is required for them to change this status (Heb. 5:12–13).

The second absolute qualification is that an elder be the husband of one wife (1 Tim. 3:2; Titus 1:6) and have believing children. It is, of course, not required that a man be married or have children in order to be a disciple of Christ. This requirement complements the first one in that the time allowed for one to bring his children to faith removes him from the possibility of being a novice.

The second category is designated *relative* because all Christians are expected to hold these qualifications to some degree, as the fourth column above shows. Since the elders are to be chosen from among the flock, all of whom are expected to manifest these qualifications, elders, like all Christians, will hold these qualities to a greater or lesser degree, depending on age, maturity, training, self-discipline, and so on. Hence, the qualifications are relative.

These two categories of qualifications assure that those chosen from the congregation to be appointed as shepherds will already be respected by the flock they are to lead. Shepherds cannot be arbitrarily forced on a flock. If the sheep do not already know and trust them, the sheep will not follow them. Cattle can be driven; sheep must be led. Literal shepherds are thus models for spiritual shepherds. This principle of choosing respected leaders from the congregation also applies to deacons, who are appointed to serve the flock.

Paul's Churches and the Church in Jerusalem

Paul's instructions for the organization and functioning of churches in the areas of his missionary work reflect much the same arrangement as the church in Jerusalem. As noted above, the Jerusalem church appointed men to assist the apostles and eventually to replace them when the apostles left Jerusalem to carry out the commission given them to go to all nations (Matt. 28:18–20). This took place about ten or fifteen years after the church was founded on Pentecost (Acts 2).

After several years of evangelizing only Jews, in accordance with Jesus' commissioning statement that they were to "go nowhere among the Gentiles, and enter no town of the Samaritans, but go rather to the lost sheep of the house of Israel" (Matt. 10:5–6), Peter was divinely sent to the house of the

Gentile Cornelius in Caesarea Maritima. Peter later said of this occasion, "God made choice among you, that by my mouth the Gentiles should hear the word of the gospel and believe" (Acts 15:7; cf. Acts 10–11).

So, when the twelve apostles left Jerusalem, the leadership of the church was left in the hands of James (probably the brother of Jesus) and the elders (Acts 21:18; cf. Acts 12:17; 15:13). In the same way that James eventually exercised authority over the leadership of the churches in Judea (Acts 15:13, 19), Paul exercised authority over the churches he established outside Judea. However, the day-to-day governing and shepherding of the churches in the towns and villages throughout the Roman Empire was placed in the hands of the elders, and the daily care of the needy was given to deacons. This twofold ministry is the only one described in the New Testament.

The Composition of Paul's Churches and the Lord's Supper

The establishment and spread of the church in the first three centuries, before Constantine, was accomplished without the construction of church buildings. When the word *church* is used in a first-century text, it does not refer to a structure on a street corner with a sign out front, a street address, a telephone number, an insurance policy, and a bank account. For the first three hundred years of its existence, until the edict of Milan in 313, Christianity was tolerated but not officially recognized, and churches could not own property.

On the other hand, Judaism was included among officially recognized religions in the Roman Empire, and Jewish groups could own property. Jewish groups were classified for legal purposes as *collegia* and protected along with other clubs, guilds, and associations. When Julius Caesar ordered all groups that did not have a long history disbanded, the synagogues were among those explicitly exempted.[22] The emperor Claudius, in the time of Paul (A.D. 41), issued a letter reconfirming the Jews' right to continue their time-honored religion without being bothered, although he denied them Roman citizenship on a community basis like that possessed by the Greeks.[23] Evidence from Sardis, Ephesus, and other cities in the Diaspora clearly demonstrates the "generally favorable policy of Rome toward the Jewish diaspora communities from Caesar until well after Constantine."[24] Ancient inscriptions, literary evidence,

22. E. Mary Smallwood, *The Jews under Roman Rule: From Pompey to Diocletian,* Studies in Judaism in Late Antiquity 20 (Leiden: Brill, 1976), 133–35.

23. Menahem Stern, *Greek and Latin Authors on Jews and Judaism,* part 1, *From Herodotus to Plutarch* (Leiden: Brill, 1974), 399–403; Avigdor Tcherikover, *Hellenistic Civilization and the Jews* (Philadelphia: Jewish Publication Society, 1961), 305–28.

24. Wayne Meeks, *The First Urban Christians: The Social World of the Apostle Paul* (New Haven, Conn.: Yale University Press, 1983), 44.

and New Testament passages (e.g., Acts 18:7) speak of synagogue buildings in the first century. Archaeological excavations in Israel have produced evidence of synagogues from the first century at Gamla, Capernaum, and Magdala, as well as renovated structures used as synagogues in Herodium and Masada.

The first converts to Christianity were Jews. When they accepted Jesus as the Messiah, they continued to attend their synagogues, as did Priscilla and Aquila in Ephesus (Acts 18:26), where they heard Apollos, who had also accepted Christ. Paul went to Damascus in an attempt to ferret Jewish Christians out of the synagogues and imprison them. Luke wrote that Paul asked the high priest "for letters to the synagogues at Damascus, so that if he found any belonging to the Way, men or women, he might bring them bound to Jerusalem" (Acts 9:2). The presence of Christians in synagogues is alluded to in James 2:2 (the word translated "assembly" is the Greek word for synagogue).

Christians had no church buildings in which to meet separately as a body of believers, so they met in homes. People like Titius Justus, a Christian whose house adjoined the synagogue he had probably attended as a God-fearer, would have welcomed others besides Paul to his home (Acts 18:7), and Crispus, the ruler of the synagogue, probably welcomed others to worship with him and his household (Acts 18:8). Priscilla and Aquila also had churches meeting in their home,[25] both in Ephesus (1 Cor. 16:19) and later in Rome (Rom. 16:5), as did Philemon in Colossae (Philem. 2), and Nympha in Laodicea (Col. 4:15). "The structure of the early Christian groups was thus linked with what was commonly regarded as the basic unit of the society," the home.[26]

The individual home that housed a small section of the composite church in a city became the "basic cell of the Christian movement."[27] The household conversions mentioned several times in the New Testament (e.g., Acts 16:15, 33; 18:8; 1 Cor. 1:16; 16:15) formed the nucleus of these "house churches." At times the entire church might meet in the home of a member like Gaius, who had a facility large enough to accommodate such meetings (Rom. 16:23). He hosted Paul and "the whole church." Paul refers on occasion to the whole church assembling in one place and worshiping together (1 Cor. 14:23). This would be a composite meeting of the house churches.

The frequency of such composite meetings is not attested in the New Testament. On the analogy of Jewish synagogue services, it might be assumed that Christians met to observe the Lord's Day every time it occurred, though

---

25. See further Jerome Murphy-O'Connor, "Priscilla and Aquila," *Bible Review* 8.6 (December 1992): 49ff.

26. Meeks, *First Urban Christians,* 75. See his discussion of households that probably served as churches.

27. Ibid.

this is not explicitly stated. One such meeting occurred on the first day of the week in Troas (Acts 20:7), and such a meeting is implied in Corinth (1 Cor. 16:1–2). The individual house groups undoubtedly met every Sunday, or even more frequently (as may be implied in Acts 2:42–46; 5:42). It was more difficult for groups to find public facilities available and large enough to accommodate large numbers.[28] An occasional meeting outside in a field would not be satisfactory in the winter or as a permanent solution to their needs.

The problem was compounded by the need to have facilities that would allow the preparation and serving of fellowship, or communal, meals. A house setting of some kind provided the culinary appurtenances necessary for these meals. Communal meals were a familiar part of ancient Greco-Roman society. They were held in pagan temples.[29] Pagan clubs or volunteer associations[30] participated in them routinely.[31] Synagogues[32] also participated in fellowship meals.[33] Major Jewish feasts were celebrated in the homes, but special occasions like circumcisions, betrothals, weddings, and even funerals[34] were held in the synagogues.[35] So whether Paul's converts came from Judaism or paganism, they were familiar with groups gathering for communal meals in domestic residences.

Table fellowship was probably the most important link between small house churches. A full meal eaten together was the paramount social event in the world of the New Testament. Sharing a meal together meant acceptance. Disfellowship of an individual meant that the church could not eat with that person

28. Ramsay MacMullen, *Paganism in the Roman Empire* (New Haven, Conn.: Yale University Press, 1981), 36. See his discussion of the difficulty in finding such facilities.

29. On the temple of Demeter and Kore in Corinth, see John McRay, *Archaeology and the New Testament* (Grand Rapids: Baker, 1991), 316. On the temple of Serapis, see Bradley Blue, "The House Church at Corinth and the Lord's Supper: Famine, Food Supply, and the Present Distress," *Criswell Theological Review* 5.2 (1991): 222ff.

30. Clubs of various kinds that met in small groups, often in homes, provided services for their members such as meaningful burials, a privilege that only the wealthy could afford. The poor were merely placed in mass public burial facilities—fields, caves, etc. See Meeks's discussion of various kinds of clubs and their provision for burials (*First Urban Christians,* 32–33).

31. D. E. Smith, "Meals and Morality in Paul and His World," in *Society of Biblical Literature Seminar Papers* (Atlanta: Scholars Press, 1981), 319–31; Meeks, *First Urban Christians,* 158 (for a discussion of the constitution of these clubs, see 31ff.). See further bibliography in Blue, "House Church," 221 nn. 2 and 3.

32. See the comparisons in Meeks, *First Urban Christians,* especially 34–35.

33. E. R. Goodenough, *Jewish Symbols in the Graeco-Roman Period,* Bollingen Series 37 (Princeton, N.J.: Princeton University Press, 1953–68), 2:108–9, and in various places in vol. 5; Martin Hengel, "Die Synagogeninschrift von Stobi," *Zeitschrift für die Neutestamentliche Wissenschaft* 57 (1966): 167–72; Blue, "House Church," 221 n. 1.

34. Bo Reicke finds evidence for Jewish memorial meals being observed prior to the development of Christian meals for the dead (*Diakonie, Festfreude, und Zelos in Verbindung mit der altchristlichen Agapenfeier,* Uppsala Universitets Årsskrift 1951, no. 5 [Uppsala: Lundequist; Wiesbaden: Harrassowitz, 1951], 263, 104–18).

35. Vincent Branick, *The House Church in the Writings of Paul* (Wilmington, Del.: Glazier, 1989), 100.

(1 Cor. 5:11). "To share food was to initiate or reinforce a social bonding which implied permanent commitment and deep ethical obligation."[36] The Lord's Supper was eaten in the context of and as a part of a regular meal at a common table. For a Jew and a Gentile to sit down together at a common meal indicated genuine acceptance based on faith in Christ and love for one another.

The Lord's Supper was celebrated by medium-sized groups (thirty to fifty) meeting either in the home of some church member who could afford to own a private house or by small groups (ten to fifteen) of poor Christians who lived in the cramped quarters of high-rise apartments. Before commenting on the nature of these fellowship meals and the Lord's Supper, it will be helpful to describe what the household facility was actually like in New Testament times, lest it be erroneously assumed that a middle class of society existed then, as now, which owned large private dwellings.[37]

In the Roman Empire in the first century, 90 percent of the free population and more than 90 percent of the slaves lived in small, crowded, high-rise apartment buildings.[38] In Rome only 3 percent of the population lived in a *domus* (private house).[39] In Pompeii less than 10 percent of the residential area was occupied by private houses.[40] Ostia, the port city of Rome, had only twenty-two private villas at this time.[41]

A large domus or a villa would be able to accommodate only about fifty people in its large atrium (open court in the center of the house) and its triclinium (dining room). Roman houses were built with solid walls facing the street, without windows (for security reasons), and with rooms arranged in a circle and opening toward the interior upon the atrium. Here in the atrium Christians might gather to worship since it was the only non-private area of the house. It was here that Romans and Greeks had worshiped their gods before becoming Christians. "The atrium, with its ancestral images, and the images of the lares and genius in the lararium, was as much a center of traditional family worship as it was a place to receive business and political clients."[42] A

36. Jerome Murphy-O'Connor, *Paul: A Critical Life* (New York: Oxford University Press, 1996), 149.

37. See further ibid., 149f.

38. Bruce Frier, *Landlords and Tenants in Imperial Rome* (Princeton, N.J.: Princeton University Press, 1980); James E. Packer, "Housing and Population in Imperial Ostia and Rome," *Journal of Roman Studies* 57 (1967): 80–95; idem, *The Insulae of Imperial Ostia,* Memoires of the American Academy in Rome 31 (Rome: American Academy in Rome, 1971).

39. Bradley Blue, "Acts and the House Church," in *The Book of Acts in Its Graeco-Roman Setting,* ed. David W. J. Gill and Conrad Gempf, BAFCS 2 (Grand Rapids: Eerdmans, 1994), 155 n. 138.

40. Ramsay MacMullen, *Roman Social Relations: 50 B.C. to A.D. 284* (New Haven, Conn.: Yale University Press, 1974), 168 n. 15.

41. Packer, "Housing and Population," 86.

42. John Clarke, *The Houses of Roman Italy: 100 B.C.–A.D. 250* (Los Angeles: University of California Press, 1991 [but actually published in 1993]), 12.

lararium was a niche carved into one or more walls of a Roman house; into these lararia were placed the family gods, called lares and genius.

The population density of the empire mandated the profusion of apartment houses. It has been estimated that there were two hundred such buildings per acre in the cities of the empire at this time,[43] and as many as three hundred per acre in the residential area of Rome.[44] This density is almost two and one-half times higher than twentieth-century Calcutta and three times as high as Manhattan Island.[45] A few Christians mentioned in the New Testament were wealthy and could own or rent villas in which a church could be invited to meet.[46] However, for most Christians in urban settings who were of the lower class of that society, the only option available was the less spacious facility of a high-rise apartment, which would accommodate only ten to fifteen people.[47] These quarters were crowded and uninviting. The first floor was usually occupied with shops. The second floor was taken by those who could pay higher rent for the privilege of having to climb only a single flight of stairs. The upper floors of high-rise buildings were rented by those who had the least income. Some buildings had larger apartments on the lower floors for the upper-class tenants and smaller ones of about thirty square feet on the upper levels for freedmen or slaves.[48]

These buildings contained no central heat, no running water, and no toilets. Tenants used the public toilets abundantly provided by the city. The only light in these apartments was furnished by lamps, which emitted fumes. A group meeting in such a facility for worship in the evening after the day's work (Paul preached till midnight, Acts 20:7) would have found it to be a very uncomfortable experience. Doubtless it was in such circumstances that Eutychus fell out of the upper-story window at night during a Lord's Supper service. There were "many lights" burning (Acts 20:8–9), and the fumes from these lamps would have been stultifying. Even though he sat in the window of this "upper chamber," he still fell into a deep sleep. Because of the heat and poor air, the windows could not be closed to keep out the noise of the carts of merchants, who were required by law to transport their goods down the narrow cobblestone streets at night.

43. Branick, *House Church,* 43.

44. James Stambaugh, *Ancient Roman City* (Baltimore: Johns Hopkins University Press, 1988), 337.

45. Robert Jewett, "Tenement Churches and Communal Meals in the Early Church: The Implications of a Form-Critical Analysis of 2 Thessalonians 3:10," *BR* 38 (1993): 26.

46. On the subject of affluent church members, see David Gill, "Acts and the Urban Elites," in *The Book of Acts in Its Graeco-Roman Setting,* ed. Gill and Gempf, 105–18.

47. See the excellent discussion of these facilities in Robert Jewett's article "Tenement Churches," 23–43. Jerome Murphy-O'Connor estimates that ten to twenty could meet in a shop space on the bottom floor of a tenement building ("Priscilla and Aquila," 49–50).

48. See Frier, *Landlords,* 15.

Given the housing situation in the empire, it is clear that the term *house church* does not convey a setting comparable to that of middle-class private homes today. Such did not exist. Only a few wealthy members had private homes in which the church met. Almost all the churches in urban settings met in small groups in small, private apartments of tenement buildings. On special occasions they would meet together as described in 1 Corinthians 14:23: "the whole church assembles ['into one place,' KJV]."[49] In these larger assemblies, no doubt held in rented rooms of various kinds, the public rules of social conduct would perhaps replace the greater freedom and responsibility of the women in the private smaller meetings, which occurred in their own apartments or homes. One of the obvious points of difference in the two kinds of meetings is that in the small group meetings at home the women had a prominent if not exclusive role in serving the meal.[50]

Three kinds of meals are discernable in these situations: (1) the regular meal taken for mere physical sustenance; (2) the agape meal (love feast, Jude 12) eaten together to promote spiritual unity; and (3) the Lord's Supper.[51] The Lord's Supper was eaten as a part of the agape meal. This provides important contextual background for 1 Corinthians 10 and 11, the only discussion of the church's observing the Supper in the New Testament.

In the tenement buildings, residents were sometimes fed from a common kitchen,[52] while others cooked over a charcoal brazier in their small apartments. In these contexts the women would have prepared and served the meals. When the small groups met together in larger assemblies, the women probably continued to serve the meals, including the Lord's Supper, which was eaten during the fellowship meal. It was a failure to properly distinguish the one from the other that led Paul to say, "When you meet together, it is not the Lord's supper that you eat. For in eating, each one goes ahead with his own meal, and one is hungry and another is drunk. What! Do you not have houses to eat and drink in? Or do you despise the church of God and humiliate those who have nothing? What shall I say to you? Shall I commend you in this? No, I will not" (1 Cor. 11:20–22).

49. The phrase (ἐπὶ τὸ αὐτό) in this verse, translated "into one place" in the KJV, may have reference to the union of the body. It occurs in Acts 1:15; 2:1, 47; 1 Cor. 11:20; 14:23 and could be translated "in church fellowship," according to Bruce Metzger, *A Textual Commentary on the Greek New Testament*, 2d ed. (Stuttgart: German Bible Society, 1994), 265. For a full discussion of the phrase with the meaning of "assembly," see Everett Ferguson, "When You Come Together: *Epi to Auto* in Early Christian Literature," *Restoration Quarterly* 16 (1973): 202–8.

50. For a recent look at the role of women, see Craig Keener, *Paul, Women, and Wives: Marriage and Women's Ministry in the Letters of Paul* (Peabody, Mass.: Hendrickson, 1992); and Bonnidell Clouse and Robert G. Clouse, eds., *Women in Ministry: Four Views* (Downers Grove, Ill.: InterVarsity, 1989), which offers four different views by evangelicals.

51. See the discussion of these three distinctions in Jewett "Tenement Churches," 32ff.

52. Frier, *Landlords*, 28.

The words *Lord's* and *his own* are placed in the emphatic position in Greek. The problem was not the same as that in a worship assembly in a large, modern church edifice where the worshipers are not "discerning" the Lord's body because they are failing to concentrate on the meaning of the observance. The word *discern* (διακρίνω, *diakrinō*) in 1 Corinthians 11:29 means "distinguish." They ate and drank condemnation upon themselves by failing to distinguish the Lord's Supper from their own supper, which they were eating on the same occasion. The Lord's Supper was being eaten in the context of another meal. This is the contextual inference.

The picture emerging from this is that when the larger group assembled in the home of a wealthy member or in a rented facility, abuses were occurring. This may be explained in two ways, first in the context of a private home and second in the context of a tenement dwelling.

First, it is possible that in the private home of a wealthy member, the elite of that society, including the wealthy and the influential, were eating in the triclinium (dining room), reclining on benches, and enjoying the best food. The lower-class members, including slaves and freedmen, were meeting out in the atrium and receiving a lesser quantity or quality of food. So when the poor, who arrived late for the communal meal, entered the atrium, they had no food. The others had already consumed the food, even to the extent of becoming drunk, while the latecomers were hungry (1 Cor. 11:21).

Paul thus instructs, "When you come together to eat, wait for one another—if anyone is hungry, let him eat at home—lest you come together to be condemned" (1 Cor. 11:33–34). The purpose of the communal agape is not to satisfy hunger but to share a sense of unity by sitting around a table and eating a meal together. Jesus said his disciples would "eat and drink" at his table in his kingdom (Luke 22:30). Table fellowship is a sign of mutual acceptance and honor: "And men will come from east and west, and from north and south, and sit at table in the kingdom of God" (Luke 13:29). Therefore, those who are hungry should go to their own residences and eat and stop making this communal agape like a pagan religious meal characterized by gluttony and drunkenness. By acting this way, they eat and drink judgment on themselves and dishonor the body and blood of the Lord (1 Cor. 11:27–29). They must examine themselves and their behavior and properly distinguish the Lord's Supper.

The second possible context for 1 Corinthians 11 is a tenement setting. In this case, the Christian host and patron who provided the meal for the believers in the wealthy private home would not be present. Some of the merchant tenement dwellers who lived on the lower levels of the insula or apartment house would have had money to help provide some of the food, but the poor would have had nothing to contribute. The poor residents of these buildings would pool their meager funds to create potluck communal meals to be eaten together in a rented facility. Sometimes they may have abused these occasions.

They may have eaten and drunk more than they should, more than they could have at home, resulting in the lack of food for the poor who happened to come late and had nothing to bring with them to share. Thus, the latecomers went hungry. Paul was instructing them that in the Lord's body, the "haves" must share with the "have-nots."

It has been suggested that in some cities Christians in tenement buildings might have regularly eaten their main meal of the day together in order to provide food for hungry brothers and sisters.[53] If some refused to work and share the fruit of their labor with those who could not work, then they would be refused a place at the communal meals. Paul reminded the Thessalonians that he and his colleagues "did not eat any one's bread without paying" (2 Thess. 3:8), and he commanded them, "If any one will not work, let him not eat" (2 Thess. 3:9–10). This sanction could not be enforced if the members were eating their food only as families in the privacy of their own homes. A communal situation is implied that was quite unlike anything with which most churches are familiar today.[54]

The Lord's Supper was celebrated in the context of such communal meals by a large proportion of Christians through the fourth century,[55] when the construction of large basilican church buildings began, and with this an emphasis on sacrament and liturgy and a corresponding diminution in the practice of communal dining.[56] In more recent times, the sacramental approach to the Lord's Supper, even by non-sacramental institutions, has replaced any real connotation of the Supper as a meal with all the fellowship implications it once carried. The first-century connotation of acceptance, fellowship, participation, and unity conveyed by sitting together at a table is totally lost in the larger setting. In a modern worship service, where most eat the Supper together, the association of the observance with a meal is almost entirely lost. Such has been the result of the evolution of the place of meeting from a household to a lecture hall.

In most locations, Christians no longer segregate minorities within the church building or exclude them. However, the real test of acceptance comes not in sitting in a building together because the law requires it, but in sitting together around a domestic dinner table. This is precisely the context in which the Lord's Supper was observed in the first century and the one that gave it the meaning our Lord intended when he instituted it: "Because there is one

---

53. Jewett, "Tenement Churches," 39–42.

54. See further Robert Banks, *Paul's Idea of Community: The Early House Churches in Their Cultural Setting,* rev. ed. (Peabody, Mass.: Hendrickson, 1994).

55. See Bo Reicke, *Diakonie, Festfreude, und Zelos.*

56. For an outline of the three-stage progression from houses (A.D. 50–150) to renovated houses (A.D. 150–250) to independently constructed basilicas (A.D.250–313) as church buildings, see Blue, *Acts and the House Church,* 124–30.

bread, we who are many are one body, for we all partake of the one bread" (1 Cor. 10:17).

In the teachings of Paul, the Lord's Supper is a fellowship, a *koinonia,* a "participation in" the process of eating and drinking (1 Cor. 10:16). It is a participatory memorial for all Christians rather than the observation of a sacramental performance by the clergy. The context of the house church in ancient times emphatically illustrated this.

The first-century Christians in Jerusalem "devoted themselves to the apostles' teaching and fellowship, to the breaking of bread and the prayers" (Acts 2:42). The frequency of meeting in the first-century church seems to have depended on the purpose of the meeting. In the months immediately after the church was founded at Pentecost, the Christians met together daily in the temple in Jerusalem and broke bread and ate together in their homes (Acts 2:46). This led to daily conversions to the Christian faith (Acts 2:47), and even a "great many of the priests were obedient to the faith" (Acts 6:7).

Whether the "breaking of bread" in Acts 2:42 refers to the Lord's Supper is arguable, since it is not unequivocally stated. The idiom of "breaking bread" is a common expression for simply having a meal. This is seen in Jesus' feeding of both the five thousand and the four thousand. In Matthew 14:19, Jesus broke the bread, and in verse 20 they all ate. In Matthew 15:36, Jesus broke bread, and in verse 37, they all ate. In Acts 20:7 the church came together "to break bread" on the first day of the week. Nothing is said of their having broken bread until the next day, after Paul preached until midnight and raised Eutychus from the dead (v. 11). Here we have idiomatic use of language. The phrase "break bread and eat" is used of a meal, of the Lord's Supper (Jesus broke the bread and said, "Take, eat," Matt. 26:26), and possibly of an agape (ἀγάπη), or love, feast, in which the Lord's Supper would be eaten in the context of another meal (1 Cor. 11:20; Jude 12). The statement in Acts 2:46 that the Jewish disciples "day by day attended the temple together and broke bread in their homes, and partook of food with glad and generous hearts" can be interpreted to refer to either common meals, the Lord's Supper, or agape meals. One eminent author on Paul sees the reference to breaking the bread in Acts 20:7 as involving all of these. He writes, "The breaking of the bread was probably a fellowship meal in the course of which the Eucharist was celebrated (cf. Acts 2:42)."[57]

In the 1 Corinthians 11:20 passage, Paul's use of Greek grammar clearly shows the meaning of the passage: "When you meet together, it is not the *Lord's* supper that you eat. For in eating, each one goes ahead with his *own* meal." The words *Lord* and *own* are both in the emphatic position in the grammatical structure of the sentence. This clarifies the meaning in verse 29 of "without discern-

57. Bruce, *The Book of the Acts,* 384. Bruce identifies breaking of bread in Acts 2:42–46 with the Lord's Supper, which he says was eaten with a common meal (73).

ing the body." The body is, of course, that of the Lord. To "discern" (διακρίνω, *diakrinō*) means to "distinguish, set apart." The Corinthians' problem was that they were eating the Lord's Supper during an agape meal, but they were not distinguishing between the two. They were even getting drunk on the wine (v. 21).

Another important question relating to Paul's breaking bread with the church in Troas is the time of its occurrence. Luke writes that the disciples there met on "the first day of the week" (Acts 20:7). This phrase is a problem for translators, who must determine whether Luke is reflecting Jewish or Roman timekeeping. On the one hand, the passage can mean that the disciples met on Saturday evening after sundown, which by *Jewish* time would be Sunday, because in Jewish culture the day changes at sundown rather than at midnight. Paul then preached until midnight, Luke says, and they broke bread after that. If this refers to the Lord's Supper, it took place on Sunday, because it was still the first day of the week. So the sequence would be (1) the disciples gathered together sometime after sundown, which was the beginning of Sunday, to break bread (i.e., eat a meal and take the Lord's Supper, Acts 20:7); (2) Paul preached until midnight; (3) the disciples then broke bread (i.e., ate the meal and took the Lord's Supper, Acts 20:11) on Sunday.

If, on the other hand, Luke is reflecting *Roman* time, according to which the day changes at midnight, then the church met on the first day of the week (i.e., Sunday) to break bread (v. 7) but did not actually eat the meal until Paul finished his preaching after midnight (v. 11), which would be Monday.

It is possible, though improbable, that "breaking bread" refers in verse 7 to the Lord's Supper and in verse 11 only to "breakfast," in which case the church ate the Lord's Supper on Sunday as they had come together to do and then ate breakfast later. This is unlikely because of the confusion it would create in the minds of Luke's readers, who would surely understand the phrase "break bread" to refer to the same thing in the same immediate context. This difficulty in conceiving time in this passage is reflected in the following translations of Acts 20:7:

Sunday

KJV	"upon the first day of the week"
LB	"on Sunday"
RSV	"on the first day of the week"
NIV	"on the first day of the week"
JB	"on the first day of the week"

Saturday

PHILLIPS	"on the Saturday"
TEV	"on Saturday evening"
NEB	"on the Saturday night"

In all probability, the early church met every Sunday because the resurrection of Jesus occurred on that day. Paul writes, "If Christ has not been raised, . . . you are still in your sins" (1 Cor. 15:17). There is no record of the church meeting regularly on the day of Christ's crucifixion. But it would have met *every* first day of the week, just as the Jews observed every seventh day, the Sabbath.

The issue remains, however, whether the Lord's Supper was observed *every* Sunday during worship. It might be argued that the Lord's Supper was observed every Sunday because Christianity has no annual festivals (there is nothing in the New Testament about the observance of Easter, Christmas, New Year's Day, etc.). The Jews observed Passover as a major annual festival, but the Lord's Supper was observed by early Jewish Christians more often than once a year on Passover. Christians in the first century seem to have operated on a weekly, not yearly, calendar. Jewish Christians like Paul, of course, observed Jewish annual festivals. For example, Paul sailed from Philippi only "after the days of Unleavened Bread" (Acts 20:6) and was in such a hurry to get to Jerusalem for Pentecost that he would not even stop in Ephesus. Instead, he went on to Miletus and called the Ephesian elders to him there, "for Paul had decided to sail past Ephesus, so that he might not have to spend time in Asia; for he was hastening to be at Jerusalem, if possible, on the day of Pentecost" (Acts 20:16).

In the phrase translated "first day of the week" (Acts 20:7), the word *day* is not in the Greek text. It is supplied on the basis of an interpretation of the Greek idiomatic phrase κατὰ μίαν σαββάτου (*kata mian sabbatou*), literally "according to first of week." However, translation is not a word-for-word reproduction of one language into another but involves a rendering of idioms as well. The word *first* (μίαν, *mian*) is an adjective, and since there is no noun stated with which it is used, the feminine adjective idiomatically implies the presence of a feminine noun, which in this case is *day.*

The interpretation of idiom is present also in the rendering of the word *every* in connection with the phrase "first day" (1 Cor. 16:2) in the following translations: LB, RSV (2d ed.), TEV, NIV, JB, NEB, and David Stern's *Jewish New Testament.* This use of the phrase may be compared to a parallel use with the word *year* (ἐνιαυτόν, *eniauton*) in Hebrews 9:25, where it refers to the high priest entering "yearly" (κατ' ἐνιαυτόν, *kat' eniauton,* according to year) into the Holy of Holies on the Day of Atonement. The idiomatic meaning here is "every year," as it is uniformly rendered in New Testament translations.[58] Also in Hebrews 7:27, the same phrase occurs using the word *day* (ἡμέρα, *hēmera*), where it states that the priest does not need to offer sacrifices

---

58. It is so rendered in all eight translations of the *Eight Translation New Testament* (Wheaton, Ill.: Tyndale House, 1974), i.e., KJV, LB, PHILLIPS, RSV, TEV, NIV, JB, NEB.

"daily" (καθ' ἡμέραν, *kath' hēmeran*). Thus, the idiom is the same whether referring to a year, a day, or a week:

κατ' ἐνιαυτόν = every year	Hebrews 9:25
καθ' ἡμέραν = every day	Hebrews 7:27
κατὰ . . . σαββάτου = every week	1 Corinthians 16:2

And when the word μίαν (one, first) is added to this last phrase, it means "the first day of every week." It seems clear, then, that Paul met with the church in Troas on the first day of the week to break bread because that was its weekly custom (Acts 20:7). And it is equally clear that a weekly meeting of the church in Corinth was the time for the Corinthians to make financial contributions, which Paul was collecting for the Jerusalem church (1 Cor. 16:3; 2 Cor. 8:8–15). The probability of the Lord's Supper being eaten every Sunday in Corinth has to be inferred from Acts 20:7 and from its divinely appropriate representation of the body of Jesus, which was crucified on Friday and resurrected on the first day of the week.

The Composition of Paul's Churches and Baptism

Baptism and the Lord's Supper are the two definitive ordinances emphatically taught by the apostle Paul and practiced by the early church. The central focus of each is the death and resurrection of Jesus. Paul's understanding of both is adequately set forth in the New Testament and clearly attests the importance he attributed to each of them. We will look first at the historical context of baptism and then at Paul's teaching about it.

Donald Guthrie has correctly observed that "it must, of course, be recognized that for Paul, as for the other early Christians, conversion and baptism were regarded as one event."[59] In the Book of Acts, baptism was the transition point in coming to Christ, the expression of one's faith in the death, burial, and resurrection of the Lord Jesus. Lars Hartman defends this perspective in his recent book on baptism in the early church: "Paul seems to be of the opinion that baptism is the focal point of the whole procedure of conversion, calling and entrance into the Christ community."[60] G. B. Caird states, "This emphasis is supported by Paul, for whom it is obvious that all Christians will be baptized at conversion."[61]

59. Donald Guthrie, *New Testament Theology* (Leicester, Eng.: Inter-Varsity, 1981), 756.
60. Lars Hartman, *'Into the Name of the Lord Jesus': Baptism in the Early Church* (Edinburgh: Clark, 1997), 67.
61. G. B. Caird, *New Testament Theology* (Oxford: Clarendon, 1994), 222.

The Background of Baptism

Baptism was not an innovation in the religious world of the first century. Jewish sectarianism had long emphasized initiatory rites and practices. Immersion in water was the initiatory rite for entrance into the Essene community at Qumran, and excavations there have produced several very large immersion vats. At Jerusalem, Masada, Jericho, and Herodion, among other places, Jewish *miqva'ot* (immersion pools) of the first century have been excavated, confirming the picture portrayed in the Mishnah of the widespread diffusion of the practice of lustral washing in first-century Judaism.

John the Baptizer appeared in the wake of these highly competitive Jewish religious movements represented by sects such as the Pharisees, Sadducees, Essenes, Herodians, and Zealots. It is quite possible that John was closely associated with the Essenes of Qumran during his earlier life.[62] His message and his practice of immersing in water were regarded by his contemporaries as being divine in origin. Contact between God and his inspired prophets, which had ceased in the days of Malachi, was renewed in the preaching of John. Malachi had spoken of God's sending Elijah the prophet, who would turn the hearts of the people to God (Mal. 4:5–6), and he was here, preaching with the authority of God and calling for repentance and immersion for the remission of sins, because the kingdom of heaven was near (Mark 1:4; Matt. 3:2). Jesus declared John to be the new Elijah (Matt. 17:11–13; Mark 9:12–13), and to him and his baptism even Jesus submitted. What John brought to the religious scene, then, was not novel. Although John's practice of immersion did not serve as an introductory rite into any institution, it was preached as a means of preparation for entrance into the rapidly approaching kingdom of heaven.

When Jesus submitted to John's baptism, it was not without some trepidation on John's part. John had been preaching what Mark described as "a baptism of repentance for the forgiveness of sins" (Mark 1:4), and people were coming to him and "confessing their sins" (Matt. 3:6). Understandably, John responded to Jesus' request by saying, "I need to be baptized by you, and do you come to me?" (Matt. 3:14).

There can, therefore, be no doubt that John and those who accepted his baptism associated the rite with moral and ethical purposes. Why then was Jesus baptized? Unlike everyone else who came to John, it was certainly not for the forgiveness of his sins! "He committed no sins" (1 Pet. 2:22). For Jesus, it would have been a rejection of the purpose of God to have refused the act. Luke wrote that "the Pharisees and the lawyers rejected the purpose of God for themselves, not having been baptized by him" (Luke 7:30).

62. John McRay, "John the Baptist and the Dead Sea Scrolls," *Restoration Quarterly* 4 (1960): 80–88.

Often overlooked in the discussions of the background of New Testament baptism, especially as practiced by John the Baptist, is the very significant fact that Jesus not only was baptized by John but also, like John, preached in the land of Judea with a group of disciples about him and baptized those who accepted his message. Jesus had a ministry of preaching and baptizing parallel to that of John.

The Gospel of John records the occasion when Jesus was in Jerusalem for the Feast of Passover and was visited by Nicodemus, a prominent Pharisaic teacher. Jesus had a discussion with him about the nature of conversion as rebirth (John 2:23–3:21), after which, John writes, Jesus remained in the land of Judea with his disciples "and baptized" (John 3:22). Indeed, all were "going to him" (John 3:26). During this time John was baptizing up north in the general region of Samaria at Aenon,[63] near Salim, "because there was much water there" (which his practice of immersion required, John 3:23). So, Jesus and John were both leading groups of disciples, preaching and baptizing at the same time in different areas of Israel. But significantly, as this Gospel reports, "Jesus was making and baptizing more disciples than John (although Jesus himself did not baptize, but only his disciples)" (John 4:1–2).

We are thus able to place Jesus' conversation with Nicodemus in the immediate context of his and John's practice of baptism: Jesus' statement to Nicodemus that he must be "born anew," or again (John 3:3), of both "water and the Spirit" (John 3:5) referred to Jesus' own practice of immersing repentant Jews in water. His requirement that Nicodemus be born anew called for immediate action, being expressed in the present tense. He must submit to the waters of baptism, and eventually he will receive the Spirit, who has not yet been given but whom John had said Jesus would soon provide (Matt. 3:11).

Although Nicodemus was puzzled by the language Jesus used about rebirth, he would no doubt have understood John's demand for repentance before baptism. The word *repent* (μετανοἶα, *metanoia*) literally means "to change one's mind." This change of mind, coupled with immersion in water, would represent to the penitent Jews who came to that baptism a rebirth of "water and spirit." This is why Mark called it "a baptism of repentance for the forgiveness of sins" (Mark 1:4). It should be noted that the identical expression of purpose, "unto the remission of sins" (εἰς ἄφεσιν ἁμαρτιῶν, *eis aphesin hamartiōn*) was used of both the baptism practiced by John and Jesus (Mark 1:4) and that commanded later by Peter at Pentecost (Acts 2:38).

The differences in these two baptisms do not, therefore, lie in the promise of the remission of sins, which was offered by both, but in two other important matters. First, the postresurrection baptism that Peter commanded for

---

63. Eusebius (*Onom.* 40.1) identified the site of Aenon as six miles south of Scythopolis (Beth Shan). Other sites have been suggested in the area east of Shechem (Nablus). See further Jerry Pattengale's article "Aenon," *ABD*, 1:87.

both Jews (Acts 2:38) and Gentiles (Acts 10:48) offered the gift of the Holy Spirit (Acts 2:38), which John's and Jesus' baptism did not. John said, "I baptize you with water for repentance, but he who is coming after me is mightier than I, whose sandals I am not worthy to carry; he will baptize you with the Holy Spirit and with fire" (Matt. 3:11).

The second difference lies in the fact that postresurrection baptism was to be done in the name of Jesus of Nazareth as the risen Lord. It was baptism in the name of this crucified and risen Savior that would confer on those who accepted it the gift of the Holy Spirit. Peter and the apostles said that God had given the Holy Spirit to "those who obey him" (Acts 5:32). In Peter's first sermon after the resurrection, he said, "Repent, and be baptized every one of you in the name of Jesus Christ for the forgiveness of your sins; and you shall receive the gift of the Holy Spirit" (Acts 2:38).

It was baptism "in the name of Jesus" that was crucial for the twelve men in Ephesus who had known only the baptism of John—which they apparently had experienced after the resurrection of Jesus, when John's baptism was no longer valid. The one to whom John had pointed, whose way he had prepared, had come (Matt. 3:3). After baptizing these disciples again, this time in the name of Jesus, Paul conferred upon them the gift of the Holy Spirit (Acts 19:1–7). They told Paul that under John's baptism they did not even know there was a Holy Spirit (Acts 19:2)!

The conversion experiences of the early church as described in Acts deepen the impression of the overriding importance attached to the name of Jesus by the apostles. Although they had been commanded in his last words to them to baptize all nations in the name of the Father, Son, and Holy Spirit (Matt. 28:18–20), there is no recorded instance of conversion in Acts employing this threefold formula, which became so important by the second century. On the other hand, several instances of immersion at conversion were stated to be by the authority of Jesus. This was undoubtedly because Jesus had prefaced his remarks about baptism with the words "all authority in heaven and on earth has been given to me." Presumably, then, baptism in the name of Jesus was inherently baptism in the name of all three.

The Importance of Baptism in the Early Church

The importance the early church placed on baptism is seen in the fact that every case of individual conversion described (not merely mentioned) in the Book of Acts included immersion in water (e.g., 2:41; 8:37–38; 10:48; 16:30–33; 22:16). Among these, the conversion of the Ethiopian nobleman is especially instructive. Luke records that he listened as Philip "preached unto him Jesus" (Acts 8:35 KJV). Then, when the chariot in which they were riding approached a place of sufficient water, it was the Ethiopian and not Philip who requested baptism. This prompts the question: Where did he learn about it? The answer is, in the sermon in which he learned about Jesus. The "preaching about Jesus" obviously included baptism. No case of conversion described in the New Testament was without it. Overemphasized, baptism becomes a liturgical tradition devoid of the understanding that led the Ethiopian to request it; but viewed from the practice of Jesus and the early church, it was and is a beautiful symbol of the most important event in the history of humanity—the resurrection of the Son of God from the grave.

Departures from this pattern of conversion experience did not appear until the second century and then only in the method, not in the purpose. As to purpose, the earliest authors outside the New Testament, such as the second-century writers Justin Martyr and the author of the *Didache*,[64] considered baptism to be essential in conversion. Justin said people "may obtain in the water the remission of sins" and that "it is received in the name of the Father, Son and Holy Spirit."[65]

The "Mode" of Baptism in the Early Church

As to method, the term *mode* as routinely used in baptismal contexts in the history of Christian thought is misleading because the word *baptize* means "immerse."[66] Actually the word *baptize* is a transliteration (a mere spelling of the Greek word letter for letter into English) rather than a translation (conveying the meaning of a word from one language to another) of the word βα-πτίζω (*baptizō*). Several words in the New Testament are so treated, often obscuring their original meaning; for example, the transliteration *deacon* (διάκονος, *diakonos*) means in translation "servant," and the transliteration *presbyter* (πρεσβύτερος, *presbyteros*) means in translation "older" or "elder."

A "mode (manner or method) of baptism" is thus, properly speaking, a "mode of immersion," and it should designate the manner in which one is immersed (e.g., face forward, backward, self-immersed, immersed by assistance, etc.). By definition it could not have meant to people in the first century a choice of pouring, sprinkling, or immersion. Immersion was the common practice among religious Jews of the first century. This is understood by the Jewish translator David Stern, who consistently renders the word *baptize* as "immerse" in his Jewish translation of the New Testament.[67]

---

64. *Did.* 7.

65. Justin Martyr, *1 Apol.* 61.

66. See βαπτίζω in BAGD, 131–32; G. W. H. Lampe, ed., *A Patristic Greek Lexicon* (Oxford: Clarendon, 1961–68); G. Abbott-Smith, *A Manual Greek Lexicon of the New Testament* (Edinburgh: Clark, 1950); LSJ 305–6; Joseph H. Thayer, *A Greek-English Lexicon of the New Testament*, 4th ed. (Edinburgh: Clark, 1901), 94.

67. David Stern, *The Jewish New Testament* (Jerusalem: Jewish New Testament Publications, 1989).

When Jewish immersions could not be performed, as preferred, in streams, they were administered in alternative ways. Six grades of water concentration that could be used for ritual purification are described in the Mishnah.[68] The sixth, and highest, grade requires running water. Specially built *miqva'ot* (plural form of *miqveh*) found in excavations throughout Israel were designed for the purpose of providing the circulation of water during the act of baptism. Over 300 are now known from the archaeological record, 150 of which have been found in Jerusalem.[69] In the opinion of William LaSor, "these *miqva'ot* undoubtedly provide the background for Christian baptism."[70]

The earliest recorded substitution for immersion is found in the Jewish Christian church manual called the *Didache,* or *Teaching of the Twelve Apostles,* which states that "you should baptize in the Name of the Father and of the Son and of the Holy Spirit, in running water; but if you have no running water, baptize in other water, and if you cannot in cold, then in warm. But if you have neither, pour water three times on the head in the Name of the Father, Son and Holy Spirit" (*Did.* 7.7).

In this Jewish Christian document, the use of cold, running water is emphasized in all probablity because it was used in the highest grade of Jewish lustral immersions, such as those performed in a *miqveh*. The evident intent of the *Didache* in substituting pouring for immersion was to compensate for situations in which only ritually impure (still) water was available. The water became living (running) water by pouring. In the Greek idiom of the day, the participle *living* (ζῶν, *zōn*) was used to express what our contemporary idiom means by *running*. It was used of "spring water in contrast to cistern water."[71] Still water was dead water. The *Didache* allowed for substitution only if running water sufficient for immersion was not available.

In early church history, the baptism of infants necessarily involved an abandonment of immersion. The word *baptize* was redefined, and the sprinkling and pouring began. In his book *The Origins of Infant Baptism,* Joachim Jeremias states unequivocally that "there is difference of opinion about the *incontrovertible fact* that *direct evidence* for the baptism of children starts only with Tertullian."[72] Sprinkling cannot be demonstrated as an alternative to immersion until the third century. It arose in clinical baptism performed by the authority of Cyprian, bishop of Carthage, in North Africa, who reasoned

---

68. See *m. Mikwa'ot* 1.1.

69. See the discussion by Ronny Reich, "The Great Mikveh Debate," *BAR* 19.2 (March–April 1993): 52.

70. William Sanford LaSor, "Discovering What Jewish Miqva'ot Can Tell Us about Christian Baptism," *BAR* 13.1 (Jan.–Feb. 1987): 52

71. BAGD, 337.

72. He then unconvincingly tries to build a case for infant baptism from indirect evidence (Joachim Jeremias, *The Origins of Infant Baptism* [Naperville, Ill.: Allenson, 1963], 9). See his further discussion on pages 64ff.

that baptism was so important that in cases of illness a substitution for immersion was better than the patient missing out on the act altogether.[73]

The problem with Cyprian's position was that without immersion, which epitomizes the burial and resurrection of Jesus, the rite lost one of its most important and fundamental characteristics—its symbolism. For any act to be recognized as symbolic, it must of necessity depict what it attempts to symbolize. Neither affusion (pouring) nor aspersion (sprinkling) is capable of providing symbolism for *resurrection* from the grave.

Paul's View of Baptism

It is against this background, then, that we must understand the teachings of the apostle Paul on baptism.[74] He stresses this symbolism of baptism, for example, when he writes: "Do you not know that all of us who have been baptized into Christ Jesus were baptized into his death? We were buried therefore with him by baptism into death, so that as Christ was raised from the dead by the glory of the Father, we too might walk in newness of life" (Rom. 6:3–4). Rising from the waters of immersion into which we were buried with Christ vividly symbolizes a resurrection from the dead. In these two verses, death and resurrection are the prominent motifs: participants in immersion, Paul says, (1) have been baptized into Christ's death, (2) have been buried with him, (3) and rise from the dead to walk in newness of life. This is emphasized in Colossians 2:12, where he writes, "You were buried with him in baptism, in which you were also raised with him through faith in the working of God, who raised him from the dead."

The later shift in Christian teaching from immersion to aspersion and affusion may also have reflected the gradual shift in Christian theology from the Jewish belief in the resurrection of the body to the Greek idea of the immortality of the soul separate from the body. With the denial of a resurrected body, there was no further motive for practicing a baptism symbolizing such a nonexistent resurrection! Paul argues to the contrary that an emphasis on the resurrection of the body necessitates a corresponding emphasis on the symbolism of that act wherein we are risen with him (Col. 2:12): "For if we have been united with him in a death like his, we shall certainly be united with him in a resurrection like his" (Rom. 6:5).

In Paul's thinking about the process of conversion, baptism is a symbol of a *burial* following spiritual death, in which the old person of sin is laid to rest, and out of his or her old self emerges the new person in Christ. "If any man be in Christ, he is a new creature: old things are passed away; behold, all things are become new," Paul insists (2 Cor. 5:17 KJV). Rising from the waters of im-

73. Cyprian, *Epistle* 75.12.
74. See the end of chapter 2 on Paul's conversion for further discussion on baptism.

mersion remains a wonderfully suited symbol for portraying this resurrection metamorphosis of the individual at conversion.

Baptism was never intended to be practiced apart from an appropriate relationship with the Divine, which requires faith, repentance, and confession. Apart from these, it can be no more than a "removal of dirt from the body" (1 Pet. 3:21). Like the intimacy between a husband and wife, baptism requires a believing and loving relationship with Christ; otherwise, it is devoid of its original and true meaning. But in such a relationship, baptism becomes a natural and spiritual experience.

SEVENTEEN

Eschatology and the Work of the Holy Spirit in Paul's Thought

Paul's entire life was motivated by the reality expressed in one of his letters: "If for this life only we have hoped in Christ, we are of all men most to be pitied" (1 Cor. 15:19). From a Christian perspective, there is nothing more fundamental to human existence than the reality that earthly life is but a ripple on the ocean of reality. An occasional visit to the cemetery corrects the apparent assumption by many of us that we will never need to deal with the reality of death. Humanity is by definition mortality. The Letter to the Hebrews states that "it is appointed for men to die once, and after that comes judgment" (Heb. 9:27). Eschatology has to do with events between the two. It is a study of the last things.

While we are not given a systematic treatise on his views of these last things, there is enough written by Paul in several of his letters to provide an inspired glimpse into this subject, which can produce hope and joyful anticipation in the hearts of those who believe him. Whether Paul's views changed with the passing of time and experience, as some suggest, is a much debated issue.[1] If so, then which were divinely inspired—his earlier views or his later views?

---

1. F. F. Bruce, *Paul: Apostle of the Heart Set Free* (Grand Rapids: Eerdmans, 1977), 340ff. (but cf. p. 312); Joseph Plevnik, *Paul and the Parousia* (Peabody, Mass.: Hendrickson, 1997), 272ff.; Ben Witherington III, *Jesus, Paul, and the End of the World* (Downers Grove, Ill.: InterVarsity, 1992), 284 n. 11.

Certainly he could not have been inspired on both ends of a contradictory spectrum.

The *Parousia* (Second Coming) of Jesus

There are many facets of the study of eschatology,[2] but we will consider in this volume only those to which Paul gives attention in his letters. Perhaps the most fundamental aspect, around which the others revolve, is Christ's return to take his faithful followers to heaven with him. This return is expressed several times by the Greek term παρουσία (*parousia*), which means "presence" and is used by Paul to refer to his own bodily presence with his disciples (2 Cor. 10:10; Phil. 2:12). It also means "coming" or "advent" and is used non-theologically of the coming of Paul's companions to be with him (1 Cor. 16:17; 2 Cor. 7:6–7) and of Paul's coming to be with them (Phil. 1:26).

Paul also uses *parousia* to refer to the return of the resurrected and ascended Lord (1 Cor. 15:23; 1 Thess. 2:19; 3:13; 4:15; 5:23; 2 Thess. 2:1, 8). It is used in this way also by other New Testament authors (James 5:7; 2 Peter 1:16; 1 John 2:28). This "coming" of Jesus is equated by Paul with the "day of the Lord" in 2 Thessalonians 2:2 (and it appears again in a variant reading in the Greek text of 1 Cor. 1:8). Second Peter 3:4, 7, 10, and 12 equates the terms "coming," "day of the Lord," "day of God," and "day of judgment," and 2 Peter 1:16 speaks of the "power and coming of our Lord Jesus Christ."

Thus, the concept of Jesus' parousia, or coming, is connected with the power that will be expressed at that time in dealing with the evil forces of the cosmos.[3] In 2 Thessalonians 2:9, Paul uses the same term when he says the coming of the lawless one is empowered by the activity of Satan. At that time, however, the Lord Jesus will slay the lawless one and "destroy him by his appearing and his coming" (2 Thess. 2:8).

This "day of the Lord" (2 Thess. 2:2), which is still in the future, cannot be predicted and will come as a "thief in the night" (1 Thess. 5:2), but it is to be anticipated by Christians, who live each day in faith, hope, and love (1 Thess. 5:8) and will not, therefore, be surprised by that day (1 Thess. 5:4). This parousia is a manifestation of Christ in glory, which is shared by his followers, who consider Jesus to be their very life (Col. 3:4). "When he comes on that day," he will "be glorified in his saints" (2 Thess. 1:10). It is their day of redemption, for which they were sealed by the Holy Spirit (Eph. 4:30).

2. See further Charles Holman, *Till Jesus Comes: Origins of Christian Apocalyptic Expectations* (Peabody, Mass.: Hendrickson, 1996).

3. See further on the relation of Christians to the cosmos in chapters 10 and 13.

Paul admonishes the Ephesians to "put on the whole armor of God" so that they will "be able to withstand in the evil day" as they struggle against the evil one and all the cosmic forces of evil (Eph. 6:11).

Before the final evil day comes, however, Paul tells the Thessalonians an apostasy or rebellion will occur that will result in the revelation of a "man of lawlessness . . . the son of perdition" who will oppose everything that is good and exalt himself above everything that is called God or that is worshiped (2 Thess. 2:3). The identity of that person is the object of endless speculation by students of the Bible. Many have been erroneously designated since Paul wrote those words, and many undoubtedly will continue to be. Paul, writing by inspiration, could have been more specific had God wanted it, but he was not. The recent entrance into the new millennium has added fuel to the fire of speculation.

What Paul stresses to his audience, and what needs to be remembered today, is the necessity of living each day according to the example and teachings of Jesus Christ and not being "quickly shaken in mind or excited, either by spirit or word, or by letter purporting to be from us, to the effect that the day of the Lord has come" (2 Thess. 2:2).

What prompted Paul to write these words to the Thessalonians was a misunderstanding in the church that either came from Paul's teaching while he was with them or was produced subsequent to his visit by someone who may have sent them a letter "purporting to be" from Paul (2 Thess. 2:2). In 1 Thessalonians, which may or may not have been written before 2 Thessalonians,[4] Paul deals with the Christians' anxiety about what will happen to their loved ones who have died before Christ's return. It should be remembered that the Thessalonians were Greeks and lived in the context of Greek philosophy, which affirmed the immortality of the soul but denied a resurrection of the body. Paul, as a Jewish Pharisee, already believed in a resurrection of the body before he became a disciple of Jesus (Acts 23:6–8; 26:5).

In 1 Thessalonians 4:13–18, Paul states that the ultimate goal of the second coming of Christ (the parousia) is to join the faithful Christians with God. He says, "through Jesus, God will bring with him [Jesus, JM] those who have fallen asleep." This means that those who are still alive at that time, "who are left until the coming of the Lord, shall not precede those who have fallen asleep." Paul says that the "dead in Christ will rise first; then we who are alive, who are left, shall be caught up together with them in the clouds to meet the Lord in the air; and so we shall always be with the Lord. Therefore comfort one another with these words." Their anxiety was to be alleviated by the awareness that at the parousia Christ will take to himself both the dead and the living.

4. The order of Paul's letters in the New Testament is based on length, not date of writing. See chapter 9 on the canon. Many scholars believe 2 Thessalonians was written first.

The Resurrection

About three years later, probably in A.D. 53,[5] Paul wrote to another church in Greece, in the city of Corinth, and dealt more fully with the question of the resurrection of the body, which he called a matter of "first importance" (1 Cor. 15:3). The issue of the resurrection from the dead is important for Paul because Christ's bodily resurrection serves as a guarantee of a future resurrection for his followers (1 Cor. 15:20; 2 Cor. 4:14). He had reminded the Thessalonians of this point in 1 Thessalonians 4:14.

Paul emphasizes the point that the resurrection of Jesus was a sign that he had the approval of God the heavenly Father. It is nowhere stated in Paul's writings or in the New Testament as a whole that Jesus raised himself from the dead,[6] although the Gospel of John records Jesus' affirmation that he will also have a part in raising the dead: "For this is the will of my Father, that every one who sees the Son and believes in him should have eternal life; and I will raise him up at the last day" (John 6:40). Paul begins his letter to the Galatians by declaring in the first verse that God the Father raised Jesus from the dead. Paul stated this in his missionary preaching (Acts 13:30) and emphasizes it in several of his letters (Rom. 8:11; 10:9; 1 Cor. 6:14; 15:15; 2 Cor. 4:14; Eph. 1:20; Col. 2:12; 1 Thess. 1:10). For Paul, this is also assurance of our future resurrection. He writes in 2 Corinthians 4:14 that "he who raised the Lord Jesus will raise us also with Jesus and bring us with you into his presence."

In his discussion of the resurrection in 1 Corinthians 15, Paul argues that if there is no resurrection from the dead:

1. Christ has not been raised (v. 13).
2. Why are people in Corinth being baptized on behalf of the dead (v. 29)? The word *dead* here is plural in Greek.
3. Why is he (Paul) in peril every hour (v. 30)?
4. Let us eat, drink, and be merry, for tomorrow we die (v. 32).

He argues further that if Christ has not been raised, the following assertions are therefore true:

1. Our preaching is vain (κένος, *kenos*), that is, without any basis, truth, or power (v. 14).
2. Our faith is also vain (v. 14).
3. Our faith is futile (μάταιος, *mataios*), that is, idle, empty, worthless, foolish (v. 17).

5. See chapter 3, where I argue that the Thessalonian letters were written in A.D. 50 and 1 Corinthians in A.D. 53.
6. Witherington, *Jesus, Paul, and the End of the World,* 186.

4. We misrepresent God (v. 15).
5. We are still in our sins (v. 17).
6. Those who have died in Christ have perished (v. 18).
7. We are of all people most to be pitied (v. 19).

A very important theological issue is raised by the fifth point. If Christ has not been raised, we are still in our sins. This means that the cross is not the only element involved in the forgiveness of sin. It took the resurrection of Christ three days later to complete the process, and without it sin would not have been removed at Calvary! This is paralleled in the annual atonement offered by the high priest in the temple at Jerusalem. Atonement was not completed when he sacrificed the animal on the altar. It also required taking the animal's blood into the Holy of Holies and sprinkling it on the mercy seat, for he made "atonement in the holy place" (i.e., Holy of Holies, Lev. 16:17). For Paul, the gospel is not limited to the cross. It also involves the resurrection, ascension, and coronation of Jesus at the right hand of God as the high priest after the order of Melchizedek. Jesus, as high priest, presented his own blood to God in the heavenly Holy of Holies. Atonement is a process rather than an event, both in the Old Testament and in the New.[7]

Paul begins his discussion in the first few verses of 1 Corinthians 15 by asserting that the gospel is to be defined as the death, burial, and resurrection of Christ. The reality of the atonement at Calvary is validated by the reality of the resurrection. Without it, people would have no reason to believe that the blood of Jesus atones for sins. Without it, Paul insists, we would still be in our sins.

But what about those who do not believe in Jesus? Will they share in the resurrection? It has been argued that "resurrection is final conformity to the likeness of Christ,"[8] and, therefore, Paul does not include nonbelievers in his understanding of the resurrection body. The argument continues that since this Christian life is an "ongoing process of being conformed to the image of the Son," one who has not participated in this process cannot be expected to get the "final installment or completion of this ongoing process later."[9] This means that those who have not believed in Jesus will not be judged in the body in which their disobedient lives were lived. But this appears to be contrary to Paul's statements in Romans 14:10–12 that "we shall all stand before the judgment seat of Christ" and in 2 Corinthians 5:10 that "we must all appear before the judgment seat of Christ, so that each one may receive good or evil, according to what he has done *in the body.*"

7. See the discussion of these points in chapter 12.
8. Witherington, *Jesus, Paul, and the End of the World,* 187.
9. Ibid.

The Nature of the Body until the Resurrection

Another important aspect of Pauline teaching on the resurrection involves the question of the nature and location of the individual between death and the second coming of Jesus, the interval referred to as the intermediate state.[10] It has been argued that Paul in his earlier letters (1 Thess. 4:13–18; 5:1–11) teaches that Christians are joined "with the Lord" at the parousia and resurrection, and that in his later letters (2 Cor. 5:5–10; Phil. 1:21–26) he shifts his view and argues that this union with Christ occurs at the time of the death of Christians.[11] If the ultimate goal of the second coming of Christ is to "bring the faithful into God's presence,"[12] then it would seem that those who have been dead for two thousand years (since the resurrection of Jesus) are not yet in his presence.

This, of course, raises the question of the relation of the immortal soul to the resurrected body. Paul addresses this question in 1 Corinthians 15:35, where he asks what kind of body the dead possess. He answers that in the eventual resurrection at the parousia, the physical body will be brought back to life, transformed from a mere physical body to a spiritual body (1 Cor. 15:44). But it is nevertheless still a *body* and not a spirit. It is buried, Paul says, as a ψυχικός (*psychikos*, physical) body. The Greek term means "pertaining to life, in this case the life of the natural world rather than the supernatural."[13] A related word refers to the first human being, Adam, who was a mere physical body composed of "dust" (1 Cor. 15:45, 47) until God breathed into his nostrils the breath of life so that he became a "living soul" (Gen. 2:7 KJV).

This suggests that upon death the soul of a human departs and leaves behind the same kind of physical body that Adam had before he was brought to life and became a "living being" (1 Cor. 15:45). At the resurrection, Paul argues, this physical body will be reunited with the soul again and, like Adam and Jesus, will become again a living, spiritual body. Paul compares this to a seed planted in the ground. We plant a hard, yellow kernel of corn in the ground, and it rises from the ground as a soft, green stalk of corn. There is a change in structure but not in content or identity. A seed of corn does not pro-

10. Herman Ridderbos, *Paul: An Outline of His Theology,* trans. J. R. DeWitt (Grand Rapids: Eerdmans, 1975), 487–508. See E. Earle Ellis, "The Structure of Pauline Eschatology (2 Corinthians 5:1–10)," in *Paul and His Recent Interpreters* (Grand Rapids: Eerdmans, 1961), 35ff.; Geerhardus Vos, *The Pauline Eschatology* (Princeton, N.J.: published by the author, 1930; reprint, Grand Rapids: Eerdmans, 1953); idem, "The Structure of the Pauline Eschatology," *Princeton Theological Review* 27 (1929); Plevnik, *Paul and the Parousia,* 272ff.; Bruce, *Paul,* 301–13.

11. Plevnik, *Paul and the Parousia,* 272–73.

12. Ibid., 75.

13. F. W. Gingrich, *Shorter Lexicon of the Greek New Testament* (Chicago: University of Chicago Press, 1965), 238.

duce a stalk of wheat, Paul insists. There is what we may call a "continuity of identity." God gives to each seed "its own body." Each kind of plant possesses a body different from other plants, a body that continues its own identity. The human body we put in the grave is not the form of the body that will be raised but is a "bare kernel" (1 Cor. 15:37) that will be transformed into a new spiritual body, while retaining its continuity of identity in the same way that a kernel of corn produces a new body of corn.

Paul is arguing that the physical body is not left in the grave to eventually disintegrate and dissolve back into the elements of nature, losing its identity forever so that God will deal henceforth only with an immortal soul. It has been argued that in the New Testament immortality is ascribed only to the resurrected body and never to the soul.[14] However, a soul does not die, cannot be buried, and therefore cannot experience resurrection, which is a return to life. This is clearly evident in the death of Jesus. His body died, but his soul was immortal and returned three days later to be united with his deceased body. James wrote that "the body apart from the spirit is dead" (James 2:26).

Of necessity, therefore, Paul is talking to the Corinthians about the resurrection of the human body and not just the immortality of the soul. Divine miracle, of course, is involved in the process, just as in the creation of Adam's body in the beginning. It was a body, but it was not alive until God breathed into it the breath of life (Gen. 2:7). Paul tells the Thessalonians that we actually consist of three elements, spirit (πνεῦμα, *pneuma*), soul (ψυχή, *psychē*), and body (σῶμα, *sōma*), and his prayer is that these might be "kept sound and blameless at the coming of our Lord Jesus Christ" (1 Thess. 5:23). Presumably, the soul is that which is created in the image of God, and the spirit is the "breath of life" that God gives to both the soul and the body.

The continuity of identity means that after an individual dies the body of that person will maintain its identity. When that body is buried in a field without a casket, it eventually disintegrates, returning to the elements in the soil in which it is buried. It may then become a part of the plants above it, which absorb those elements into their roots, but those elements do not cease to exist. And then when an animal eats the plants, those elements become a part of the body of that animal. It would seem that the dead person has thus become nonexistent. However, God's miraculous power can preserve the continuity of identity, restore those precise elements, and recreate the same body again when he raises it from the dead at the parousia of Jesus. This is equally true of a person whose body has been eaten by cannibals. Even though its elements have become a part of other human bodies, God can reproduce those elements and maintain the continuity of identity.

Likewise, bodies that have been blown apart or reduced to the elements of nature by an atomic blast can be recreated by God's power and rejoined to

14. Bruce, *Paul*, 311.

their souls at the parousia. This miraculous continuity of identity is seen in Paul's use of the word *it* in 1 Corinthians 15:42–44: "So is it with the resurrection of the dead. What is sown is perishable, what is raised is imperishable. *It* is sown in dishonor, *it* is raised in glory. *It* is sown in weakness, *it* is raised in power. *It* is sown a physical body, *it* is raised a spiritual body. If there is a physical body, there is also a spiritual body" (italics added).

So, Paul is saying to the Greek Corinthians, Do not let your philosophy of the immortality of the soul blind you to the reality of the resurrection of the body, which will be joined to the immortal soul to become a new spiritual body. It is fundamental to Paul's theology that "the dead will be raised imperishable, and we shall be changed" (1 Cor. 15:52). But it is equally inherent in his thought that this change consists in the mortal becoming immortal and the perishable becoming imperishable (1 Cor. 15:53). The change does not entail a loss of identity.

When the body of Jesus was raised from the dead, it did not immediately undergo complete transformation. He told some of his disciples who supposed he was a spirit when they saw him, "A ghost does not have flesh and bones, as you see that I have" (Luke 24:39 NIV). To demonstrate this he ate fish in their presence (Luke 24:43). There are eschatological questions that remain unanswered. Was this body of flesh and bones in which the disciples saw Jesus ascend to heaven (Acts 1:9) transformed into the kind of spiritual body of which Paul speaks in 1 Corinthians 15, or did he return to his preincarnate state after his ascension? When he returns "in the same way" (Acts 1:11) they saw him leave, will he return in the same *form?* Or will he then be in his preincarnate form of existence?

Paul touches this question only briefly when he says that "just as we have borne the image of the man of dust [Adam], we shall also bear the image of the man of heaven [Jesus]." Paul's point is that "flesh and blood cannot inherit the kingdom of God, nor does the perishable inherit the imperishable" (1 Cor. 15:49–50). What is that "image of the man of heaven" that we shall bear? The body of Jesus after his resurrection and before his ascension still consisted of flesh and bones at that time, but the question remains as to the nature of his ascended body forty days later.

If the ascended Jesus, whom Paul calls the "man of heaven" (1 Cor. 15:47–48), is not composed of "flesh and blood" (which cannot inherit the kingdom of heaven, 1 Cor. 15:50), then Jesus' body must have changed from its post-resurrection form (which still contained "flesh and bones," Luke 24:39) into some kind of new spiritual form. What then is the nature of the body of Jesus now? Has he now reverted to the mode of his preincarnate existence as "the Word of God" (John 1:1–14)? Or, conversely, did he keep a body like ours, in which he lived during his incarnate existence and which has now been transformed as ours will be into the new "spiritual body" of which Paul speaks (1 Cor. 15:44)?

The question concisely stated, then, is whether Jesus, after his ascension, reverted to the mode in which he existed before he came to the earth or whether he now lives in a resurrected and transformed body. Of course, being the Word of God who was in the beginning with God and through whom all things were created (John 1:3), he is exceptional among his creation. But even if we could understand the nature of Jesus' body during the period between his resurrection and ascension, would this mean that our future "spiritual bodies" will be like his during that time? Or, if he possesses a different kind of body now after his ascension, will ours be like that one? Paul declared that "we await a Savior, the Lord Jesus Christ, who will change our lowly body to be like his glorious body, by the power which enables him even to subject all things to himself" (Phil. 3:21). But what is that glorious body? Paul gives us no answer, perhaps because it lies beyond the understanding of mortal beings. It is enough to know that we shall be like him and "like his glorious body."

The Intermediate State

Paul writes in 2 Corinthians 5:1 that we presently live in an earthly house that, when it is destroyed, will be replaced by a building from God, a house not made with hands, which in the next verse he calls a "heavenly building." The Greek word οἰκία (*oikia*), used by Paul twice in verse 1 for "house," is rendered differently in some translations (RSV, NIV, etc.), which use "tent" for the first occurrence and "house" for the second to emphasize the temporal nature of the first, earthly body.

Paul's statement in 2 Corinthians 5:8 that "we would rather be away from the body and at home with the Lord" could be understood to imply an intermediate state of existence for those who are now dead and living in a disembodied state until the resurrection. But the fact that he says the earthly body will be replaced by the *heavenly body* suggests to some commentators that the replacement is immediate and there is no intermediate state.[15] However, this is not an inherent implication. Paul is speaking about the body in which we now live in contrast to the one that will be ours eternally. How soon after death that transition occurs is not stated. Indeed, for some living when Christ returns, it will not even necessitate death—"we shall not all sleep [die], but we shall all be changed" (1 Cor. 15:51).

It has been mistakenly asserted by a recent author on Paul that in 1 Thessalonians 4:16–17 Paul "had said that the dead would be restored to life, and would be with the Lord, *only at the Second Coming*."[16] This means that the

15. This is the view of Herman Ridderbos, *Paul*, 504ff.
16. Jerome Murphy O'Connor, *Paul: A Critical Life* (New York: Oxford University Press, 1997), 221, italics added.

dead are not now alive because they still have to be restored to life. However, when Paul says the dead in Christ will be resurrected, he is referring to the body, not the soul, since the soul does not die. It is the body, not the soul, that has to be restored to life.

F. F. Bruce argues that those who die before the parousia of Jesus receive at death some kind of body that he calls a "new body" and are not, therefore, disembodied immortal souls. Speaking of immortality, he says, "It is always of the resurrection body that it is predicated, never of the soul."[17] He argues that in the New Testament there is no such thing as an immortal soul without some kind of body. Immortality is granted to the body and soul together, not to the soul alone. He then contrasts this "new body" given to people at death with what he calls a "spiritual body" that will be granted to people still living at the parousia of Jesus. This spiritual body will then be their eternal body. Thus, according to Bruce, there are two different kinds of bodies for people in two different situations—those who are alive at Jesus' coming and those who have died—but in no case does Bruce allow for the existence of a disembodied immortal soul.

So where are the dead prior to the resurrection?

1. Are they, as Bruce suggests, living a conscious existence with the Lord in a new spiritual body given to them immediately upon death, which will have no participation in a resurrection of their old physical bodies at the parousia?
2. Are they living with the Lord in a disembodied soul awaiting the final resurrection of and unification with their bodies at the parousia?
3. Are they being kept, with or without a spiritual body, in a state of unconscious existence (soul sleep) awaiting the parousia?
4. Are they living with the Lord in a new spiritual body, which at the parousia will be joined to their old physical body and molded into a still different kind of eternal, spiritual body?

Paul does not answer this question. He states only that "the dead in Christ will rise first" (1 Thess. 4:16). However, Bruce is correct in his assertion that "in order to benefit by resurrection one must continue to exist; otherwise it [resurrection] would be the creation of an entirely new being,"[18] and this, of course, would negate the continuity of identity discussed above.

It is probably true that "speculation on how Paul conceived the so-called 'intermediate state' is pointless."[19] However, Paul emphatically asserts that following his death, Jesus continued to live for three days in an intermediate

17. Bruce, *Paul*, 312–13.
18. Ibid.
19. Ibid.

state until his resurrection (1 Cor. 15:4). Therefore, whether it is three days or three thousand years, the existence of an intermediate state between death and resurrection is only a question of time, not of existence, a question of duration, not of reality.

Although the nature of that intermediate state is not developed in Scripture, Paul's desire to "depart and be with Christ" (Phil. 1:23) need not mean that being with Christ would occur immediately, but only that it would happen in the appropriate sequence of time that God appoints. If, however, Paul does mean that he desires to be with Christ immediately after death, he would be referring to his entering into an indefinite period of disembodied existence, like that of Jesus during the three days between his death and resurrection. Such a postulated immediate presence with Jesus after death would not necessarily negate Paul's eventual participation in the coming reunion of his soul and body at the general resurrection. Eternal presence with God is the privileged destiny of all resurrected believers in Christ, who is the "first fruits of those who have fallen asleep" (1 Cor. 15:20). "We . . . who have the first fruits of the Spirit . . . wait for . . . the redemption of our bodies" (Rom. 8:23) because one day Jesus Christ will "change our lowly body to be like his glorious body" (Phil. 3:21).

At this point in our inquiry, we cannot escape contemplation of the philosophical question about the relation between time and eternity. Whether there is or is not activity in an intermediate period, we must ask whether time is passing in the heavenly realm in the same way it is passing here on earth. Were Moses and Elijah hundreds of years older when they appeared and talked to Jesus at his transfiguration (Matt. 17:3)? Is Paul two thousand years older now than when he wrote his letters? Or does time exist in eternity? Is it measured by the passing of years? Is it possible that beyond the realm of human existence in this cosmos life is not measured by the passing of time? Are the elements that constituted the body of Paul aging with the passage of time, or have they actually ceased to exist? If they have ceased to exist, will they not have to be recreated for Paul's resurrection and reunification with that body? Otherwise, will there not be a completely new body created for him and a consequent loss of the "continuity of identity" with the Paul of the first century? The reader of Paul's letters cannot but wonder about questions such as these, and since he does not provide his readers with answers to these and related questions, it may be assumed that they are not essential to the life of faith and the joy of living in expectation of the ultimate resurrection of the body and reunion with Jesus Christ.

Inherent to this issue, however, is the necessity of the presence of the resurrected body at the parousia of Jesus and the day of judgment. The purpose of our bodies being resurrected is that "we must all appear before the judgment seat of Christ, so that each one may receive good or evil, according to what he has done in the body" (2 Cor. 5:10). When Paul argues in 1 Corinthians 6:14 that God will "raise us up," he is referring to our human bodies, which he specifically names in the preceding and following verses. The judgment will not occur until after the general resurrection of human bodies from death (those that have been buried and are still in the grave will rise from their graves, and those that have decomposed will be re-created).[20] Such is the continuity expressed in the repetition of the pronoun *it* in 1 Corinthians 15:43. "It," the pre-resurrected body that has died, will be raised, and "it" will be raised not just as a spirit but as a "spiritual body" (1 Cor. 15:44). "It is sown a physical body, it is raised a spiritual body." Thus, Paul is not speaking of a fleshly body becoming a spirit but of "two modes of bodily existence."[21] There is an earthly body, and there is a heavenly, spiritual body. Paul emphasizes that this earthly body should be used to glorify God (1 Cor. 6:20) in anticipation of its being transformed into a spiritual body. There is a difference in Paul's thought between the flesh and the body. The "flesh is doomed to die," whereas the "body is destined for immortality."[22]

We are left, then, with the question of the nature of our existence immediately after death. If we are not merely disembodied spirits but possessors of a new kind of body, what kind is it? Obviously, it could not include the earthly, physical body that is still in the grave. Equally obvious is the fact that it could not be the postresurrection "spiritual body" because the resurrection has not yet occurred. This has led some to argue that we are taken directly to the presence of Jesus at death and continue there until the general resurrection as disembodied spirits. In this perspective the "spiritual body" referred to by Paul in 1 Corinthians 15:44 is merely a metaphorical reference to the immortal soul of man to contrast it with the "physical body."

From this perspective Paul is referring to a bodiless soul when he speaks of desiring to not be *naked* (2 Cor. 5:3). However, in the next verse he says that while he is living in this body, he is anxious not to be *unclothed* when he dies. Rather, he wants to be *further clothed* (2 Cor. 5:4). In these verses he also uses the analogy of a building in which he now lives and a new building that will be his "heavenly dwelling." In both comparisons he is exchanging one metaphor for the other, one kind of clothing for a new kind, one kind of dwelling for another kind. He is not saying he is leaving this earth and his physical body for a naked or homeless state—in essence, to live as a disembodied soul. It has been argued that "the soul is nowhere spoken of in this context as the subject of continued existence after death," by which is meant the immortality of the soul apart from some kind of body. But it is also argued that after death we are "not yet to live in the glorified body."[23]

---

20. Ridderbos denies that "the resurrection of those already dead would take place in the same body as that in which they had lived before" (*Paul*, 535).

21. Ibid., 543.

22. Bruce, *Paul*, 206.

23. Ridderbos, *Paul*, 507, see also 503.

This means, then, that some kind of "body," "tent," or "clothing" characterizes the postmortem state of existence, but we are left with the question, What is it? The author of the above quotations concludes that it is "thus for us an inconceivable mode of human existence."[24] Some have dubbed this period between death and resurrection as a time of "soul sleep," a kind of spiritual hypnosis.[25]

Others have thought that at death we are caught up to be with Christ in the heavenly region forever.[26] Still others have argued that we are caught up into the heavenly realm to be with Christ in order to come back to earth with him.[27]

Millennialism

This last approach raises the question of the purpose of Christ's returning to the earth. If he returns to the earth, will it be to establish a millennial reign? If this is true, why does he not come to the earth, raise the dead, and remain here with them? Why are they called up to meet him in the air only to return again to the earth for another thousand years? The question of a literal millennial (thousand-year) reign of Christ has been an issue of considerable interest throughout the history of the church,[28] and the recent transition into the third millennium after Christ at the year 2001 has brought a renewed interest in the topic. However, some major works on Paul omit the subject,[29] and this is not without some justification, because Paul makes no mention of a thousand-year reign of Jesus. The conjecture that he alludes to it is based on the introduction of the idea of the millennial kingdom from Revelation 20 into Paul's discussion of the end-time events in 1 Corinthians 15:22–28.[30]

In Revelation, the millennial reign of Christ is ended by Satan's release from his prison, after which he deceives the nations until he is finally thrown into the lake of fire and brimstone to be tormented day and night forever and ever (Rev. 20:1–10). How this relates to the parousia has been and continues

24. Ibid.
25. "On the intermediate state between death and resurrection the New Testament gives us no explicit information. It is thought of as a sleep unless the various authors suggest other conceptions" (Rudolf Bultmann, "Θάνατος," *Theological Dictionary of the New Testament,* ed. G. Kittel and G. Friedrich; trans. G. W. Bromiley [Grand Rapids: Eerdmans, 1964–76], 3:17).
26. Vos, *Pauline Eschatology,* 138.
27. Ridderbos, *Paul,* 535.
28. See the brief discussions in Ridderbos, *Paul,* 556–62; and Plevnik, *Paul and the Parousia,* 129.
29. E.g., Bruce, *Paul;* and Murphy-O'Connor, *Paul: A Critical Life.*
30. Ridderbos, *Paul,* 557.

to be intensely debated. However, Paul does not discuss such an apocalyptic event and makes no specific, unquestionable allusion to it or to a rapture.

A Possible Sequence of Eschatological Events

Looking at the thoughts of the passages as a whole in which Paul discusses the eschatological events, which for him (and for us two thousand years later) still lie in the future, we can perhaps construct the following scenario. This construction is admittedly based on an assumption of Paul's inspiration, which does not allow for his being mistaken in his early years of ministry and then developing different ideas as time progressed.[31] I will add some statements from other New Testament authors for additional clarification at times.

1. The End of the Times. The preexistent Word of God came to the earth and lived in the realm of humanity as the incarnate Son of God, who eventually was crucified, buried, and raised from the dead for the sins of the world. Paul writes that "in fact Christ has been raised from the dead, the first fruits of those who have fallen asleep" (1 Cor. 15:20; cf. Acts 13:30). Peter agrees with Paul, asserting that Christ "was destined before the foundation of the world but was made manifest at the end of the times for your sake" (1 Pet. 1:20). This manifestation of Jesus is here declared to be "at the end of the times" (ἐσχάτου τῶν χρόνων, *eschatou tōn chronōn*), which begins with his first coming, not a later event.

2. The Present Interval. The interval between Christ's ascension and his future return is a period during which God has made Christ "sit at his right hand in the heavenly places, far above all rule and authority and power and dominion" (Eph. 1:20–21). During this time in which we now live, Peter assures the recipients of his letter, "through him you have confidence in God, who raised him from the dead and gave him glory, so that your faith and hope are in God" (1 Pet. 1:21). Jesus now reigns in heaven with God, and we live in joyful anticipation of his return.

However, the unseen, evil powers of the universe, though they are subject to Christ, are still free to exercise some power and to tempt humans to turn

---

31. Bruce speaks of a "progression in his thoughts and language" on the subject of the life to come but says "his central belief and teaching do not appear to have undergone any essential change throughout his career." He then adds, "It would be surprising if his experiences had no influence at all on his outlook on the future" (*Paul,* 305). A few pages later he comments: "It is when we come to 2 Corinthians that we are conscious of a change of perspective on Paul's part. . . . Whatever other changes this experience [facing death on occasions, JM] occasioned in his outlook, it modified his perspective on death and resurrection. For one thing, he henceforth treats the prospect of his dying before the parousia as more probable than otherwise" (310).

from God. Peter says that Christ "has gone into heaven and is at the right hand of God, with angels, authorities, and powers subject to him" (1 Pet. 3:22). Paul further clarifies this, saying that Jesus will eventually destroy these cosmic powers and that he "must reign until he has put all his enemies under his feet. The last enemy to be destroyed is death" (1 Cor. 15:25–26). And so, until Christ returns, we live with sickness and death as present realities.

During this interval, as we await that return, the unrighteous dead are being kept "under punishment [or, 'while continuing their punishment,' NIV] until the day of judgment" (2 Pet. 2:9). This was emphatically illustrated by Jesus in the story of the rich man and Lazarus, both of whom had died (Luke 16:19–31). The ungodly rich man was in Hades (ᾅδης, *hadēs*), the unseen realm of the dead, where he was in torment because of his sins, while Lazarus was in a state of happiness called "Abraham's bosom." During this time people were still living on earth, and the rich man asked Abraham to send Lazarus back to earth to warn his five brothers still living there (Luke 16:28). If this is meant to give some insight into the situation after death, then it should be noted that (1) the evil are being tormented, (2) the righteous are being blessed, (3) there is an impassable chasm between the two so that their situation is unchangeable (Luke 16:26), and (4) final judgment has obviously not occurred. Jesus appears to be speaking of an interval period.

Not only humans but also angels who sinned at some point in the past have been "sent . . . to hell" and "put into gloomy dungeons to be held for judgment" (2 Pet. 2:4 NIV). The heavens and the earth that now exist are also being kept until that "day of judgment and destruction of ungodly men" (2 Pet. 3:7).

During this interval period, the "dead in Christ" (1 Thess. 4:16)—those Christians who have "fallen asleep"—have not perished (1 Cor. 15:6, 18; 1 Thess. 4:13, 15); they are dead but not destroyed. Christ's resurrection is the guarantee that he is the "first fruits" of those who have "fallen asleep" (1 Cor. 15:20).

3. The Great Apostasy. Paul assures the Thessalonians that there will be a "coming of our Lord Jesus Christ" (2 Thess. 2:1), but it will not occur until the "rebellion" comes first and the "man of lawlessness," the "son of perdition," is revealed (2 Thess. 2:3, 7–9). A "mystery of lawlessness," as Paul calls it in verse 7, was "already at work" when he was writing the letter, but it was being restrained by someone (v. 6) until the "lawless one" would be revealed and destroyed by the Lord Jesus (v. 8). Who or what this restrainer is has been endlessly speculated about and shown to be beyond indisputable identification. Everything and everyone from the Roman Empire to a Roman emperor to an ancient or modern political or religious leader has been suggested. What is indisputably obvious is that the earth is still populated, still functioning, and still awaiting the parousia of Christ. He has not yet returned! What is important to understand is Paul's admonition that people should "love the truth

. . . believe the truth . . . and [have no] pleasure in unrighteousness" (2 Thess. 2:10–12). But what is the truth? Apart from him who is "the way, and the truth, and the life" (John 14:6), there is no assurance of what it is. And even though students of Paul and his life (and other New Testament authors) may not always know the answer to doctrinal or hypothetical questions, it must be remembered that when Paul in 1 Corinthians 13:13 compares the things that are permanent and eternal with those that are temporary, he does not say "So faith, hope, love abide, . . . but the greatest of these is *knowledge.*" He says "The greatest of these is *love.*"

4. *The Coming Parousia of Christ.* Paul clearly declares a future coming of Christ (1 Cor. 15:23) and states that it is "near" (ἐγγύς, *engys,* Phil. 4:5), as does James (James 5:8). Peter used the same Greek word to state that "the end of all things is at hand [near]" (ἤγγικεν, *ēngiken,* 1 Pet. 4:7), having already stated that Jesus was revealed at these end times (1 Pet. 1:20). Thus, the parousia of Jesus is a part of the "end of all things." Paul states that "then comes the end, when he delivers the kingdom to God the Father after destroying every rule and every authority and power" (1 Cor. 15:24). This is called "the day of the Lord" and is said to come without anyone being able to predict it, "like a thief in the night. When people say, 'There is peace and security,'" then it will happen (1 Thess. 5:2–3). The last enemy to be destroyed is death (1 Cor. 15:26; 2 Tim. 1:10), which necessarily includes "him who has the power of death, that is, the devil" (Heb. 2:14). In the apocalyptic picture portrayed in the Book of Revelation, "Death and Hades gave up the dead in them, and all were judged by what they had done. Then Death and Hades were thrown into the lake of fire. This is the second death, the lake of fire; and if any one's name was not found written in the book of life, he was thrown into the lake of fire" (Rev. 20:13–15).

5. *The Resurrection of Believers.* The resurrection of believers comes next. Paul assures the Thessalonians, who were concerned about the status of loved ones who had died, that "the dead in Christ will rise first" (1 Thess. 4:16). About believers who have "fallen asleep in Christ" (1 Cor. 15:18), Paul says Christ is "the first fruits of those who have fallen asleep" (1 Cor. 15:20). The sequence of resurrection includes Christians first: "In Christ shall all be made alive. But each in his own order: Christ the first fruits, then at his coming those who belong to Christ. Then comes the end" (1 Cor. 15:22–24).

It is not stated whether the judgment of the living and the dead (1 Pet. 4:5) occurs immediately upon the resurrection of the body (the "flesh and bones" body like that of Jesus after his resurrection, Luke 24:40) or after the change into the new "imperishable" body (1 Cor. 15:52). Paul simply states that "we shall all be changed, . . . and the dead will be raised imperishable, and we shall be changed" (1 Cor. 15:51–52). He says the dead in Christ and the living Christians will "be caught up together . . . to meet the Lord in the air; and so we shall always be with the Lord" (1 Thess. 4:17).

6. The Resurrection of Unbelievers. Since the coming judgment will be for the deeds done in the body, whether good or evil, the unbelievers will also be resurrected in anticipation of that event. Paul tells the Romans that "we shall all stand before the judgment seat of God. . . . So each of us shall give account of himself to God" (Rom. 14:10–12). He writes similarly to the Corinthians that "we must all appear before the judgment seat of Christ, so that each one may receive good or evil, according to what he has done in the body" (2 Cor. 5:10).

7. The Judgment of All People. In Jesus' description of the judgment scene in Matthew 25:31–46, he said the Son of Man will come in all his glory and all the angels with him. He will sit on his glorious throne, and before him will be gathered all the nations. They will be separated into two categories, the sheep and the goats. The sheep, who will be placed at his right hand, will be those who have lived as Jesus taught them. The goats at his left hand will be those who have not. To them he will say, "Depart from me, you cursed, into the eternal fire prepared for the devil and his angels." Paul also writes to the Thessalonians about the judgment, telling them that the Lord will inflict "vengeance upon those who do not know God and upon those who do not obey the gospel of our Lord Jesus. They shall suffer the punishment of eternal destruction and exclusion from the presence of the Lord and from the glory of his might, when he comes on that day to be glorified in his saints, and to be marveled at in all who have believed" (2 Thess. 1:8–10).

Judgment will "begin with the household of God" and include those who "do not obey the gospel of God" (1 Pet. 4:17). Peter calls it a "day of judgment and destruction of ungodly men" (2 Pet. 3:7). Both Peter (1 Pet. 1:17) and Paul (2 Cor. 5:10) declare that the judgment will be made on the basis of the deeds done in the body.

At this time all things, except God, will be subjected to Christ (1 Cor. 15:27–28). The disobedient angels, who have been *tartarized* and committed "to pits of nether gloom [ζόφος, *zophos*] to be kept until the judgment" (2 Pet. 2:4; Jude 6) will be punished by "eternal fire" (Jude 7). I have transliterated the Greek participle *tartarize* here because its exact meaning is debatable. It is translated "hell" in both the RSV and the NIV, but this is its only occurrence in the New Testament, and it is not a noun. The Greek text literally says that God "delivered them to pits of nether gloom ["gloomy dungeons," NIV], having *tartarized* them [ταρταρώσας, *tartarōsas*]." Whether a final state of punishment or an interim state of punishment is indicated here is not specified. However, it is clear that the punishment is currently in progress and will continue until the parousia and the final day of judgment. Jude states that godless people who are licentious and deny Jesus Christ (Jude 4) and defile the flesh (Jude 8) will experience this "nether gloom of darkness" (Jude 13; "blackest darkness," NIV). Peter also writes that this "nether gloom of darkness" (2 Pet.

2:17) is reserved for the unrighteous who "have eyes full of adultery" and never stop sinning (2 Pet. 2:14).

On this "day of the Lord . . . the heavens will pass away, with a loud noise, and the elements will be dissolved with fire, and the earth and the works that are in it will be burned up" (2 Pet. 3:10). Two verses later Peter speaks of this as the "day of God," on which God will "bring about the destruction of the heavens by fire, and the elements will melt in the heat" (2 Pet. 3:12 NIV). This "day of the Lord," Paul says, will come like a thief in the night after the rebellion and the revelation of the man of lawlessness, the son of perdition (1 Thess. 5:2; 2 Thess. 2:2–3).

8. *The Return of the Lord to Heaven.* After the resurrection and judgment of the righteous and the wicked, and the consignment of each to the appropriate position of reward or punishment, the righteous are caught up to meet the Lord in the air (1 Thess. 4:17). Then will follow the destruction of the cosmos by fire (2 Pet. 3:12), including the destruction of every rule and every authority and power, and the kingdom will be delivered to God the Father (1 Cor. 15:24). And when all things are subjected to God, then the Son himself will also be subjected to him (1 Cor. 15:28).

When the Perfect Comes

Few phrases from the pen of Paul have occasioned more controversy than his comment in 1 Corinthians 13:10 that spiritual gifts will be done away with when the perfect (τὸ τέλειον, *to teleion*) has come. The validity of present-day claims to possession of the spiritual gifts (i.e., charismatic gifts, χαρίσματα, *charismata*) depends upon the meaning of this phrase. The variation given it in translation raises the question of whether the statement was meant by Paul to be historical or apocalyptic, present or future. It has been rendered as "that which is perfect" (KJV), "the perfect" (RSV), "the Complete" (PHILLIPS), "wholeness" (NEB), "the time of fulfillment" (KNOX), "that which is mature" (Cotton Patch Version), "when we have been made perfect and complete" (LB), and "perfection" (JB).

Determining what Paul means by the term τέλειος (*teleios*) in 1 Corinthians requires an investigation of the entire corpus attributed to Paul in the New Testament since aspects of his theology are to be found in each book bearing his name. Even those who reject Pauline authorship of such books as Ephesians, Colossians, and the Pastoral Epistles must recognize within such books the earliest understanding of Paul's thinking outside the generally recognized Pauline corpus. The meaning of the phrase *to teleion,* "the perfect," is as problematical in interpretation as in translation. Possible meanings for the phrase include:

1. The completed or perfected New Testament canon.[32] James 1:25, where the law of liberty is designated as *teleios,* has been seen as evidence for this understanding. Paul refers to the "good and acceptable and perfect [*teleios*]" will of God in Romans 12:2.

2. The perfect unity of the church as expressed in the concept of love. Support for this meaning may be found in the emphasis on *agapē* in the immediate context of the chapter, though *to teleion* (that which is perfect) is neuter, and *agapē* (love) is feminine. It may also be noted that 1 John 4:18 states that *teleios* (perfect) love casts out fear.

3. The perfection or sinlessness of the individual (which in its absolute sense could apply in this life only to Jesus). For this view, appeal has been made to Matthew 5:48, where Jesus says, "Be perfect [*teleios*], as your heavenly Father is perfect." It may also be noted that Jesus commanded the rich young ruler to sell all his possessions and follow Jesus if he wanted to be "perfect" (*teleios*) (Matt. 19:21). A number of times the term is given the ethical sense of maturity in Christian wisdom (1 Cor. 2:6; 14:20; Phil. 3:15; Heb. 5:14; James 1:4).

4. The ultimate reward of heaven.[33] The general picture of the perfection of heaven presented in Revelation 21 has suggested this meaning to many interpreters of Paul. In heaven perfection comes when the "former things" (τὰ πρῶτα, *ta prōta*) have passed away (Rev. 21:4) and in 1 Corinthians 13, the *teleios* comes when the "imperfect," or "partial" (ἐκ μέρους, *ek merous*), things have passed away.

All of these interpretations, however, suffer from the same weakness; they impose a meaning on *teleios* that the various contexts do not warrant:

1. Neither in James nor in Paul is the canon of the New Testament under consideration in the general context. The "perfect" (*teleion*) law of which James speaks, in the context, more likely describes a law involving both faith and works in contrast to one that does not. The implication in both James 1:25 and Romans 12:2 is that such a law has already been given and only needs to be accepted and followed.

2. First Corinthians 13, in which Paul speaks of love with such emphasis, cannot be divorced from its relation to both the preceding and the following chapters, which have charismatic gifts as their theme. The thirteenth chapter is injected by Paul as a moderating influence

32. David Lipscomb, *A Commentary on the New Testament,* vol. 2, *First Corinthians* (Nashville: Gospel Advocate, 1935), 184; W. E. Vine, *First Corinthians* (London: Oliphants, 1961), 200–201.

33. The overwhelming majority of commentators take this view: e.g., Bultmann, Godet, Beet, Stanley, McGarvey, Moffatt, Meyer, Hodge, Barnes, Clarke, Craig, Cambridge Greek Testament.

on the inordinate desire of the Corinthians to exercise their spiritual gifts. The love of which he speaks, therefore, must not be taken in the absolute sense of an *agapē* (the highest kind of love) that in its perfection allows no dissension. It must rather be understood as in some way bearing directly on the prevailing tension in Corinth over the use of *charismata* and must be within the possibility of attainment by those who possess these gifts. Furthermore, if "love" were intended by the words *to teleion,* the phrase would more naturally have been in the feminine gender agreeing with *agapē,* rather than in the neuter.

3. While considerable discussion *is* given to the need for ethical or moral *teleiōtēs* (maturity) in individual Christians, it should also be noted that James, who regards a *teleios* person as one who does not stumble in speech (James 3:2), nevertheless declares that "no one can tame the tongue" (James 3:8). He thus affirms that *teleios* is less than human perfection. Moreover, in 1 Corinthians 13 Paul discusses the ethical implications of *agapē* in the context of spiritual gifts, not in the context of one person's general ethical and moral behavior. When Jesus used the term *teleios* in affirming that his disciples should be "perfect" as their "heavenly Father is perfect," the context of his words defined *teleios* as loving those who do not love you. Paul uses the term in the specific context of charismatic conduct, and we must therefore look for its meaning in light of that special discussion.

4. The identification of *to teleios* as heaven involves the application of a secondary meaning to the term. The English term *perfect* should be used to translate *teleios* only if the context demands such a meaning, because the term *perfect* in contemporary usage carries with it the idea of flawlessness and infallibility rather than the original connotation of completeness, fullness, or maturity. But even without this misleading translation of the term here in 1 Corinthians, there is nothing in the context of Paul's discussion that justifies equating heaven with *to teleion.*

In short, we may observe that the general procedure employed in defining *to teleion* in 1 Corinthians 13 has been to assign it a meaning consistent with its use elsewhere in some New Testament text that is clearer than the one in this chapter. While this procedure is basically sound, for contexts are more important than dictionaries in defining words, we must look not simply for other usages of the term *teleios* in Pauline material but, more important, for usages in contexts *similar* to the one in this chapter. Only then can we be confident we are assigning the word the meaning that best suits the author's intentions.

The use of the term in the Septuagint,[34] the Apostolic Fathers,[35] and the papyri[36] supports its basic meaning in the New Testament as "full grown, mature, total, complete, or final." Such is also the normal meaning in Hebrew of both *tāmim* and *shālēm,* for which *teleios* stands in the Septuagint.[37] There is an instance in the papyri where the phrase ἀλεκτόρων τελείων τεσσάρων occurs, meaning "four *full-grown* roosters."[38] It is this sense, with the meaning of maturity, that the word almost always bears in the New Testament. Of nineteen occurrences, three appear in Matthew (5:48 [twice]; 19:21), two in Hebrews (5:14; 9:11), five in James (1:4 [twice], 17, 25; 3:2), one in 1 John 4:18, and the remaining six in the Pauline corpus (Rom. 12:2; 1 Cor. 2:6; 13:10; 14:20; Eph. 4:13; Phil. 3:15; Col. 1:28; 4:12).[39]

The majority of these occurrences are in contexts contrasting *teleios* with babes (Heb. 5:14; 1 Cor. 13:10; 14:20; Eph. 4:13),[40] immature wisdom (1 Cor. 2:6–7),[41] something that is lacking (Col. 1:24, 28),[42] or something that is partial (1 Cor. 13:10).[43] The verb form of this word, τελειόω (*teleioō*), appears twenty-three times in the New Testament with the meaning of "accomplish or complete." Nine of these occurrences are in the Book of Hebrews (Heb. 2:10; 5:9; 7:19, 28; 9:9; 10:1, 14; 11:40; 12:23),[44] where the verb is used of the *complete* obedience manifested by Jesus in his work as high priest. Included in this concept is the complete or final nature of his law and his sacrifice in contrast to those of Moses.

Thus, more than 50 percent of the occurrences of the noun and verb appear in the section of the New Testament designated historically as Pauline. The breadth of meaning given to the word is such that it does not appear to be a technical term. We must, therefore, turn to similar contexts to establish

34. Edwin Hatch and Henry A. Redpath, *A Concordance to the Septuagint,* 2d ed. (Grand Rapids: Baker, 1998), 1342.

35. Herm. *Sim.* 5.3.6; Herm. *Vis.* 1.2.1; *Did.* 1.4; 6.2; *1 Clem.* 1.2; 44.2, 5; 55.6; 56.1; *Barn.* 1.5; 4.3, 11; 5.11; 8.1; 13.7; Ign. *Pol.* 1.3; Ign. *Eph.* 15.2; Ign. *Smyrn.* 10.2; 11.1, 2, 3; 4.2; Ign. *Phld.* 1.2.

36. Moulton and Milligan, *Vocabulary,* 629.

37. Francis Brown, S. R. Driver, and C. A. Briggs, *A Hebrew and English Lexicon of the Old Testament* (Oxford: Clarendon, 1957), 1071, 1023–24.

38. Moulton and Milligan, *Vocabulary,* 629.

39. H. Bachmann and W. A. Slaby, eds., *Concordance to the Novum Testamentum Graece,* 3d ed. (Berlin: De Gruyter, 1987), 1777.

40. Two words for *babes* are used in the contrasts: νήπιος (*nēpios*) is used in all these passages except 1 Cor. 14:20, where παιδία (*paidia*) is used.

41. A number of different words are used: σοφία, *sophia* (1 Cor. 2:6–7; James 1:4–5); φρήν, *phrēn* (1 Cor. 14:20); φρονέω, *phroneō* (Phil. 3:15); ἐπίγνωσις, *epignōsis* (Eph. 4:13); γινώσκω, *ginōskō;* and βλέπω, *blepō* (1 Cor. 13:9, 12).

42. ὑστερήματα, *hysterēmata* (Col. 1:24, 28); ὑστερέω, *hystereō* (Matt. 19:20); λειπόμενοι, *leipomenoi* (James 1:4).

43. τὸ ἐκ μέρους, *to ek merous* (1 Cor. 13:10).

44. The other occurrences are in Luke 2:43; 13:32; John 4:34; 5:36; 17:4, 23; 19:28; Acts 20:24; Phil. 3:12; James 2:22; 1 John 2:5; 4:12, 17, 18.

its meaning. If we can establish that two contexts are identical and successfully define the meaning of *to teleion* in one of them, we shall have made as strong a case as can be made for the meaning of the phrase in the other context.

Such identical contexts are to be found in 1 Corinthians 12–14 and Ephesians 4. This may be seen in a comparative table:

Table 17.1 Ephesians and 1 Corinthians Compared

Ephesians	1 Corinthians
1. Jew-Gentile discussion (2:11; 3:1; 4:17 [22])	1. Gentiles (12:2); Greeks (12:13)
2. Emphasis on "all"	2. "All in all" (12:6, 12)
3. Emphasis on "oneness and unity" (4:4–6; 2:16–22)	3. Emphasis on "one, one and the same" giver of the gifts (12:4–14)
unity of the Spirit (4:3)	*same* Spirit (12:4); *same* Lord (12:5)
one body, *one* Spirit, *one* hope (4:4)	*same* God (12:6); *same* Spirit (12:8)
one Lord, *one* faith, *one* baptism (4:5)	*same* spirit, *one* Spirit (12:9)
one God and Father of all (4:6)	*one* and the *same* Spirit (12:11)
one body (2:16); *one* Spirit (2:18)	*one* body (12:12); *one* Spirit, *one* body, *one* Spirit (12:13)
4. Divine gifts (4:7–11)	4. Divine gifts (12:4–11, 27–31; 13:1–3, 8–13; 14:1–10)
5. Human body illustration of unity (4:12–16)	5. Human body illustration (12:12–13, 14–26)
6. Human growth illustrates progress of the spiritual body (church) (4:13–16)	6. Paul's growth illustrates Corinthian progress (13:11)
7. *Teleios* (4:13)	7. *Teleios* (13:10)

The analysis of 1 Corinthians 12–14 must be made on the basis of the entire argument of Ephesians. The theological development of Ephesians is clear;[45] the Gentiles are shown to be included in the church on equal grounds with the Jews as a part of "salvation history." Chapter 1 shows the Jews to be the predestined *hagioi* (saints) of God who bring salvation into the world. Paul includes himself as a Jew in these discussions by using the first-person pronouns *we, us,* and *our.* In 1:13, a transition from the Jews is made, and the Gentiles have been included. They are referred to with the second-person pronoun *you* throughout Ephesians; this is clear in 2:11. The Gentiles' concern for the welfare of Jewish Christians is mentioned in 1:15.

Chapter 2 begins with a discussion of the previous pagan Gentile life of Gentile Christians, climaxing in verses 13 and following with the statement that the Gentiles have nevertheless been included with the Jews in the work

---

45. See the discussion in chapter 13.

of Christ; Christ reconciled them "both [Jew and Gentile, JM] to God in one body through the cross" (Eph. 2:16). They "*both* have access in one Spirit to the Father" (Eph. 2:18). The result is that the Gentiles are no longer strangers and sojourners but are "fellow citizens" with the Jewish Christians (Eph. 2:19). As such, they are part of the "household of God" and are built upon the foundation of Jewish apostles and prophets (Eph. 2:20).

The author begins chapter 3 by reminding his Gentile audience that it is for this very purpose (i.e., his work among the Gentiles in bringing them into the house of God) that he is a prisoner of Christ. As he says in Ephesians 2:22, the Gentiles *also* are "builded together [with the Jews] for an habitation of God through the Spirit" (KJV). In fact, the very mystery of the gospel itself involves the inclusion of the Gentiles with the status of *fellow* heirs, *fellow* members of the body, and *fellow* partakers of the promise given to Abraham that *all* nations would be blessed through his seed (Eph. 3:4–6; Gal. 3:16). Paul's discussion of this point in Galatians 3:7–14 identifies Christ as the promised seed of Abraham and connects the promise with the inclusion of the Gentiles. Galatians 3:13–14 says, "Christ redeemed us . . . that in Christ Jesus the blessing of Abraham might come upon the Gentiles; that we might receive the promise of the Spirit through faith." The promise mentioned in Ephesians 3:6 has already been identified in 1:13 with the guarantee given the Gentiles by the Holy Spirit of their inclusion into the plan of God. Thus, in Ephesians 3:14 Paul bows before the Father of both Jew and Gentile, of both earthly and heavenly families.

It is then, within the framework of this Jew-Gentile discussion and indeed on the basis of it, that chapter 4 begins "I therefore, a prisoner for the Lord." It is precisely because the author of Ephesians is a prisoner on behalf of the Gentiles that he exhorts them to keep the unity of the Spirit, who guarantees their inclusion (Eph. 4:2–3). The unity pleaded for is, thus, the willingness of the Jew and Gentile to accept the fact that for *both* of them there is only *one* body, *one* Spirit, *one* hope, *one* Lord, *one* faith, *one* baptism, and certainly from the viewpoint of a Jewish monotheist, *one* God and Father of *all*, who is over *all*, and through *all*, and in *all*. There cannot be one God for the Jew and another for the Gentile. The issue is clear in Romans 3:29–30 that if there is one God, he is the God of the Gentile as well as the Jew.[46]

Continuing in Ephesians 4, the author next asserts that divine gifts have been imparted to this newly created body so that it can achieve the purpose for which it was created. Verse 12 states this purpose, and if we note the special Jewish meaning of the word *saints* in this letter and the distinction in the prepositions in Greek, we may loosely translate it as follows: "The gifts have been given to equip the Jewish Christians to do their work of ministering, which is to include the Gentiles into the body of Christ." The next verse states

---

46. George Howard, "Romans 3:21–31 and the Inclusion of the Gentiles," *HTR* 63 (1970): 223–33.

that this work is to continue until a level of faith and knowledge may be achieved that can be characterized as *teleios,* "a *full-grown* man." In the total context of the discussion, *teleios* can only mean *the maturity of the church as evidenced in the Jewish acceptance of the inclusion of the Gentiles into the one divine body,* which for at least a decade belonged only to the Jews.

If this is the correct understanding of the argument of Ephesians, then the identical context in 1 Corinthians, as well as the identical development of the argument (as outlined in table 17.1 above), establishes the same meaning for *to teleion* in 1 Corinthians 13:10—*the inclusion of the Gentiles.* When this had been achieved, "that which is in part" was done away with, since the gifts were given to achieve this goal. Careful comparison of these two contexts shows that the gifts (*charismata*) were given to both Jews and Gentiles (1 Cor. 12:13; Eph. 4:12–13) primarily to show divine acceptance of both on equal terms into the one body.

The context of 1 Corinthians 12–14 is identical to that of Ephesians. The discussion of charismatic gifts is opened with a reference to the Gentile past of the Corinthians (1 Cor. 12:2), and 12:13 shows that both Jews and Greeks were made to drink of the one Spirit, who gave the gifts to both elements of the early church (12:11). The presence of Jews in the Corinthian church is affirmed in Acts 18:4, which states that Paul "argued in the synagogue every sabbath, and persuaded Jews and Greeks." Acts 18:8 states that Crispus, the ruler of the synagogue, believed, along with all of his house. In 1 Corinthians 1:23, Paul testifies to the presence of both Jew and Greek in the church in Corinth. He says the crucified Christ is foolishness to Greeks and a stumbling block to Jews. The point of chapter 12, then, is not that there are many different kinds of gifts, but rather that, even with the many different kinds of gifts, there is but one giver.

This may be noted in table 17.1. It is the one Spirit, the same Spirit, who gives the gifts to both Jew and Gentile (1 Cor. 12:4–14). As in Ephesians 4, so also in 1 Corinthians Paul illustrates the point with the metaphor of the human body and the process of growth to maturity (*teleios*). In view of these identical contexts, we expect to find identical meanings for *teleios.* In 1 Corinthians 13:10, as in Ephesians 4:13, *teleios* refers to the inclusion of the Gentiles. They too have been made recipients of these divine *charismata* to show God's intention of including them on equal terms into the one body. Peter said in Acts 11:17 that God gave the Gentiles at the house of Cornelius (Acts 10) the same gift that he had given to Jewish believers at Pentecost.

Ephesians 1:13–14 asserts that the Gentiles were sealed with the Holy Spirit as a "guarantee" (ἀρραβών, *arrabōn,* a down payment) of their possession by God, and 1 Corinthians 12:13 affirms that both Jews and Greeks drank of one Spirit and were by one Spirit baptized into one body. The addition of "slave and free" here, and "slave and free, male and female" in Galatians 3:28, is a necessity if God has indeed created one new body. Whether these Jews and Greeks are slaves or free, men or women, barbarian or Scythian, circumcised or uncircumcised (Col. 3:11), they are fully accepted by God and must therefore accept each other. The point is that God has given the *charismata* to all, regardless of social status, sex, or nationality. In 1 Corinthians 11, Paul establishes the right of women to exercise their gifts in prayer and prophecy if properly veiled, and Acts 21:9 says that Philip had four virgin daughters who prophesied.

A primary purpose of the *charismata,* according to Ephesians 4 and 1 Corinthians 12–14, was to weld these diverse elements together into one body with a recognition of one God for both and the observance of one ethical system based upon this relationship. Paul contrasts "that which is perfect" (*to teleion*) with "that which is in part" (*to ek merous*) in 1 Corinthians 13:10. The latter phrase occurs in the Greek New Testament only in 1 Corinthians 12–13, where it appears five times. Perhaps the four occurences in 1 Corinthians 13:9, 10, and 12 are to be understood in the same way as the fifth instance in 1 Corinthians 12:27, where it means "individually." If so, then *to teleion* would mean "complete" in contrast to the possession and exercise of the *charismata* by individuals, whether they are, in Paul's words, "Jews or Greeks, males or females, slaves or free persons." When the church became complete or mature by its equal acceptance before God of every kind of individual, then the partial (individual) possession of the gifts ceased because they had achieved their individual purpose of creating this one new body. For Paul, this purpose primarily involves the inclusion of the Gentiles. God had fulfilled his promise in blessing *all* the nations through the seed of Abraham.

A look at the context in Ephesians 4:17–24 shows a further striking connection with Paul's letter to Rome and may indicate that certain patterns of thought prevailed when the subject of the Gentiles was discussed. In a point-by-point comparison with Romans 1:13–32, it can clearly be seen that not only is the general subject matter the same but that the progression of the thought pattern is identical.

Table 17.2 Ephesians and Romans Compared

Ephesians		Romans	
4:17	Gentiles	1:13, 16	Gentiles, Greeks
4:17	Vanity in their understanding	1:21	Vain in their reasonings
4:18	Darkened in their understanding	1:21	Senseless minds darkened
4:18	Ignorance that is in them	1:22	Professing wisdom, became fools
4:18	Alienated from life of God	1:23	Exchanged glory of God
4:18	Hardening of their heart	1:24	Lust of their heart
4:19	Being past feeling	1:26–27	Changed natural use
4:19	Gave themselves up to lasciviousness, uncleanness, greediness	1:29–32	Filled with all manner of wickedness

These comparative charts show that Paul sometimes wrote with a definite pattern in mind, and when such identical patterns can be found, identical meanings may be assigned to words within those contexts.

More specifically, the time envisioned by the phrase "that which is perfect" (*to teleion*) is, in the Pauline corpus, tied to the work of Paul himself. It was his God-appointed purpose in life to bring the Gentiles into the church. He declares that he was separated from his mother's womb to preach Christ to the Gentiles (Gal. 1:15). He informed King Agrippa that his conversion was a divine call to preach to the Gentiles (Acts 26:17–18). Just as God sent Peter to the Jews, Paul insists that God sent him to the Gentiles (Gal. 2:8). All that Christ did through him was for the obedience of the Gentiles (Rom. 15:16–18). His apostleship to Gentiles meant that he must suffer for them, as Christ suffered for the Jews (Rom. 15:8, 16; Col. 1:24). He filled up on his part that which was lacking in Christ's afflictions (Col. 1:24).

This does not mean that he regarded himself as a messiah to the Gentiles, as has been erroneously asserted.[47] Rather, both Christ and Paul are part of the suffering assigned to Israel on behalf of the Gentiles (Rom. 11:7, 11, 28; Eph. 3:8; Col. 1:24–25). It is through the hardening, rejection, and suffering of Israel that the promise of Abraham is to be fulfilled and *all nations* blessed in his seed. The work of Christ among the Jews was not *complete* without the work of Paul among the Gentiles. Paul, in fact, considered his apostleship to be a spiritual "miscarriage" (ἔκτρωμα, *ektrōma,* 1 Cor. 15:8), in that he experienced an "untimely birth" for his special work among the Gentiles,[48] just as the twelve apostles had been sent to the Jews, the lost sheep of the house of Israel. The separation from his mother's womb, mentioned in Galatians 1:15, refers to the same thing as his "miscarriage" among the apostles in 1 Corinthians 15:8—his calling to preach to the Gentiles. Therefore, when this ministry had been completed and the church throughout the empire had accepted its implications, "that which is perfect" (*to teleion*) came.

It is in this same light that the contribution for the saints in Jerusalem must be viewed. The chronology of the work of Paul indicates that the time covered in collecting the money involved too many years for it to be considered a purely benevolent gesture.[49] Anyway, did Paul not describe the people who gave to the poor saints as being themselves in "extreme poverty" (2 Cor. 8:2)? Rather, Paul regards the contribution as having a theological purpose and dis-

---

47. Hugh Schonfield, *The Jew of Tarsus: An Unorthodox Portrait of Paul* (New York: Macmillan, 1947).

48. Gingrich, *Shorter Lexicon,* 66.

49. John Hurd Jr., "Pauline Chronology and Pauline Theology," in *Christian History and Interpretation: Studies Presented to John Knox,* ed. W. R. Farmer et al. (Cambridge: Cambridge University Press, 1967), 225ff.; George Ogg, *The Chronology of the Life of Paul* (London: Epworth, 1968); Jack Finegan, *Handbook of Biblical Chronology* (Princeton, N.J.: Princeton University Press, 1964).

cusses it in the context of his work among Gentiles (Rom. 15:27). A contribution of material things made by poverty-stricken Gentile Christians and accepted by poverty-stricken Jewish Christians in appreciation for the spiritual benefit granted the Gentiles through the Jews would constitute a seal on the ministry of Paul in the east, thus enabling him to travel westward to Rome (Rom. 15:28). From Paul's point of view, this would be a significant indication that *to teleion* had indeed come—the Gentiles had been included on equal terms with the Jews. He could then say, "I have finished my course and kept the trust given me" (2 Tim. 4:6–8, author's translation).

In summary, the Epistle to the Ephesians develops a theology of the inclusion of the Gentiles. In chapter 4, the inclusion of the Gentiles into the one body is illustrated with the metaphor of a man who is designated *teleios*. The chapter shows that charismatic gifts were given to Jewish Christians to implement this union and assure both Jew and Gentile that God had created of the two one new person. First Corinthians 12–14 discusses the charismatic gifts in an identical context to that of Ephesians, indicating a well-developed and often-used outline of such presentations by Paul. In the thirteenth chapter, Paul uses the same analogy to illustrate the same point he makes in Ephesians. In verses 8–12, he contrasts the individual stage of the Corinthian church with the corporate stage, using *teleios* to mean the corporate stage, the inclusion of the Gentiles, to whom God has also granted charismatic gifts. *To teleion,* therefore, refers to the concluding stages of Paul's work as an apostle to the Gentiles.[50] The generation upon whom he laid his hands and imparted *charismata* experienced *to teleion.* An interesting final note to the story occurred about A.D. 95 when Clement of Rome wrote to this same church in Corinth, employing some of Paul's terminology from 1 Corinthians 13: "ἐν τῇ ἀγάπῃ ἐτελειώθησαν πάντες οἱ ἔκκλεκτοι τοῦ θεοῦ" (*en tē agapē eteleiōthēsan pantes hoi ekklektoi tou theou,* In *love* were all the elect people of God made perfect).[51]

And so I suggest that Paul's phrase "the perfect" in 1 Corinthians 13:10 and Ephesians 4:13 is historical and not eschatological. It refers to the anticipated full and equal inclusion of the Gentiles into the Jewish roots of the church by the time of the deaths of the charismatically gifted apostles.

---

50. On the recent emphasis on this aspect of Pauline studies, see George Howard, "Notes and Observations on the 'Faith of Christ,'" *HTR* 60 (October 1967): 459–84; idem, "Romans 3:21–31," 223–33; John Knox, "Romans 15:14–33 and Paul's Conception of His Apostolic Mission," *JBL* (1964): 1–11; Krister Stendahl, "The Apostle Paul and the Introspective Conscience of the West," *HTR* 56 (1963): 199–215; Eduard Schweizer, "The Church as the Missionary Body of Christ," *NTS* 8 (1961): 1–11; Johannes Munck, *Paul and the Salvation of Mankind* (Atlanta: John Knox, 1977); idem, *Christ and Israel: An Interpretation of Romans 9–11* (Philadelphia: Fortress, 1967); Oscar Cullmann, *Salvation in History* (London: SCM, 1967), 248–68.

51. *1 Clem.* 49.5.

EIGHTEEN

Paul in Recent Study

Paul before Schweitzer

William Ramsay, the intrepid Mediterranean traveler and follower in Paul's footsteps, once wrote: "The life of Paul partakes of the uncertainty that envelopes all ancient history."[1] The perusal of Pauline studies in modern times only corroborates this century-old assessment. In many ways the study of Paul is more complex and farther from consensus today than it ever has been. Putting Paul in his place has become a complex, if not virtually impossible, task in modern scholarship. Victor Furnish stated in his 1993 presidential address to the annual meeting of the Society of Biblical Literature that "if Paul commands attention still, it is not because he is or ever can be fully understood, nor because anybody can ever succeed in putting him in his place."[2]

Older studies on Paul focused on him as an antinomian, one who was opposed to the law of Moses and who is best understood as an opponent of first-century Judaism. He was seen as one who converted from Judaism to Christianity and became a defender of the doctrine of salvation by faith only, as opposed to the meritorious works of the law demanded by the Judaism of Paul's day. These studies argued that there was a fundamental antithesis between Paul and Judaism, whether Palestinian or Hellenistic, and that this an-

---

1. *St. Paul the Traveller and the Roman Citizen* (London: Hodder and Stoughton, 1908), 30.
2. Victor Furnish, "On Putting Paul in His Place," *JBL* 113.1 (spring 1994): 17.

tithesis was the core, the functional center, of Paul's understanding of re-demptive history.

The argument was that in reaction to a Jewish system that offered salvation by human works of merit, Paul taught justification by faith alone as the only appropriate response to God's extended grace in Christ. One system of religion was contrasted with the other, Judaism with Christianity, works with faith. The greatest proponent of this perspective was considered to be Martin Luther, whose reaction to the medieval Catholic system of selling meritorious indulgences sparked the Protestant Reformation and emphatically empha-sized the doctrine of justification by faith alone, despite the fact that the only place in the New Testament where the phrase "faith alone" occurs specifically states that one is not justified "by faith alone" (James 2:24). The endless peri-ods of self-denial and mortification Luther spent in his cell as an Augustinian monk, futilely attempting to procure the feeling of satisfaction that he had earned God's acceptance, had driven Luther to the diametrically opposite conclusion that God's favor cannot be earned.

The conclusion was inescapable: his own Catholic Church was requiring the impossible. The works it demanded were no different in essence from those works required by Paul's Jewish opponents, who also erroneously taught a system of salvation by human merit. This, Luther concluded, was what Paul referred to when he wrote, "For by grace you have been saved through faith; and this is not your own doing, it is the gift of God" (Eph. 2:8). Thus was ignited in Luther the spark that blazed into the Reformation movement, the conviction that a person is justified by faith alone.

Rudolf Bultmann, Ernst Käsemann, and F. C. Baur, three of the most in-fluential European New Testament scholars in recent history, championed this perspective. Baur saw Paul from a Hegelian perspective. Hegel divided history into recurring phases that he delineated as thesis, antithesis, and syn-thesis. Baur saw Paul as a representative of the antithesis in Hegel's dialectical reconstruction of historical development. Jewish Christianity (the earliest ex-pression of Christianity) was the thesis, Paul's Gentile Christianity was the an-tithesis, and the amalgamation of the two later became the synthesis. Baur saw this synthesis in Acts and Ephesians as well as in other books that he dated late in the first century.

Before Albert Schweitzer wrote his *Mysticism of Paul the Apostle* in 1931, it was normative to look at Paul through the eyes of Luther and see the doctrine of justification by faith as the heart of Pauline teaching. Since Judaism was viewed as a religion through which righteousness was attained by works, Paul was predictably postured as antinomian.

Arguments by liberals, neoorthodox scholars, Bultmannians, and post-Bultmannians, therefore, tended to focus on Paul's understanding of salva-tion as the product of faith and not of obedience to law. Paul was widely viewed as a first-century Protestant theologian, who held authority to lie in

Scripture rather than the church and taught that righteousness before God was to be found in believing Scripture rather than in doing the works of the church.[3]

Many scholars who did not believe that Paul's Jewish heritage continued to be a significant factor in his thinking after he became a Christian minimized the Jewishness of Paul and emphasized his exposure to Hellenistic religions, which they thought were more influential on his thought.[4] The failure to contextualize Paul's teaching in its first-century milieu was as old as the postapostolic church.[5]

Paul since Schweitzer

After Albert Schweitzer wrote *Paul and His Interpreters* in 1911, the scenario changed.[6] In this study, Schweitzer rooted Paul squarely in the matrix of Judaism rather than that of Protestant-Catholic history, and his book became a pivotal point in the history of Pauline studies.

Schweitzer later wrote *The Mysticism of Paul the Apostle,*[7] in which he depicted Paul as a mystic and argued that "cosmic mysticism" was the meaning of Paul's expression "in Christ." Paul meant that the believer is united with Christ in a mystical way, just as the elect are understood to be one with their Messiah. Adolf Deissmann had argued from essentially the same perspective,[8] but the greater impact was made by Schweitzer.

Schweitzer saw a strong distinction between Palestinian (Semitic) Judaism and Diaspora (Hellenistic) Judaism. He further divided Palestinian Judaism into rabbinic and apocalyptic categories. He put Paul, as he had placed Jesus, in the latter category. Thus Paul was dissociated from legal issues relating to

3. See also J. Christiaan Beker's references to "the catholic Paul" in *Heirs of Paul: Paul's Legacy in the New Testament and in the Church Today* (Minneapolis: Fortress, 1991), 33–34, 94.

4. H. J. Holtzmann, *Lehrbuch der neutestamentlichen Theologie,* ed. A. Jülicher and W. Bauer, 2d ed. (Tübingen: Mohr, 1911); W. Bousset, *Die Religion des Judentums im späthellenistischen Zeitalter,* ed. H. Gressmann (Tübingen: Mohr, 1926); Richard Reitzenstein, *Die hellenistischen Mysterienreligionen nach ihren Grundgedanken und Wirkungen,* 3d ed. (Leipzig: Teubner, 1927) (the English translation is *Hellenistic Mystery-Religions: Their Basic Ideas and Significance,* trans. John E. Steely [Pittsburgh: Pickwick, 1978]).

5. See Martinus C. de Boer, "Images of Paul in the Post-Apostolic Period," *CBQ* 42 (1980): 359–80; William S. Babcock, ed., *Paul and the Legacy of Paul* (Dallas: Southern Methodist University Press, 1990); Ernst Dassman, *Das Stachel im Fleisch: Paulus in der frühchristlichen Literatur bis Irenäus* (Münster: Aschendorff, 1979).

6. *Paul and His Interpreters: A Critical History,* trans. W. Montgomery (London: Black, 1912), from the 1911 German edition.

7. Published in German in 1930. English edition published in 1931; reprinted by Macmillan, 1956.

8. *Paul: A Study in Social and Religious History,* trans. William E. Wilson, 2d ed. (London: Hodder and Stoughton, 1926).

the Pharisaism manifested later in rabbinic Judaism and was viewed from a different perspective.

By putting Paul in the apocalyptic category of Jewish religious thought, Schweitzer relocated the center of Paul's theology to a concern with the future rather than the present—to questions about eschatology rather than justification by faith as opposed to works of law, where Luther had placed it. The impact of Schweitzer's approach was to shift Pauline concern from the removing of the pangs of conscience to the problem of redirecting the cosmos, of uniting Jew and Gentile into one cosmic body. Thereby he refocused attention from present concerns over sin on a personal level to the problem of sin on a cosmic scale and highlighted Paul's unique role as a first-century Jewish apostle working among Gentiles. This represented a significant change from the emphasis of normative studies on Paul before Schweitzer.

However, since Schweitzer wrote his book on Paul, the essential difference he saw between the two kinds of Judaism (Diaspora and Palestinian) has been largely disproved by two basic factors. First, Gershom Scholem,[9] among other authors, has demonstrated that there was a mystical and proto-Gnostic element within Palestinian Judaism itself. Second, the Dead Sea Scrolls have further demonstrated that concepts that had been thought to be mystical, dualistic, Hellenistic, or Gnostic (and therefore of the Diaspora) may actually have been Palestinian and Semitic.[10]

---

9. *Major Trends in Jewish Mysticism* (Jerusalem: Schocken, 1941).

10. See recent evaluations of Qumran in James VanderKam, *The Dead Sea Scrolls Today* (Eerdmans, 1994); Norman Golb, *Jerusalem and the Origin of the Dead Sea Scrolls* (New York: Macmillan, 1993); Ed Cook, *The Rediscovery of the Dead Sea Scrolls* (Grand Rapids: Zondervan, 1993); Neil Asher Silberman, *The Hidden Scrolls: Christianity, Judaism, and the War for the Dead Sea Scrolls* (New York: Putnam, 1994); Hershel Shanks, ed., *Understanding the Dead Sea Scrolls: A Reader* (New York: Random House, 1992); Hershel Shanks, J. VanderKam, K. McCarter, and J. Sanders, *The Dead Sea Scrolls after Forty Years* (Biblical Archaeology Society, 1992); Joseph Fitzmyer, *The Dead Sea Scrolls: Major Publications and Tools for Study*, rev. ed., Sources for Biblical Study 20 (Atlanta: Scholars Press, 1990); and Lawrence H. Schiffman and James C. VanderKam, eds., *Encyclopedia of the Dead Sea Scrolls*, 2 vols. (New York: Oxford University Press, 2000). For a recent questionable evaluation of the Dead Sea Scrolls, see Robert Eisenmann and Michael Wise, *The Dead Sea Scrolls Uncovered* (New York: Penguin, 1994). This is a translation and interpretation of fifty key documents. The authors argue that Christianity arose directly from Qumran. Their viewpoint is rejected by Alan Segal in his review of their work: "A First Look at Key Scrolls," *BAR* 19.1 (January–February 1993): 60–61. See also Michael Wise et al., eds., *Methods of Investigation of the Dead Sea Scrolls and the Khirbet Qumran Site: Present Realities and Future Prospects* (New York: New York Academy of Sciences, 1994). A translation of all the known scrolls and fragments is now available in paperback, translated into English from Spanish: Florentino García Martínez, *The Dead Sea Scrolls Translated: The Qumran Texts in English*, trans. Wilfred Watson, 2d ed. (Leiden: Brill; Grand Rapids: Eerdmans, 1996).

The Scrolls reveal a community of Judeans, perhaps Essenes, though this is disputed,[11] that was ardently devoted to the law but also manifestly eschatological in its orientation—a circumstance unknown at the time Schweitzer wrote. His premise then, is no longer tenable. Nevertheless, Schweitzer's concentration on the Jewishness of Paul and the nature of the Judaism he represented produced conclusions that continue to influence Pauline studies today.

More Recent Studies on Paul

In recent studies by an increasing number of scholars, the center of Pauline thought is being shifted from justification by faith to the essential meaning of his Jewishness and his commission as apostle to the Gentiles.[12] The impact of

11. Frank Cross writes, "The scholar who would 'exercise caution' in identifying the sect of Qumran with the Essenes places himself in an astonishing position: he must suggest seriously that two major parties formed communistic religious communities in the same district of the desert of the Dead Sea and lived together in effect for two centuries, holding similar bizarre views, performing similar or rather identical lustrations, ritual meals, and ceremonies. He must suppose that one, carefully described by classical authors, disappeared without leaving building remains or even potsherds behind; the other, systematically ignored by the classical sources, left extensive ruins, and indeed a great library. I prefer to be reckless and flatly identify the men of Qumran with their perennial houseguests, the Essenes" ("The Dead Sea Scrolls and the People Who Wrote Them," *BAR* 3.1 [March 1977]: 29). A strong case against identifying these as Essenes is now being made by various scholars. Recent suggestions have included:

1. a breakaway sect of Sadducees (Lawrence Schiffman, *Reclaiming the Dead Sea Scrolls* [Jewish Publication Society, 1994]);
2. militant Jews who were being crushed by the Romans (Silberman, *Hidden Scrolls*);
3. a military fortress (Norman Golb, "Khirbet Qumran and the Manuscripts of the Judean Wilderness: Observations on the Logic of Their Investigation," *Journal of Near Eastern Studies* 49.2 [April 1990]: 102–14; idem, *Jerusalem and the Origin of the Dead Sea Scrolls*);
4. a commercial entrepôt (Alan Crown and Lena Cansdale, "Qumran, Was It an Essene Settlement?" *BAR* 20.5 [Sept.–Oct. 1994]: "Qumran was not an Essene settlement but a customs post, an entrepôt for goods and a resting stop for travelers crossing the Salt Sea" [74]); and
5. a winter villa (Robert Donceel and Pauline Donceel-Voûtre, "The Archaeology of Khirbet Qumran," in Wise, *Methods of Investigation;* see Hershel Shanks, "The Qumran Settlement—Monastery, Villa, Fortress," *BAR* 19.3 [May–June 1993]: 63. Also mentioned by Crown and Cansdale, "Qumran, Was It an Essene Settlement?" 31).

12. For informative surveys of current trends see James D. G. Dunn, "The New Perspective on Paul," *Bulletin of the John Rylands University Library* 65.2 (spring 1983); Scott J. Hafemann, "Paul and His Interpreters," in *Dictionary of Paul and His Letters,* ed. Gerald F. Hawthrone et al. (Downers Grove, Ill.: InterVarsity, 1993), 666–79; Stephen Westerholm, *Israel's Law and the Church's Faith: Paul and His Recent Interpreters* (Grand Rapids: Eerdmans, 1988); Frank Thielman, "Paul, the Law, and Judaism: The Creation and Collapse of a Theological Consensus," in *Paul and the Law: A Contextual Approach* (Downers Grove, Ill.: InterVarsity, 1994), 14–47; E. Earle Ellis, *Paul and His Recent*

the shift has been great enough to capture the attention of the media. *Newsweek* carried a brief article on Paul that states: "A new generation of Scripture scholars is challenging many of the commonplace assumptions about who Paul was and what his teachings meant."[13]

The "new look" focuses directly on Paul and Judaism, rather than on Luther's problems of dealing with personal guilt inherited through Adam. Francis Watson explains Paul's attitudes toward Judaism, the law, and Gentiles as part of his attempt to legitimate the social reality of sectarian Gentile Christian communities in which the law was not observed.[14] Philip Cunningham argues that Paul remained a faithful Jew throughout his life, never conceived himself as an opponent of Judaism, and thought of his call and conversion as a mission to preach to Gentiles.[15] A book edited by Richard Horsley sees Paul's gospel and mission as being set over against the Roman Empire, not Judaism. He argues that Paul never said anything to indicate that he was abandoning Judaism or Israel.[16] David Wenham, in a comprehensive survey of the question of how Paul related to Jesus, argues that Paul was very dependent upon the teachings of Jesus and that his "gospel" is much more like the works of Matthew, Mark, and Luke than has usually been recognized.[17]

Jewish scholars have entered into the discussion of Paul, just as they have into the discussion of Jesus.[18] Geza Vermes, in a recently published book on

---

Interpreters (Grand Rapids: Eerdmans, 1961); Victor Furnish, "Pauline Studies," in *The New Testament and Its Modern Interpreters,* ed. Eldon J. Epp and George MacRae, (Philadelphia: Fortress; Atlanta: Scholars Press, 1989), 321–50; Donald Hagner, "Paul and Judaism: Issues in the Current Debate," *BBR* 3 (1993): 111–30; idem, "Paul in Modern Jewish Thought," in *Pauline Studies: Essays Presented to Professor F. F. Bruce on His 70th Birthday,* ed. Donald A. Hagner and Murray J. Harris (Exeter, Eng.: Paternoster; Grand Rapids: Eerdmans, 1980), 143–68; idem, "Paul's Quarrel with Judaism," in *Anti-Semitism and Early Christianity: Issues of Polemic and Faith,* ed. Craig Evans and Donald Hagner (Minneapolis: Fortress, 1993), 128–50; H. Hübner, "Paulusforschung seit 1945: Ein kritischer Literaturbericht," in *ANRW,* 2.25.4:2649–80; Johannes Munck, "Pauline Research since Schweitzer," in *The Bible in Modern Scholarship,* ed. J. P. Hyatt (Nashville: Abingdon, 1965), 166–77; Schweitzer, *Paul and His Interpreters.*

13. Kenneth Woodward, "How to Read Paul, 2,000 Years Later," *Newsweek,* 29 February 1988, 65.

14. *Paul, Judaism, and the Gentiles: A Sociological Approach,* Society for New Testament Studies Monograph series 56 (Cambridge: Cambridge University Press, 1986).

15. Philip A. Cunningham, *Jewish Apostle to the Gentiles: Paul As He Saw Himself* (Mystic, Conn.: Twenty-Third Publications, 1986).

16. Richard Horsley, ed., *Paul and Empire: Religion and Power in Roman Imperial Society* (Harrisburg, Pa.: Trinity Press International, 1997).

17. David Wenham, *Paul: Follower of Jesus or Founder of Christianity? A New Look at the Question of Paul and Jesus* (Grand Rapids: Eerdmans, 1995). William Simmons finds a much stronger connection between Paul and the teachings of Jesus than merely a few parallel statements (*A Theology of Inclusion in Jesus and Paul* [Lewiston, N.Y.: Mellen Biblical Press, 1996]).

18. Significant works on Paul by Jewish scholars include the following: Joseph Klausner, *From Jesus to Paul,* trans. William F. Stinespring (New York: Macmillan, 1943); Pinchas Lapide and Peter Stuhlmacher, *Paul: Rabbi and Apostle,* trans. Lawrence W. Denef (Minneap-

Jesus, writes that Paul was "the true founder of Christianity" and "was a poetic and mystical genius capable of construing a multifarious, impressive and exciting theological complex. Without any doubt, Paul was the most imaginative and creative writer among the authors of the New Testament, even though his ingenuity often resulted in twisting and sometimes undoing the genuine message of Jesus. But he was also a brilliantly gifted organizer without whose contribution Christianity would not exist or would be something totally different."[19] Claude G. Montefiore takes Schweitzer's dichotomy between Palestinian Judaism and Hellenism as valid and argues that if Paul, the Diaspora Jew, had known the superior Judaism of Palestine, he would never have embraced the gospel.[20] This view is also espoused by Joseph Klausner,[21] and later the argument is essentially repeated and defended by Samuel Sandmel. Sandmel roots his study squarely in the Jewish background of Paul, which he views as fundamentally Hellenistic.[22]

In 1961 Westminster Press published an English translation of a major book on Paul written by Hans J. Schoeps, a Jewish professor at Erlangen University in Germany.[23] The book was hailed by W. D. Davies as "the most sig-

---

olis: Augsburg, 1984), a dialogue between a Christian and a Jew; Claude G. Montefiore, *Judaism and St. Paul: Two Essays* (London: Goschen, 1914; reprint, New York: Arno, 1973); Richard L. Rubenstein, *My Brother Paul* (New York: Harper and Row, 1972); Samuel Sandmel, *A Jewish Understanding of the New Testament* (Cincinnati: Hebrew Union College Press, 1956); idem, *The Genius of Paul: A Study in History* (New York: Farrar, Straus & Cudahy, 1958; reprinted with a new introduction, New York: Schocken, 1970); Hans J. Schoeps, *Paul: The Theology of the Apostle in the Light of Jewish Religious History,* trans. Harold Knight (Philadelphia: Westminster, 1961); Alan F. Segal, *Paul the Convert: The Apostolate and Apostasy of Saul the Pharisee* (New Haven, Conn.: Yale University Press, 1990). On Jewish aspects of Pauline study by non-Jewish scholars see Jürgen Becker, *Paul, Apostle to the Gentiles* (Louisville: Westminster/John Knox, 1993); Cunningham, *Jewish Apostle to the Gentiles;* W. D. Davies, *Jewish and Pauline Studies* (Philadelphia: Fortress, 1984); idem, *Paul and Rabbinic Judaism,* 4th ed. (New York: Harper & Row, 1980); idem, "Paul and Judaism," in *The Bible in Modern Scholarship,* ed. J. Philip Hyatt (Nashville: Abingdon, 1965), 178–86; Hagner, "Paul in Modern Jewish Thought," 143–68; Martin Hengel, *The Pre-Christian Paul* (London: SCM Press; Philadelphia: Trinity Press International, 1991); George Howard, *Paul: Crisis in Galatia* (Cambridge: Cambridge University Press, 1979); Helmut Koester, "Paul and Hellenism," in *The Bible in Modern Scholarship,* ed. Hyatt, 187–95; Gerd Luedemann, *Opposition to Paul in Jewish Christianity,* trans. M. Eugene Boring (Minneapolis: Fortress, 1989); Johannes Munck, *Paul and the Salvation of Mankind,* trans. Frank Clarke (Atlanta: John Knox, 1977); E. P. Sanders, *Paul, the Law, and the Jewish People* (Philadelphia: Fortress, 1983); idem, *Paul and Palestinian Judaism* (Philadelphia: Fortress, 1977); Thomas Schreiner, *The Law and Its Fulfillment* (Grand Rapids: Baker, 1993); W. C. Van Unnik, *Tarsus or Jerusalem?* (London: Epworth, 1962).

19. Geza Vermes, *The Changing Faces of Jesus* (Middlesex, Eng.: Penguin, 2001), 60, 71.

20. *Judaism and St. Paul* (1914).

21. *From Jesus to Paul* (1939).

22. *A Jewish Understanding of the New Testament* (1956), 44.

23. *Paul: The Theology of the Apostle* (first published as *Paulus: Die Theologie des Apostels im Lichte der jüdischen Religionsgeschichte* [Tübingen: Mohr, 1959]).

nificant contribution to Pauline studies since the appearance of J. Munck's *Paulus und die Heilsgeschichte* (1954)."[24] The work is highly critical of Paul as a Jew but works from the premise that he must be understood as a Jew, primarily a Hellenistic Jew of the first century, and not treated as though he were a Gentile Reformation theologian.

Alan Segal, a Jewish author, argues in a recent book on Paul that most Jewish authors have ignored Paul, treating him as no more than an "antagonistic apostate who broke completely with his Jewish past."[25] On the contrary, he thinks that Paul's Jewishness must be taken seriously. He argues that "Paul's goal was the creation of a new community of Jews and Gentiles. He used Pharisaic legal methodology, learned in his past, to resolve issues that separated Jew from Christian in this community. Thus he was not writing systematic theology but was reacting to individual issues and trying to define proper practice."[26]

Johannes Munck writes: "Looking back on Pauline research in the last decades there is one trend which is generally accepted in international scholarship, namely that *Paul is a Jew,* and that he must be understood on the background of Judaism and the O.T."[27]

Munck elsewhere attacks the lingering theology of the nineteenth-century German Tübingen school, which argued that Christianity was the product of Pauline teaching that was later than and different from Judaism in kind as well as degree.[28] Paul, Munck argues, belongs in the center of primitive Christianity, and if we place him there, we will see him as he was—a Jew, and an apostle with a mission to Israel and to the Gentiles.

He argues further that Christianity was not a revision of Judaism that became a religion for Gentiles, but rather that Jewish Christianity existed from the beginning as a new phenomenon. It was different from Judaism from the start, and this was due to the work of Jesus himself. It was not Paul but *the unbelief of the Jews that altered the course of Christianity,* Munck insists.[29]

Ernst Käsemann, another prominent German scholar, argues (contrary to the majority of other German scholars) that the teaching on justification by faith in Paul's writings has to do not so much with individual conscience as with the inclusion of the Gentiles in the true Israel.[30] In his commentary on Romans,[31] he continues the move away from Bultmann and anchors the justifica-

---

24. *NTS* 10.2 (January 1964): 295.
25. *Paul the Convert.*
26. Ibid., from the cover.
27. "Pauline Research," 174.
28. "The Tübingen School and Paul," in *Paul and the Salvation of Mankind,* 59ff.
29. "Pauline Research," 174.
30. "Gottesgerichtigkeit bei Paulus," *Zeitschrift für Theologie und Kirche* 58 (1961): 367–78.
31. *Commentary on Romans* (Grand Rapids: Eerdmans, 1980). This is a fourth edition and translation of his German original *An die Römer,* published in 1974.

tion or righteousness of God in the Old Testament, finding it expressed also in the Dead Sea Scrolls. Distancing himself from Bultmann, he finds justification to be concentrated not on the individual but on God's reclaiming of the world, which highlights the cosmic implications of Paul's preaching as Schweitzer did.

Munck has further argued that Paul thought of himself as a kind of second messiah to the Gentiles when he wrote in Colossians 1:24: "Now I rejoice in my sufferings for your sake, and in my flesh I complete what is lacking in Christ's afflictions for the sake of his body, that is, the church."[32] This view is shared by Oscar Cullmann.[33] They both argue that "the one who restrains" in 2 Thessalonians 2:6–7 is none other than Paul, who delays the second coming of Christ by preaching to Gentiles.

In 1963 Krister Stendahl wrote a watershed article arguing that the teaching that a Christian inherently lives with a guilty conscience became prominent only in later church history.[34] Stendahl maintained that Luther, as an Augustinian monk, inherited the idea through medieval theology from Augustine's *Confessions* and interpreted Romans in the light of his own problems rather than those that actually confronted Paul as a Jew. In contrast to Luther, neither Paul nor his ancestors lived with a guilty conscience. This may be seen from statements attributed to Paul in Acts 23:1 ("Brethren, I have lived before God in all good conscience up to this day") and in 2 Timothy 1:3 ("I thank God whom I serve with a clear conscience, as did my fathers").

Käsemann argues the same point, suggesting that Paul's idea of justification by faith has nothing to do with individual conscience but with the inclusion of the Gentiles.[35] George Howard continues the discussion in several journal articles and in his book *Paul: Crisis in Galatia,* showing that when Paul discussed justification by faith as opposed to works, he meant to refer not to works of merit but to Jewish performances of the works required by the law—in essence, doing what the law required.[36]

W. D. Davies accepted Schweitzer's and Montefiore's separation of Judaism into apocalyptic and rabbinic categories, but against Montefiore he argued that Paul must be understood as a Hebrew of Hebrews who reflected a background of rabbinic Judaism. Davies believed that although it was to be expected that the Judaism of the Diaspora and that of Palestine would present variations, "it is erroneous to over emphasize the differences between them as does Montefiore."[37]

---

32. *Paul and the Salvation of Mankind,* 41.

33. "Le caractère eschatologique du devoir missionaire et de la conscience apostolique de St. Paul: Étude sur le κατέχον (-ων) de II Thess. 2:6–7," *Revue d'Histoire et de Philosophie Religieuses* 16 (1936): 210–45.

34. "Paul and the Introspective Conscience of the West," *HTR* 56 (1963): 199–215.

35. "Gottesgerichtigkeit bei Paulus," 367–78.

36. For further bibliography, see the notes in chapter 15 on Paul's view of the law.

37. *Paul and Rabbinic Judaism: Some Rabbinic Elements in Pauline Theology,* 2d ed. with additional notes (1st ed., 1948; London: S.P.C.K., 1955), 5.

However, E. P. Sanders takes issue with the conclusions of Schweitzer, Montefiore, and Davies in one of the most influential books on Paul written in our generation, *Paul and Palestinian Judaism* (1977). He argues that Paul does not really represent either rabbinic or apocalyptic Judaism but rather something essentially different. Paul's basic view of Judaism is expressed in the term *covenantal nomism,* while Christianity is best described by the term *participationist eschatology.* In Judaism, to be justified by faith is to *remain* in the covenant by keeping its laws and rules. In Christianity, to be justified by faith is to *transfer* from one domain into another, to participate for the first time in the eschatological kingdom.

Jews, Sanders argues, are born into covenant relationship; Christians must be transferred into it. Both the Christian transfer and the Jewish birth into the covenant are by God's grace, but once they are in that relationship, God rewards their good works and punishes their evil ones. According to Sanders, Jews entertain no thoughts of entering the covenant because they have been born into it; their only concern is maintaining the relationship established by the covenant.

Christians, on the other hand, enter into a new covenant by conversion and must maintain the relationship by an obedient faith, just as the Jews. The point to emphasize here is that Sanders, in a tremendously erudite and heavily documented work, roots the study of Paul squarely in the Judaism of his day rather than in the existentialism of Reformation and post-Reformation theology.

James D. G. Dunn, in a lengthy critique of Sanders, observes that until recently Paul has been understood as "the great exponent of the central Reformation doctrine of justification by faith" and that it has been almost universally assumed that there is a "fundamental antithesis between Paul and Judaism."[38] This assumption is challenged by Dunn in his commentary on Romans, where he writes:

> Paul's negative thrust against the law is against the law taken over too completely by Israel, the law misunderstood by a misplaced emphasis on boundary-marking ritual. . . . Freed from that too narrowly Jewish perspective, the law still has an important part to play in "the obedience of faith."[39]

Dunn argues in a later article that Paul continued to identify with the Judaism he had espoused but also embraced the apocalyptic element in Christ's

---

38. This was stated in the Manson memorial lecture at Manchester University in 1982 and later published as "The New Perspective on Paul," *Bulletin of the John Rylands University Library* 65.2 (spring 1983): 98 (the full article is pp. 95–122). It also appears with an "additional note" in *Jesus, Paul, and the Law: Studies in Mark and Galatians* (Louisville: Westminster/John Knox, 1990), 183–214.

39. *Romans 1–8,* Word Biblical Commentary 38 (Dallas: Word, 1988), lxxii.

role and teaching. What was new in Paul was a "fresh and final unfolding of ancient promise." There was "continuity in the discontinuity." It was the "apocalyptic climax of the salvation-history which constituted the heart of his gospel."[40]

An international seminar on Paul associated with the Society of Biblical Literature has tried without success to define a core of Pauline theology upon which its participants can agree. The failure of that effort has been acknowledged by Jouette Bassler, a member of the seminar, who proposes moving in a new direction on the presuppositional level. She charges that the effort to find a consistent theology in Paul by attempting to discover "the theology" of each individual letter and then adding them together as the core of "Pauline theology" is flawed in methodology. She proposes another model for construing Paul's theology, which is to move in the direction of discerning what Paul assumes in his letters to be "self-evidently good and desirable" and, in this "quest for convictions," to find what motivated and guided Paul, though she says we probably will never be able to speak confidently of finding "*the* center of Paul's theology. It no longer seems completely accurate to speak of his theology in this way."[41]

Indeed, Heikki Räisänen has recently argued that Paul was consistently self-contradictory in his theology and that the law "was not a direct divine revelation to Moses."[42] Victor Furnish believes that the theological task of an interpreter of Paul "is not to delineate the apostle's theological system, because he had none."[43]

Richard Hays has argued that Paul, in his responses to local problems in the churches to which he wrote, consciously integrated his reactions into a previously conceived "narrative" of God's redemptive plan for humanity. This narrative runs from Abraham to the parousia of Christ at the end of time. He says that "the coherence in Paul's thought is to be found not in a system of theological presuppositions . . . but in the kerygmatic story of God's action through Jesus Christ."[44]

---

40. James D. G. Dunn, "How New Was Paul's Gospel? The Problem of Continuity and Discontinuity," in *Gospel in Paul: Studies on Corinthians, Galatians, and Romans for Richard N. Longenecker,* ed. L. Ann Jervis and Peter Richardson, Journal for the Study of the New Testament Supplement Series 108 (Sheffield: Sheffield Academic Press, 1994), 388.

41. "Paul's Theology: Whence and Whither?" in *Pauline Theology,* vol. 2, *1 and 2 Corinthians,* ed. David M. Hay (Minneapolis: Fortress, 1993), 13, 17.

42. *Paul and the Law,* Wissenschaftliche Untersuchungen zum Neuen Testament 29 (Tübingen: Mohr, 1983; Philadelphia: Fortress, 1986), 266, 268.

43. "On Putting Paul in His Place," 14. See also his "Paul the Theologian," in *The Conversation Continues: Studies in Paul and John: In Honor of Louis Martyn,* ed. Robert T. Fortna and Beverly Roberts Gaventa (Nashville: Abingdon, 1990), 19–34.

44. Richard Hays, "Crucified with Christ: A Synthesis of the Theology of 1 and 2 Thessalonians, Philemon, Philippians, and Galatians," in *Pauline Theology,* vol. 1, *Thessalonians, Philippians, Galatians, Philemon,* ed. Jouette M. Bassler (Minneapolis: Fortress, 1991), 231–32.

Paul and the Law

Recent scholarship has also concentrated on the question of how Paul viewed the law of Moses and what its implications are for the relation of Jewish Christians to Gentile Christians. This is discussed in chapter 15 on Paul and the law, but it should be noted here that a number of important publications, both articles[45] and books,[46] have appeared dealing with this subject.

---

45. For selective bibliography, see the notes in chapter 15 on Paul's view of the law.

46. These are selective. For a fuller list see my chapter on Paul and the law. Thomas R. Schreiner, *The Law and Its Fulfillment* (Grand Rapids: Baker, 1993); Westerholm, *Israel's Law and the Church's Faith* (see especially his survey of recent scholarship on pp. 13–31); Thielman, *Paul and the Law;* E. P. Sanders, *Jewish Law from Jesus to the Mishnah: Five Studies* (London: SCM Press; Philadelphia: Trinity Press International, 1992); idem, *Paul, the Law, and the Jewish People;* James D. G. Dunn, *The Parting of the Ways: Between Christianity and Judaism and Their Significance for the Character of Christianity* (London: SCM Press; Philadelphia: Trinity Press International, 1991). Heikki Räisänen in his *Paul and the Law,* argues that Paul delivers no reliably systematic understanding of the law.

Subject Index

Author Index

Scripture Index